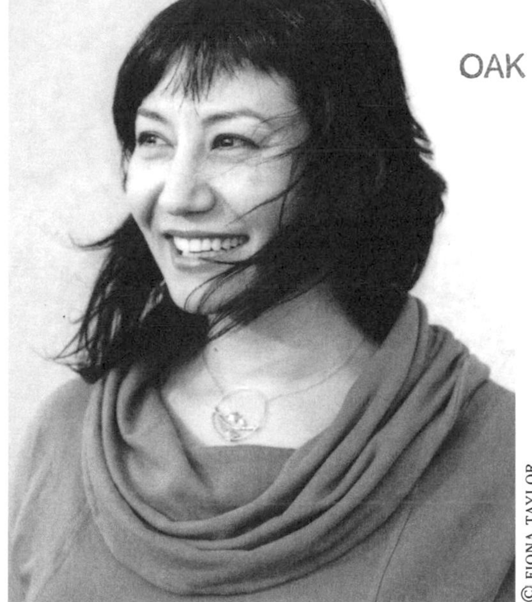

© FIONA TAYLOR

About the Author

MariNaomi is the author and illustrator of *Estrus Comics,* which she has been self-publishing since 1998. Her work has appeared in such publications as *The Comics Journal, Not My Small Diary* and *Action Girl Comics.* Mari has been exhibiting her artwork since 2002 and has exhibited and done live painting in such venues as the De Young Museum, Yerba Buena Center for the Arts, Varnish Fine Arts and 111 Minna. She works and lives in San Francisco, California, with her husband, Gary, and their nonhuman companions. Visit her website at www.marinaomi.com.

Kiss & Tell

A Romantic Résumé, Ages 0 to 22

MariNaomi

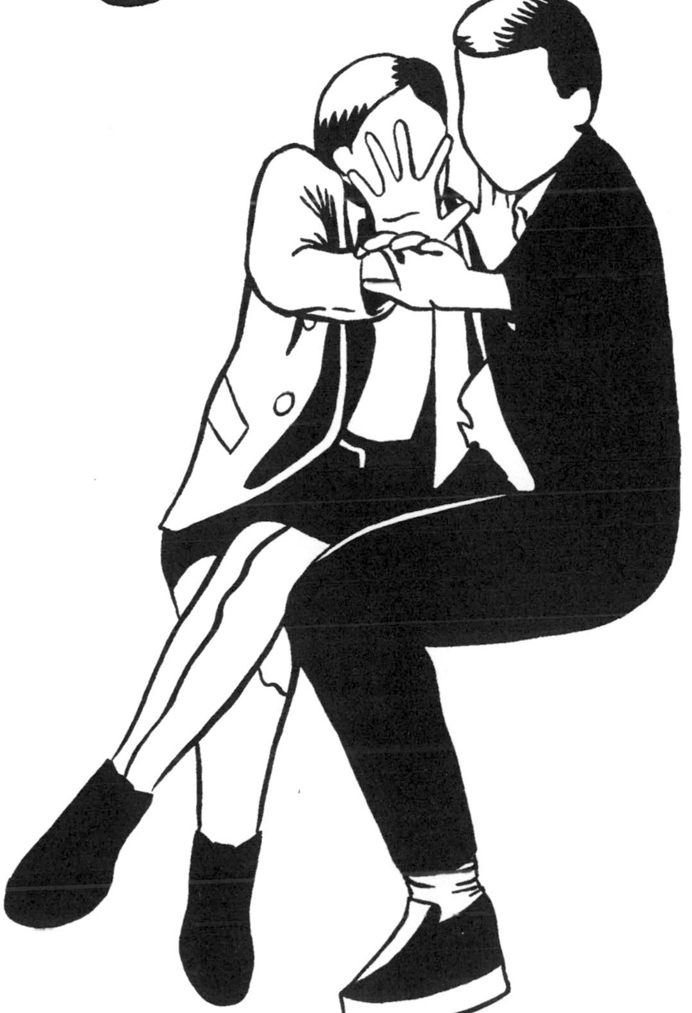

HARPER PERENNIAL

NEW YORK • LONDON • TORONTO • SYDNEY • NEW DELHI • AUCKLAND

This is dedicated to my parents, who I pray will still speak to me after they read the contents of this book.

HARPER PERENNIAL

Some names, faces and details have been changed to protect the innocent (and the not-so-innocent, as the case may be). Aside from that, this is about as honest a memoir as you're going to get. Enjoy!

HarperCollins books may be purchased for educational, business, or sales promotional use. For information please write: Special Markets Department, HarperCollins Publishers, 10 East 53rd Street, New York, NY 10022.

FIRST EDITION

Library of Congress Cataloging-in-Publication Data is available upon request.

ISBN 978-0-06-200923-4

11 12 13 14 15 ID/QGP 10 9 8 7 6 5 4 3 2 1

Prologue

Stage 1: EGG

Protective hard outer shell (chorion), inside is lined with waxlike substance.

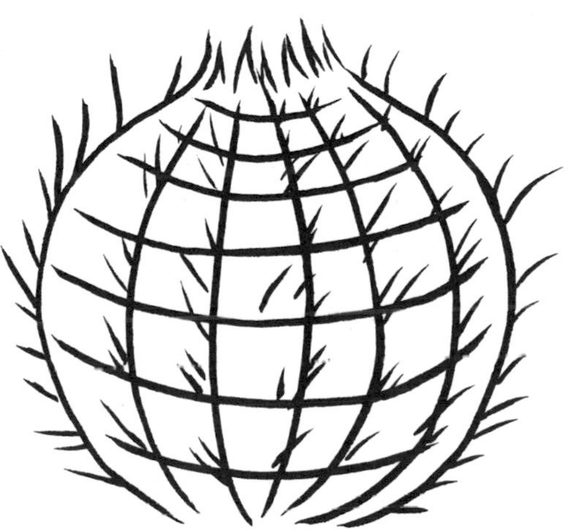

IN 1968, MY FATHER, AN OFFICER IN THE U.S. ARMY, WENT TO JAPAN TO TEACH ENGLISH.

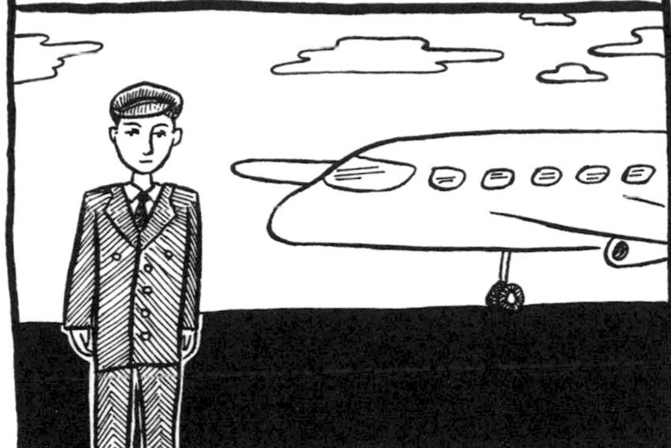

MY MOTHER WAS ONE OF HIS STUDENTS. SHE WAS SIXTEEN AND HE WAS TWENTY-FIVE.

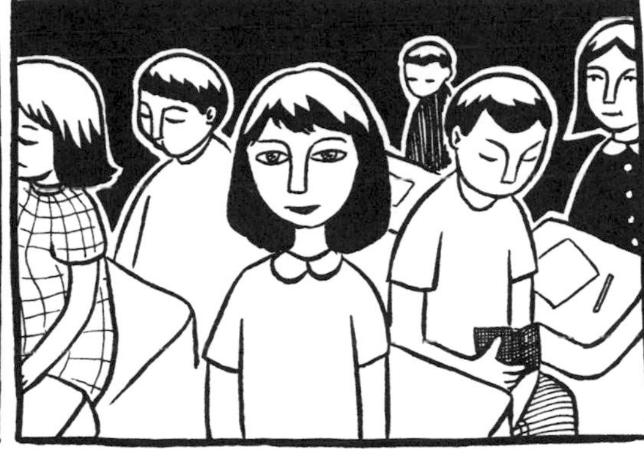

IN JAPAN, VALENTINE'S DAY IS LIKE SADIE HAWKINS, WHERE THE GIRLS ASK OUT THE BOYS. SO SHE ASKED HIM OUT ON A DATE.

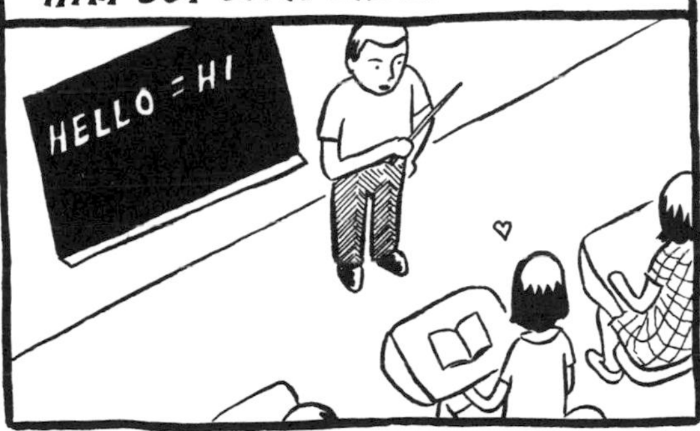

THEY WENT OUT ON A FEW CHAPERONED DATES, HER SISTER IN TOW.

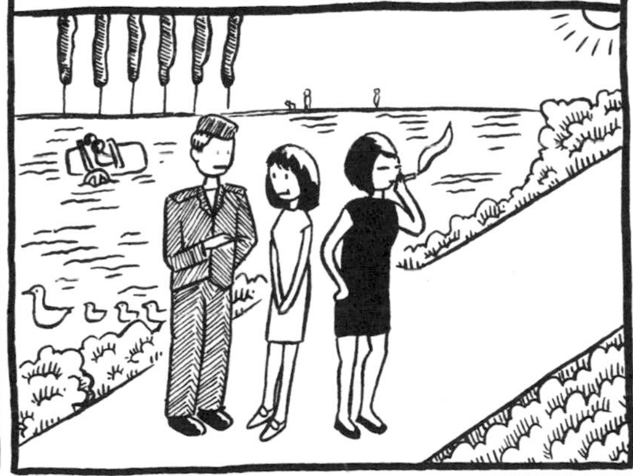

MY DAD RETURNED TO THE U.S. BUT THEY STILL KEPT IN TOUCH.

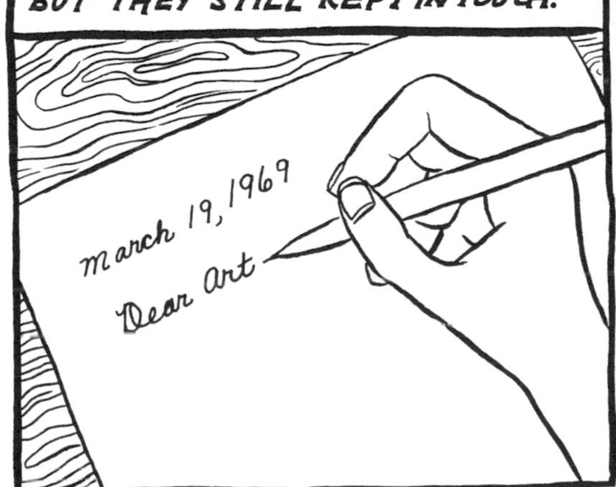

THE LETTERS, OVER TIME, BECAME ROMANTIC.

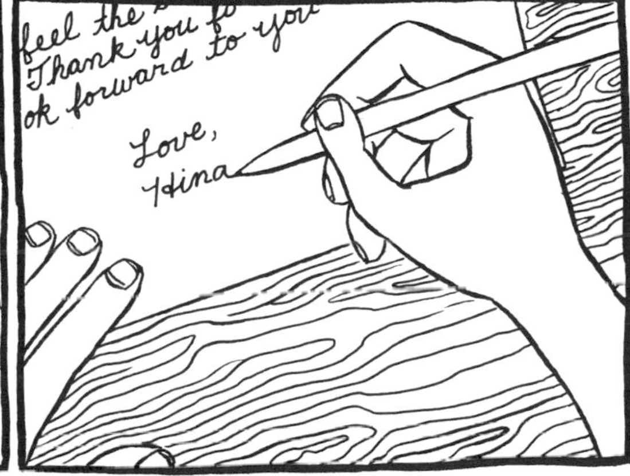

WHEN MY MOM WAS NINETEEN, SHE FLEW TO THE STATES TO MARRY MY DAD, DESPITE PARENTAL OPPOSITION.

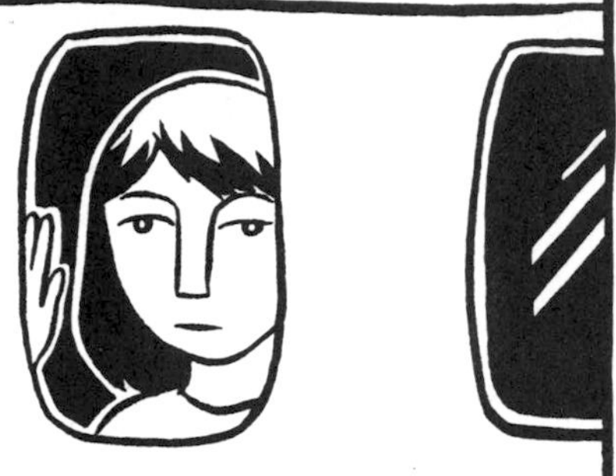

MY GRAMPA, WHO HAD PREVIOUSLY THREATENED TO DISOWN MY DAD WERE HE TO MARRY A JAPANESE WOMAN, ADORED HER THE MOMENT THEY MET.

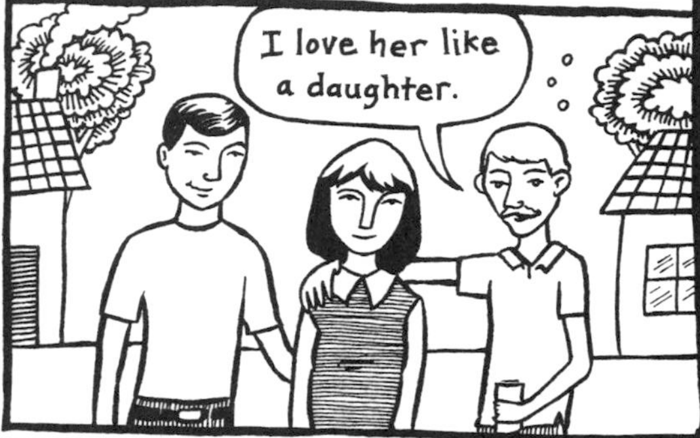

IT WAS A FAIRY-TALE ROMANCE WITH A VERY HAPPY ENDING.

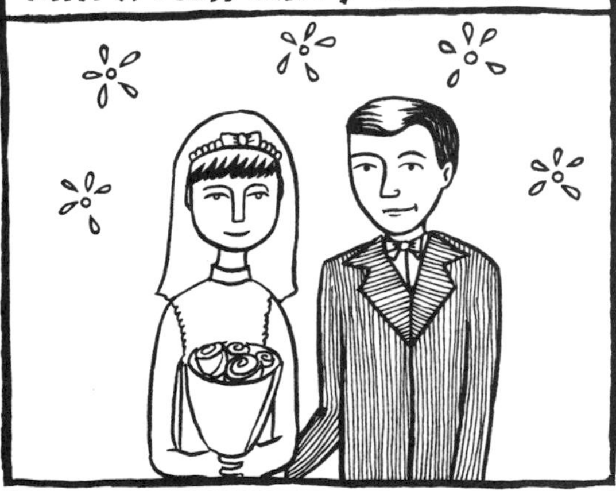

THEY BOUGHT A HOME IN TEXAS.

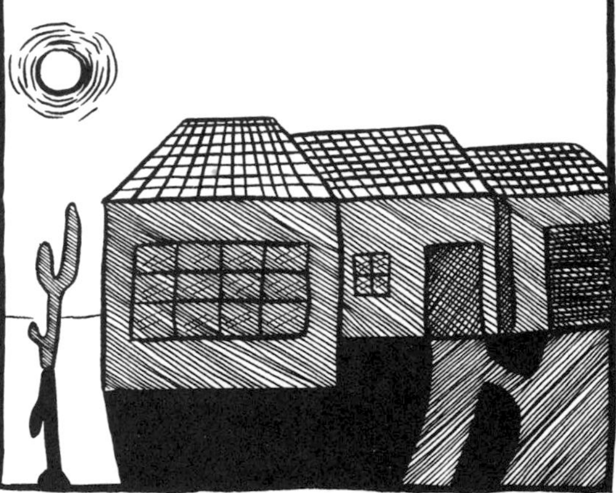

IN 1973, WHEN MY MOM WAS TWENTY-ONE AND MY DAD WAS THIRTY, I WAS BORN.

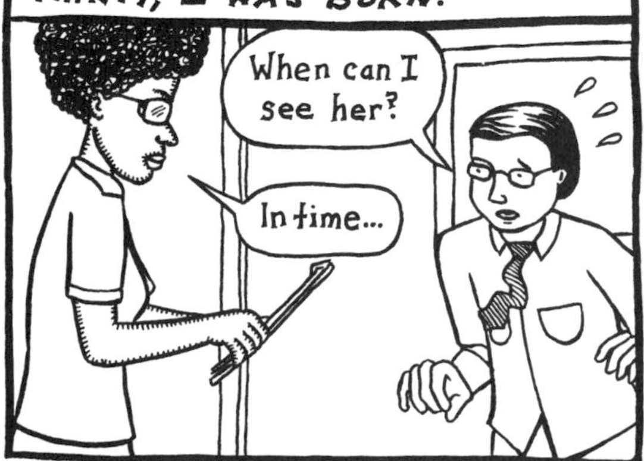

ALL THEY EVER WANTED FOR ME WAS TO FIND LOVE LIKE THEY HAD.

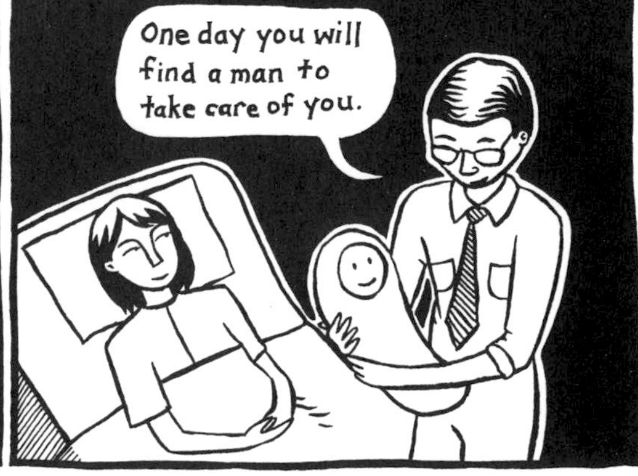

The most beautiful
penis I've ever seen

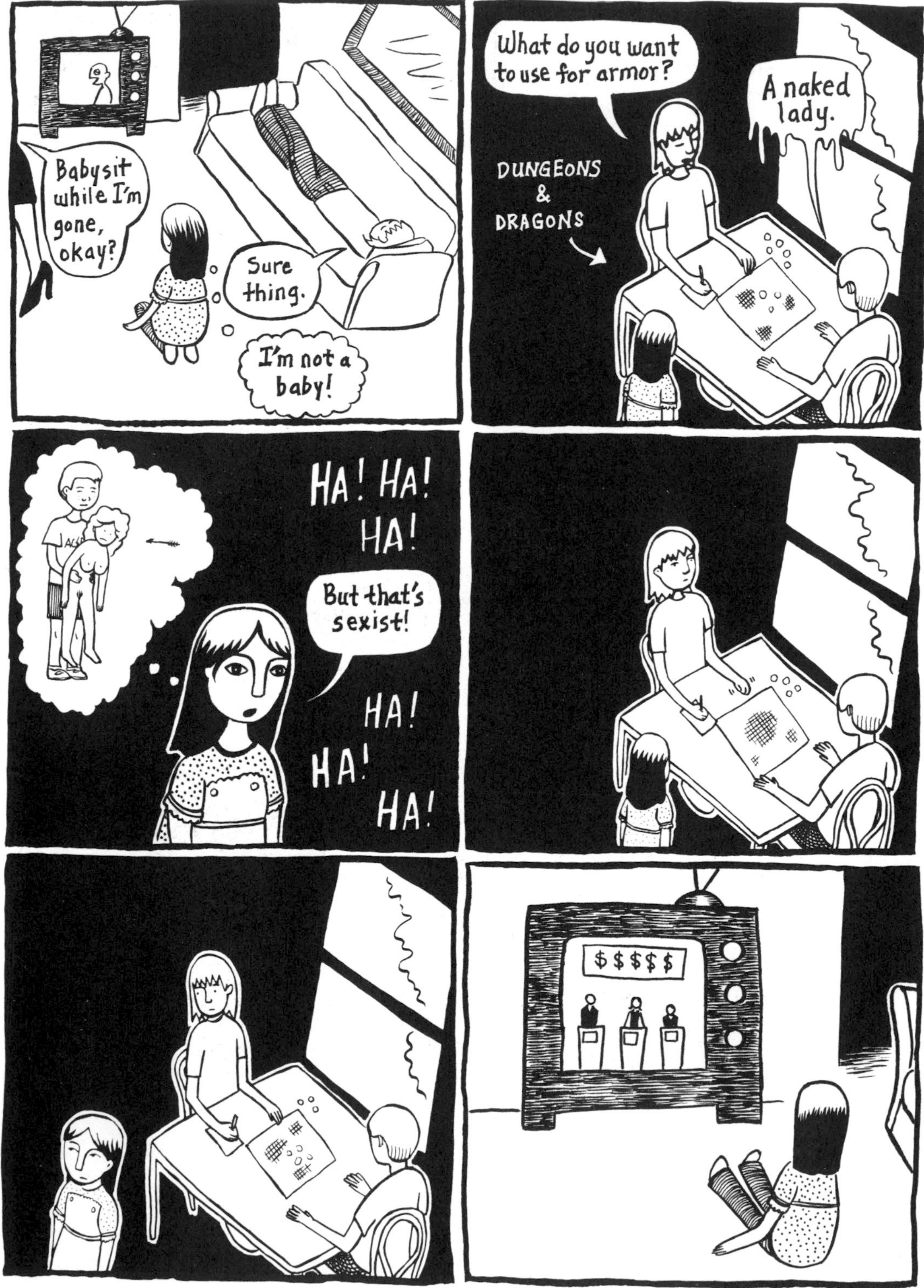
Baby sit while I'm gone, okay?
Sure thing.
I'm not a baby!
What do you want to use for armor?
A naked lady.
DUNGEONS & DRAGONS
HA! HA! HA!
But that's sexist!
HA! HA! HA!
$ $ $ $ $

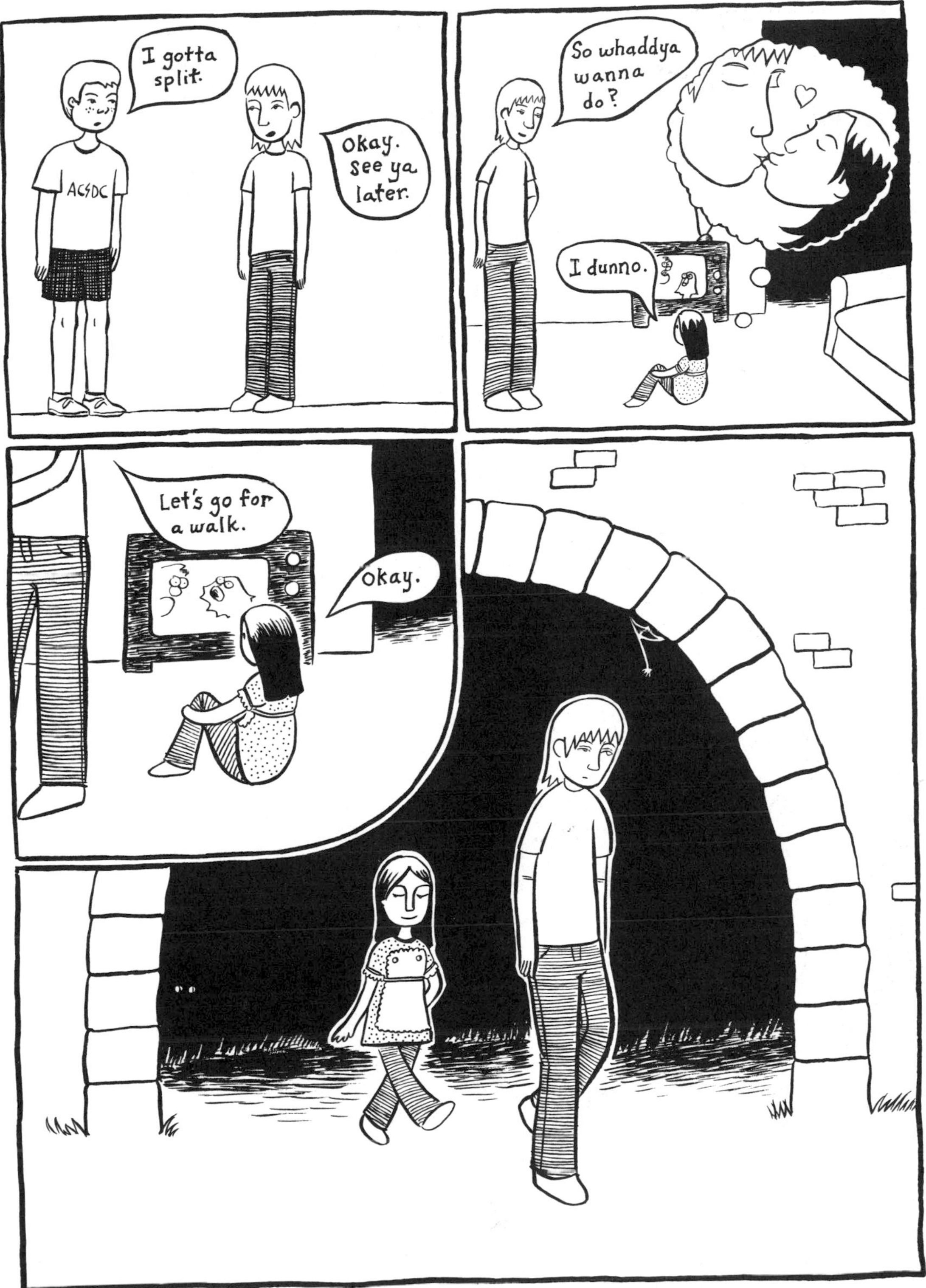
I gotta split.
ACDC
Okay. see ya later.
So whaddya wanna do?
I dunno.
Let's go for a walk.
Okay.

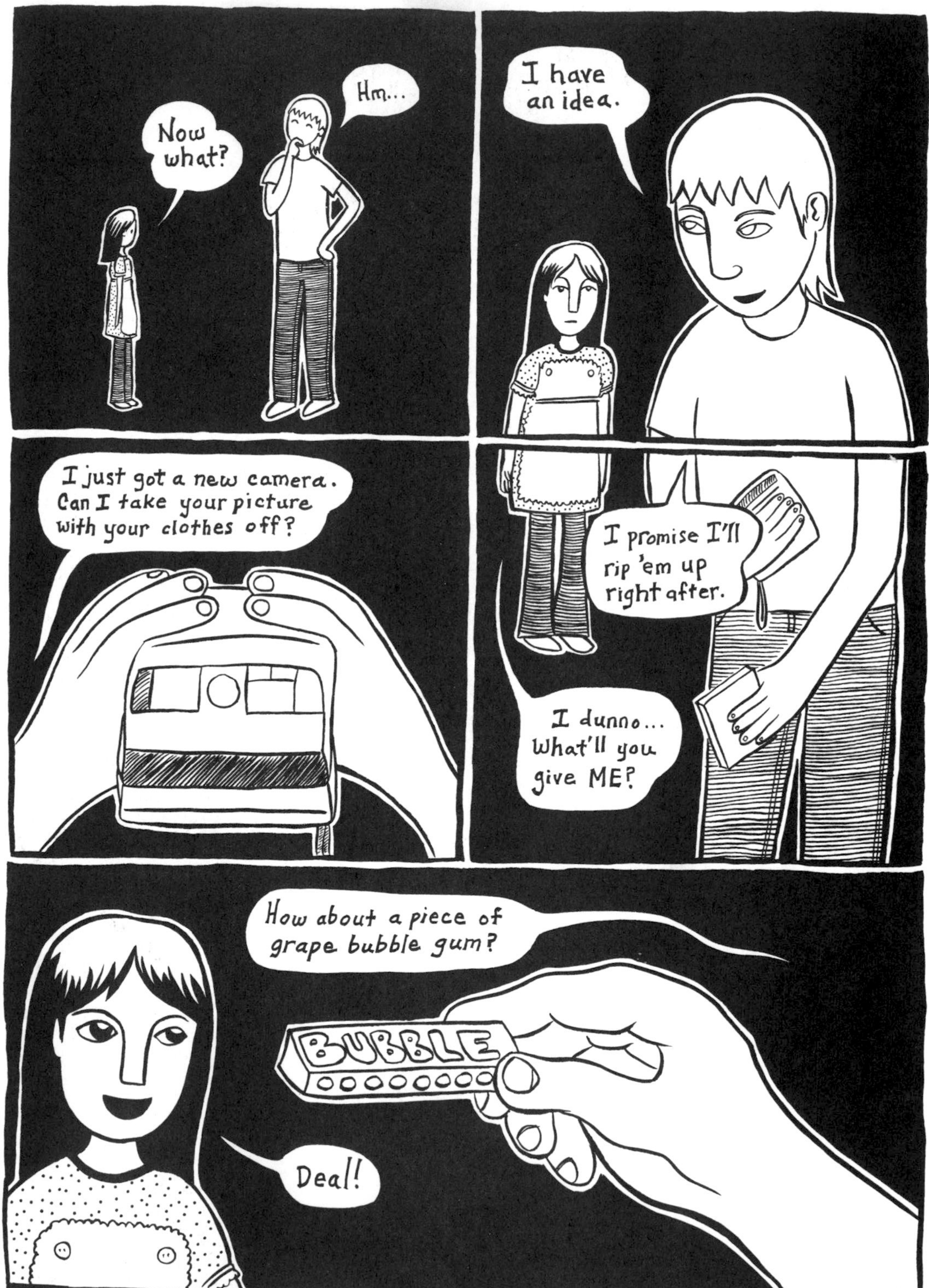
Now what?
Hm...
I have an idea.
I just got a new camera. Can I take your picture with your clothes off?
I promise I'll rip 'em up right after.
I dunno... What'll you give ME?
How about a piece of grape bubble gum?
BUBBLE
Deal!

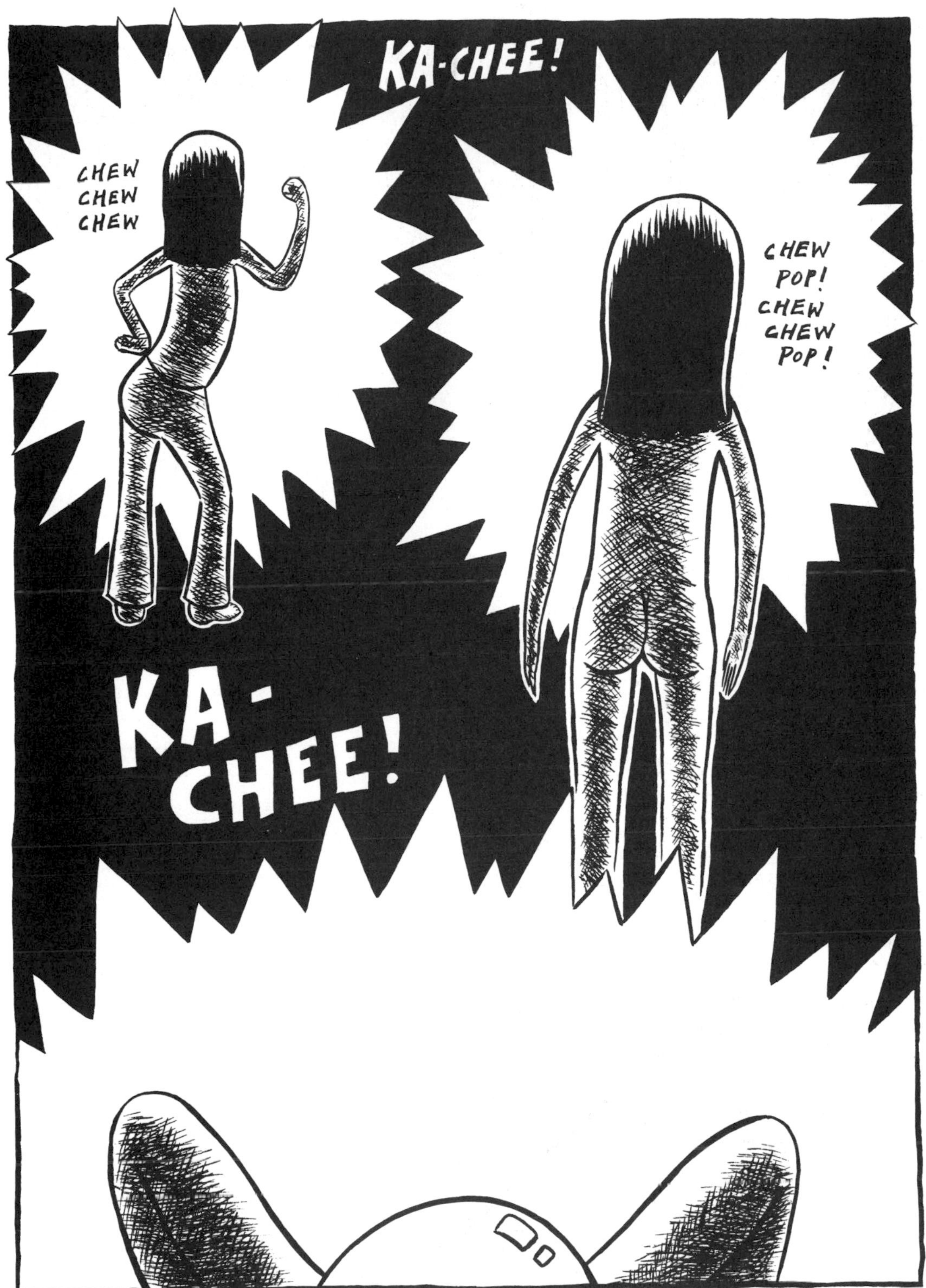
KA-CHEE!
CHEW
CHEW
CHEW
CHEW
POP!
CHEW
CHEW
POP!
KA-
CHEE!

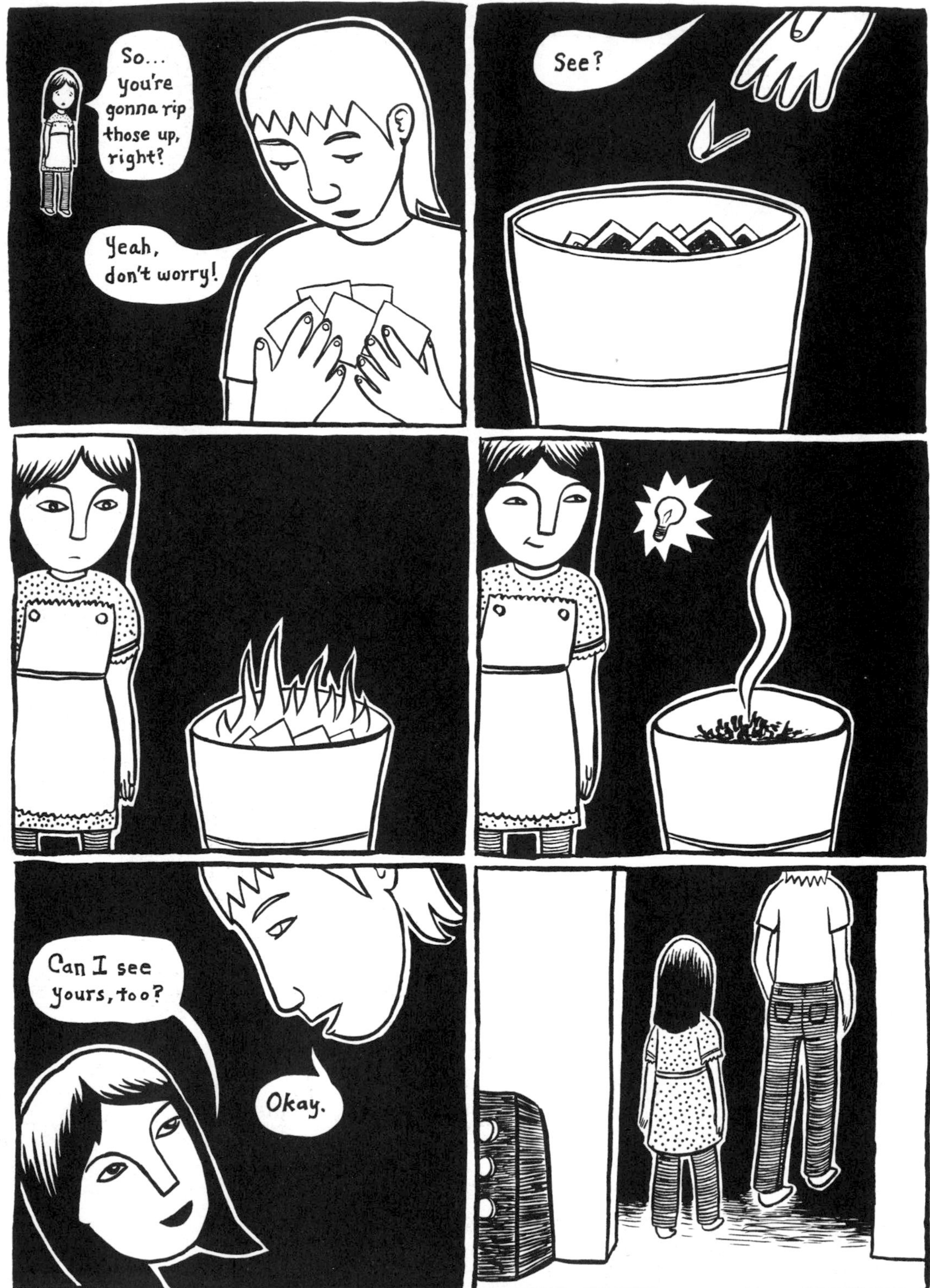
So... you're gonna rip those up, right?
Yeah, don't worry!
See?
Can I see yours, too?
Okay.

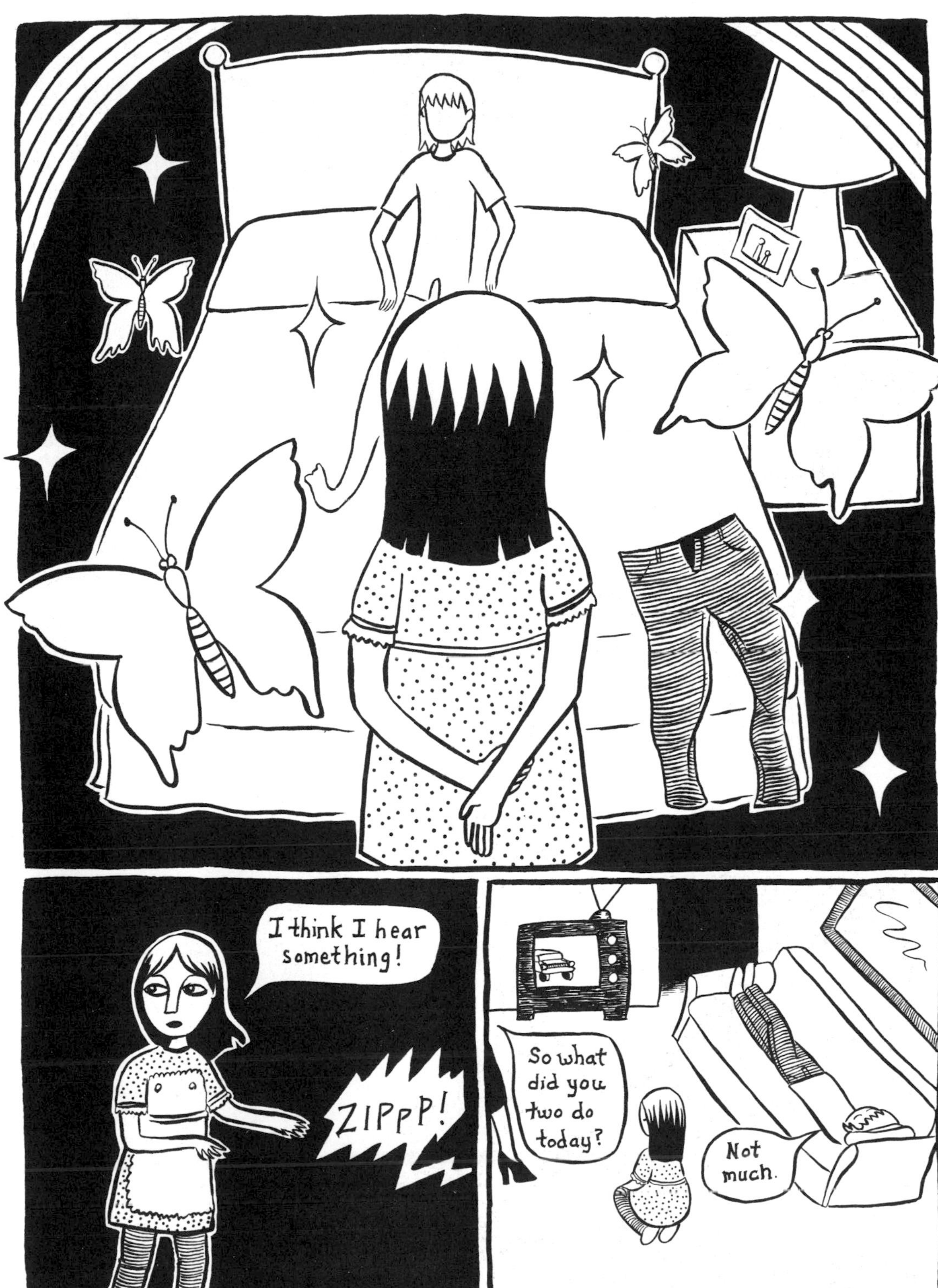
I think I hear something!
ZIPPP!
So what did you two do today?
Not much.

Book One

1978
age 5

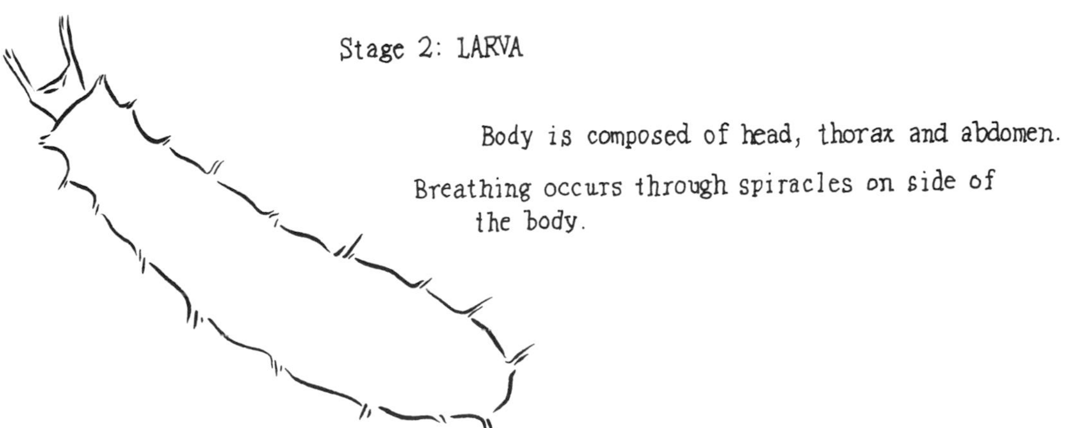
Stage 2: LARVA
Body is composed of head, thorax and abdomen.
Breathing occurs through spiracles on side of the body.
Has five false legs (prolegs).

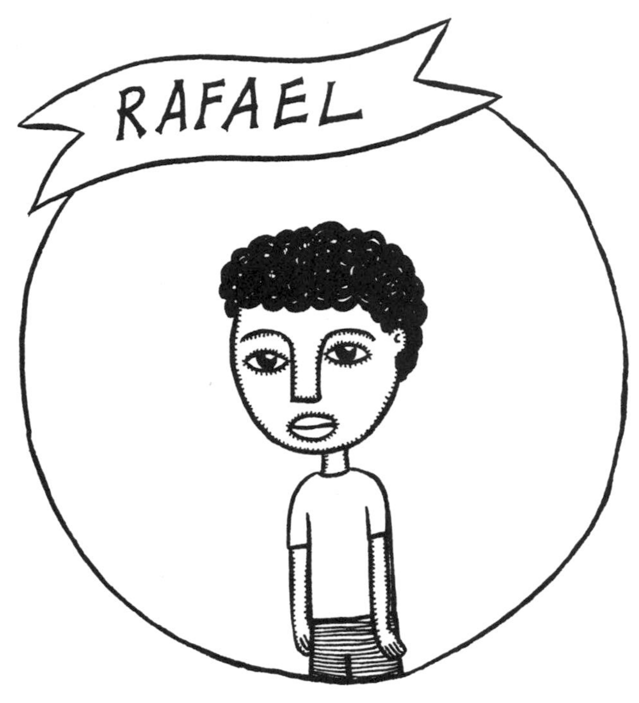
RAFAEL

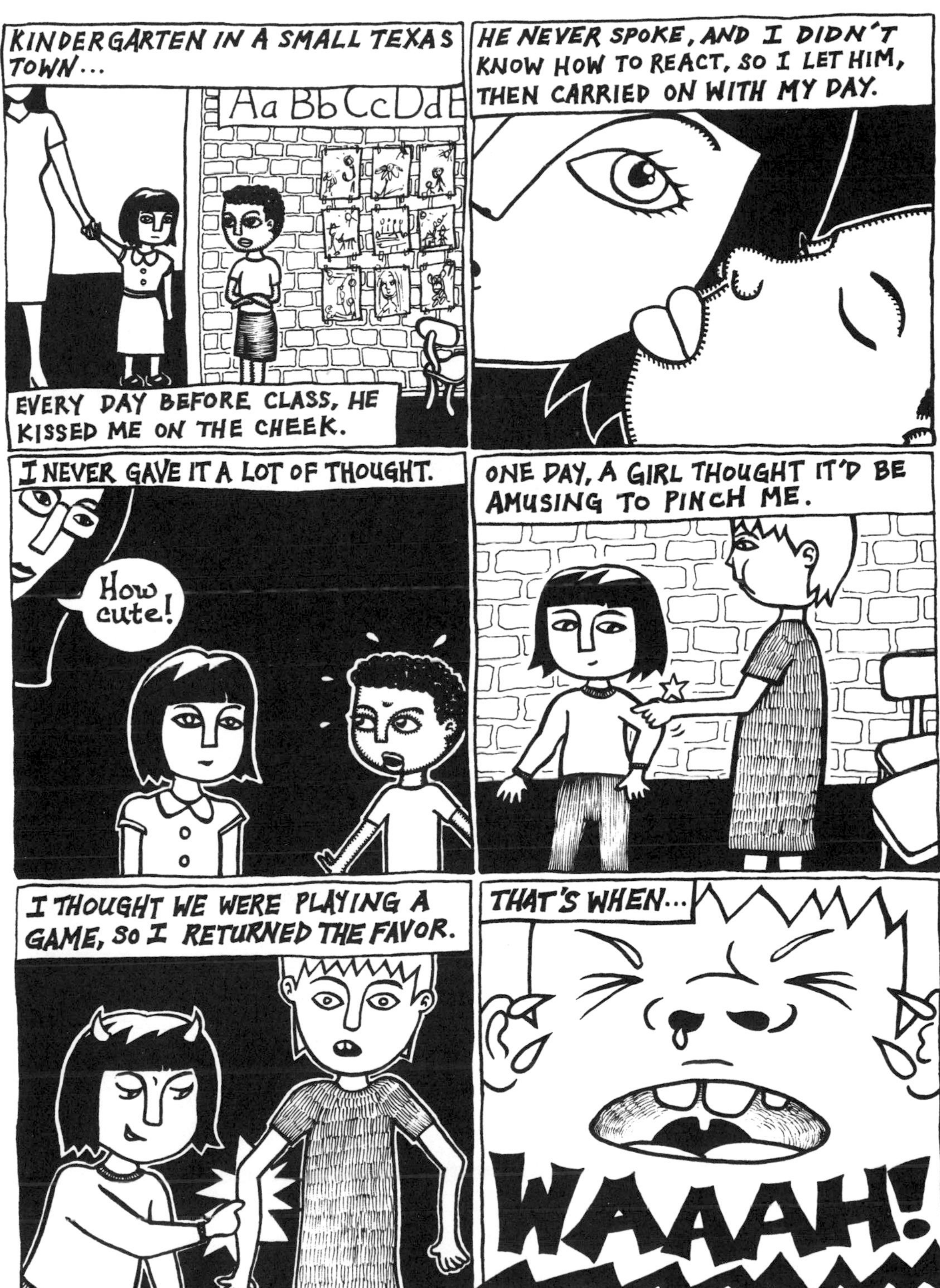
KINDERGARTEN IN A SMALL TEXAS TOWN...
Aa Bb Cc Dd E
EVERY DAY BEFORE CLASS, HE KISSED ME ON THE CHEEK.
HE NEVER SPOKE, AND I DIDN'T KNOW HOW TO REACT, SO I LET HIM, THEN CARRIED ON WITH MY DAY.
I NEVER GAVE IT A LOT OF THOUGHT.
How cute!
ONE DAY, A GIRL THOUGHT IT'D BE AMUSING TO PINCH ME.
I THOUGHT WE WERE PLAYING A GAME, SO I RETURNED THE FAVOR.
THAT'S WHEN...
WAAAH!

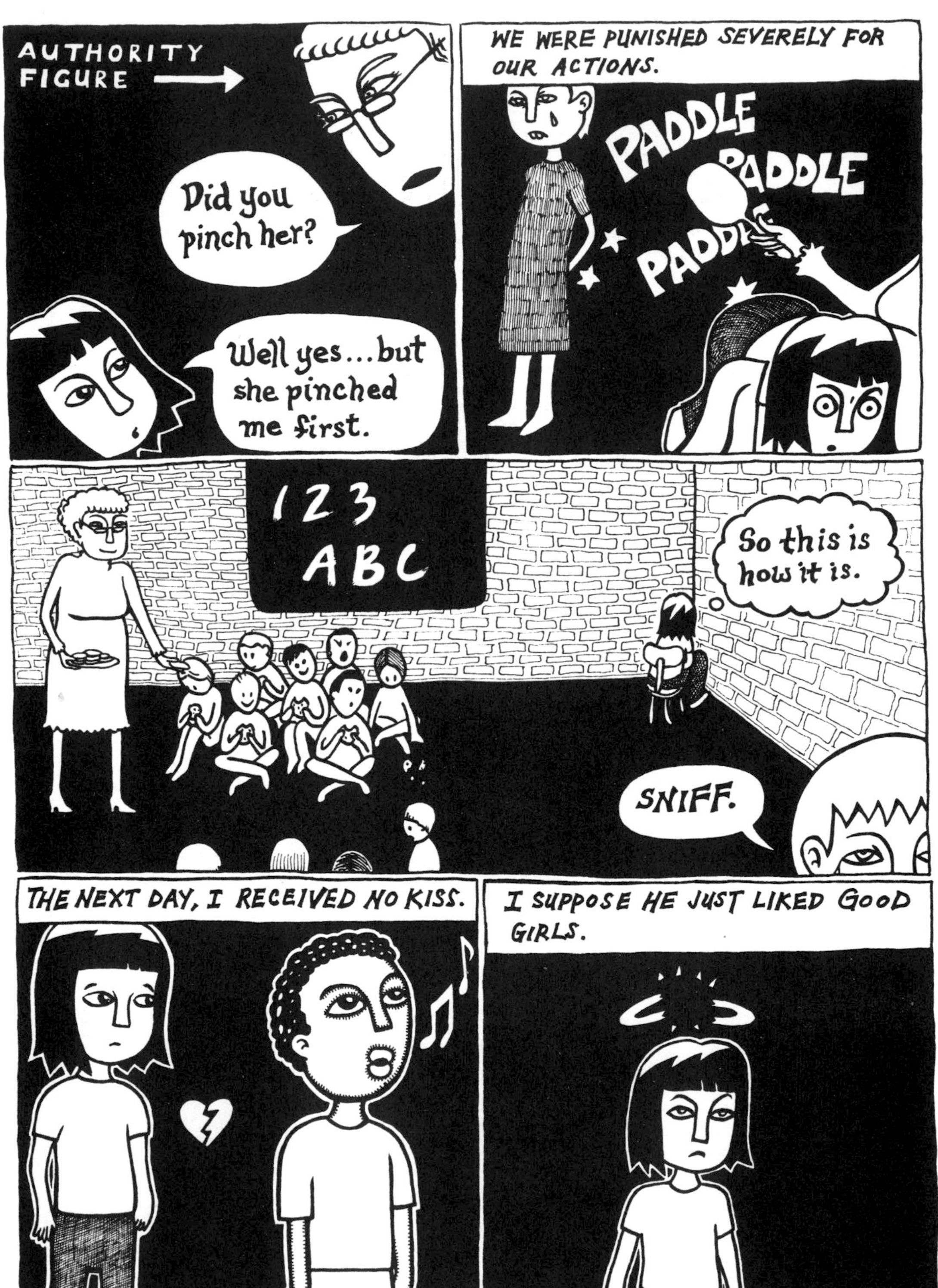
AUTHORITY FIGURE
Did you pinch her?
Well yes... but she pinched me first.
WE WERE PUNISHED SEVERELY FOR OUR ACTIONS.
PADDLE
PADDLE
PADDLE
123
ABC
So this is how it is.
SNIFF.
THE NEXT DAY, I RECEIVED NO KISS.
I SUPPOSE HE JUST LIKED GOOD GIRLS.

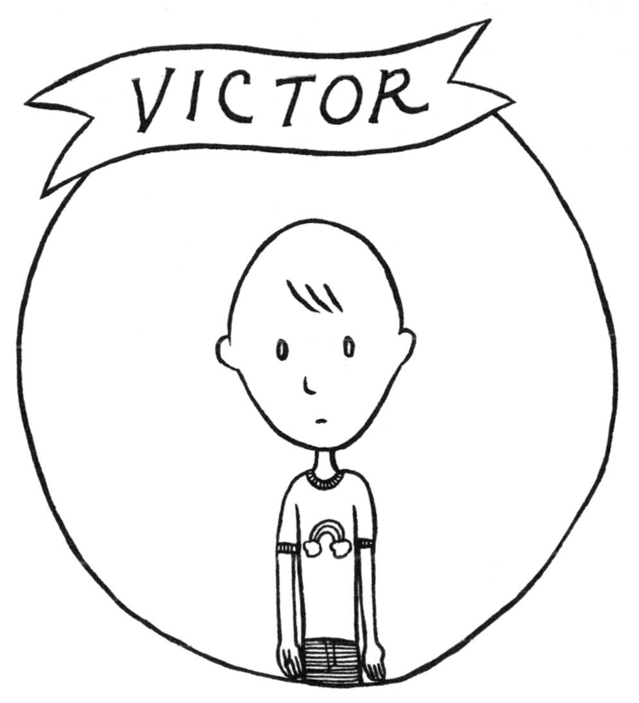
VICTOR

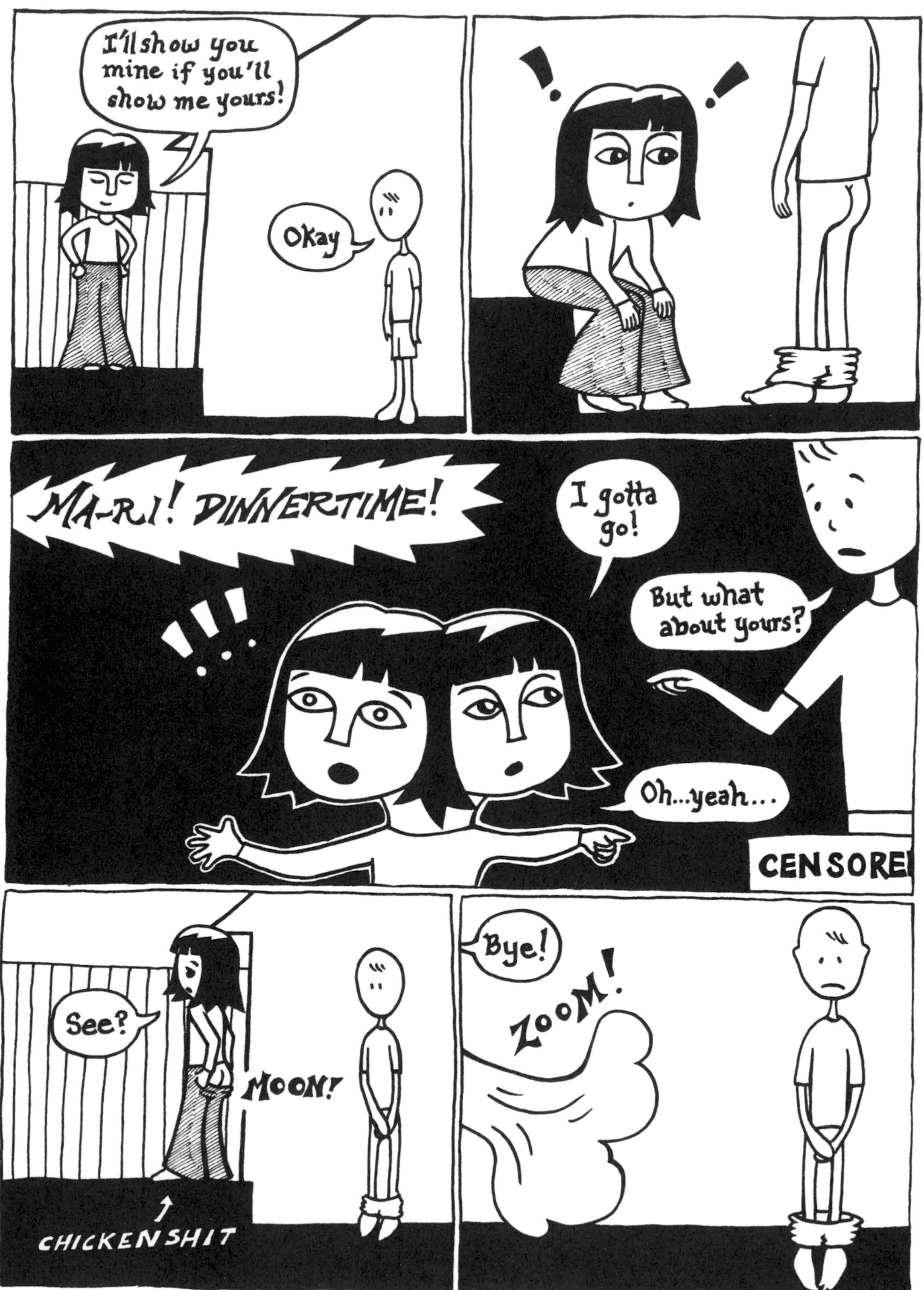
I'll show you mine if you'll show me yours!
Okay
MA-RI! DINNERTIME!
I gotta go!
But what about yours?
Oh...yeah...
CENSORE
See?
MOON!
CHICKENSHIT
Bye!
ZOOM!

1980

age 6

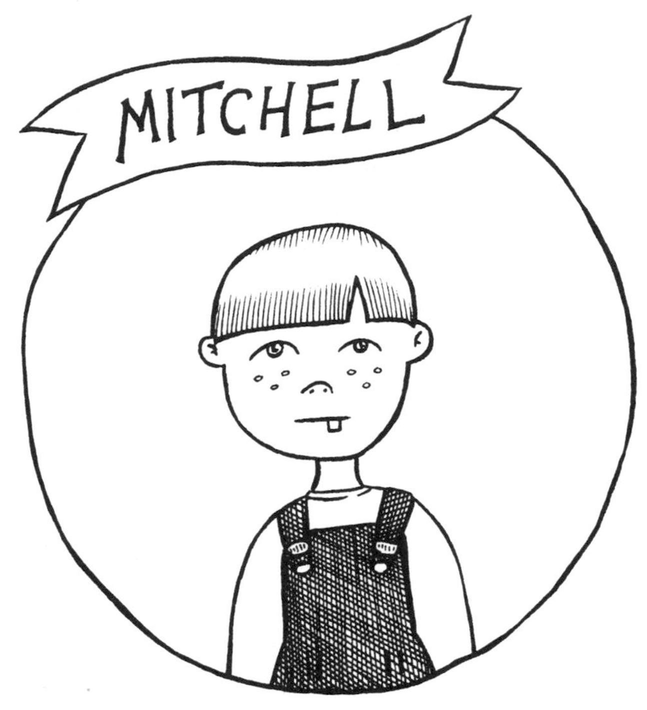
MITCHELL

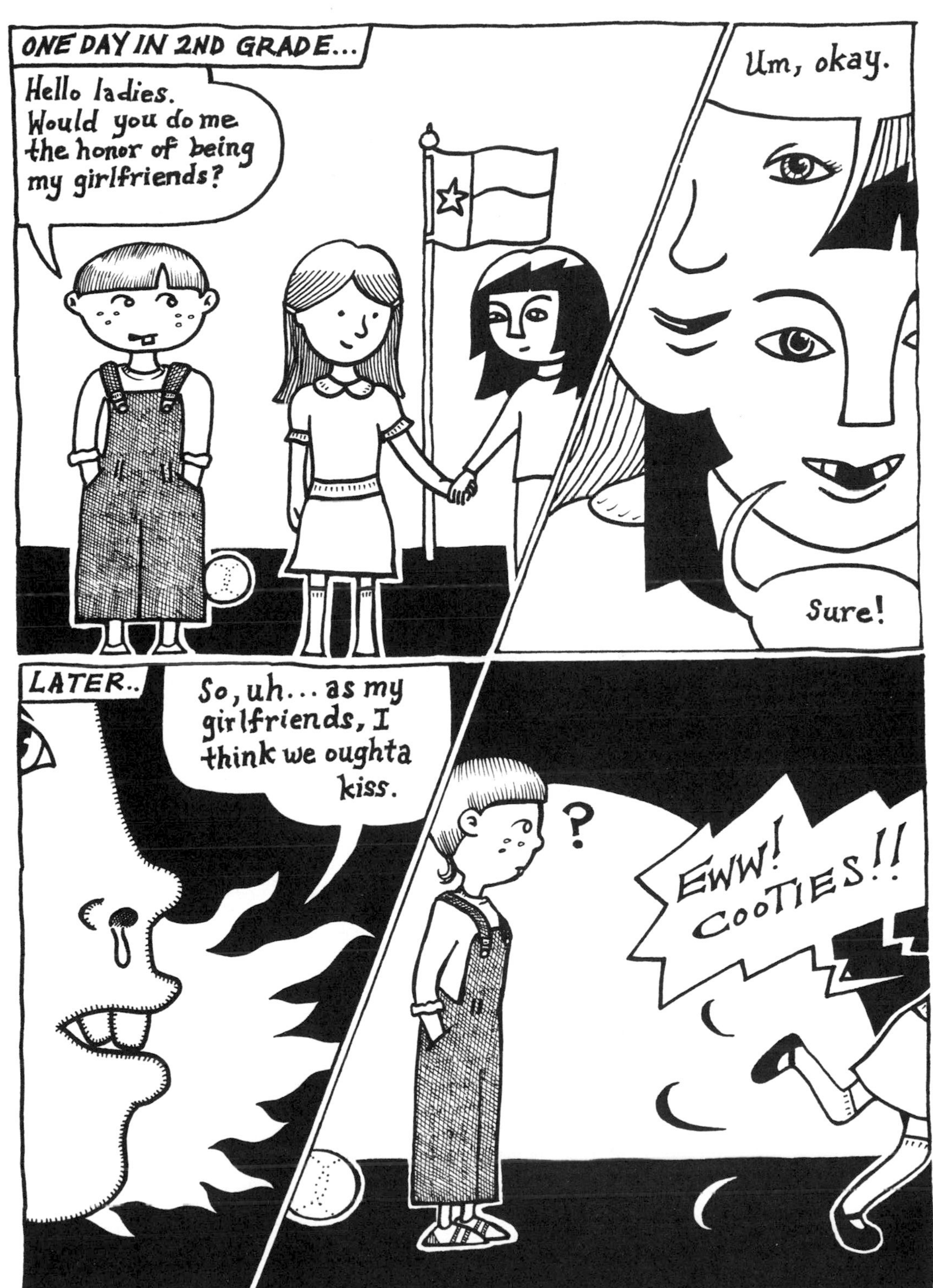
ONE DAY IN 2ND GRADE...
Hello ladies. Would you do me the honor of being my girlfriends?
Um, okay.
Sure!
LATER..
So, uh... as my girlfriends, I think we oughta kiss.
?
EWW! COOTIES!!

1981

age 7

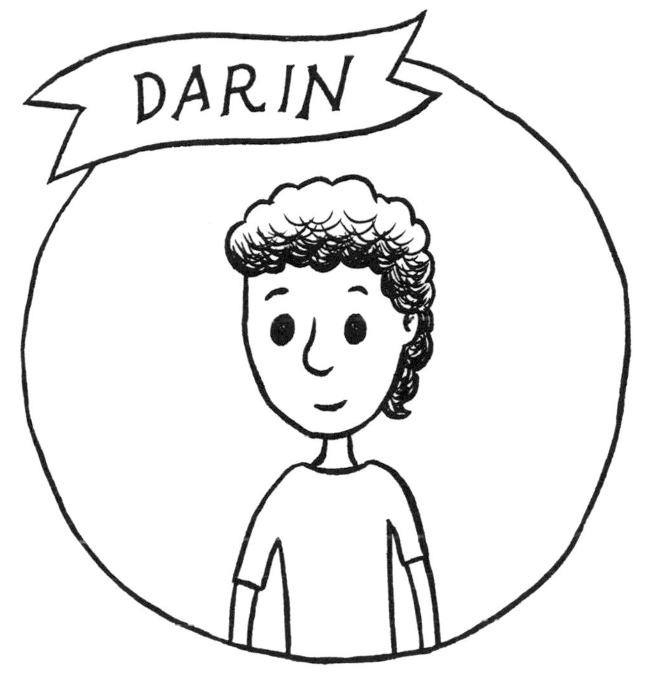
DARIN

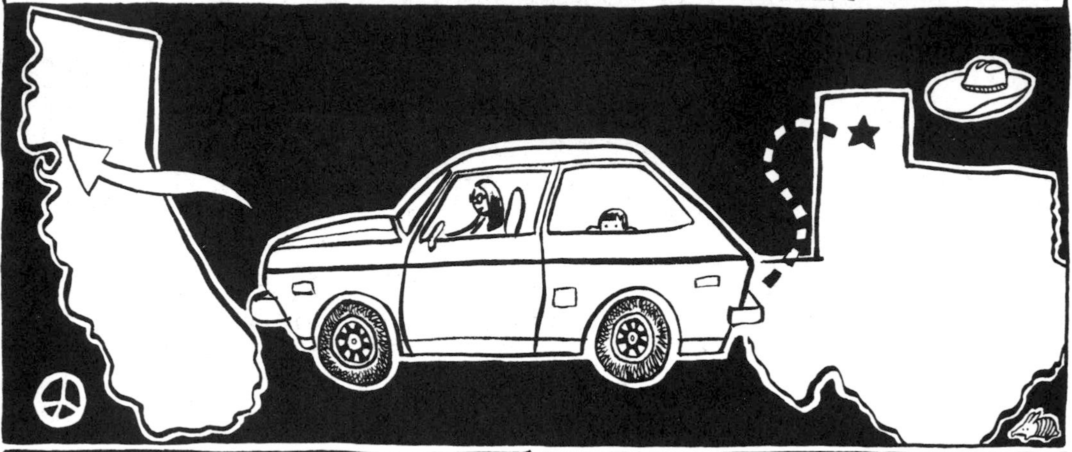
SHORTLY BEFORE I TURNED 8, MY FAMILY MOVED TO NORTHERN CALIFORNIA.

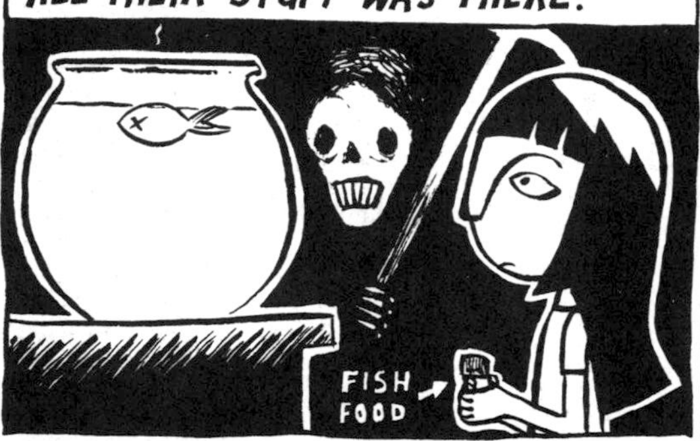
WE WERE SUBLETTING A HOUSE FROM A VACATIONING FAMILY UNTIL THE PURCHASE OF OUR HOME WENT THROUGH. ALL THEIR STUFF WAS THERE.
FISH FOOD

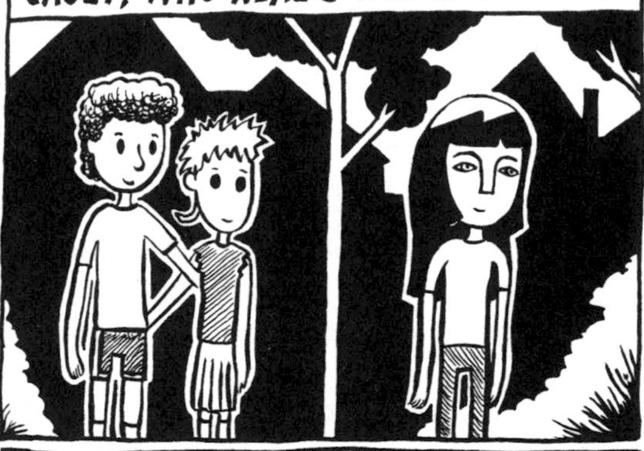
I HUNG OUT WITH THE NEIGHBORHOOD KIDS, INCLUDING DARIN AND CASEY, WHO WERE JOINED AT THE HIP.

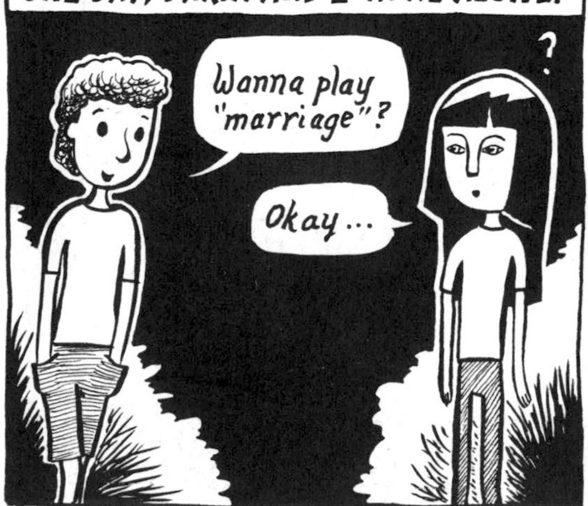
ONE DAY, DARIN AND I WERE ALONE.
Wanna play "marriage"?
?
Okay...

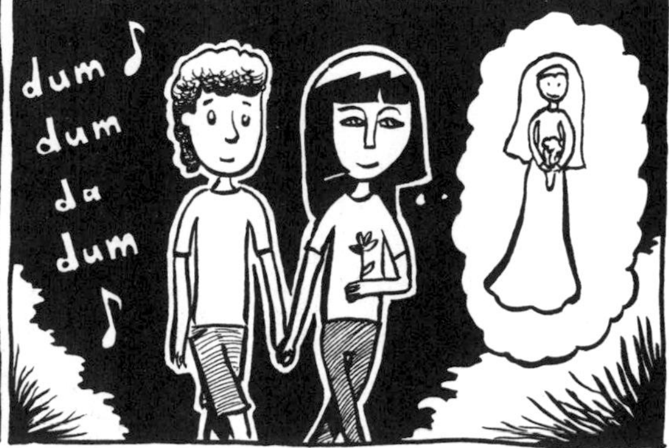
WE PRACTICED WALKING DOWN THE "AISLE" TOGETHER IN MY TEMPORARY BACK YARD.
dum dum da dum

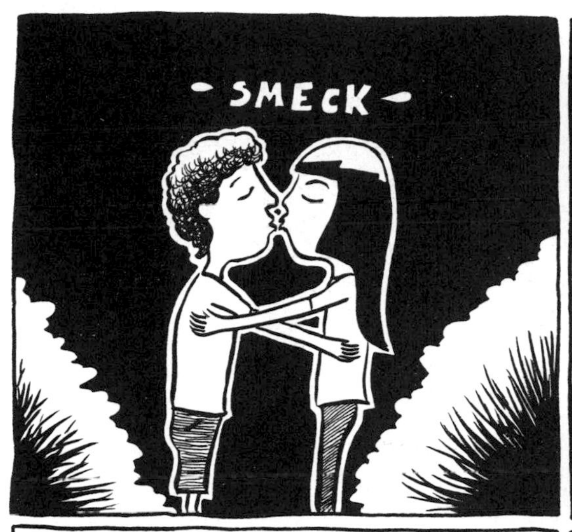
SMECK

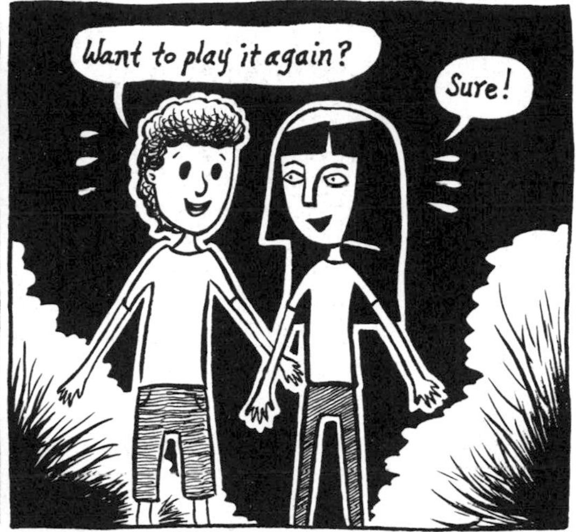
Want to play it again?
Sure!

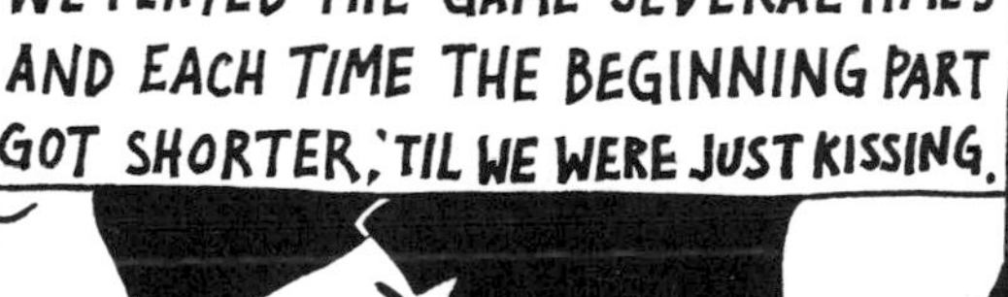
WE PLAYED THE GAME SEVERAL TIMES AND EACH TIME THE BEGINNING PART GOT SHORTER, 'TIL WE WERE JUST KISSING.

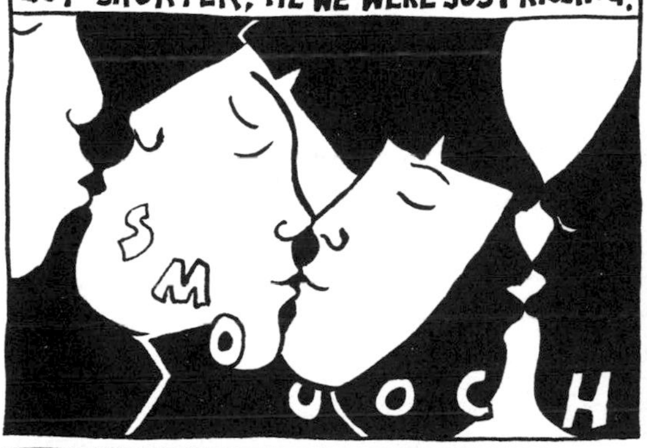
SMOOOCH

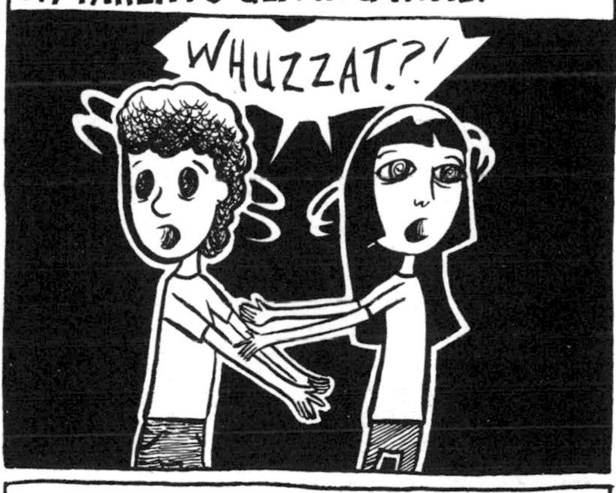
THE GAME ENDED WHEN WE HEARD MY PARENTS GETTING HOME.
WHUZZAT?!

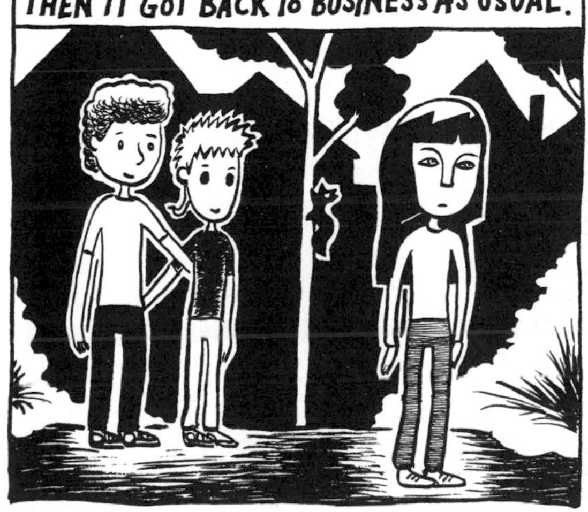
THEN IT GOT BACK TO BUSINESS AS USUAL.

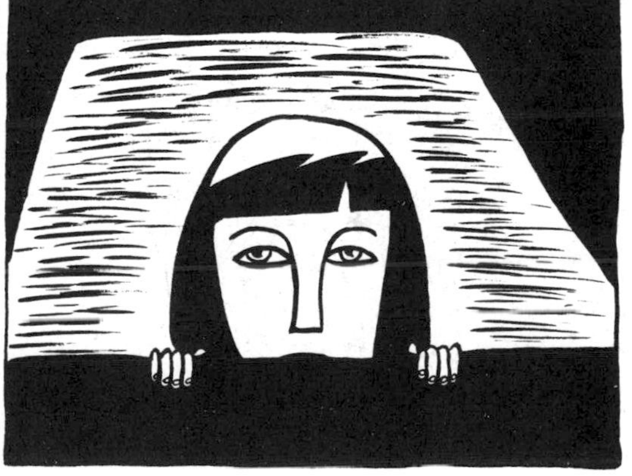
WE MOVED AWAY TO OUR REAL HOME SHORTLY THEREAFTER.

1982
age 8

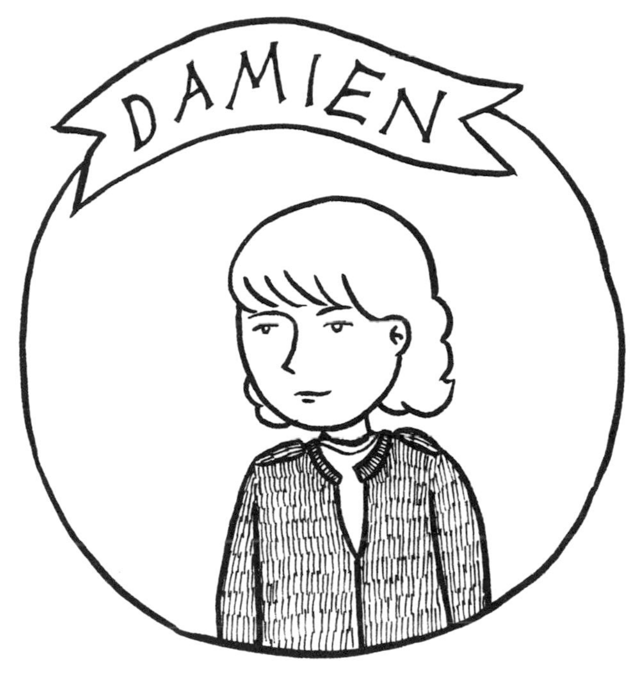
DAMIEN

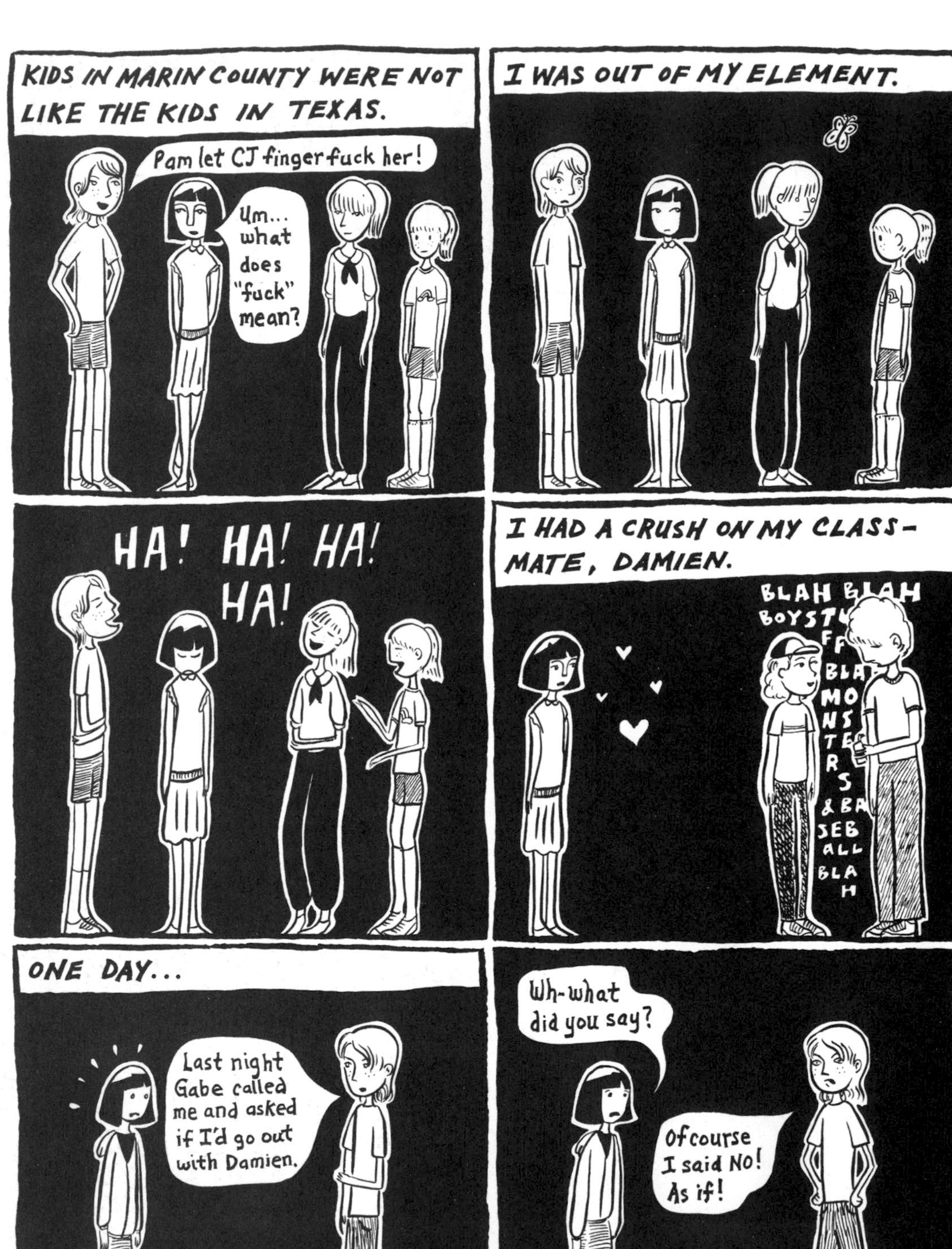

KIDS IN MARIN COUNTY WERE NOT LIKE THE KIDS IN TEXAS.
Pam let CJ finger fuck her!
Um... what does "fuck" mean?
I WAS OUT OF MY ELEMENT.
HA! HA! HA! HA!
I HAD A CRUSH ON MY CLASS-MATE, DAMIEN.
BLAH BLAH
BOYSTUFF
MONSTERS & BASEBALL
BLAH
ONE DAY...
Last night Gabe called me and asked if I'd go out with Damien.
Wh-what did you say?
Of course I said NO! As if!

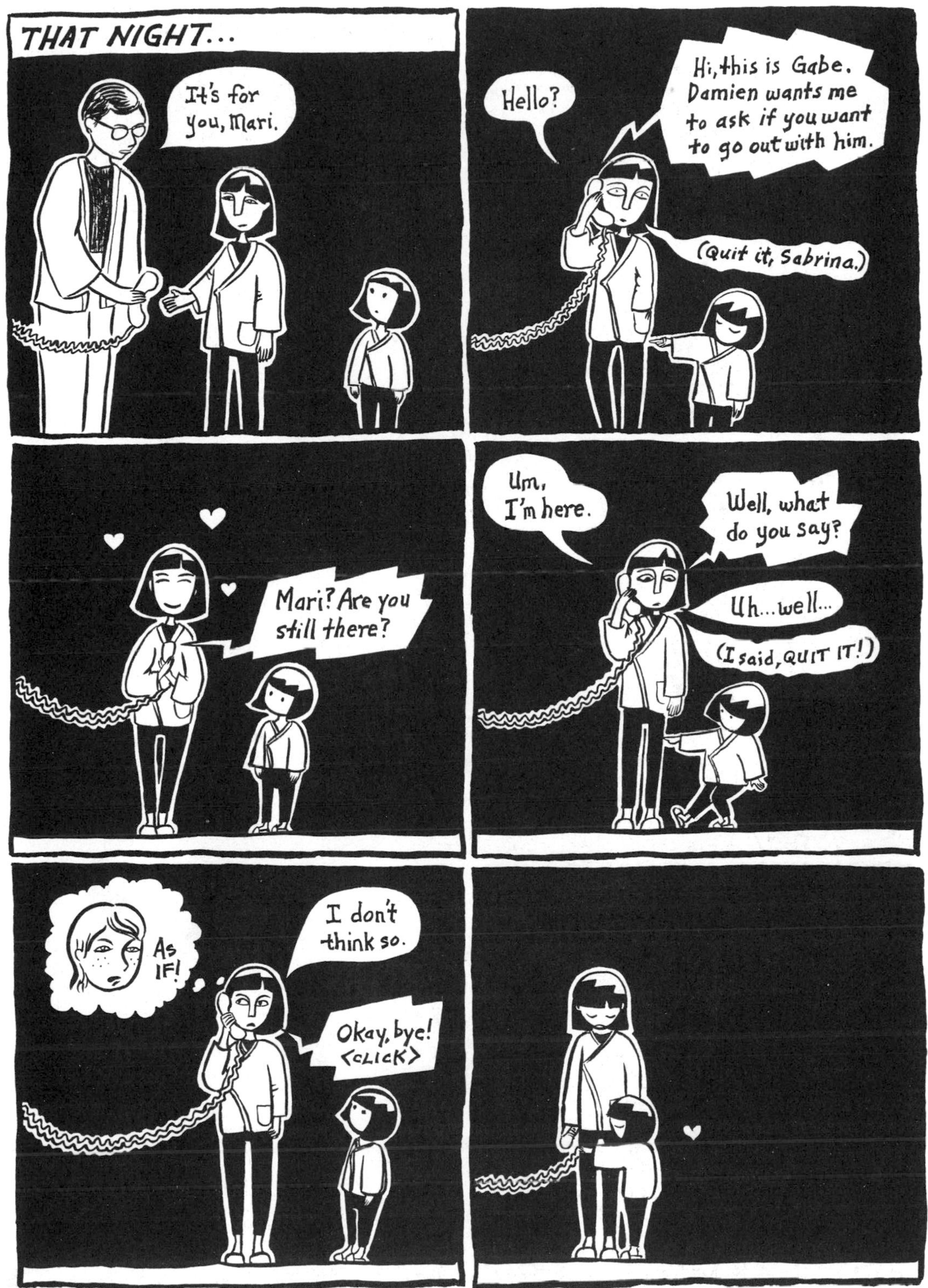
THAT NIGHT...
It's for you, Mari.
Hello?
Hi, this is Gabe. Damien wants me to ask if you want to go out with him.
(Quit it, Sabrina.)
Mari? Are you still there?
Um, I'm here.
Well, what do you say?
Uh...well...
(I said, QUIT IT!)
As IF!
I don't think so.
Okay, bye! <CLICK>

Wishful thinking

Featuring Mirabai

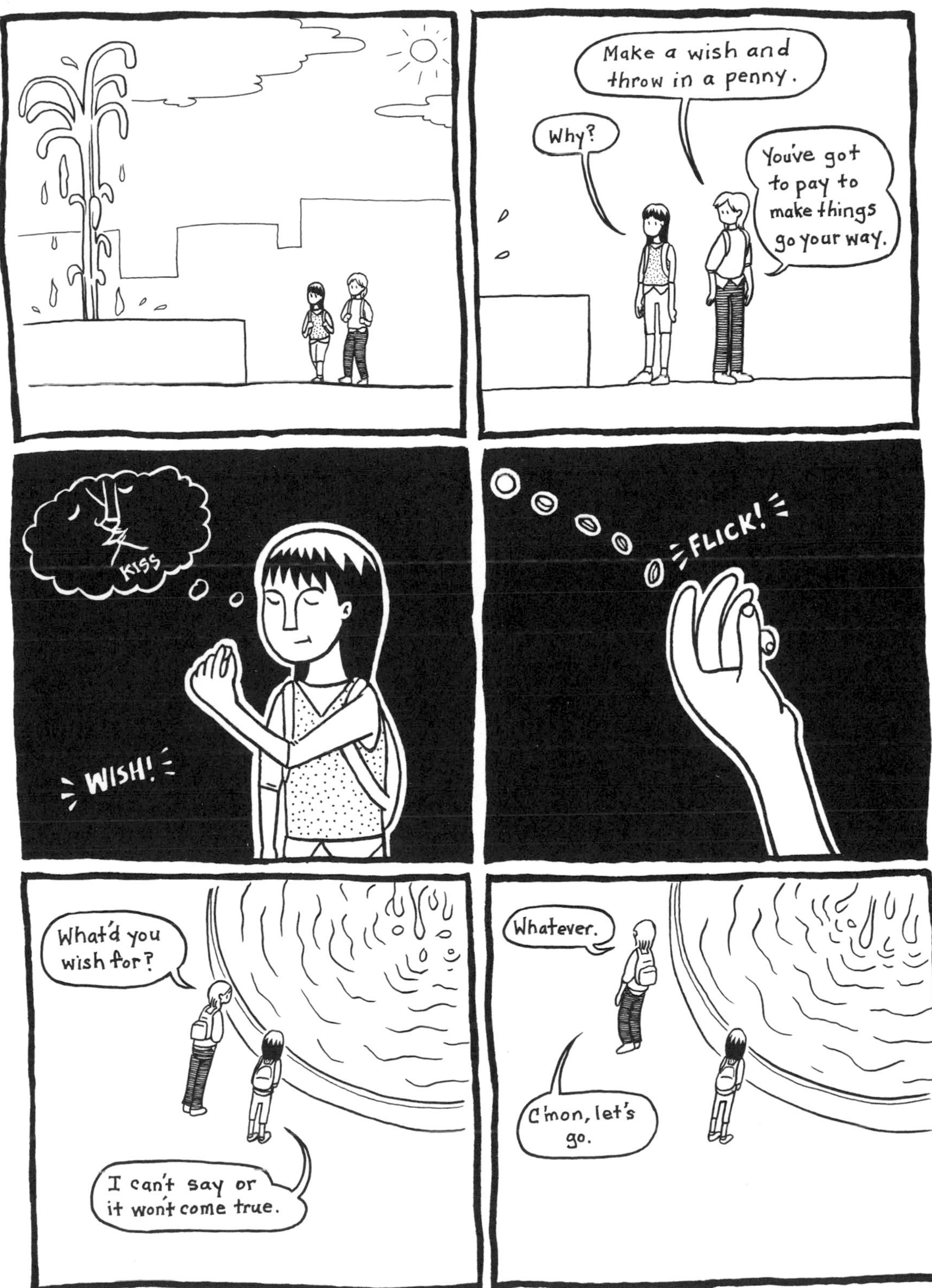
Make a wish and throw in a penny.
Why?
You've got to pay to make things go your way.
KISS
WISH!
FLICK!
What'd you wish for?
I can't say or it won't come true.
Whatever.
C'mon, let's go.

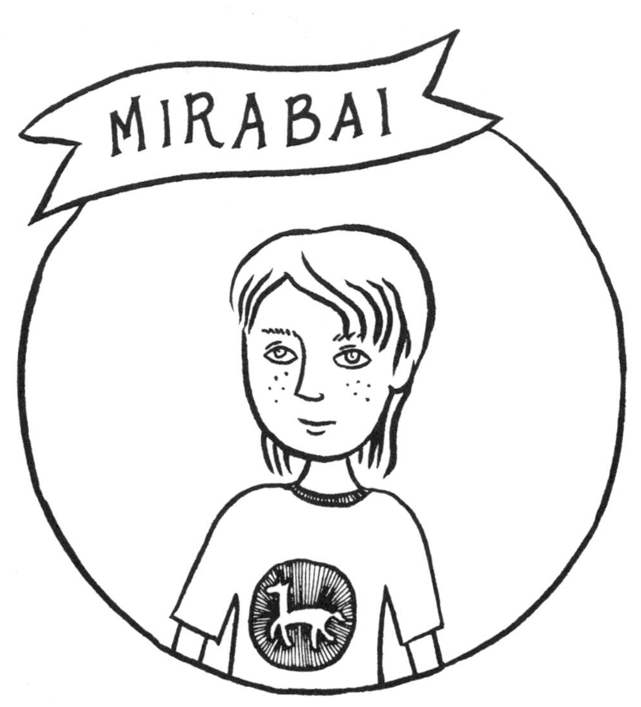
MIRABAI

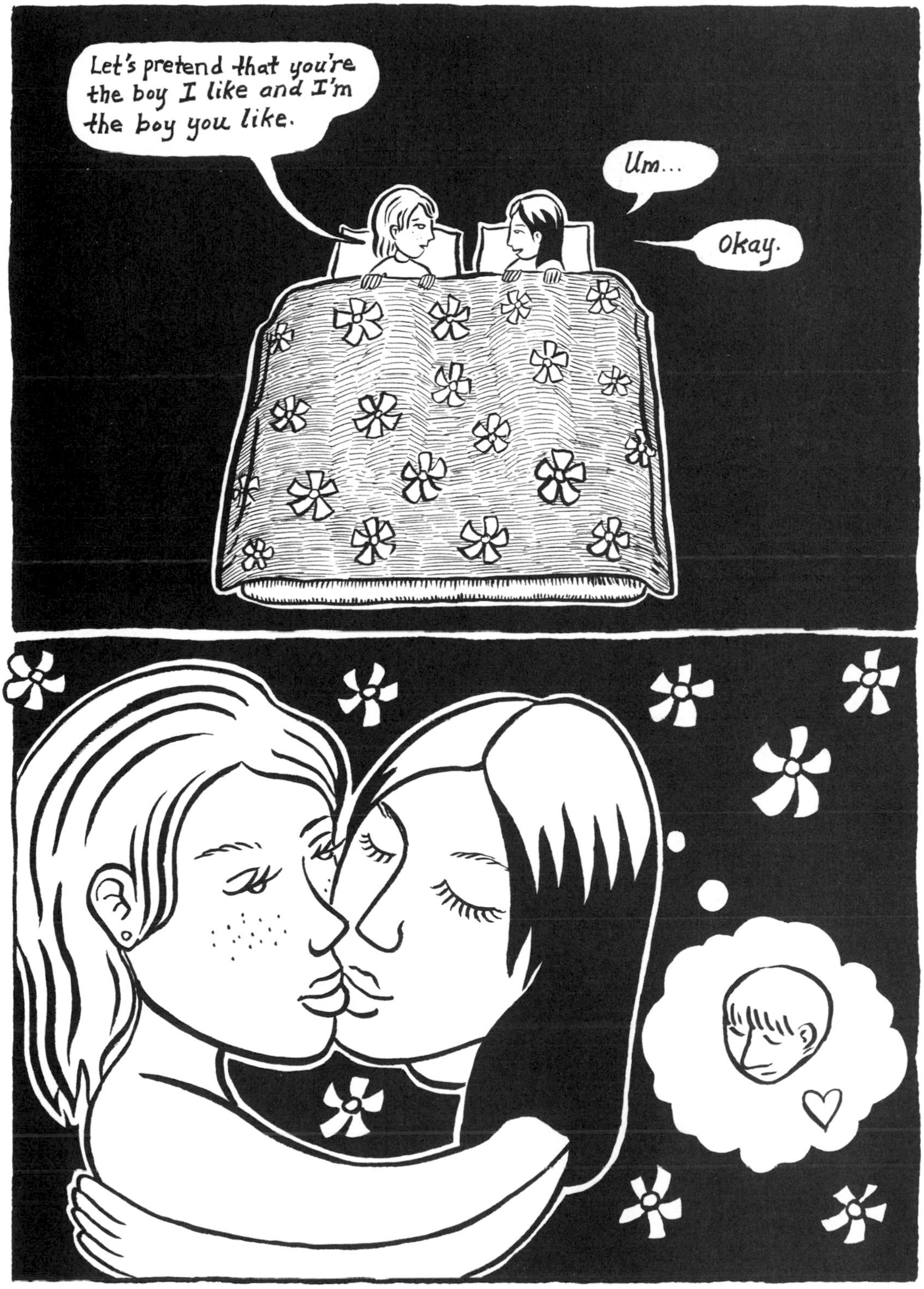

Let's pretend that you're the boy I like and I'm the boy you like.

Um...

Okay.

Call me "sir"

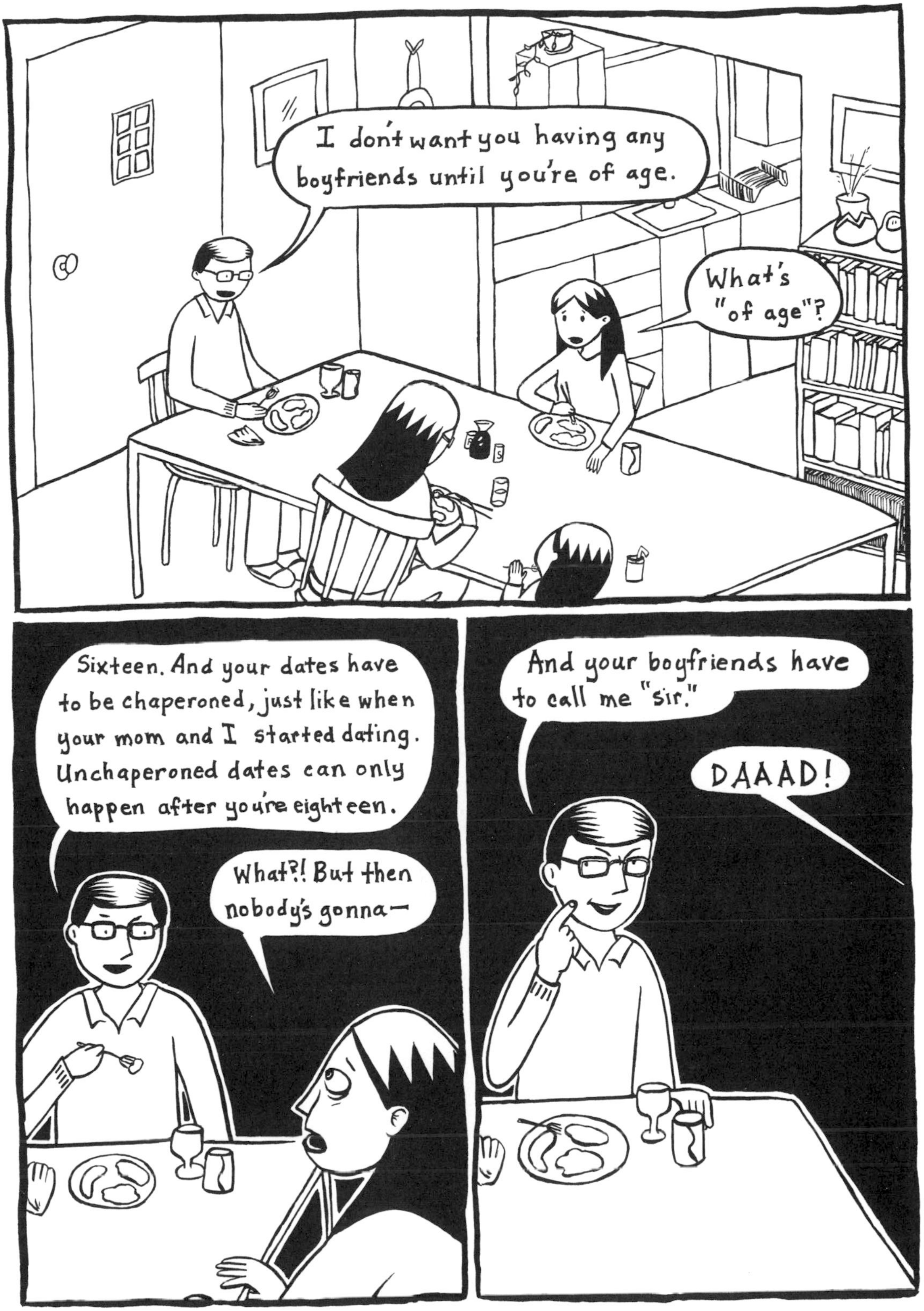

I don't want you having any boyfriends until you're of age.

What's "of age"?

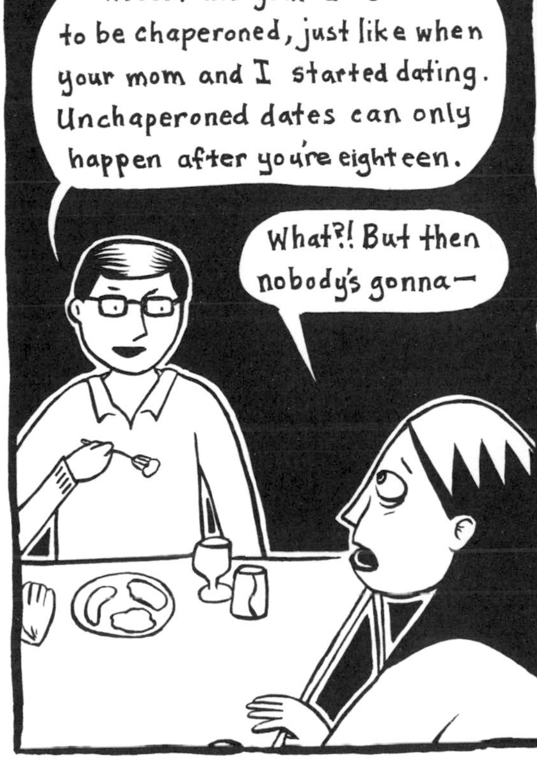

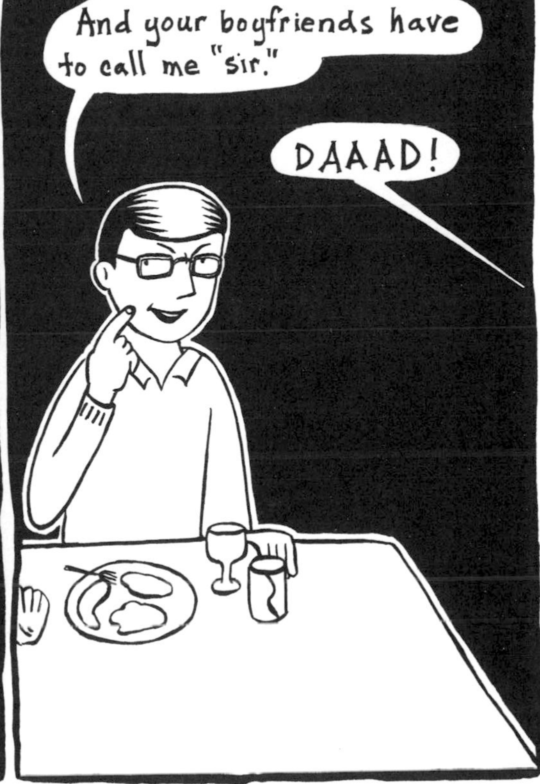

1984

ages 10 ~ 11

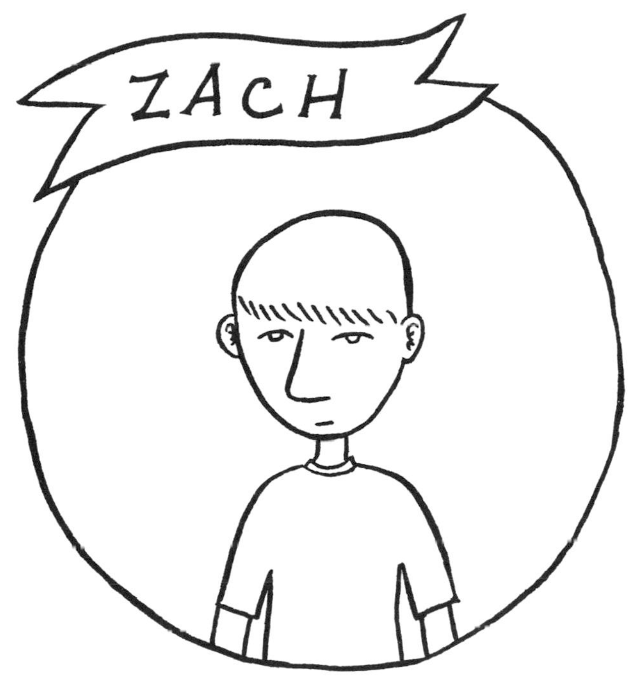
ZACH

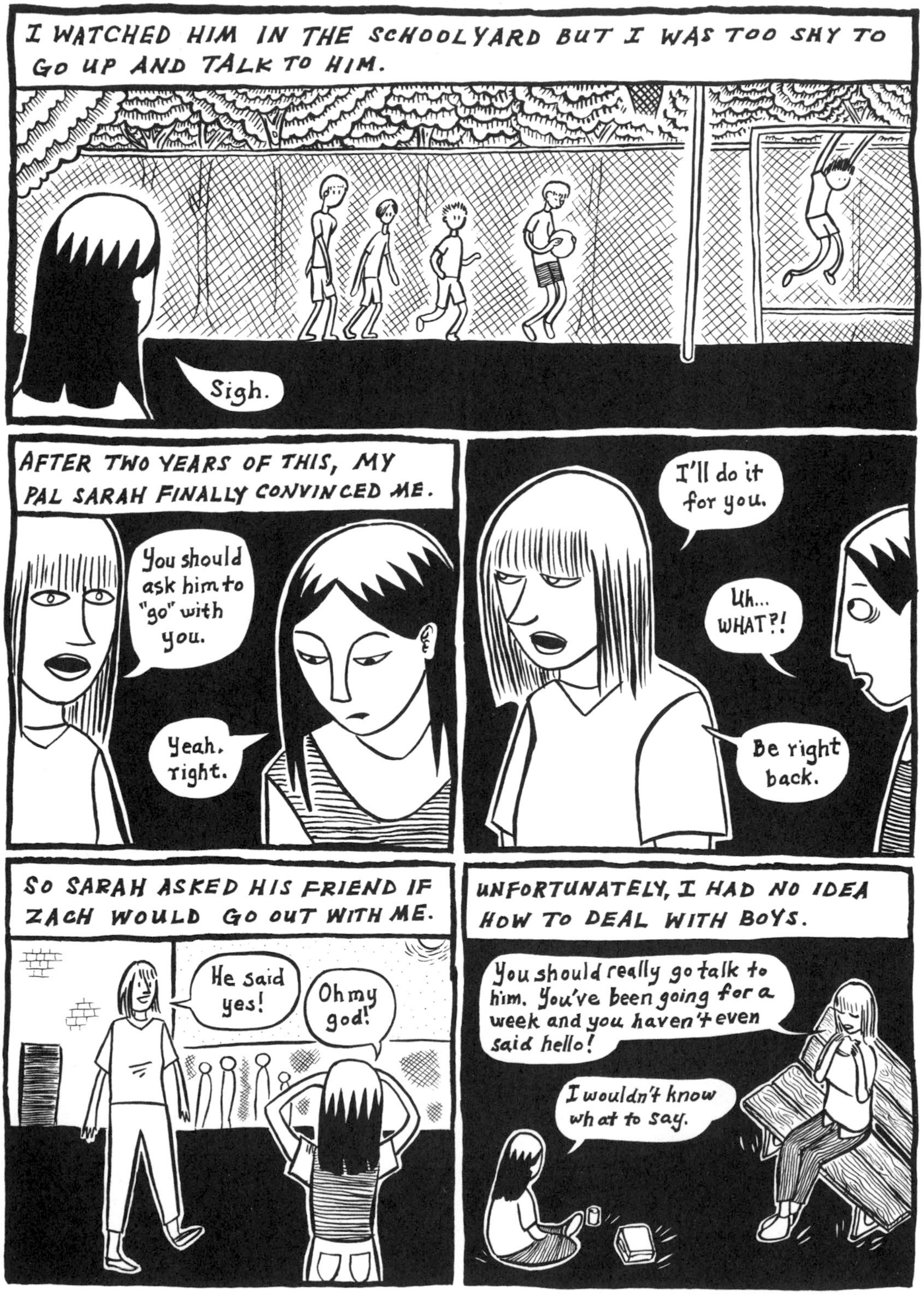

I WATCHED HIM IN THE SCHOOLYARD BUT I WAS TOO SHY TO GO UP AND TALK TO HIM.

Sigh.

AFTER TWO YEARS OF THIS, MY PAL SARAH FINALLY CONVINCED ME.

You should ask him to "go" with you.

Yeah. right.

I'll do it for you.

Uh... WHAT?!

Be right back.

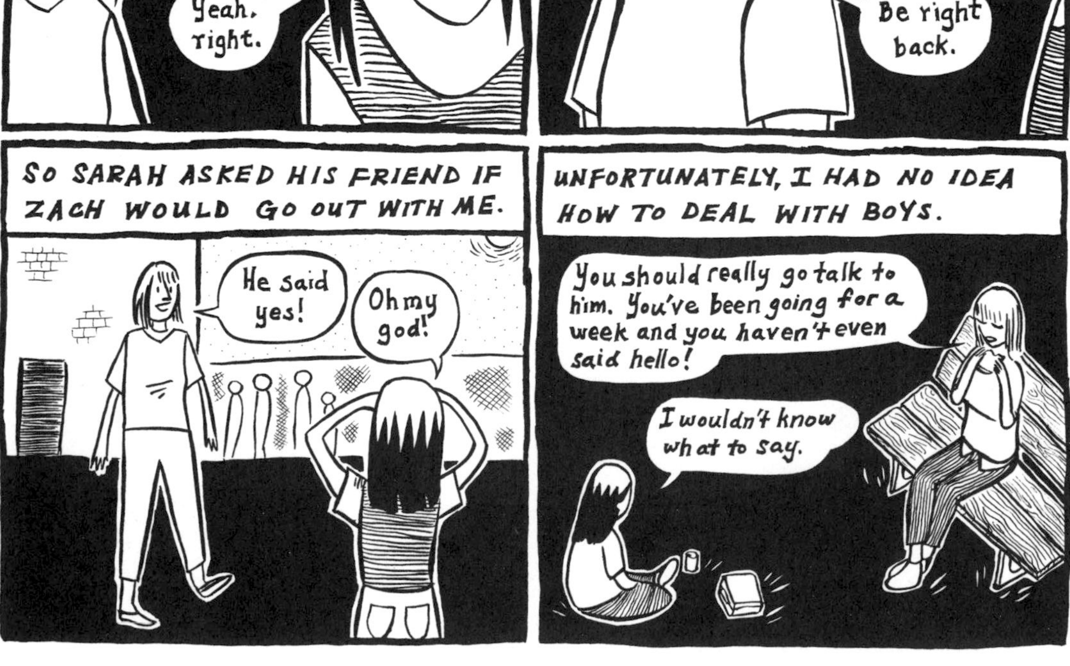

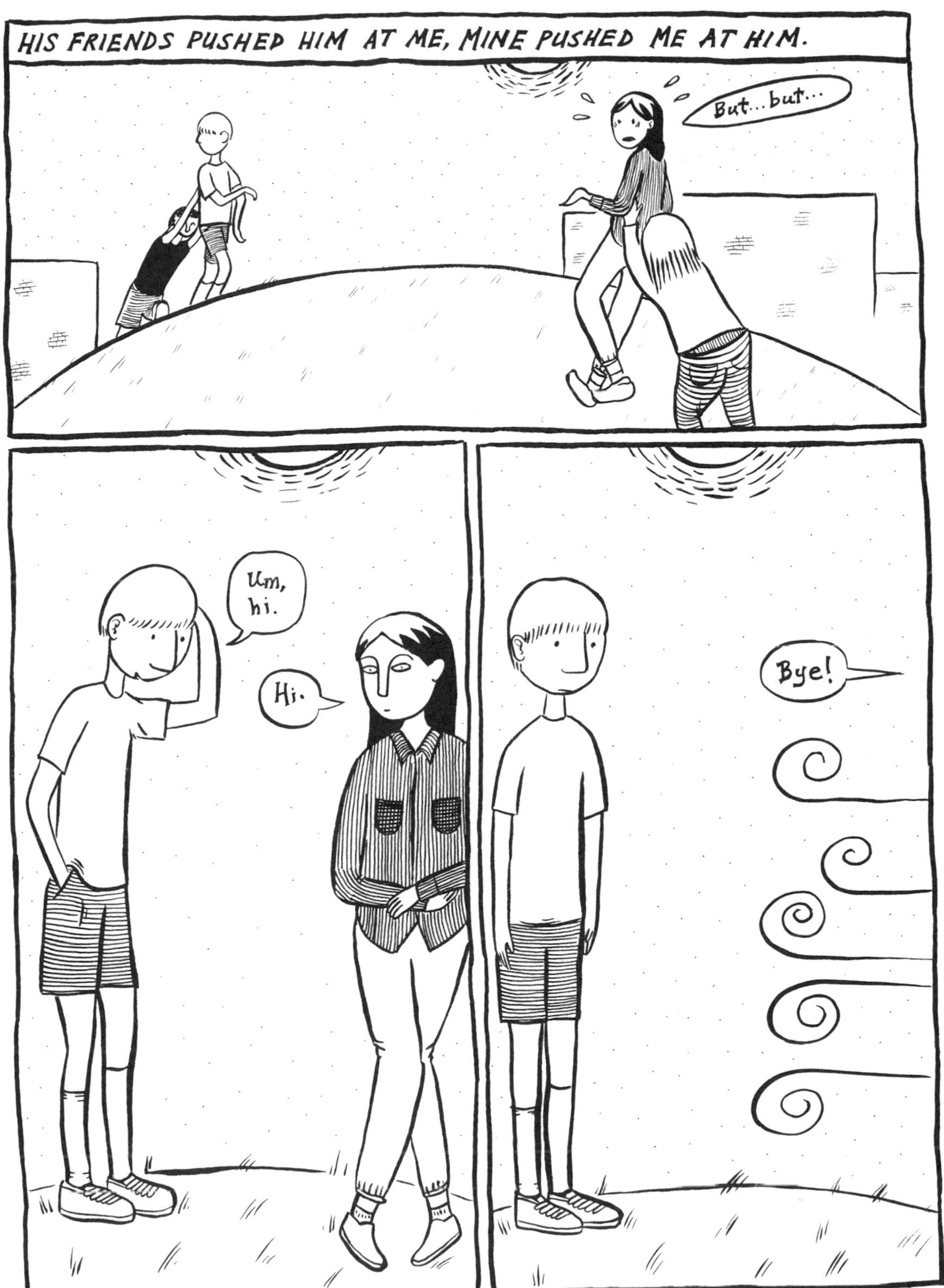
HIS FRIENDS PUSHED HIM AT ME, MINE PUSHED ME AT HIM.
But... but...
Um, hi.
Hi.
Bye!

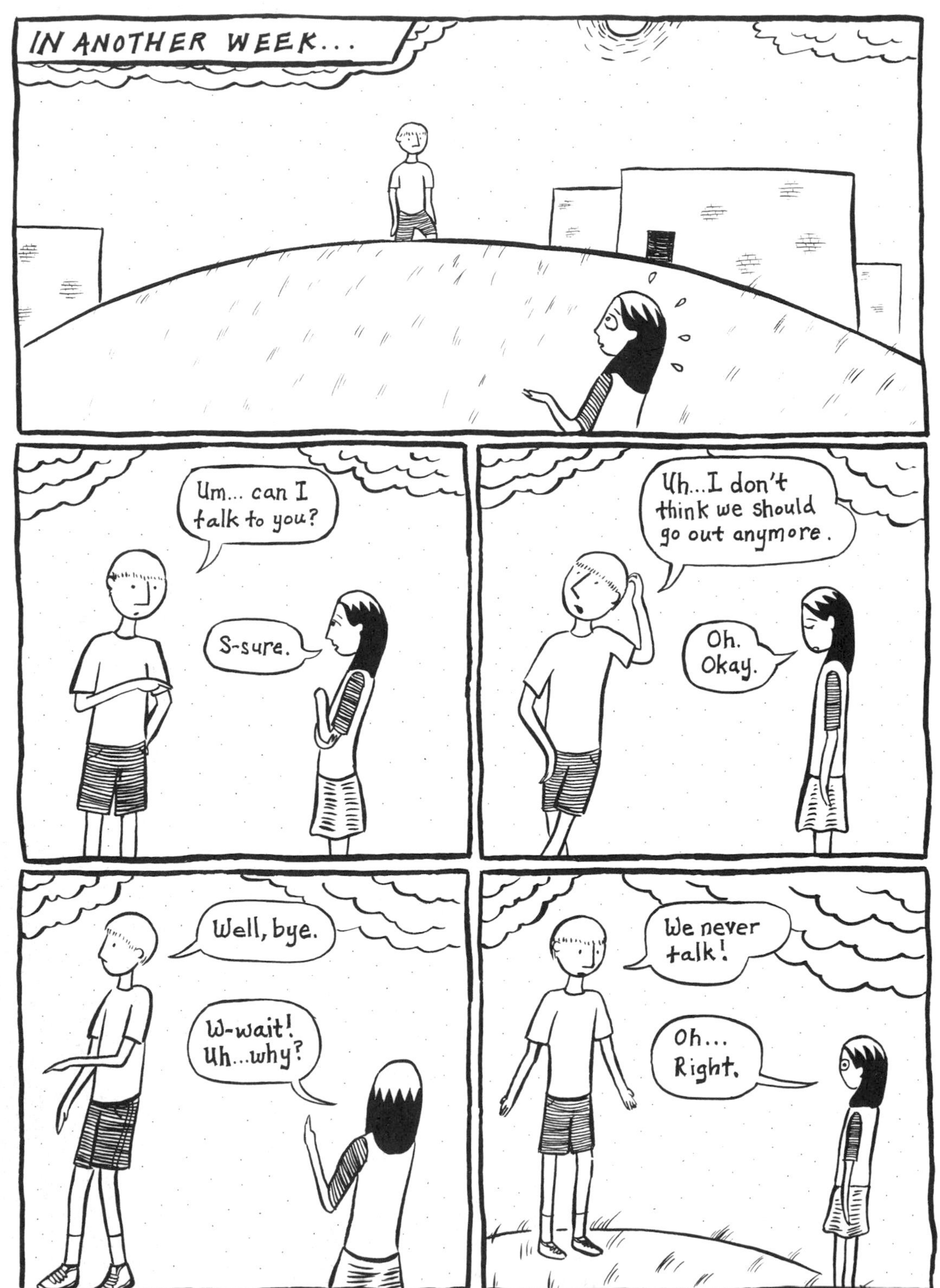
IN ANOTHER WEEK...
Um... can I talk to you?
S-sure.
Uh...I don't think we should go out anymore.
Oh. Okay.
Well, bye.
W-wait! Uh...why?
We never talk!
Oh... Right.

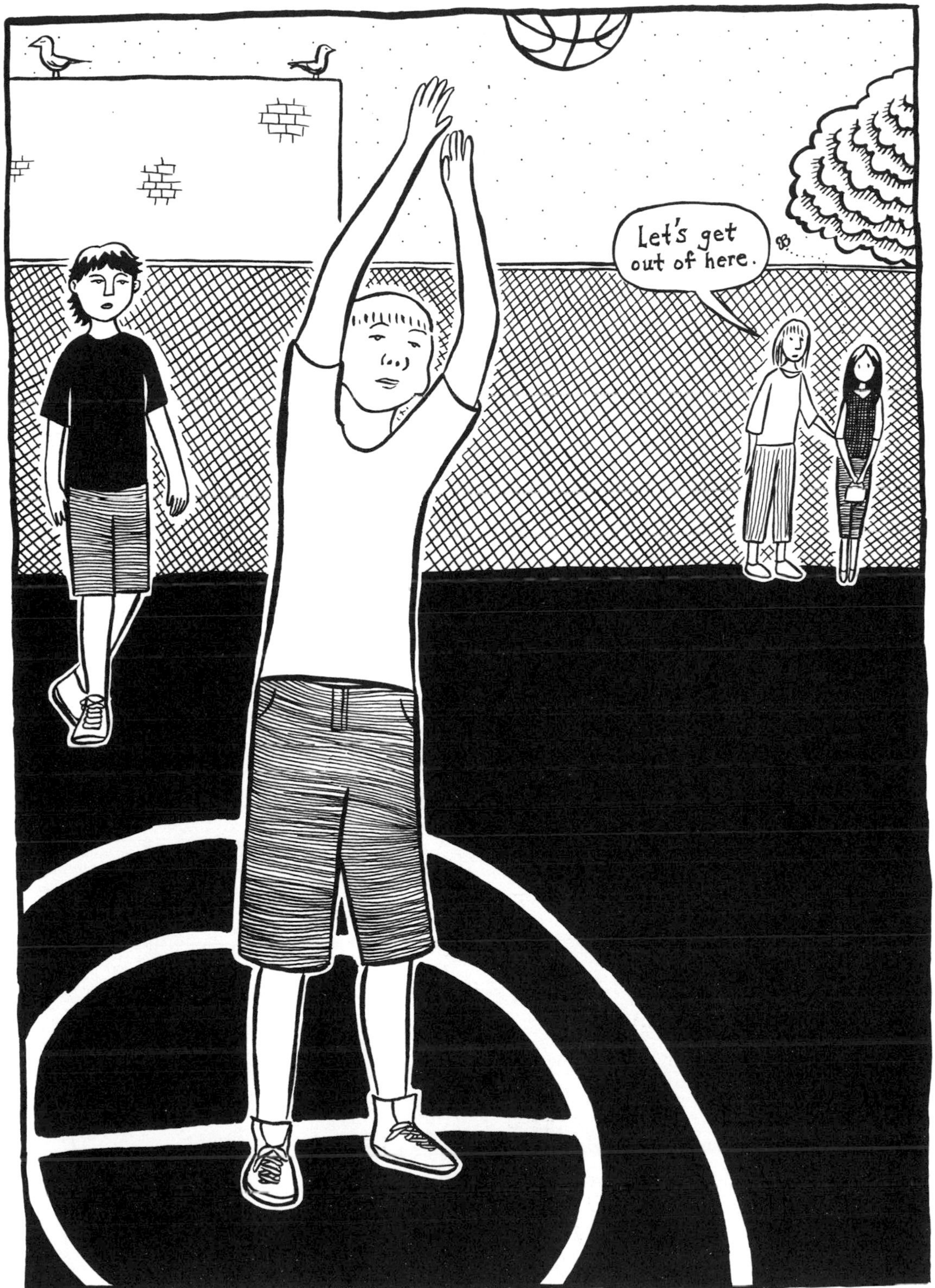
Let's get out of here.

A woman's work

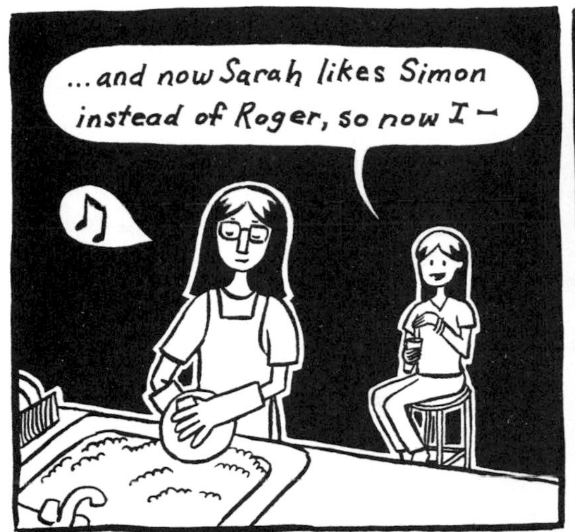
...and now Sarah likes Simon instead of Roger, so now I—
♪
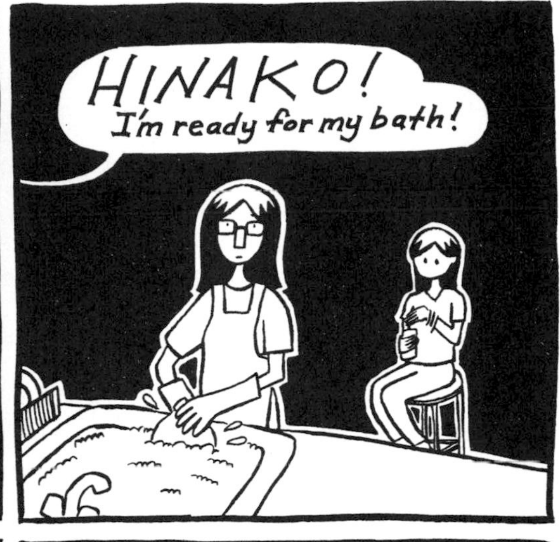
HINAKO! I'm ready for my bath!
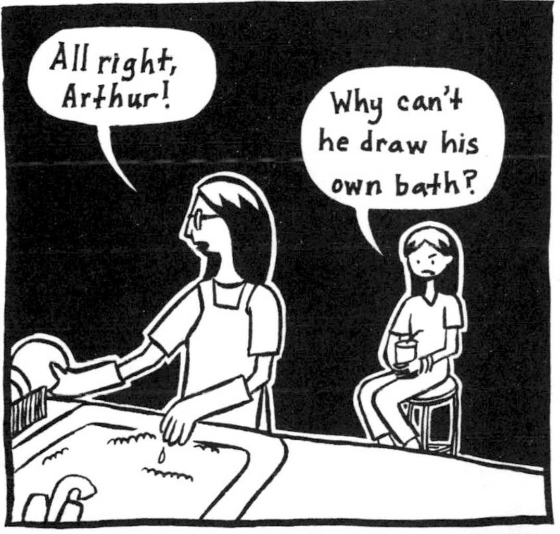
All right, Arthur!
Why can't he draw his own bath?
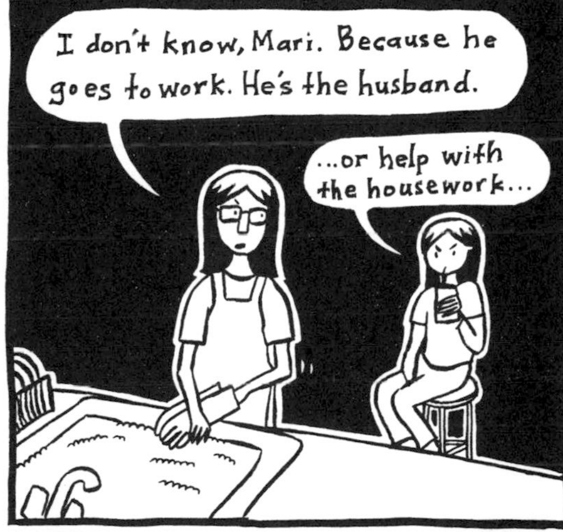
I don't know, Mari. Because he goes to work. He's the husband.
...or help with the housework...
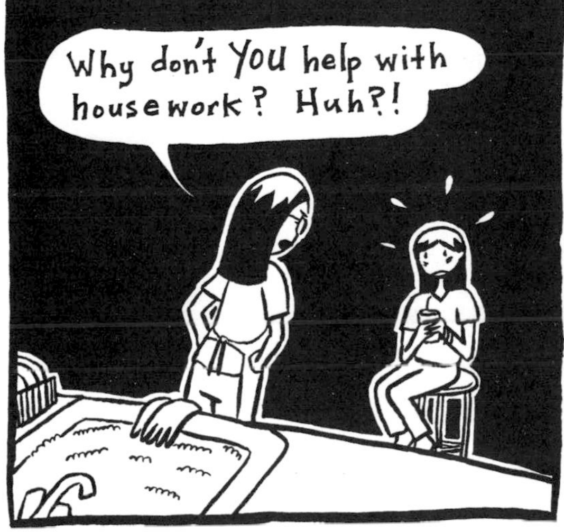
Why don't YOU help with housework? Huh?!
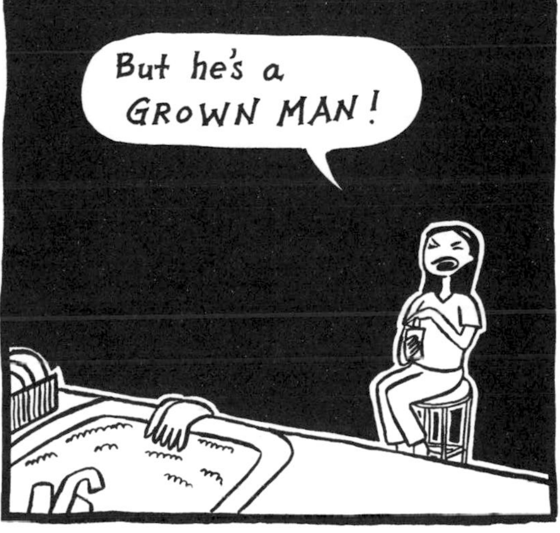
But he's a GROWN MAN!

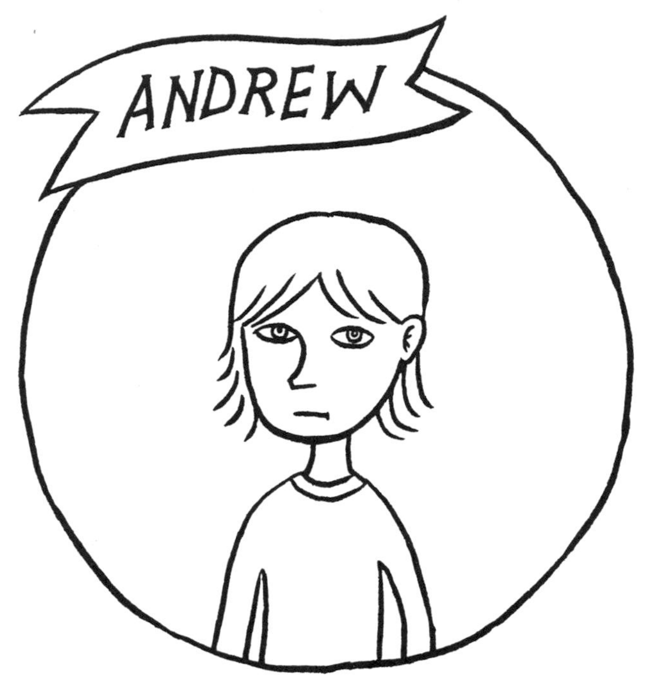
ANDREW

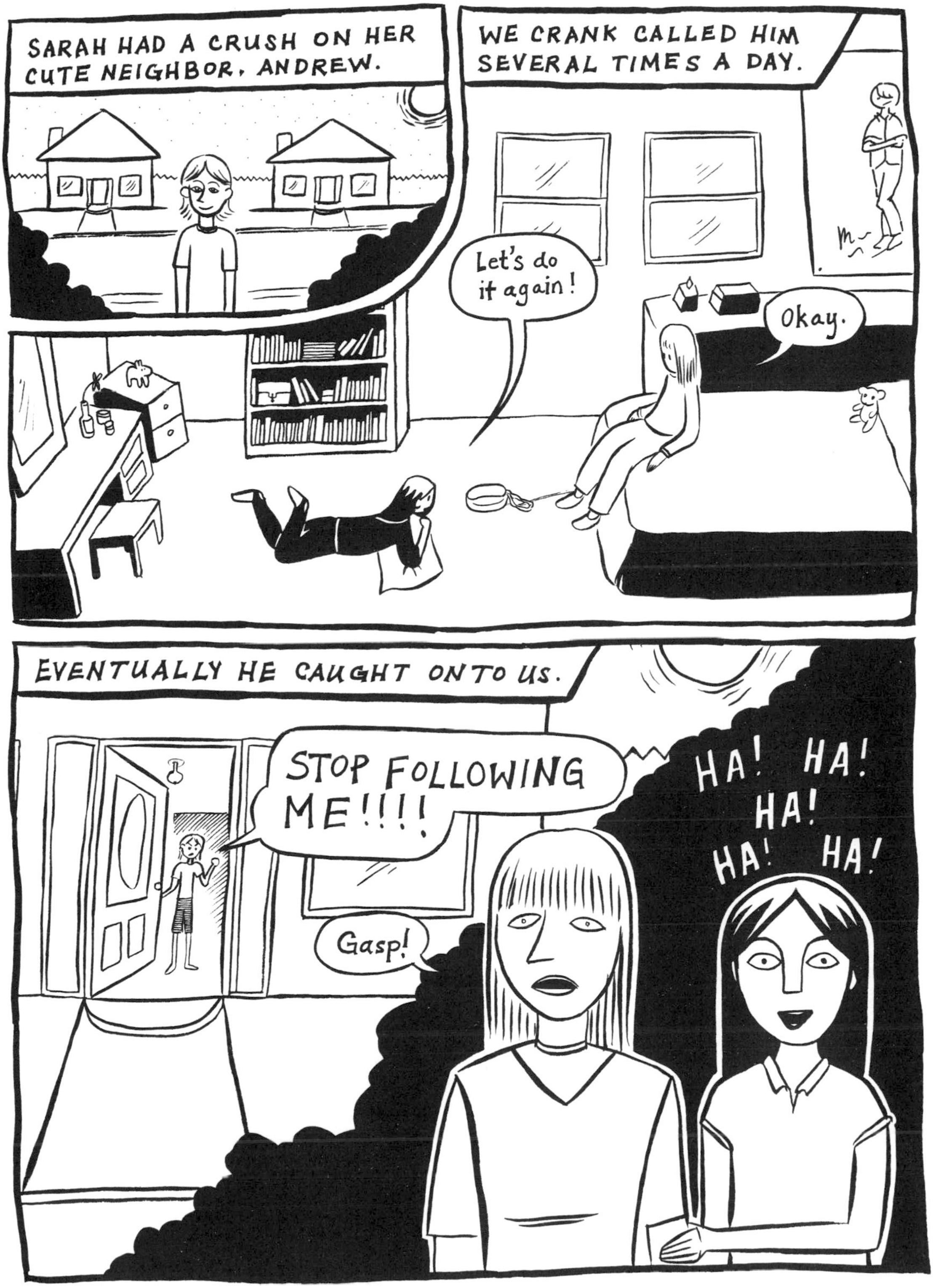

SARAH HAD A CRUSH ON HER CUTE NEIGHBOR, ANDREW.

WE CRANK CALLED HIM SEVERAL TIMES A DAY.

Let's do it again!

Okay.

EVENTUALLY HE CAUGHT ONTO US.

STOP FOLLOWING ME!!!!

HA! HA! HA! HA! HA!

Gasp!

Girl talk

Featuring Sarah

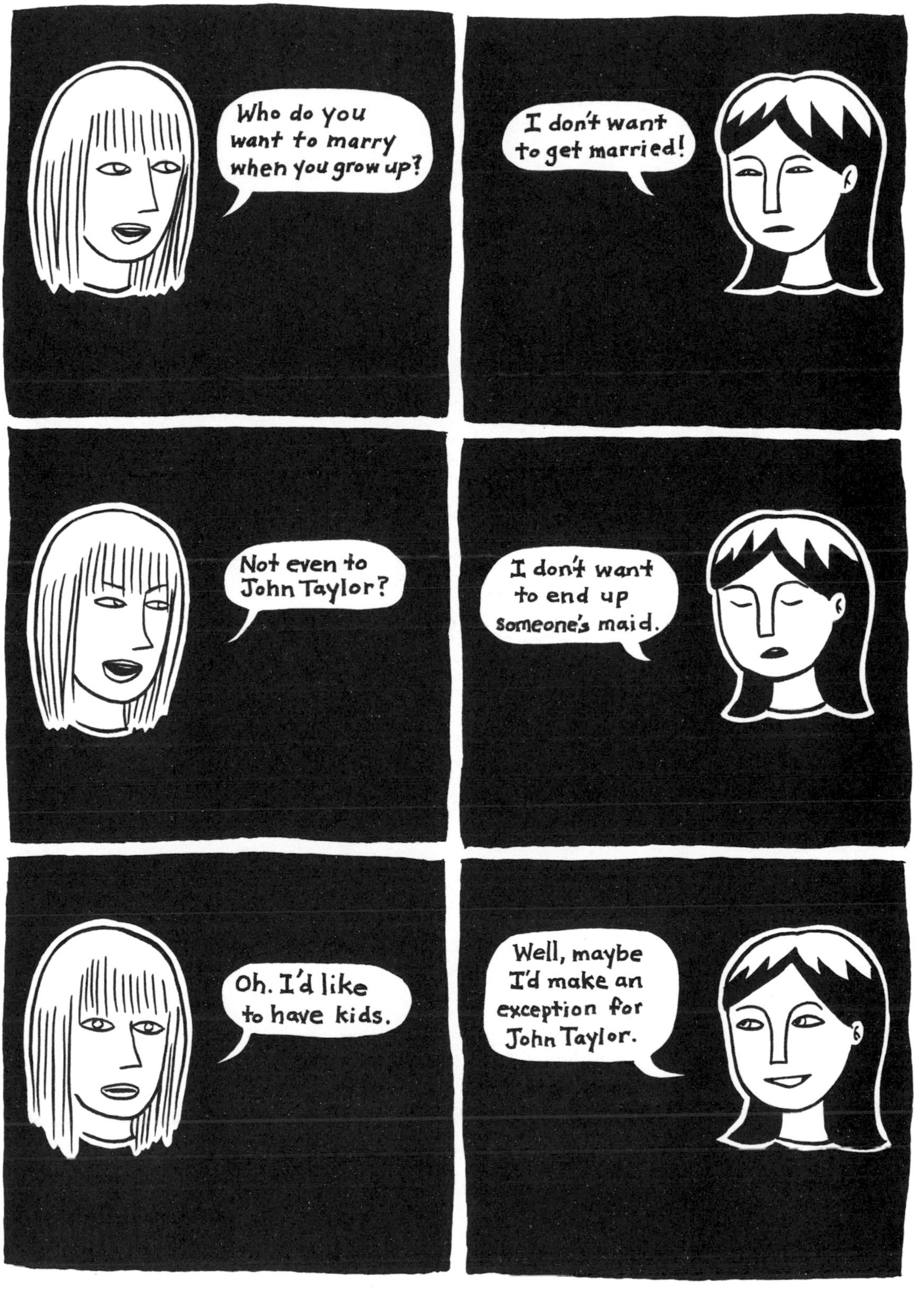

Who do you want to marry when you grow up?
I don't want to get married!
Not even to John Taylor?
I don't want to end up someone's maid.
Oh. I'd like to have kids.
Well, maybe I'd make an exception for John Taylor.

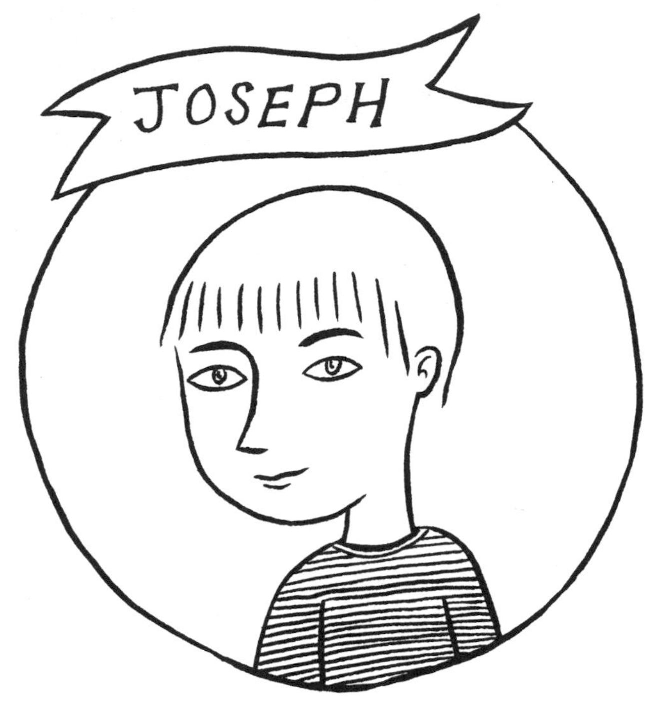
JOSEPH

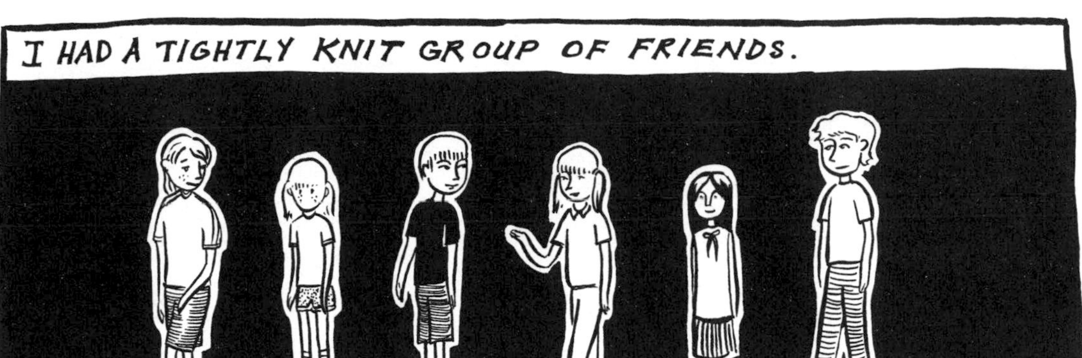

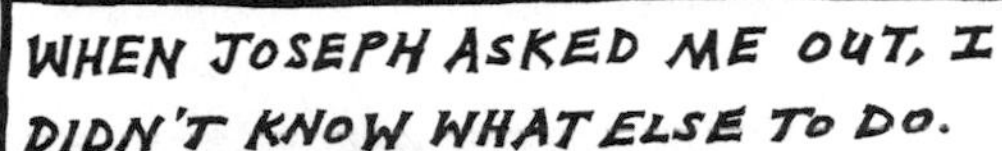

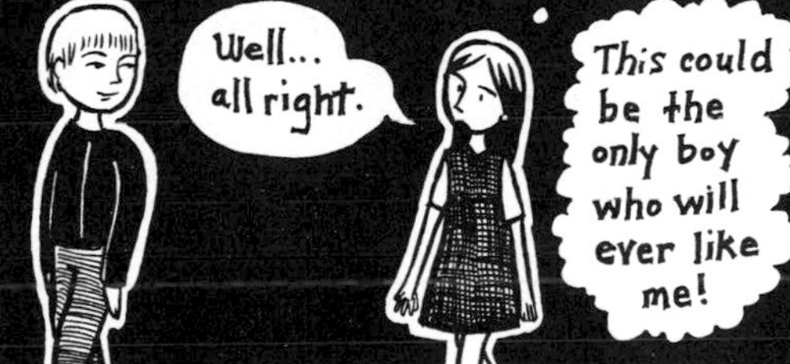

NOT A LOT CHANGED BETWEEN US. WE STILL HUNG OUT WITH THE GANG EVERY DAY.

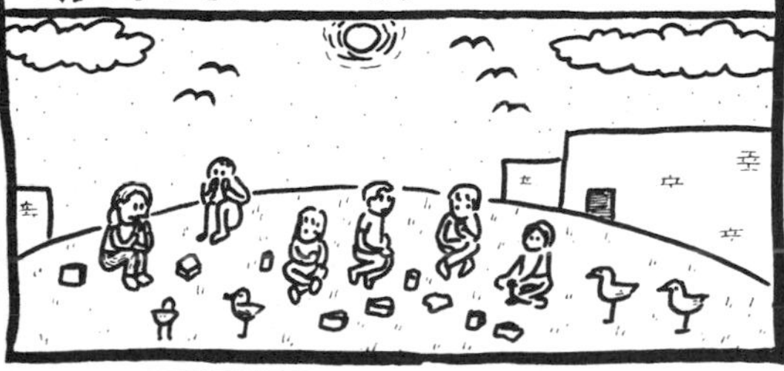

ONLY NOW HE DID ROMANTIC THINGS FOR ME.

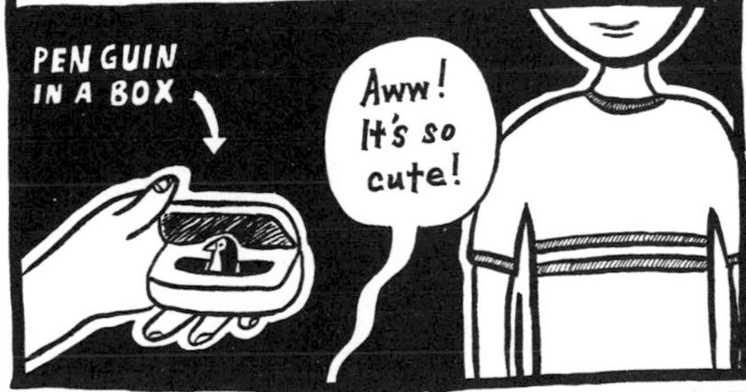

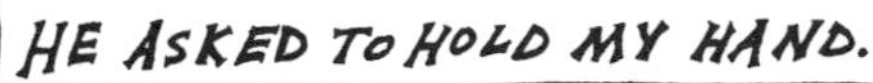

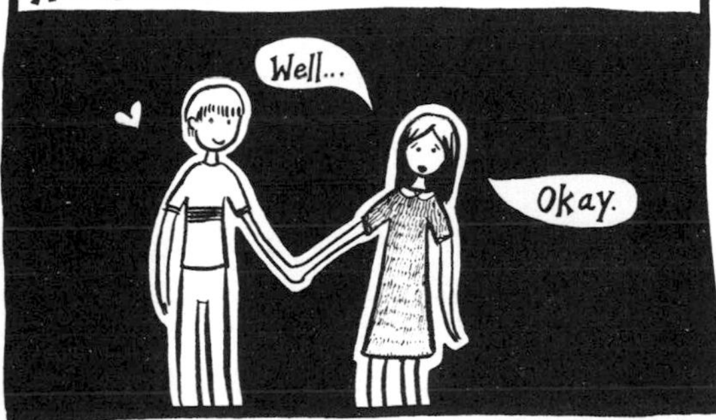

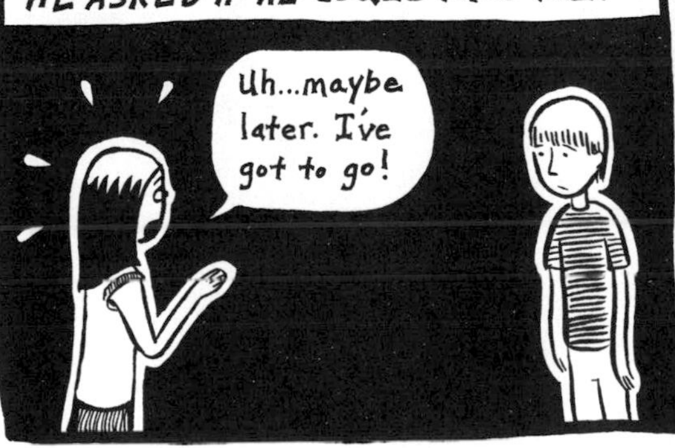

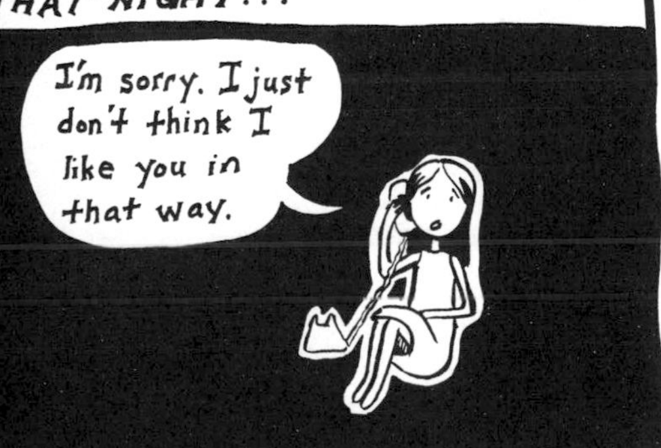

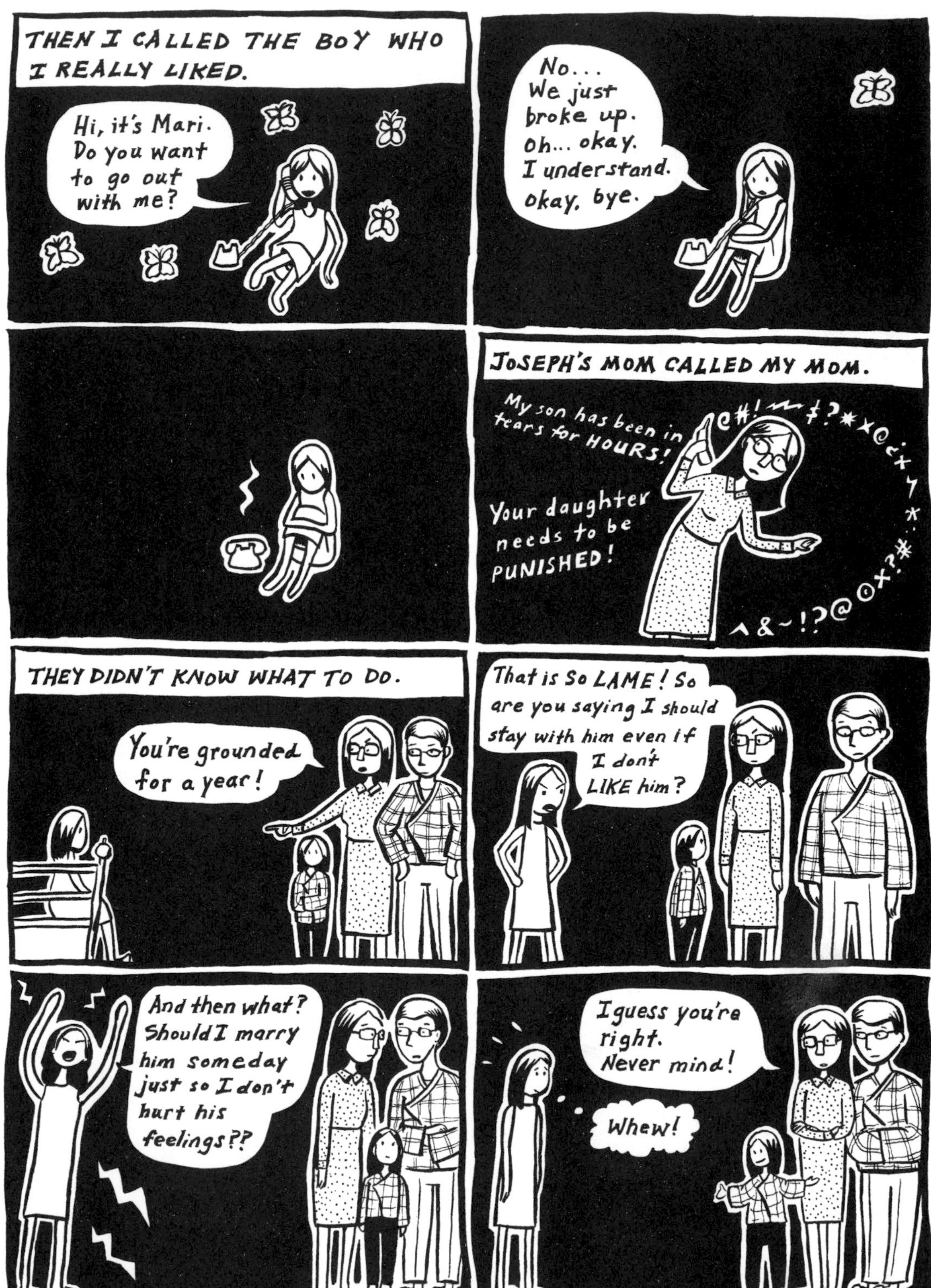
THEN I CALLED THE BOY WHO I REALLY LIKED.
Hi, it's Mari. Do you want to go out with me?
No... We just broke up. Oh... okay. I understand. okay, bye.
JOSEPH'S MOM CALLED MY MOM.
My son has been in tears for HOURS!
Your daughter needs to be PUNISHED!
THEY DIDN'T KNOW WHAT TO DO.
You're grounded for a year!
That is So LAME! So are you saying I should stay with him even if I don't LIKE him?
And then what? Should I marry him someday just so I don't hurt his feelings??
I guess you're right. Never mind!
Whew!

1985
age 12

More girl talk

Featuring Sarah

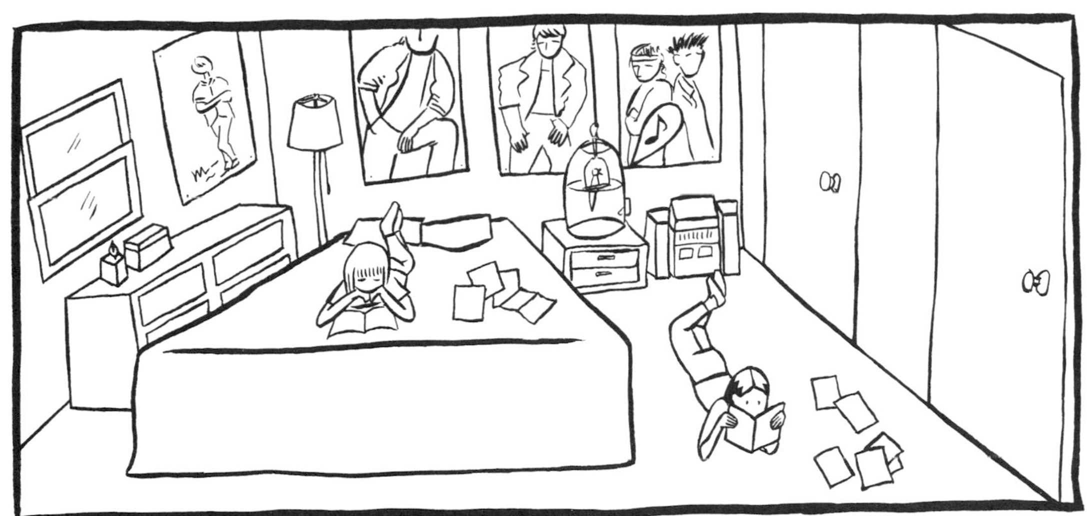

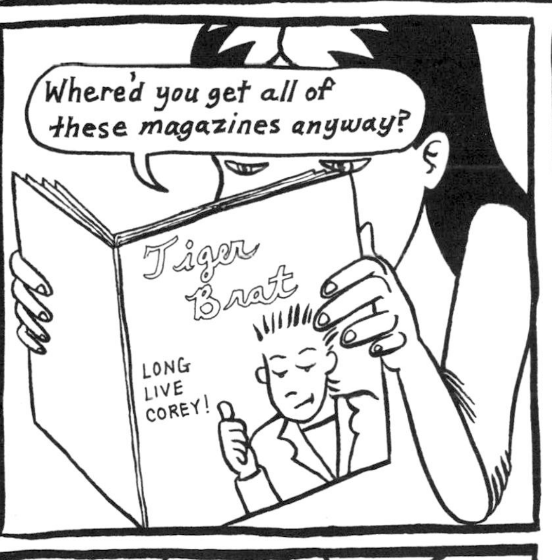
Where'd you get all of these magazines anyway?
Tiger Brat
LONG LIVE COREY!

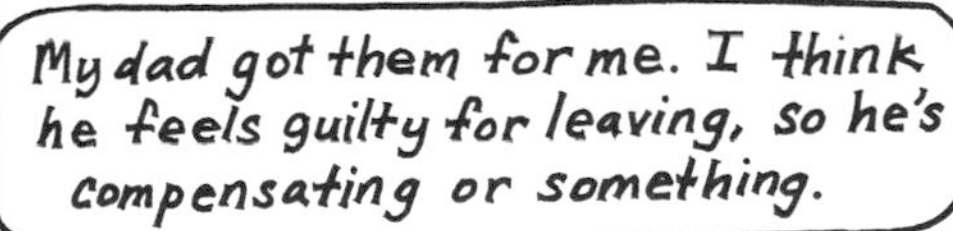
My dad got them for me. I think he feels guilty for leaving, so he's compensating or something.

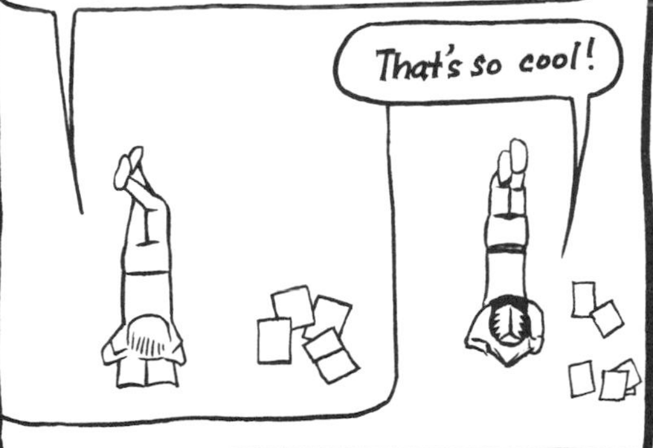
That's so cool!

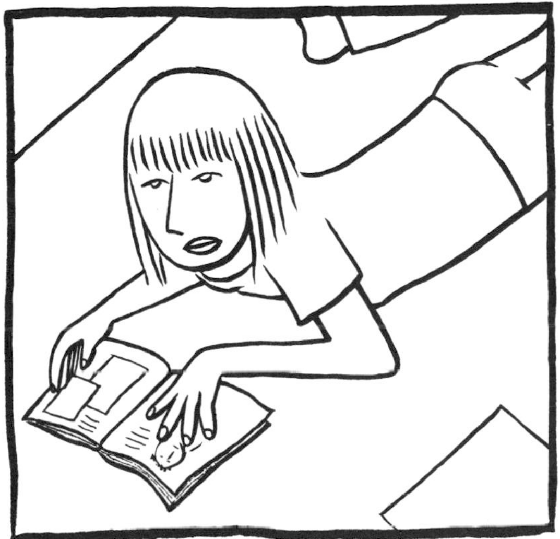

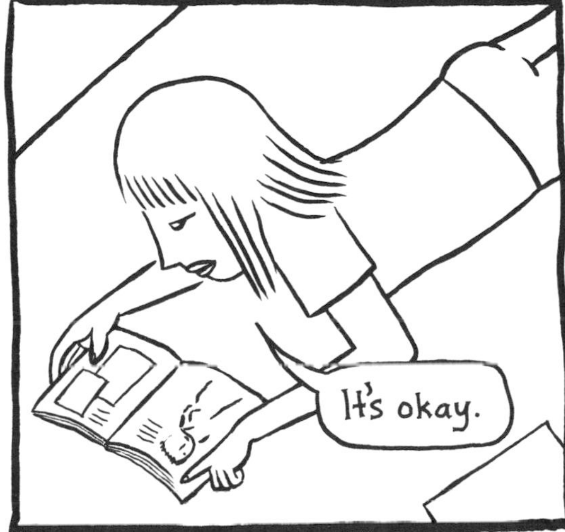
It's okay.

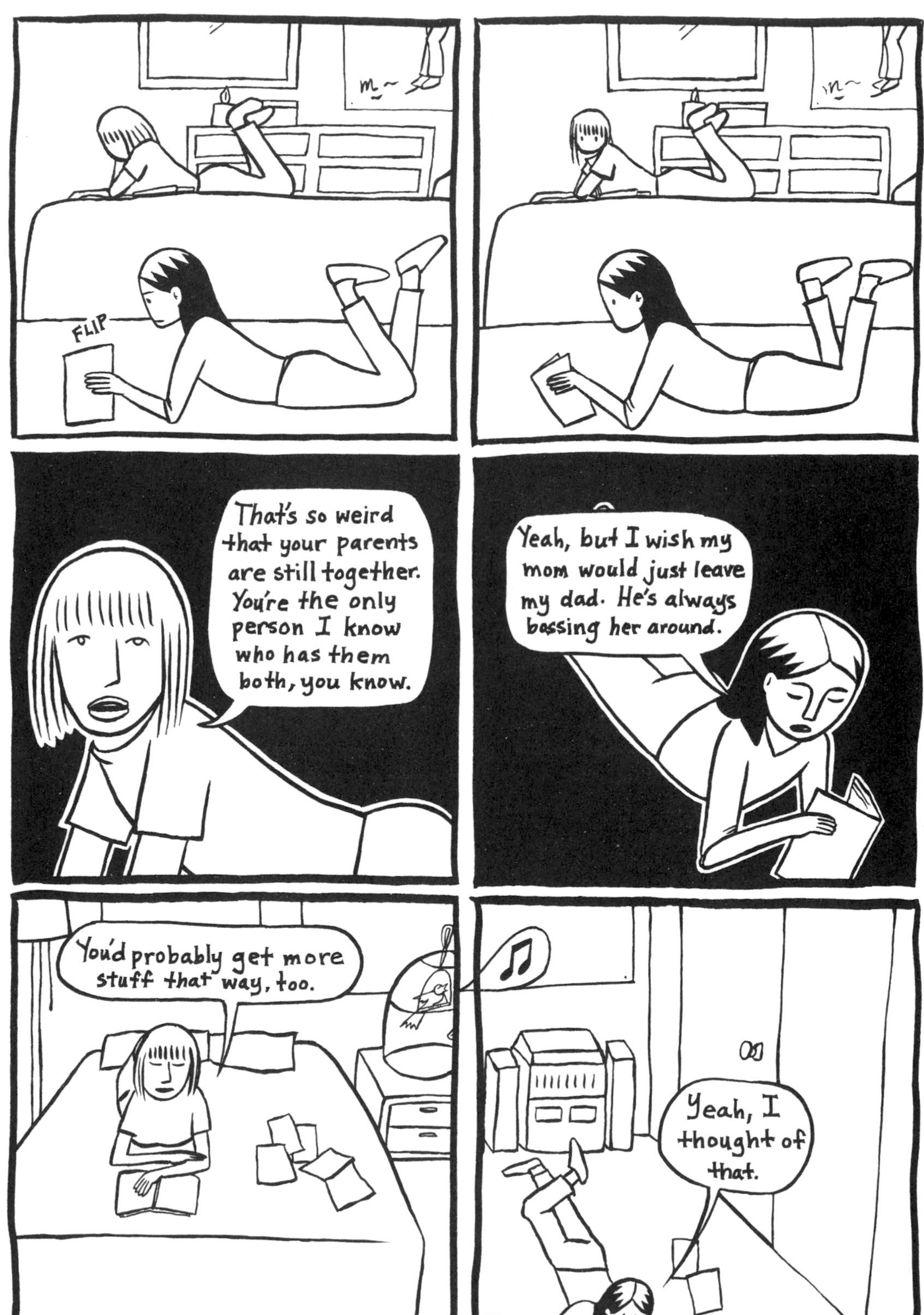
FLIP
That's so weird that your parents are still together. You're the only person I know who has them both, you know.
Yeah, but I wish my mom would just leave my dad. He's always bossing her around.
You'd probably get more stuff that way, too.
Yeah, I thought of that.

1986

ages 12 ~ 13

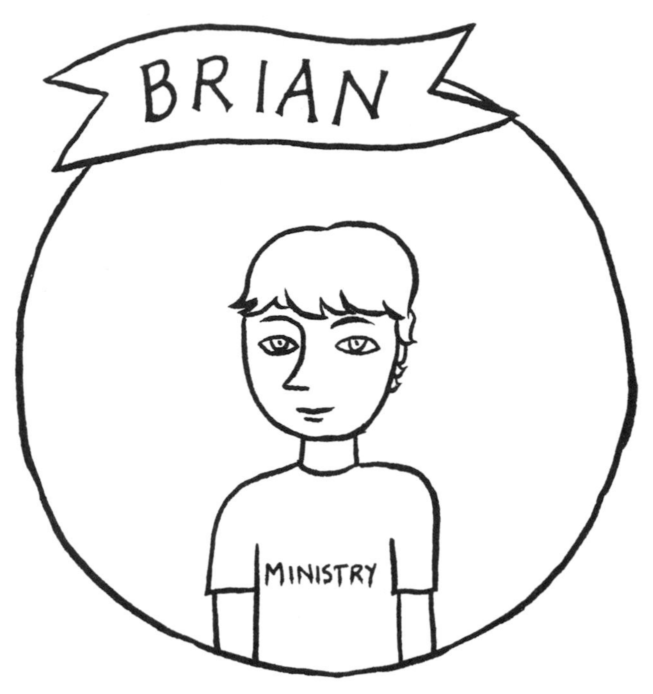
BRIAN
MINISTRY

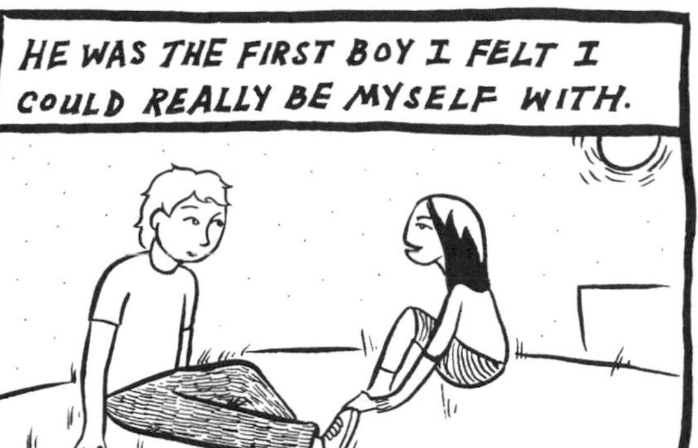
HE WAS THE FIRST BOY I FELT I COULD REALLY BE MYSELF WITH.

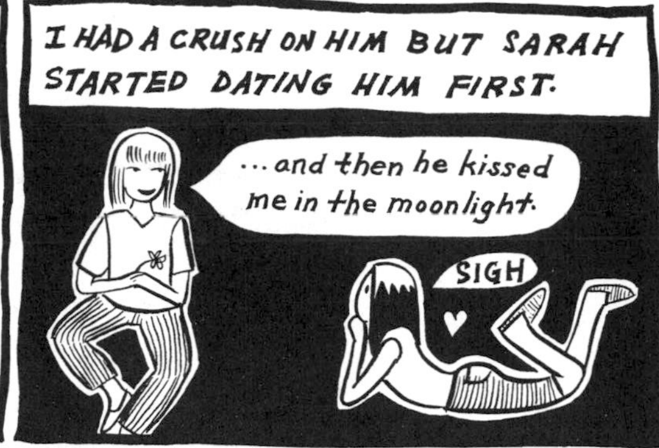
I HAD A CRUSH ON HIM BUT SARAH STARTED DATING HIM FIRST.
...and then he kissed me in the moonlight.
SIGH

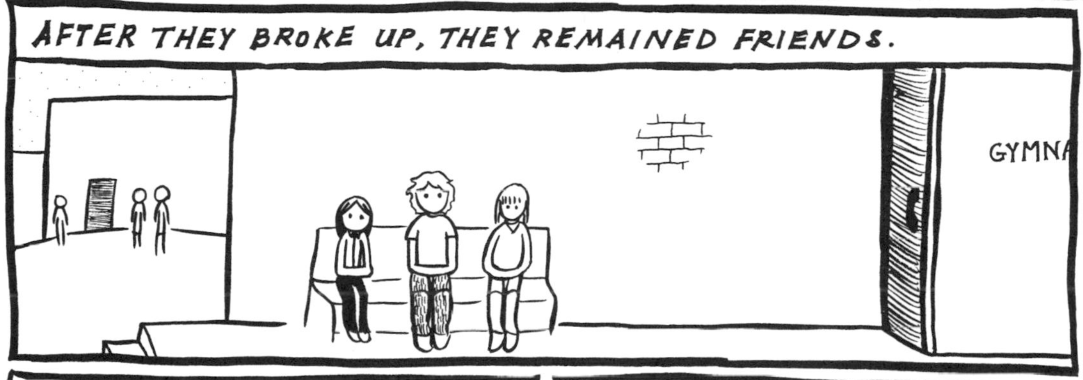
AFTER THEY BROKE UP, THEY REMAINED FRIENDS.
GYMNA

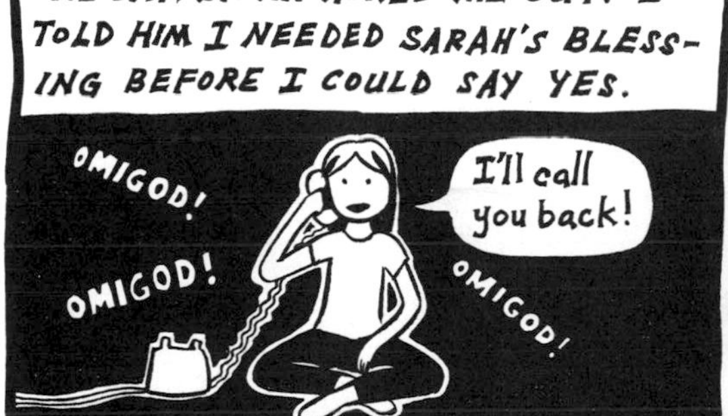
ONE DAY, BRIAN ASKED ME OUT. I TOLD HIM I NEEDED SARAH'S BLESS-ING BEFORE I COULD SAY YES.
OMIGOD!
OMIGOD!
I'll call you back!
OMIGOD!

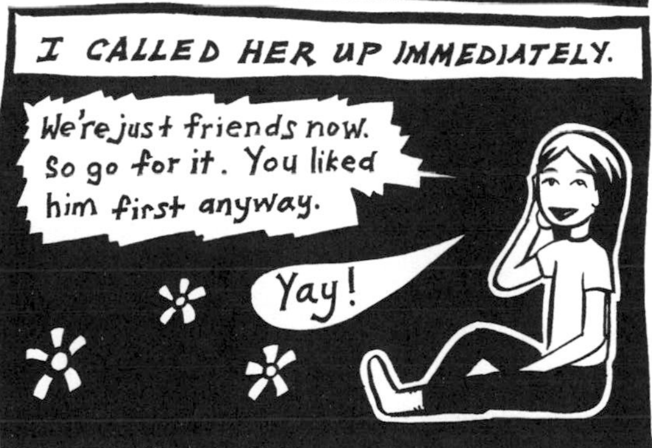
I CALLED HER UP IMMEDIATELY.
We're just friends now. So go for it. You liked him first anyway.
Yay!

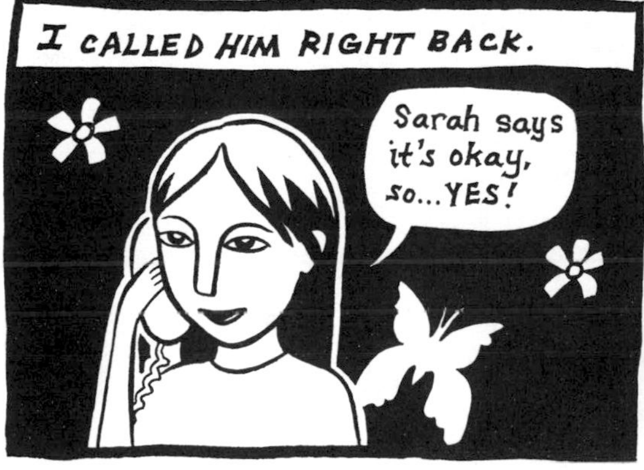
I CALLED HIM RIGHT BACK.
Sarah says it's okay, so...YES!

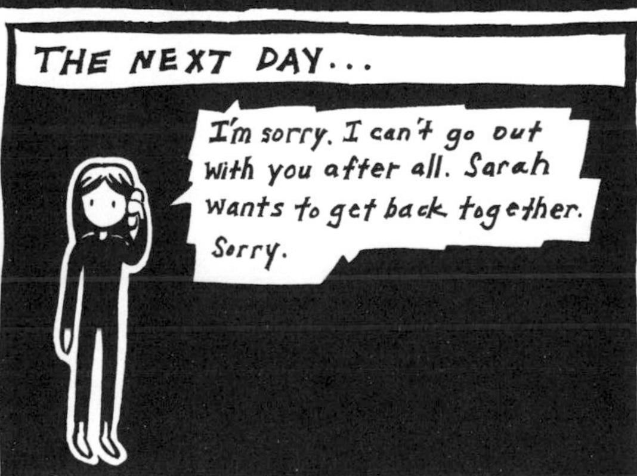
THE NEXT DAY...
I'm sorry. I can't go out with you after all. Sarah wants to get back together. Sorry.

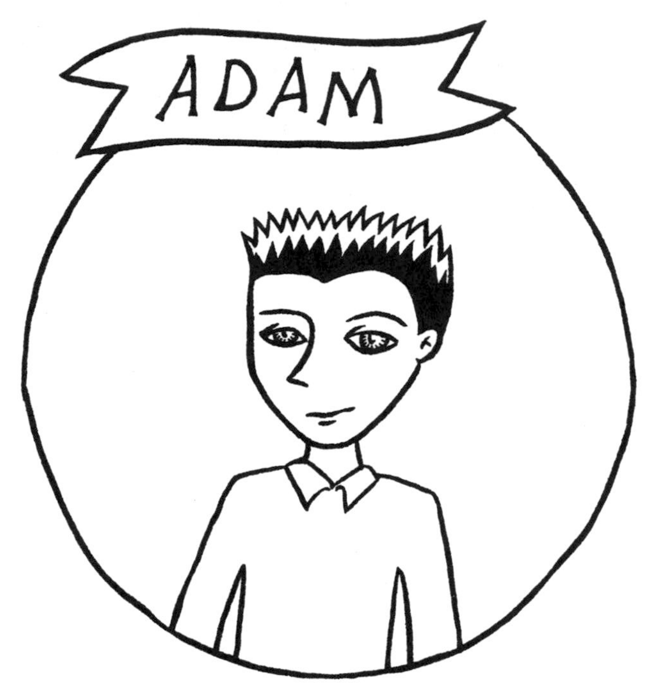
ADAM

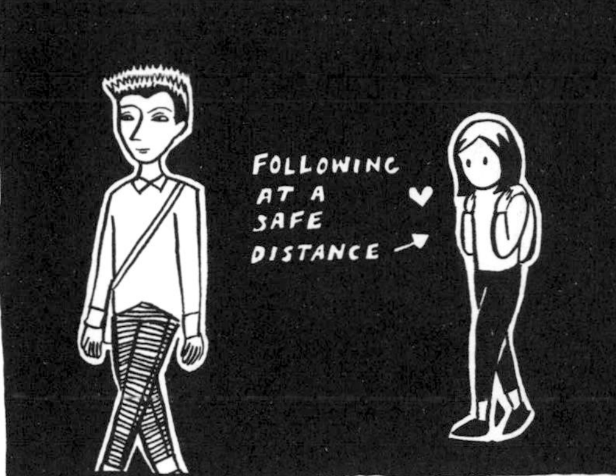
HE WAS THE FIRST BOY I'D MET WHO HAD A SENSE OF STYLE.
FOLLOWING AT A SAFE DISTANCE

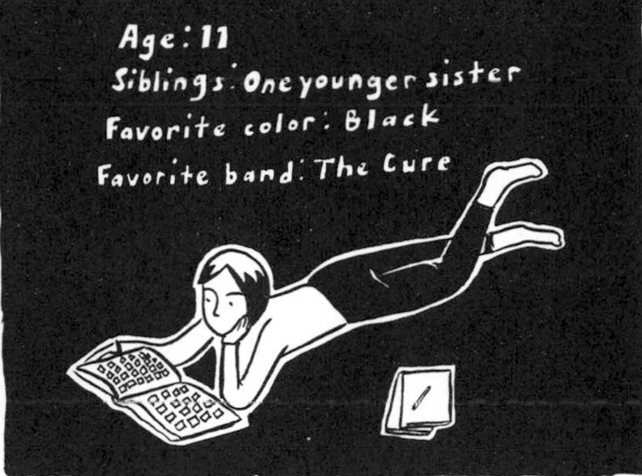
I OBSESSED OVER HIM IN TIGER BEAT STALKER FASHION.
Age: 11
Siblings: One younger sister
Favorite color: Black
Favorite band: The Cure

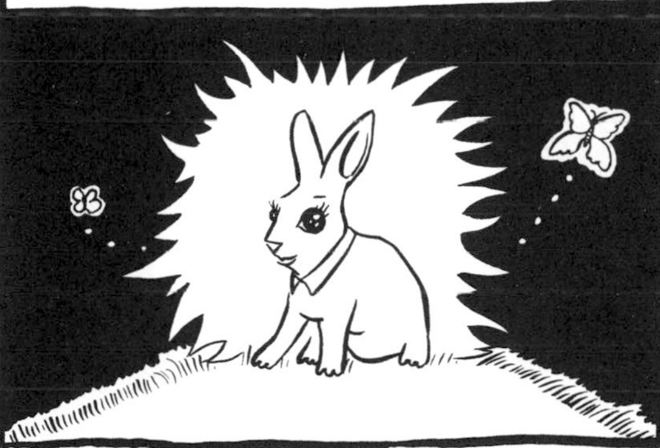
MY NICKNAME FOR HIM WAS FRITH, THE RABBITS' GOD IN THE BOOK WATERSHIP DOWN.

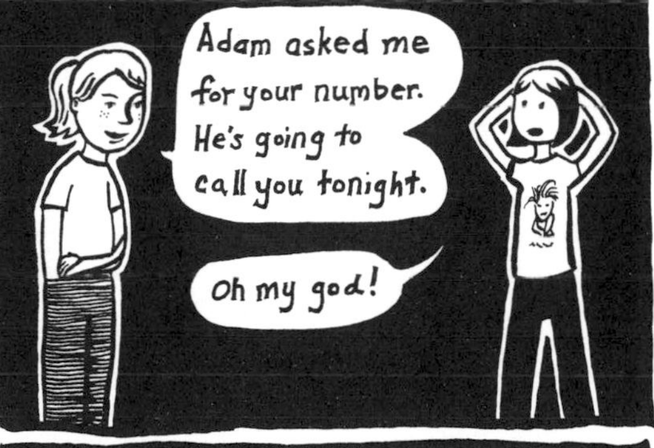
AFTER A FULL YEAR OF CRUSHING ON HIM, SOMEONE MUST HAVE TOLD HIM I LIKED HIM.
Adam asked me for your number. He's going to call you tonight.
Oh my god!

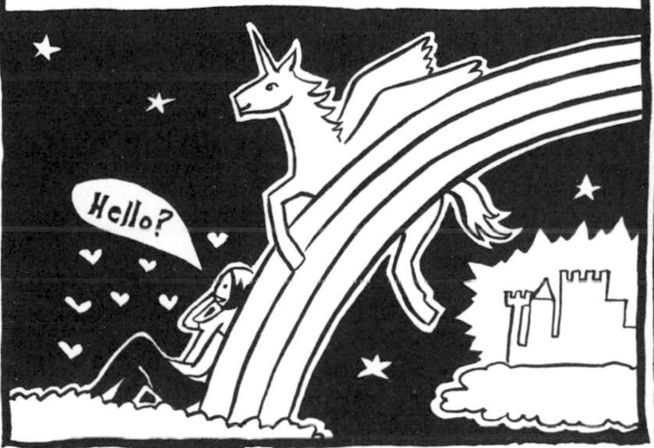
I DON'T REMEMBER WHAT WAS SAID WHEN HE CALLED BUT WHEN I GOT OFF THE PHONE I WAS OVER THE MOON.
Hello?

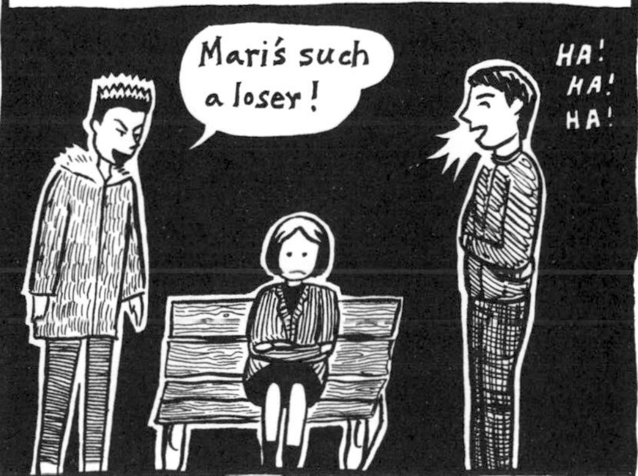
I GUESS HE DIDN'T THINK IT WENT SO WELL, BECAUSE THE NEXT DAY...
Mari's such a loser!
HA! HA! HA!

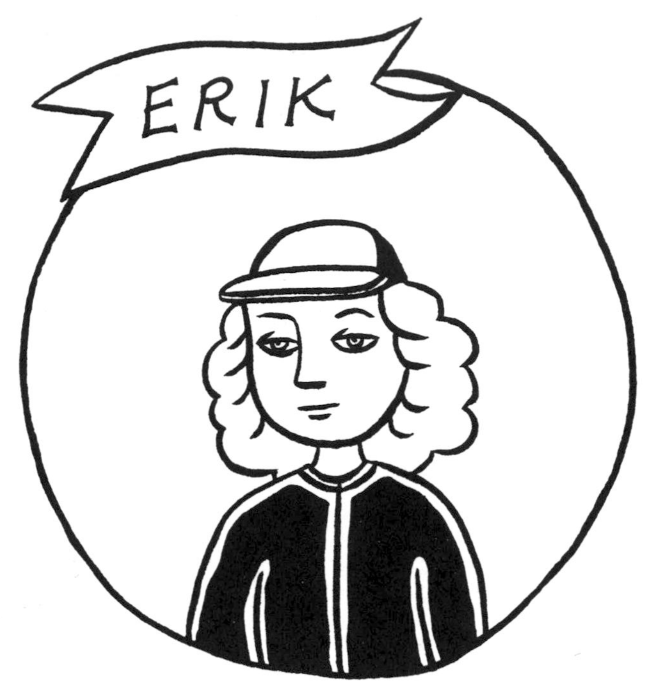
ERIK

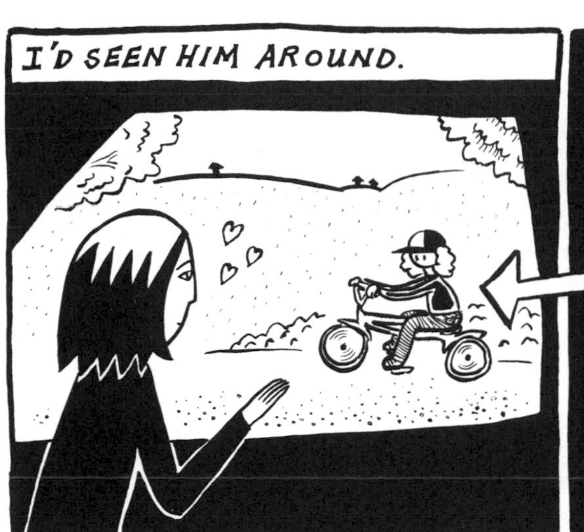
I'D SEEN HIM AROUND.

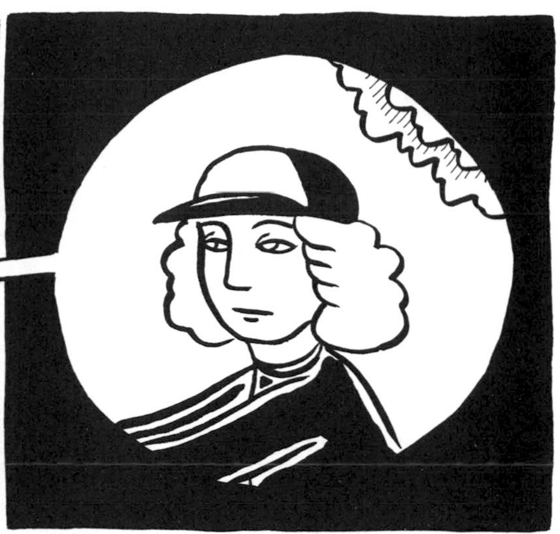

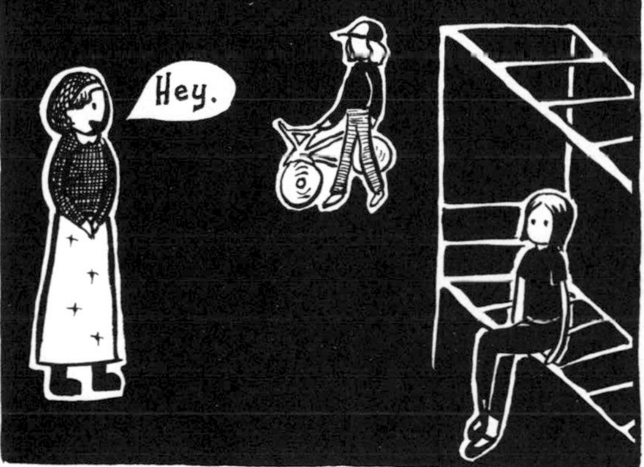
ONE DAY I WAS HANGING OUT AT MY OLD GRADE SCHOOL WITH MIRABAI.
Hey.

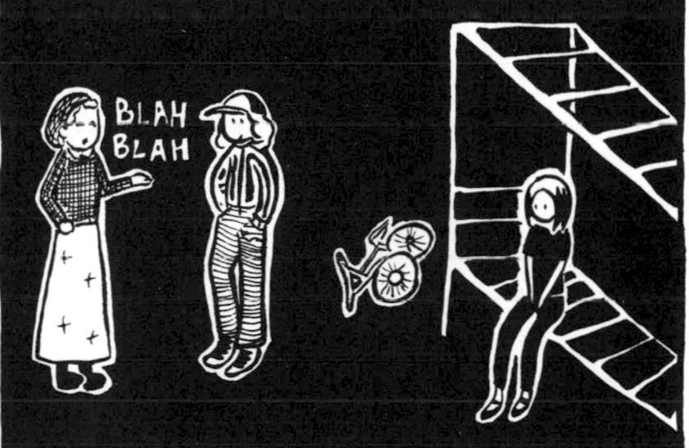
MIRABAI WAS A PEOPLE PERSON WHO HAD NO PROBLEM TALKING TO NEW PEOPLE, BUT I WAS PAINFULLY SHY.
BLAH BLAH

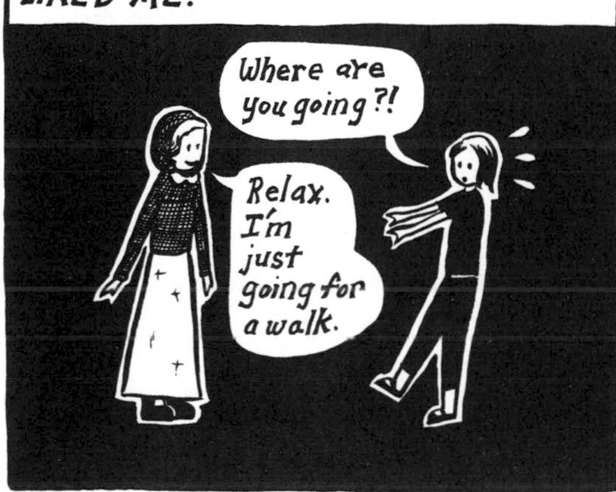
MIRABAI COULD SENSE THAT HE LIKED ME.
Where are you going?!
Relax. I'm just going for a walk.

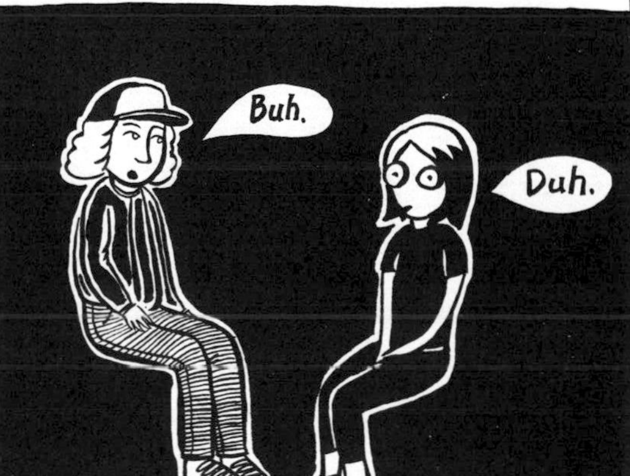
I DON'T REMEMBER WHAT WE SAID.
Buh.
Duh.

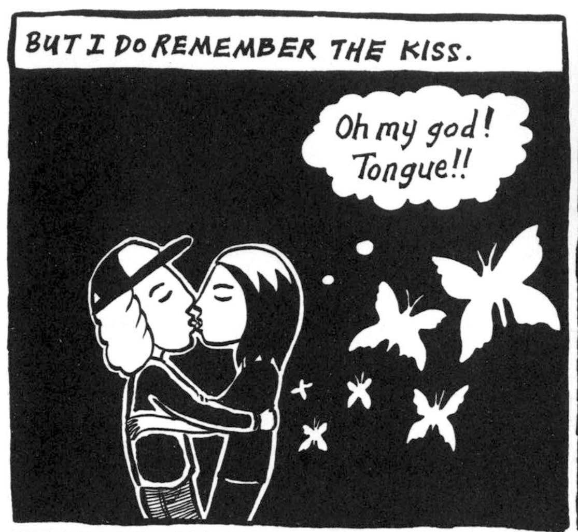
BUT I DO REMEMBER THE KISS.
Oh my god! Tongue!!

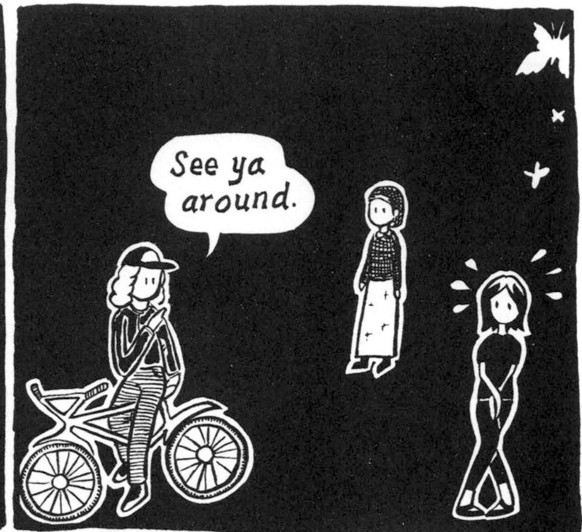
See ya around.

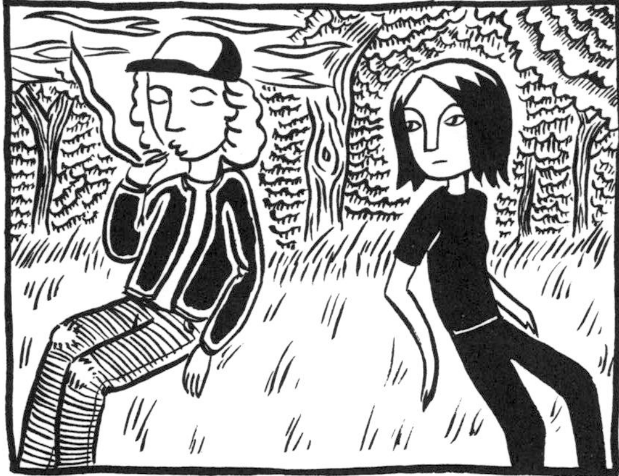
ON ANOTHER DAY WE MANAGED TO MEET AGAIN, THIS TIME ALONE.

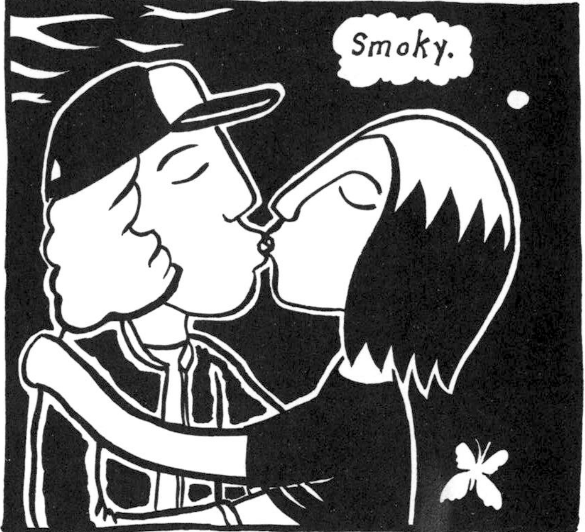
Smoky.

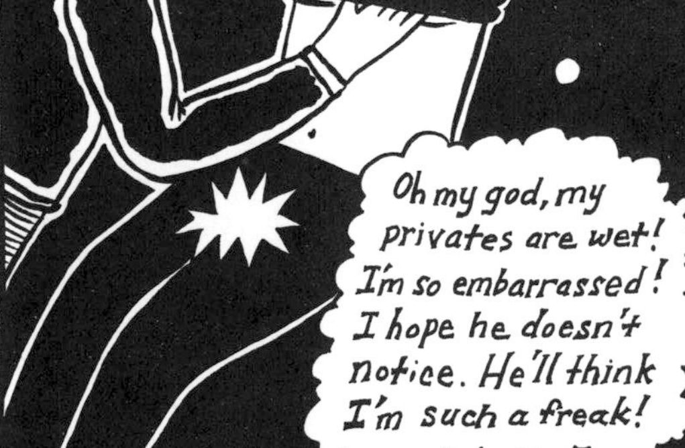
I DIDN'T KNOW WHAT TO DO WITH MYSELF.
Oh my god, my privates are wet! I'm so embarrassed! I hope he doesn't notice. He'll think I'm such a freak!

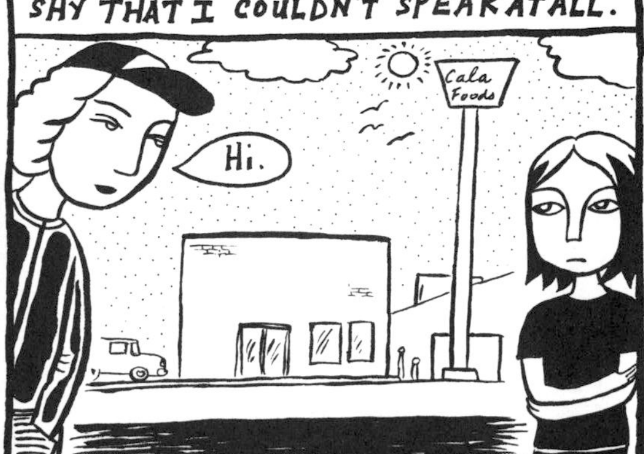
WHEN I SAW HIM AGAIN I WAS SO SHY THAT I COULDN'T SPEAK AT ALL.
Cala Foods
Hi.

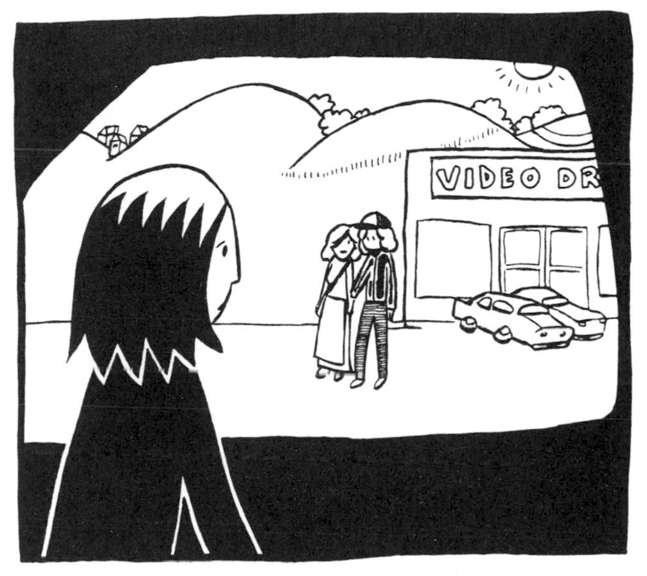
VIDEO DR

1987

age 14

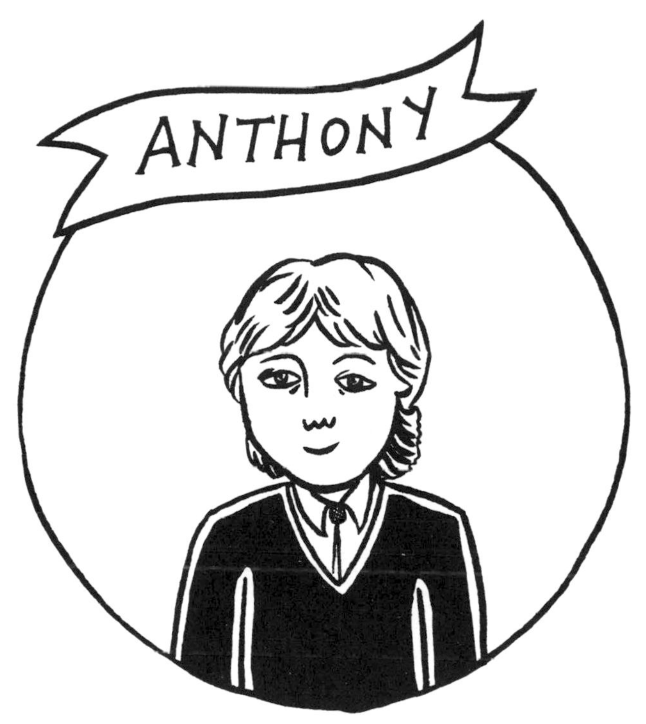
ANTHONY

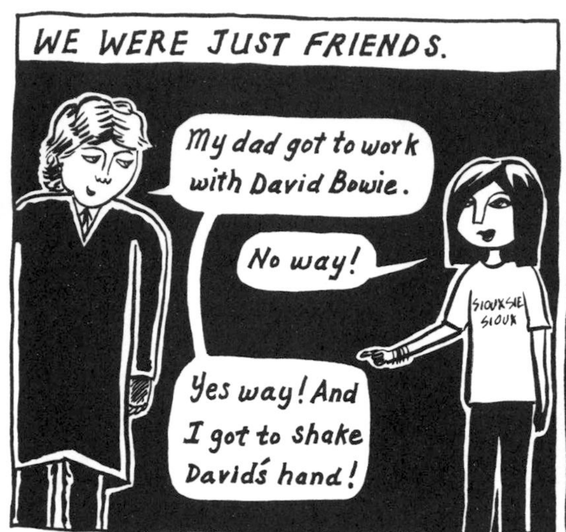

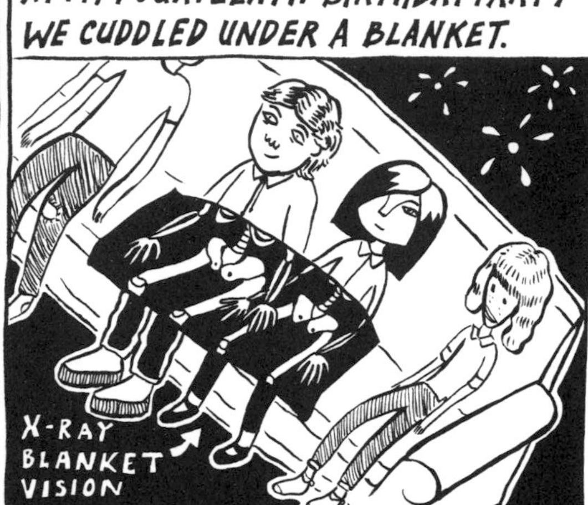

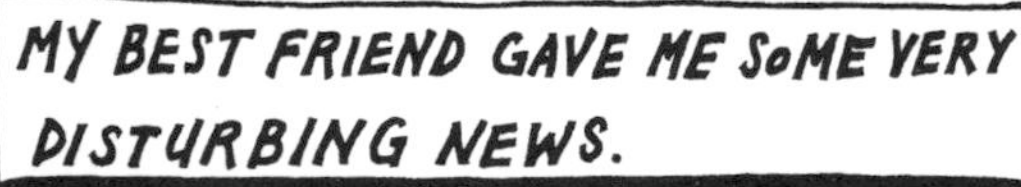

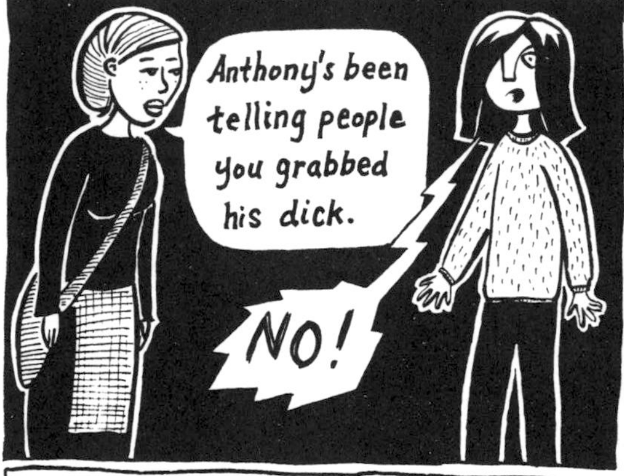

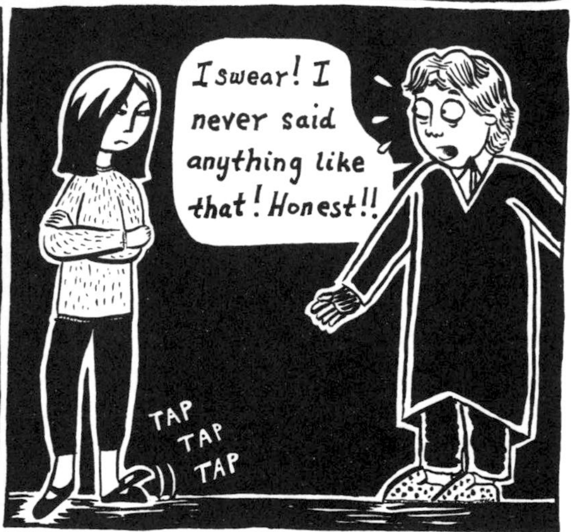

I WOULDN'T TAKE HIS CALLS AND EVENTUALLY HE STOPPED TRYING TO CONVINCE ME HE WAS INNOCENT.

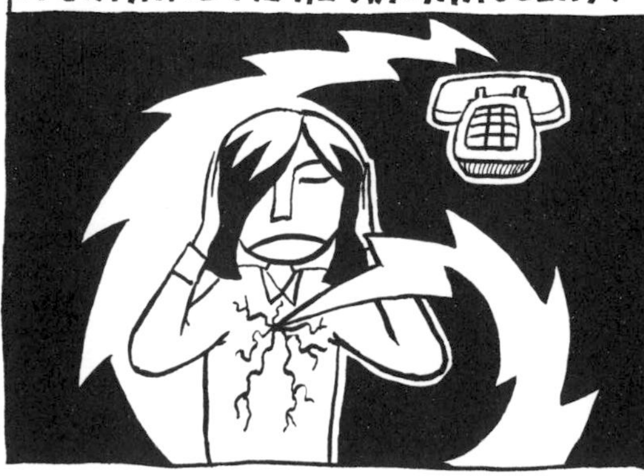

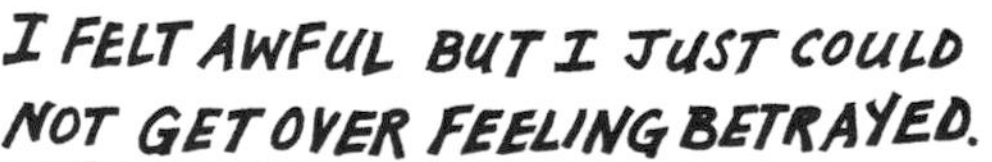

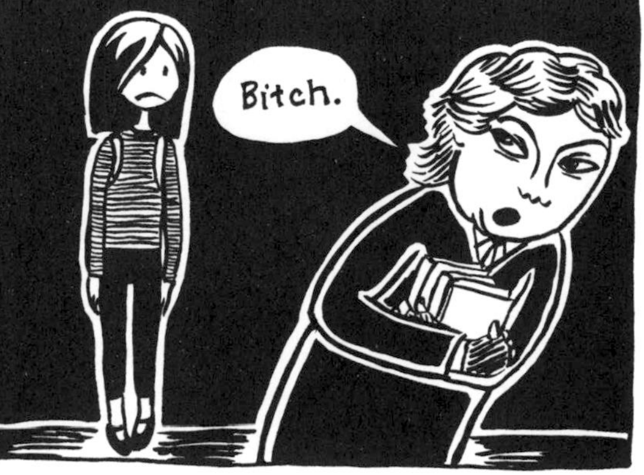

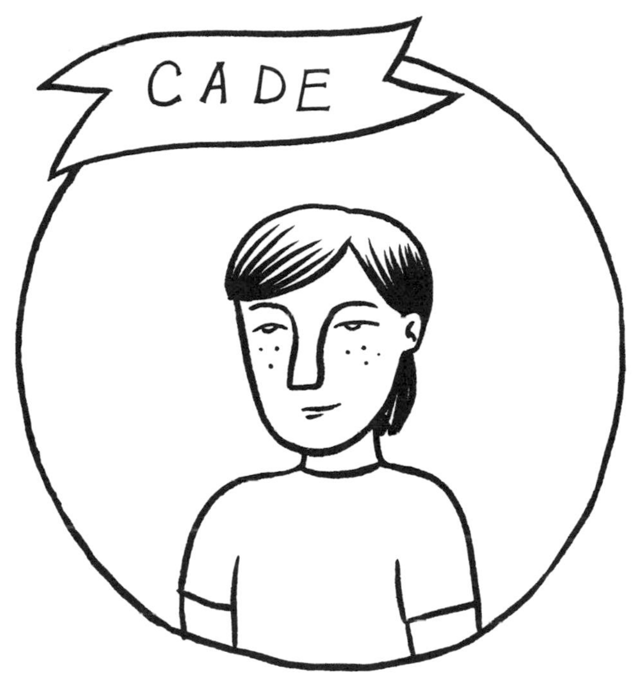
CADE

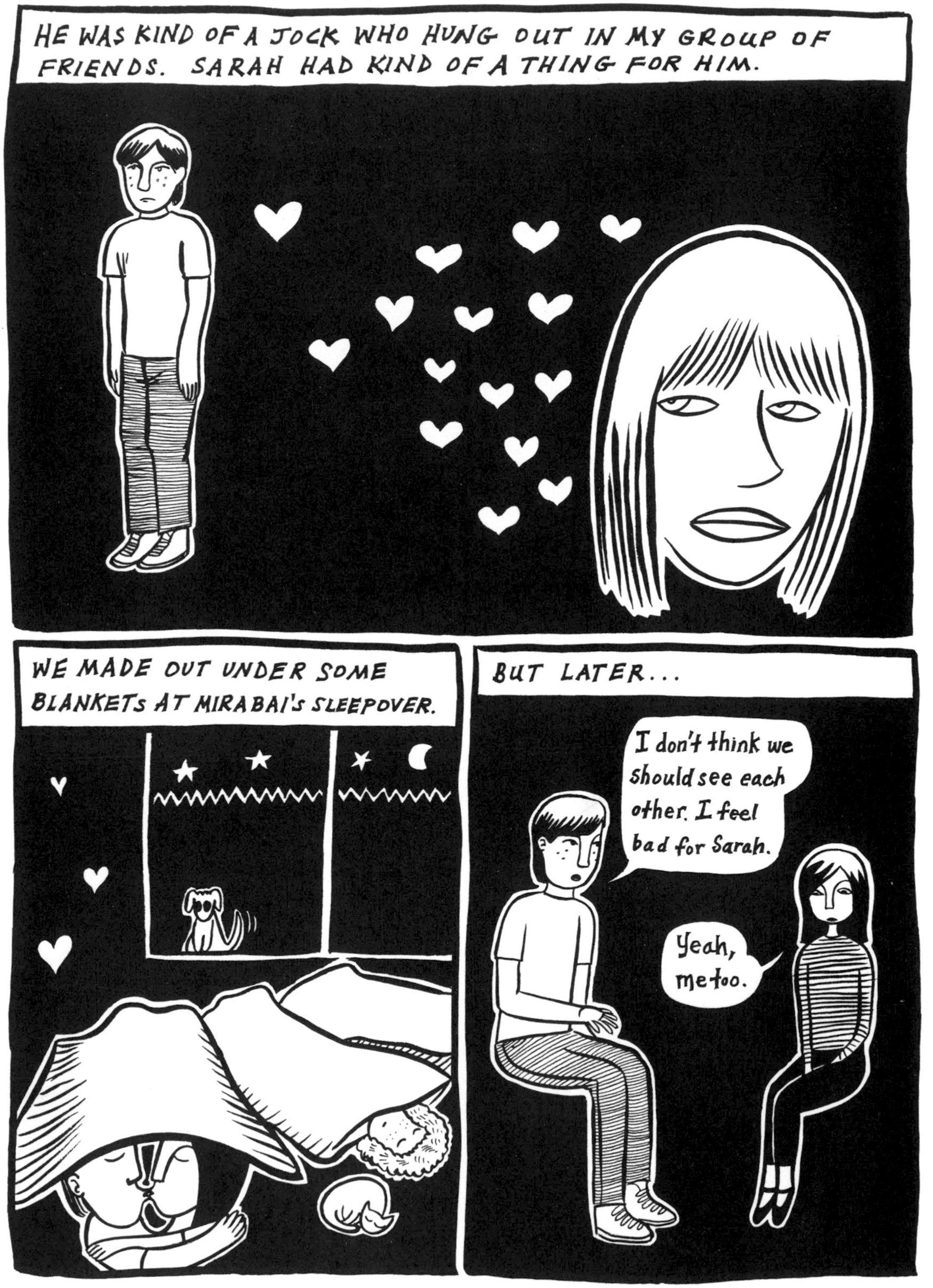

HE WAS KIND OF A JOCK WHO HUNG OUT IN MY GROUP OF FRIENDS. SARAH HAD KIND OF A THING FOR HIM.

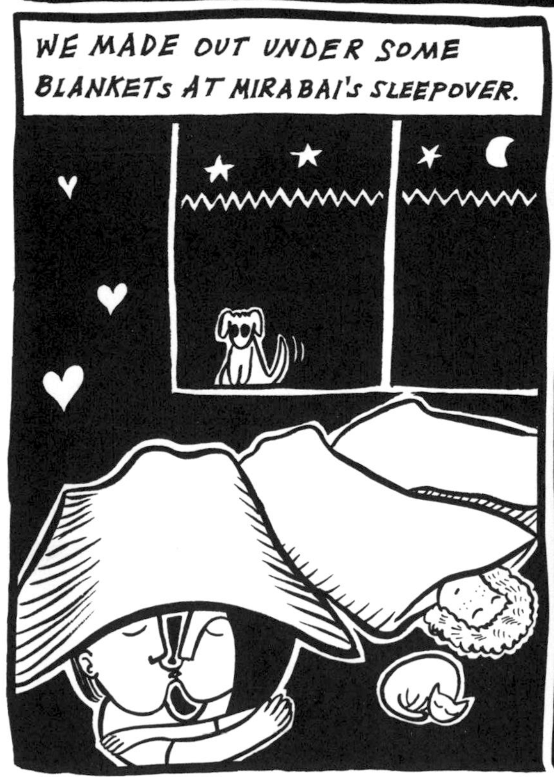

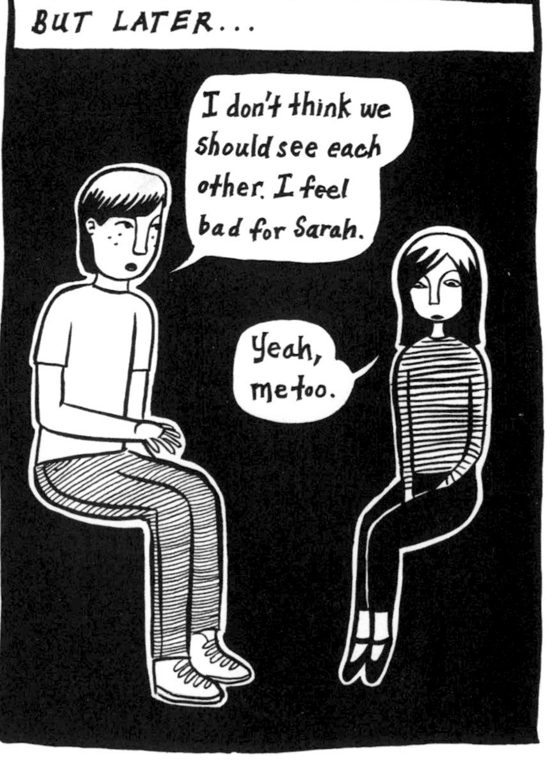

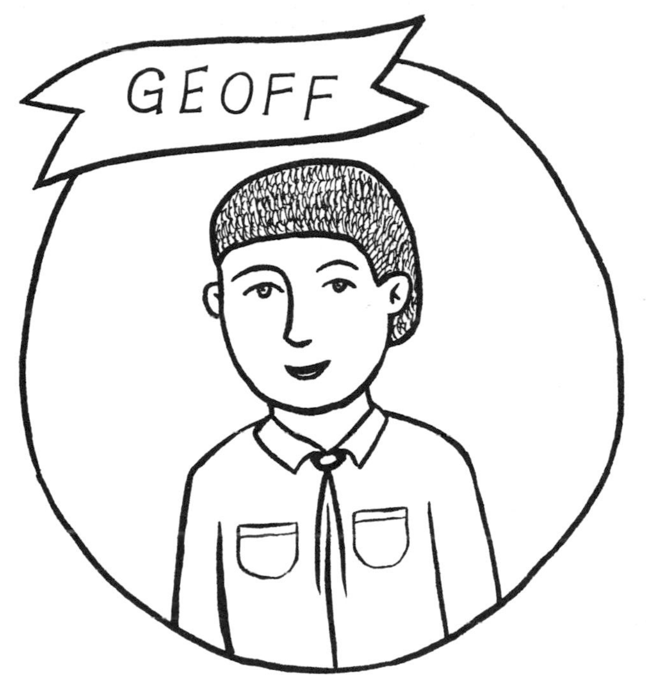
GEOFF

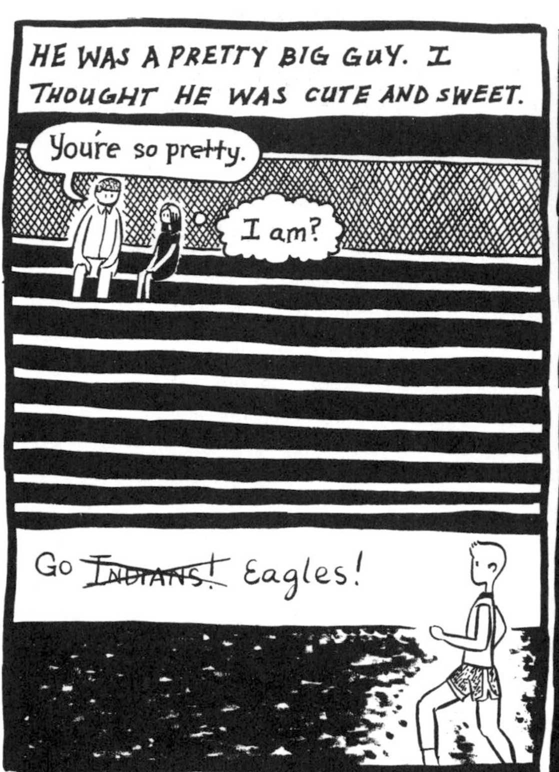
HE WAS A PRETTY BIG GUY. I THOUGHT HE WAS CUTE AND SWEET.
You're so pretty.
I am?
Go ~~INDIANS!~~ Eagles!

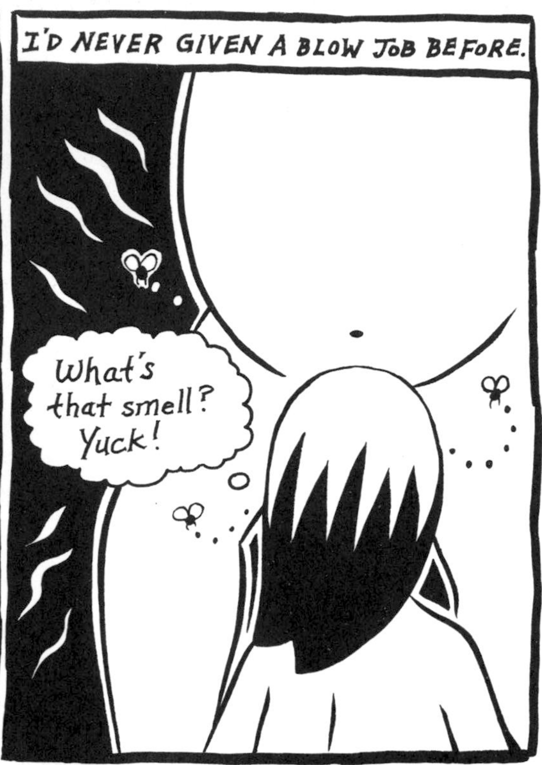
I'D NEVER GIVEN A BLOW JOB BEFORE.
What's that smell? Yuck!

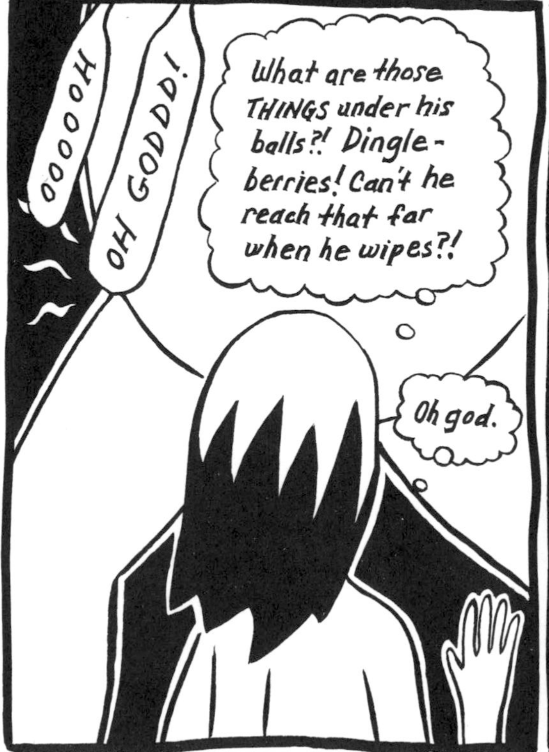
HOOOOOO
OH GODDD!
What are those THINGS under his balls?! Dingle-berries! Can't he reach that far when he wipes?!
Oh god.

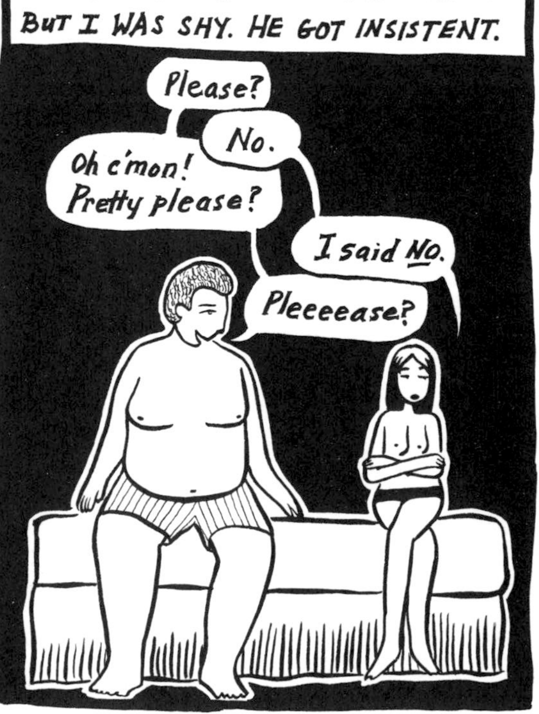
HE WANTED TO RETURN THE FAVOR BUT I WAS SHY. HE GOT INSISTENT.
Please?
No.
Oh c'mon! Pretty please?
I said NO.
Pleeeease?

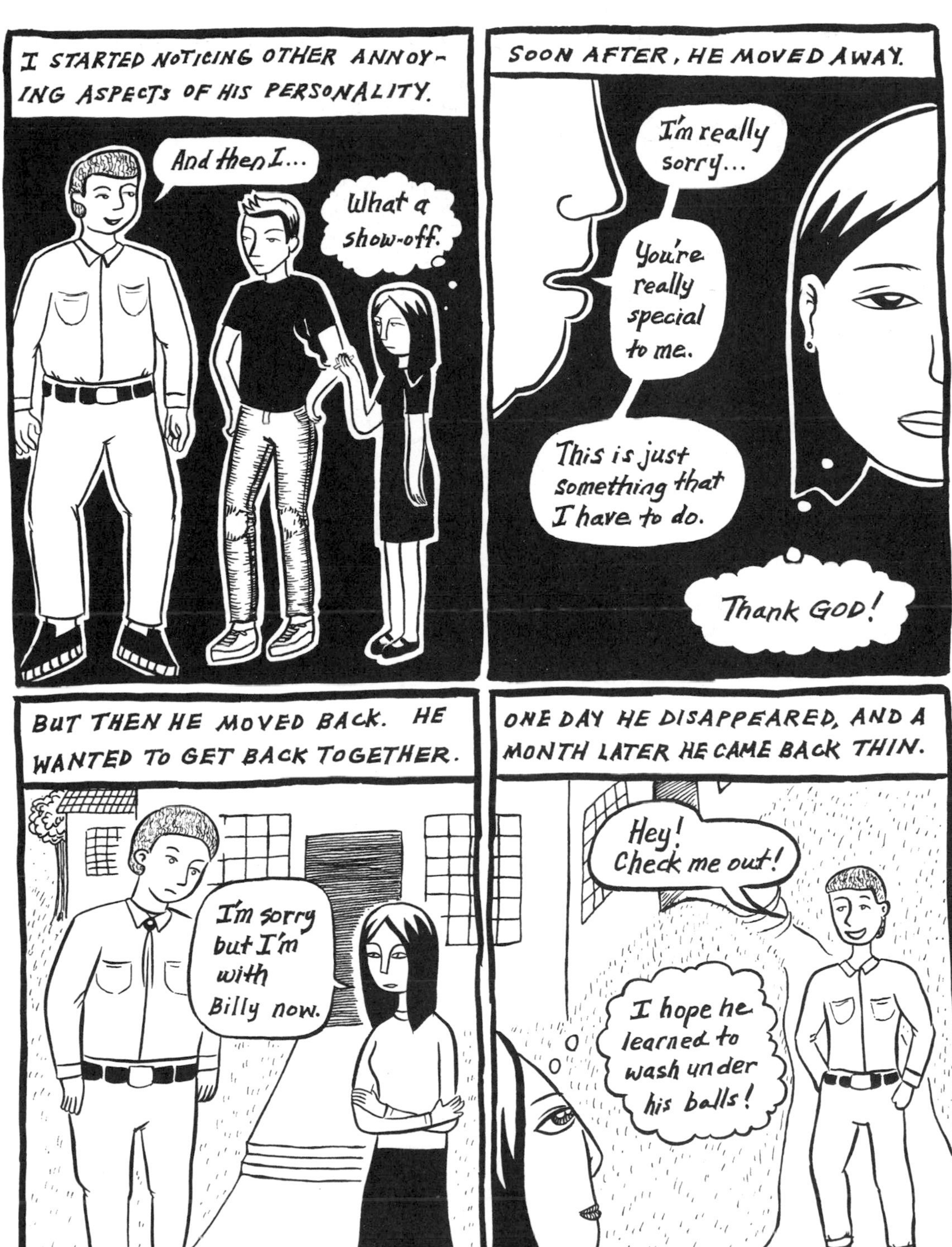
I STARTED NOTICING OTHER ANNOY-ING ASPECTS OF HIS PERSONALITY.
And then I...
What a show-off.
SOON AFTER, HE MOVED AWAY.
I'm really sorry...
You're really special to me.
This is just something that I have to do.
Thank GOD!
BUT THEN HE MOVED BACK. HE WANTED TO GET BACK TOGETHER.
I'm sorry but I'm with Billy now.
ONE DAY HE DISAPPEARED, AND A MONTH LATER HE CAME BACK THIN.
Hey! Check me out!
I hope he learned to wash under his balls!

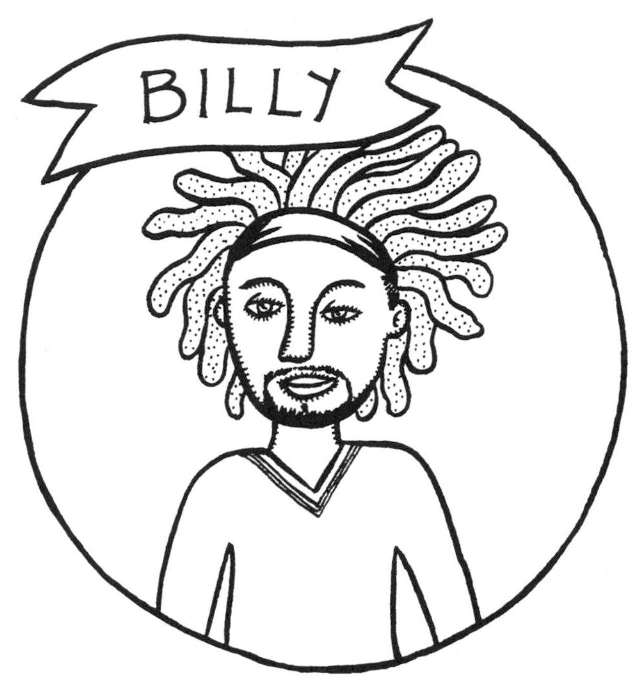
BILLY

MY BOYFRIEND GEOFF WAS LEAVING TOWN AND I WAS ON THE PROWL.

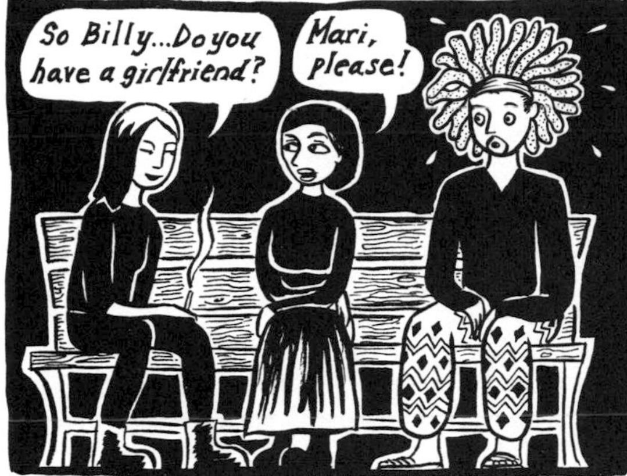

BILLY TOOK ME TO KEG PARTIES THAT GOT BUSTED BY THE COPS.

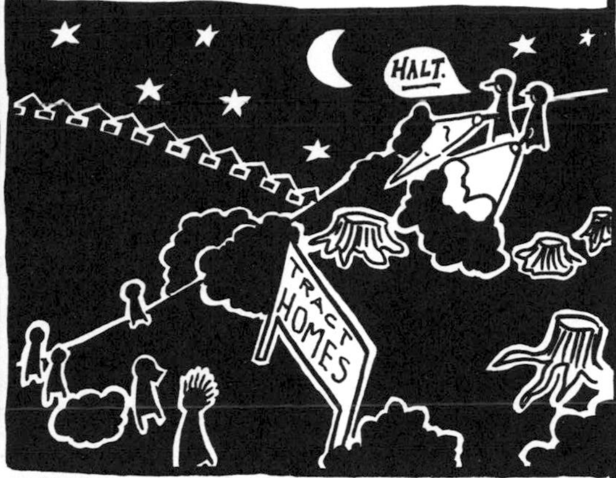

HE WAS "QUITTING POT" AND SUCKED ON LICORICE ROOT INSTEAD. HIS MOUTH TASTED SWEET AND HE DROOLED A LOT.

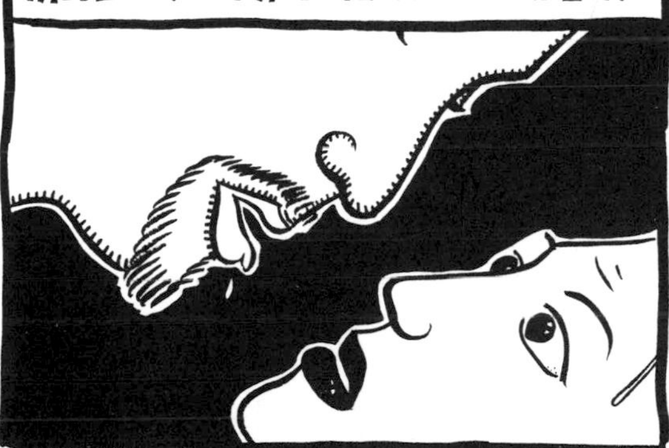

HE WENT DOWN ON ME OFTEN BUT WE NEVER WENT ALL THE WAY. I DIDN'T THINK HIS PENIS WOULD FIT IN ME.

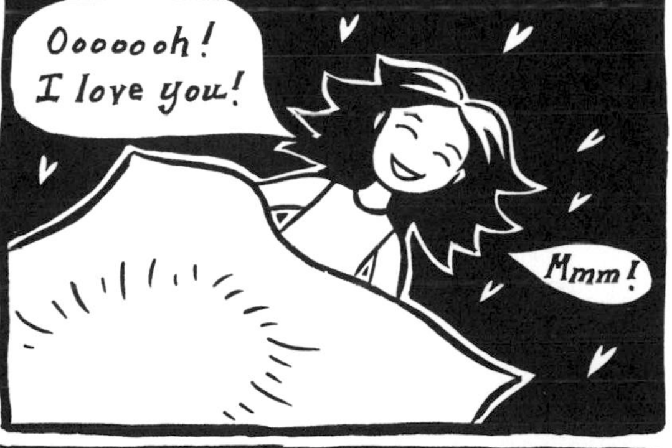

HE WAS MOSTLY NICE BUT SOMETIMES WHEN HE GOT CRANKY HE GOT MEAN.

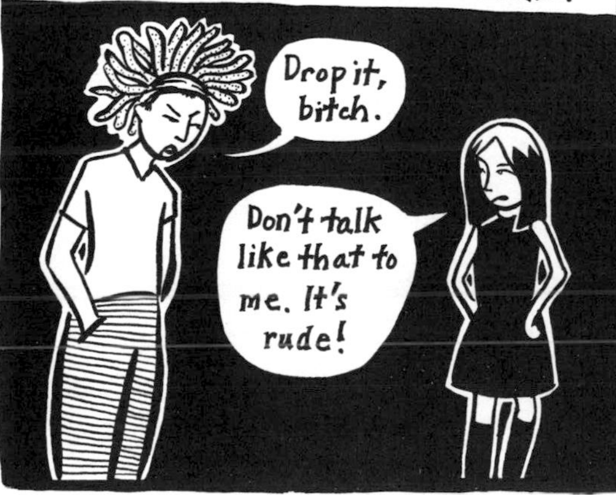

I GOT TIRED OF HIS MOODINESS AND DUMPED HIM AFTER A FEW MONTHS.

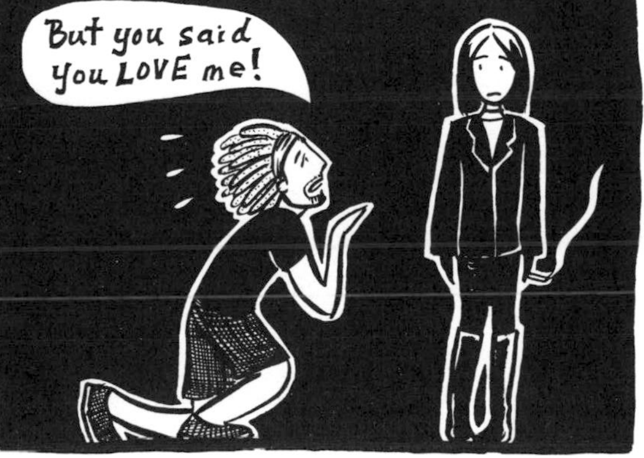

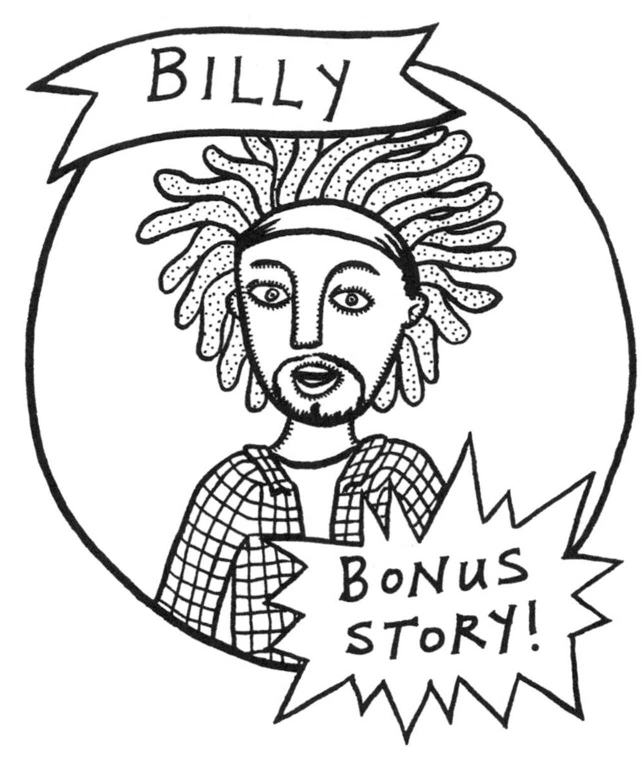
BILLY
BONUS STORY!

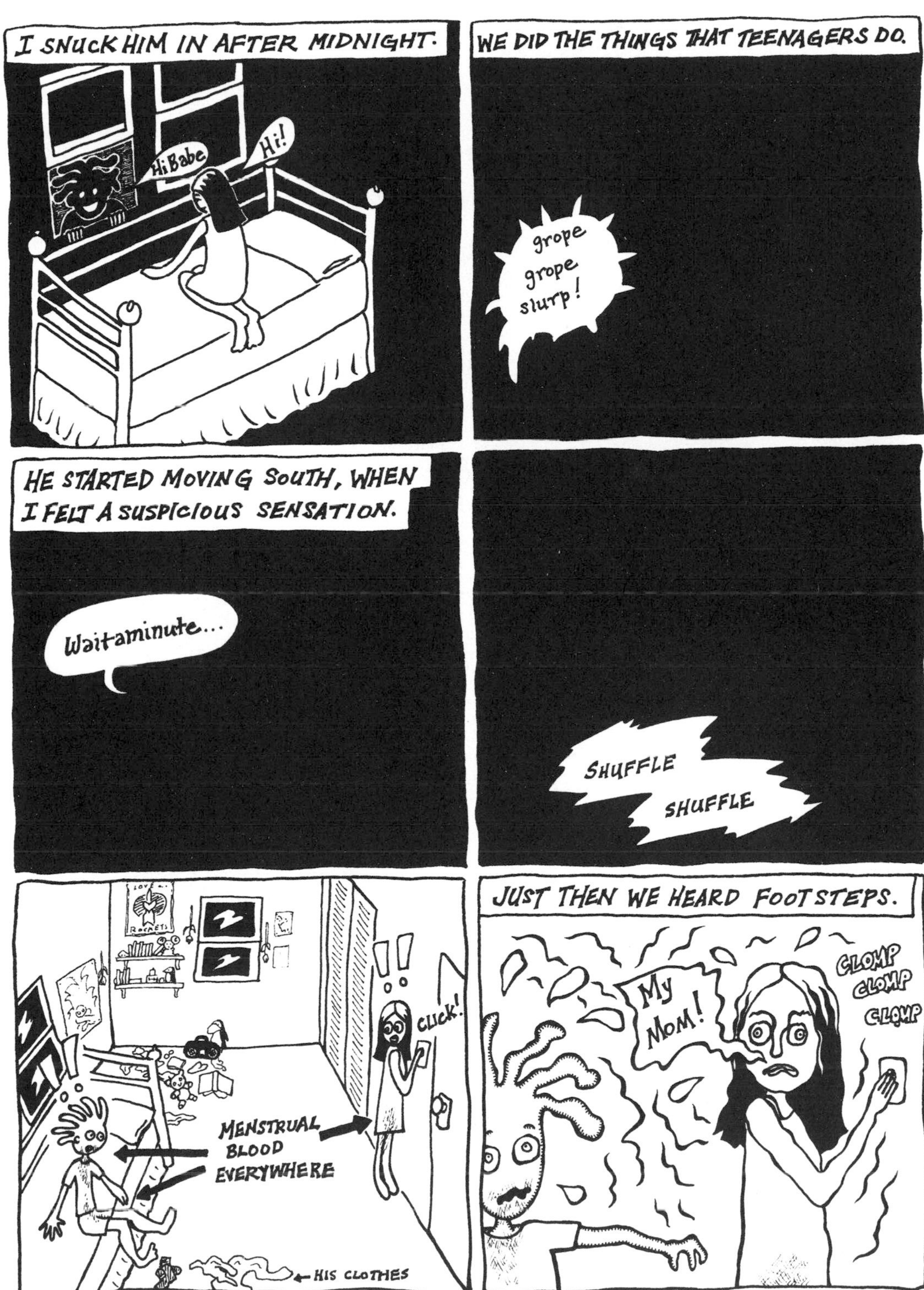
I SNUCK HIM IN AFTER MIDNIGHT.
Hi Babe
Hi!
WE DID THE THINGS THAT TEENAGERS DO.
grope grope slurp!
HE STARTED MOVING SOUTH, WHEN I FELT A SUSPICIOUS SENSATION.
Waitaminute...
SHUFFLE
SHUFFLE
ROCKETS
!!
CLICK!
!
MENSTRUAL BLOOD EVERYWHERE
HIS CLOTHES
JUST THEN WE HEARD FOOTSTEPS.
My MOM!
CLOMP
CLOMP
CLOMP

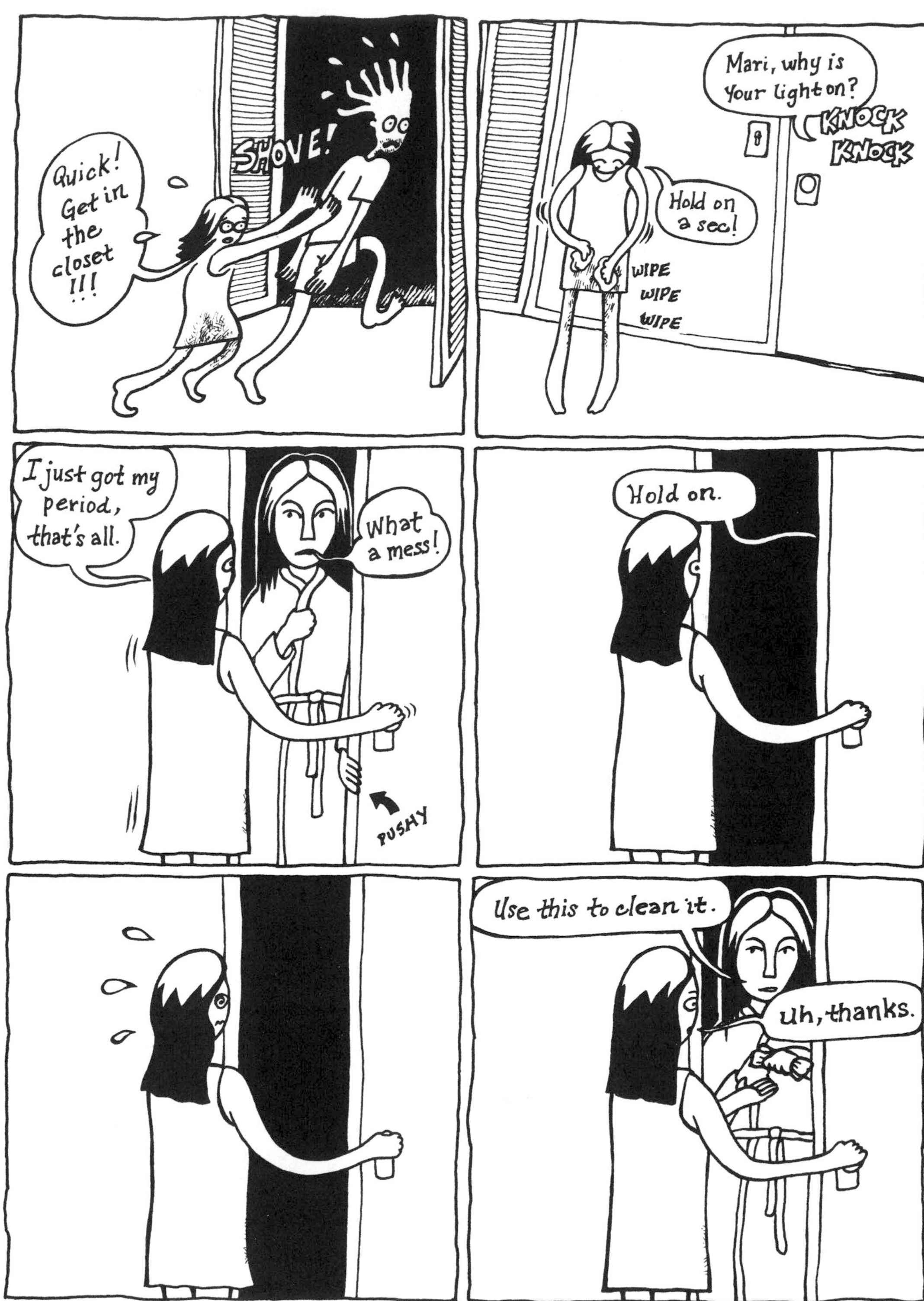
Quick! Get in the closet !!!
SHOVE!
Mari, why is your light on?
KNOCK KNOCK
Hold on a sec!
WIPE WIPE WIPE
I just got my period, that's all.
What a mess!
PUSHY
Hold on.
Use this to clean it.
uh, thanks.

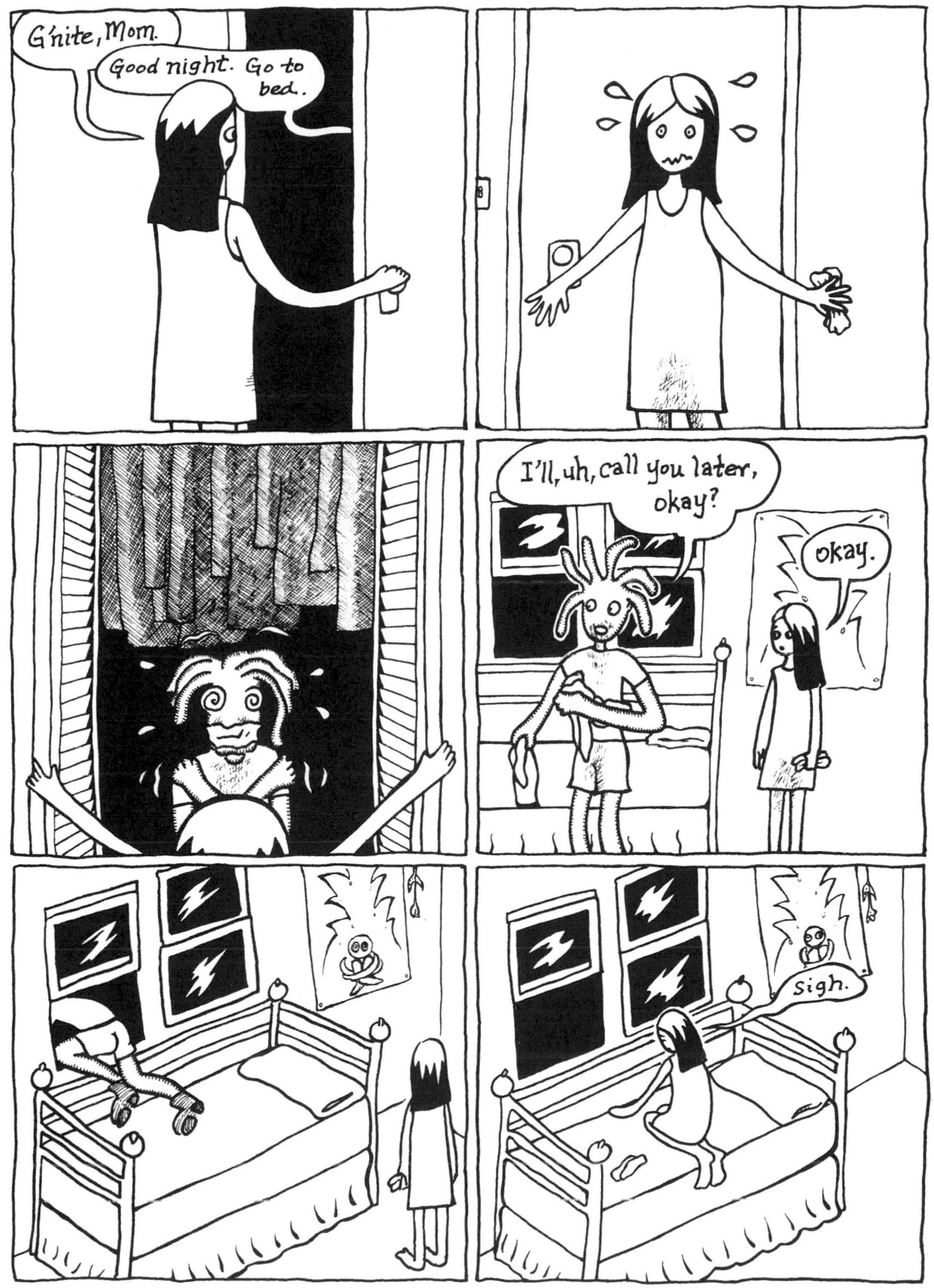
G'nite, Mom.
Good night. Go to bed.
I'll, uh, call you later, okay?
Okay.
Sigh.

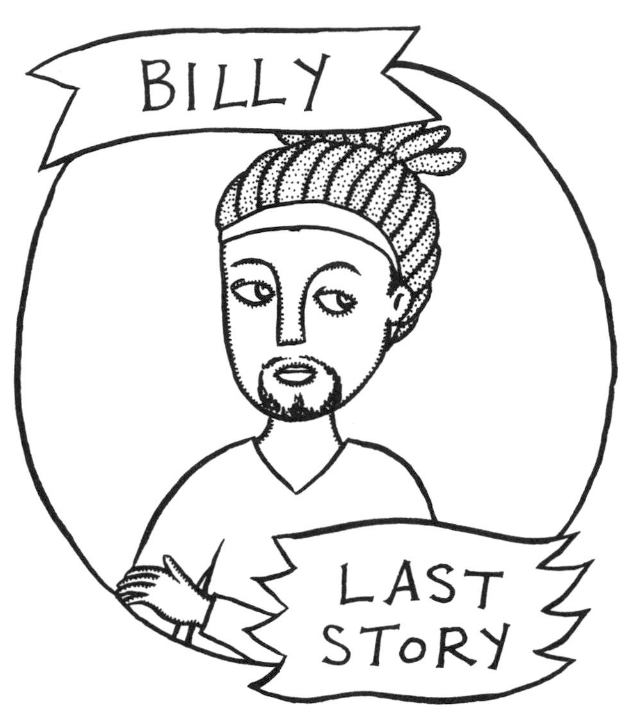
BILLY
LAST STORY

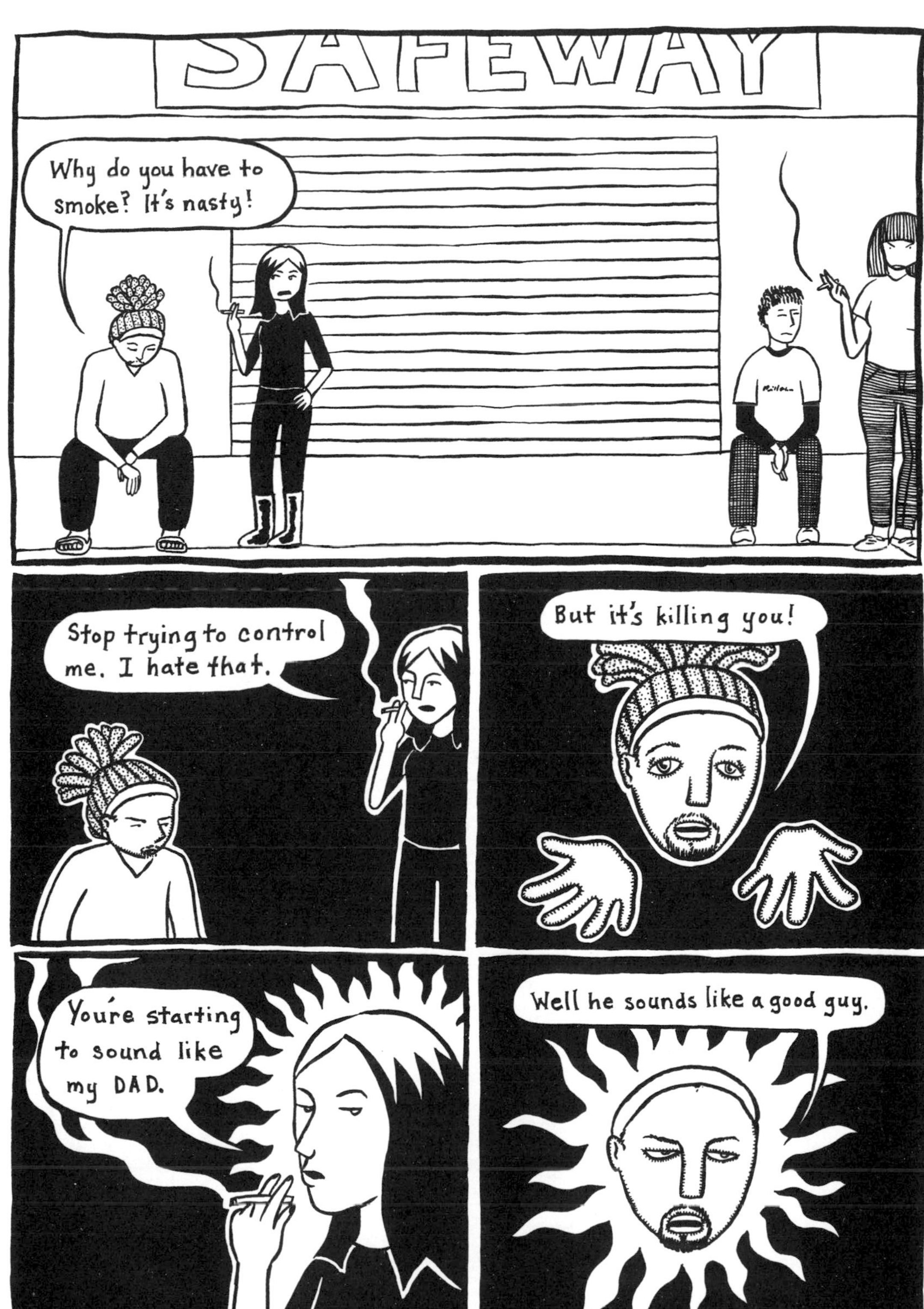
SAFEWAY
Why do you have to smoke? It's nasty!
Stop trying to control me. I hate that.
But it's killing you!
You're starting to sound like my DAD.
Well he sounds like a good guy.

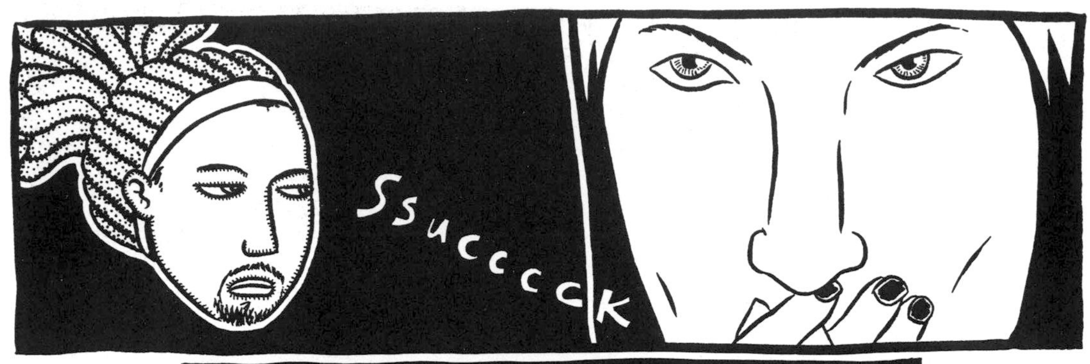
Ssuccccck

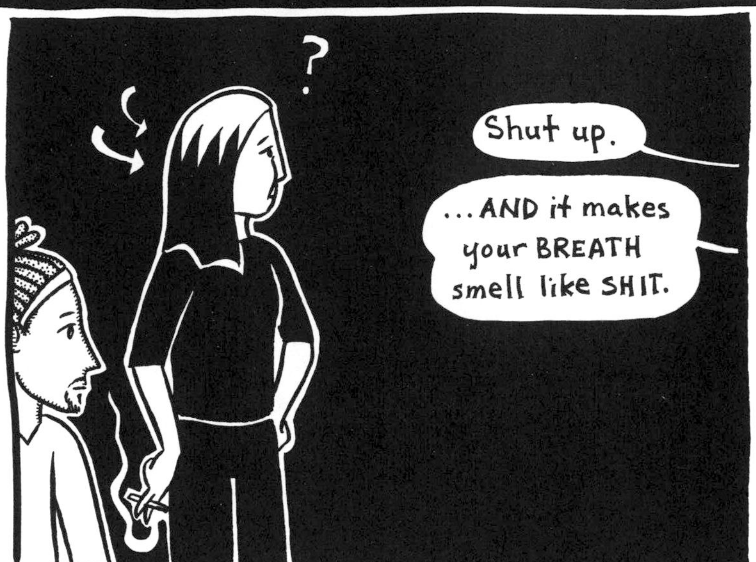
?
Shut up.
...AND it makes your BREATH smell like SHIT.

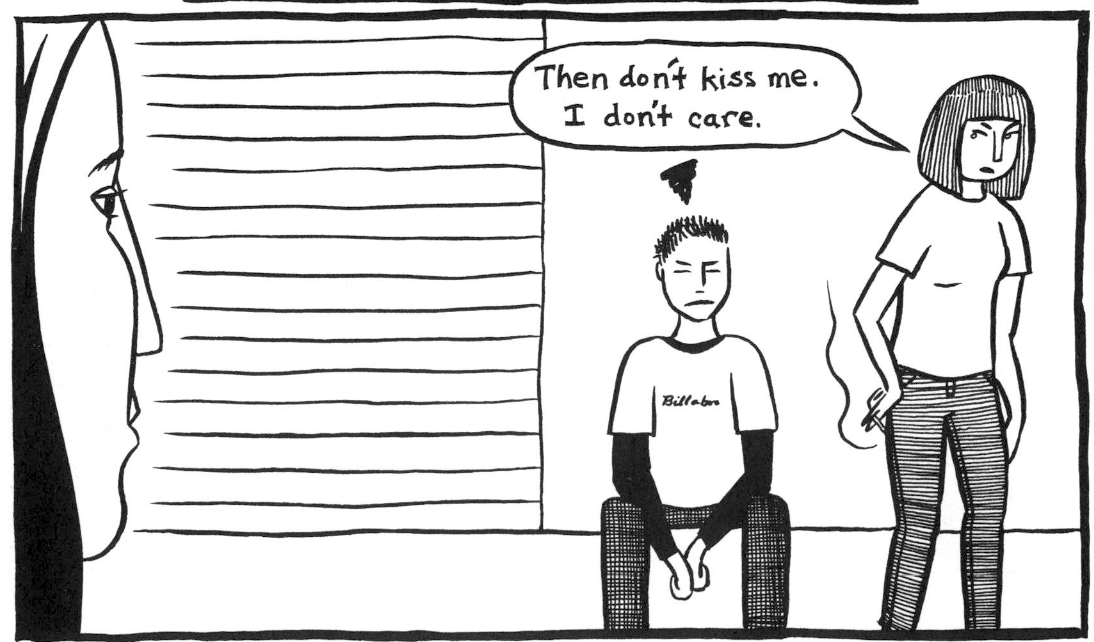
Then don't kiss me. I don't care.
Billabo

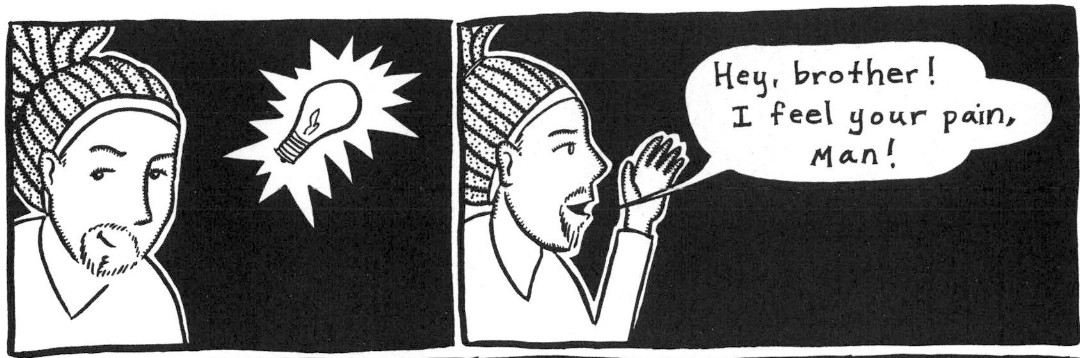
Hey, brother!
I feel your pain, Man!

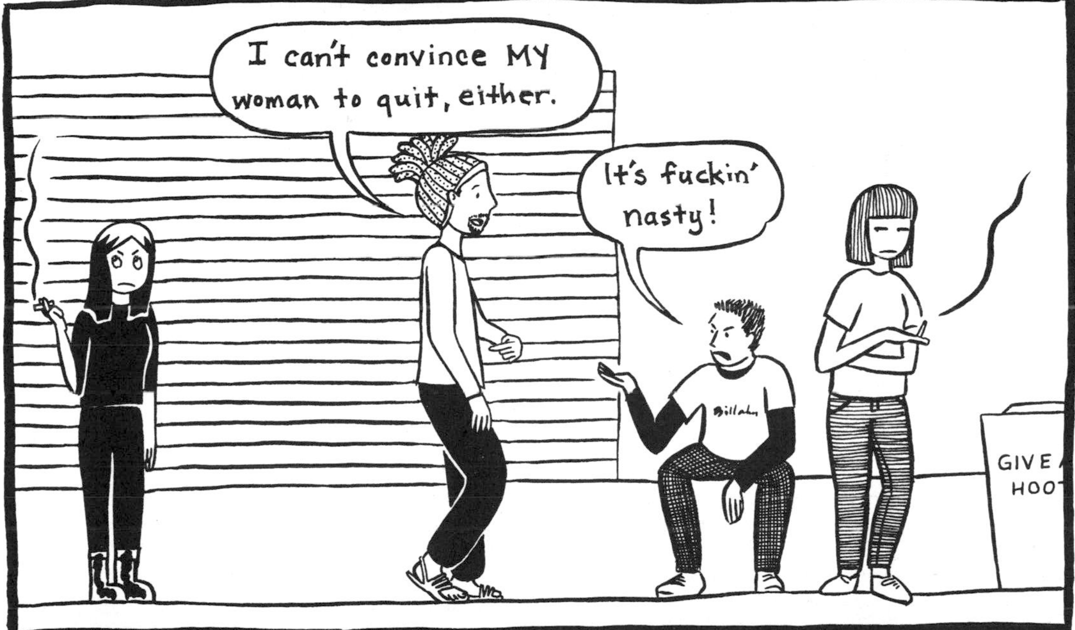
I can't convince MY woman to quit, either.
It's fuckin' nasty!
Billabo
GIVE
HOO

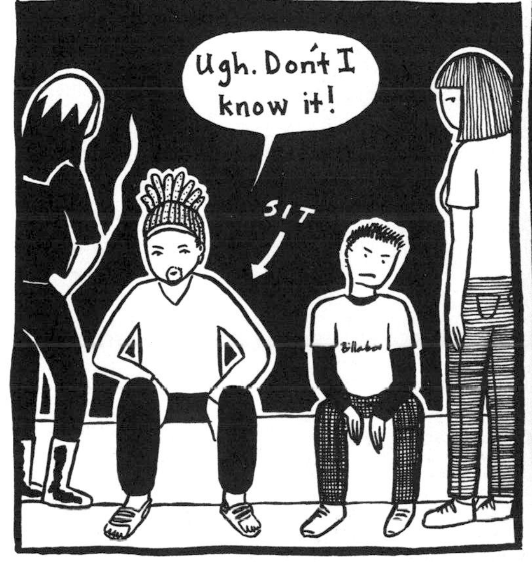
Ugh. Don't I know it!
SIT
Billabo

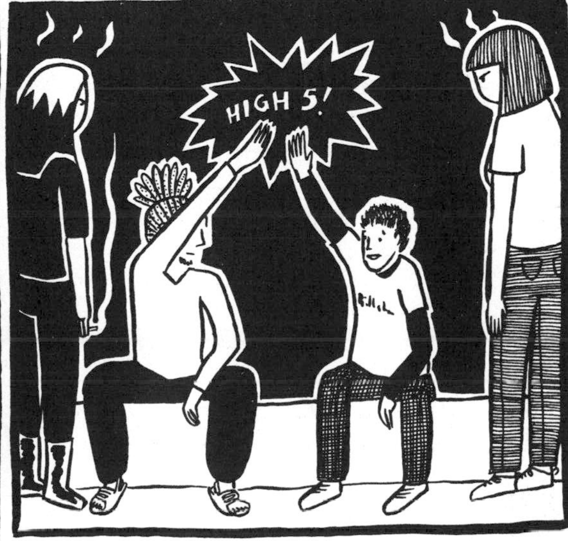
HIGH 5!

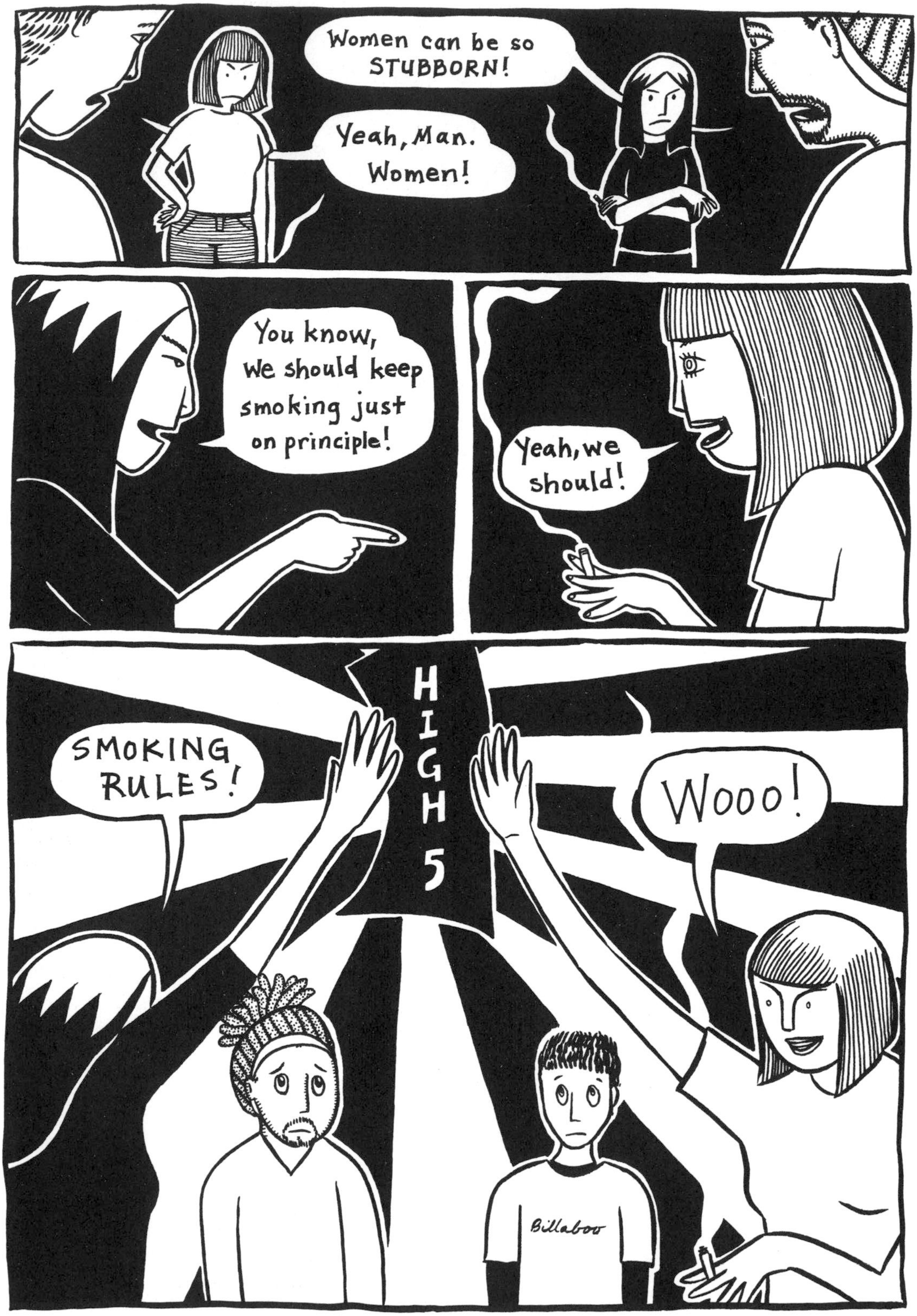

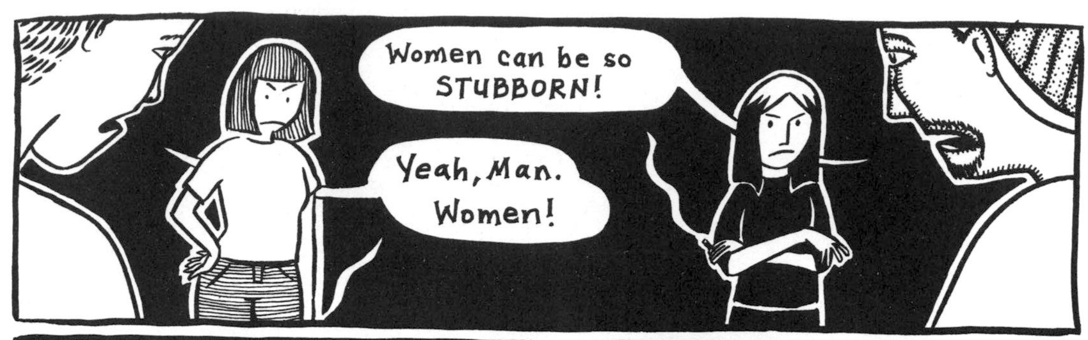
Women can be so STUBBORN!
Yeah, Man. Women!

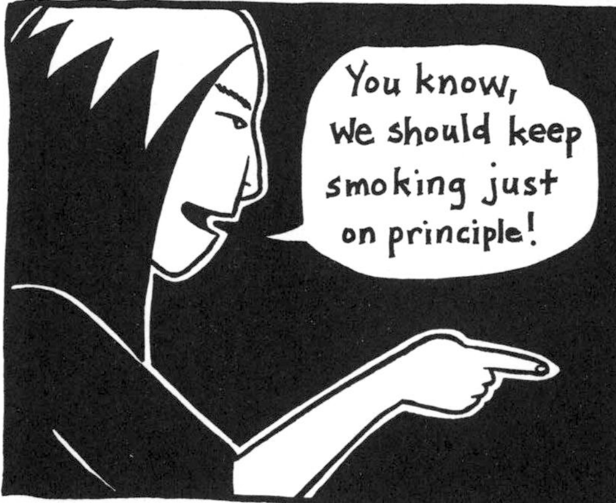
You know, we should keep smoking just on principle!

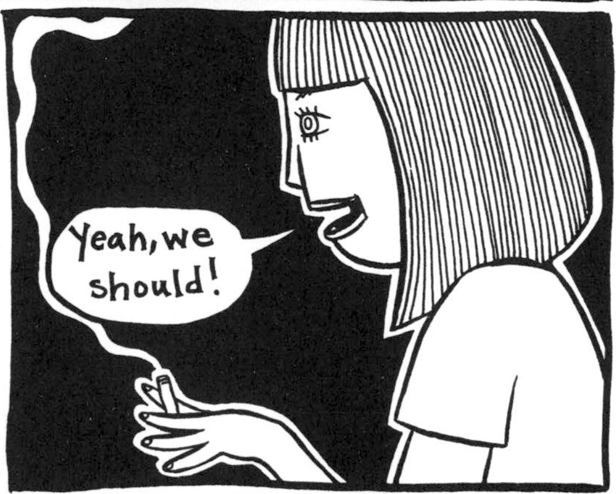
Yeah, we should!

SMOKING RULES!
HIGH 5
Wooo!
Billabong

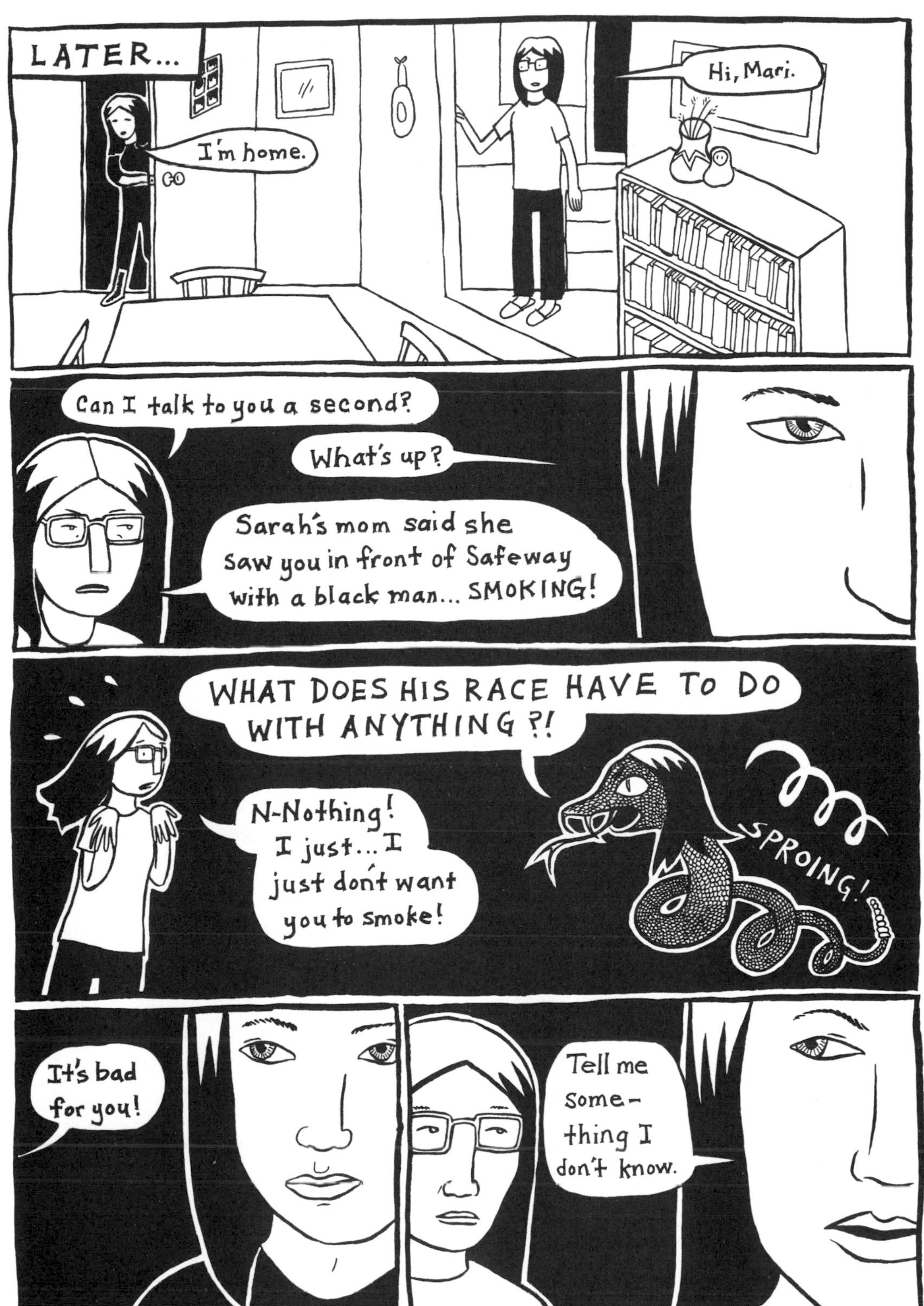
LATER...
I'm home.
Hi, Mari.
Can I talk to you a second?
What's up?
Sarah's mom said she saw you in front of Safeway with a black man... SMOKING!
WHAT DOES HIS RACE HAVE TO DO WITH ANYTHING?!
N-Nothing! I just... I just don't want you to smoke!
SPROING!
It's bad for you!
Tell me some-thing I don't know.

Drug talk

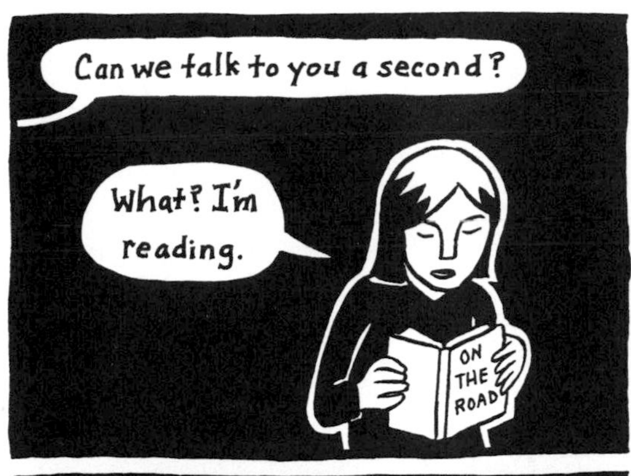
Can we talk to you a second?
What? I'm reading.
ON THE ROAD

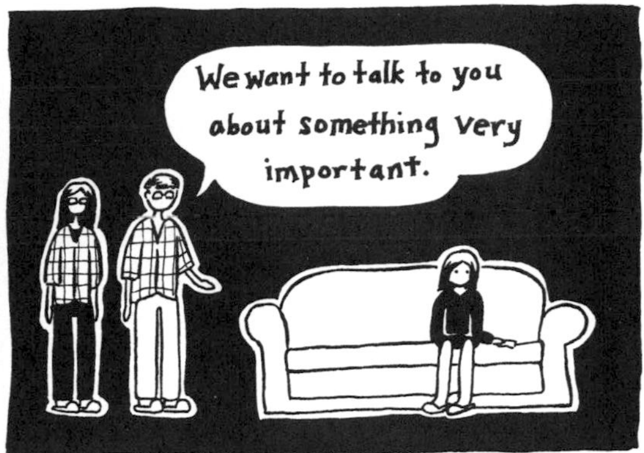
We want to talk to you about something very important.

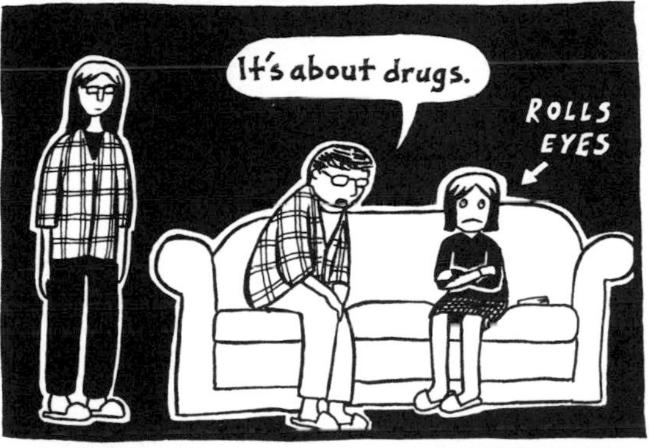
It's about drugs.
ROLLS EYES

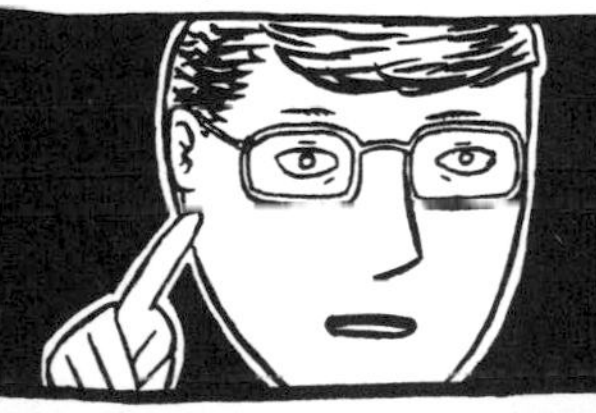
One time, your mom and I went to a party. One of the party-goers offered us marijuana. We said, "No, thanks" and then we left.

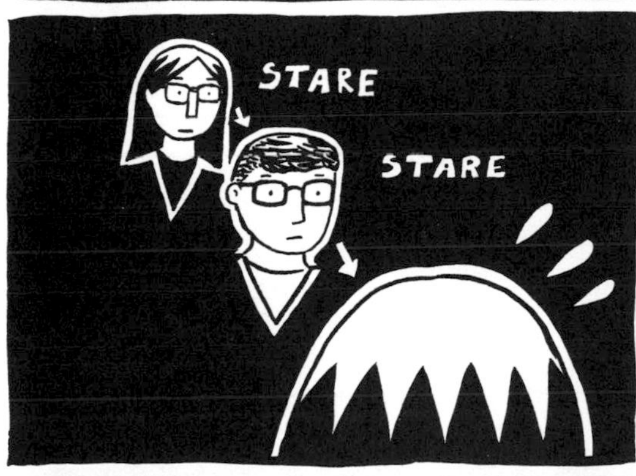
STARE
STARE

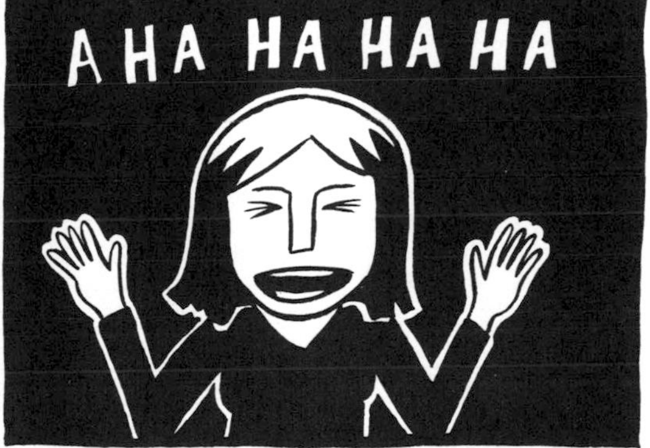
AHA HA HA HA HA

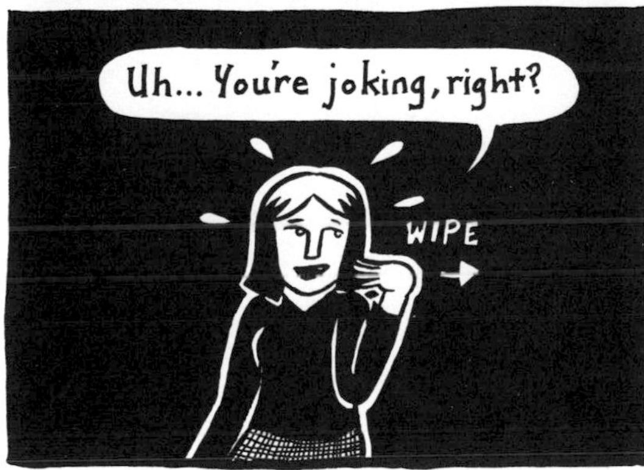
Uh... You're joking, right?
WIPE

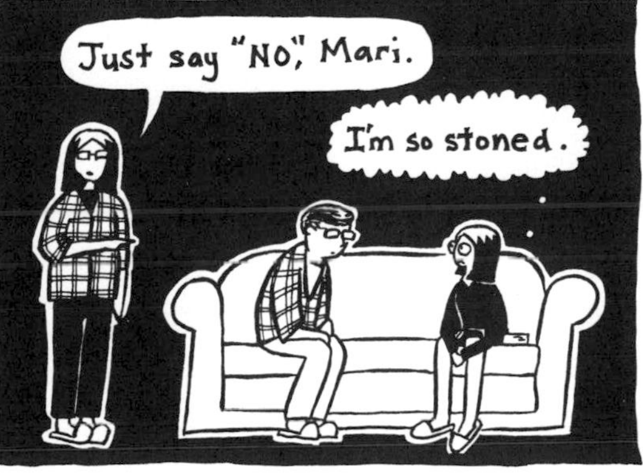
Just say "NO," Mari.
I'm so stoned.

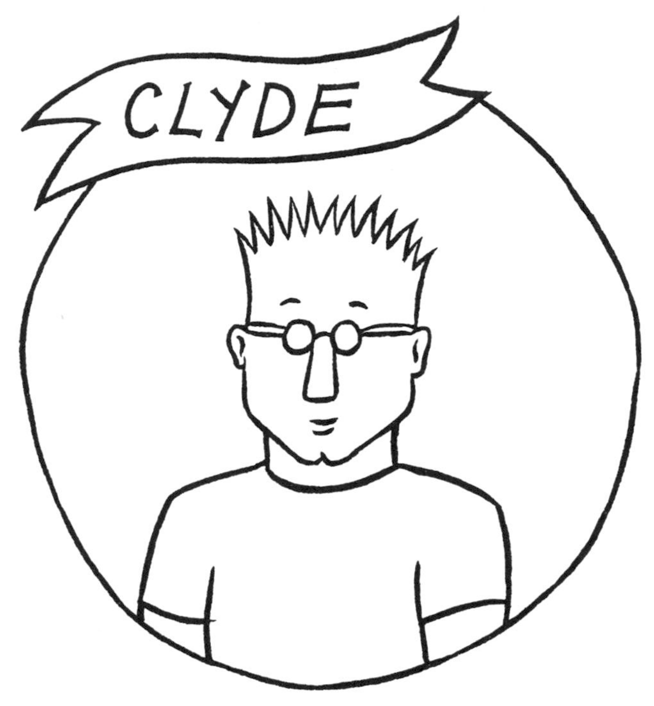
CLYDE

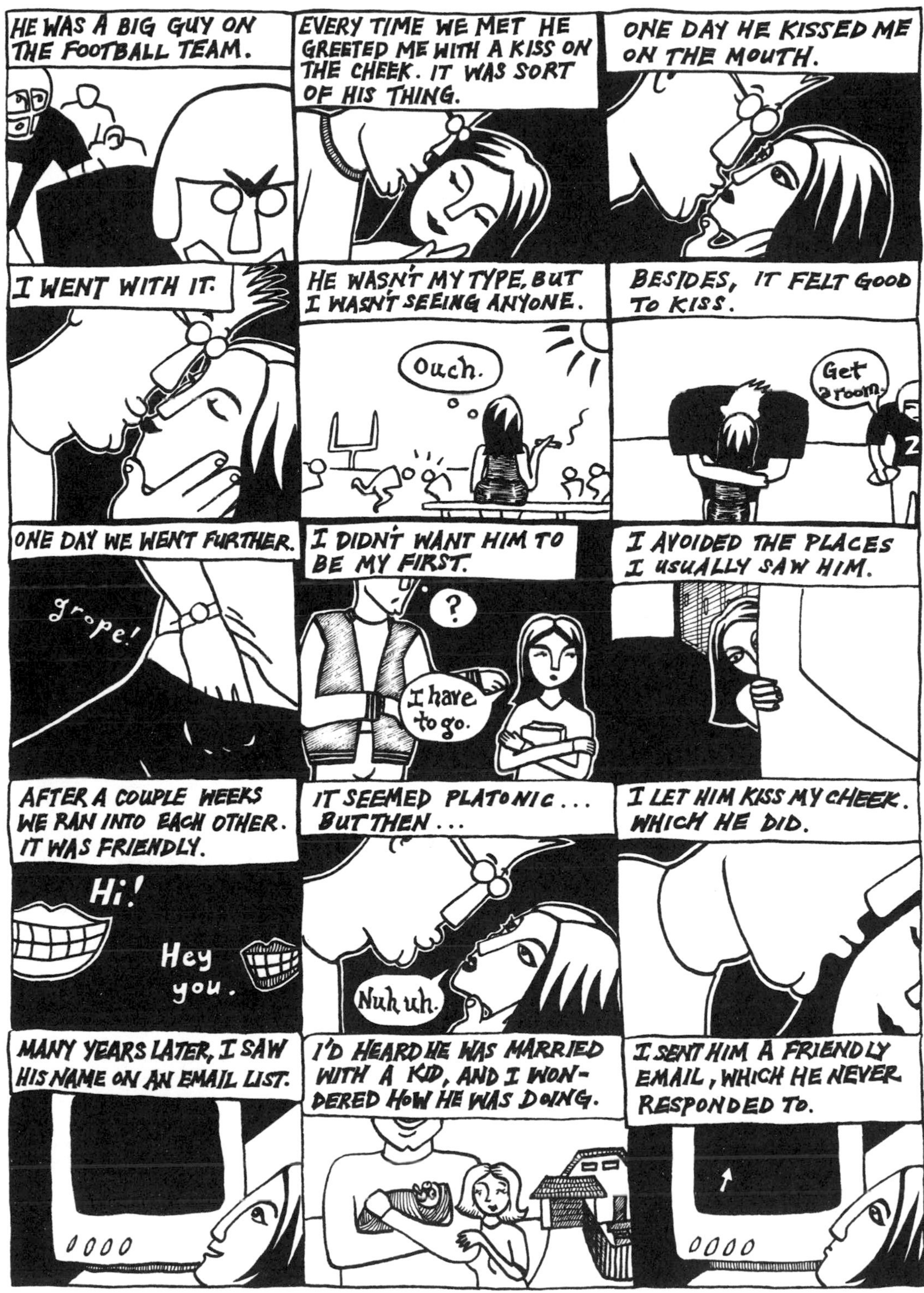
HE WAS A BIG GUY ON THE FOOTBALL TEAM.
EVERY TIME WE MET HE GREETED ME WITH A KISS ON THE CHEEK. IT WAS SORT OF HIS THING.
ONE DAY HE KISSED ME ON THE MOUTH.
I WENT WITH IT.
HE WASN'T MY TYPE, BUT I WASN'T SEEING ANYONE.
Ouch.
BESIDES, IT FELT GOOD TO KISS.
Get a room.
ONE DAY WE WENT FURTHER.
grope!
I DIDN'T WANT HIM TO BE MY FIRST.
?
I have to go.
I AVOIDED THE PLACES I USUALLY SAW HIM.
AFTER A COUPLE WEEKS WE RAN INTO EACH OTHER. IT WAS FRIENDLY.
Hi!
Hey you.
IT SEEMED PLATONIC... BUT THEN...
Nuh uh.
I LET HIM KISS MY CHEEK. WHICH HE DID.
MANY YEARS LATER, I SAW HIS NAME ON AN EMAIL LIST.
I'D HEARD HE WAS MARRIED WITH A KID, AND I WONDERED HOW HE WAS DOING.
I SENT HIM A FRIENDLY EMAIL, WHICH HE NEVER RESPONDED TO.

My dad is so naïve!

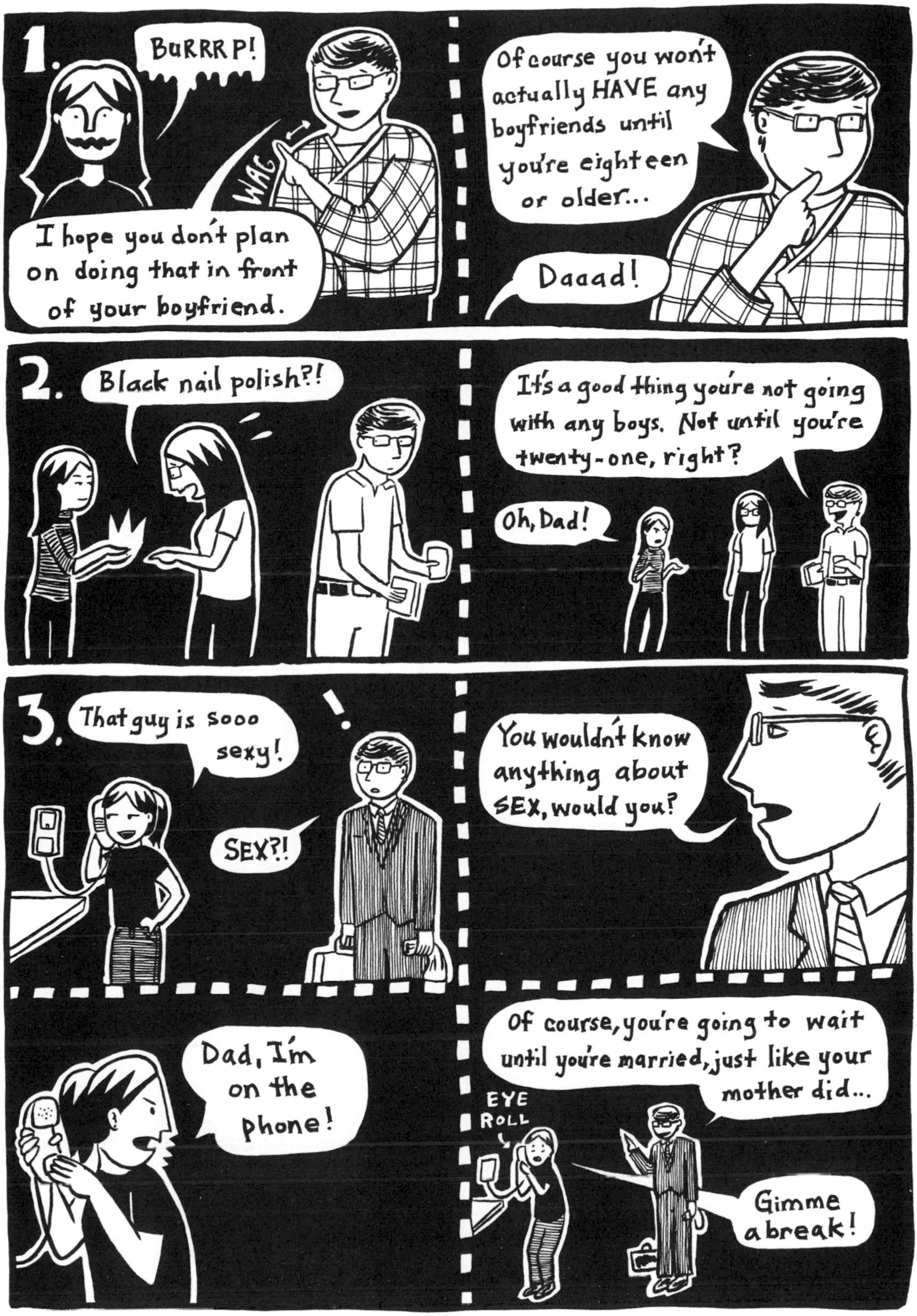

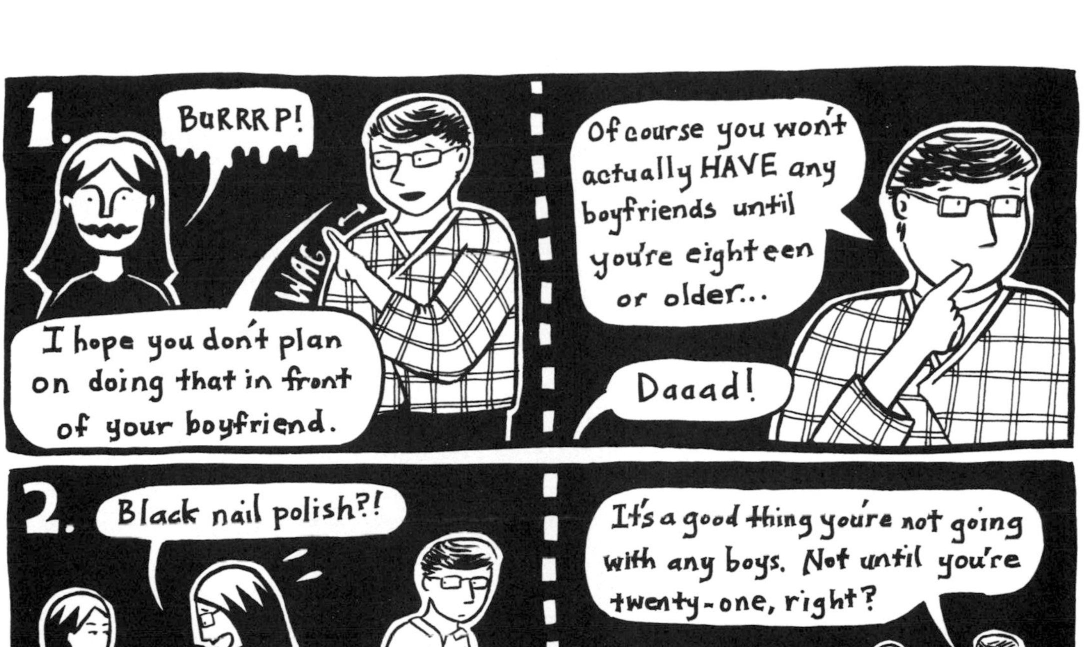

2.

Black nail polish?!

It's a good thing you're not going with any boys. Not until you're twenty-one, right?

Oh, Dad!

3.

That guy is sooo sexy!

!

SEX?!

You wouldn't know anything about SEX, would you?

Dad, I'm on the phone!

Of course, you're going to wait until you're married, just like your mother did...

EYE ROLL

Gimme a break!

1988

ages 14 ~ 15

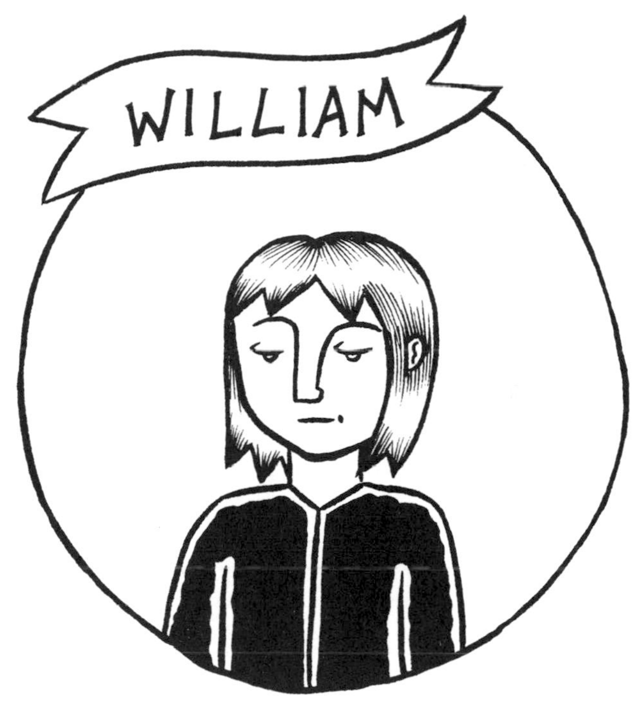
WILLIAM

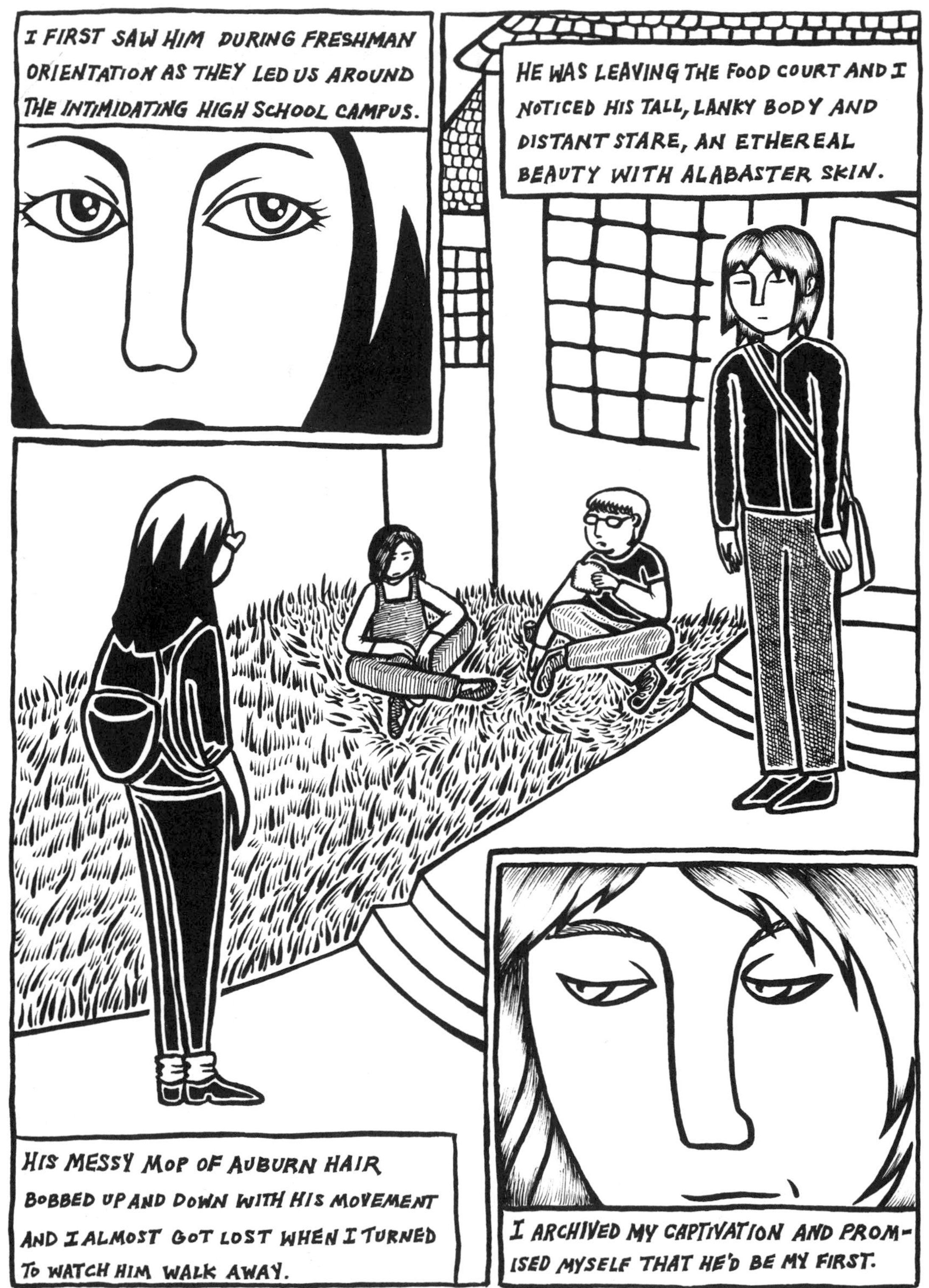
I FIRST SAW HIM DURING FRESHMAN ORIENTATION AS THEY LED US AROUND THE INTIMIDATING HIGH SCHOOL CAMPUS.
HE WAS LEAVING THE FOOD COURT AND I NOTICED HIS TALL, LANKY BODY AND DISTANT STARE, AN ETHEREAL BEAUTY WITH ALABASTER SKIN.
HIS MESSY MOP OF AUBURN HAIR BOBBED UP AND DOWN WITH HIS MOVEMENT AND I ALMOST GOT LOST WHEN I TURNED TO WATCH HIM WALK AWAY.
I ARCHIVED MY CAPTIVATION AND PROMISED MYSELF THAT HE'D BE MY FIRST.

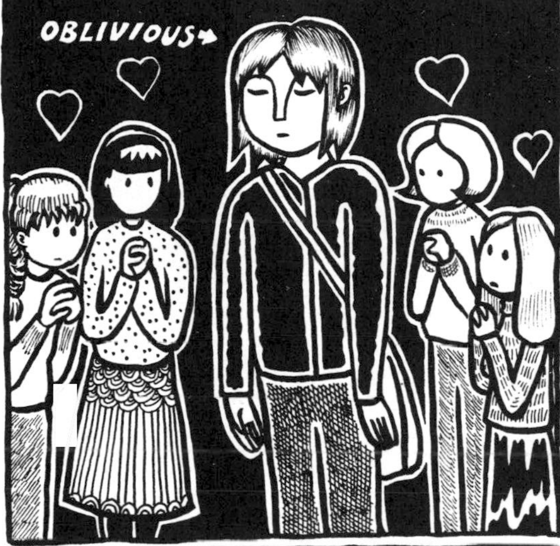
A YEAR LATER HE WAS THE "IT" BOY AND I WAS NOBODY SPECIAL YET. ALL THE GIRLS AVOIDED HIM BECAUSE HE WAS JUST TOO CUTE. PLUS IT WAS WELL KNOWN THAT HE HAD A CRUSH ON MY BEST FRIEND.
OBLIVIOUS

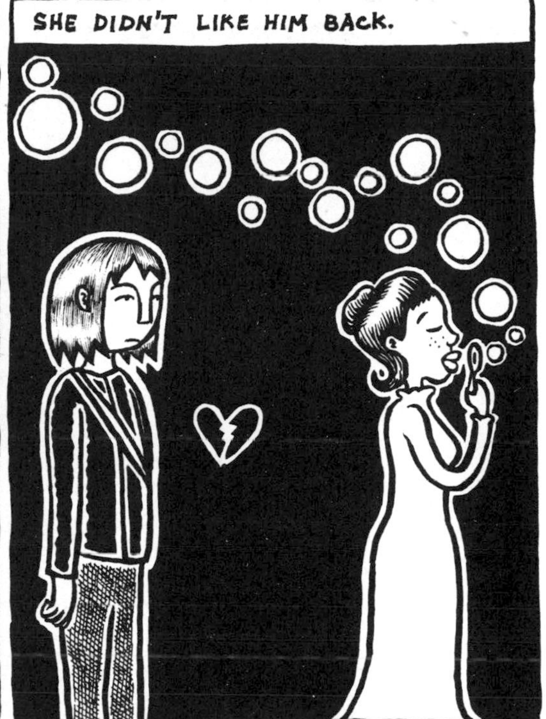
SHE DIDN'T LIKE HIM BACK.

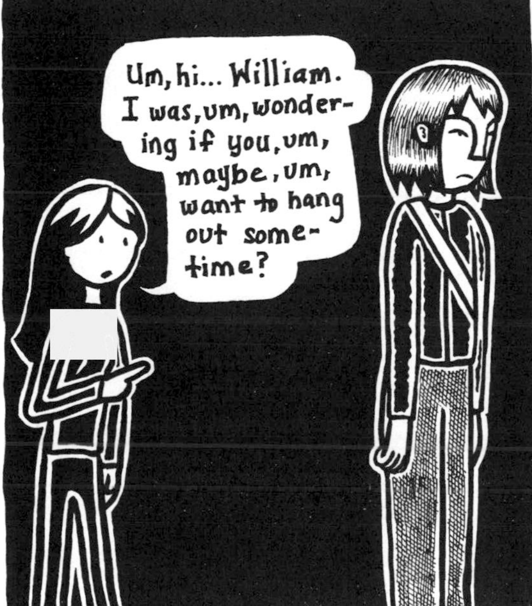
WITH MY EGO PRIMED BY MONTHS OF FOOLING AROUND WITH BOYS, I GATHERED THE NERVE AND MADE MY MOVE.
Um, hi... William. I was, um, wondering if you, um, maybe, um, want to hang out sometime?

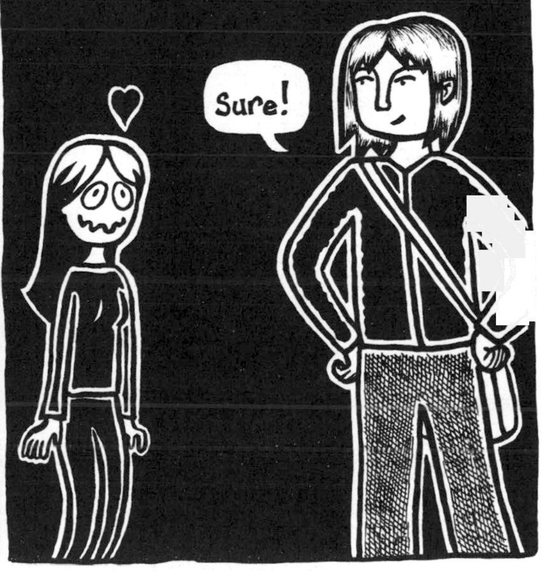
WHEN HE RESPONDED FAVORABLY, THE SURPRISE I FELT MANIFESTED ITSELF IN THE QUEER SENSATION OF MY STOMACH FALLING WAY BELOW MY FEET.
Sure!

HE TOOK ME TO HIS HOUSEBOAT.

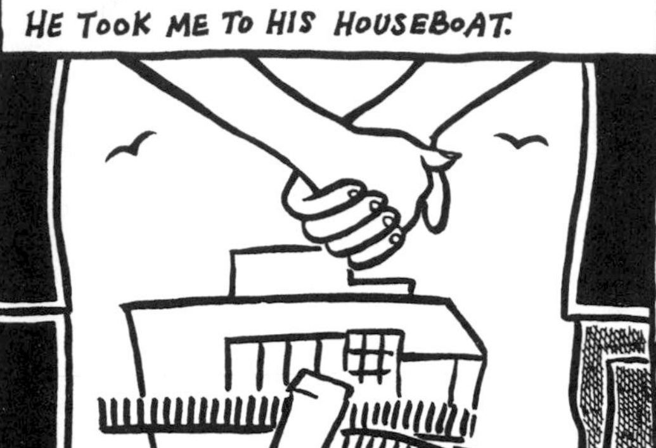

BY NOW WE'D KISSED. HE HAD THIN, TIGHT LIPS AND AN AWKWARD, CHOPPY KISSING STYLE.

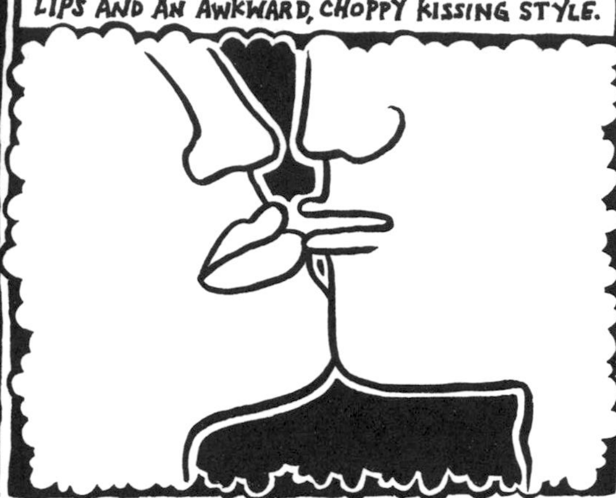

HE LIVED WITH HIS DAD, A MUSICIAN WHO SOLD POT. THEY THREW HUGE PARTIES FULL OF KIDS WHO GREW UP PUMPING BILGES AND WHO KNEW HOW TO RAISE A SAIL.

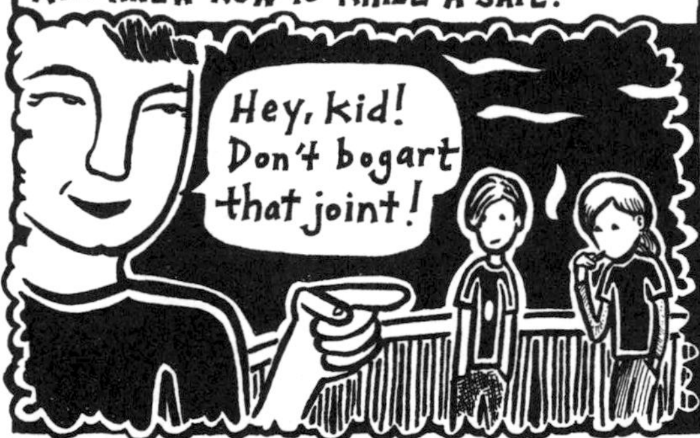

NOT RICH KIDS BUT GRIMY, SEXY ADOLESCENTS WHO HAD AN ALOOF AIR TO THEM INHERITED FROM DISTANT, WILD PARENTS.

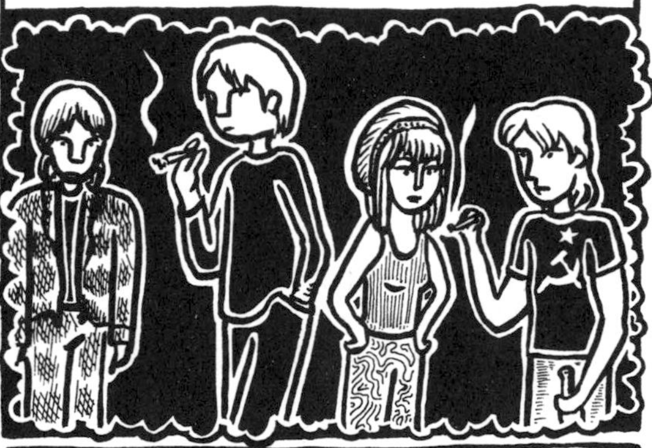

THE OLD FERRY BOAT HE AND HIS DAD LIVED ON WAS A LABYRINTH FILLED WITH BIZARRE ARTIFACTS, INCLUDING A COSTUME WORN BY A LITTLE PERSON IN "THE WIZARD OF OZ."

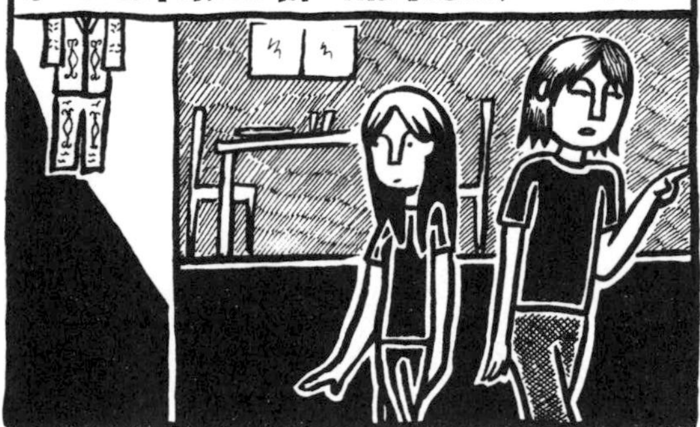

I STUDIED THE FADED GREEN EMBROIDERY, WISHING I COULD RUN MY HANDS DOWN IT BUT NOT DARING TO.

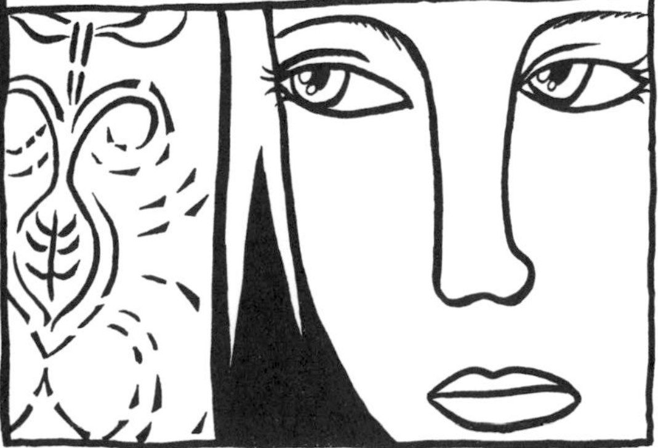

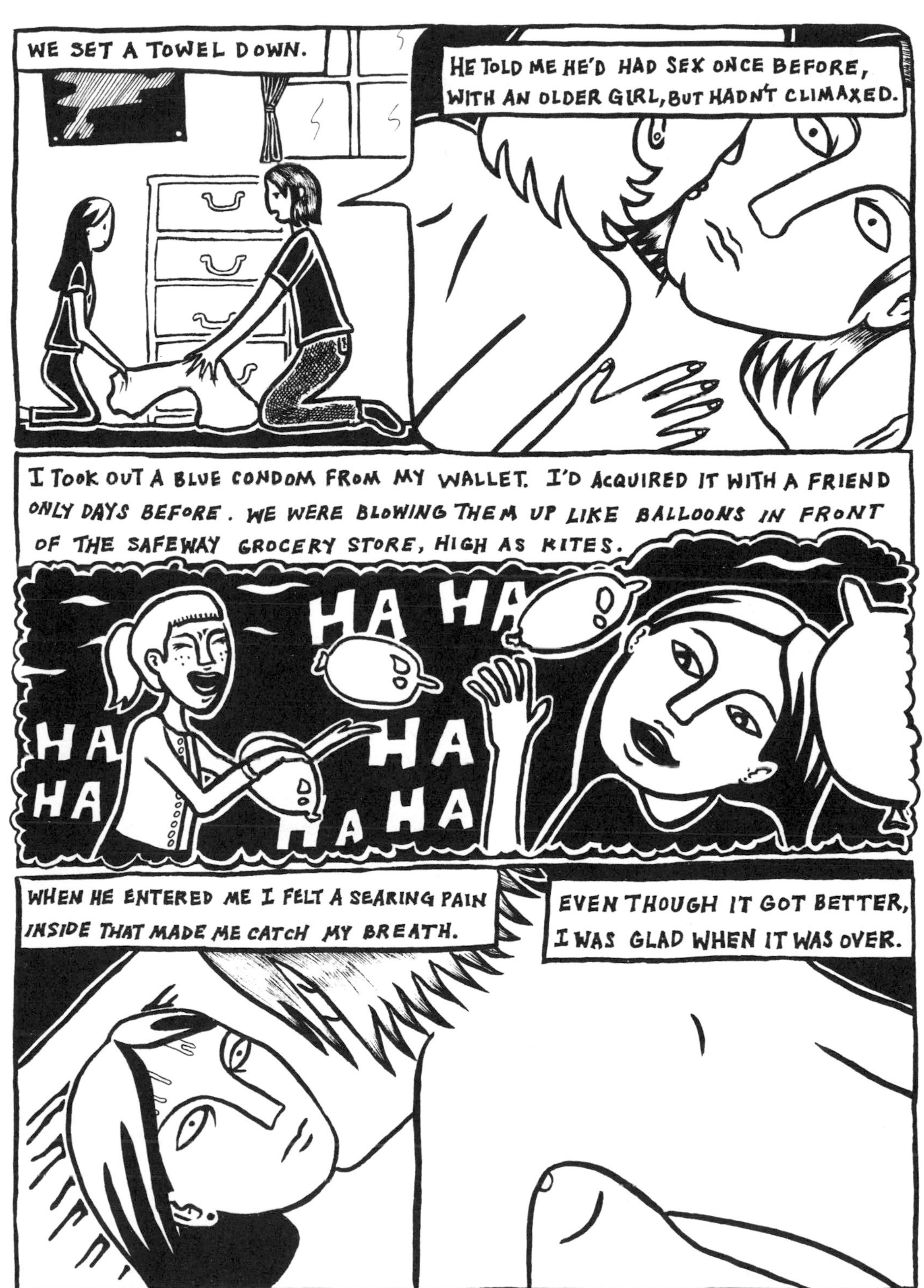
WE SET A TOWEL DOWN.
HE TOLD ME HE'D HAD SEX ONCE BEFORE, WITH AN OLDER GIRL, BUT HADN'T CLIMAXED.
I TOOK OUT A BLUE CONDOM FROM MY WALLET. I'D ACQUIRED IT WITH A FRIEND ONLY DAYS BEFORE. WE WERE BLOWING THEM UP LIKE BALLOONS IN FRONT OF THE SAFEWAY GROCERY STORE, HIGH AS KITES.
HA HA
HA
HA
HA
HA
HA HA
WHEN HE ENTERED ME I FELT A SEARING PAIN INSIDE THAT MADE ME CATCH MY BREATH.
EVEN THOUGH IT GOT BETTER, I WAS GLAD WHEN IT WAS OVER.

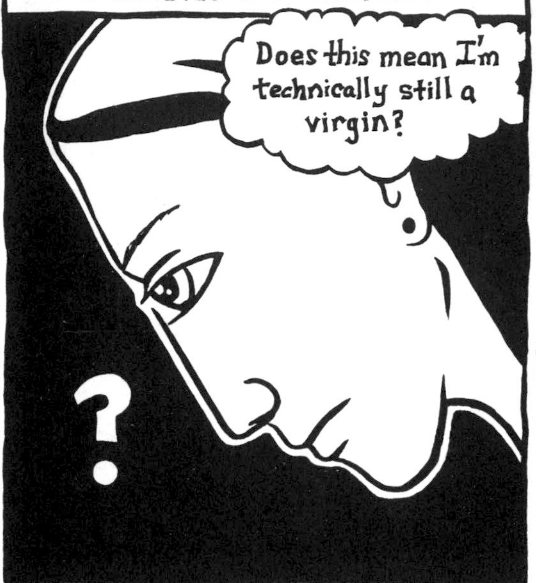
HE ROLLED OVER AND I SEARCHED FOR A BLOOD STAIN ON THE TOWEL. WHEN I FOUND NO CHERRY, I WAS SIMULTANEOUSLY RELIEVED AND DISAPPOINTED.
Does this mean I'm technically still a virgin?
?

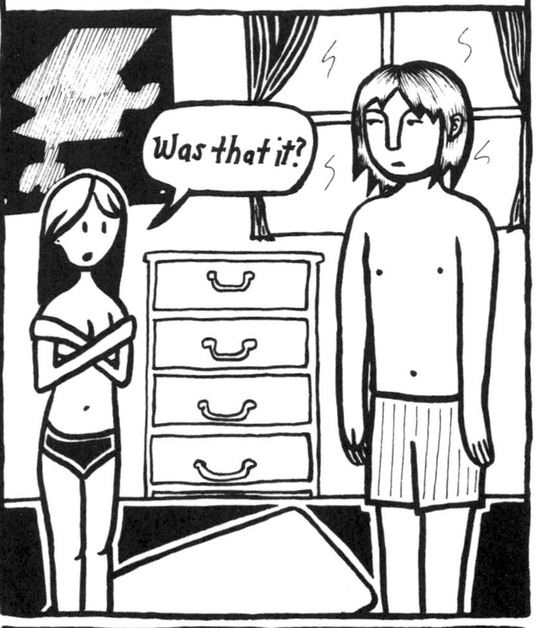
I WANTED TO SOUND COOL BUT I WAS ALSO A LITTLE BIT WORRIED THAT PERHAPS WE'D DONE IT WRONG.
Was that it?

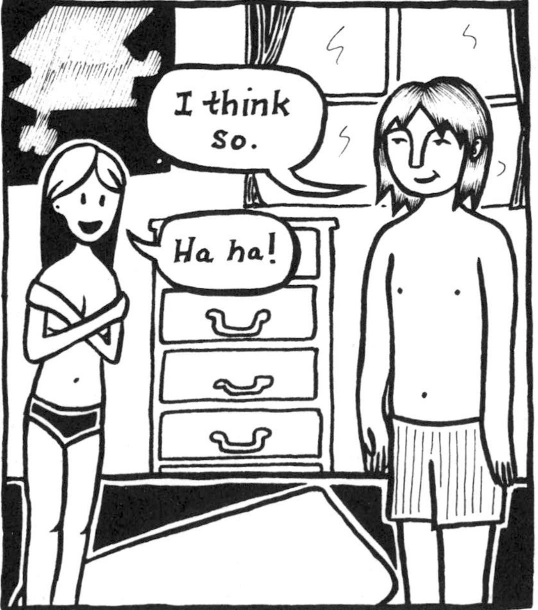
SUDDENLY WE WERE FRIENDS, COMMISERATING ON OUR UNREALISTIC EXPECTATIONS AND OUR SHARED DISAPPOINTMENT.
I think so.
Ha ha!

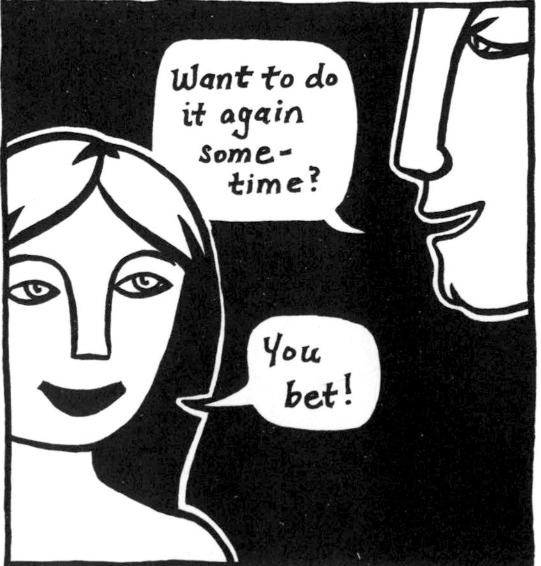
WE AGREED THAT WE'D SOMEHOW BEEN MISLED TO BELIEVE THAT SEX WAS SUPPOSED TO BE THE END-ALL-BE-ALL. BUT AFTER A RESPECTFUL PAUSE...
Want to do it again some-time?
You bet!

A COUPLE OF DAYS LATER I WAS PERCHED ON THE HANDLE BARS OF HIS BICYCLE. SCHOOL HAD JUST GOTTEN OUT, IT WAS A BEAUTIFUL DAY AND WE WERE LOOKING FOR A PLACE TO HAVE SEX.

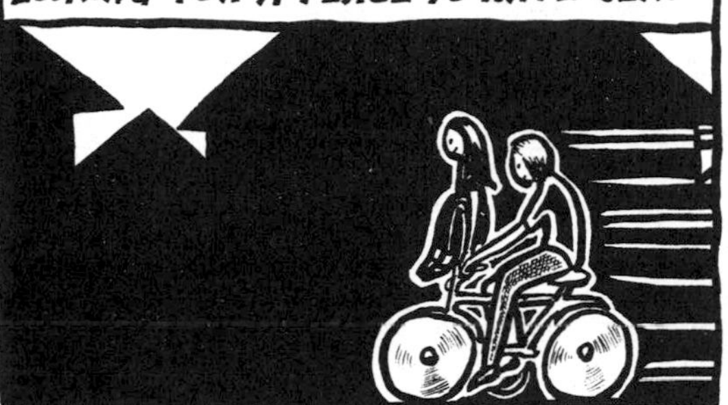

BUT THERE SEEMED TO BE NOWHERE FOR A COUPLE OF TEENS TO FORNICATE, SO OUR EYES WANDERED TO A NEARBY MARSHLAND.

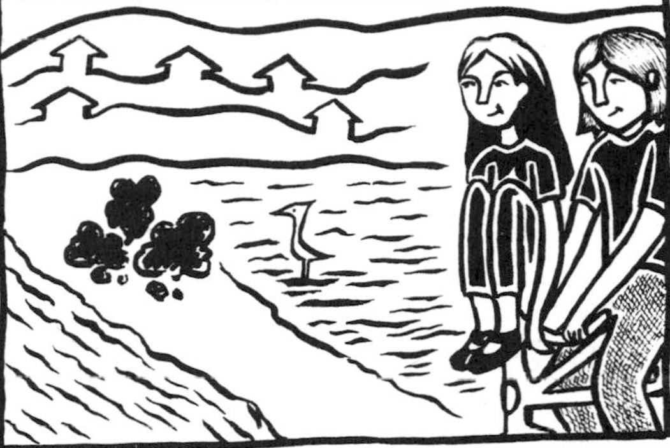

WE SET UP CAMP UNDER A LOW-LYING BUSH, PULLED OFF MY BLACK LEGGINGS AND WENT AT IT. IT HURT AGAIN BUT NOT AS MUCH AS LAST TIME AND I WAS CONVINCED I'D CERTAINLY SHED MY VIRGINITY BY NOW.

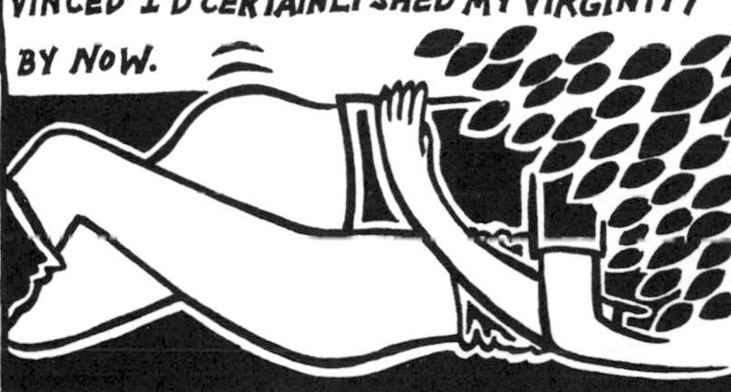

I CLIMBED DELICATELY BACK ON HIS HANDLEBARS, TAKING CARE NOT TO JOSTLE MY TENDER PRIVATE PARTS.

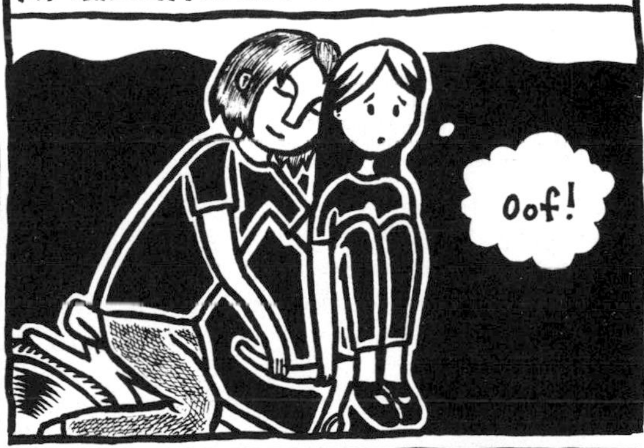

AS WE RODE AWAY I GLANCED BACK AND WAS ALARMED WHEN I REALIZED OUR SECRET PLACE WAS FULLY VISIBLE FROM THE ROAD.

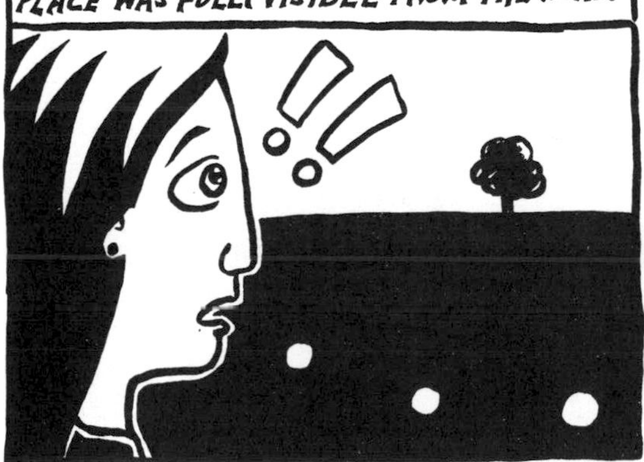

I WONDERED IF MY MOM HAD DRIVEN BY AND NOTICED THE KIDS HUMPING UNDER THE BUSH IN THE MARSH.

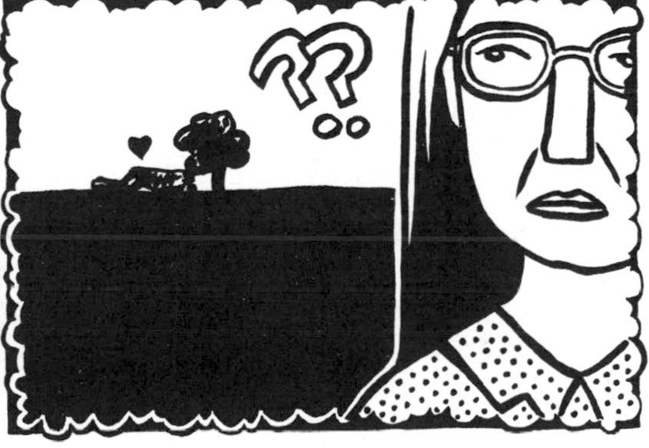

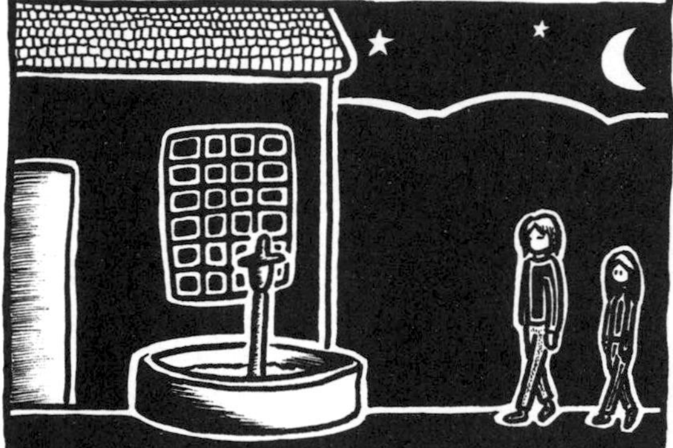
SOME EVENINGS LATER, HE AND I WERE WALKING THROUGH THE EMPTY GROUNDS OF OUR HIGH SCHOOL.

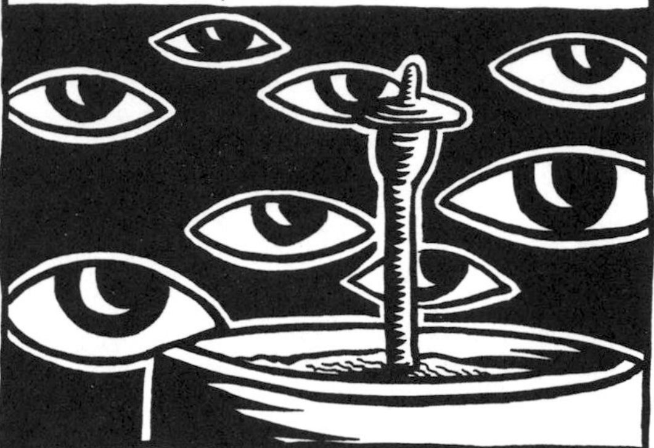
THE MOON SHONE ON THE FOUNTAIN IN THE MIDDLE OF CAMPUS, GIVING IT A COLD, UNEARTHLY GLOW, LIKE THE LOOK IN HIS EYES.

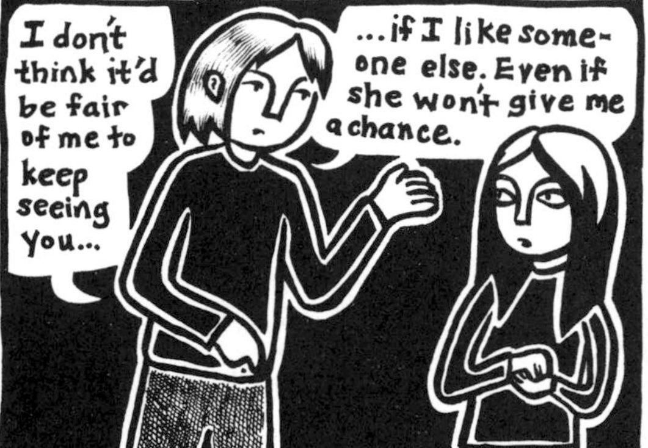
HE WAS GIVING ME THE TALK AND I WAS TAKING IT. HE STILL LIKED MY FRIEND, HE SAID.
I don't think it'd be fair of me to keep seeing you...
...if I like someone else. Even if she won't give me a chance.

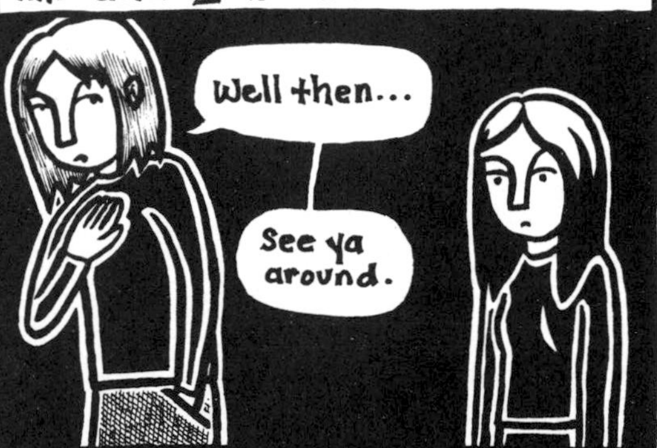
I LISTENED AND NODDED, SECRETLY HOPING THAT HE'D CHANGE HIS MIND AND GIVE ME A CHANCE.
Well then...
See ya around.

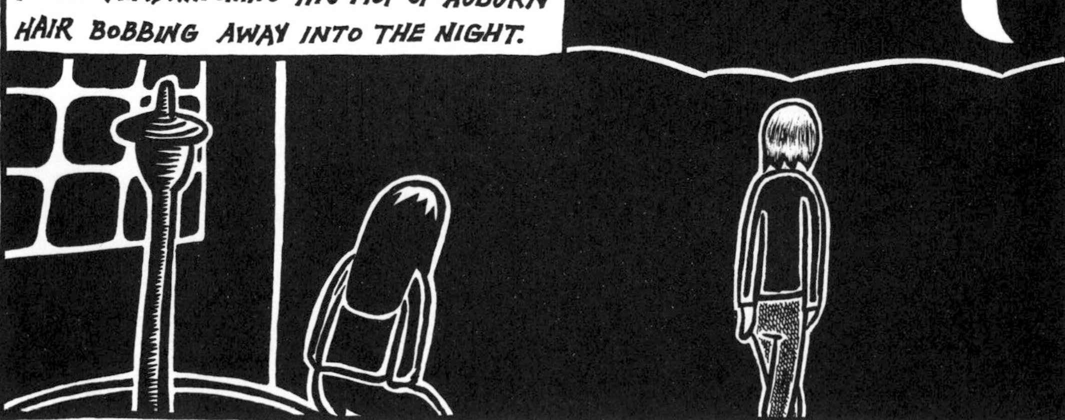
AS WE PARTED, I SAT AT THE LIP OF THE FOUNTAIN, WATCHING HIS MOP OF AUBURN HAIR BOBBING AWAY INTO THE NIGHT.

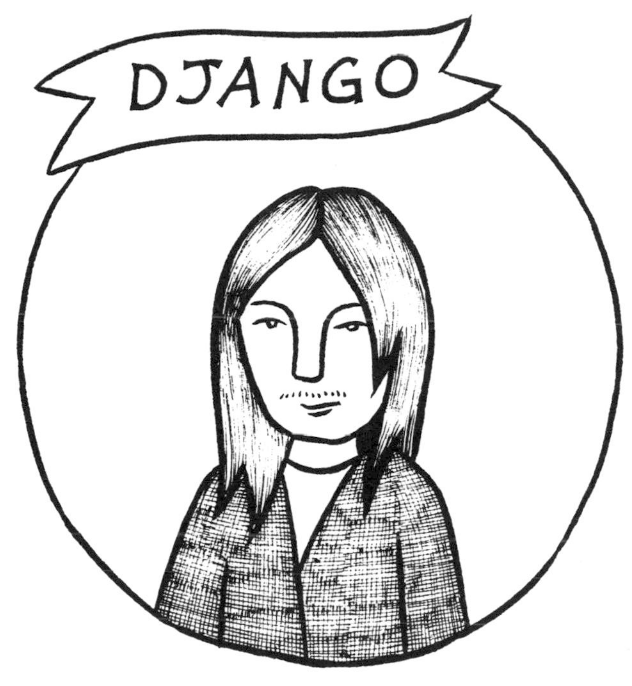
DJANGO

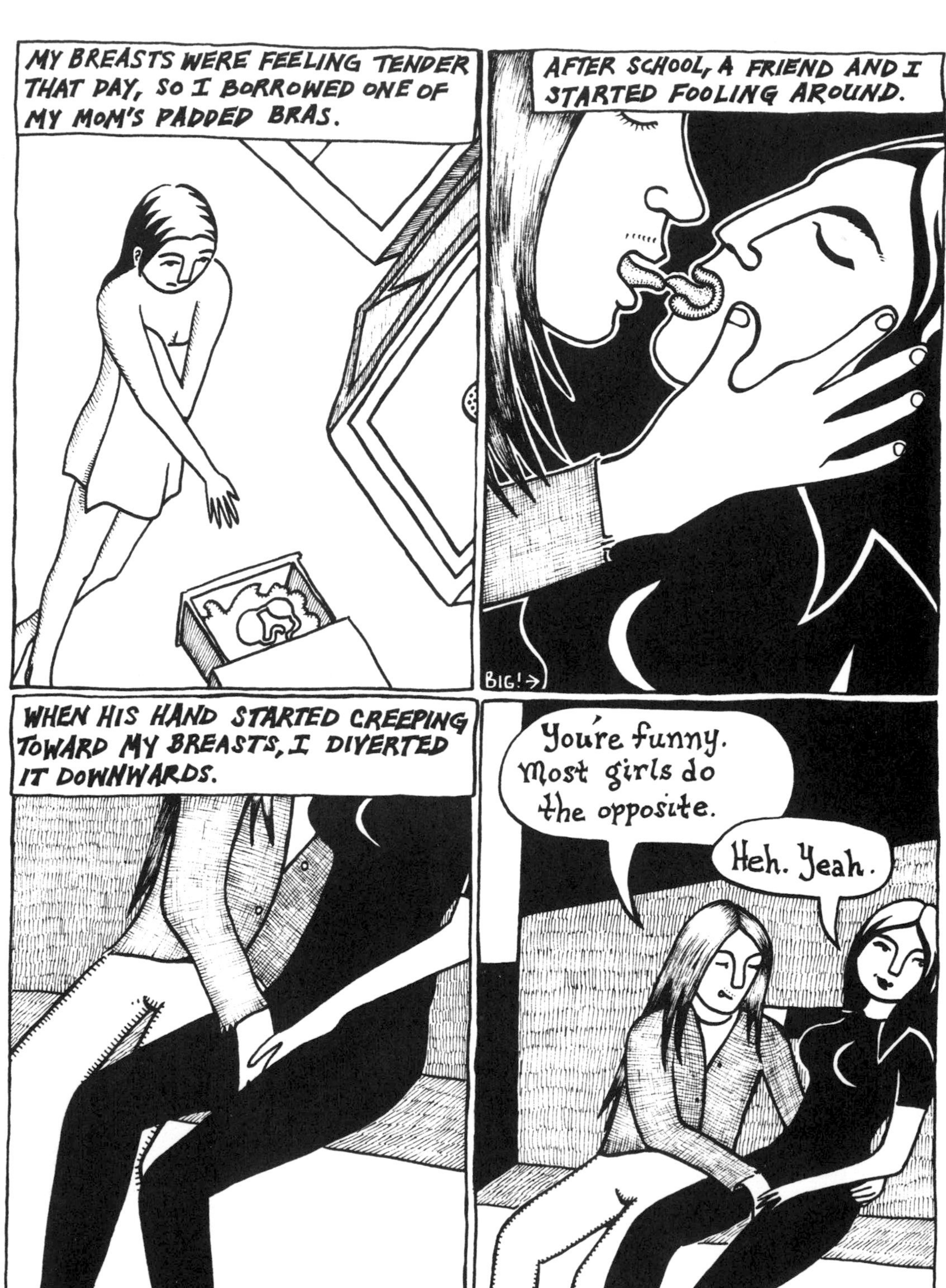
MY BREASTS WERE FEELING TENDER THAT DAY, SO I BORROWED ONE OF MY MOM'S PADDED BRAS.
AFTER SCHOOL, A FRIEND AND I STARTED FOOLING AROUND.
BIG! →
WHEN HIS HAND STARTED CREEPING TOWARD MY BREASTS, I DIVERTED IT DOWNWARDS.
You're funny. Most girls do the opposite.
Heh. Yeah.

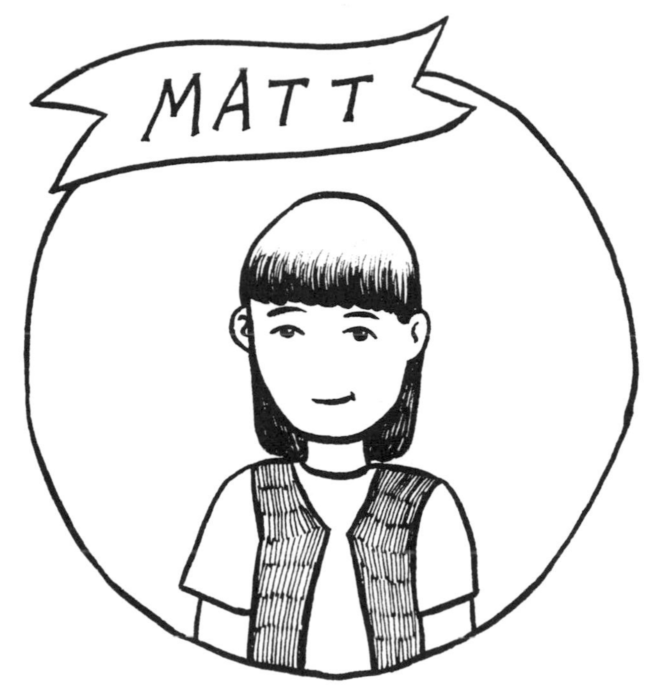
MATT

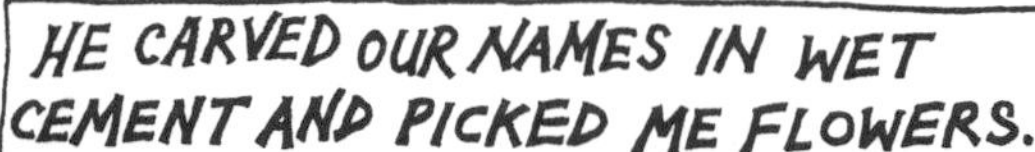

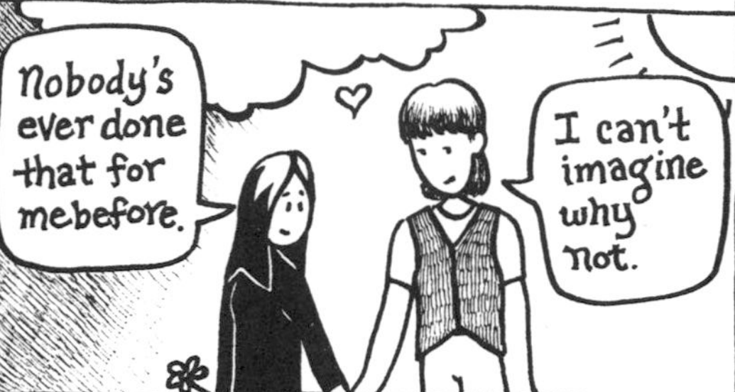

I WAS EXCITED SINCE IT WAS FEBRUARY AND I'D NEVER HAD A BOYFRIEND ON VALENTINE'S DAY.

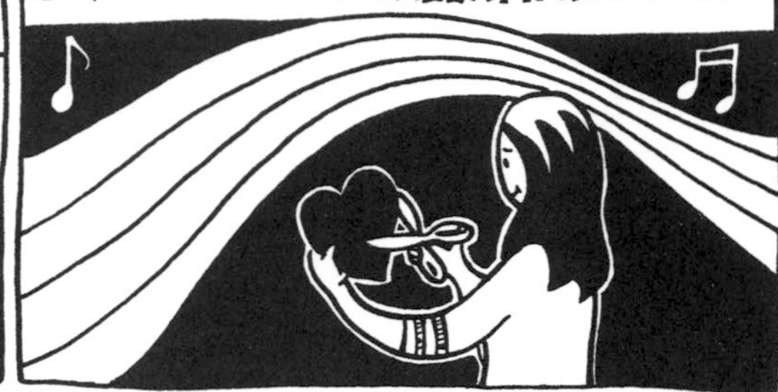

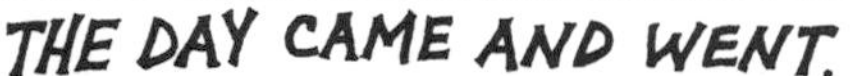

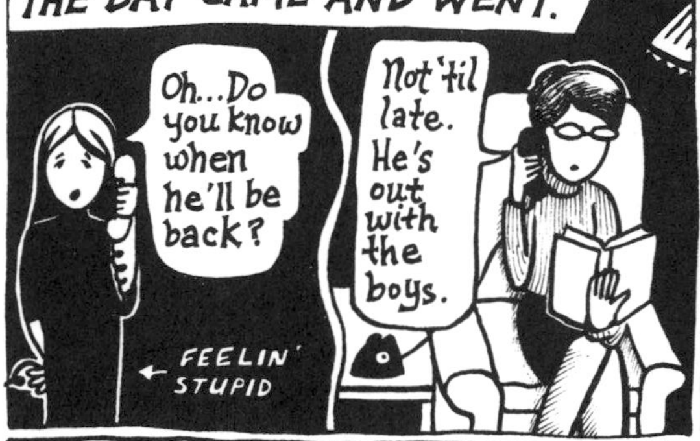

AND THEN...

I think we should be friends. I'm not over my ex yet.

OUR DRAMA DEPARTMENT HAD A DANCE-A-THON TO RAISE MONEY.

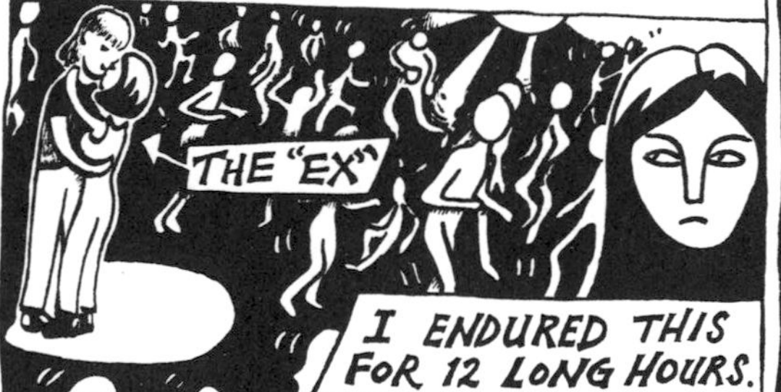

OVER THE YEARS WE MADE OUT AT VARIOUS PARTIES.

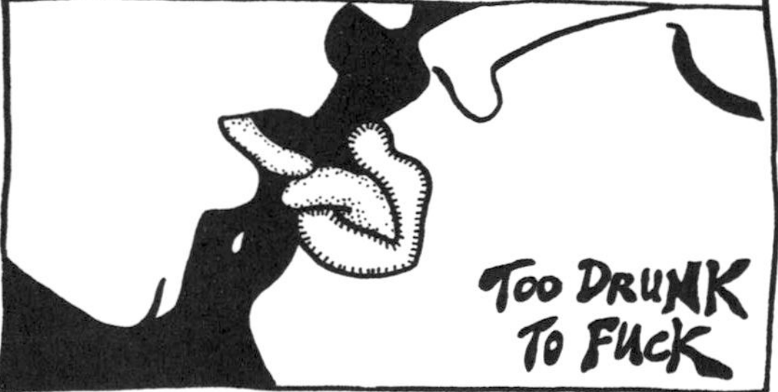

WHEN I WAS 17 WE CONSUMMATED OUR FRIENDSHIP, FINALLY.

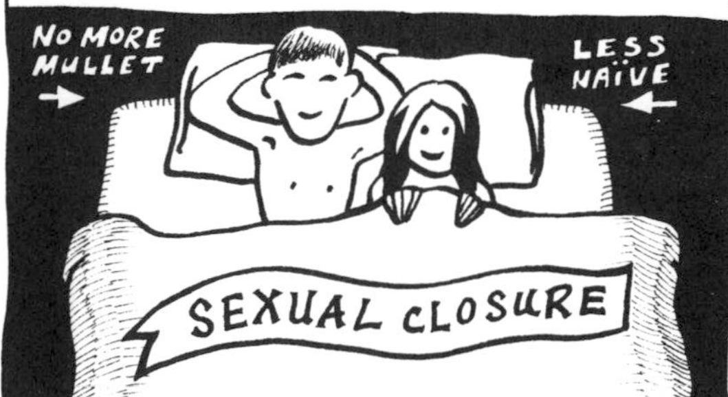

A DECADE LATER, I RAN INTO HIS EX AT A LESBIAN CLUB.

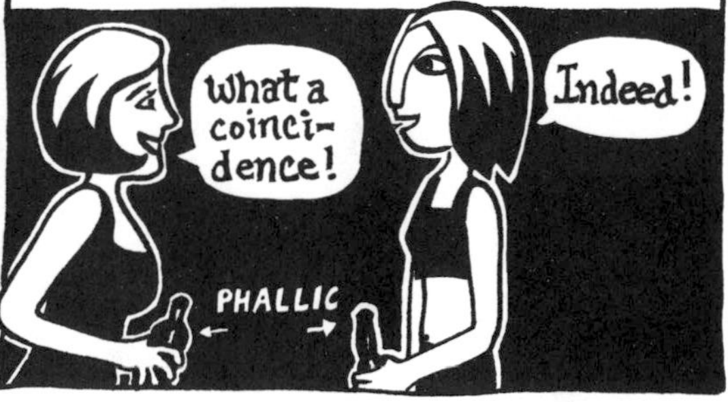

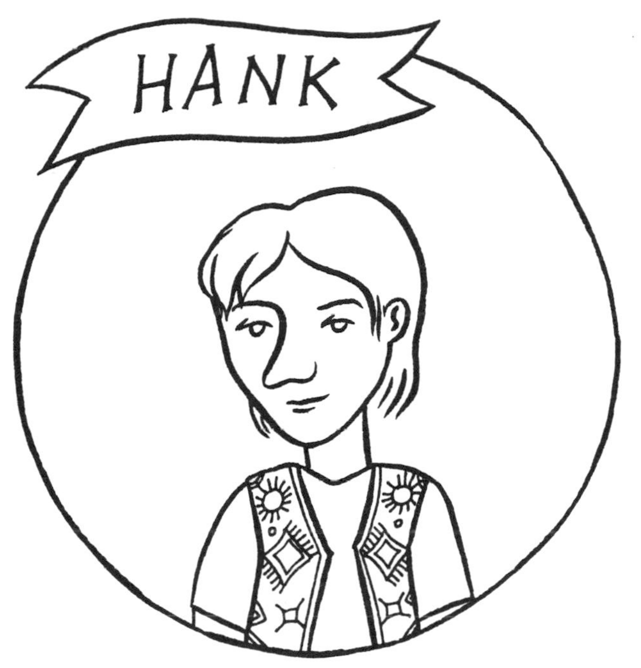
HANK

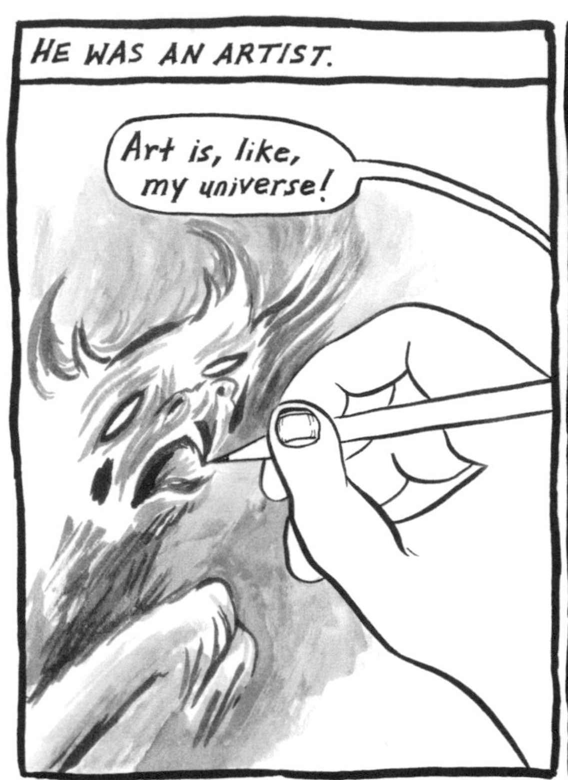
HE WAS AN ARTIST.
Art is, like, my universe!

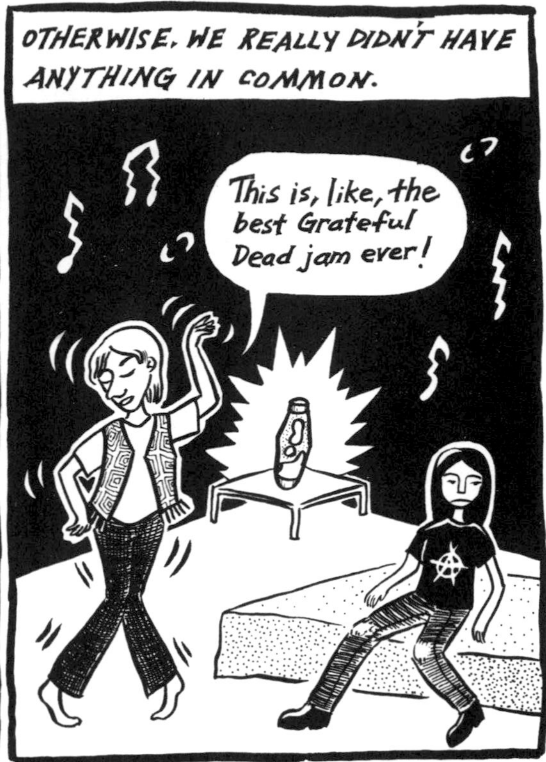
OTHERWISE, WE REALLY DIDN'T HAVE ANYTHING IN COMMON.
This is, like, the best Grateful Dead jam ever!

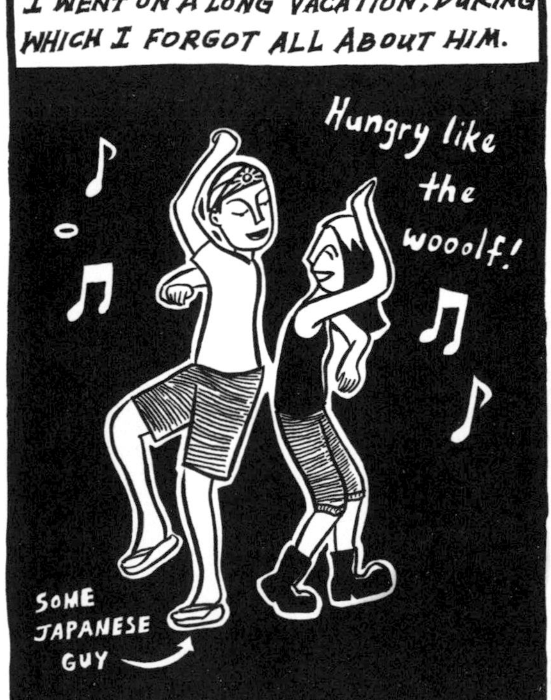
I WENT ON A LONG VACATION, DURING WHICH I FORGOT ALL ABOUT HIM.
Hungry like the wooolf!
SOME JAPANESE GUY

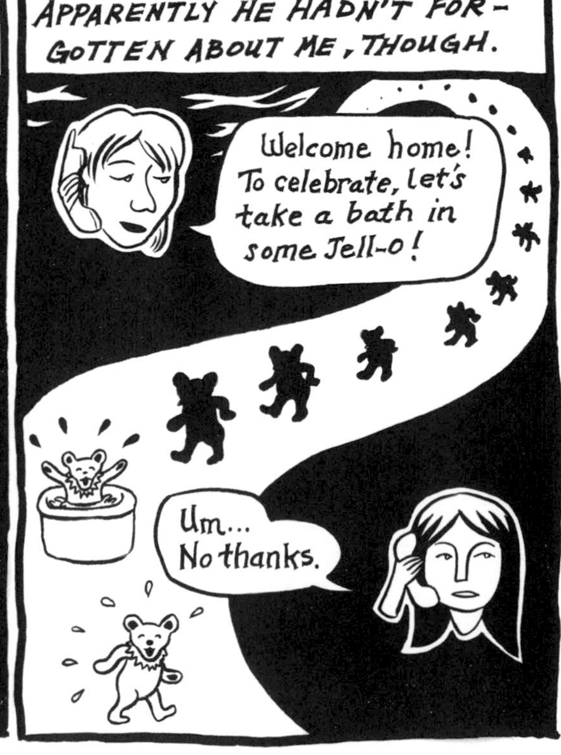
APPARENTLY HE HADN'T FOR-GOTTEN ABOUT ME, THOUGH.
Welcome home! To celebrate, let's take a bath in some Jell-o!
Um... No thanks.

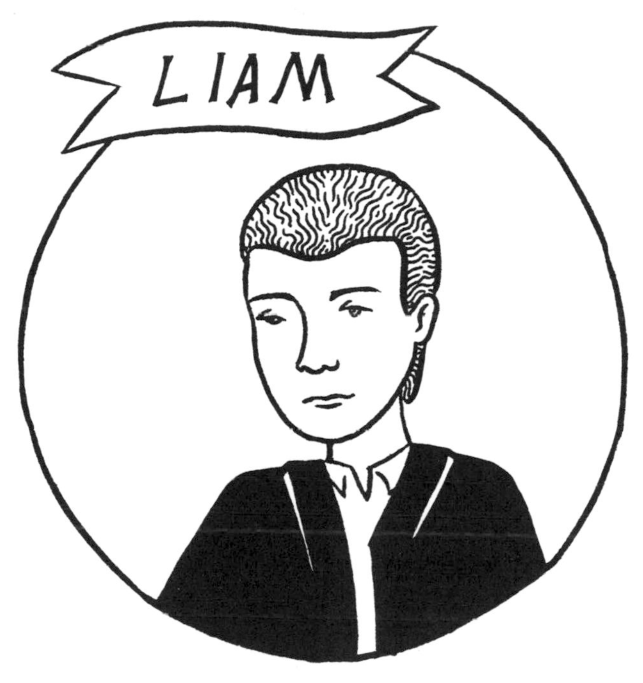
LIAM

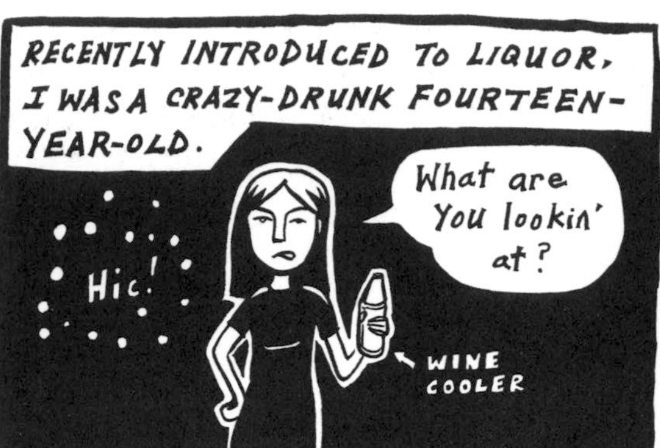
RECENTLY INTRODUCED TO LIQUOR, I WAS A CRAZY-DRUNK FOURTEEN-YEAR-OLD.
Hic!
What are you lookin' at?
WINE COOLER

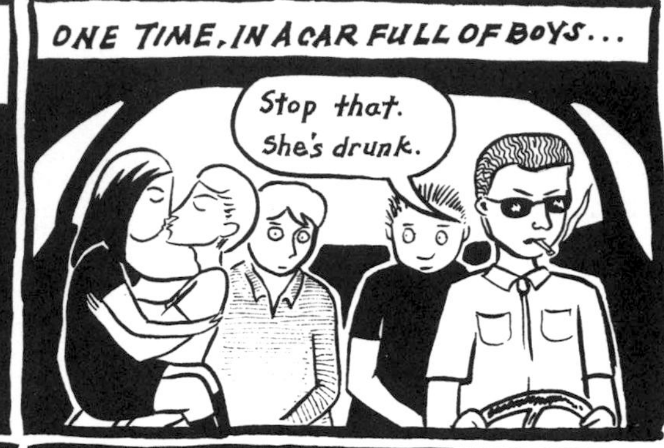
ONE TIME, IN A CAR FULL OF BOYS...
Stop that. She's drunk.

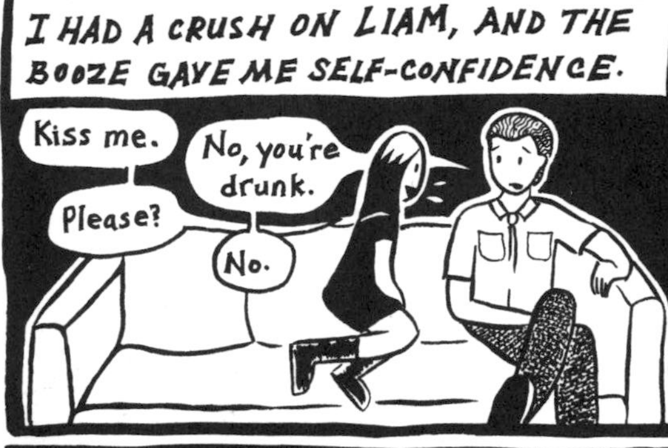
I HAD A CRUSH ON LIAM, AND THE BOOZE GAVE ME SELF-CONFIDENCE.
Kiss me.
No, you're drunk.
Please?
No.

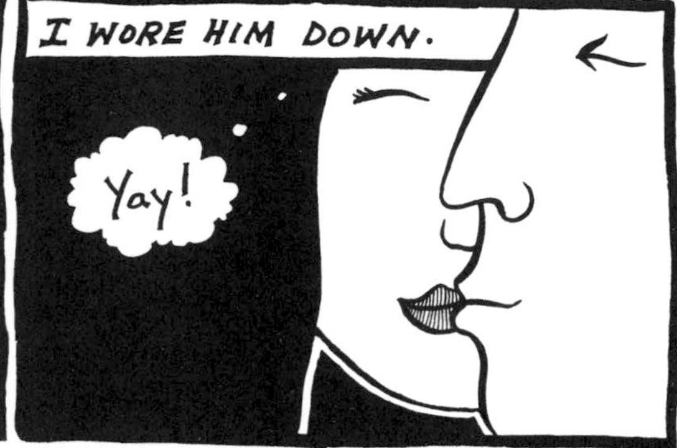
I WORE HIM DOWN.
Yay!

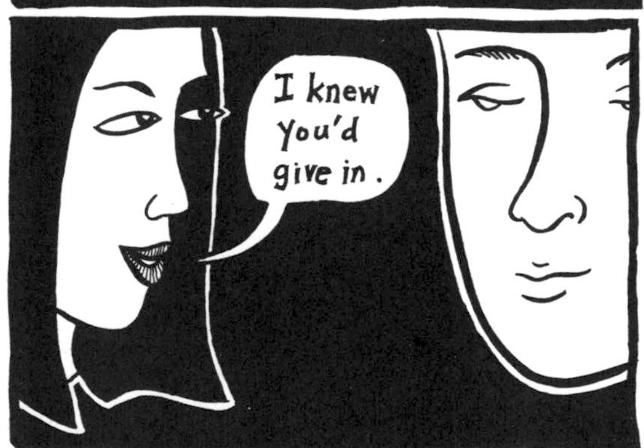
I knew you'd give in.

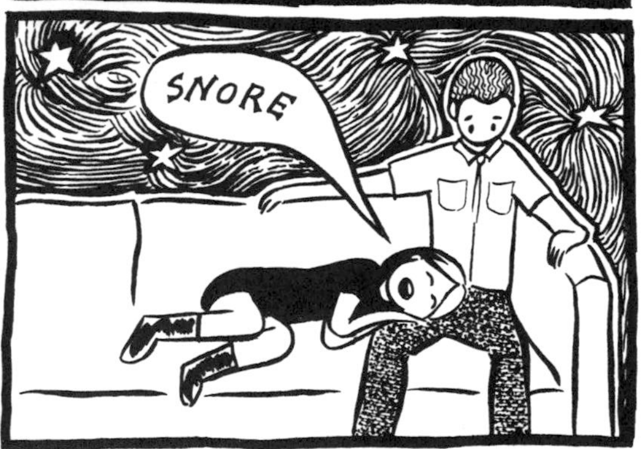
SNORE

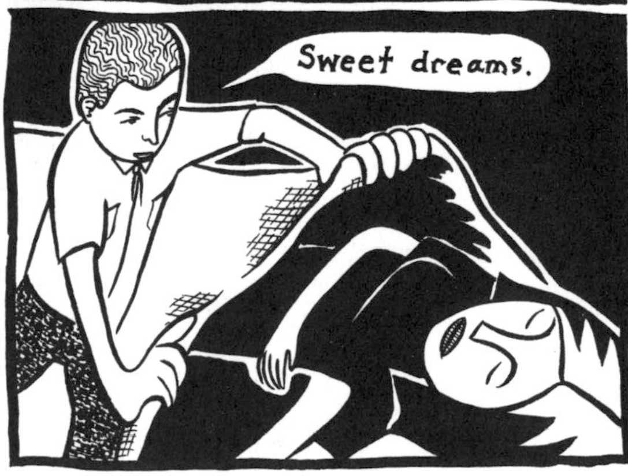
Sweet dreams.

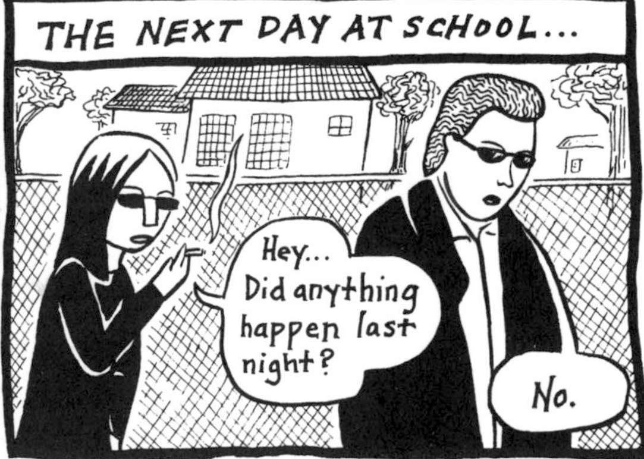
THE NEXT DAY AT SCHOOL...
Hey... Did anything happen last night?
No.

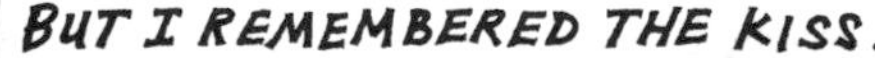

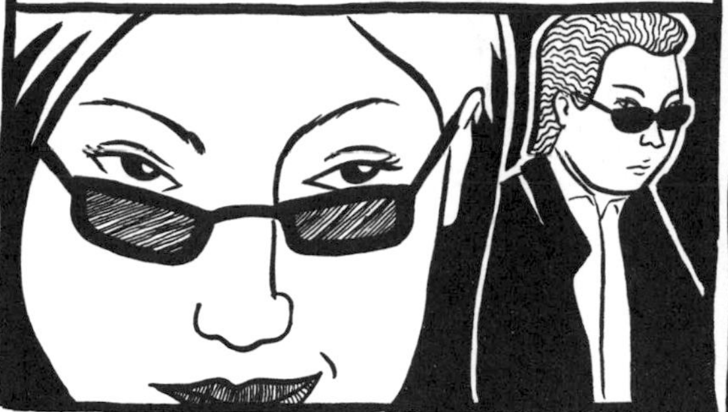

FOUR DAYS LATER, WE WERE AN ITEM.

HE HAD A CERTAIN CHARISMA THAT DREW ME TO HIM, DESPITE HIS ACID-WASHED JEANS. AND HIS CAMARO. AND HIS COMPULSIVE LYING.

!!

♫ SOME KIND OF STRANGER COME INSIIIDE ♪

The Sisters of Mercy STOLE this song from me. I wrote it when we JAMMED together when I was thirteen.

SUMMER CAME. HE WENT TO THE EAST COAST TO VISIT FAMILY AND I RAN AWAY FROM MINE. WE HAD NO MEANS TO REACH EACH OTHER.

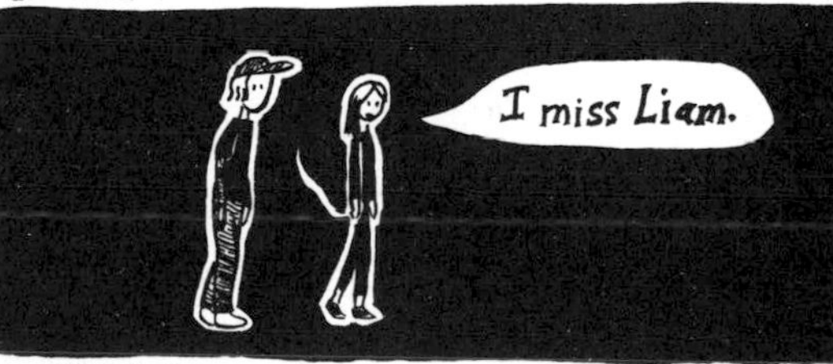

A RUMOR SPREAD AROUND.

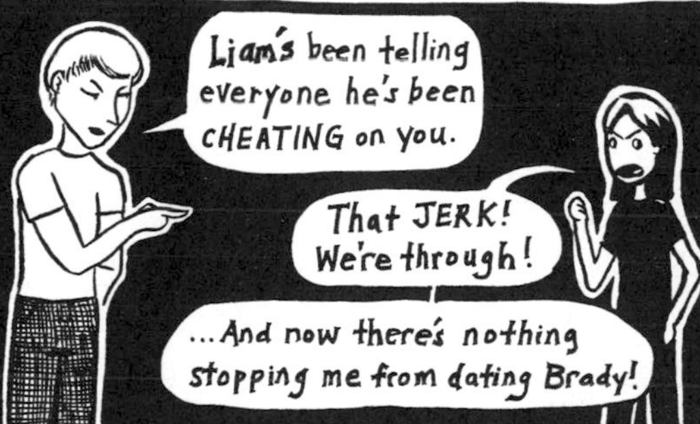

WHEN LIAM RETURNED, I REALLY LET HIM HAVE IT.

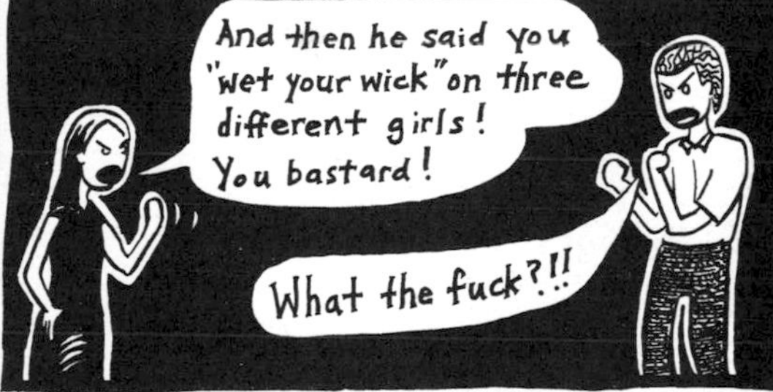

I'D NEVER SEEN HIM SO UPSET.

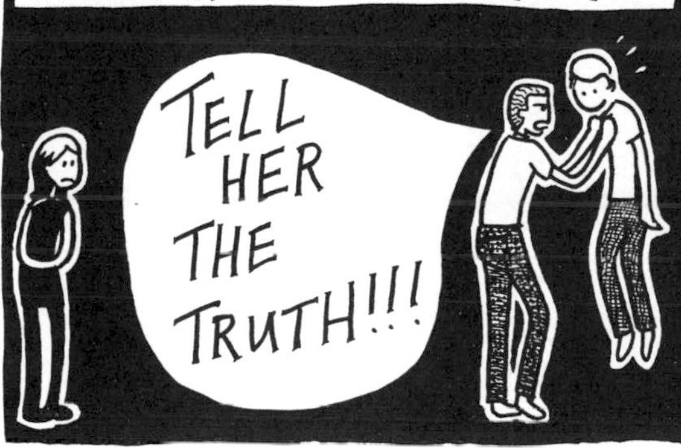

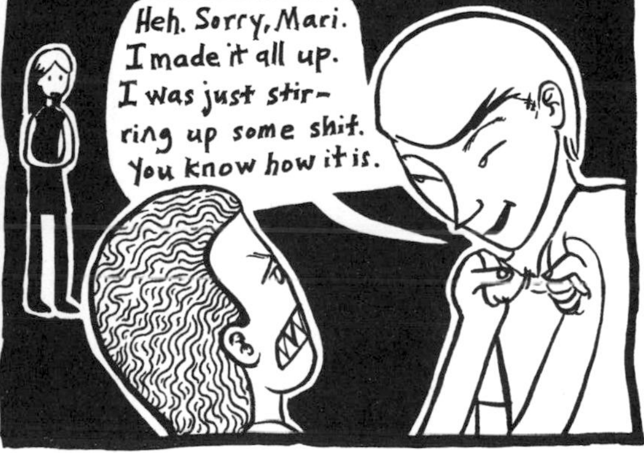

The blackout

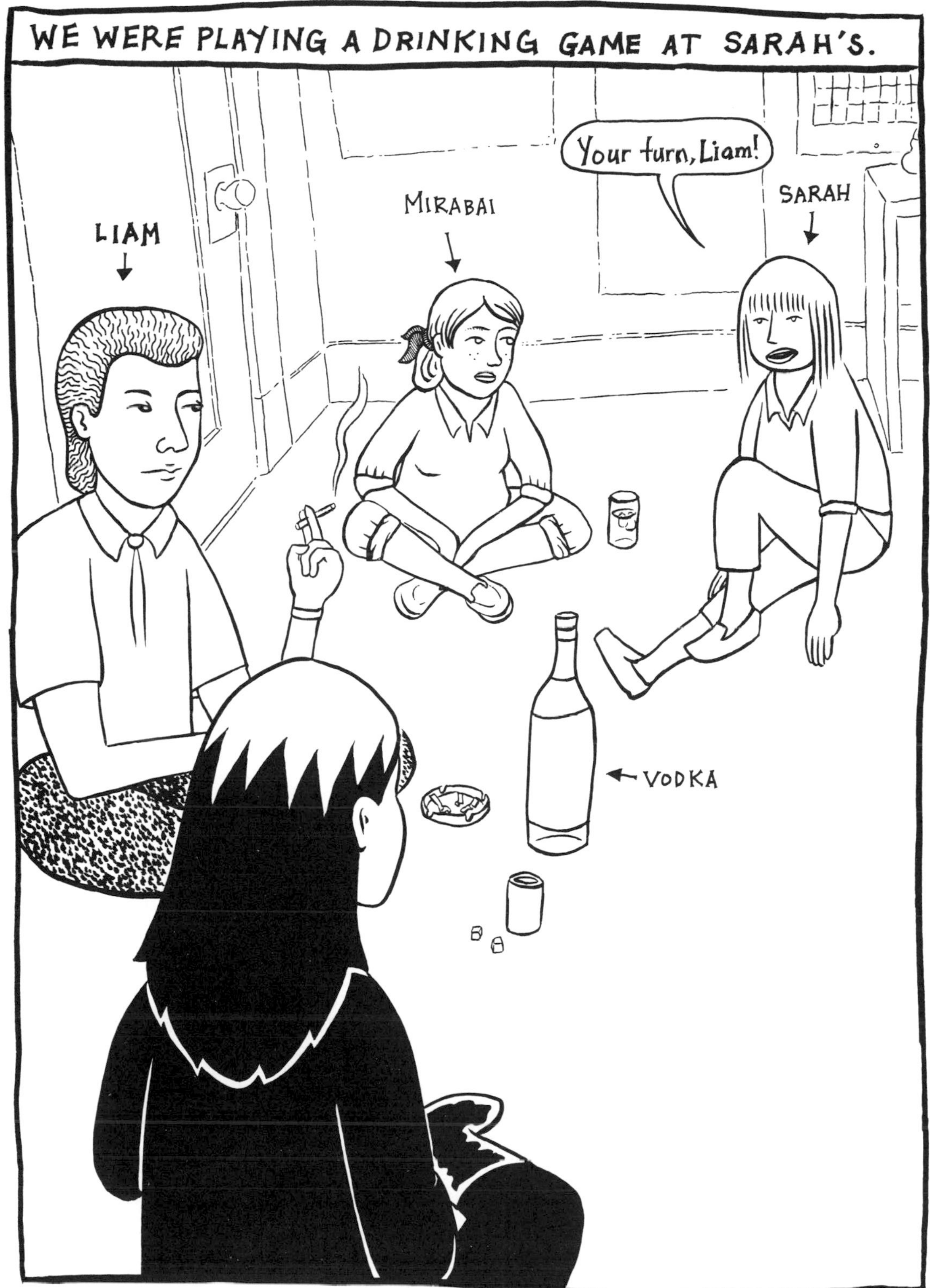
WE WERE PLAYING A DRINKING GAME AT SARAH'S.
Your turn, Liam!
LIAM
MIRABAI
SARAH
VODKA

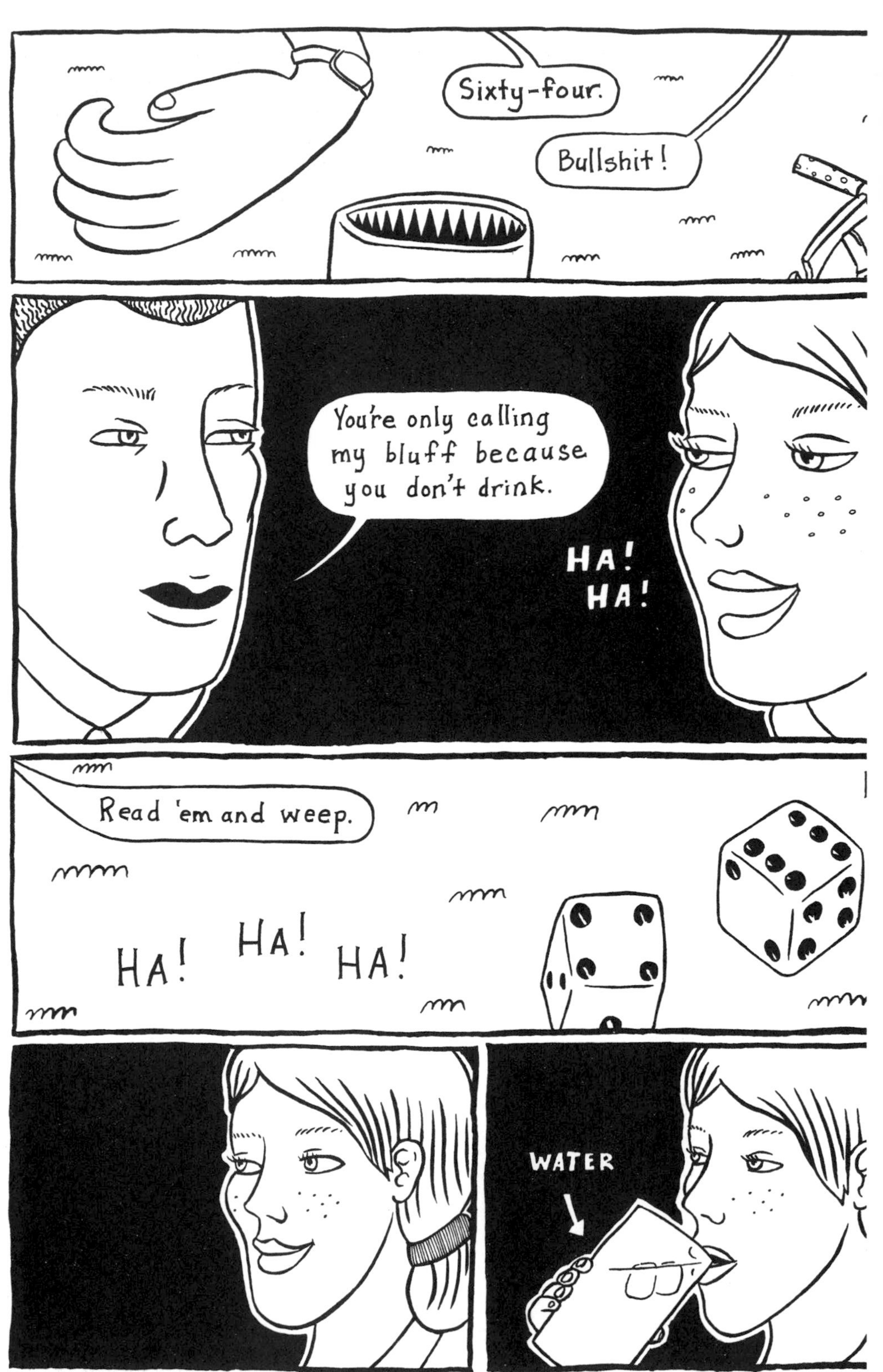
Sixty-four.
Bullshit!
You're only calling my bluff because you don't drink.
HA! HA!
Read 'em and weep.
HA! HA! HA!
WATER

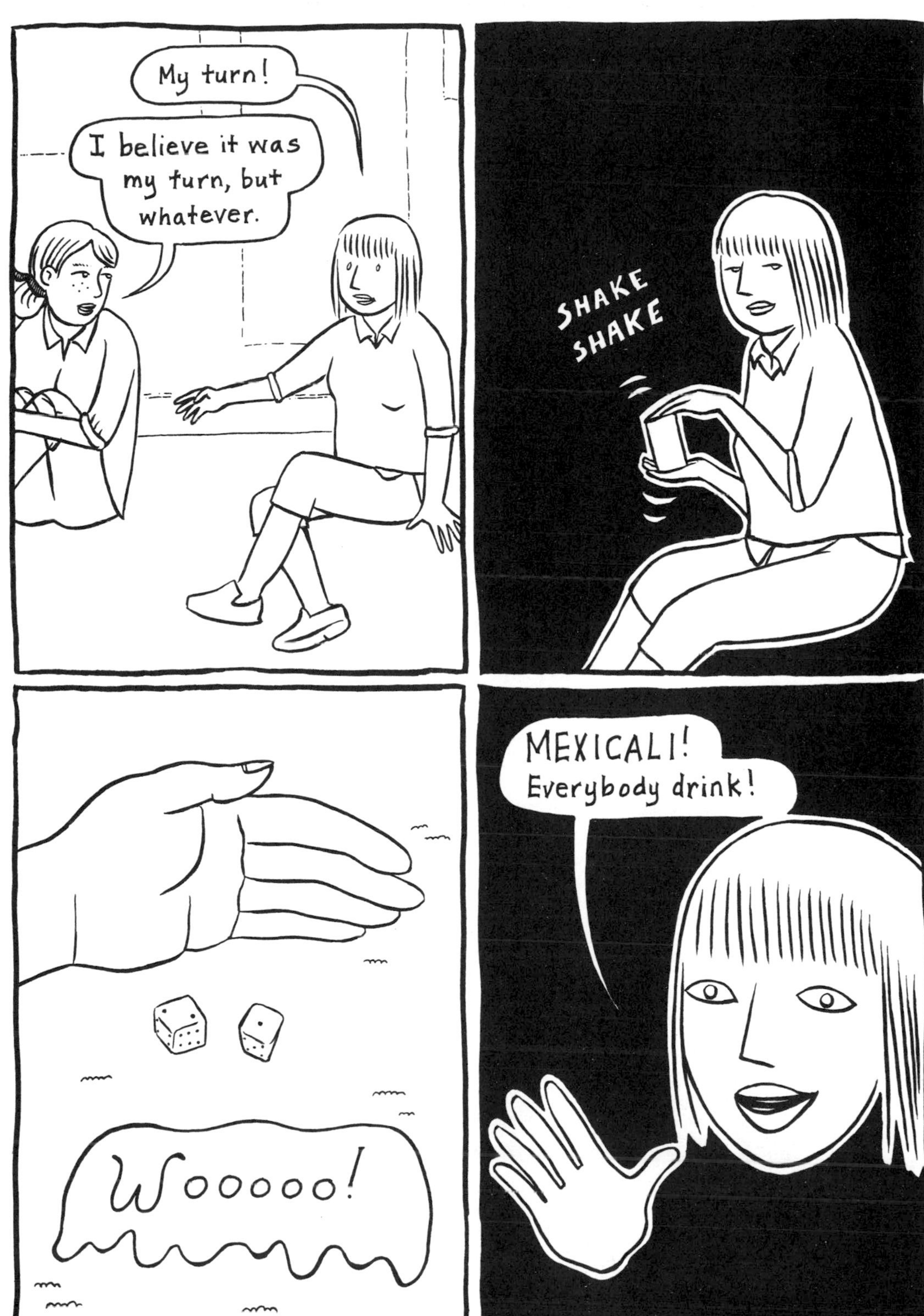
My turn!
I believe it was my turn, but whatever.
SHAKE SHAKE
Wooooo!
MEXICALI! Everybody drink!

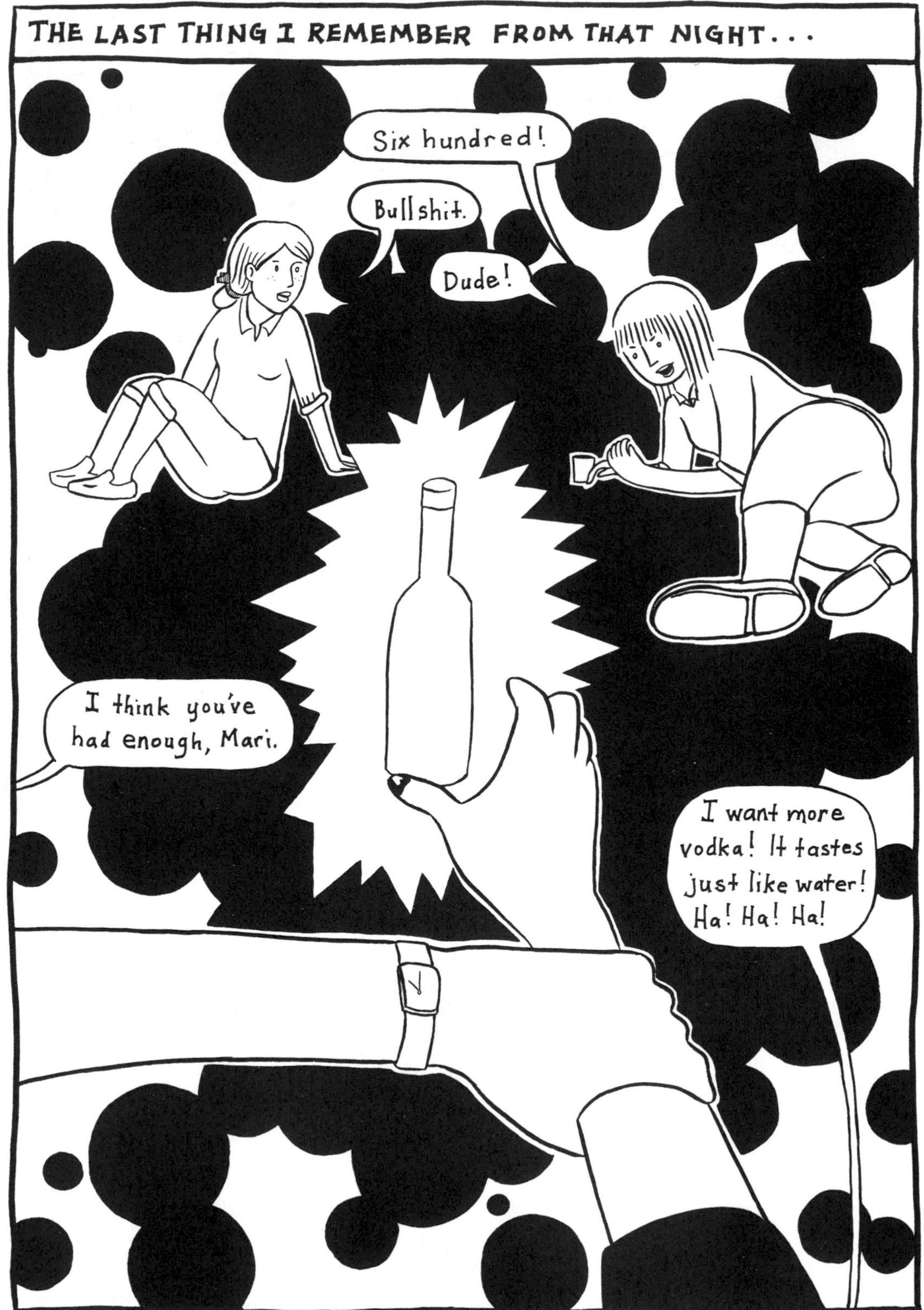
THE LAST THING I REMEMBER FROM THAT NIGHT...
Six hundred!
Bullshit.
Dude!
I think you've had enough, Mari.
I want more vodka! It tastes just like water! Ha! Ha! Ha!

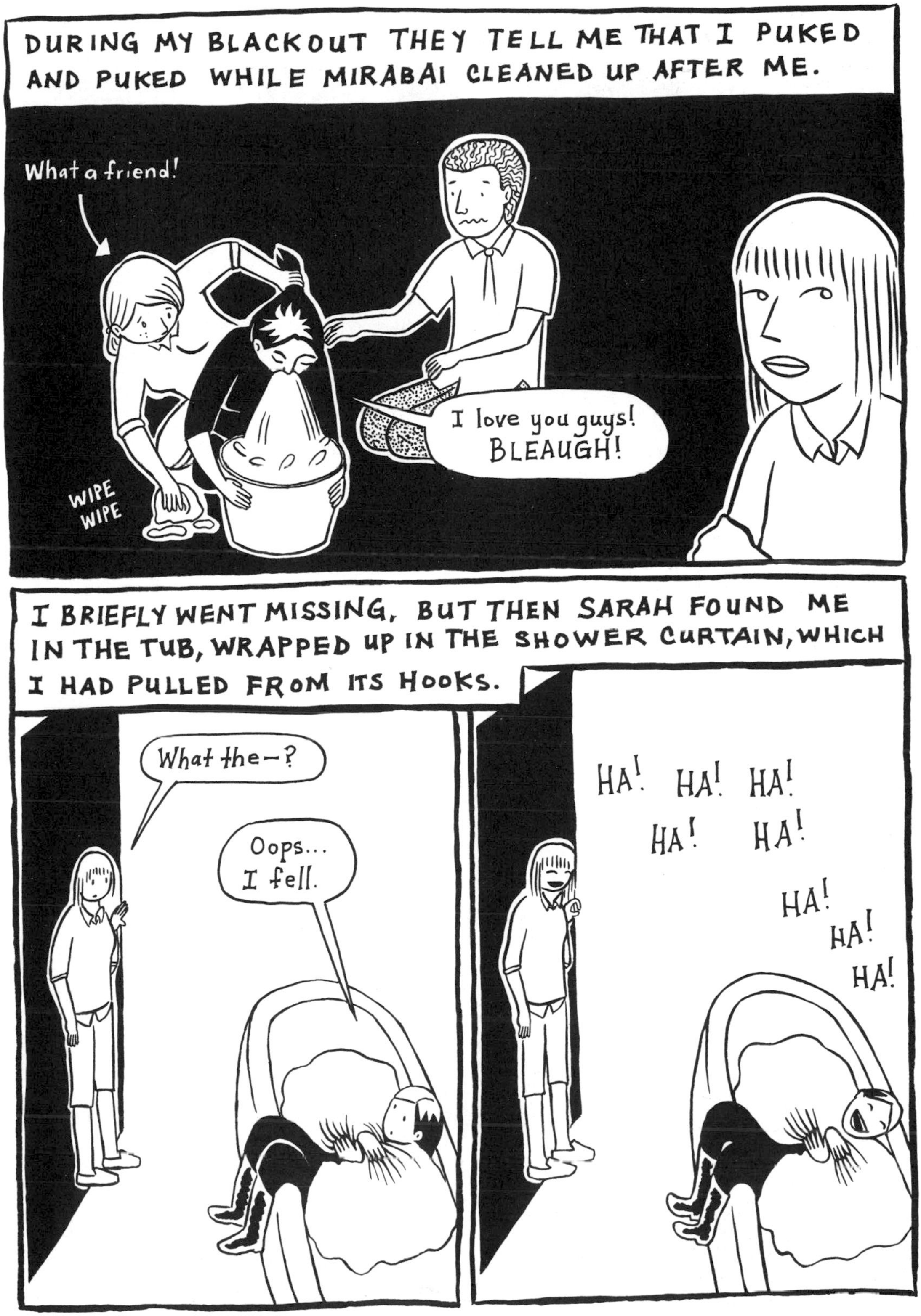

DURING MY BLACKOUT THEY TELL ME THAT I PUKED AND PUKED WHILE MIRABAI CLEANED UP AFTER ME.

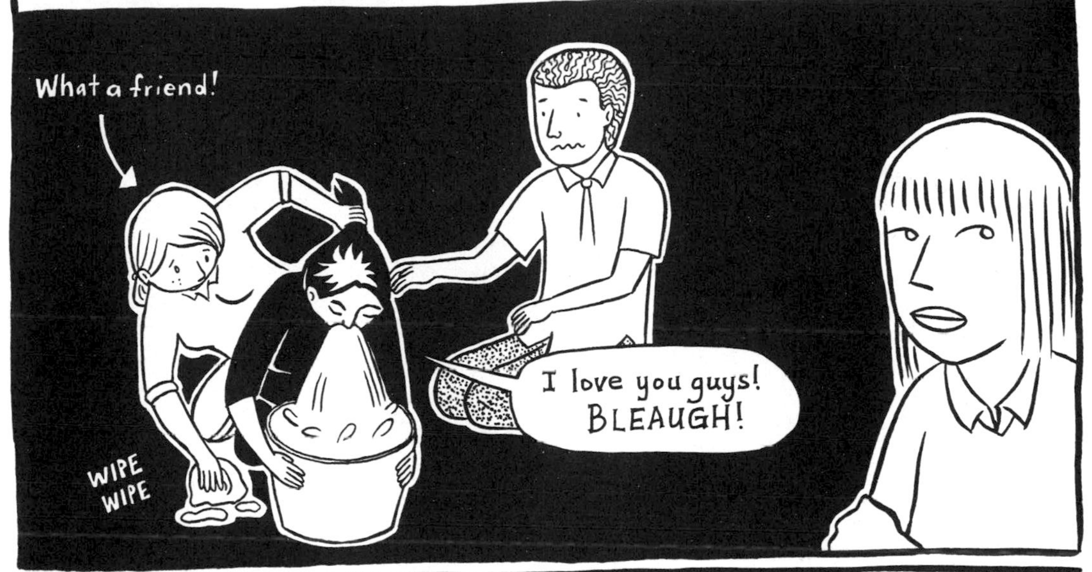

I BRIEFLY WENT MISSING, BUT THEN SARAH FOUND ME IN THE TUB, WRAPPED UP IN THE SHOWER CURTAIN, WHICH I HAD PULLED FROM ITS HOOKS.

What the—?

Oops... I fell.

HA! HA! HA! HA! HA!

HA! HA! HA!

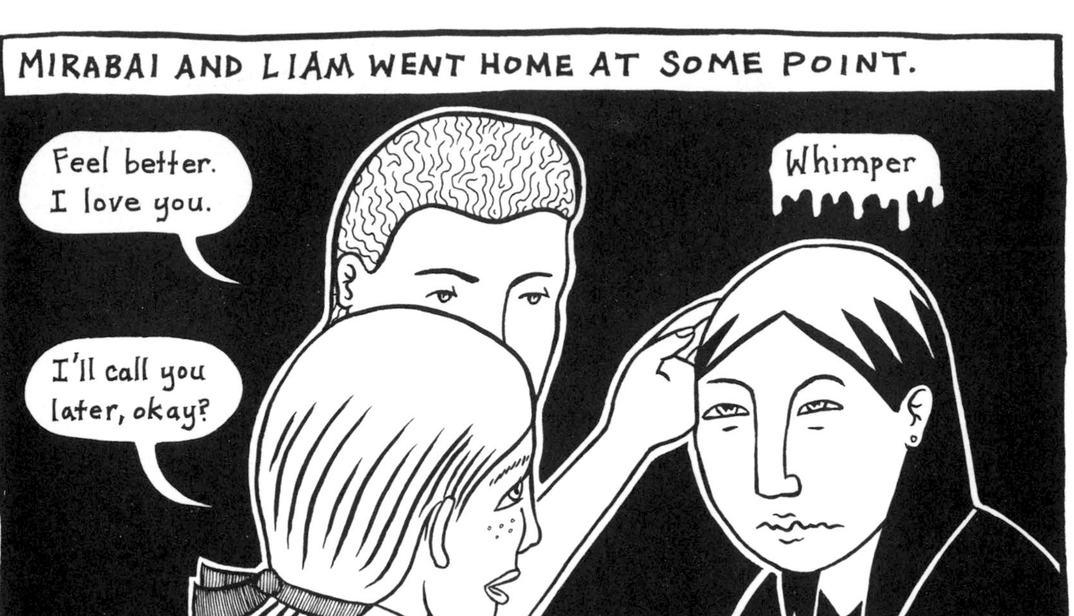
MIRABAI AND LIAM WENT HOME AT SOME POINT.
Feel better. I love you.
I'll call you later, okay?
Whimper

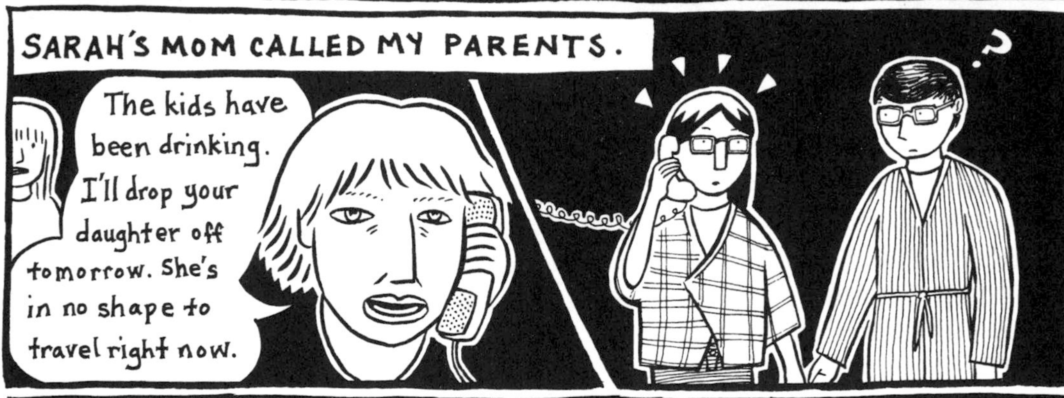
SARAH'S MOM CALLED MY PARENTS.
The kids have been drinking. I'll drop your daughter off tomorrow. She's in no shape to travel right now.
?

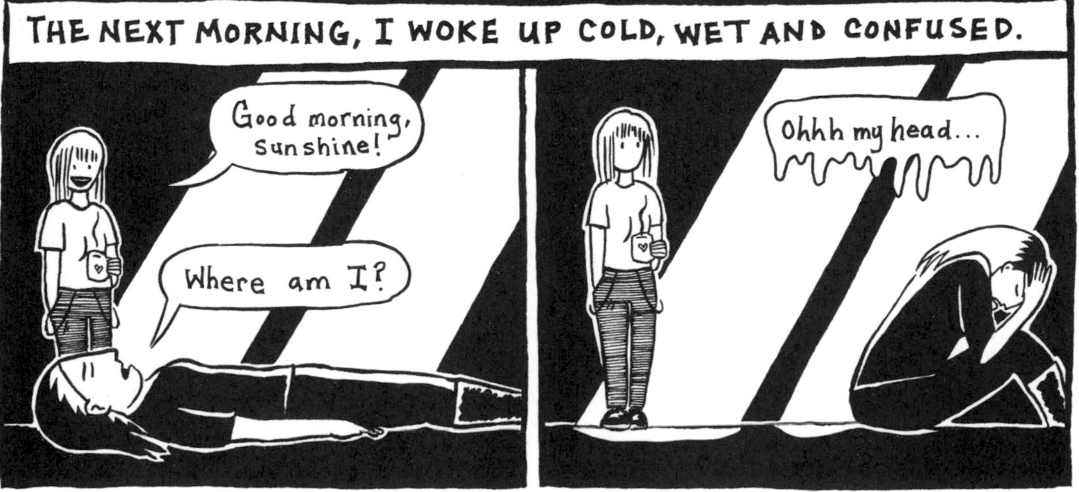
THE NEXT MORNING, I WOKE UP COLD, WET AND CONFUSED.
Good morning, sunshine!
Where am I?
Ohhh my head...

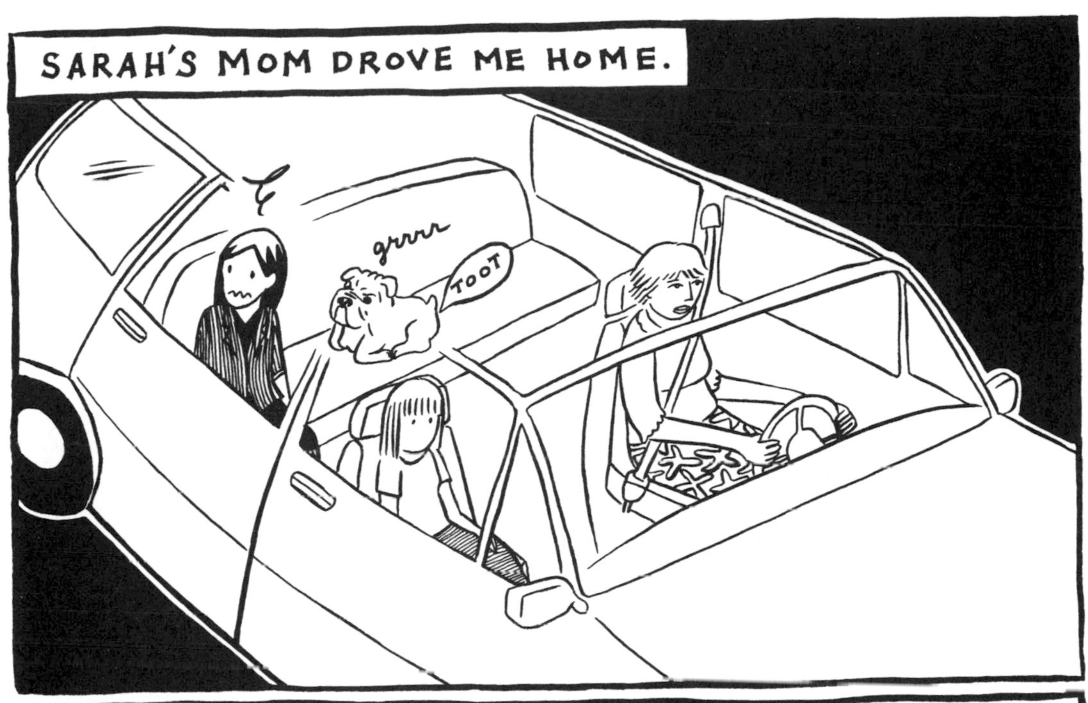
SARAH'S MOM DROVE ME HOME.
grrrr
TOOT

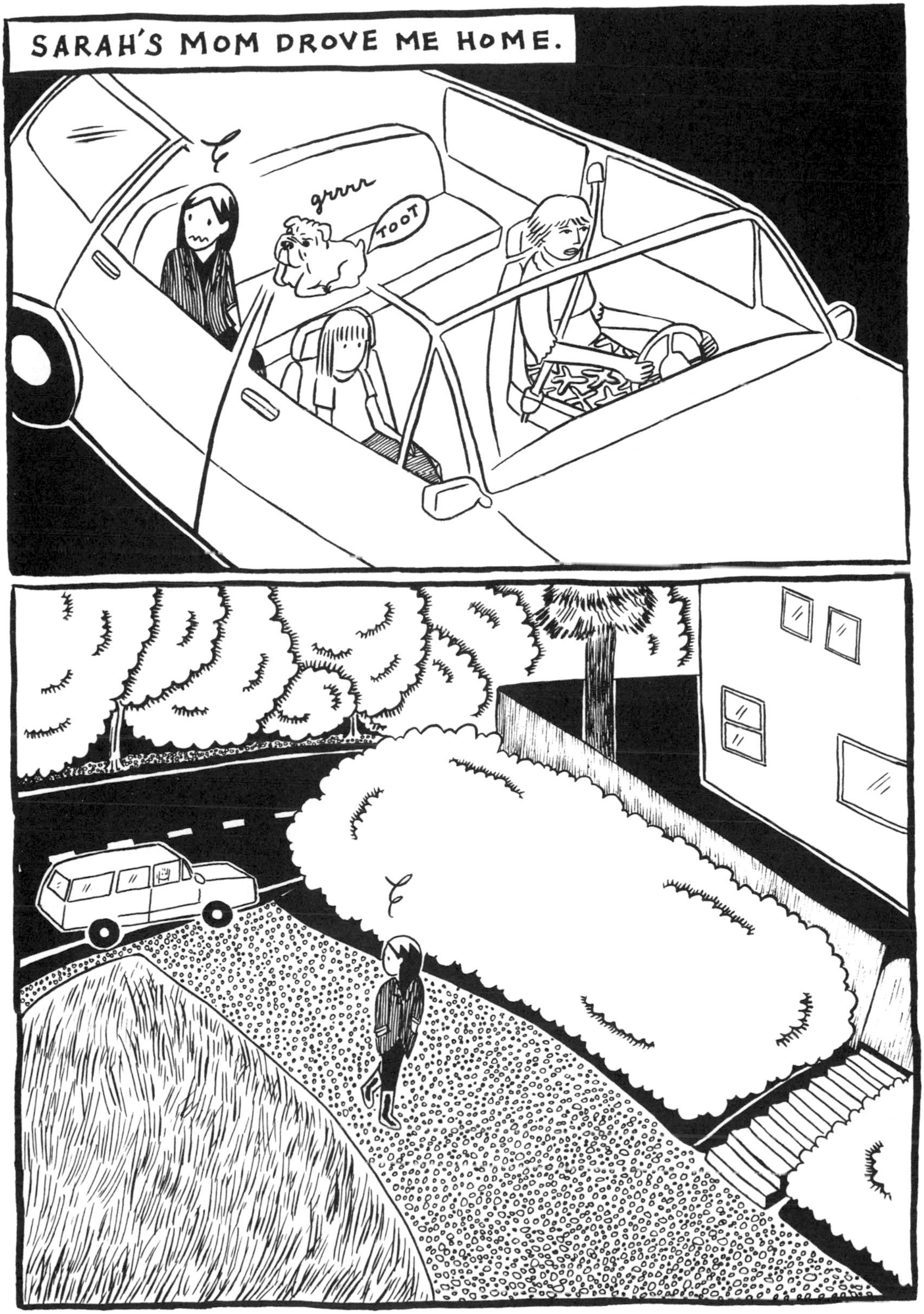

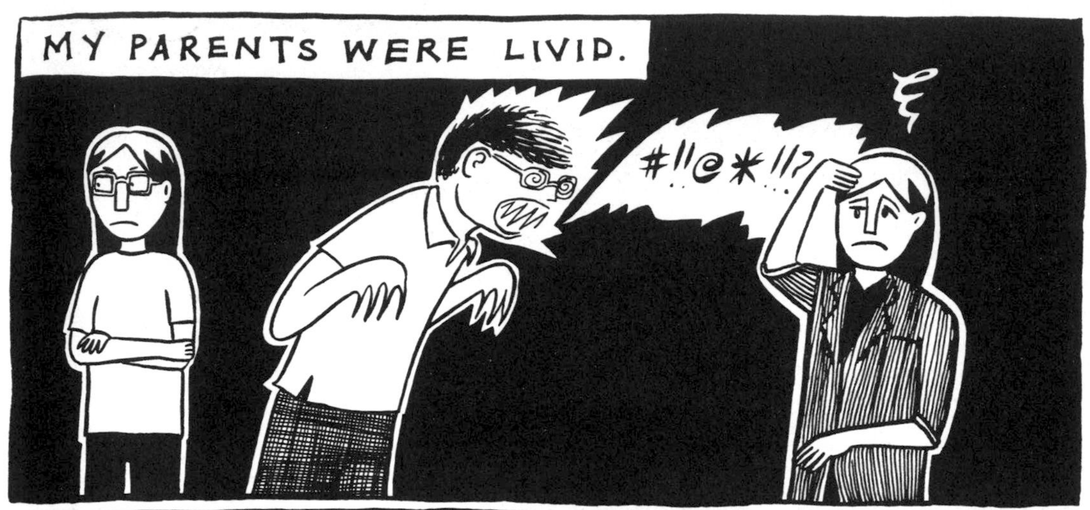

LIAM AND MIRABAI HAD LEFT ME A SWEET NOTE.

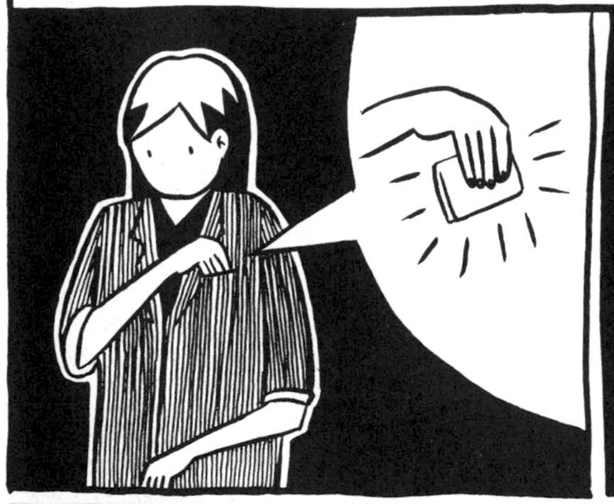

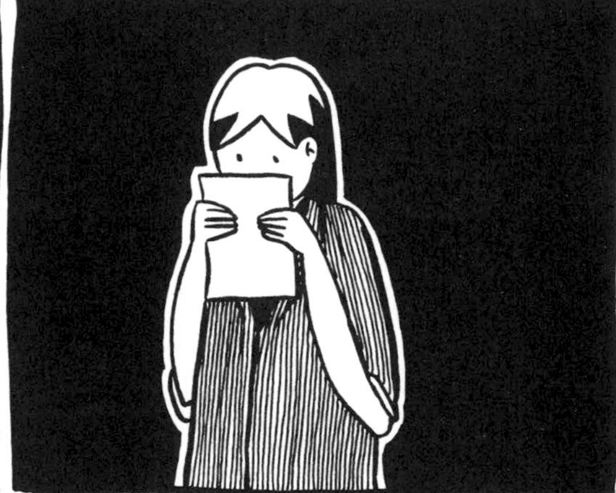

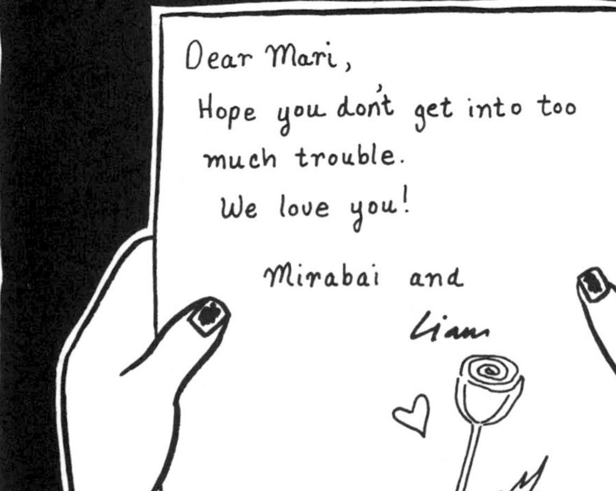

It doesn't matter since I'll probably never get to see them again. Or anyone else for that matter.

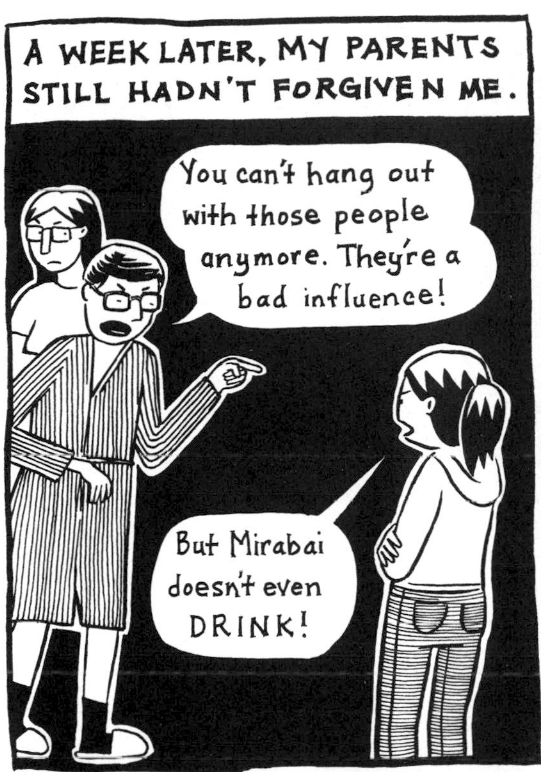
A WEEK LATER, MY PARENTS STILL HADN'T FORGIVEN ME.
You can't hang out with those people anymore. They're a bad influence!
But Mirabai doesn't even DRINK!

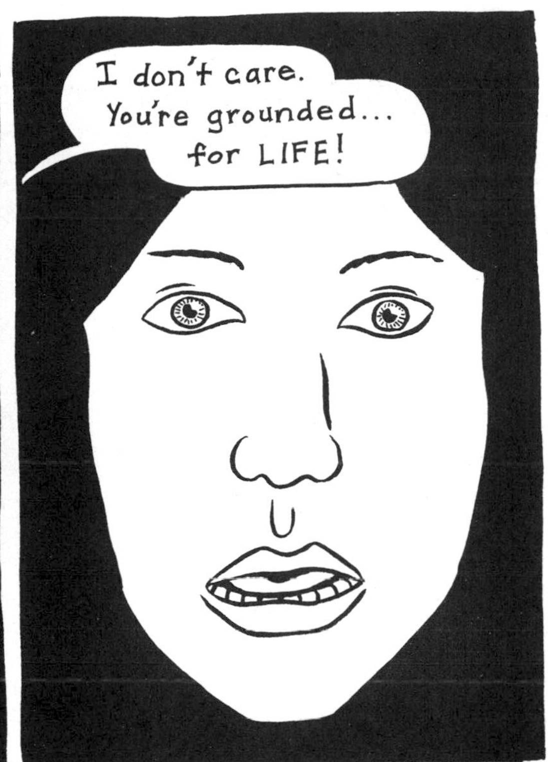
I don't care. You're grounded... for LIFE!

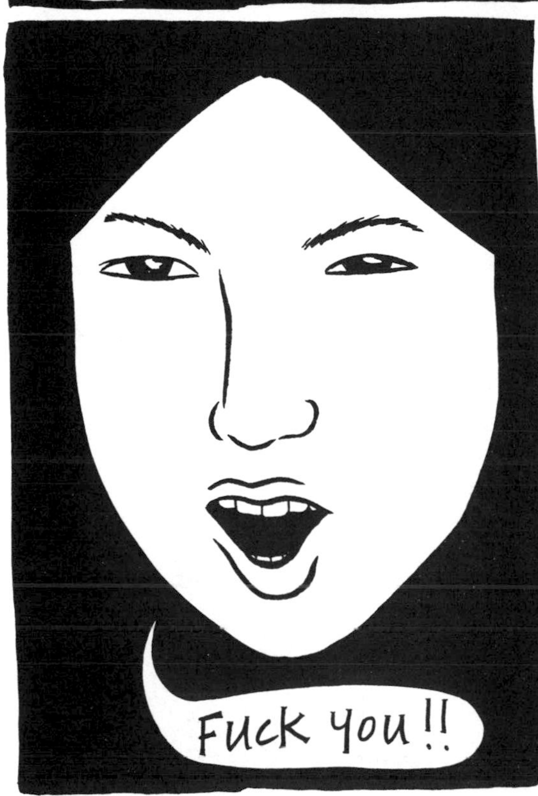
FUCK YOU!!

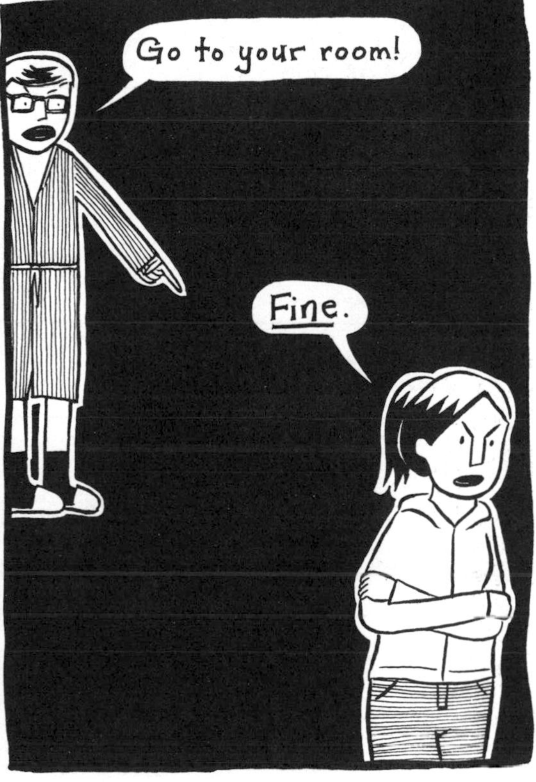
Go to your room!
Fine.

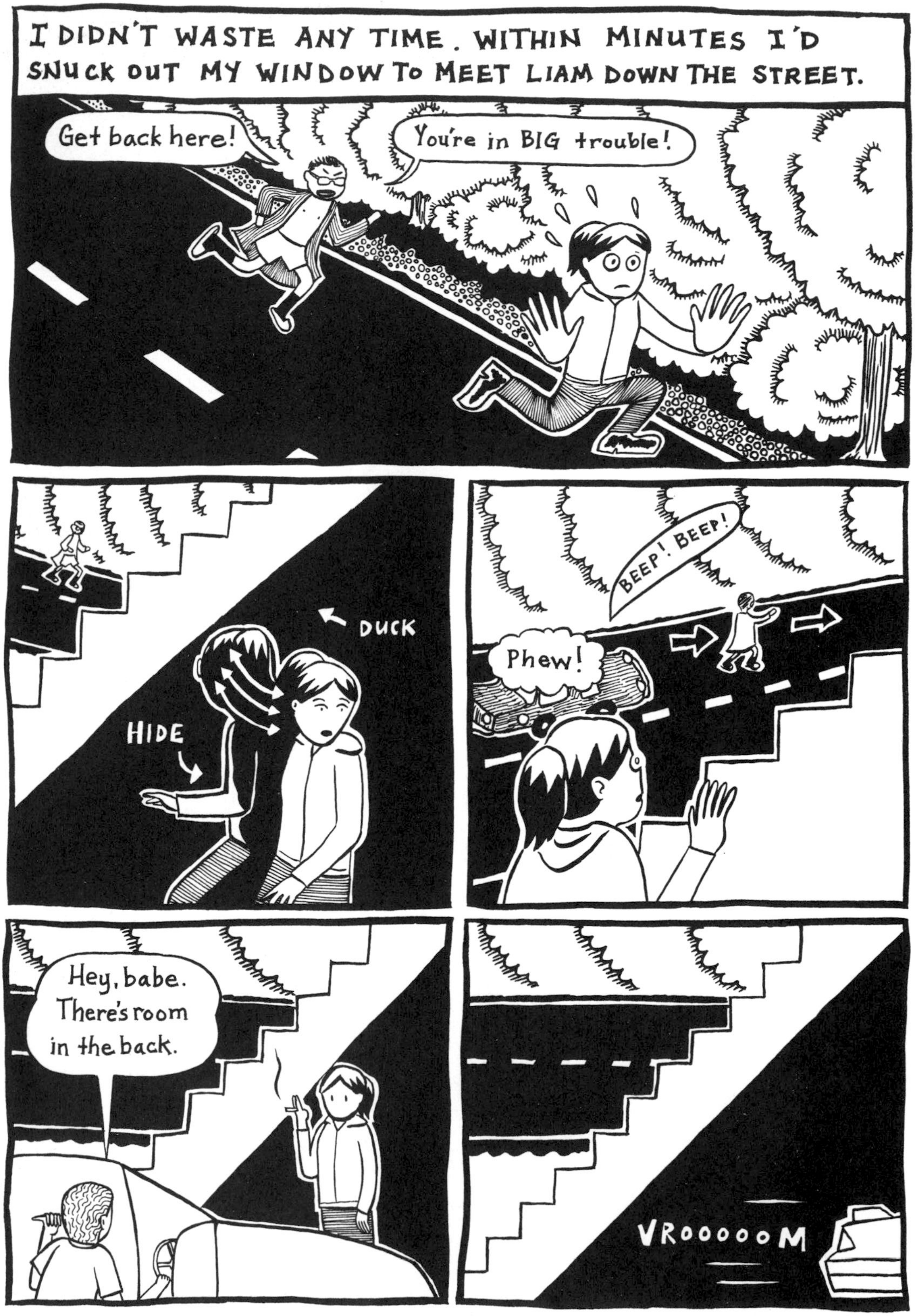

I DIDN'T WASTE ANY TIME. WITHIN MINUTES I'D SNUCK OUT MY WINDOW TO MEET LIAM DOWN THE STREET.

Get back here!

You're in BIG trouble!

DUCK

HIDE

BEEP! BEEP!

Phew!

Hey, babe. There's room in the back.

VROOOOOM

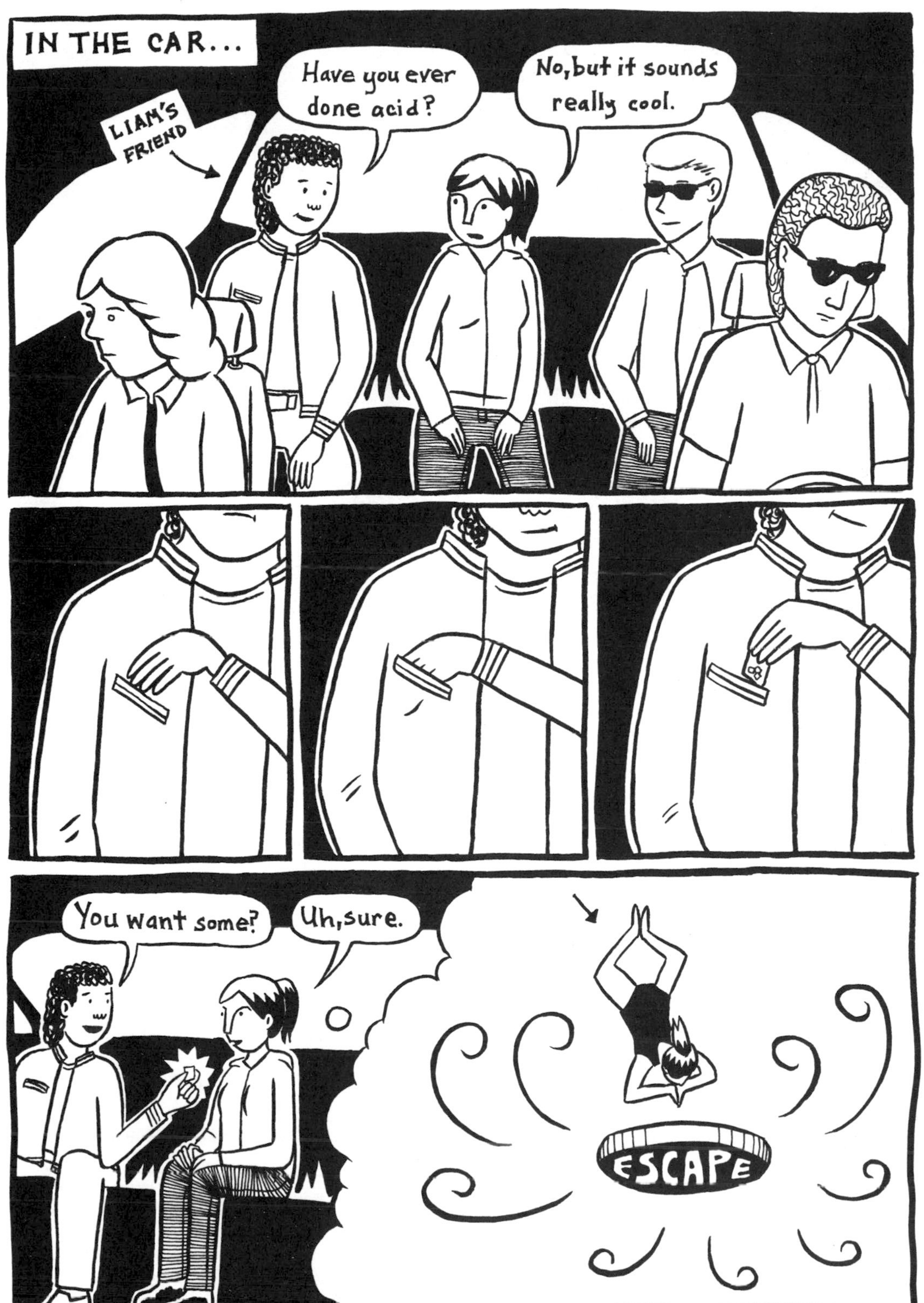
IN THE CAR...
LIAM'S FRIEND
Have you ever done acid?
No, but it sounds really cool.
You want some?
Uh, sure.
ESCAPE

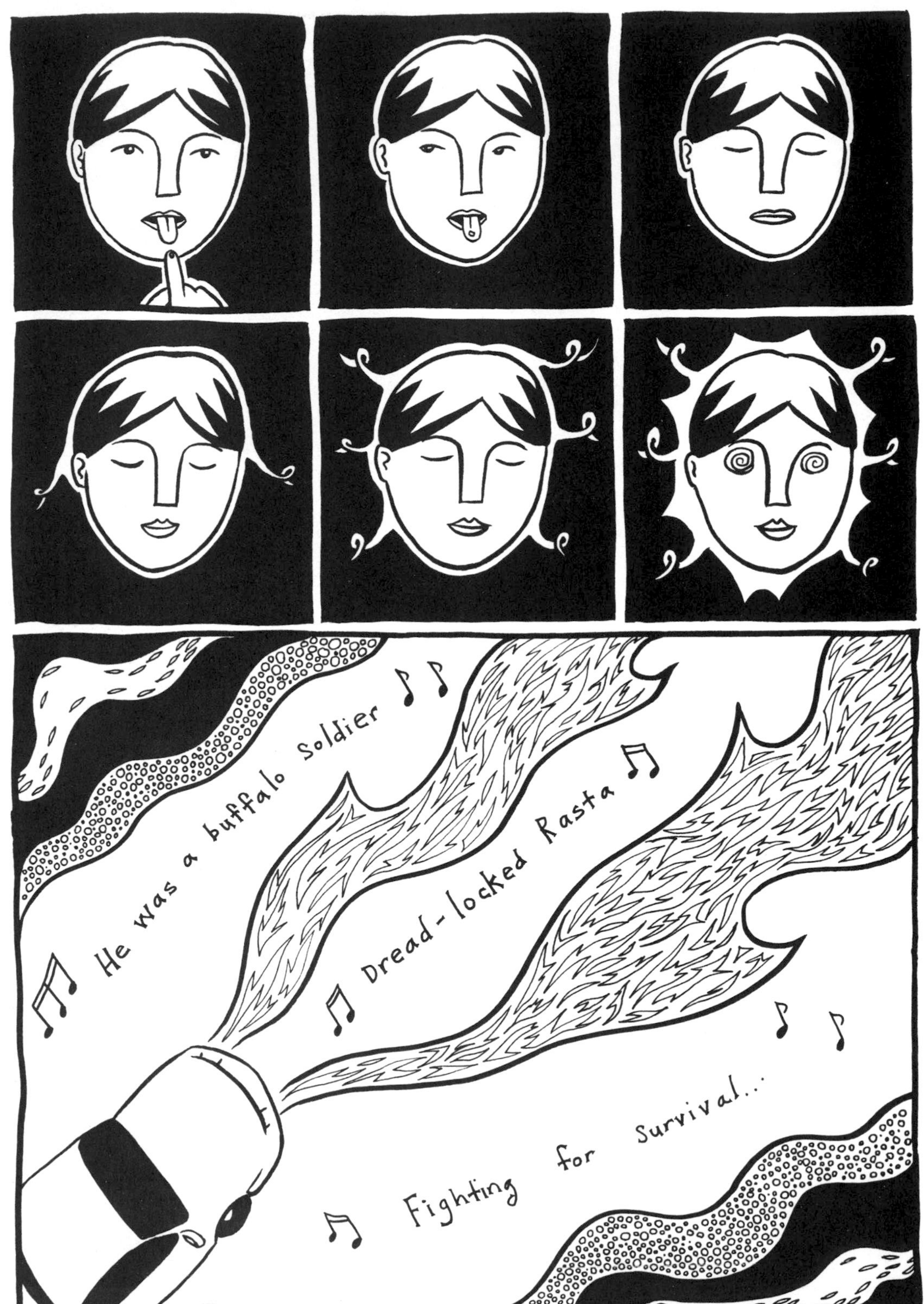
He was a buffalo soldier
Dread-locked Rasta
Fighting for survival...

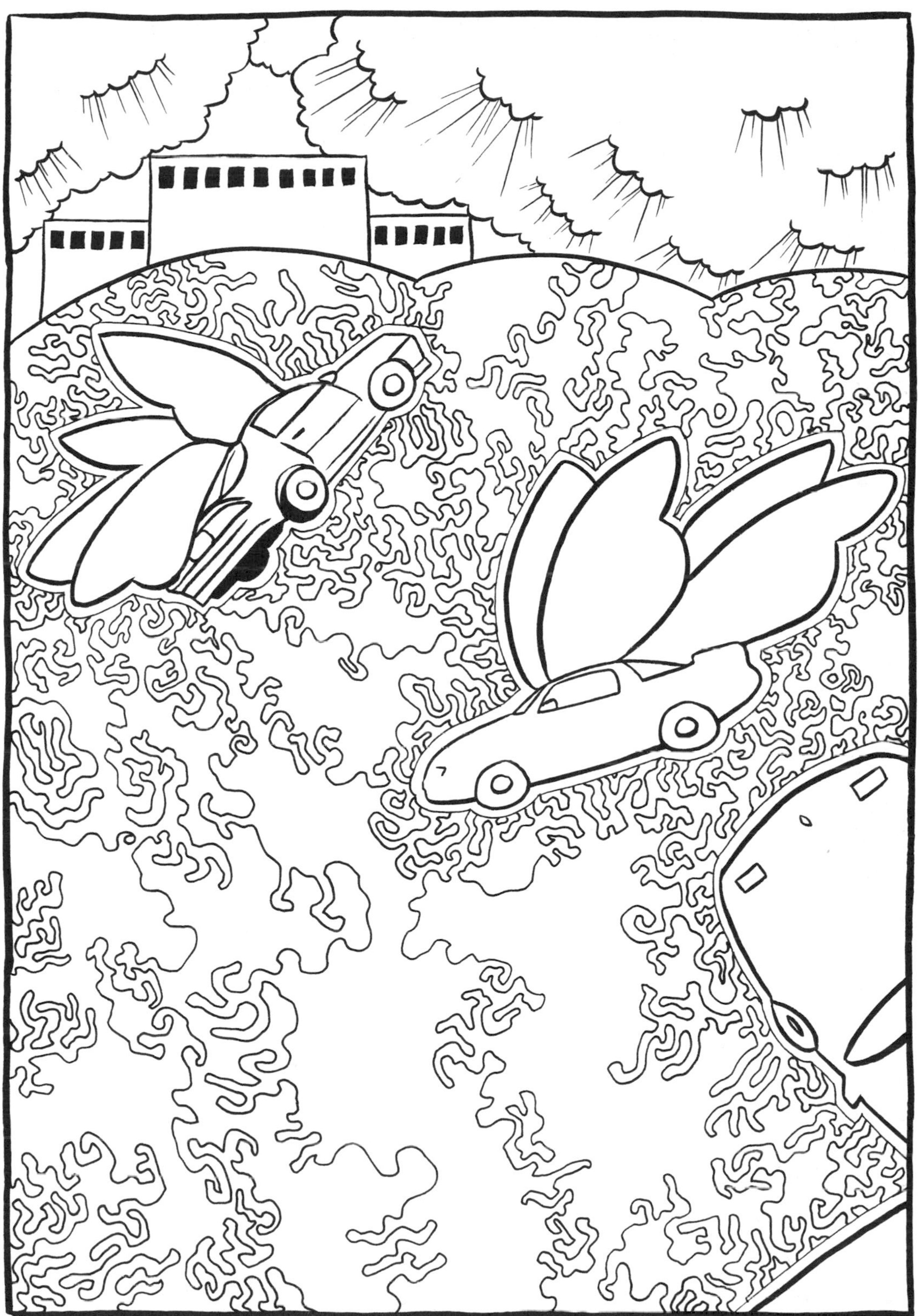

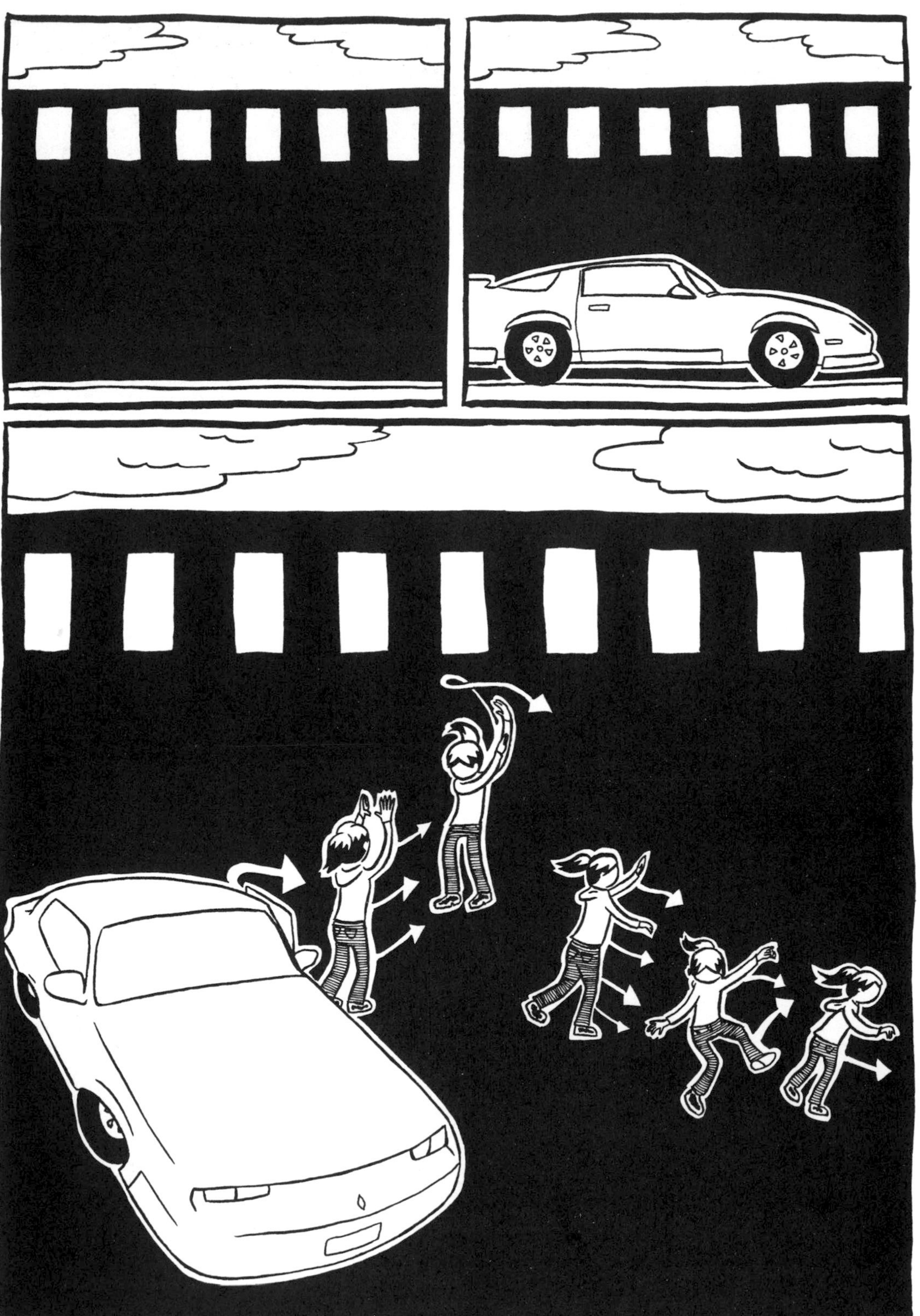

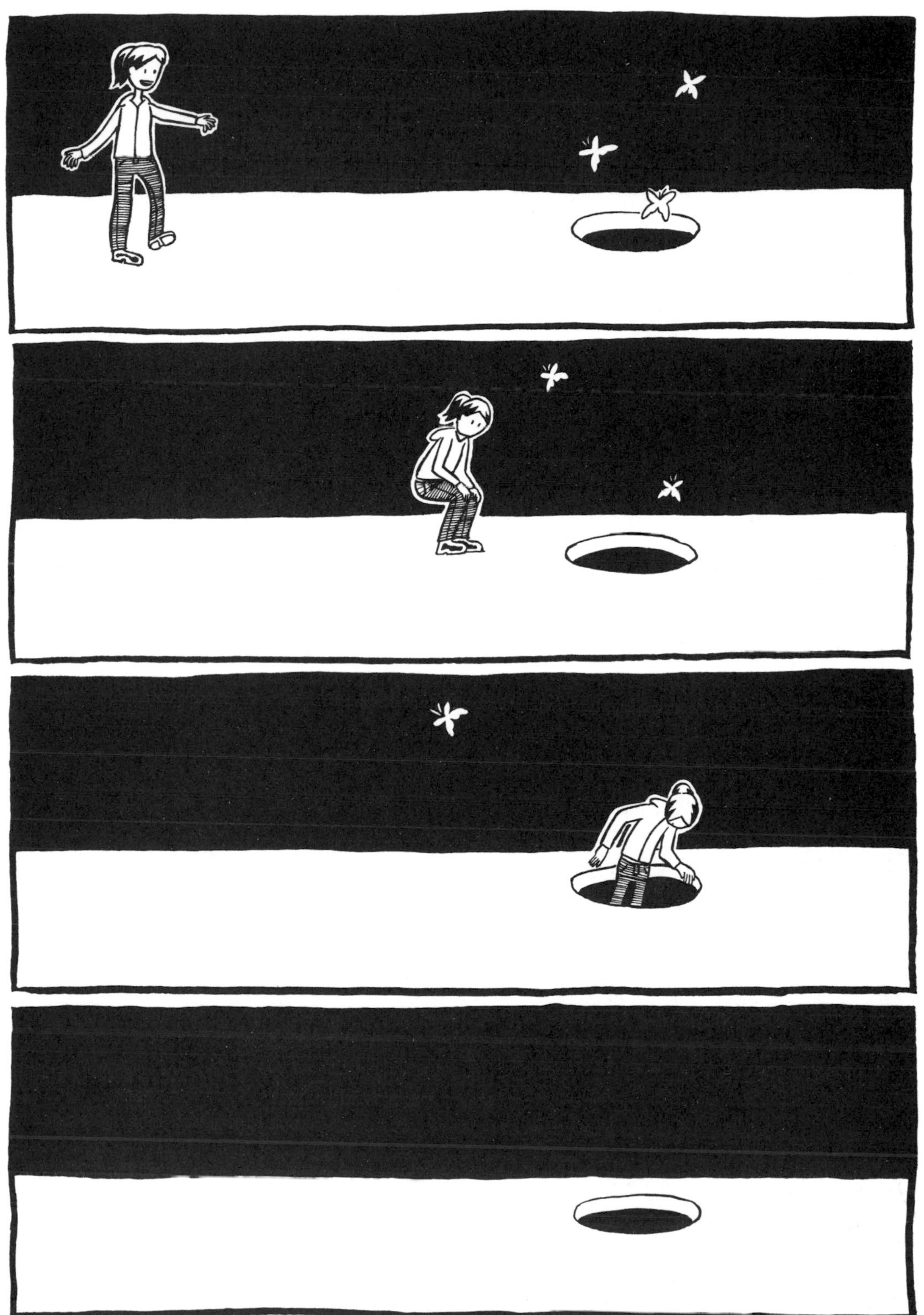

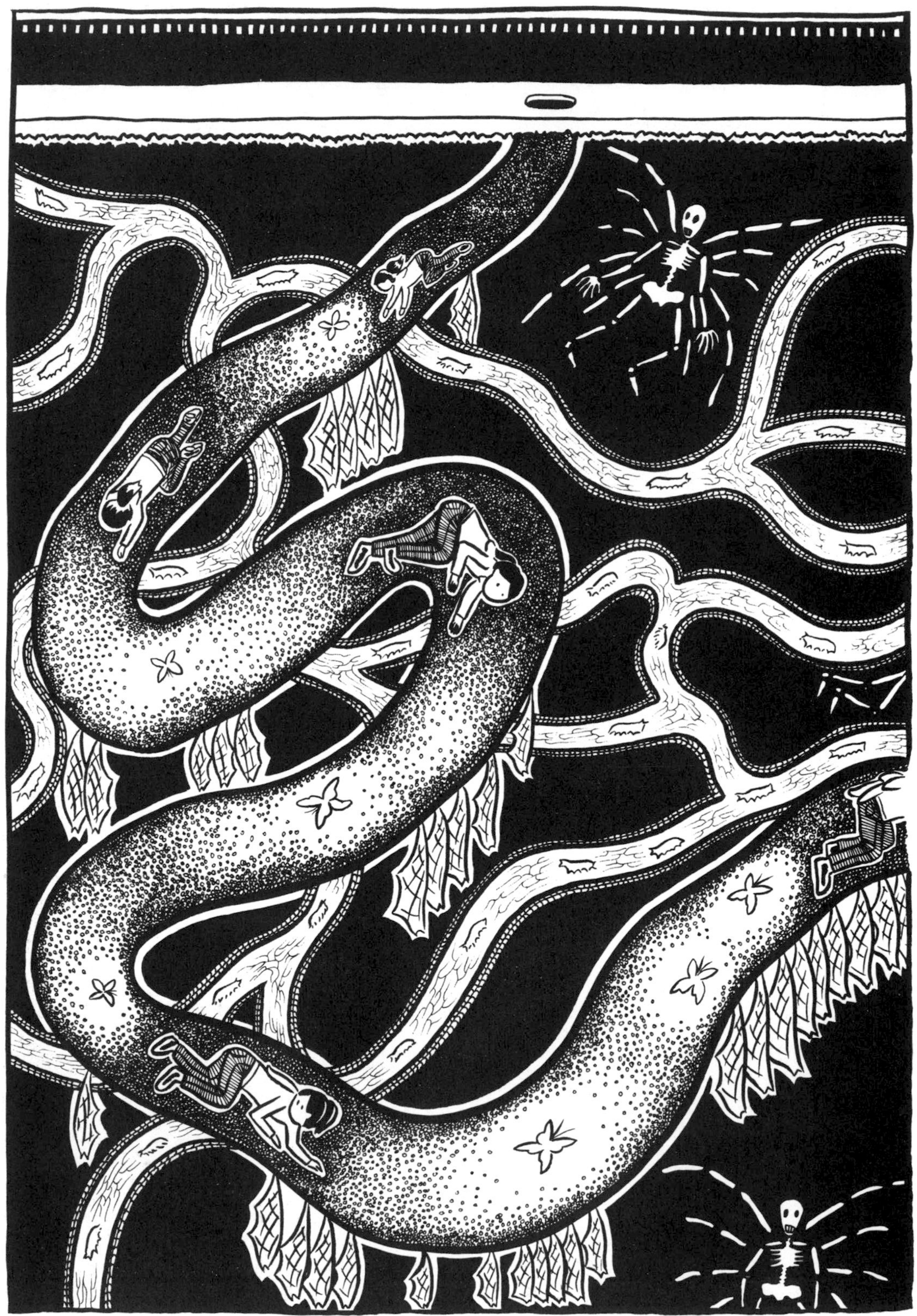

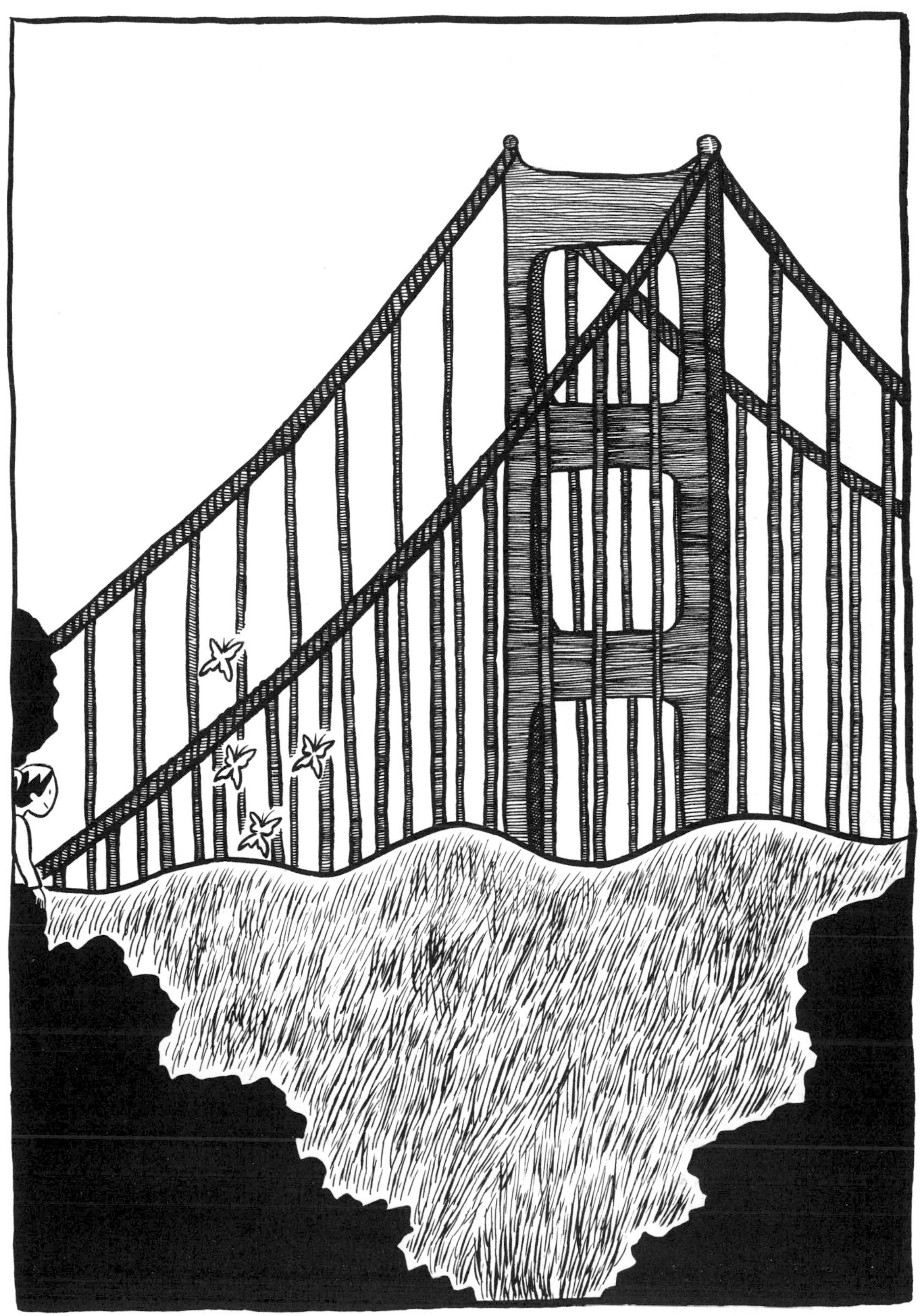

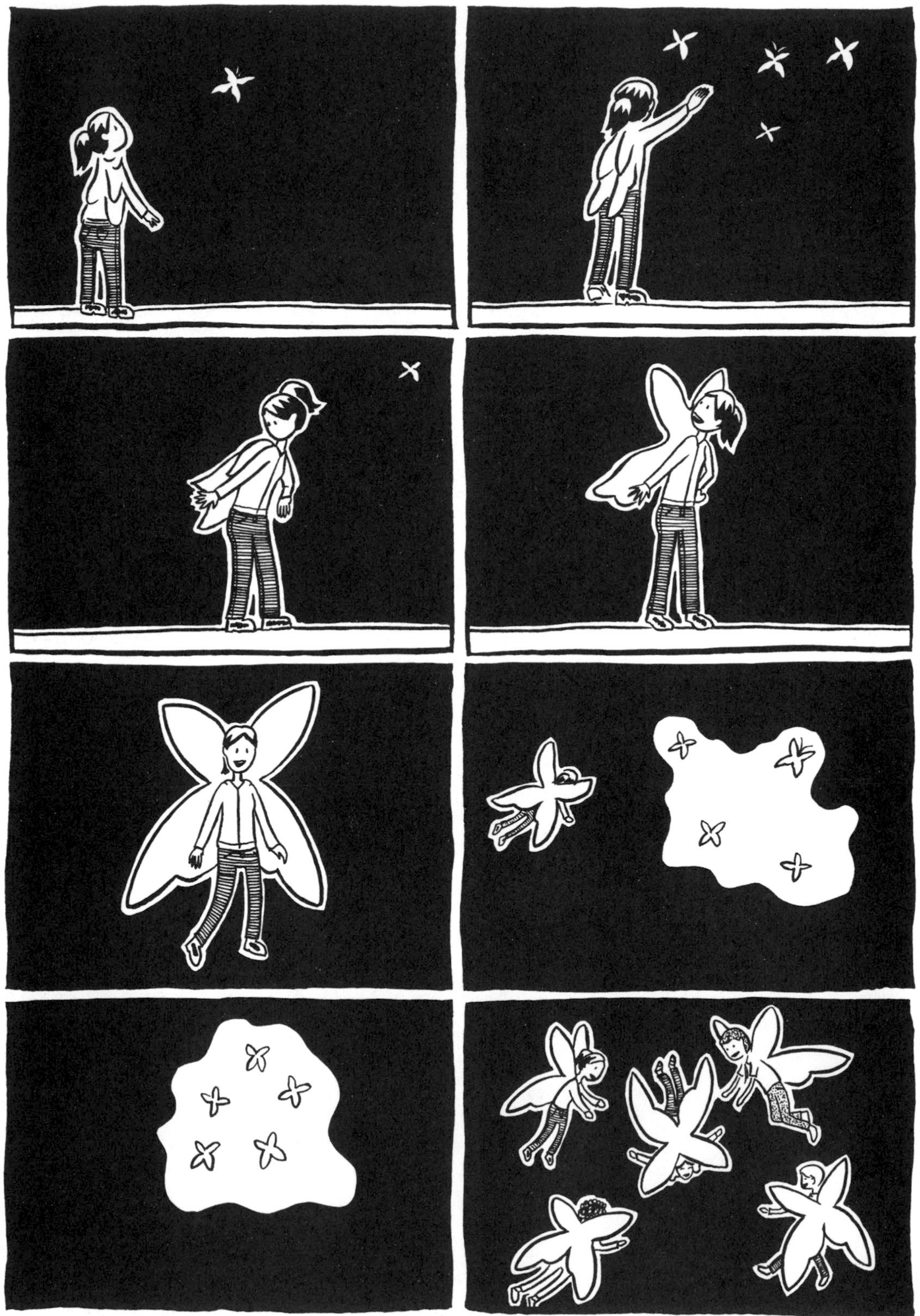

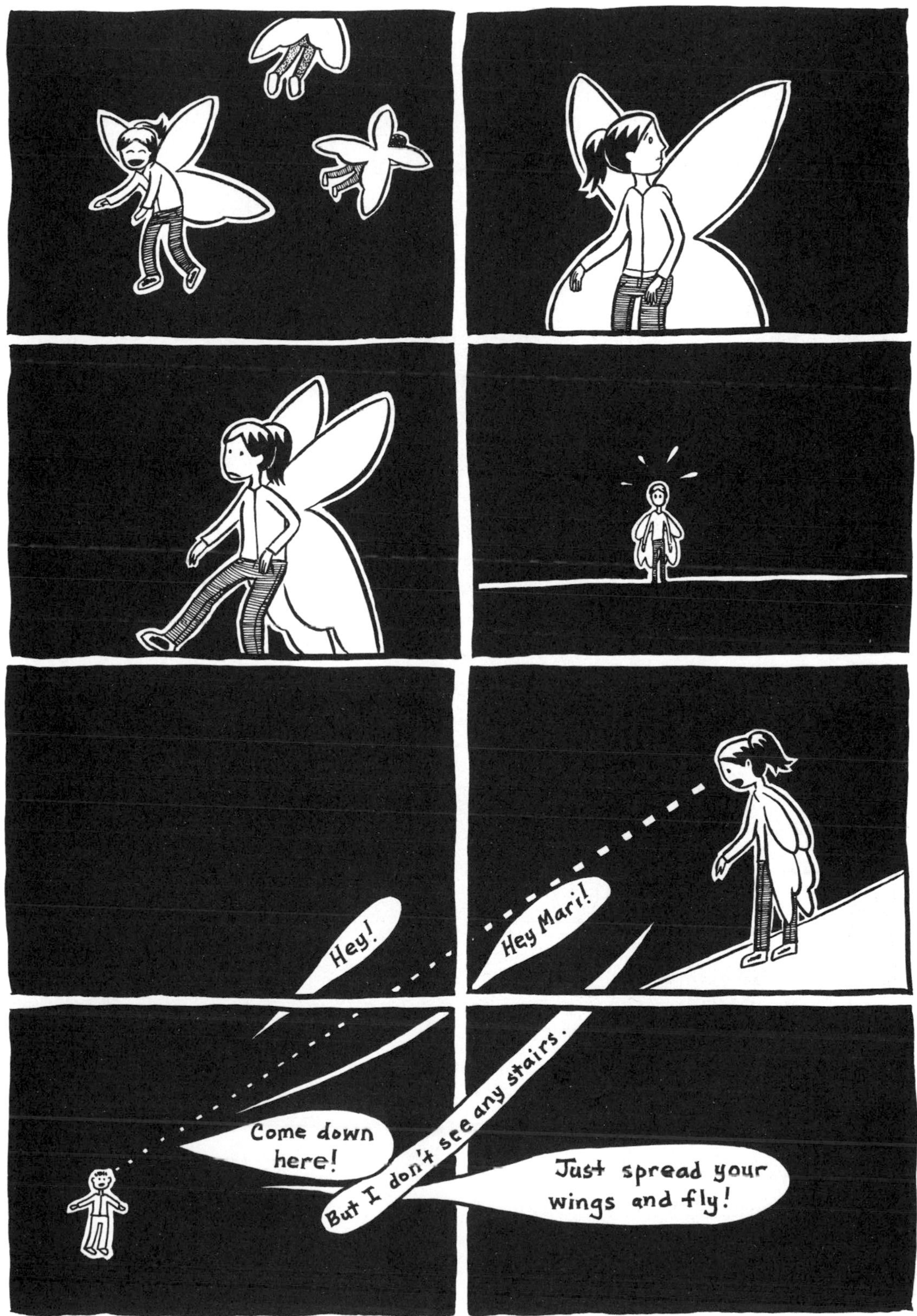
Hey!
Hey Mari!
Come down here!
But I don't see any stairs.
Just spread your wings and fly!

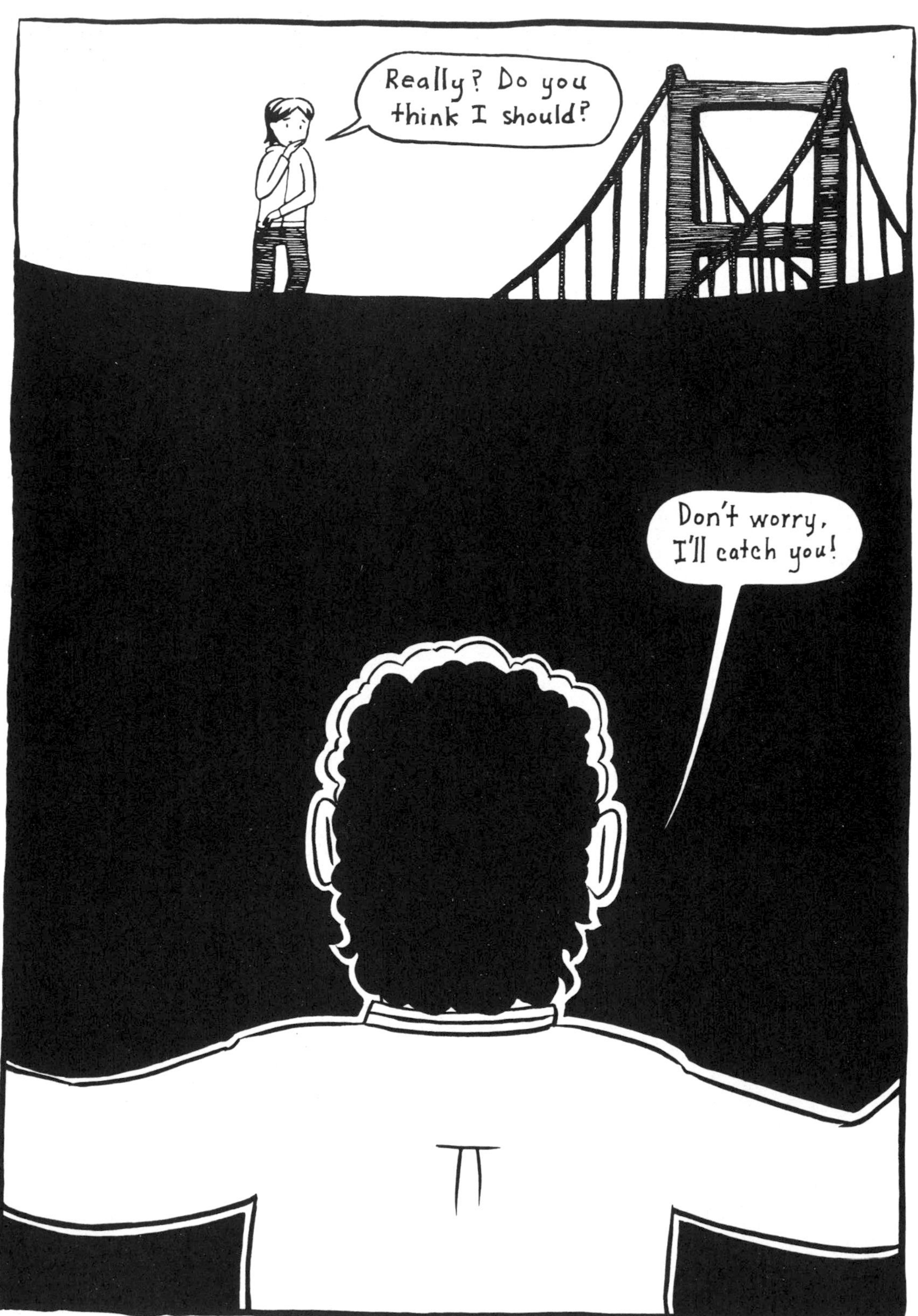
Really? Do you think I should?
Don't worry, I'll catch you!

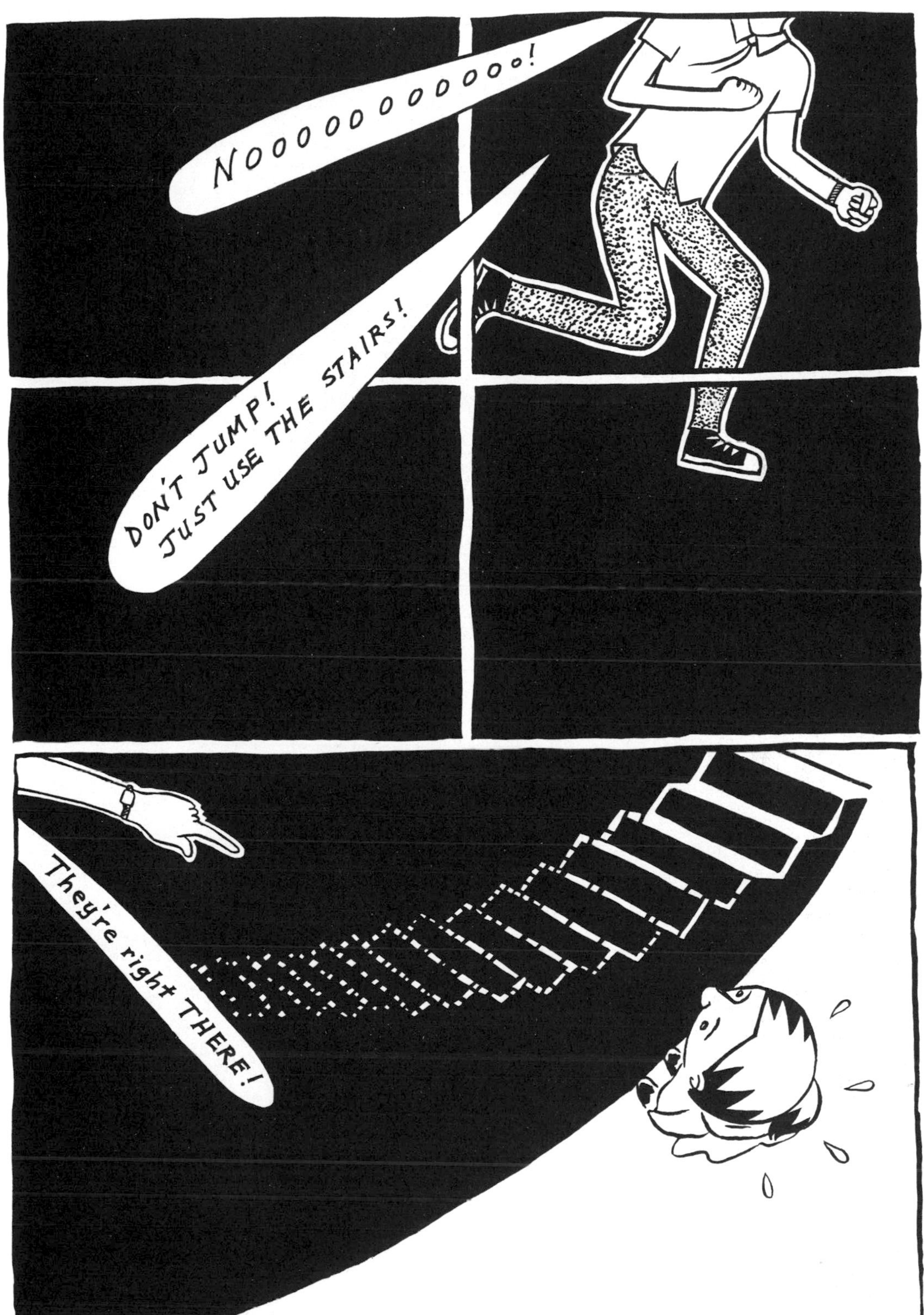
Nooooooooooooo!
DON'T JUMP! JUST USE THE STAIRS!
They're right THERE!

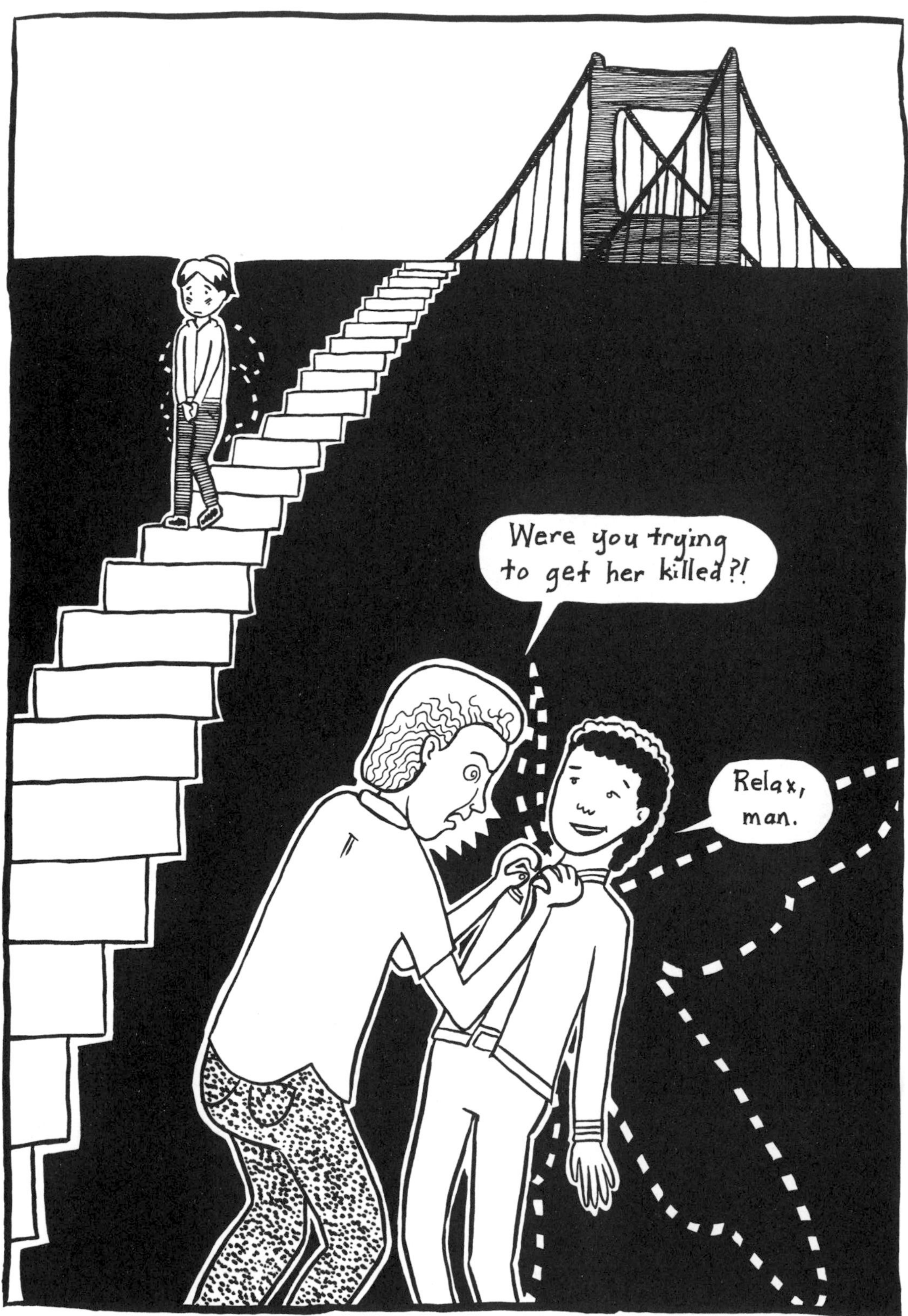
Were you trying to get her killed?!
Relax, man.

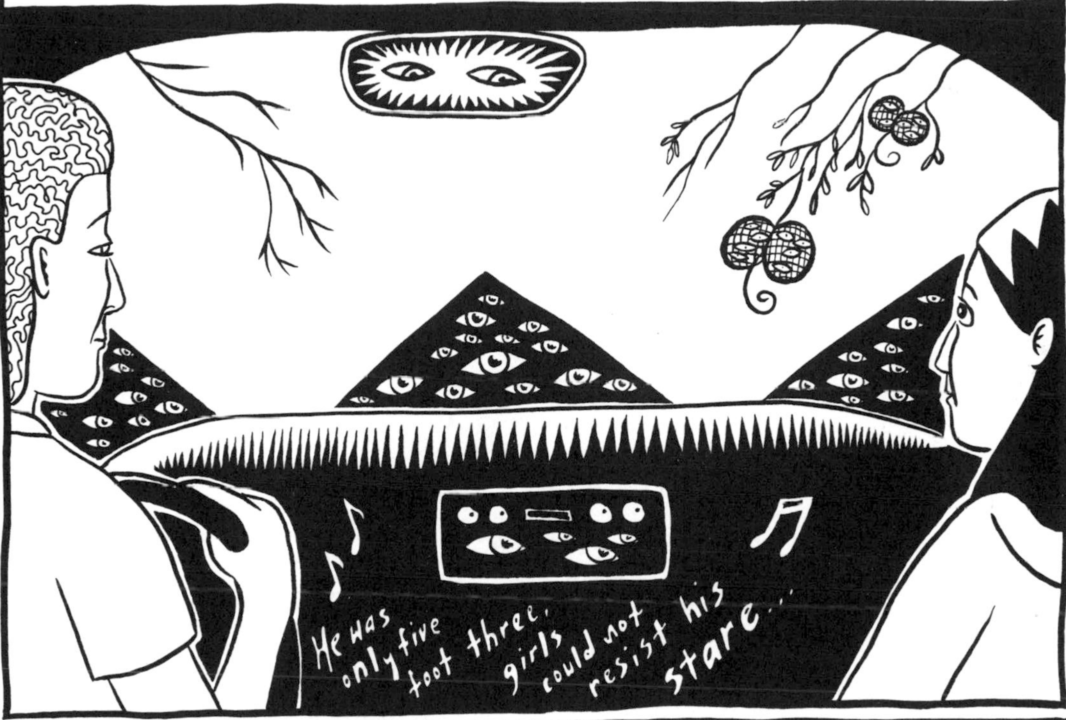
NIGHT FELL AND THINGS FELT A BIT CREEPIER.
He was only five foot three, girls could not resist his stare...

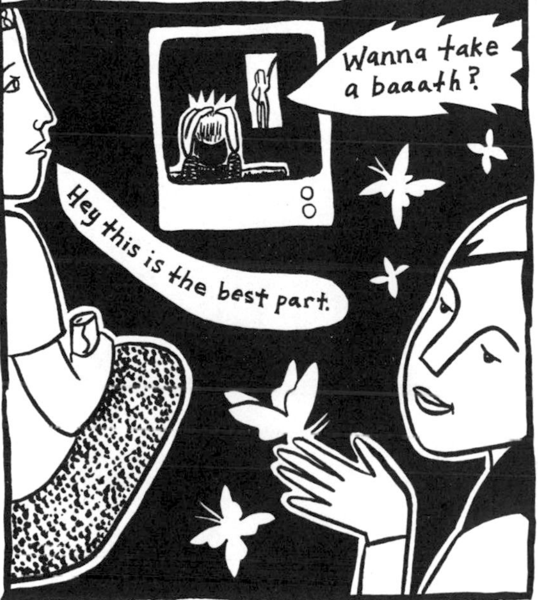
LIAM TOOK ME TO HIS HOUSE TO WATCH A MOVIE BUT I WAS TOO DISTRACTED.
Wanna take a baaath?
Hey this is the best part.

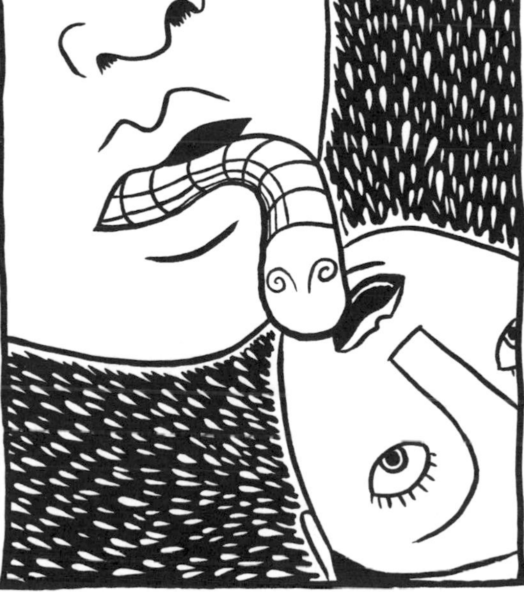
WHEN HE KISSED ME, I DIDN'T GET THE WARM FUZZIES LIKE USUAL.

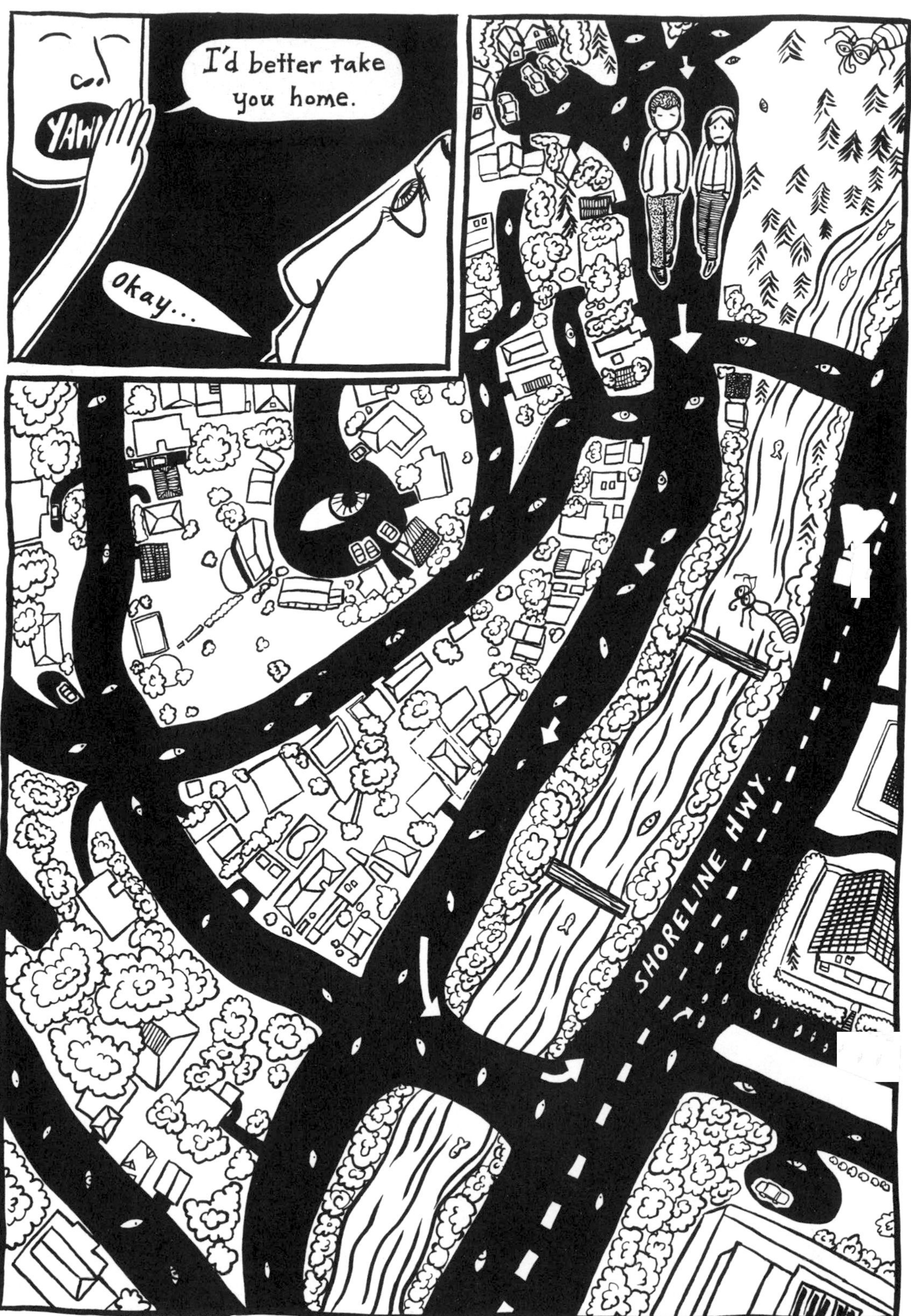
YAWN
I'd better take you home.
Okay...
SHORELINE HWY.

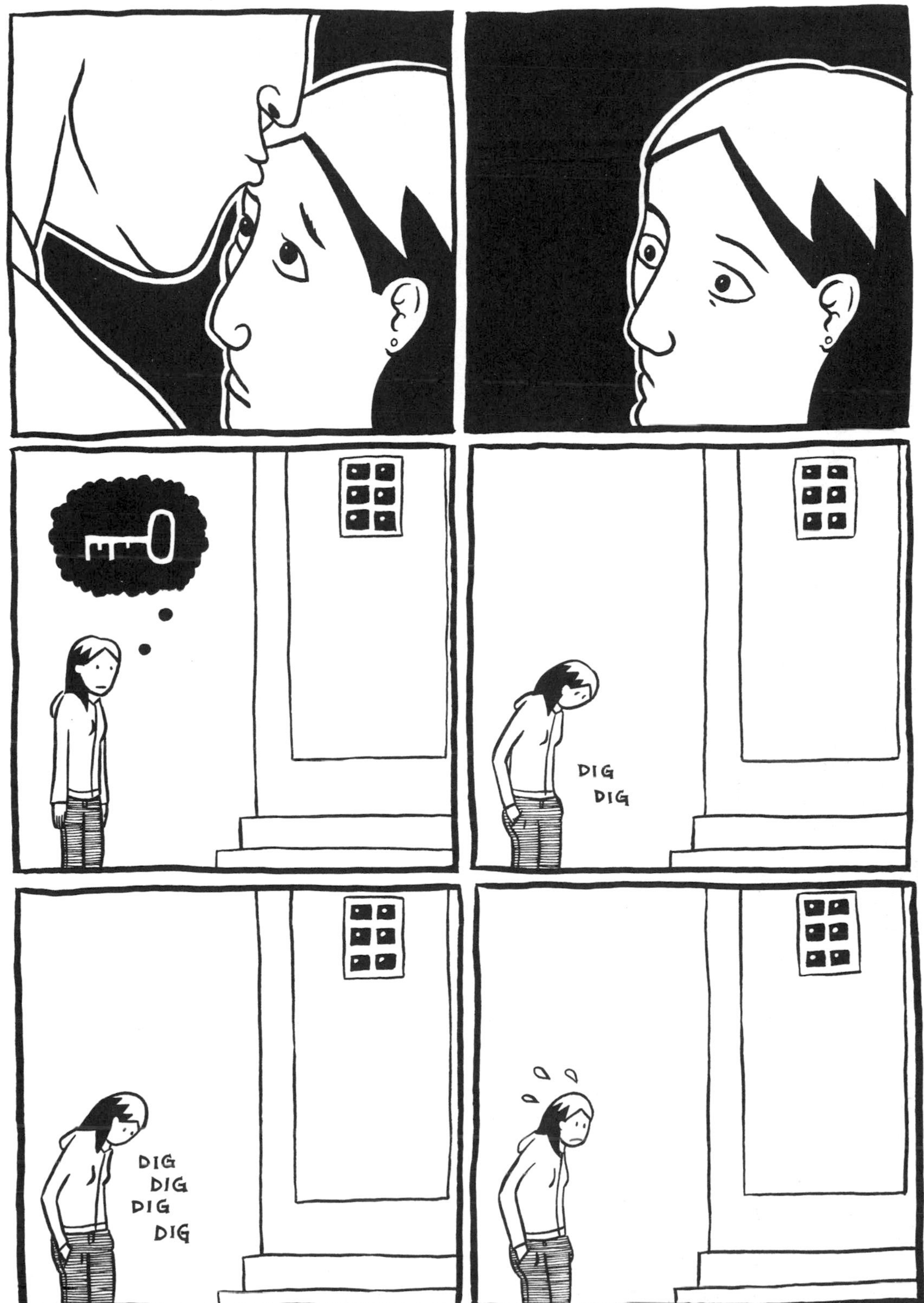
DIG
DIG
DIG
DIG
DIG
DIG

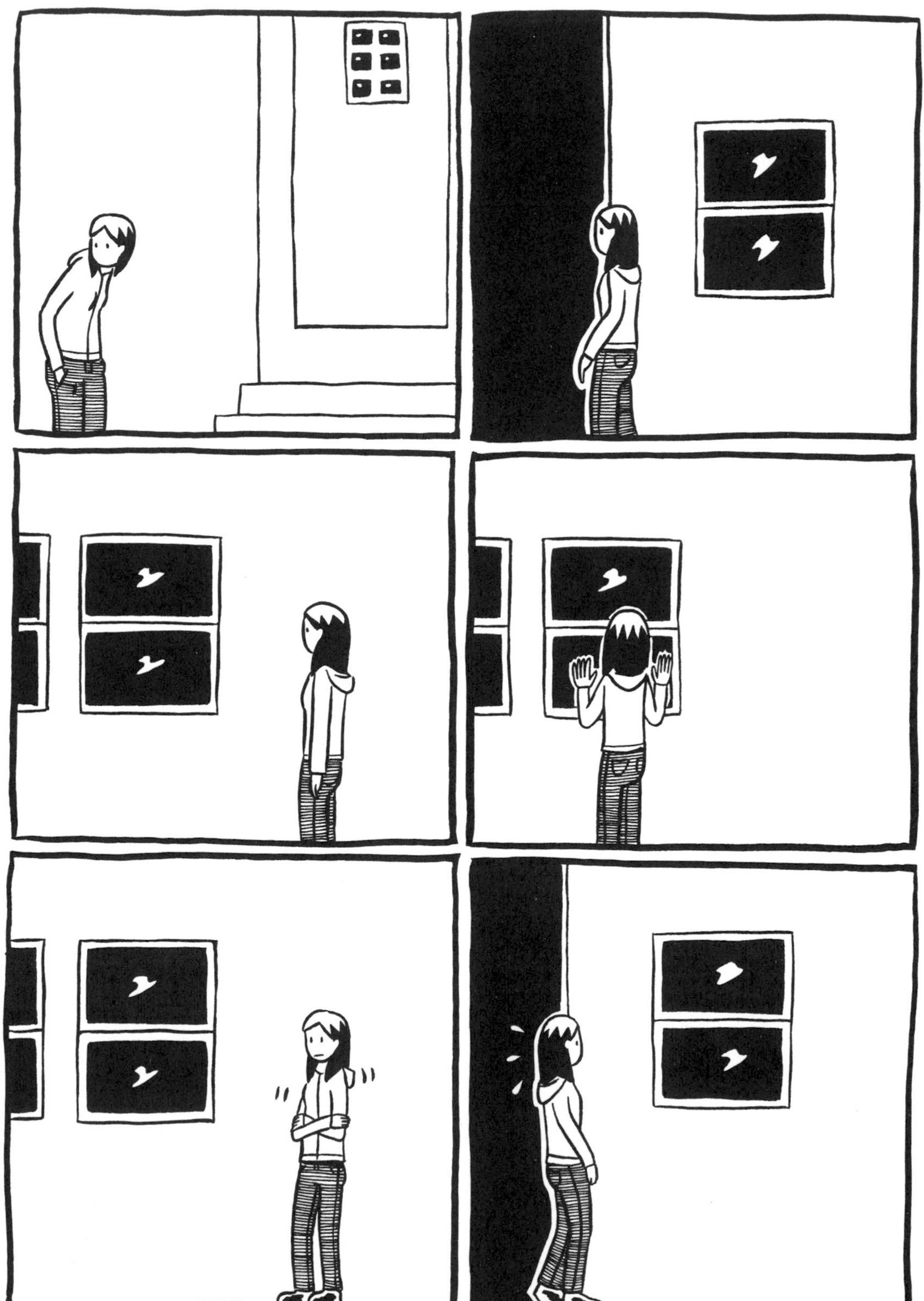

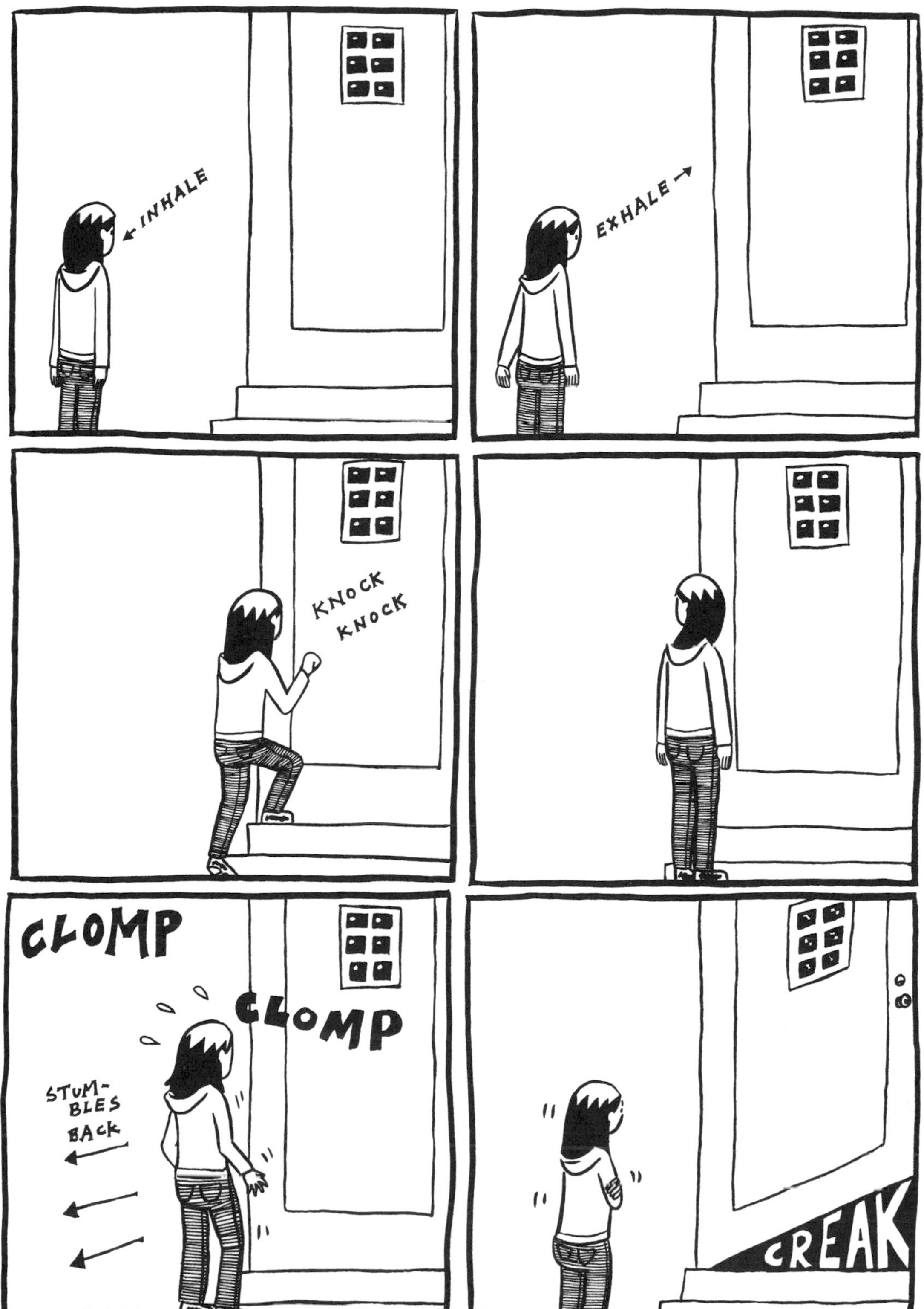
INHALE
EXHALE
KNOCK
KNOCK
CLOMP
CLOMP
STUM-
BLES
BACK
CREAK

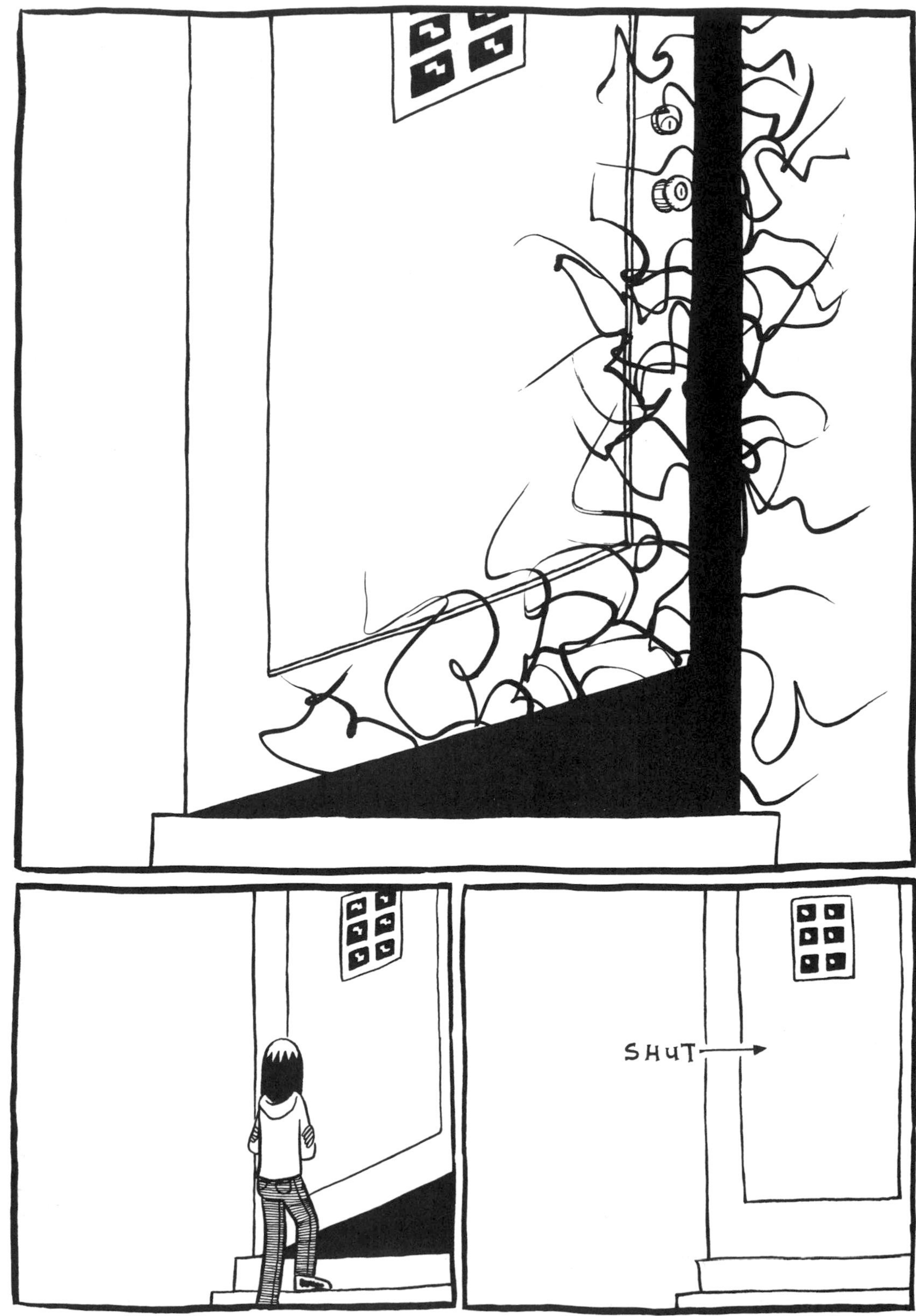
SHUT

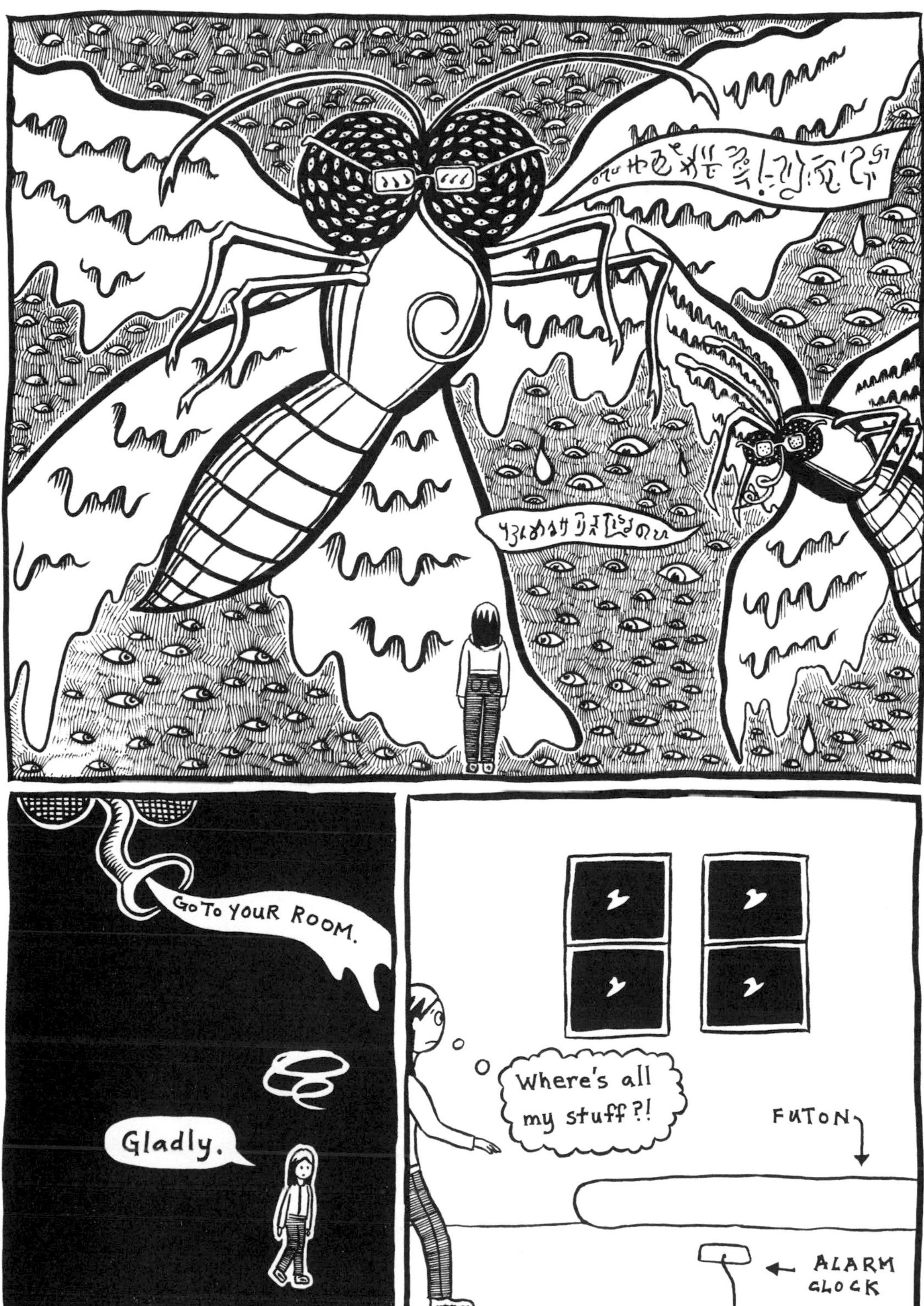
GO TO YOUR ROOM.
Gladly.
Where's all my stuff?!
FUTON
ALARM CLOCK

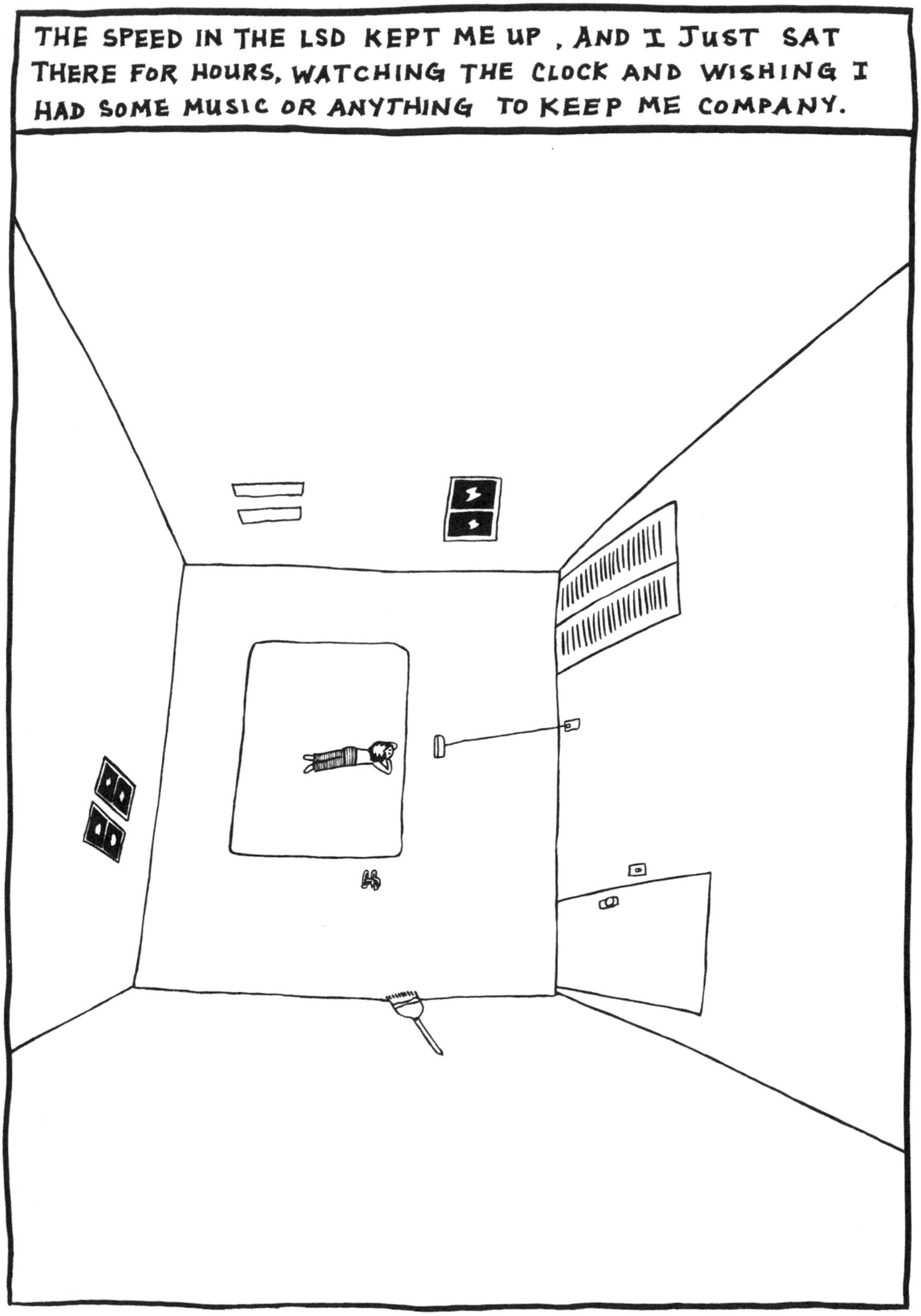

THE SPEED IN THE LSD KEPT ME UP, AND I JUST SAT THERE FOR HOURS, WATCHING THE CLOCK AND WISHING I HAD SOME MUSIC OR ANYTHING TO KEEP ME COMPANY.

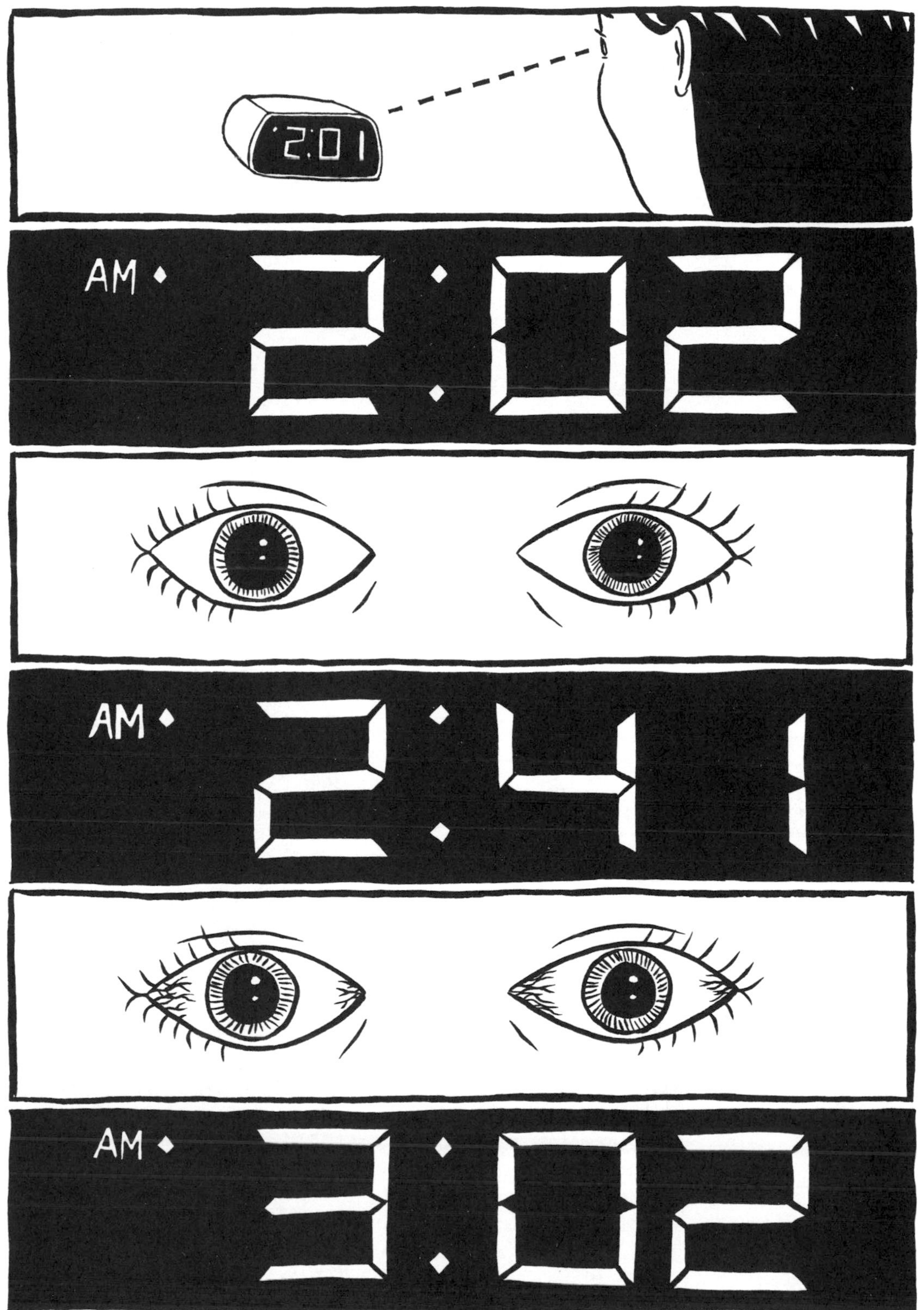
2:01
AM
2:02
AM
2:41
AM
3:02

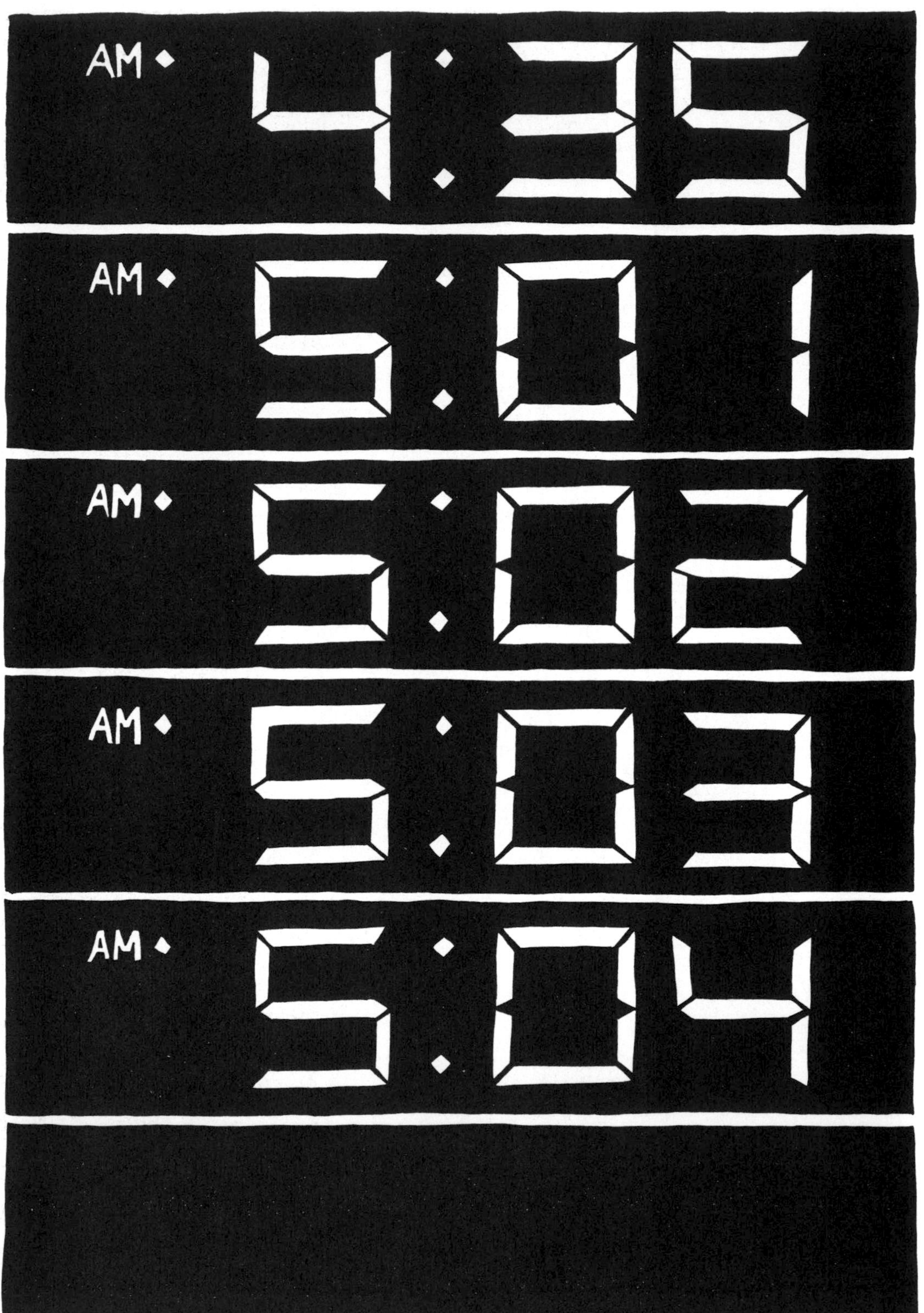
AM 4:35
AM 5:01
AM 5:02
AM 5:03
AM 5:04

POKE

POKE
POKE

POKE POKE
POKE

Why won't they stop it? I just want to be left alone.

I BLINDLY GRABBED WHAT WAS NEAREST TO ME AND FOUGHT BACK AT WHATEVER IT WAS THAT WAS ACCOSTING ME.

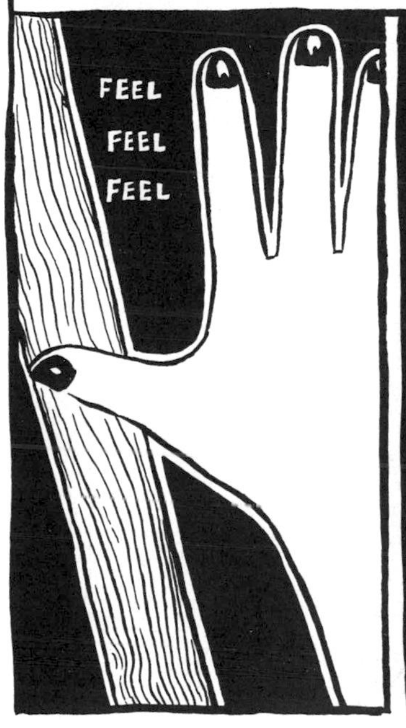

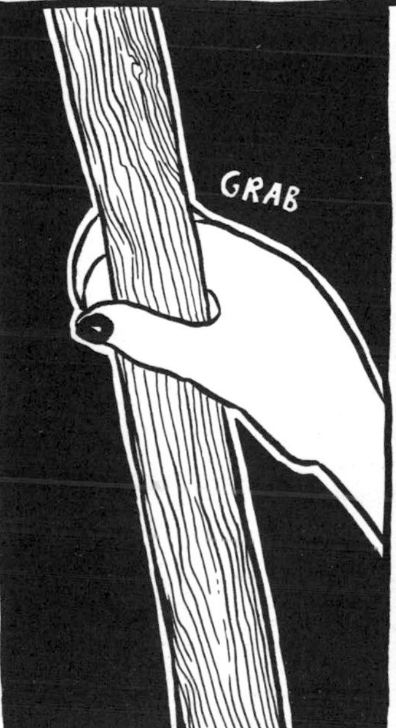

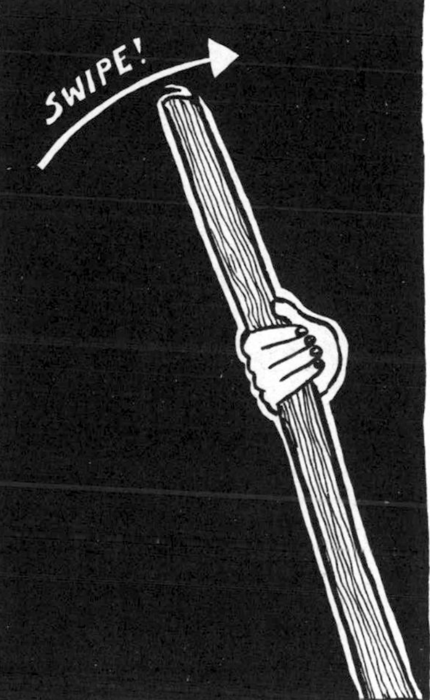

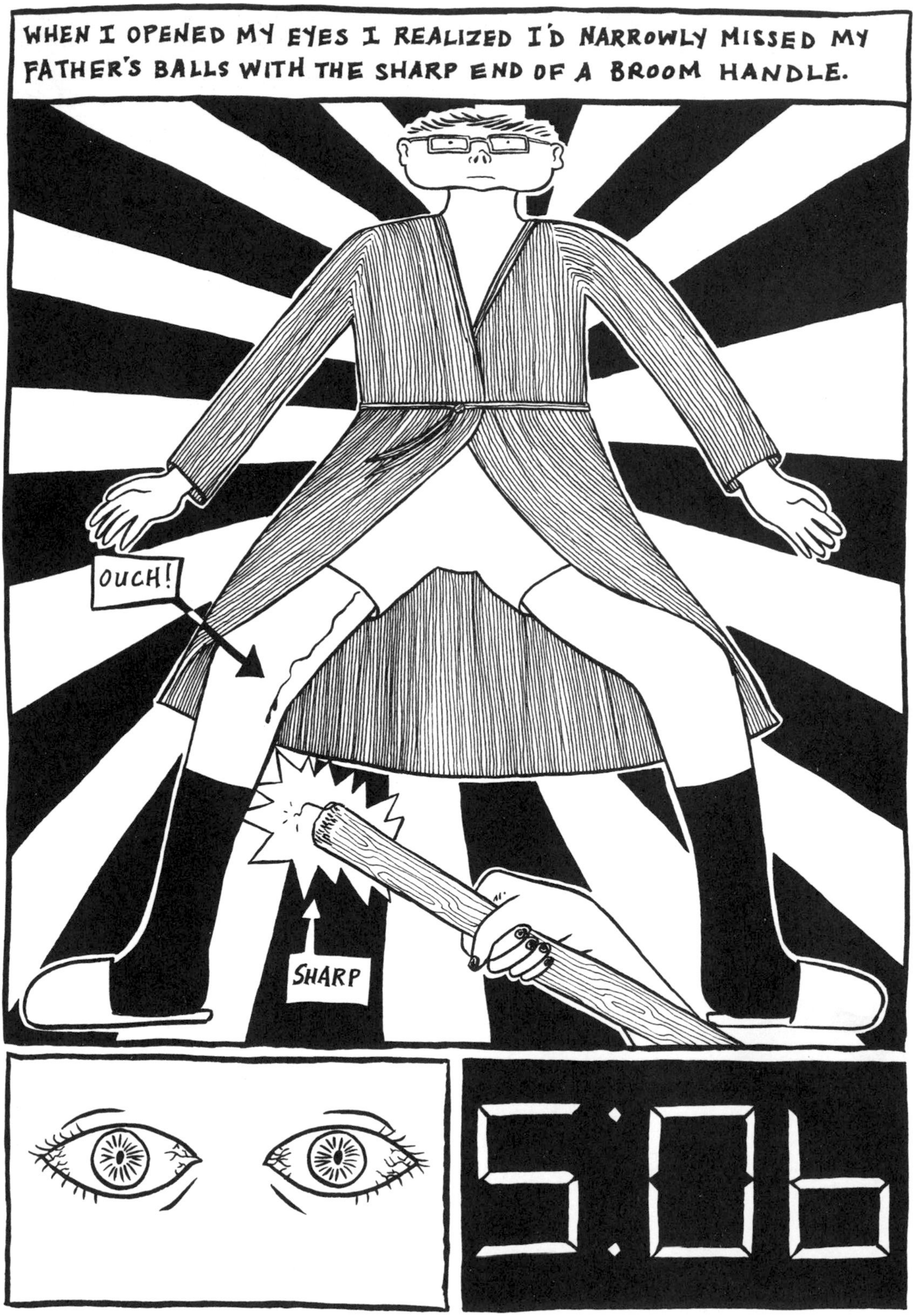

WHEN I OPENED MY EYES I REALIZED I'D NARROWLY MISSED MY FATHER'S BALLS WITH THE SHARP END OF A BROOM HANDLE.

OUCH!

SHARP

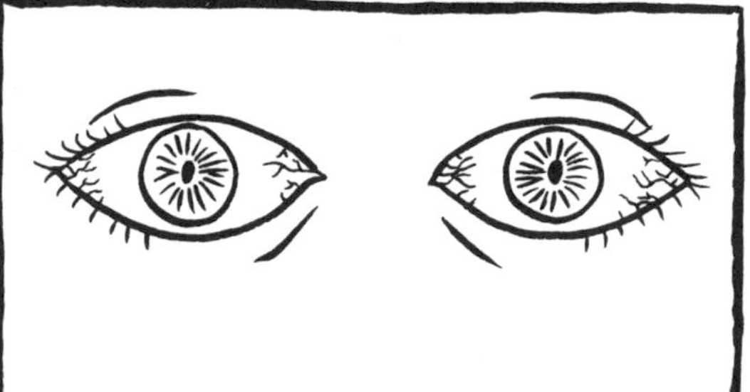

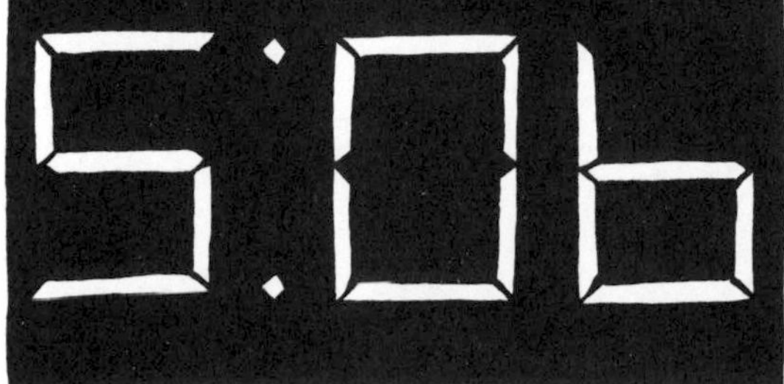

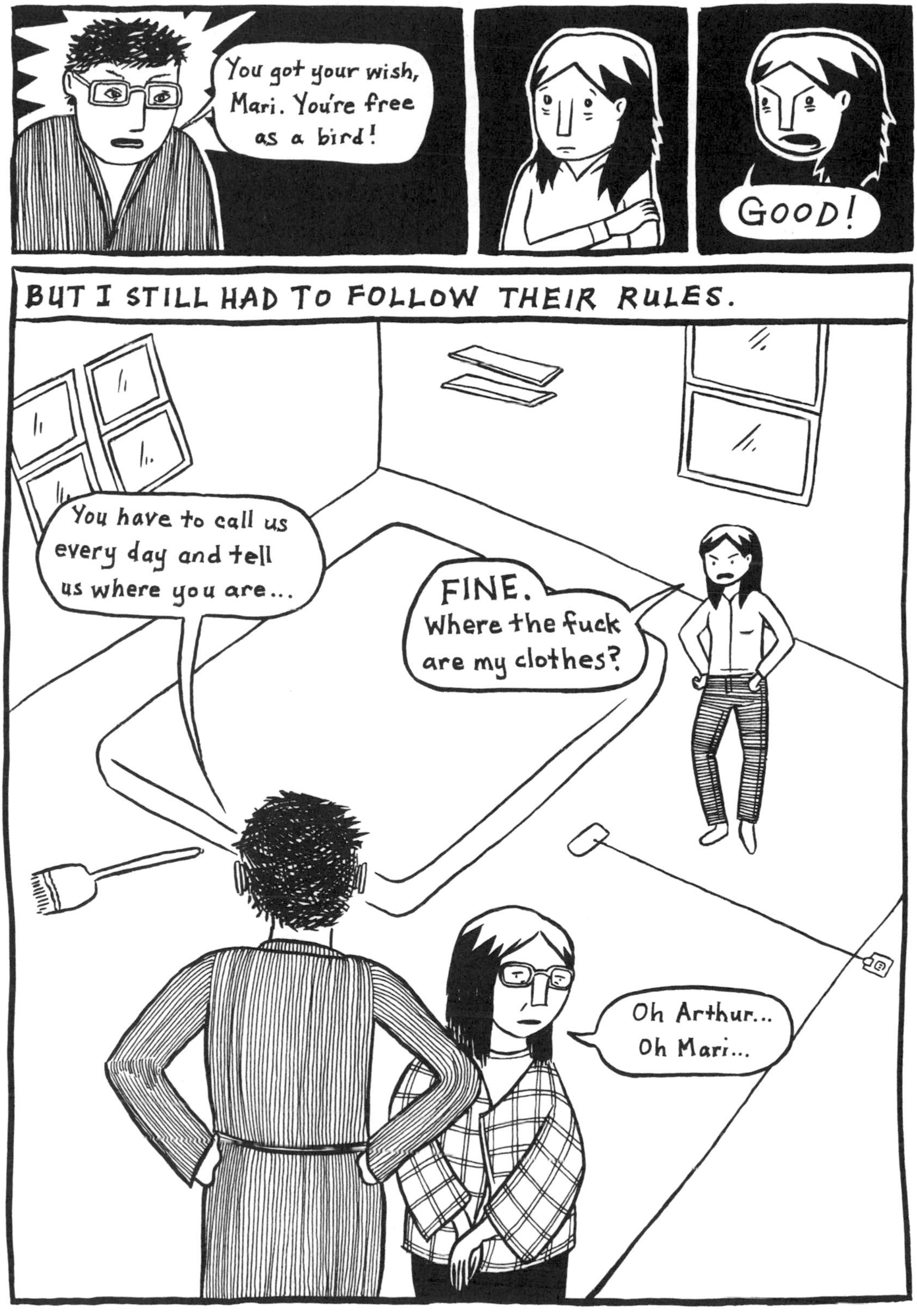

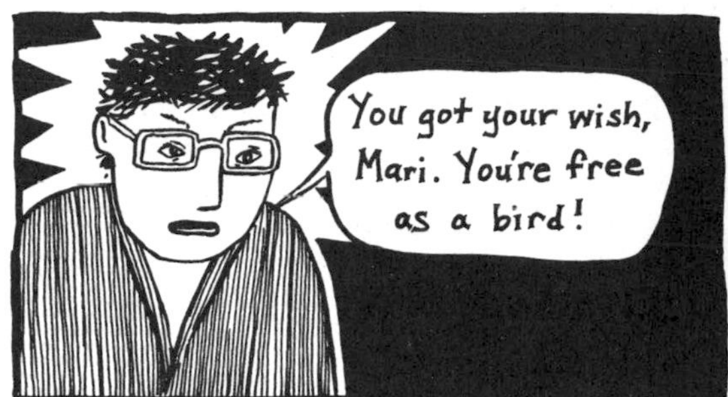

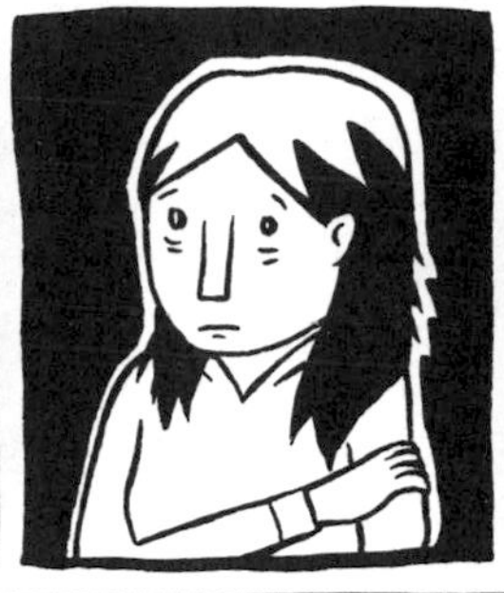

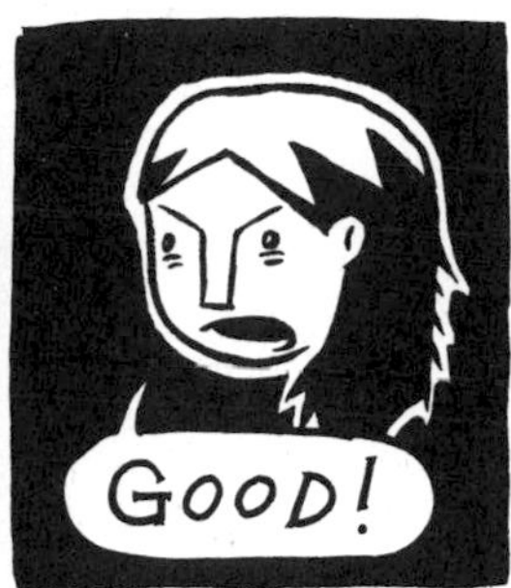

BUT I STILL HAD TO FOLLOW THEIR RULES.

You have to call us every day and tell us where you are...

FINE. Where the fuck are my clothes?

Oh Arthur... Oh Mari...

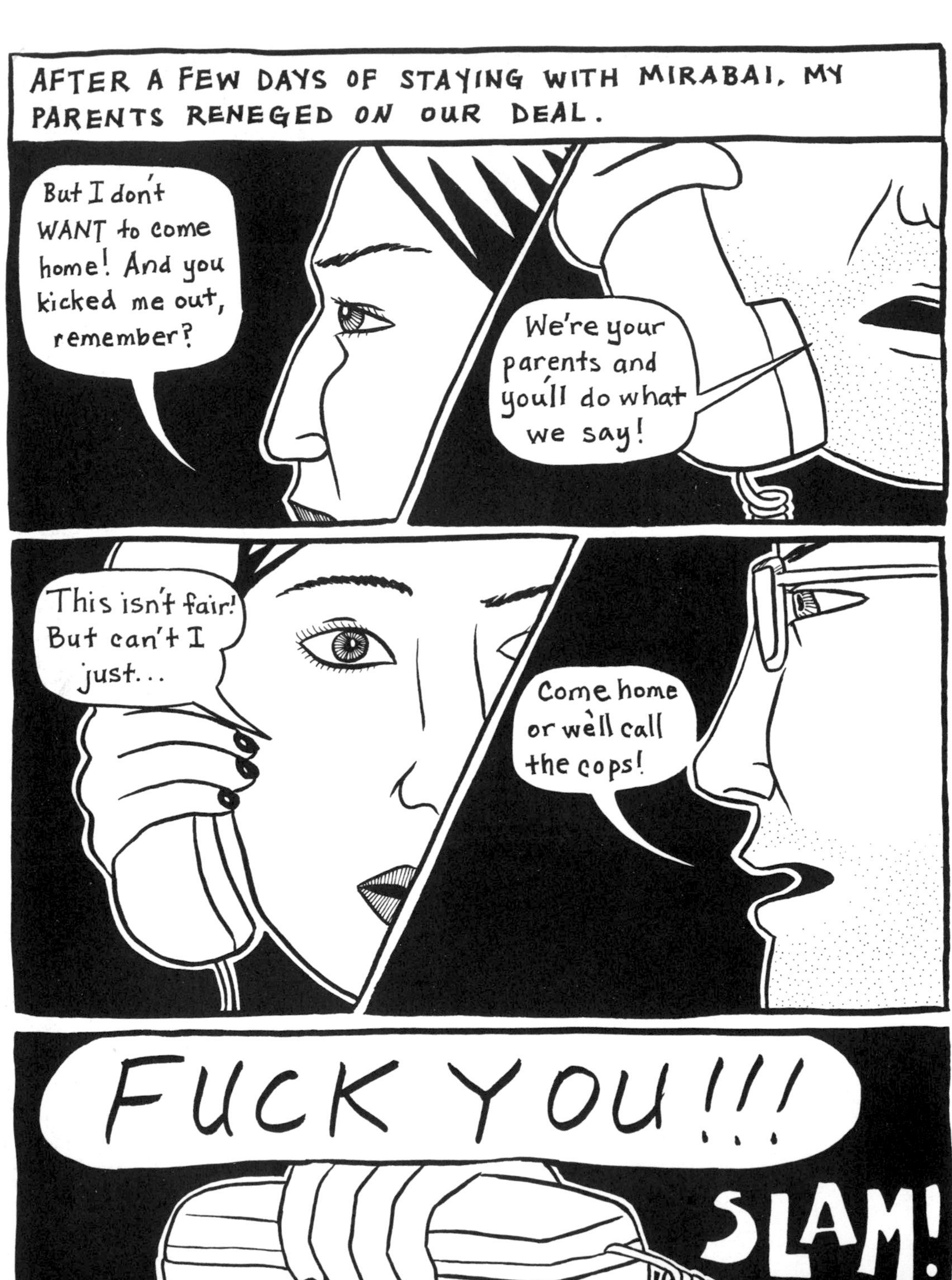
AFTER A FEW DAYS OF STAYING WITH MIRABAI, MY PARENTS RENEGED ON OUR DEAL.
But I don't WANT to come home! And you kicked me out, remember?
We're your parents and you'll do what we say!
This isn't fair! But can't I just...
Come home or we'll call the cops!
FUCK YOU!!!
SLAM!

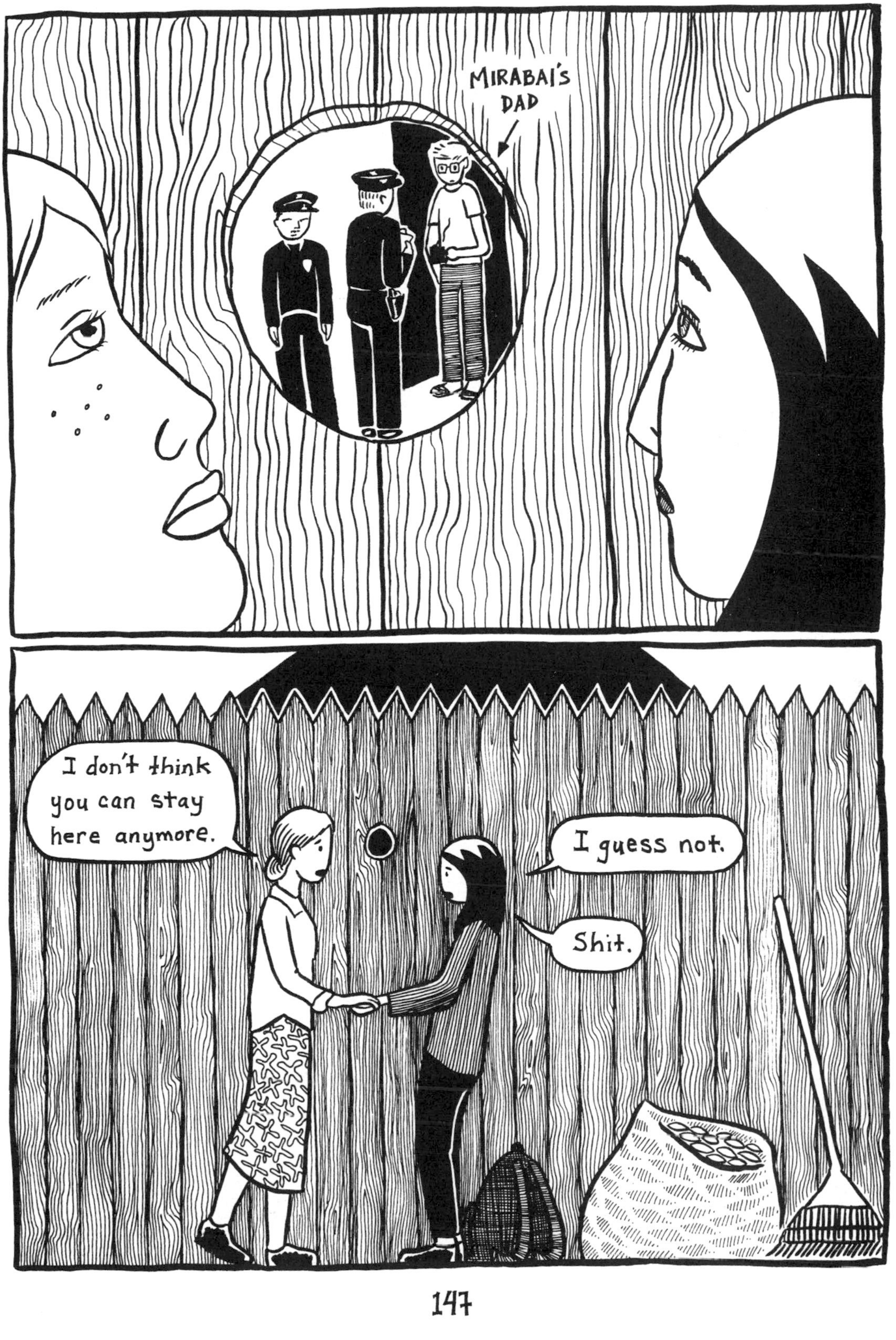

MIRABAI'S DAD

I don't think you can stay here anymore.

I guess not.

Shit.

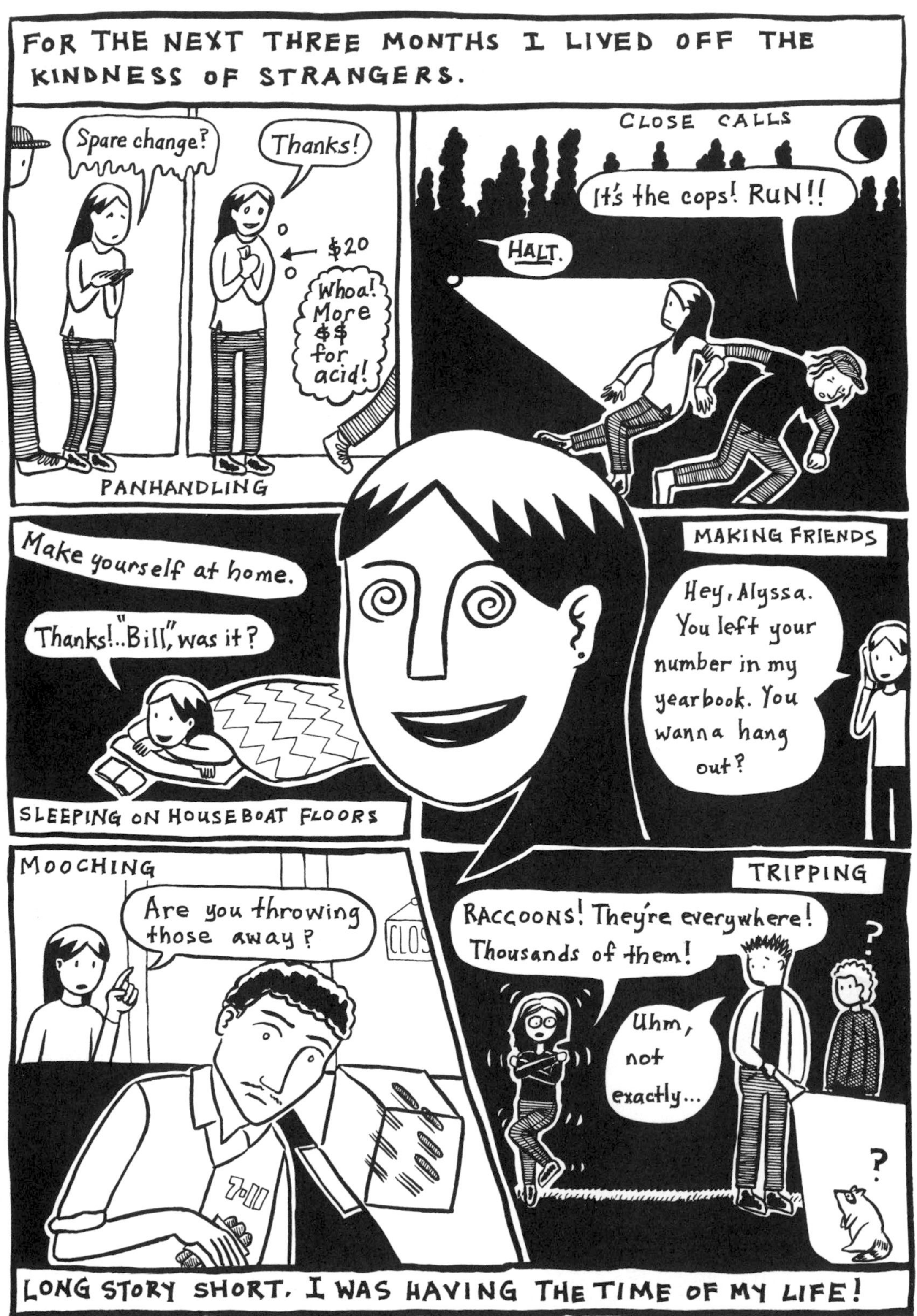
FOR THE NEXT THREE MONTHS I LIVED OFF THE KINDNESS OF STRANGERS.
Spare change?
Thanks!
$20
Whoa! More $$ for acid!
PANHANDLING
CLOSE CALLS
It's the cops! RUN!!
HALT.
Make yourself at home.
Thanks!.."Bill," was it?
SLEEPING ON HOUSEBOAT FLOORS
MAKING FRIENDS
Hey, Alyssa. You left your number in my yearbook. You wanna hang out?
MOOCHING
Are you throwing those away?
CLOS
7-11
TRIPPING
RACCOONS! They're everywhere! Thousands of them!
Uhm, not exactly...
?
?
LONG STORY SHORT, I WAS HAVING THE TIME OF MY LIFE!

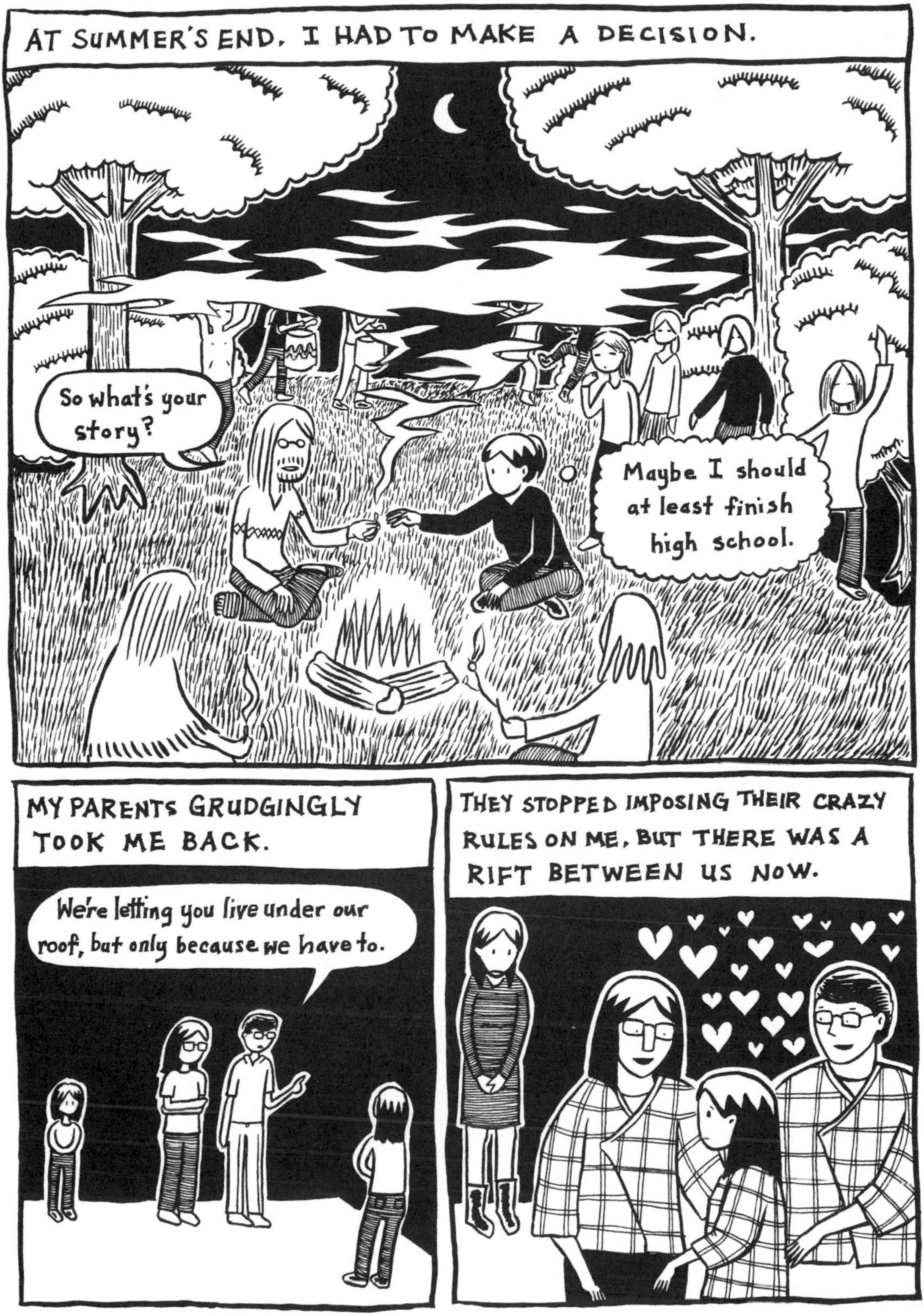

AT SUMMER'S END, I HAD TO MAKE A DECISION.

So what's your story?

Maybe I should at least finish high school.

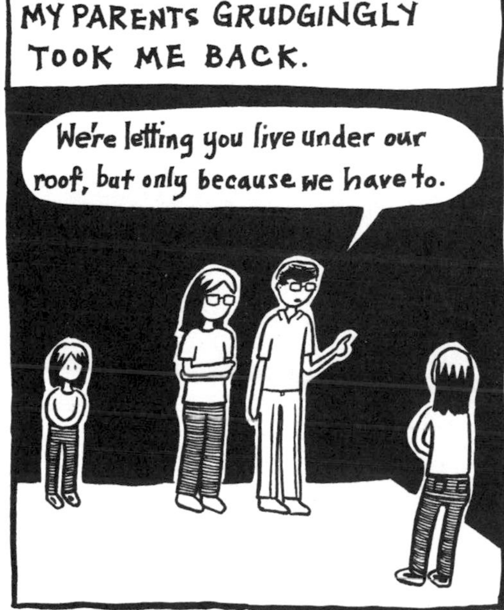

THEY STOPPED IMPOSING THEIR CRAZY RULES ON ME, BUT THERE WAS A RIFT BETWEEN US NOW.

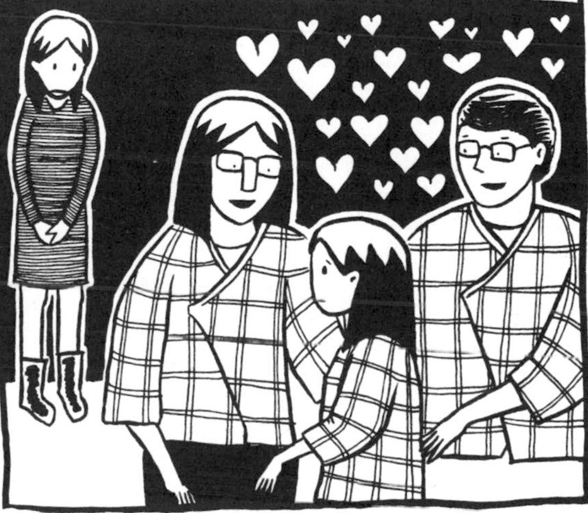

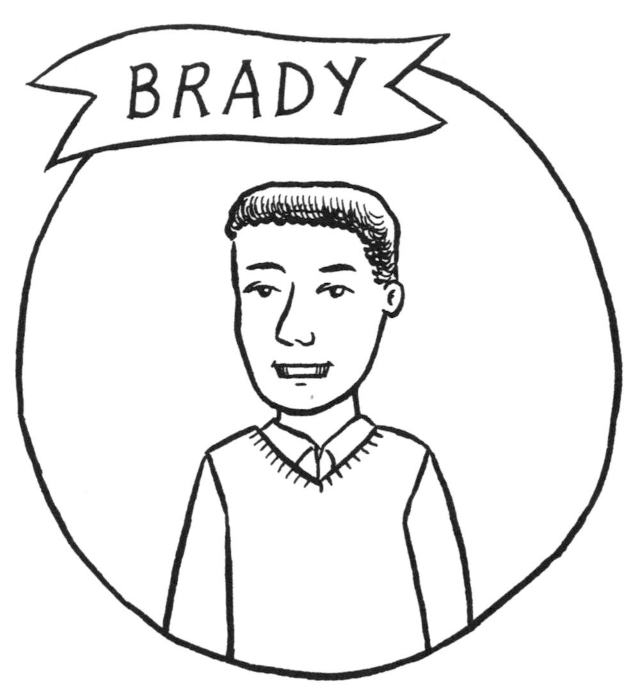
BRADY

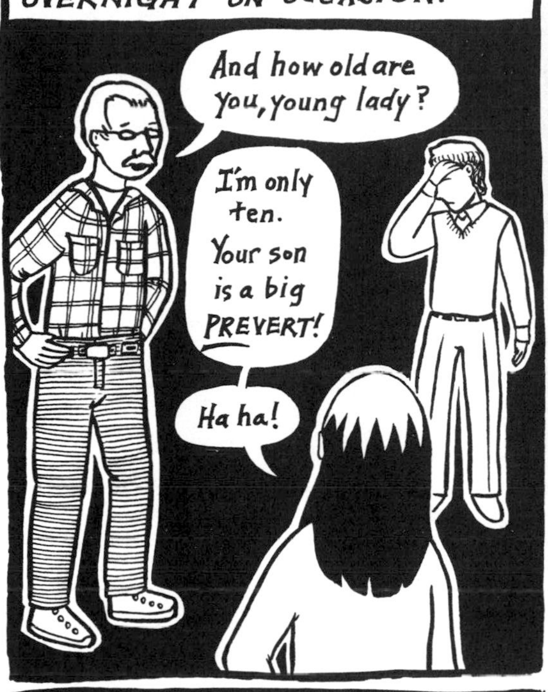
HE LIVED WITH HIS DAD. I STAYED OVERNIGHT ON OCCASION.
And how old are you, young lady?
I'm only ten. Your son is a big PREVERT!
Ha ha!

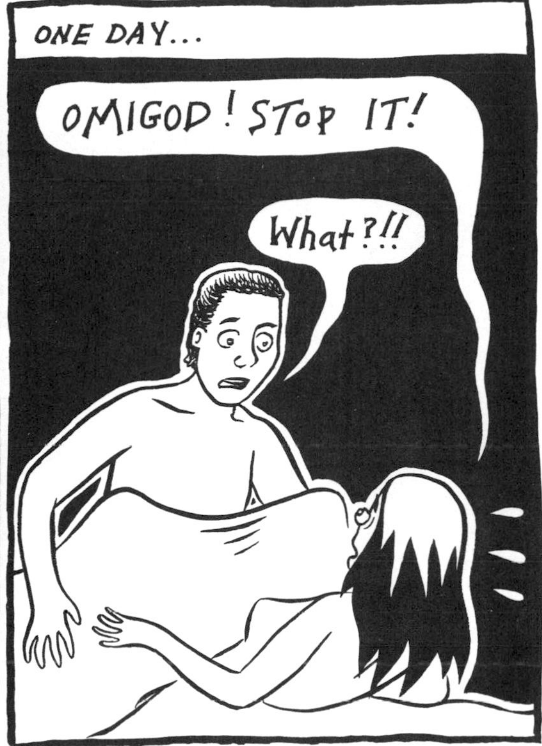
ONE DAY...
OMIGOD! STOP IT!
What?!!

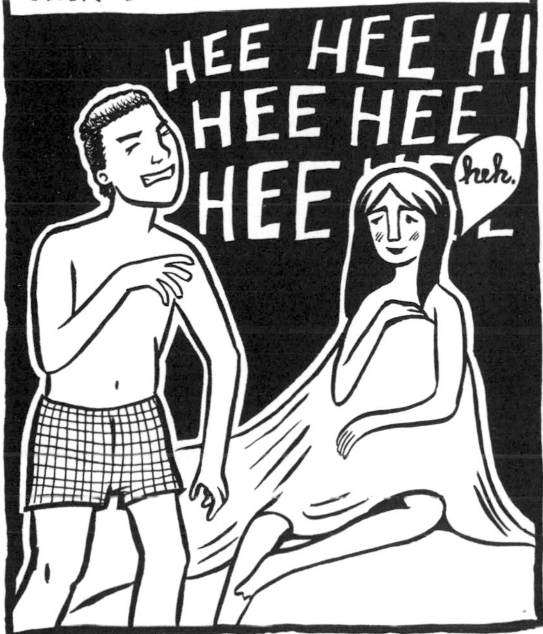
AFTER SOME DISCUSSION, WE REALIZED I'D JUST HAD MY VERY FIRST ORGASM.
HEE HEE
HEE HEE
HEE
heh.

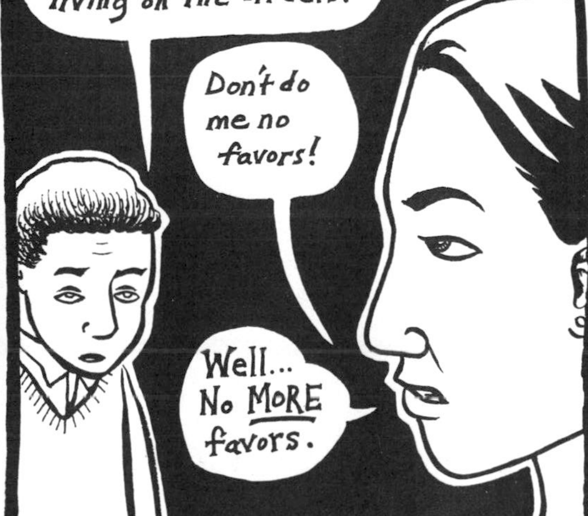
AFTER ABOUT A MONTH HE TURNED EIGHTEEN AND THEN PROMPTLY BROKE UP WITH ME.
You're just too young for me. And now that you're back at your parents', I won't have to worry about you living on the streets.
Don't do me no favors!
Well... No MORE favors.

THE VERY NEXT WEEK...

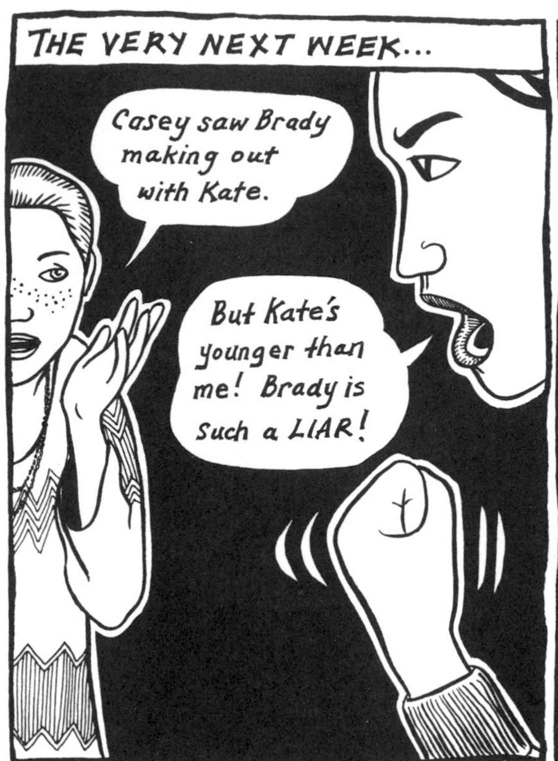

THIS MESSED ME UP FOR MANY YEARS TO COME.

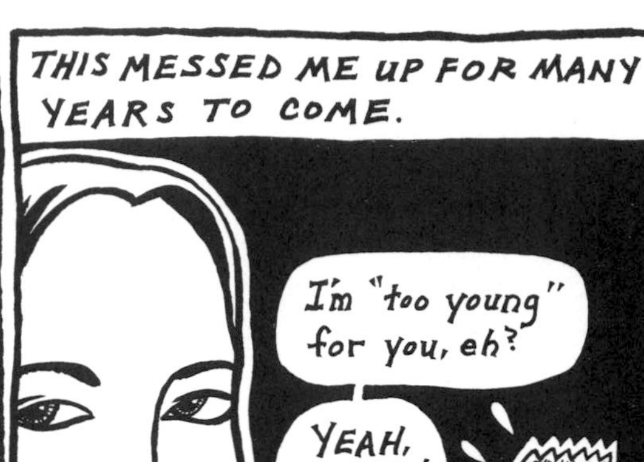
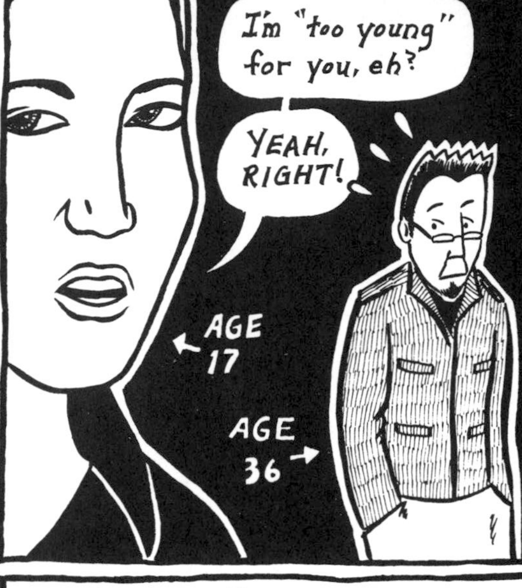

ALMOST TWENTY YEARS LATER, WE GOT IN TOUCH ONLINE.

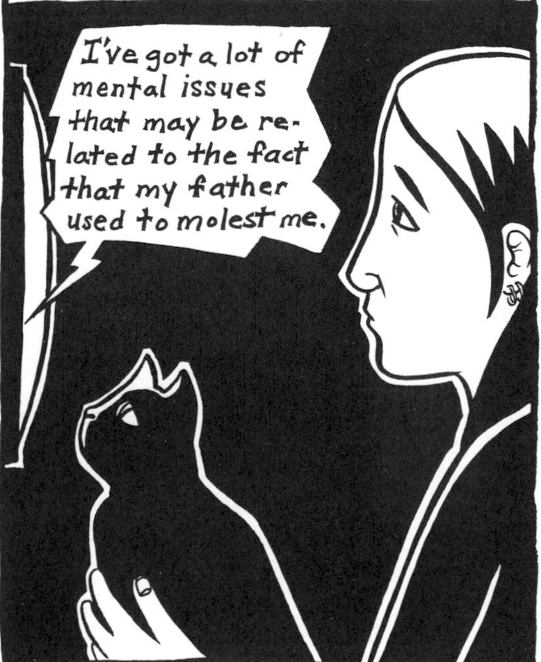

APPARENTLY HE HAD A LOT OF LEFTOVER BAGGAGE TOO.

brady: i'm so sorry i took advantage of you.
Mari: No way! :) You gave me my first orgasm. I've always been grateful. Ha ha.
brady: ha ha
Mari: But what was the deal with you making out with Kate right after you said I was too young for you? She was a year younger than me!
brady: i never did that.
Mari: Huh? Are you sure?
brady: i'm positive. i was wracked with guilt after you. i didn't so much as kiss another girl for years.
Mari: . . .
Mari: Huh.
Mari: Weird.

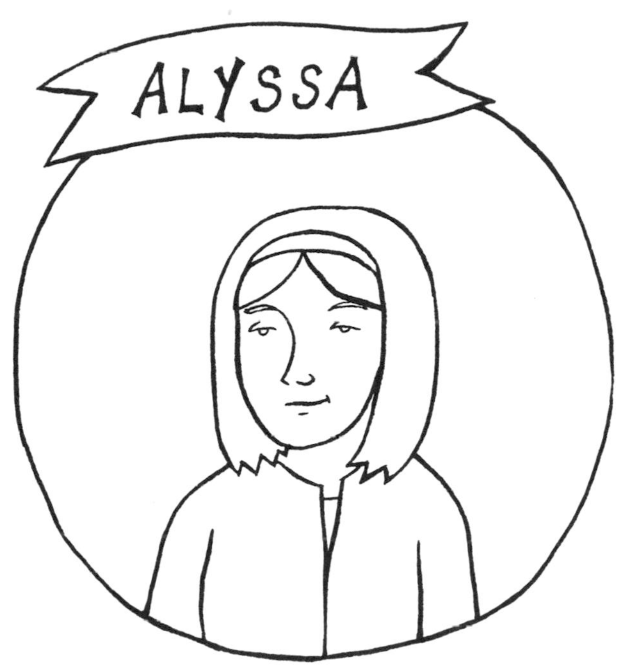
ALYSSA

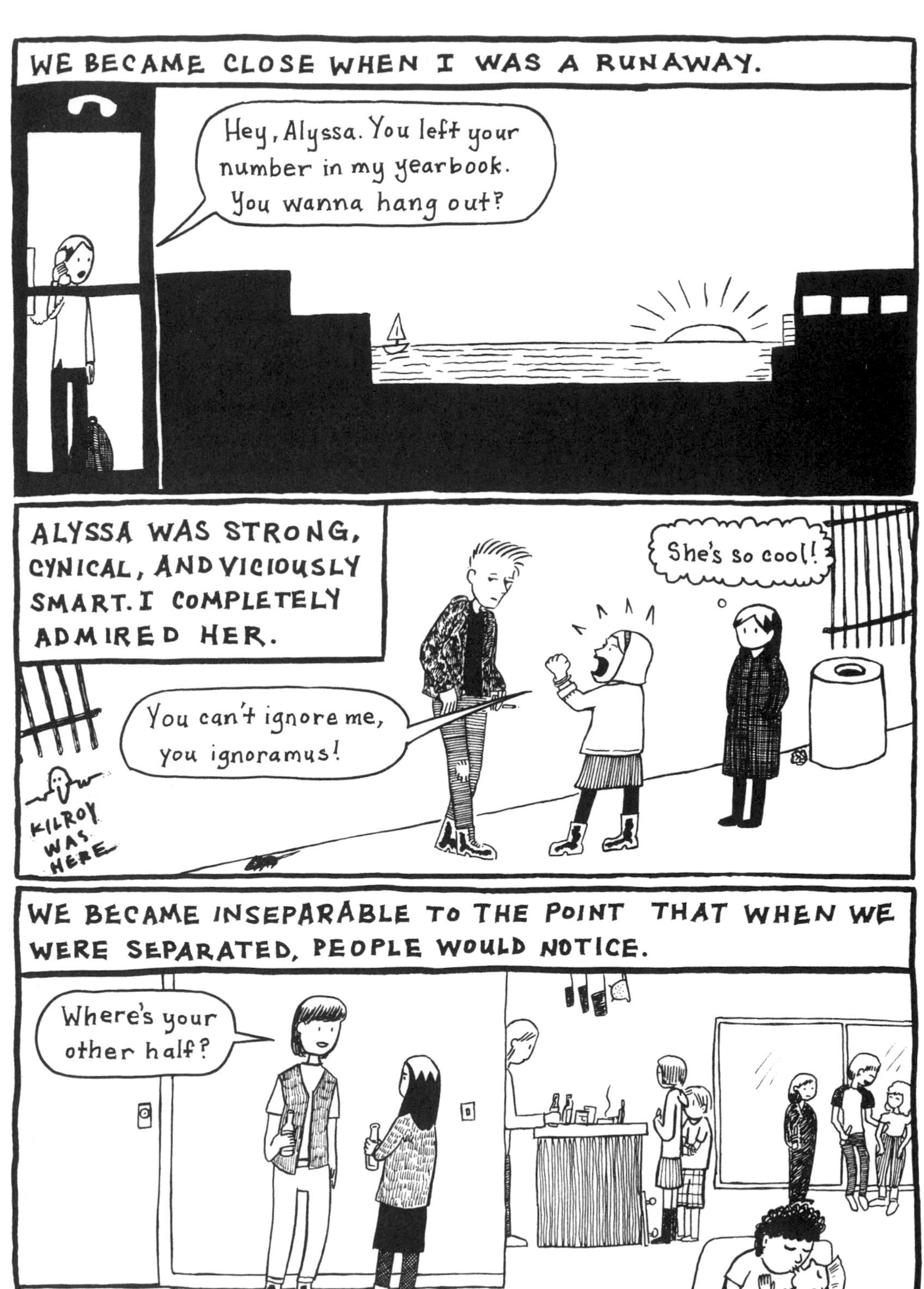
WE BECAME CLOSE WHEN I WAS A RUNAWAY.
Hey, Alyssa. You left your number in my yearbook. You wanna hang out?
ALYSSA WAS STRONG, CYNICAL, AND VICIOUSLY SMART. I COMPLETELY ADMIRED HER.
She's so cool!
You can't ignore me, you ignoramus!
KILROY WAS HERE
WE BECAME INSEPARABLE TO THE POINT THAT WHEN WE WERE SEPARATED, PEOPLE WOULD NOTICE.
Where's your other half?

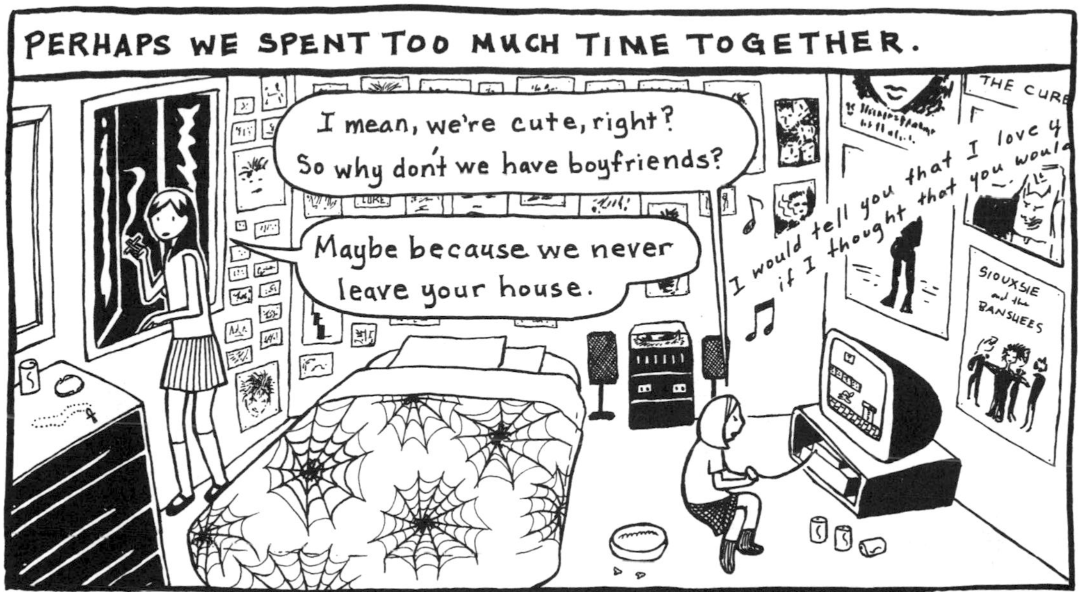

PERHAPS WE SPENT TOO MUCH TIME TOGETHER.
I mean, we're cute, right? So why don't we have boyfriends?
Maybe because we never leave your house.
THE CURE
I would tell you that I love y
if I thought that you woul
SIOUXSIE and the BANSHEES

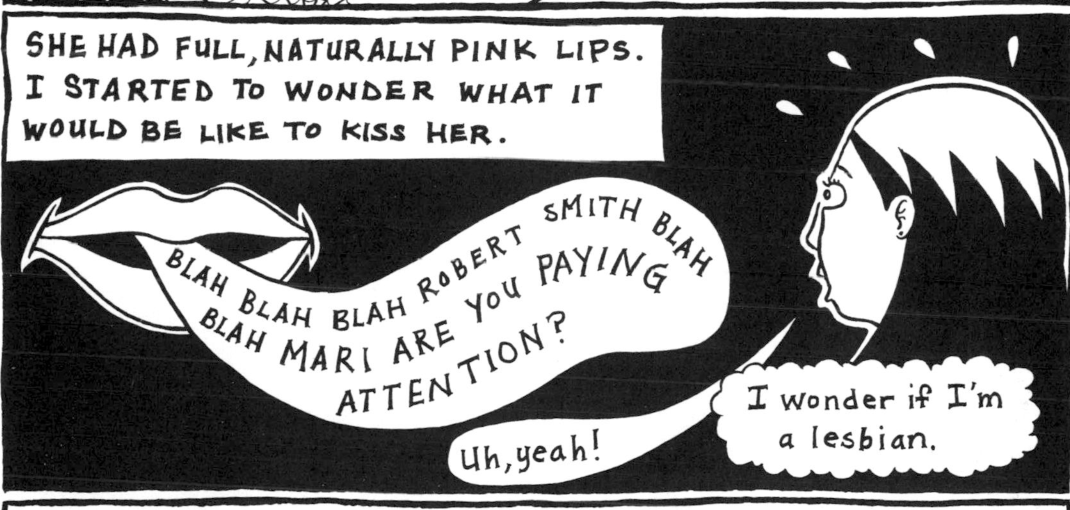

SHE HAD FULL, NATURALLY PINK LIPS. I STARTED TO WONDER WHAT IT WOULD BE LIKE TO KISS HER.
BLAH BLAH BLAH ROBERT SMITH BLAH BLAH MARI ARE YOU PAYING ATTENTION?
Uh, yeah!
I wonder if I'm a lesbian.

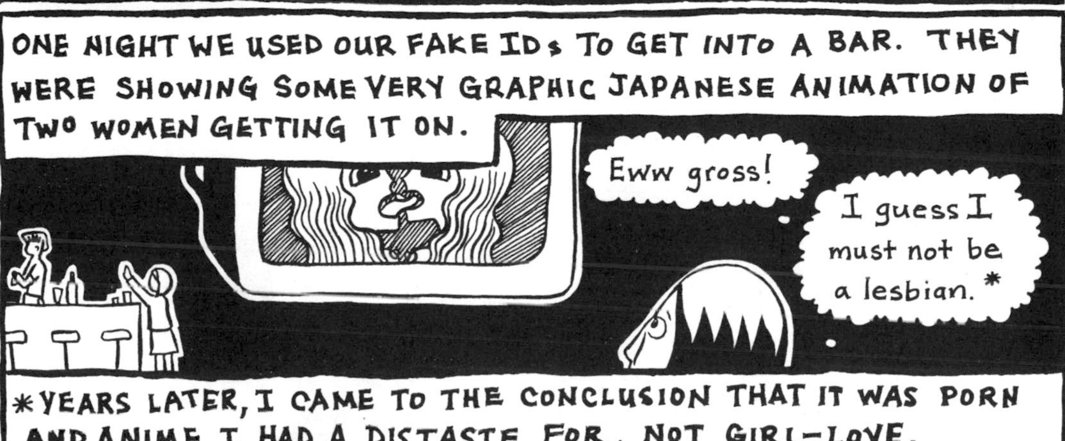

ONE NIGHT WE USED OUR FAKE IDs TO GET INTO A BAR. THEY WERE SHOWING SOME VERY GRAPHIC JAPANESE ANIMATION OF TWO WOMEN GETTING IT ON.
Eww gross!
I guess I must not be a lesbian.*
*YEARS LATER, I CAME TO THE CONCLUSION THAT IT WAS PORN AND ANIME I HAD A DISTASTE FOR, NOT GIRL-LOVE.

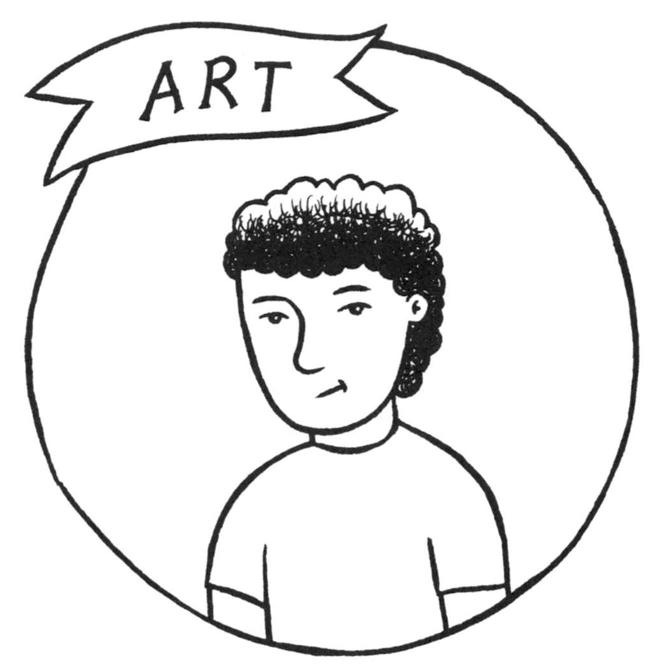
ART

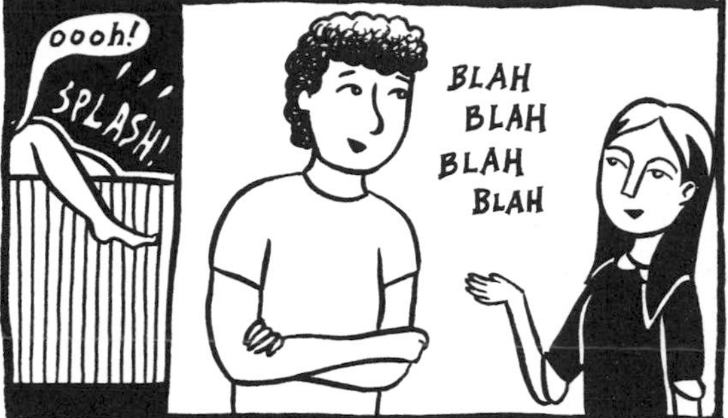
I WAS AT MY EX-BOYFRIEND MATT'S PARTY. MY FRIEND ALYSSA WAS GETTING IT ON WITH SOME GUY IN THE HOT TUB, SO ART AND I STARTED TALKING.
oooh!
SPLASH!
BLAH BLAH BLAH BLAH

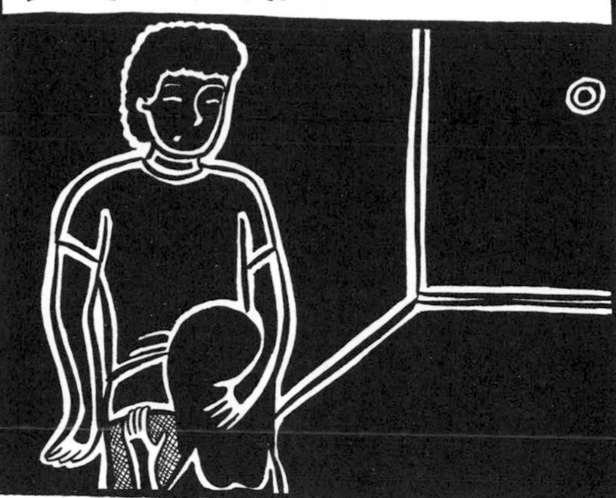
THE TALKING SOON PROGRESSED TO OTHER THINGS.

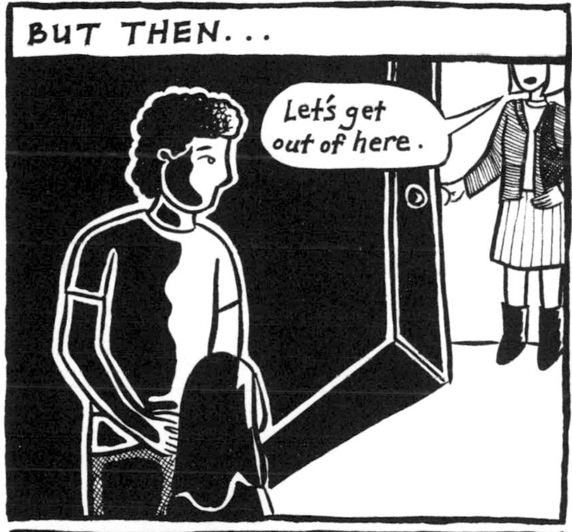
BUT THEN...
Let's get out of here.

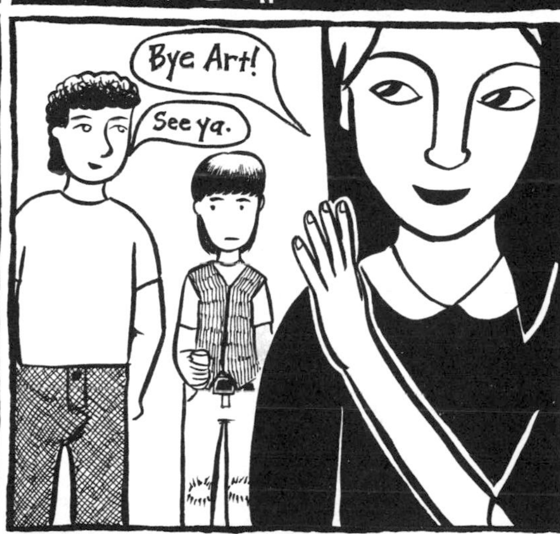
Bye Art!
See ya.

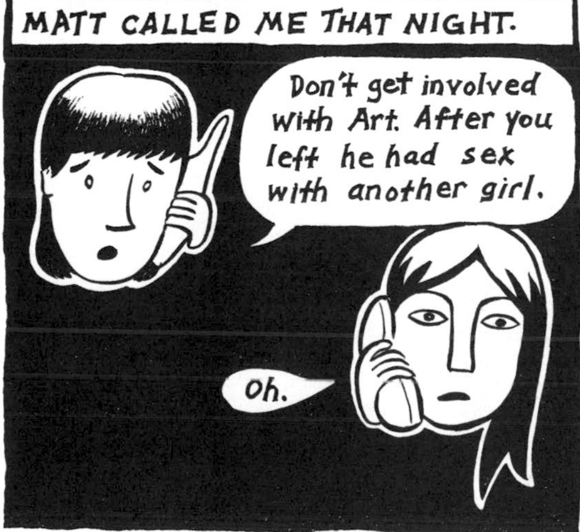
MATT CALLED ME THAT NIGHT.
Don't get involved with Art. After you left he had sex with another girl.
Oh.

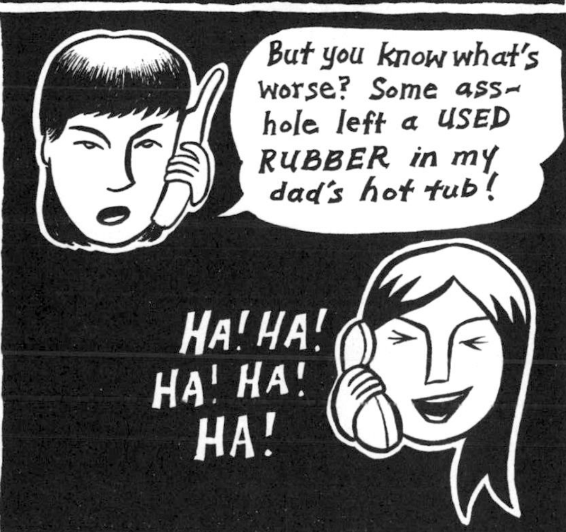
But you know what's worse? Some ass-hole left a USED RUBBER in my dad's hot tub!
HA! HA! HA! HA! HA!

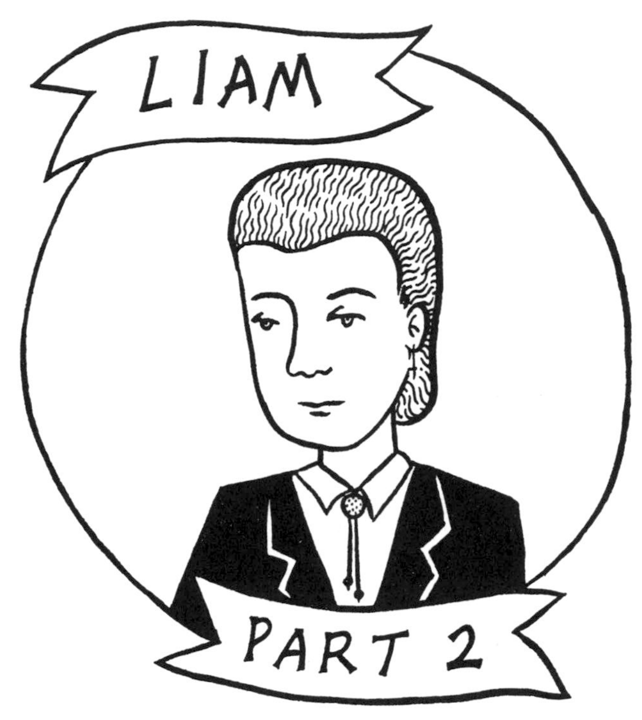
LIAM
PART 2

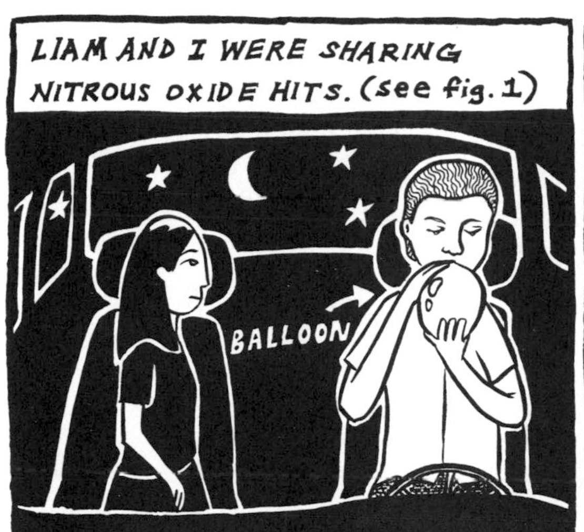

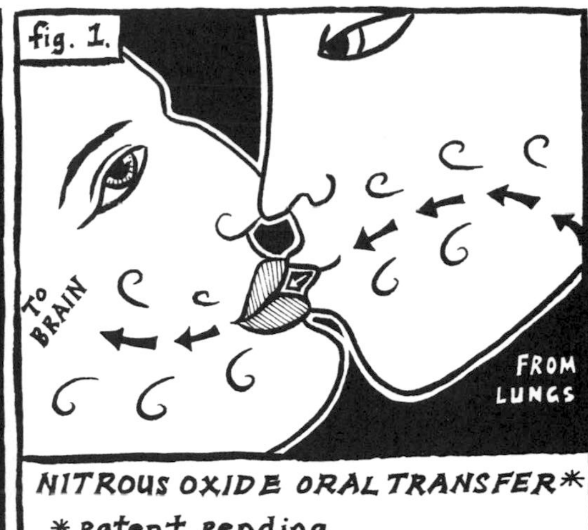

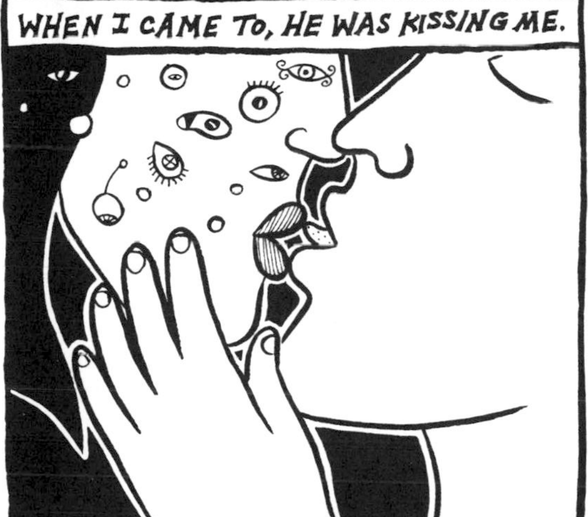

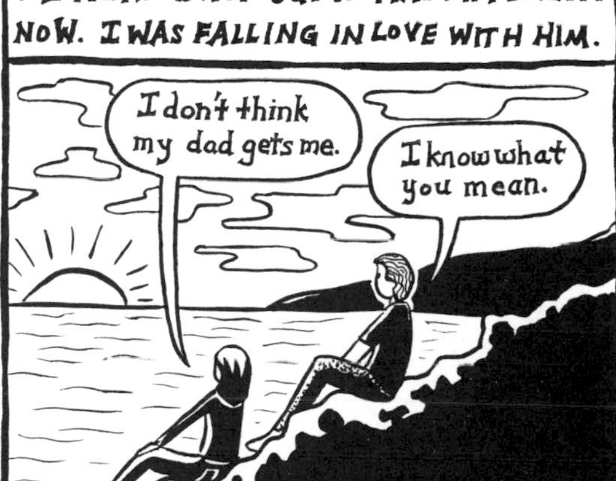

BUT HE TREATED ME DIFFERENTLY IN PUBLIC THAN IN PRIVATE.

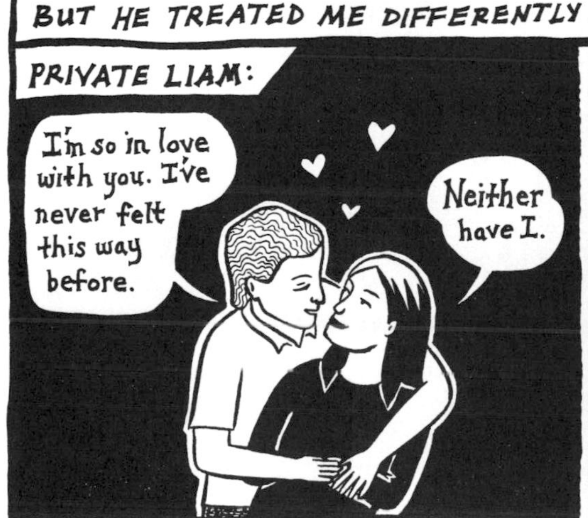

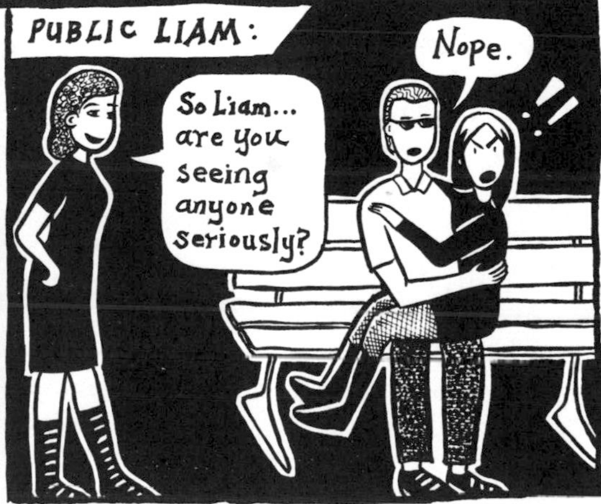

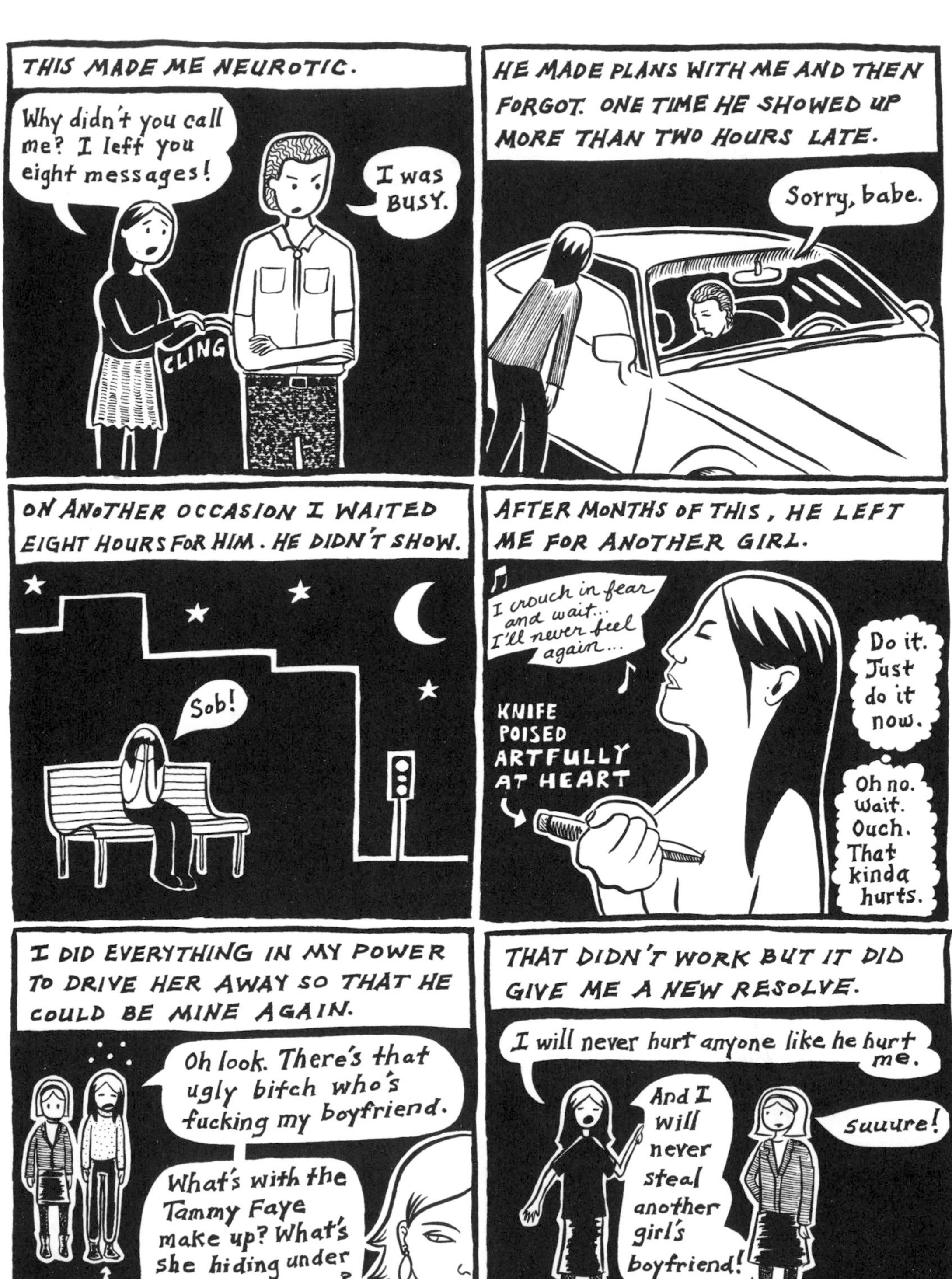
THIS MADE ME NEUROTIC.
Why didn't you call me? I left you eight messages!
I was BUSY.
CLING
HE MADE PLANS WITH ME AND THEN FORGOT. ONE TIME HE SHOWED UP MORE THAN TWO HOURS LATE.
Sorry, babe.
ON ANOTHER OCCASION I WAITED EIGHT HOURS FOR HIM. HE DIDN'T SHOW.
Sob!
AFTER MONTHS OF THIS, HE LEFT ME FOR ANOTHER GIRL.
I crouch in fear and wait... I'll never feel again...
KNIFE POISED ARTFULLY AT HEART
Do it. Just do it now.
Oh no. Wait. Ouch. That kinda hurts.
I DID EVERYTHING IN MY POWER TO DRIVE HER AWAY SO THAT HE COULD BE MINE AGAIN.
Oh look. There's that ugly bitch who's fucking my boyfriend.
What's with the Tammy Faye make up? What's she hiding under all those layers?
DRUNK + MEAN
THAT DIDN'T WORK BUT IT DID GIVE ME A NEW RESOLVE.
I will never hurt anyone like he hurt me.
And I will never steal another girl's boyfriend!
Suuure!

Postmortem

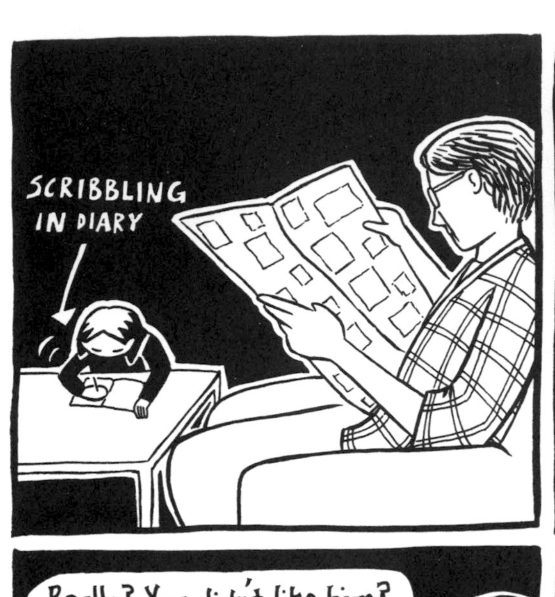
SCRIBBLING IN DIARY

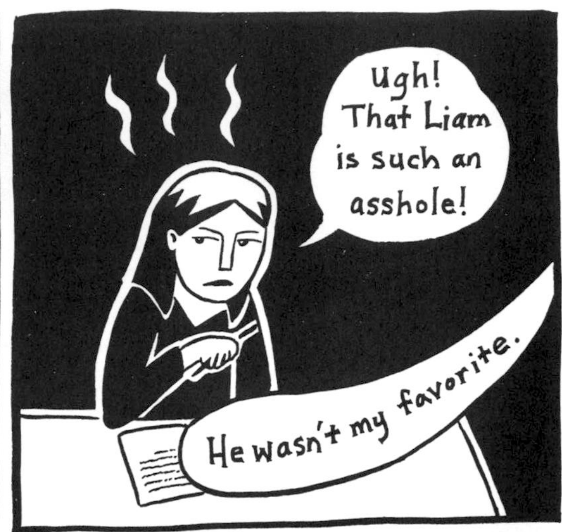
Ugh! That Liam is such an asshole!
He wasn't my favorite.

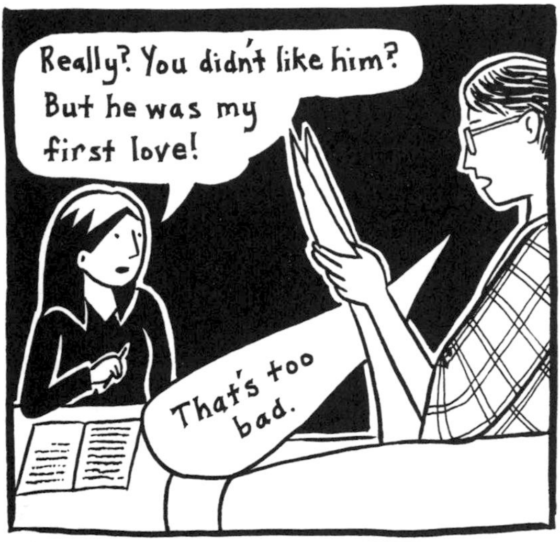
Really? You didn't like him? But he was my first love!
That's too bad.

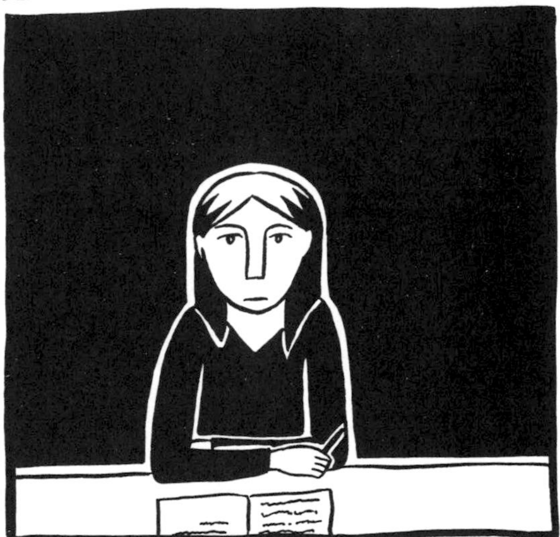

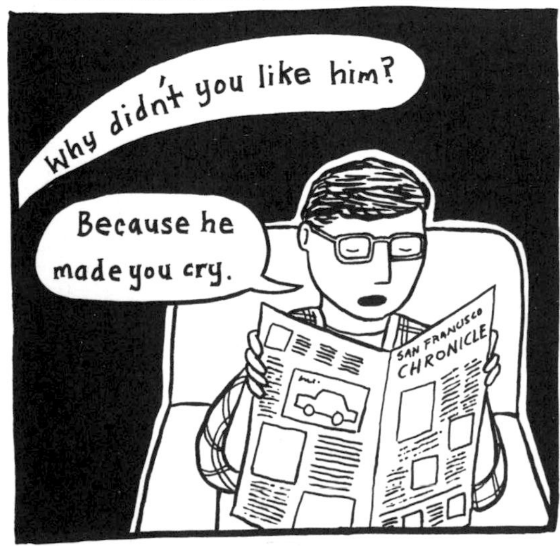
Why didn't you like him?
Because he made you cry.
SAN FRANCISCO CHRONICLE

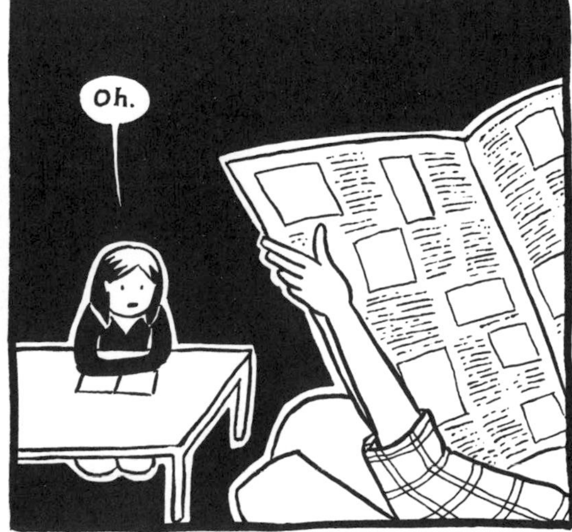
Oh.

1989
ages 15 ~ 16

Stage 3: PUPA

Larval skin is shed, exposing the cremaster, from which the young butterfly hangs until maturity.

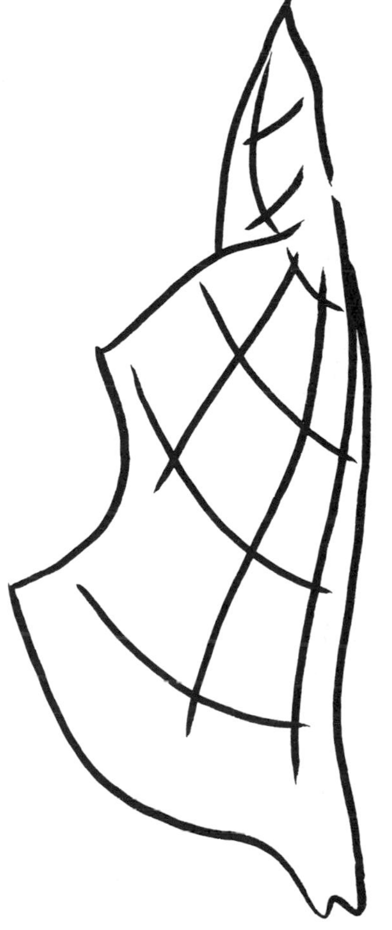

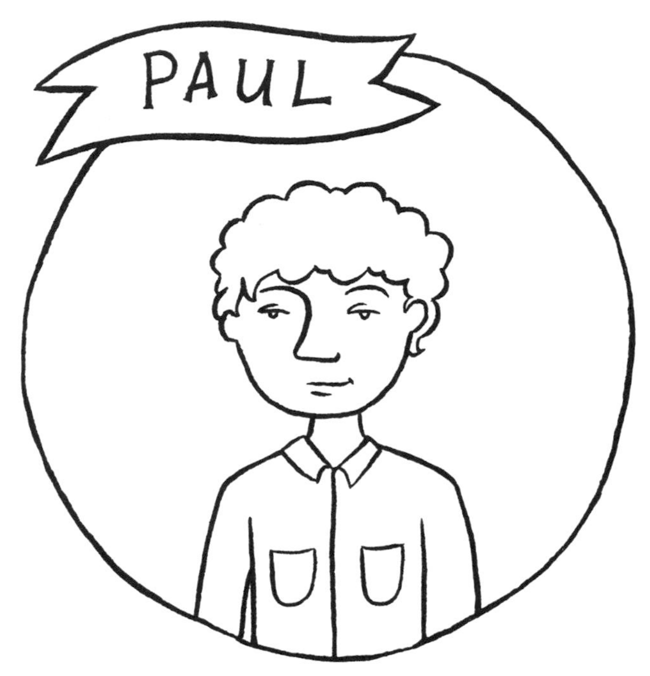
PAUL

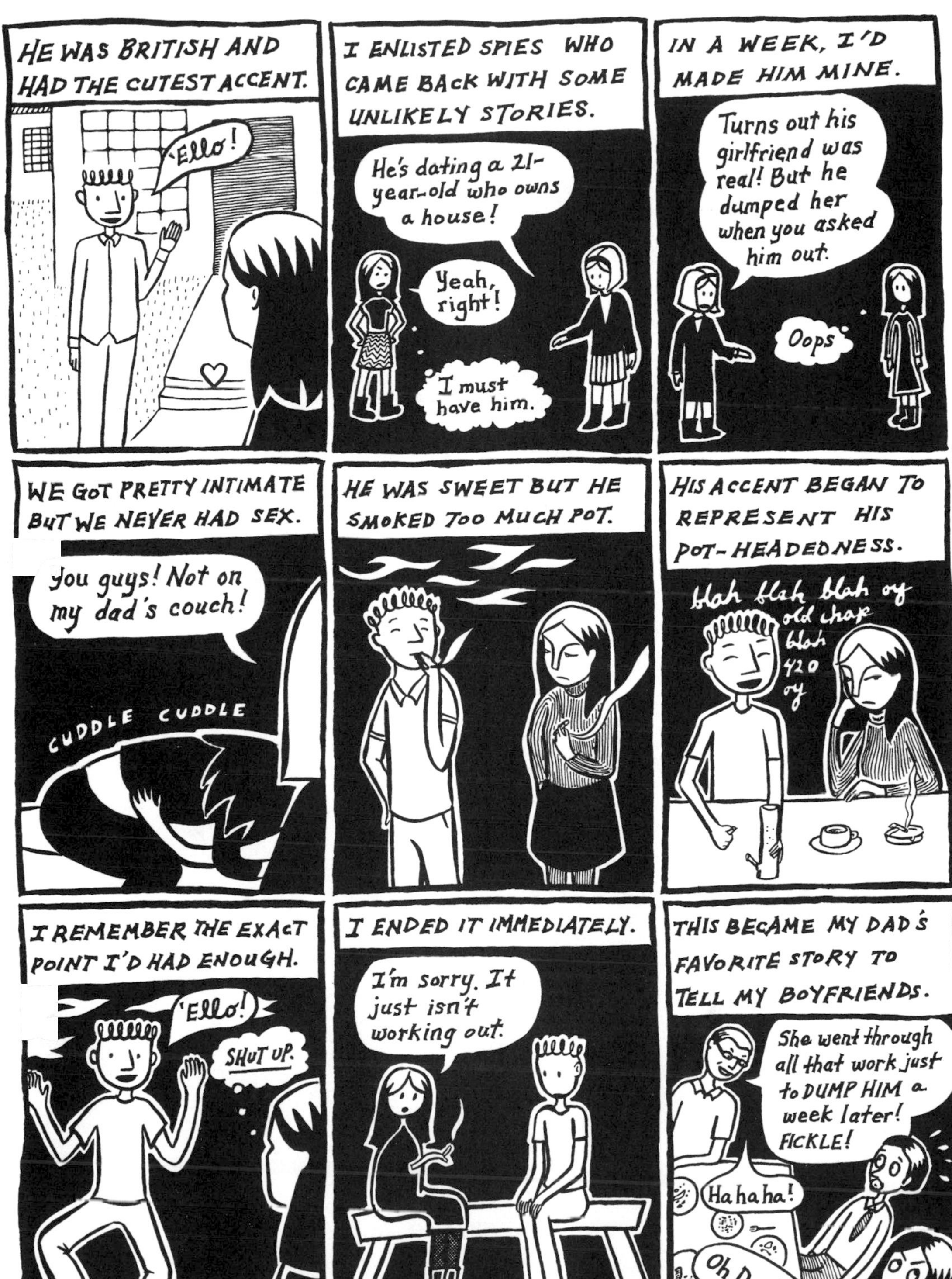
HE WAS BRITISH AND HAD THE CUTEST ACCENT.
'Ello!
I ENLISTED SPIES WHO CAME BACK WITH SOME UNLIKELY STORIES.
He's dating a 21-year-old who owns a house!
Yeah, right!
I must have him.
IN A WEEK, I'D MADE HIM MINE.
Turns out his girlfriend was real! But he dumped her when you asked him out.
Oops
WE GOT PRETTY INTIMATE BUT WE NEVER HAD SEX.
You guys! Not on my dad's couch!
CUDDLE CUDDLE
HE WAS SWEET BUT HE SMOKED TOO MUCH POT.
HIS ACCENT BEGAN TO REPRESENT HIS POT-HEADEDNESS.
blah blah blah oy
old chap
blah
420
oy
I REMEMBER THE EXACT POINT I'D HAD ENOUGH.
'Ello!
SHUT UP.
I ENDED IT IMMEDIATELY.
I'm sorry. It just isn't working out.
THIS BECAME MY DAD'S FAVORITE STORY TO TELL MY BOYFRIENDS.
She went through all that work just to DUMP HIM a week later! FICKLE!
Ha ha ha!
Oh Dad!

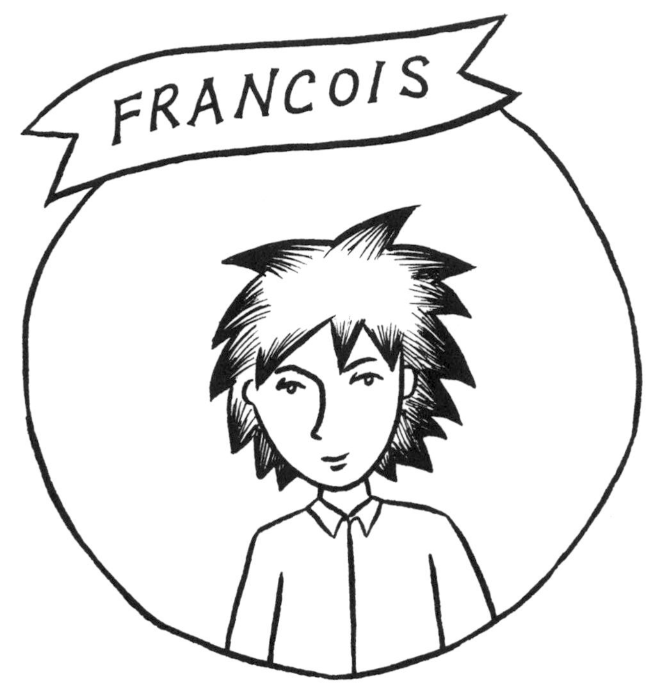
FRANCOIS

IT WAS A FRENCH-AMERICAN PARTY AND HE WAS KISSING ALL THE GIRLS.

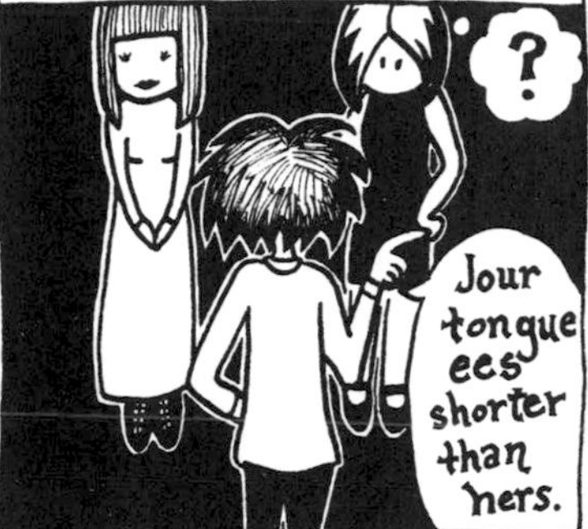

HIS ENGLISH WAS PRETTY HORRIBLE, BUT HE STILL MADE ME LAUGH.

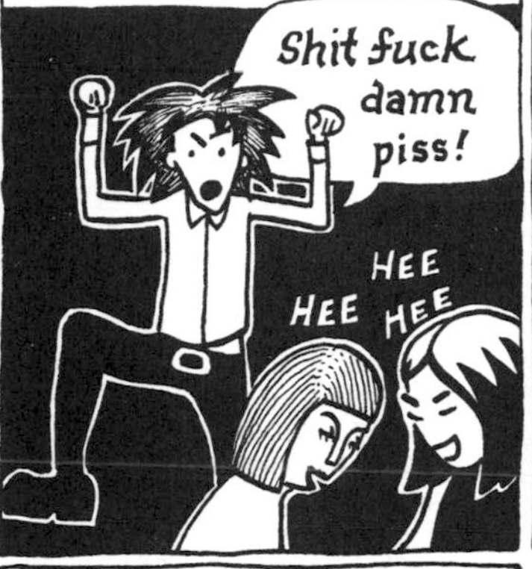

HE WAS THE PERFECT CANDIDATE FOR MY FIRST ONE-NIGHTER.

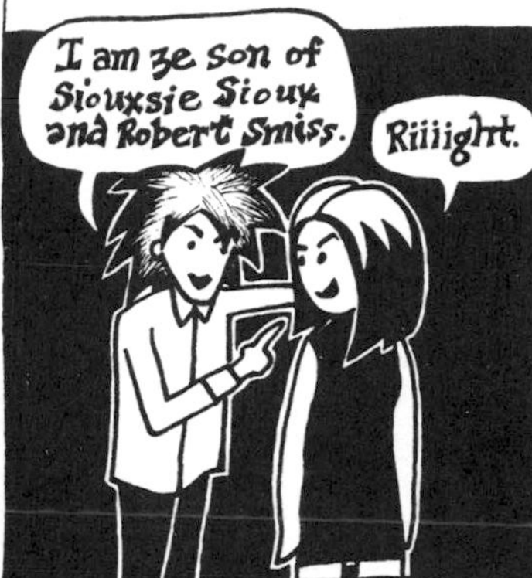

SO WE DID IT.

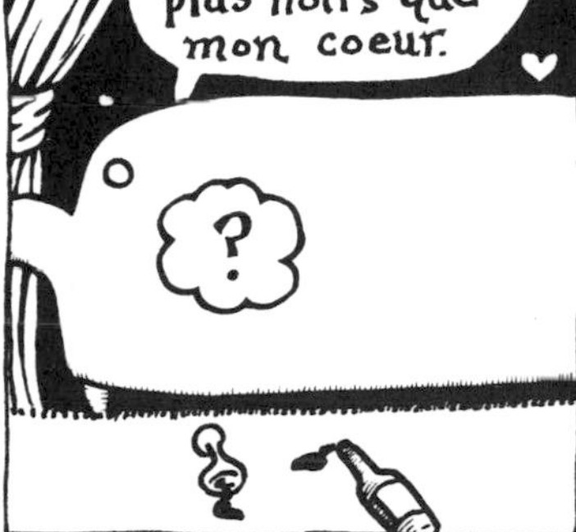

I GOT WHAT I WANTED, BUT HE WAS TAKING FOREVER, SO FINALLY...

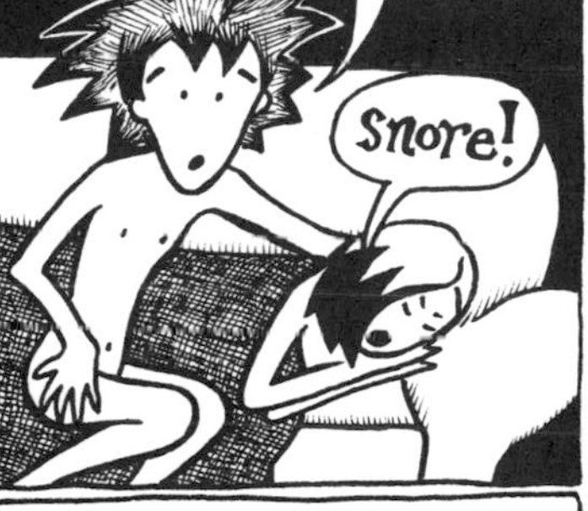

THE NEXT DAY:

No attachment, no nothing! I never hafta hear from him again since we don't even speak the same language!

Uhm, I hate to break it to you, but...

He spent all day at school talking about you. He calls you his new American girlfriend. Apparently you devirginized him.

NO!!

SOMEHOW HE GOT MY NUMBER. AND HE USED IT EVERY DAY!

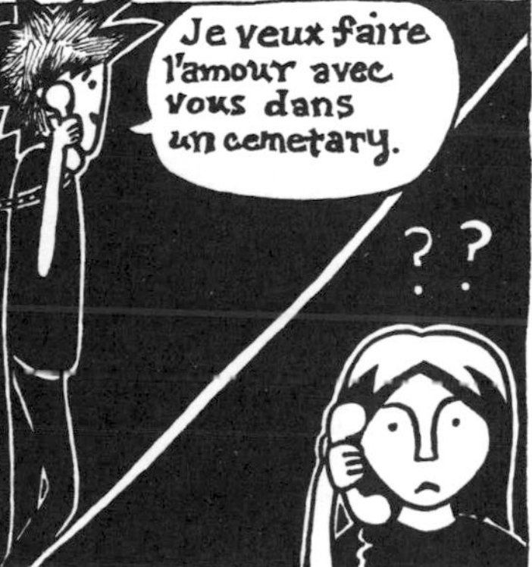

I HAD NO CHOICE.

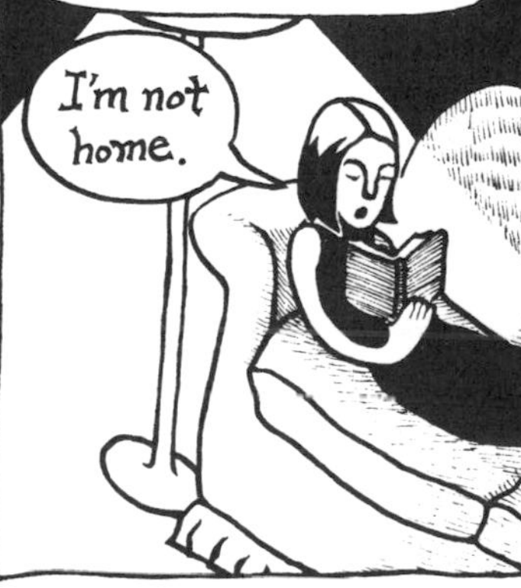

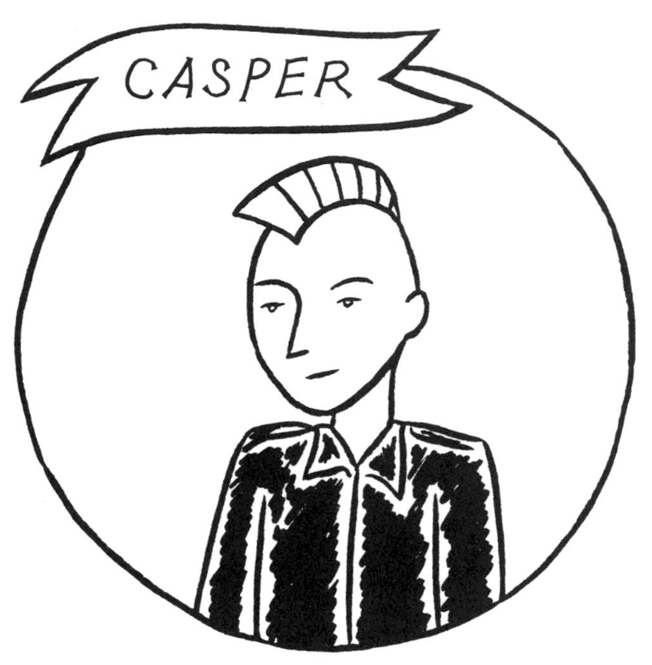
CASPER

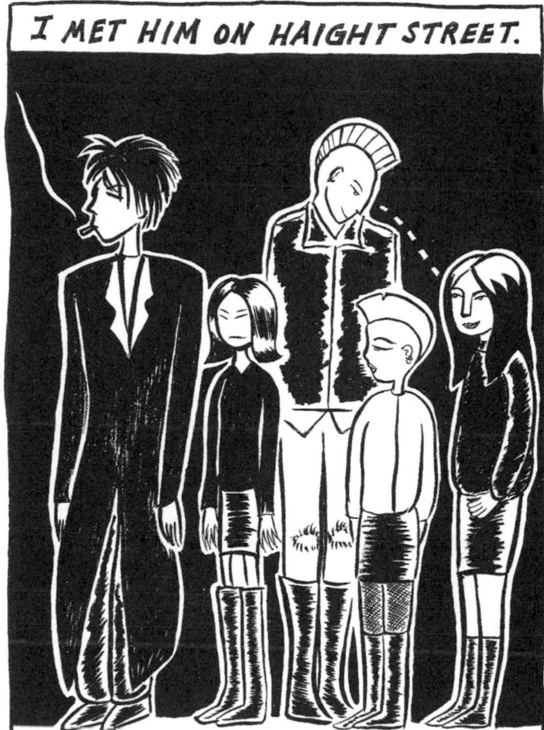
I MET HIM ON HAIGHT STREET.

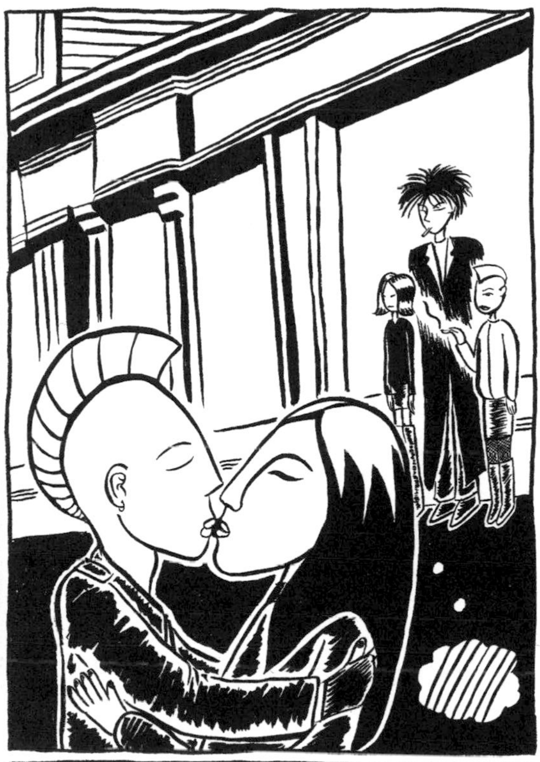

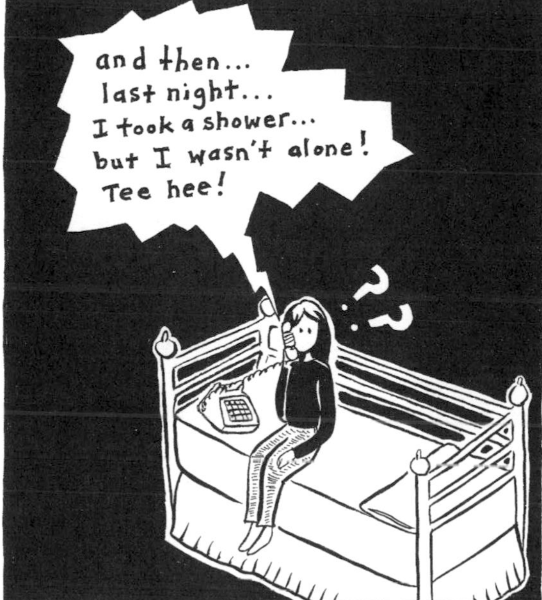
WHEN WE TALKED ON THE PHONE I COULDN'T TELL IF HE WAS TRYING TO IMPRESS ME OR REPEL ME.
and then... last night... I took a shower... but I wasn't alone! Tee hee!
??

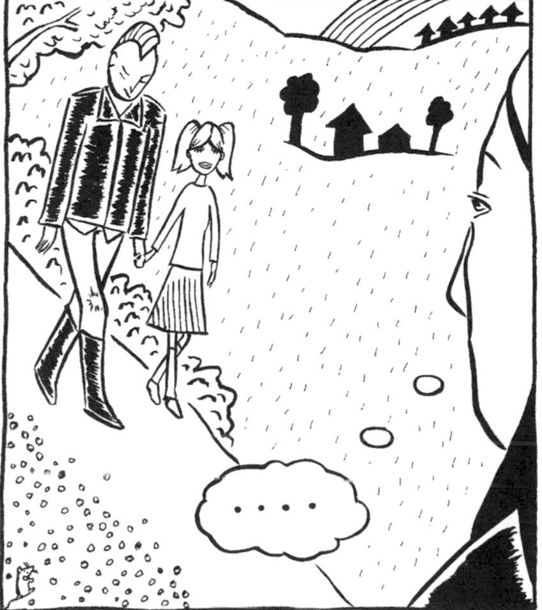
ONE DAY I SPOTTED HIM IN MILL VALLEY WALKING HAND-IN-HAND WITH A CHEERLEADER.
....

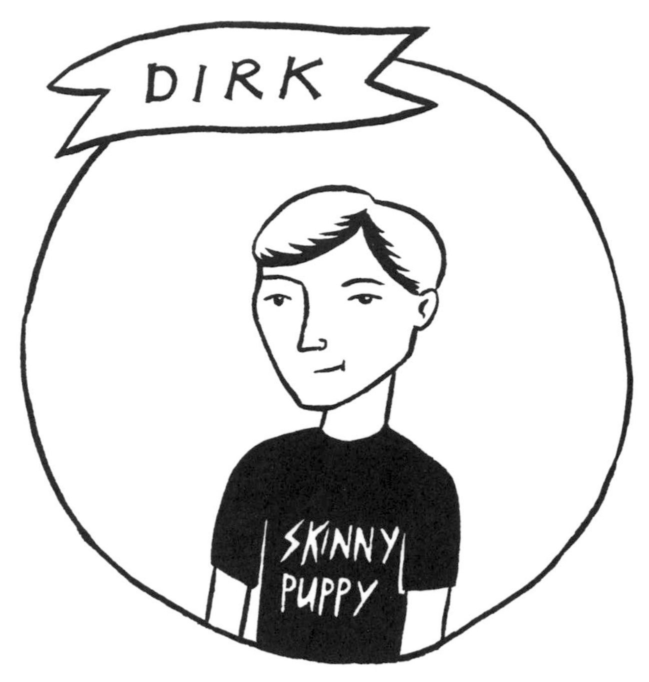
DIRK
SKINNY PUPPY

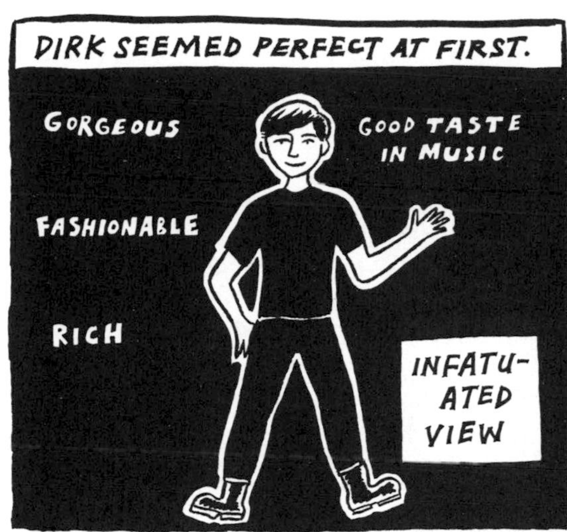
DIRK SEEMED PERFECT AT FIRST.
GORGEOUS
GOOD TASTE IN MUSIC
FASHIONABLE
RICH
INFATUATED VIEW

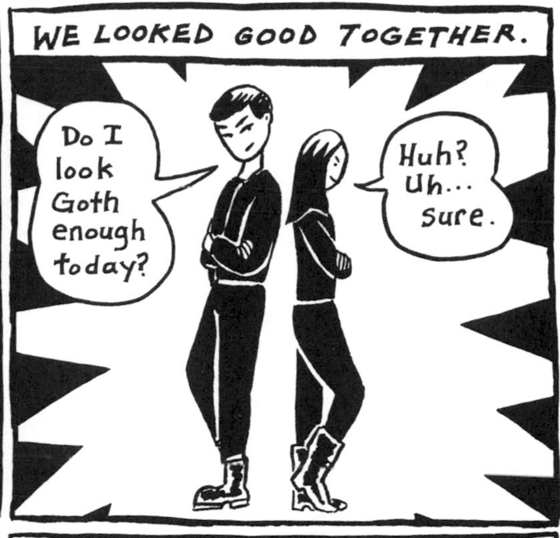
WE LOOKED GOOD TOGETHER.
Do I look Goth enough today?
Huh? Uh... Sure.

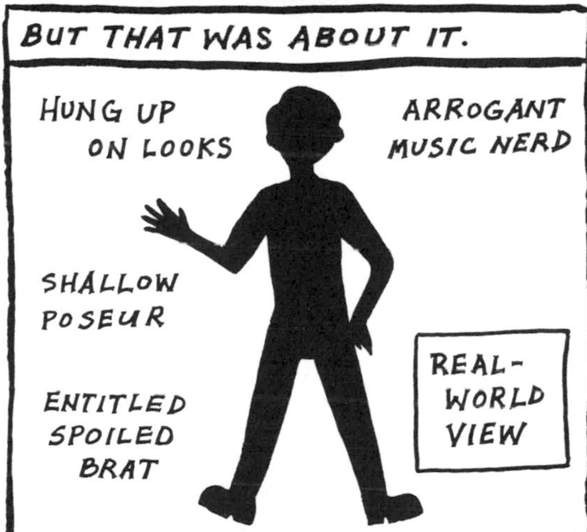
BUT THAT WAS ABOUT IT.
HUNG UP ON LOOKS
ARROGANT MUSIC NERD
SHALLOW POSEUR
ENTITLED SPOILED BRAT
REAL-WORLD VIEW

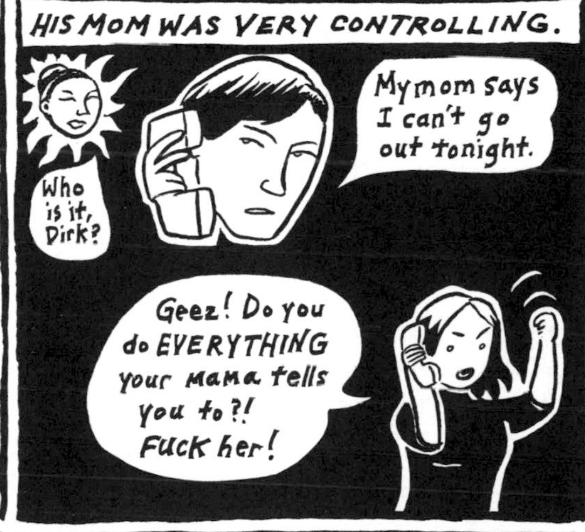
HIS MOM WAS VERY CONTROLLING.
Who is it, Dirk?
My mom says I can't go out tonight.
Geez! Do you do EVERYTHING your mama tells you to?! Fuck her!

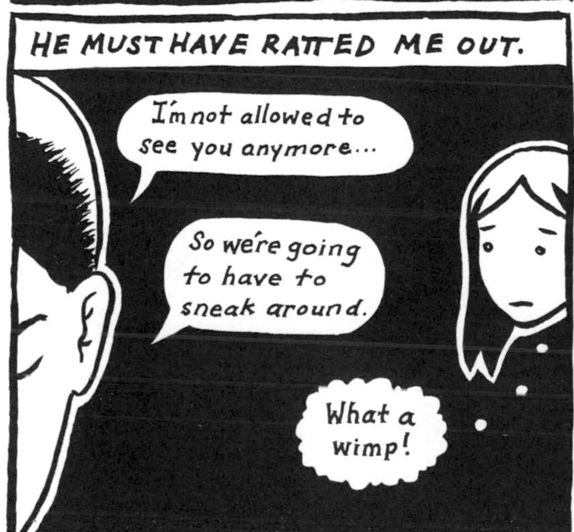
HE MUST HAVE RATTED ME OUT.
I'm not allowed to see you anymore...
So we're going to have to sneak around.
What a wimp!

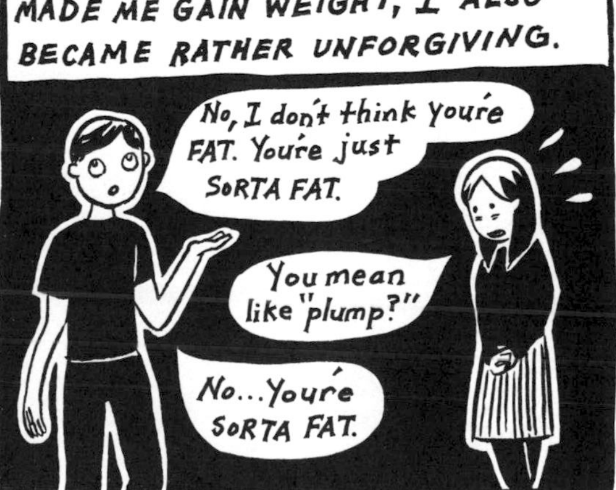
I WAS ON THE PILL, WHICH NOT ONLY MADE ME GAIN WEIGHT, I ALSO BECAME RATHER UNFORGIVING.
No, I don't think you're FAT. You're just SORTA FAT.
You mean like "plump?"
No... You're SORTA FAT.

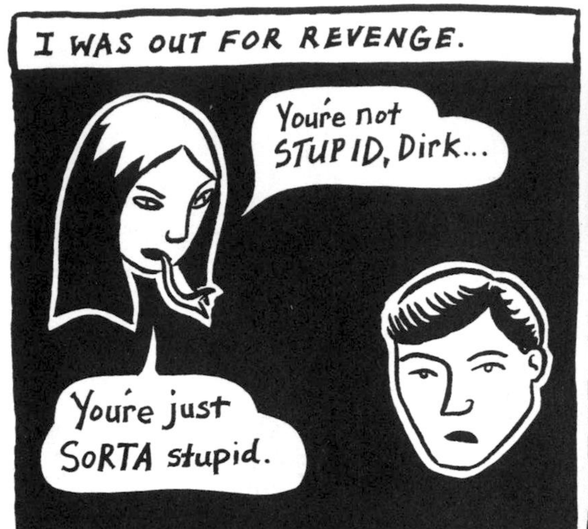
I WAS OUT FOR REVENGE.
You're not STUPID, Dirk...
You're just SORTA stupid.

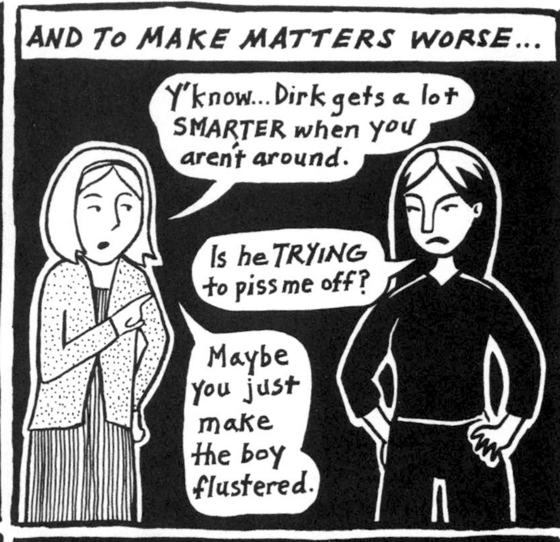
AND TO MAKE MATTERS WORSE...
Y'know... Dirk gets a lot SMARTER when you aren't around.
Is he TRYING to piss me off?
Maybe you just make the boy flustered.

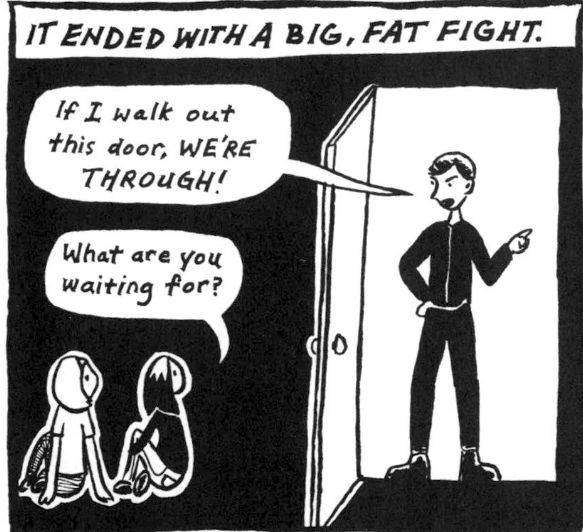
IT ENDED WITH A BIG, FAT FIGHT.
If I walk out this door, WE'RE THROUGH!
What are you waiting for?

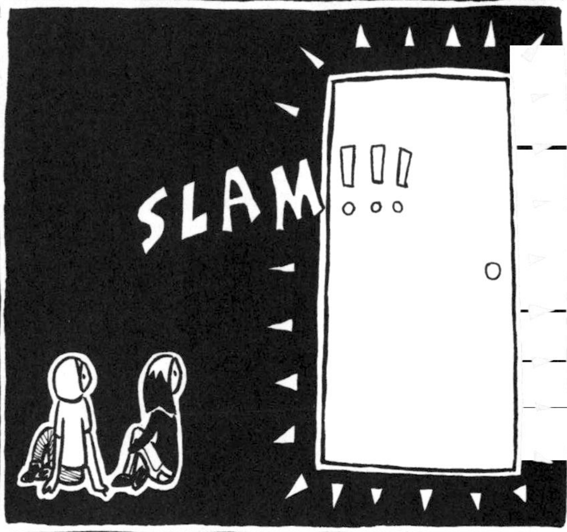
SLAM!!!

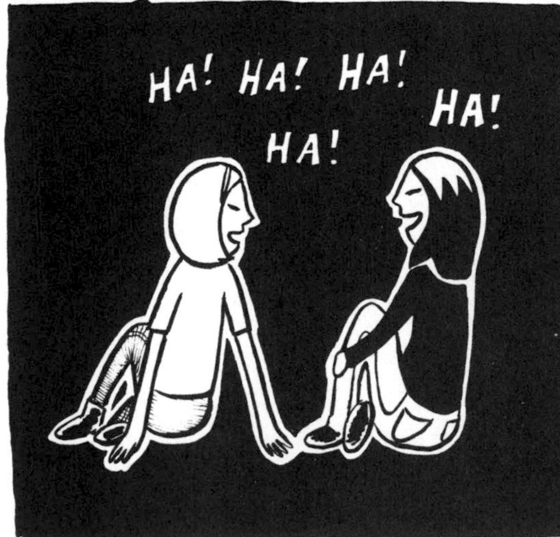
HA! HA! HA! HA! HA!

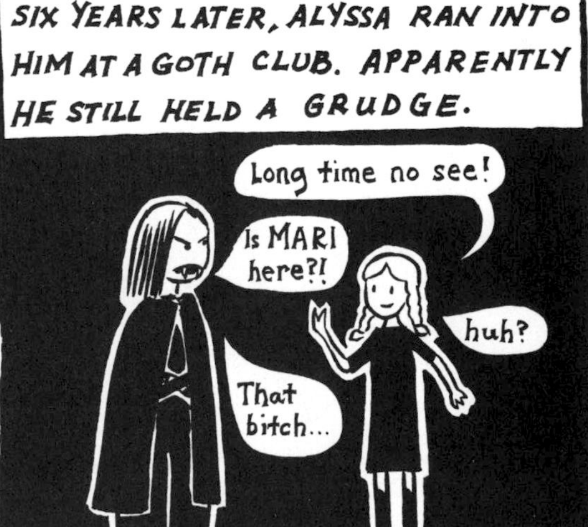
SIX YEARS LATER, ALYSSA RAN INTO HIM AT A GOTH CLUB. APPARENTLY HE STILL HELD A GRUDGE.
Long time no see!
Is MARI here?!
huh?
That bitch...

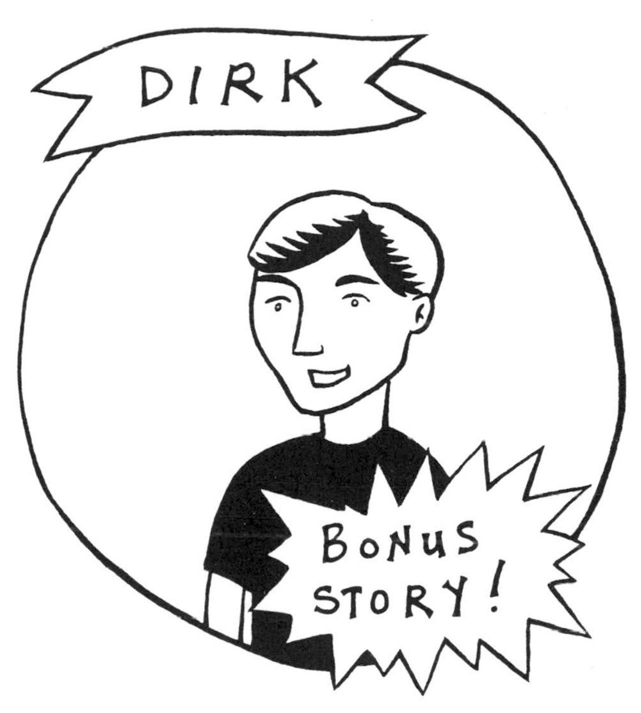
DIRK
BONUS STORY!

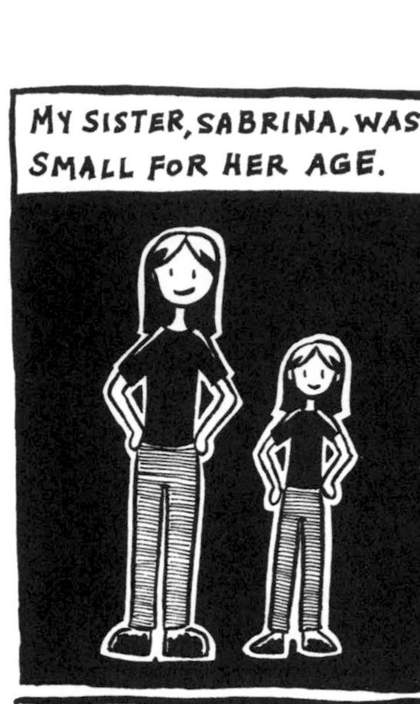
MY SISTER, SABRINA, WAS SMALL FOR HER AGE.

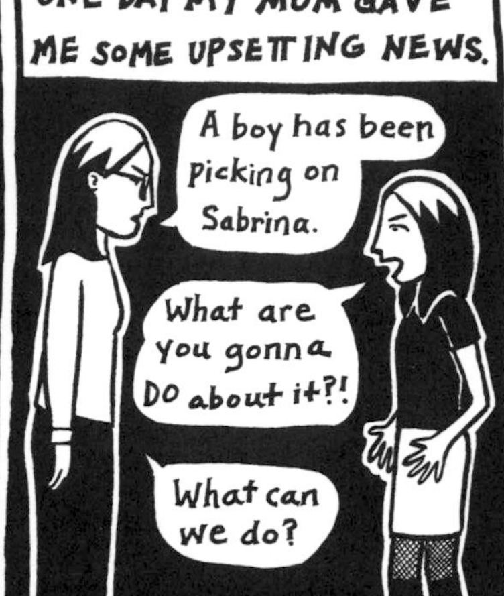
ONE DAY MY MOM GAVE ME SOME UPSETTING NEWS.
A boy has been picking on Sabrina.
What are you gonna DO about it?!
What can we do?

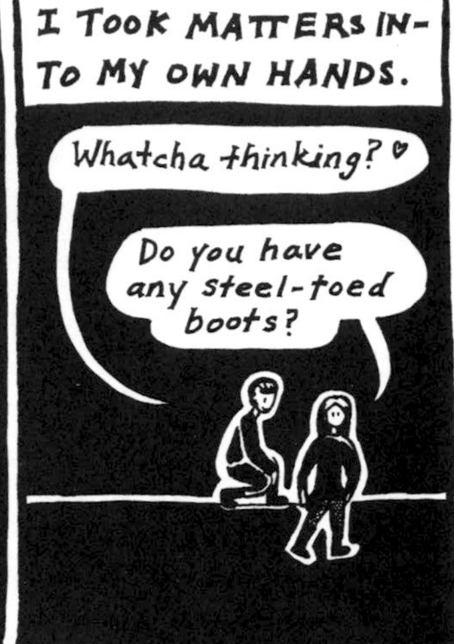
I TOOK MATTERS INTO MY OWN HANDS.
Whatcha thinking? ♥
Do you have any steel-toed boots?

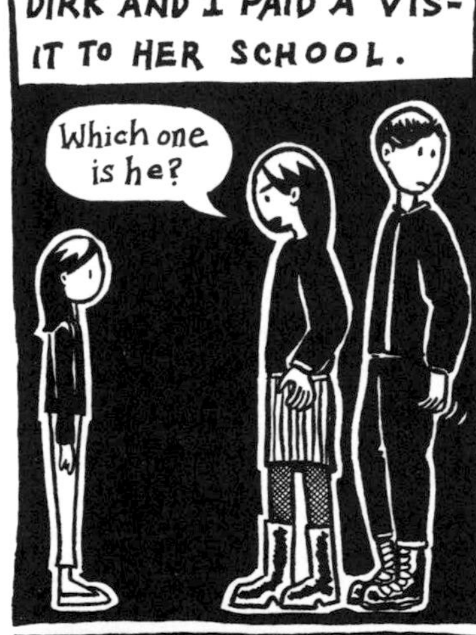
DIRK AND I PAID A VISIT TO HER SCHOOL.
Which one is he?

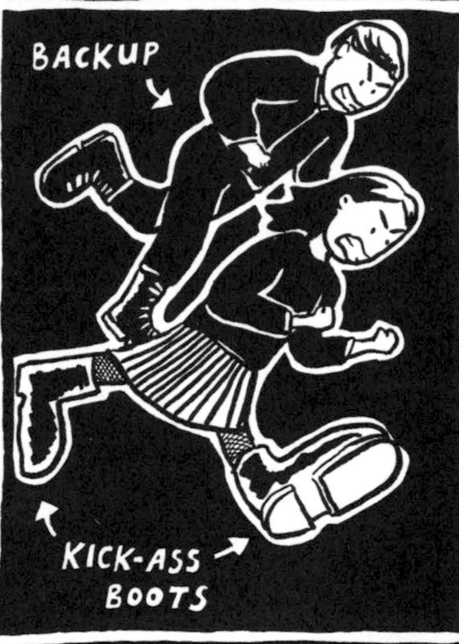
BACKUP
KICK-ASS BOOTS

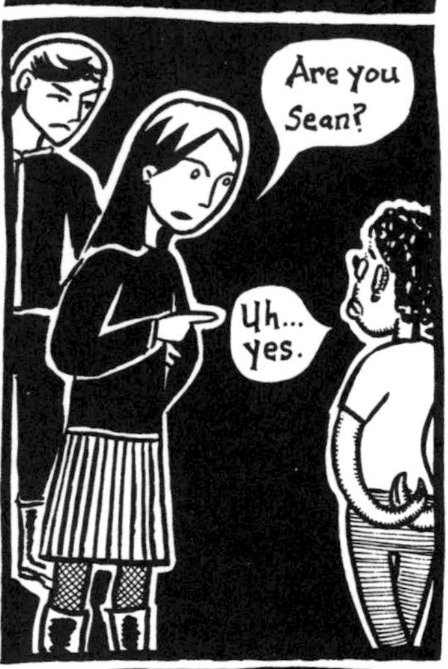
Are you Sean?
Uh... yes.

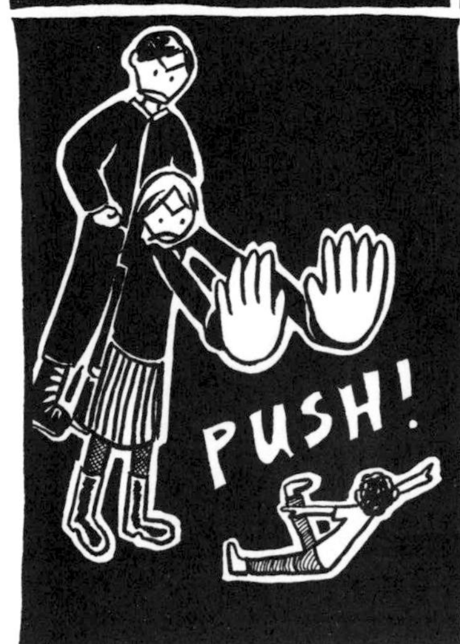
PUSH!

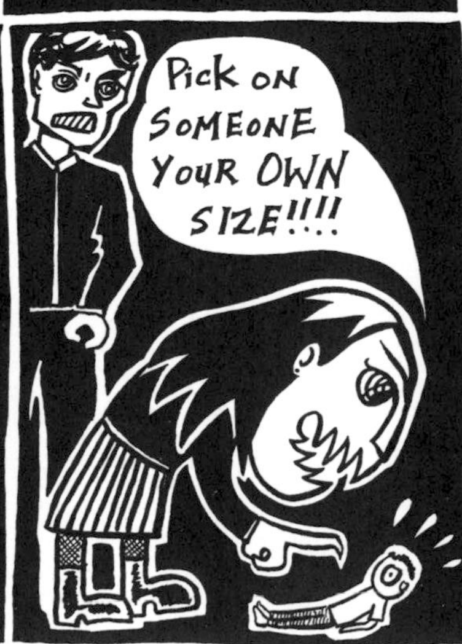
Pick on SOMEONE YOUR OWN SIZE!!!!

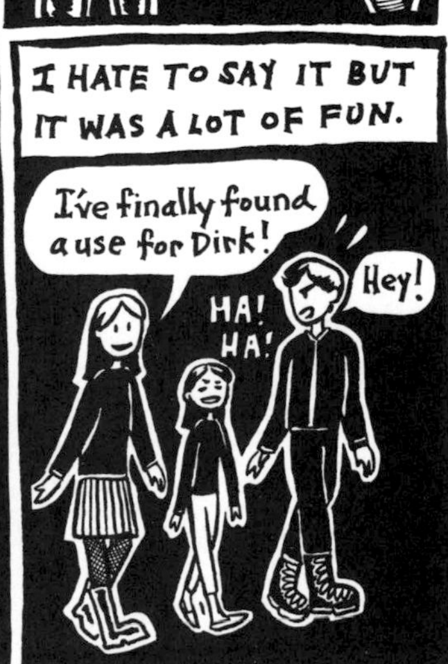
I HATE TO SAY IT BUT IT WAS A LOT OF FUN.
I've finally found a use for Dirk!
HA! HA!
Hey!

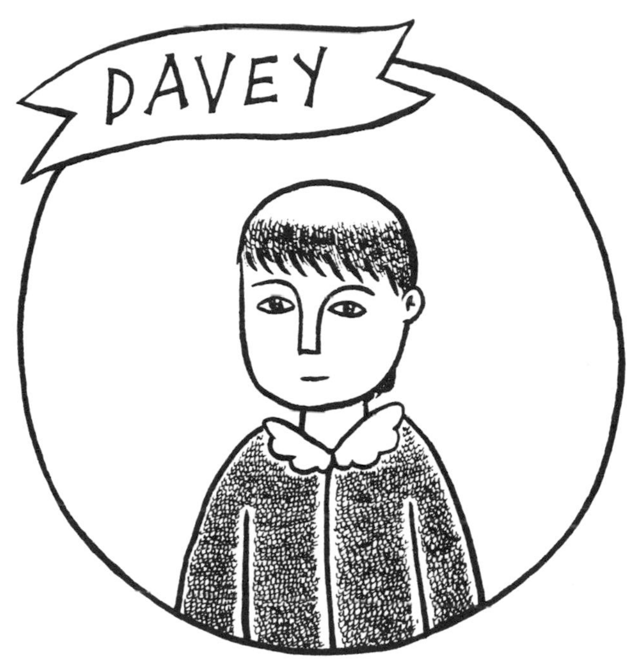
DAVEY

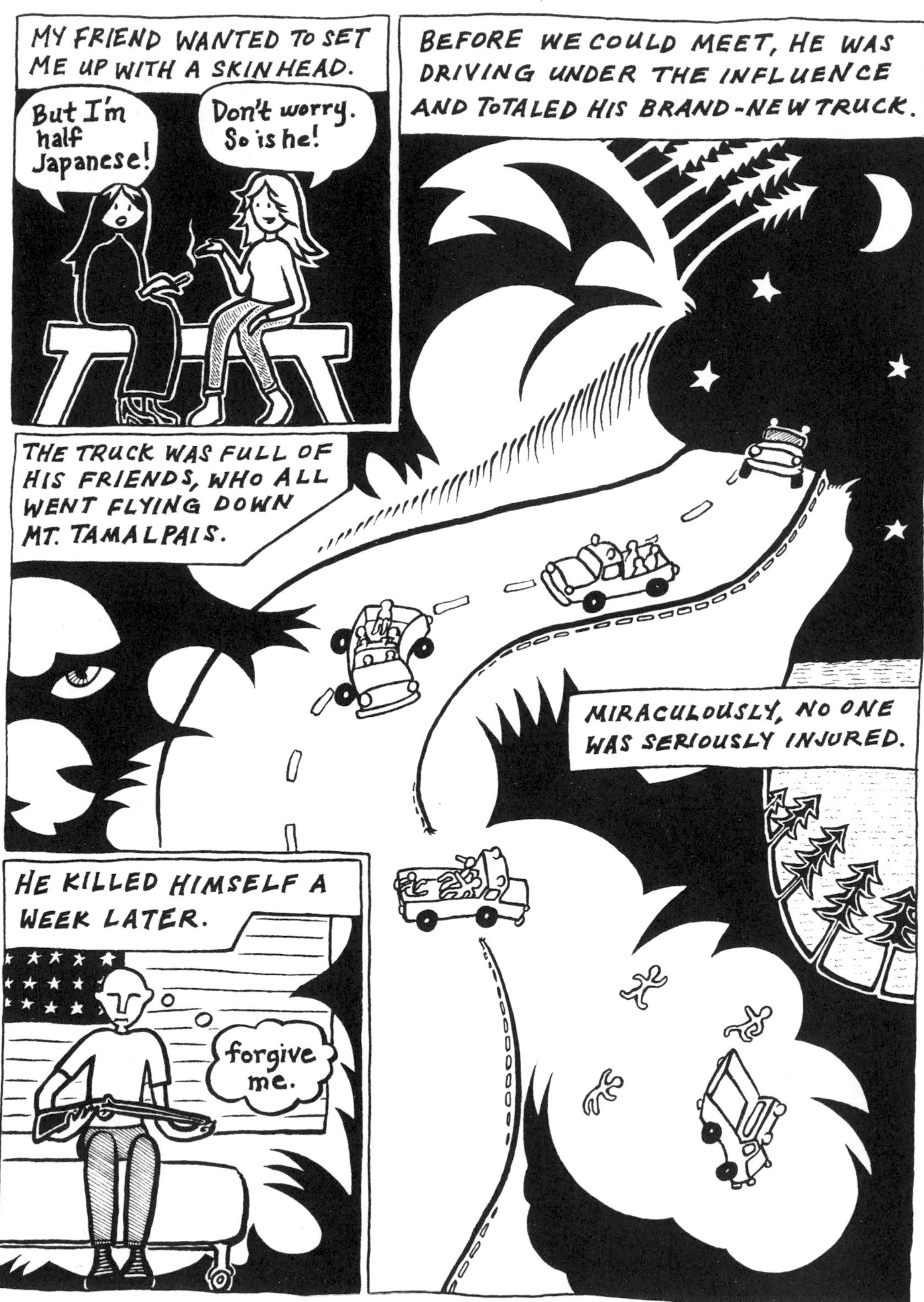
MY FRIEND WANTED TO SET ME UP WITH A SKINHEAD.
But I'm half Japanese!
Don't worry. So is he!
BEFORE WE COULD MEET, HE WAS DRIVING UNDER THE INFLUENCE AND TOTALED HIS BRAND-NEW TRUCK.
THE TRUCK WAS FULL OF HIS FRIENDS, WHO ALL WENT FLYING DOWN MT. TAMALPAIS.
MIRACULOUSLY, NO ONE WAS SERIOUSLY INJURED.
HE KILLED HIMSELF A WEEK LATER.
forgive me.

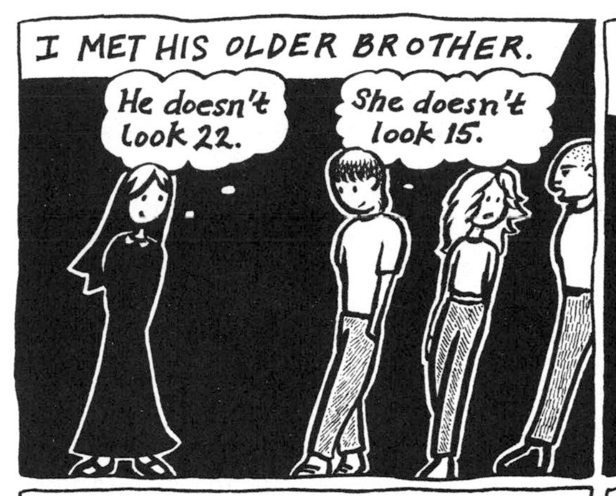
I MET HIS OLDER BROTHER.
He doesn't look 22.
She doesn't look 15.

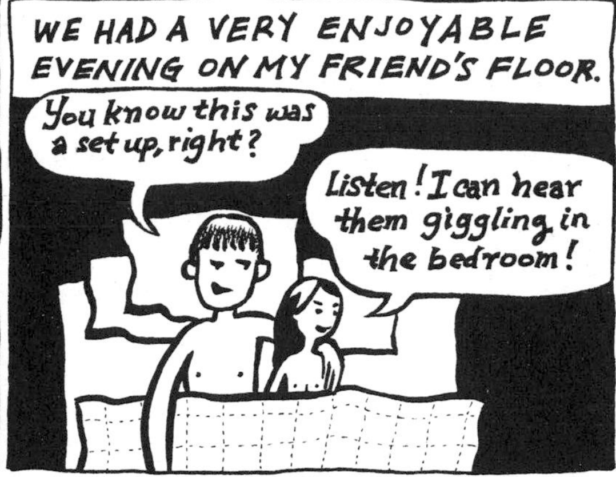
WE HAD A VERY ENJOYABLE EVENING ON MY FRIEND'S FLOOR.
You know this was a set up, right?
Listen! I can hear them giggling in the bedroom!

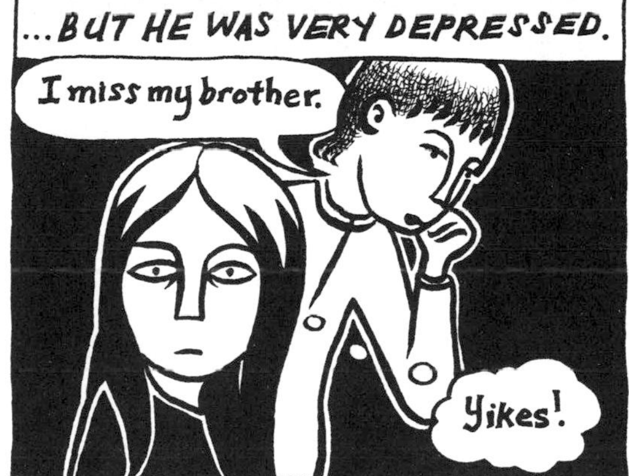
...BUT HE WAS VERY DEPRESSED.
I miss my brother.
Yikes!

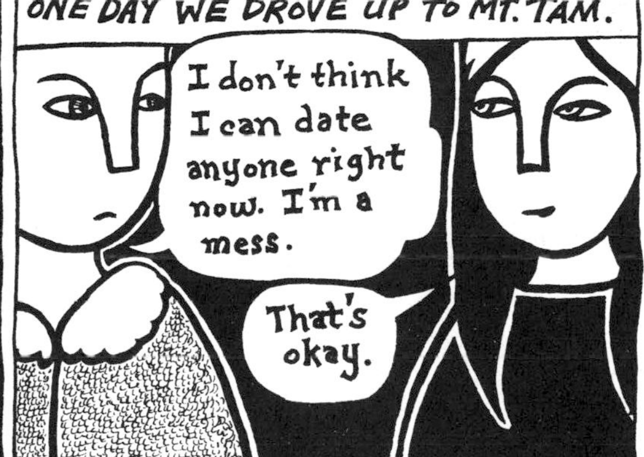
ONE DAY WE DROVE UP TO MT. TAM.
I don't think I can date anyone right now. I'm a mess.
That's okay.

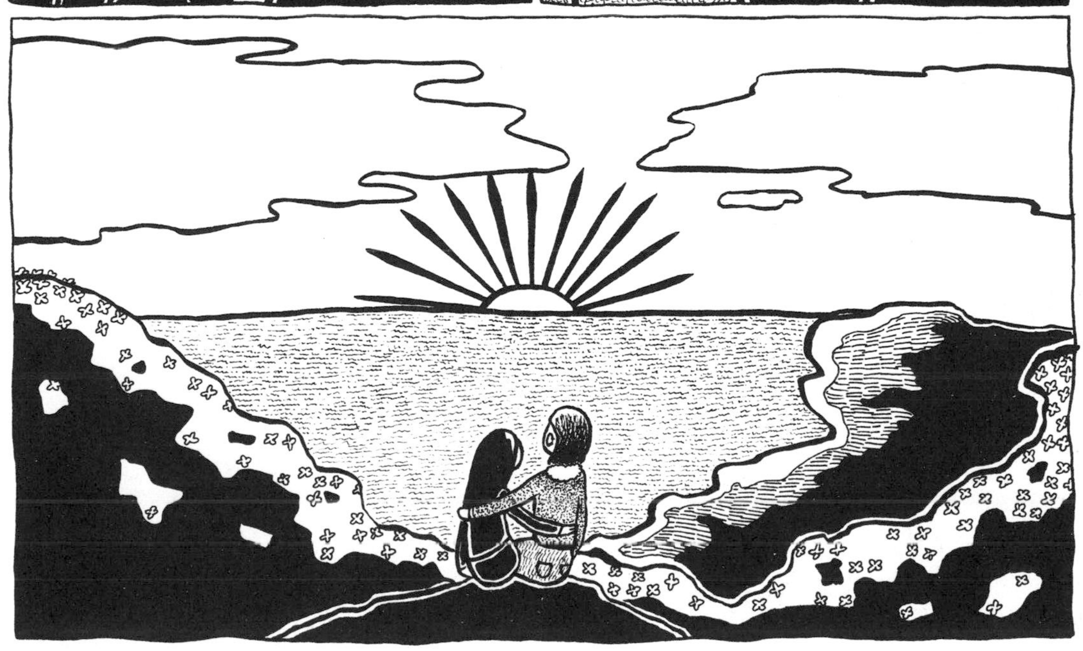

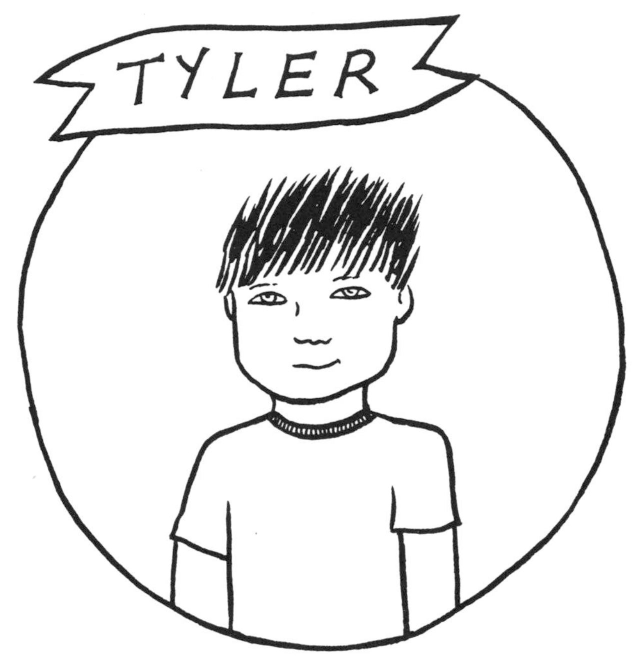
TYLER

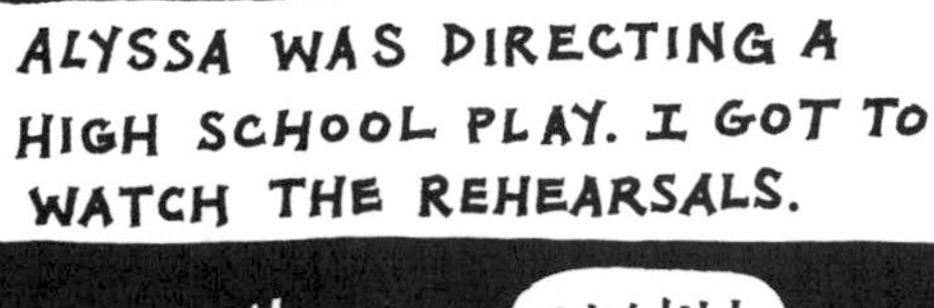
ALYSSA WAS DIRECTING A HIGH SCHOOL PLAY. I GOT TO WATCH THE REHEARSALS.

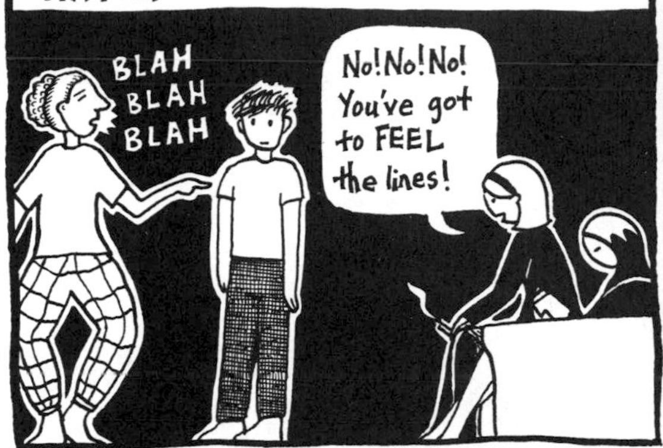
BLAH BLAH BLAH
No! No! No! You've got to FEEL the lines!

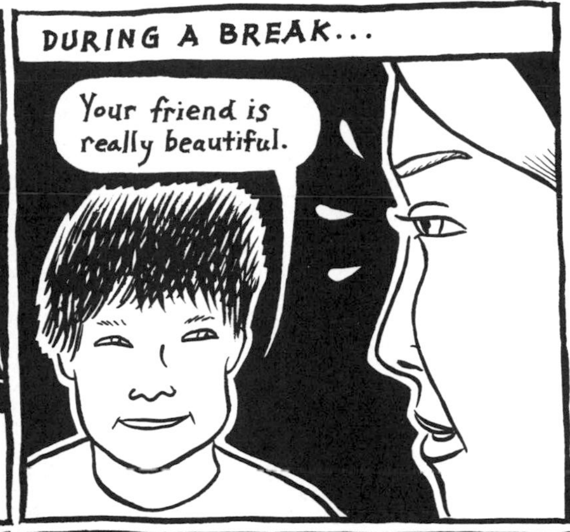
DURING A BREAK...
Your friend is really beautiful.

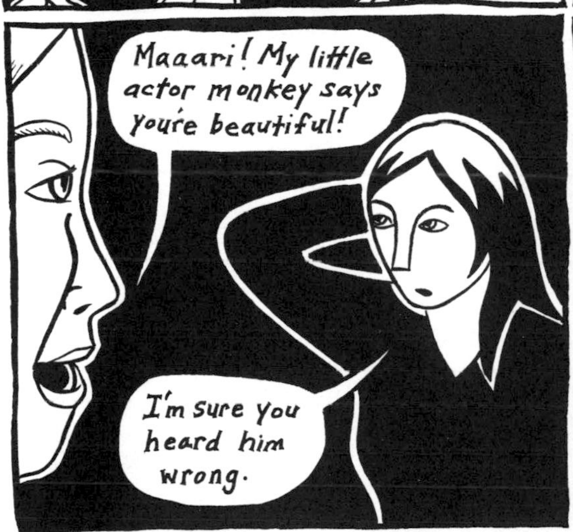
Maaari! My little actor monkey says you're beautiful!
I'm sure you heard him wrong.

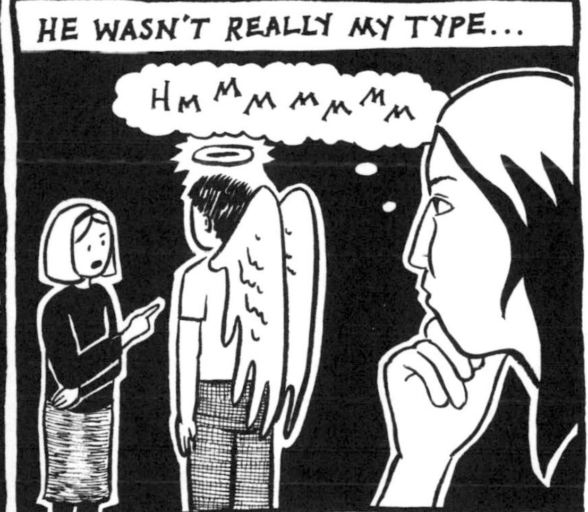
HE WASN'T REALLY MY TYPE...
HMMMMMMMM

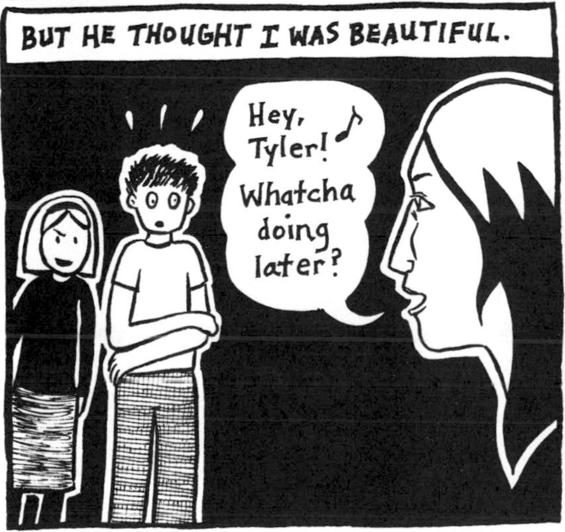
BUT HE THOUGHT I WAS BEAUTIFUL.
Hey, Tyler! ♪ Whatcha doing later?

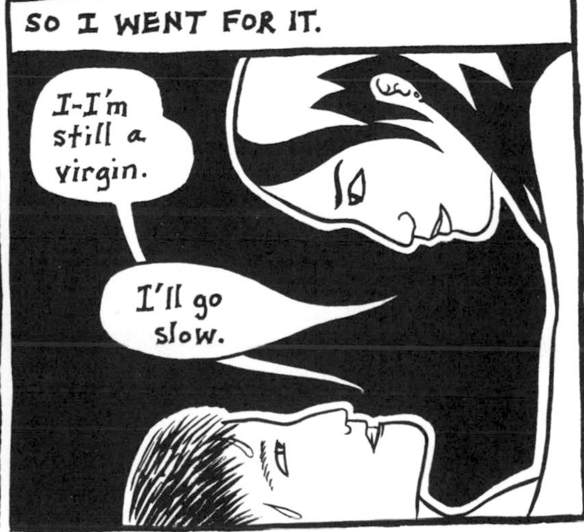
SO I WENT FOR IT.
I-I'm still a virgin.
I'll go slow.

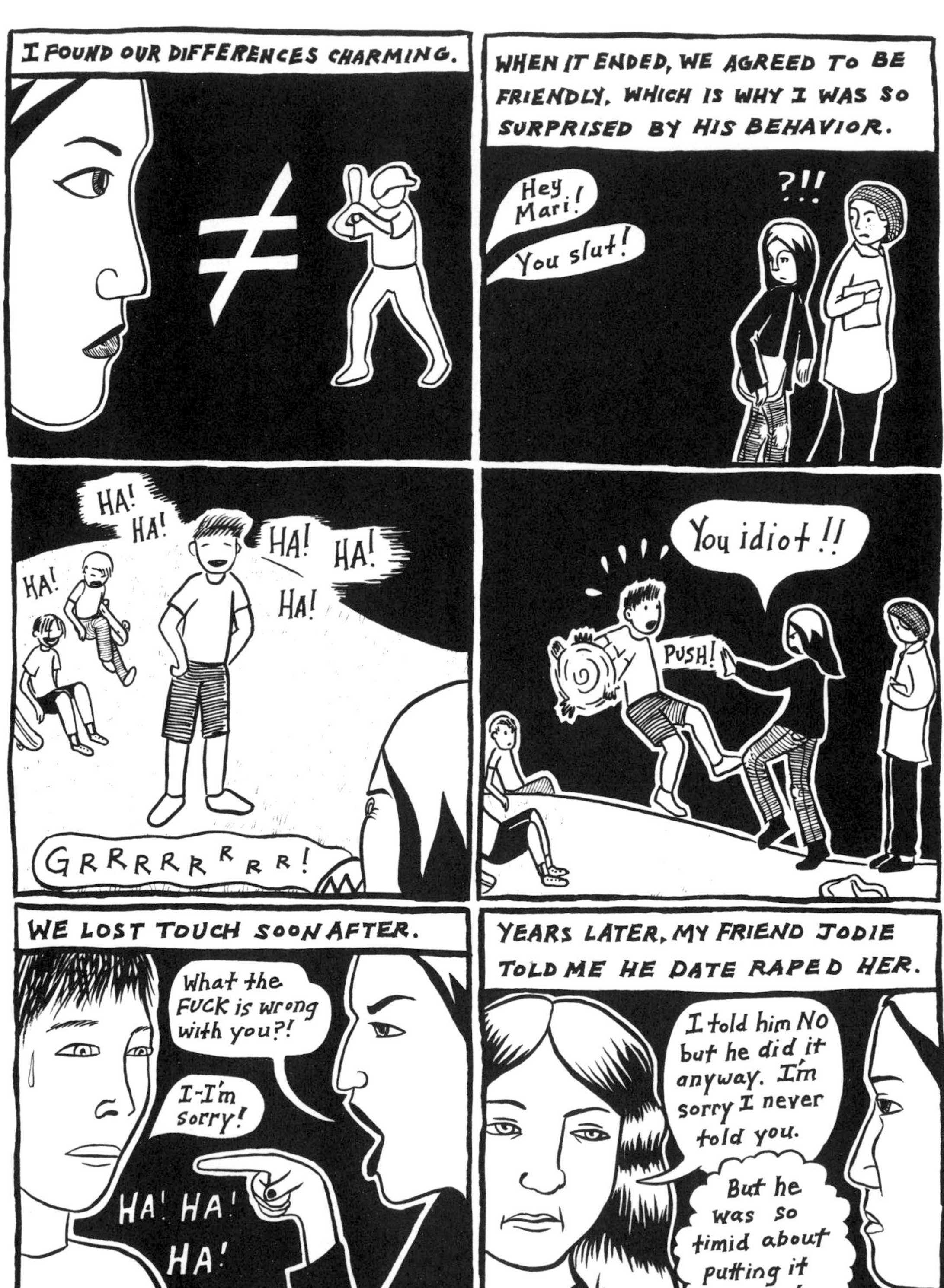
I FOUND OUR DIFFERENCES CHARMING.
≠
WHEN IT ENDED, WE AGREED TO BE FRIENDLY, WHICH IS WHY I WAS SO SURPRISED BY HIS BEHAVIOR.
Hey Mari!
You slut!
?!!
HA! HA!
HA!
HA! HA!
HA!
GRRRRRRRR!
You idiot!!
PUSH!
WE LOST TOUCH SOON AFTER.
What the FUCK is wrong with you?!
I-I'm sorry!
HA! HA! HA! HA!
YEARS LATER, MY FRIEND JODIE TOLD ME HE DATE RAPED HER.
I told him NO but he did it anyway. I'm sorry I never told you.
But he was so timid about putting it in me!

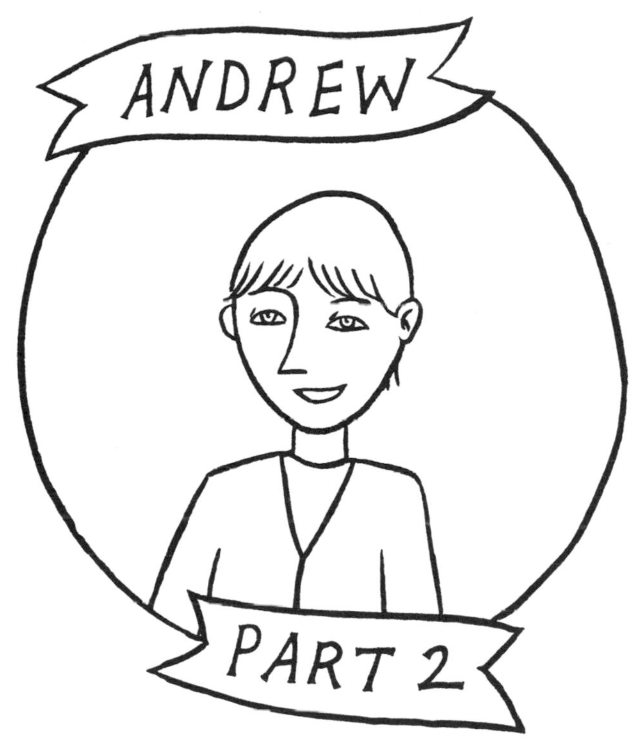
ANDREW
PART 2

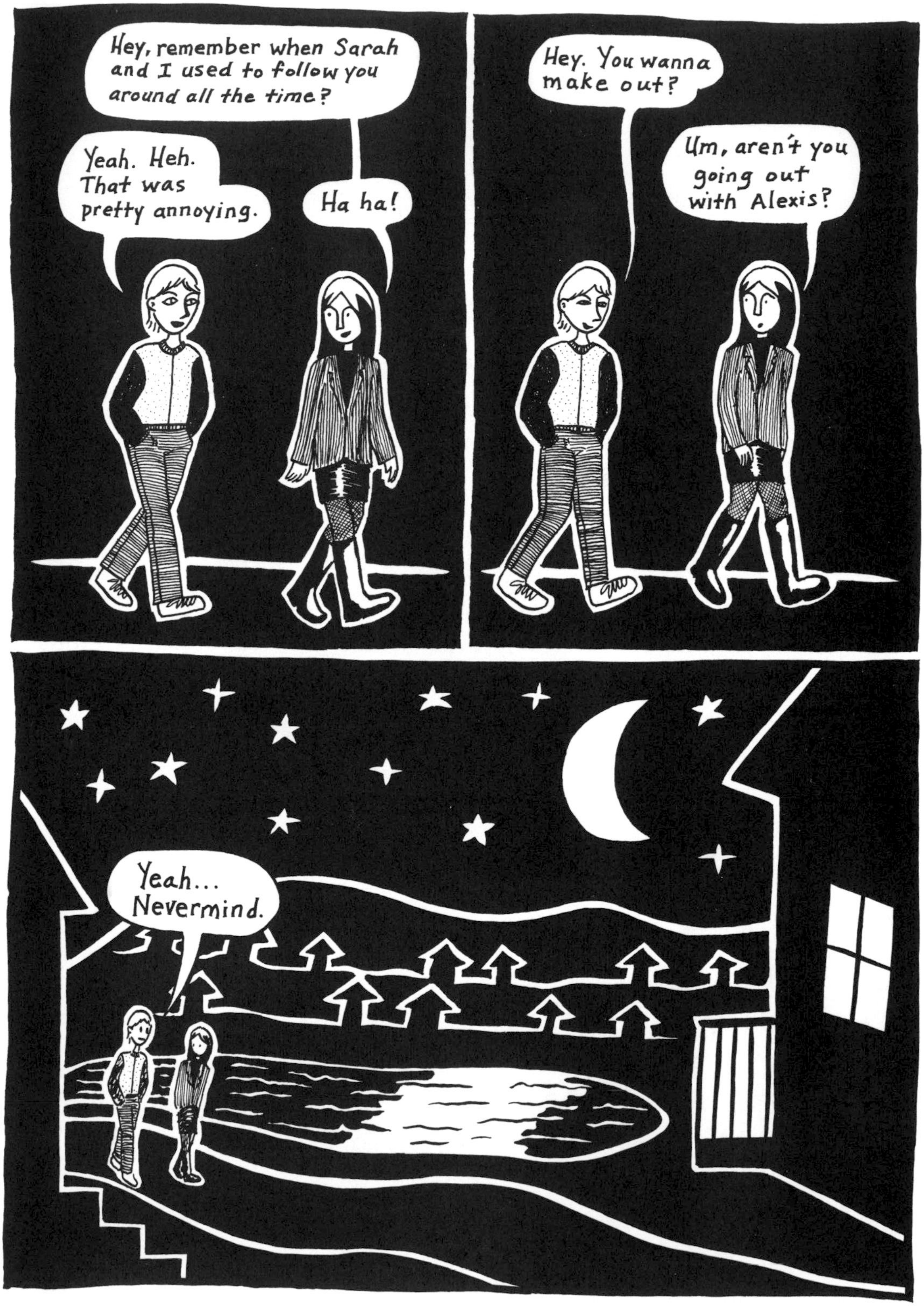

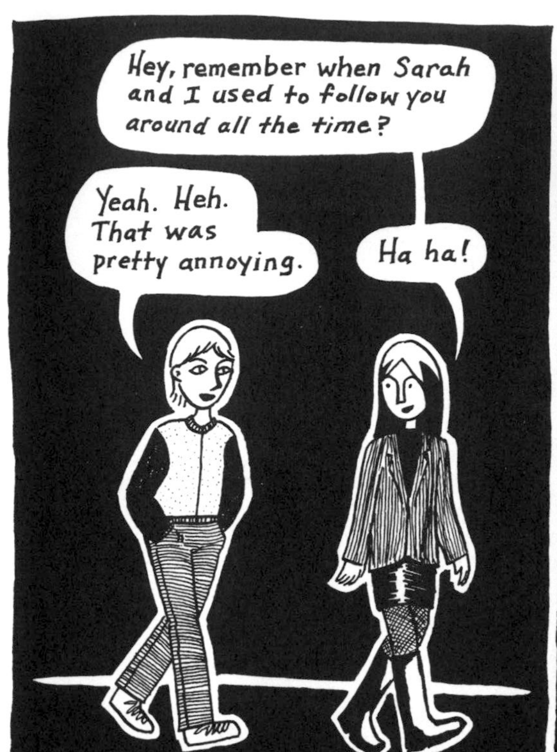
Hey, remember when Sarah and I used to follow you around all the time?
Yeah. Heh. That was pretty annoying.
Ha ha!

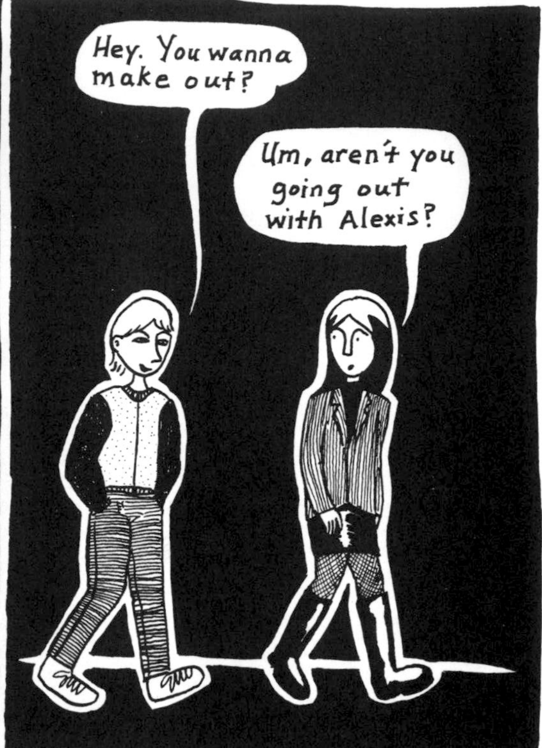
Hey. You wanna make out?
Um, aren't you going out with Alexis?

Yeah... Nevermind.

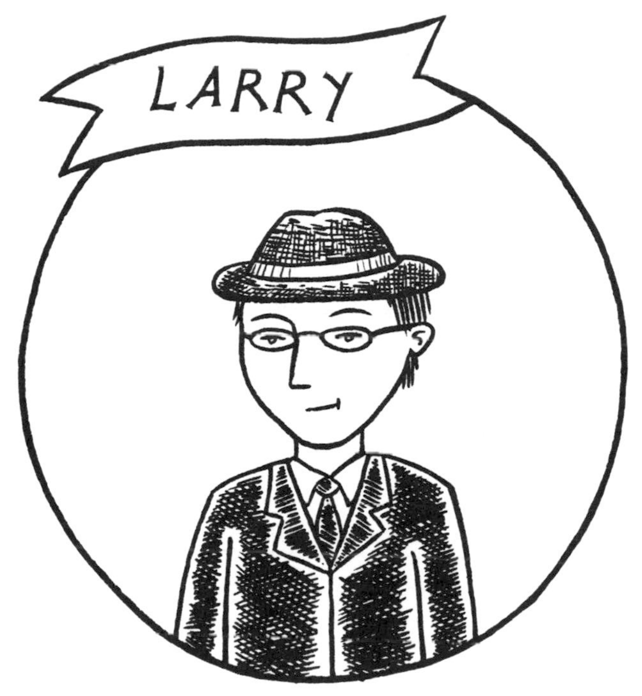
LARRY

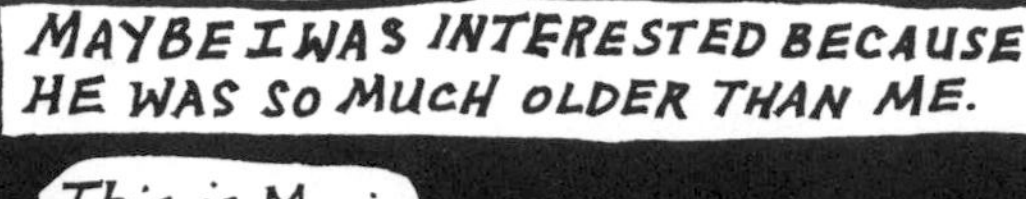

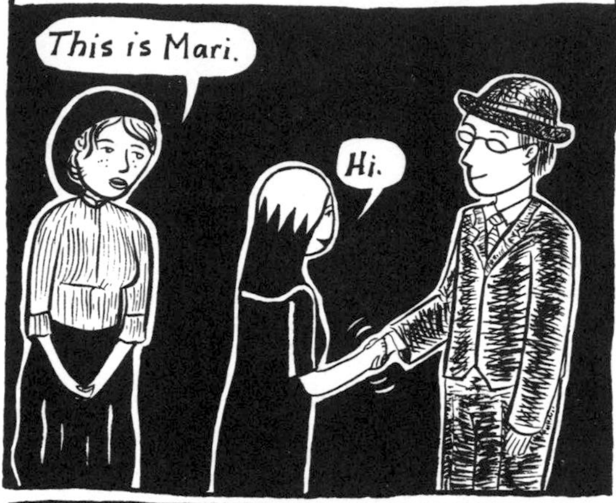

MAYBE IT WAS HIS TASTE IN MUSIC.

I think you'll like this.

Cool!

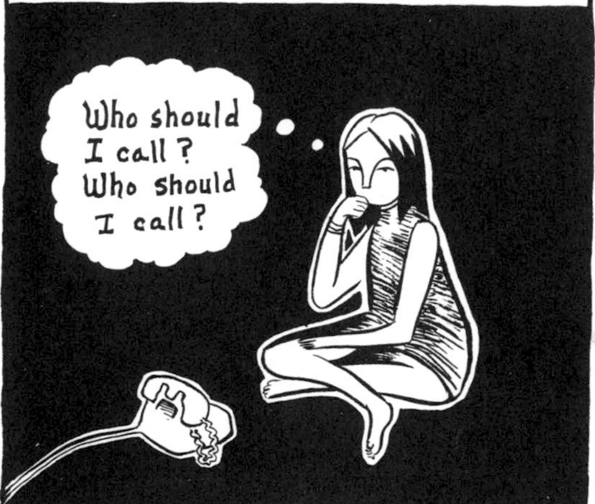

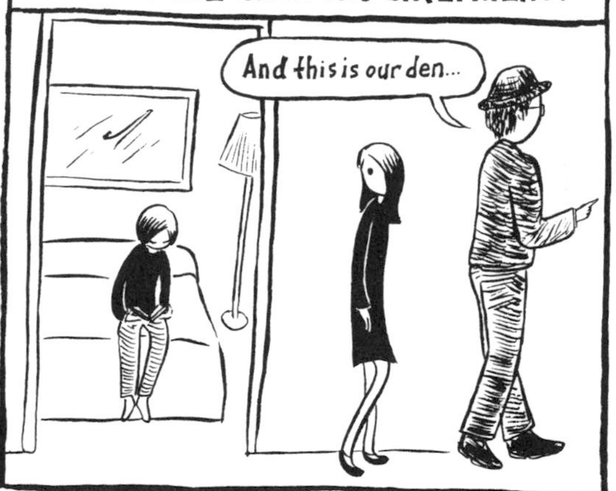

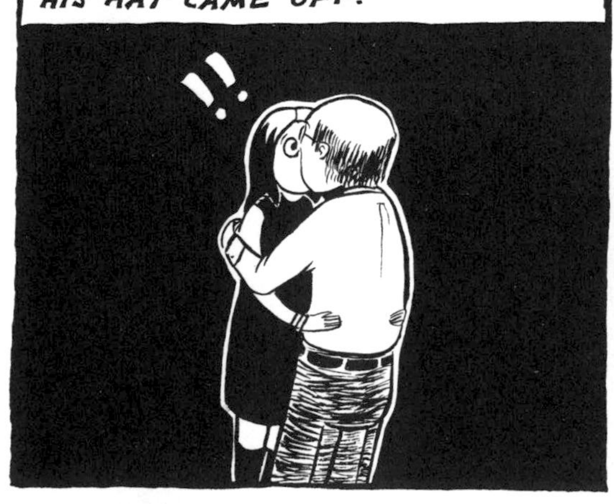

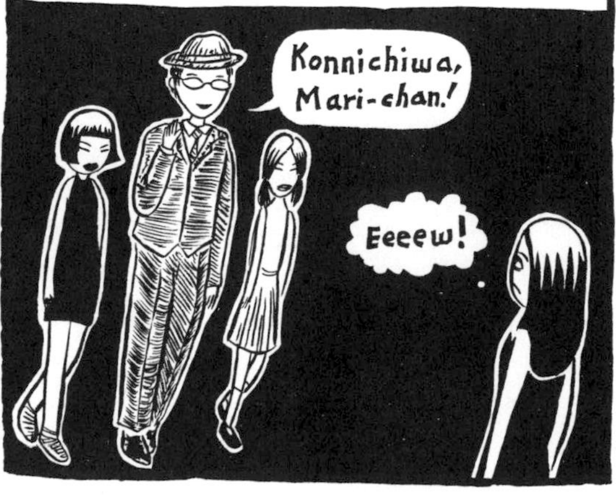

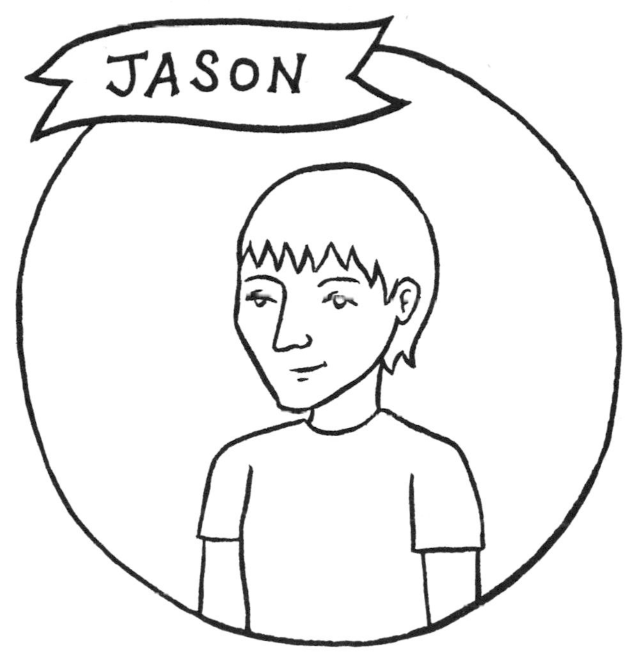
JASON

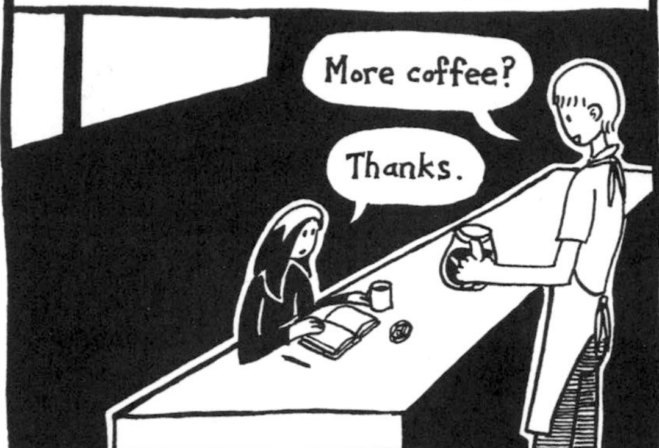
I MET HIM AT DENNY'S. I SPENT MANY A LATE, SOLITARY HOUR THERE, WRITING UNTIL THE SUN CAME UP.
More coffee?
Thanks.

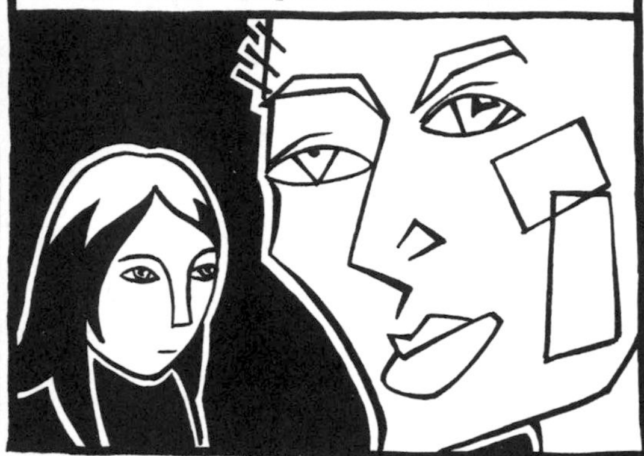
HE WAS A MODEL AS WELL AS A WAITER. HE WAS PHOTOGENIC BUT HE LOOKED STRANGE IN PERSON.

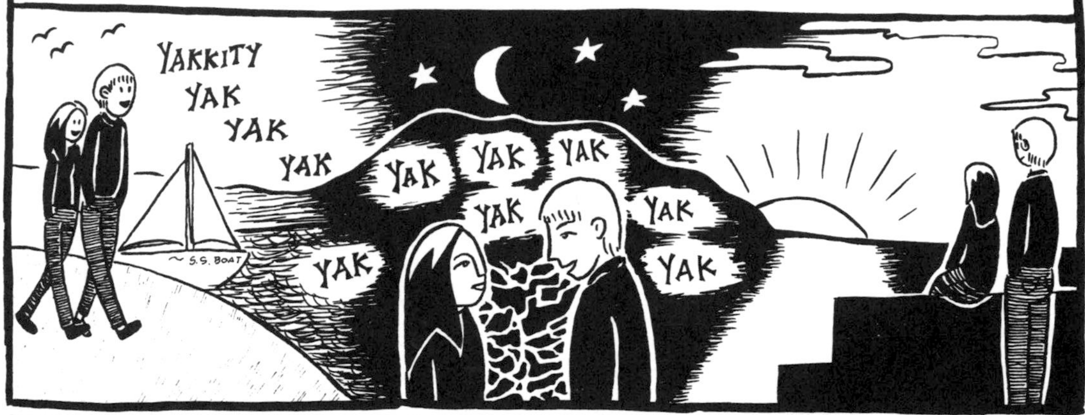
WE SPENT ALL DAY IN SAUSALITO, JUST BUMMING AROUND, THEN THE NIGHT, AND THEN WATCHED THE SUNRISE, BUT IT WAS INNOCENT. WE JUST TALKED.
YAKKITY
YAK
YAK
YAK
S.S. BOAT
YAK
YAK
YAK
YAK
YAK
YAK
YAK

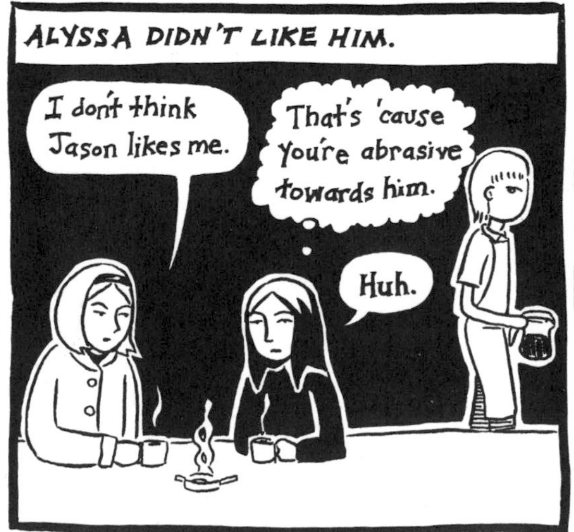
ALYSSA DIDN'T LIKE HIM.
I don't think Jason likes me.
That's 'cause you're abrasive towards him.
Huh.

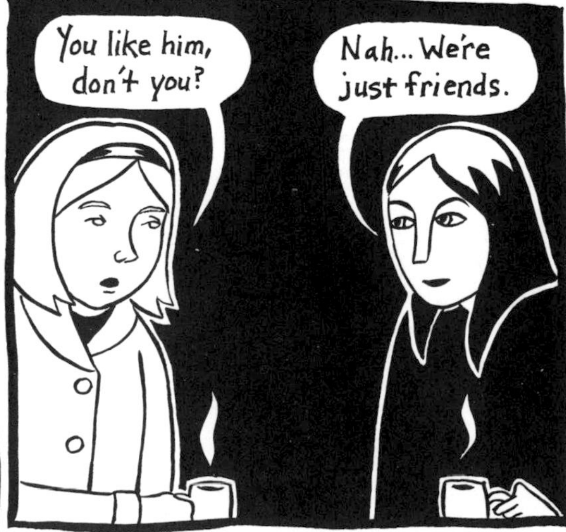
You like him, don't you?
Nah... We're just friends.

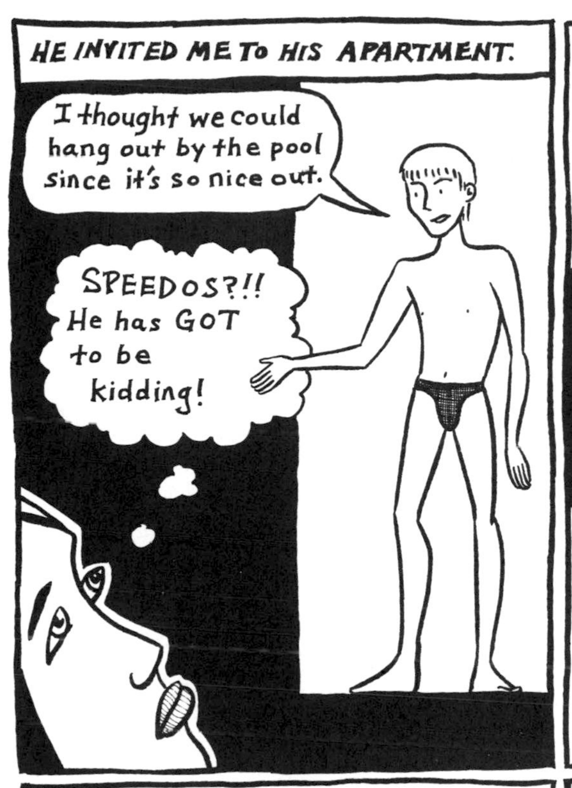
HE INVITED ME TO HIS APARTMENT.
I thought we could hang out by the pool since it's so nice out.
SPEEDOS?!! He has GOT to be kidding!

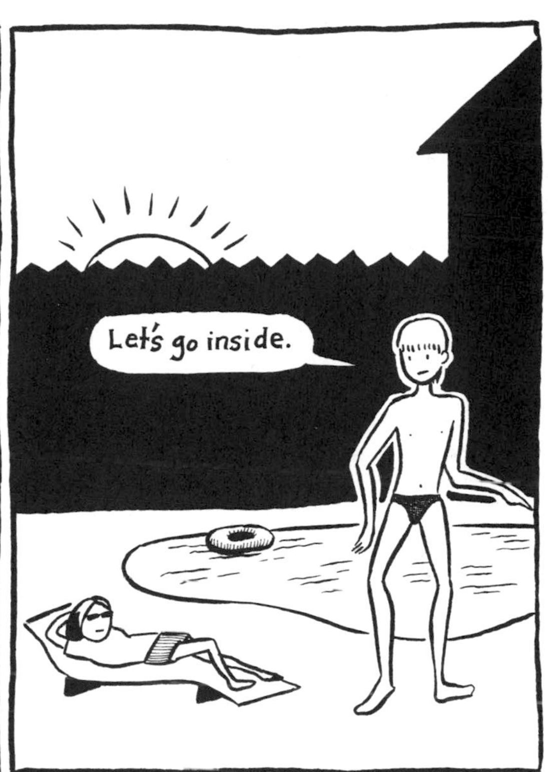
Let's go inside.

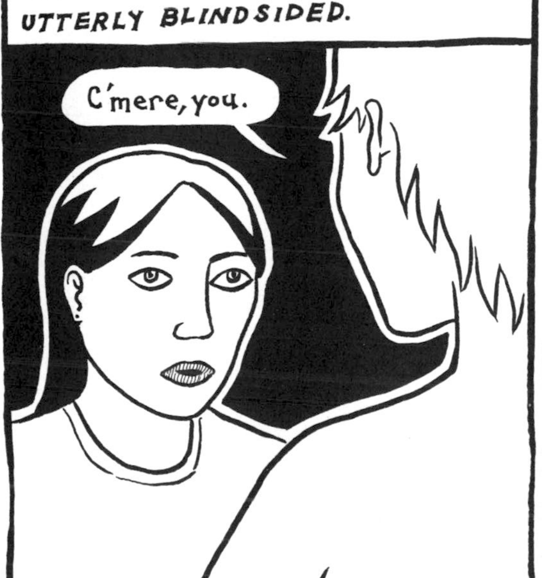
WHEN HE KISSED ME, I WAS UTTERLY BLINDSIDED.
C'mere, you.

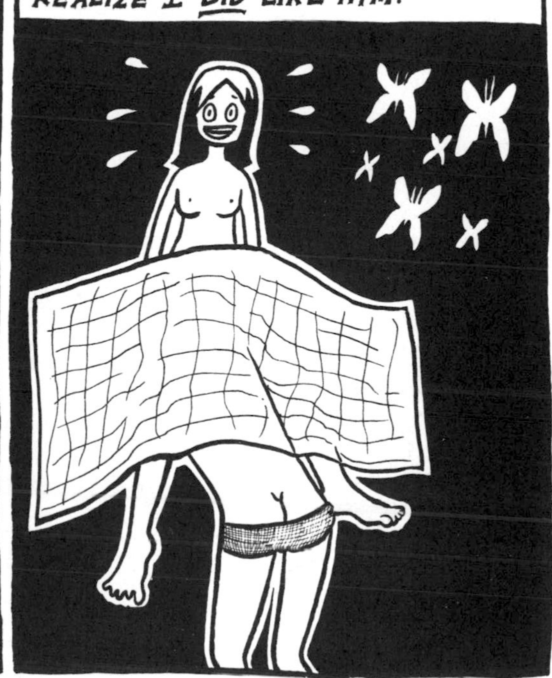
BUT IT DIDN'T TAKE ME LONG TO REALIZE I DID LIKE HIM.

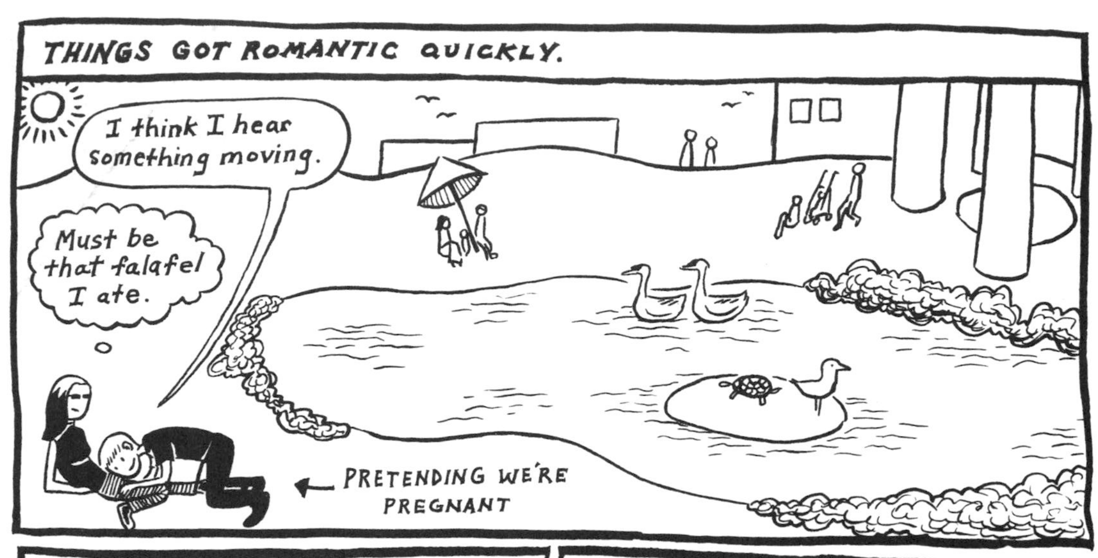
THINGS GOT ROMANTIC QUICKLY.
I think I hear something moving.
Must be that falafel I ate.
PRETENDING WE'RE PREGNANT

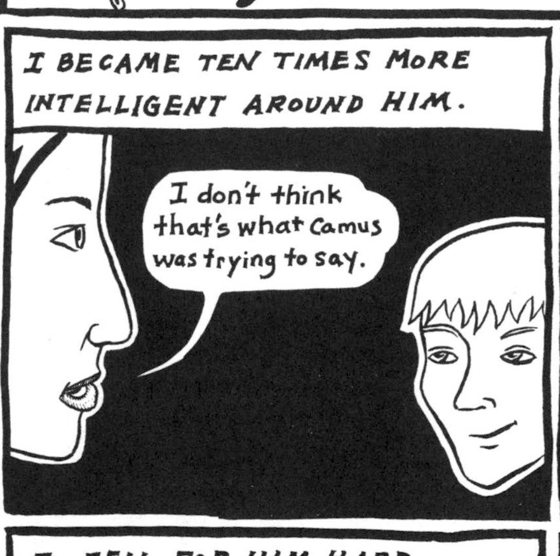
I BECAME TEN TIMES MORE INTELLIGENT AROUND HIM.
I don't think that's what Camus was trying to say.

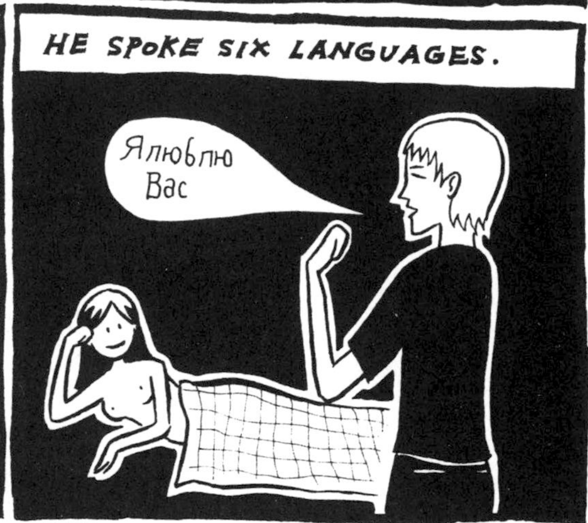
HE SPOKE SIX LANGUAGES.
Ялюблю Вас

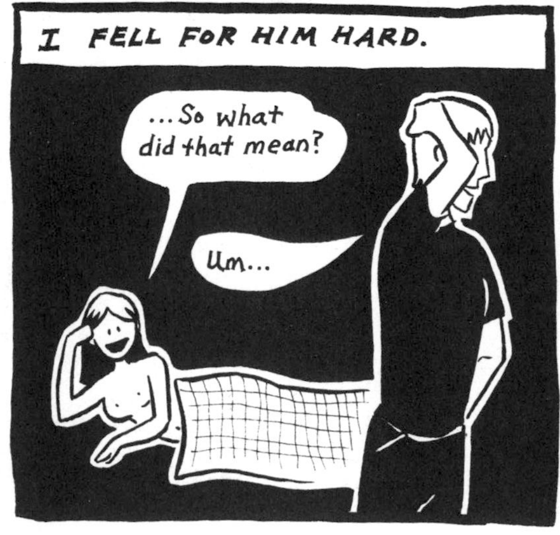
I FELL FOR HIM HARD.
...So what did that mean?
Um...

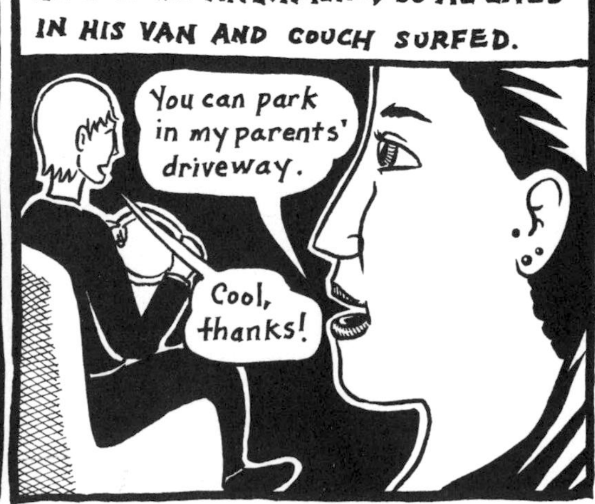
HE LOST HIS APARTMENT, SO HE LIVED IN HIS VAN AND COUCH SURFED.
You can park in my parents' driveway.
Cool, thanks!

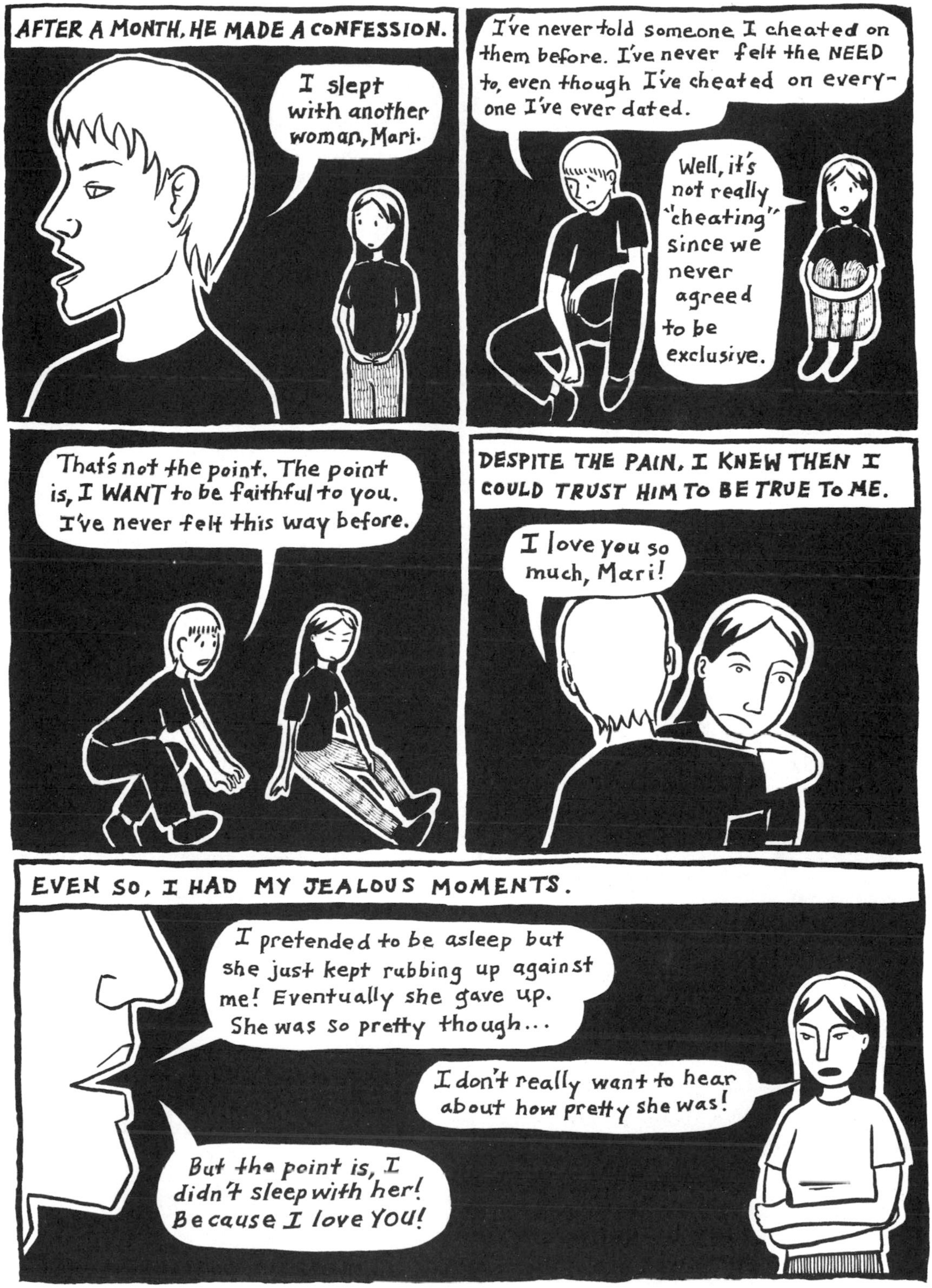

AFTER A MONTH, HE MADE A CONFESSION.

I slept with another woman, Mari.

I've never told someone I cheated on them before. I've never felt the NEED to, even though I've cheated on everyone I've ever dated.

Well, it's not really "cheating" since we never agreed to be exclusive.

That's not the point. The point is, I WANT to be faithful to you. I've never felt this way before.

DESPITE THE PAIN, I KNEW THEN I COULD TRUST HIM TO BE TRUE TO ME.

I love you so much, Mari!

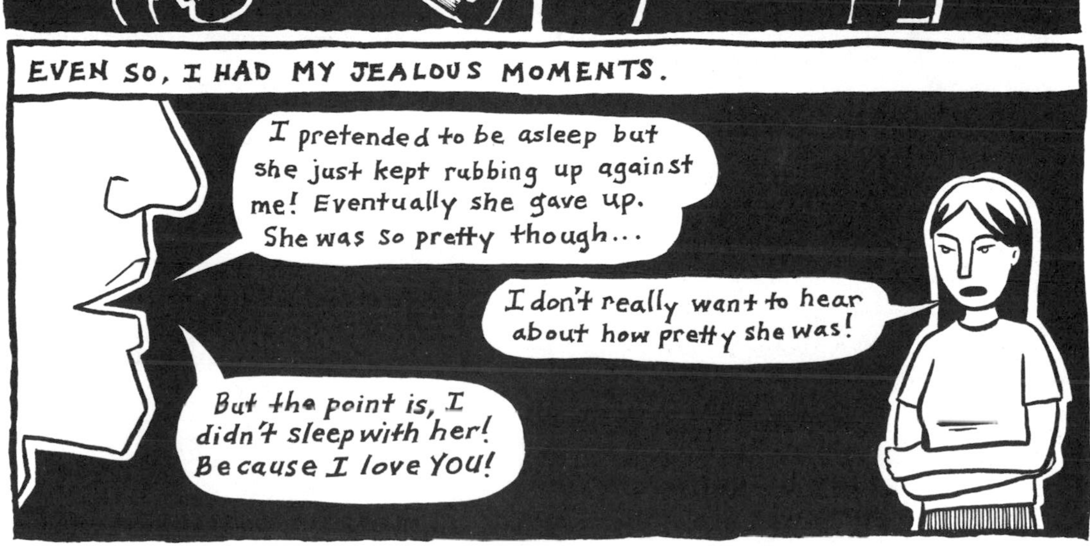

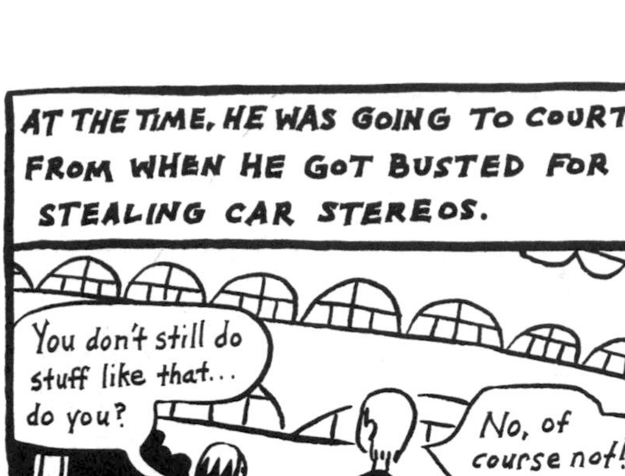
AT THE TIME, HE WAS GOING TO COURT FROM WHEN HE GOT BUSTED FOR STEALING CAR STEREOS.
You don't still do stuff like that... do you?
No, of course not!

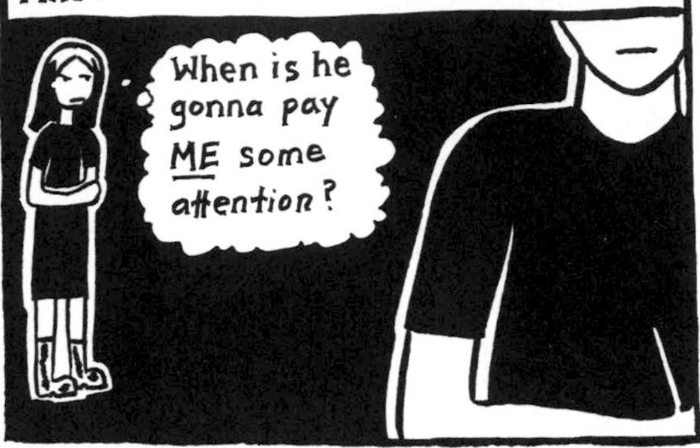
IT MADE HIM VERY DEPRESSED THAT HE'D LED A LIFE OF CRIME, AND HE SUBMERGED HIMSELF IN DRAWING MAPS FOR A ROLE-PLAYING GAME.
When is he gonna pay ME some attention?

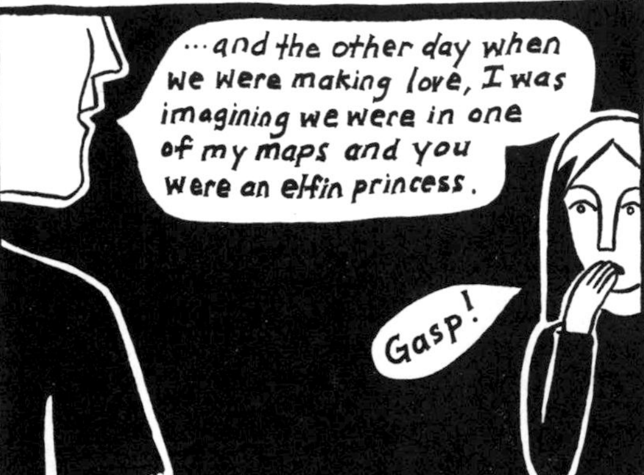
IT GOT KIND OF WEIRD EVERY TIME HE CONFESSED SOMETHING NEW.
...and the other day when we were making love, I was imagining we were in one of my maps and you were an elfin princess.
Gasp!

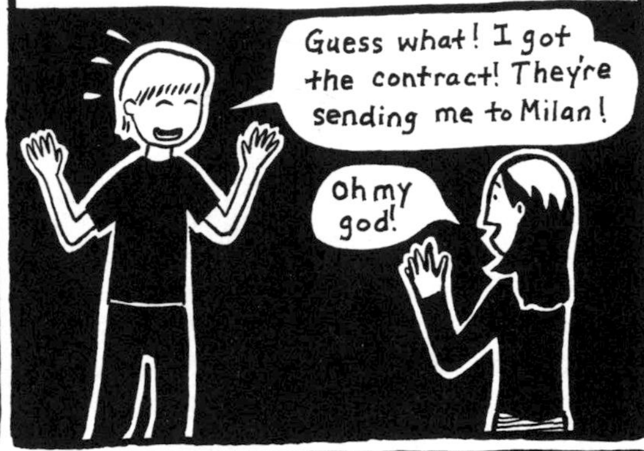
HIS MODELING WAS TAKING HIM PLACES. HIS DREAMS OF INTERNATIONAL TRAVEL WERE ABOUT TO COME TRUE.
Guess what! I got the contract! They're sending me to Milan!
Oh my god!

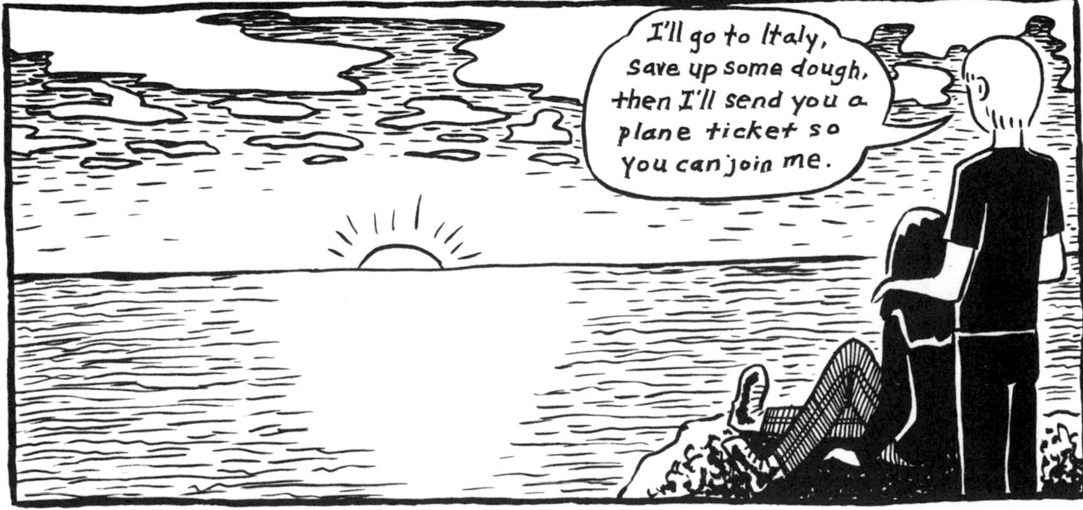
I'll go to Italy, save up some dough, then I'll send you a plane ticket so you can join me.

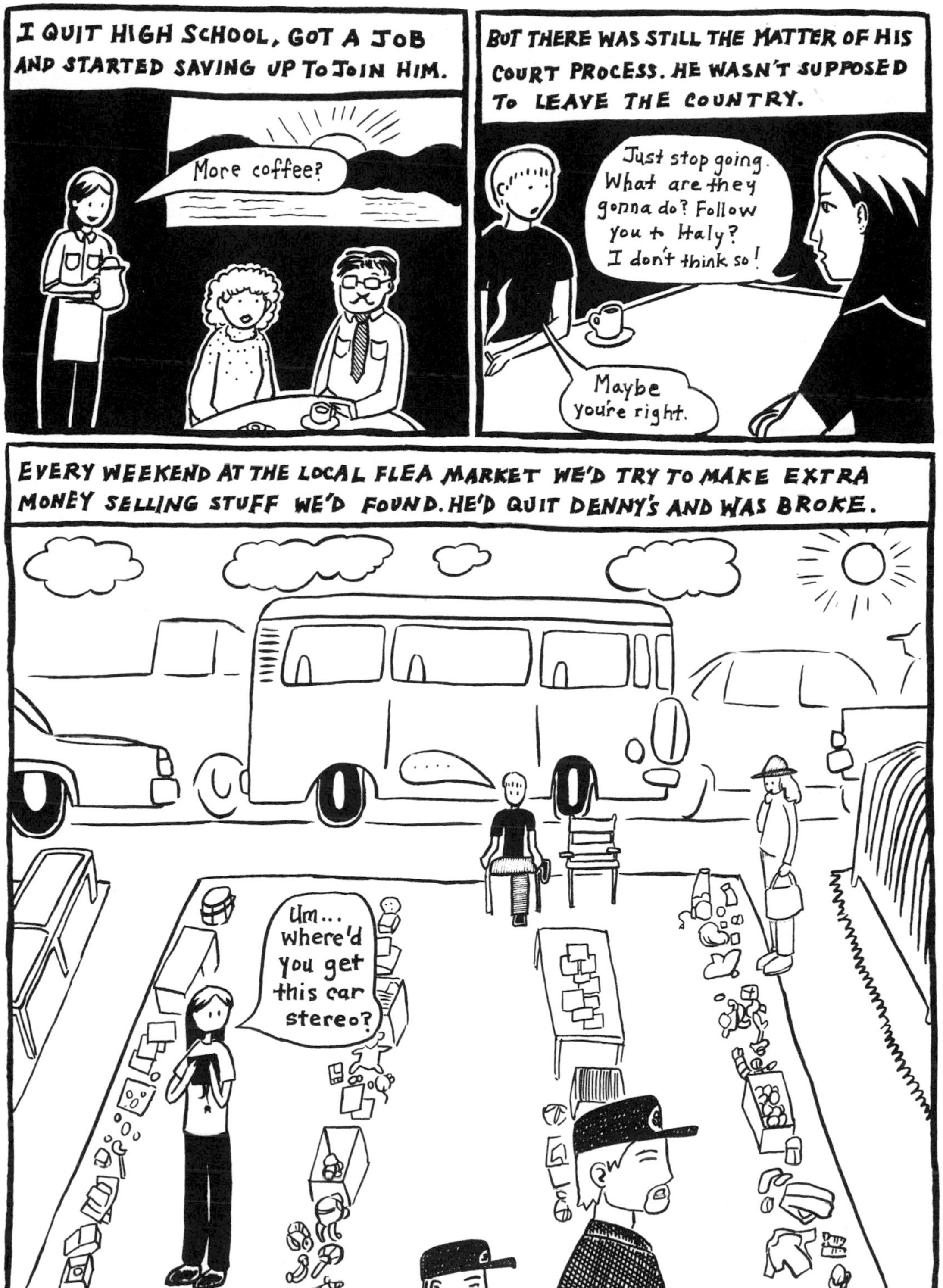

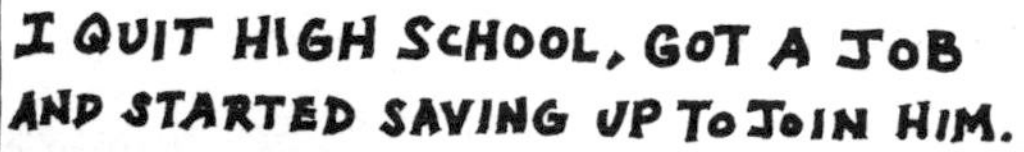

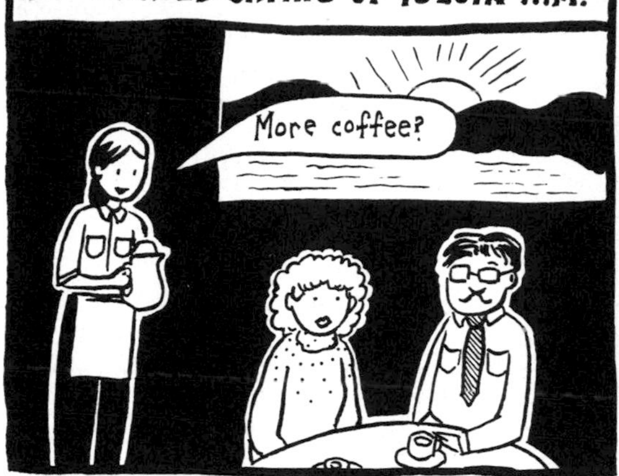

BUT THERE WAS STILL THE MATTER OF HIS COURT PROCESS. HE WASN'T SUPPOSED TO LEAVE THE COUNTRY.

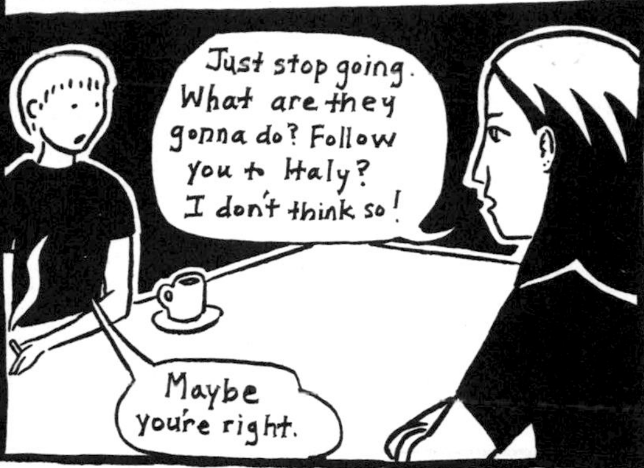

EVERY WEEKEND AT THE LOCAL FLEA MARKET WE'D TRY TO MAKE EXTRA MONEY SELLING STUFF WE'D FOUND. HE'D QUIT DENNY'S AND WAS BROKE.

Um... where'd you get this car stereo?

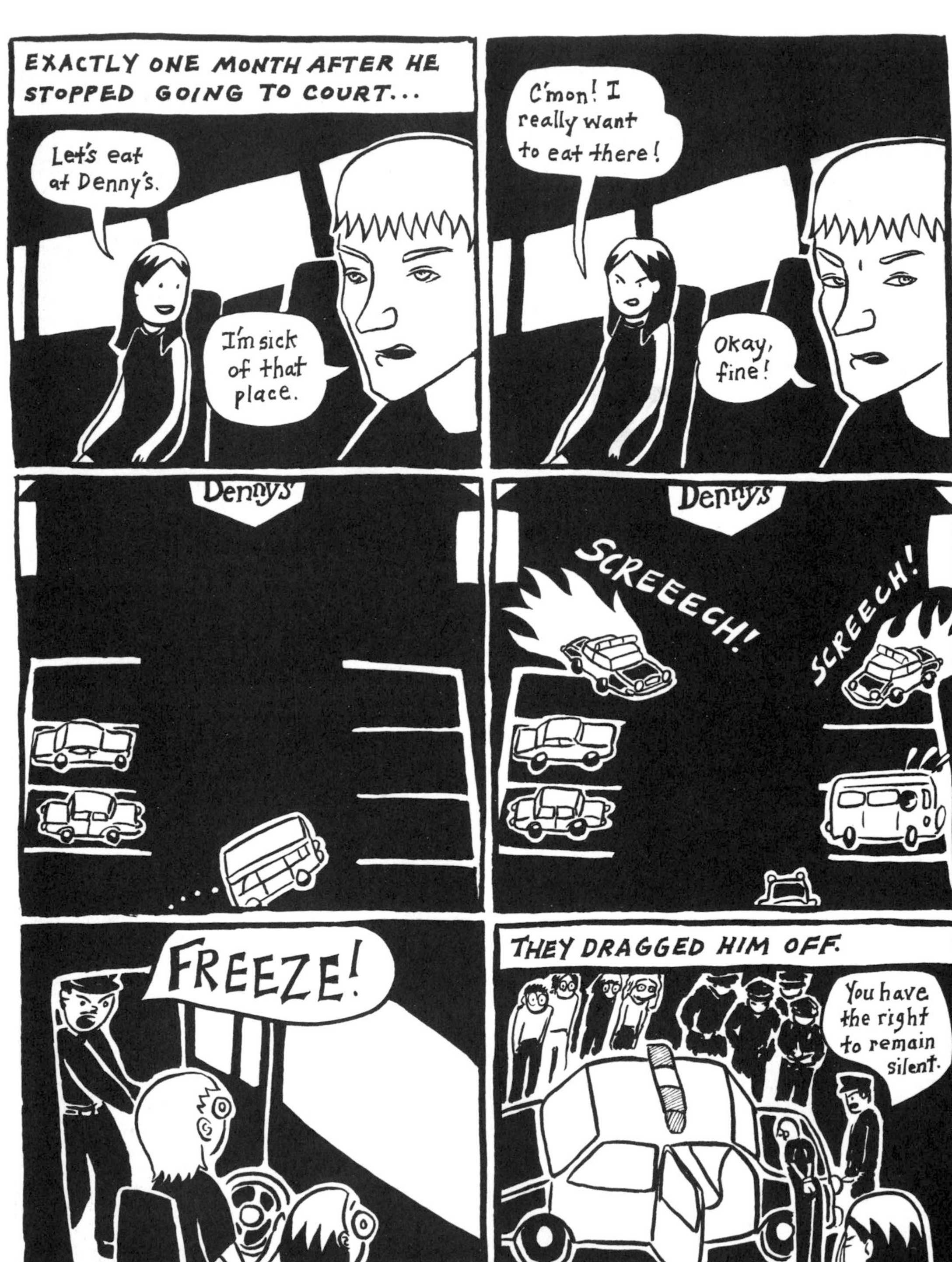
EXACTLY ONE MONTH AFTER HE STOPPED GOING TO COURT...
Let's eat at Denny's.
I'm sick of that place.
C'mon! I really want to eat there!
Okay, fine!
Denny's
Denny's
SCREEEECH!
SCREECH!
FREEZE!
THEY DRAGGED HIM OFF.
You have the right to remain silent.
SOB!

I WAS DEVASTATED. NOT ONLY WAS MY JASON GONE BUT SO WERE MY DREAMS OF ESCAPE. THE FUTURE LOOKED GRIM.

No education...No direction... I want to write for a living but I have no idea where to begin. What should I do? What should I do?

I WAS TOO YOUNG TO BE GOOD AT ANYTHING BUT RESTAURANT WORK. AND I WASN'T VERY GOOD AT THAT, EITHER.

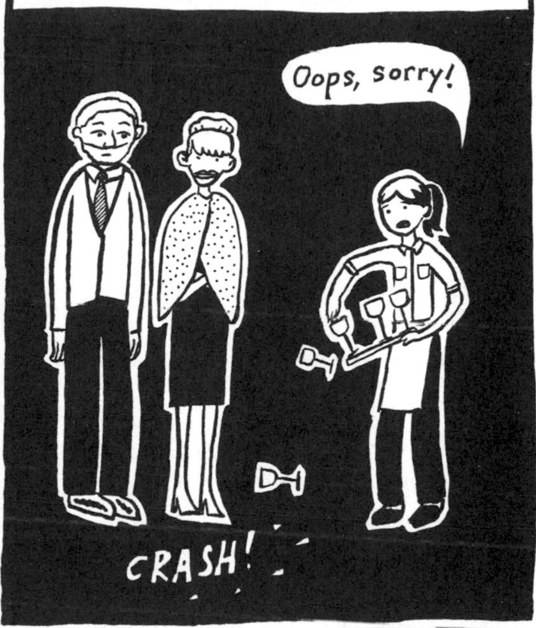

MY PARENTS DROVE ME TO SEE JASON IN JAIL ONCE A WEEK.

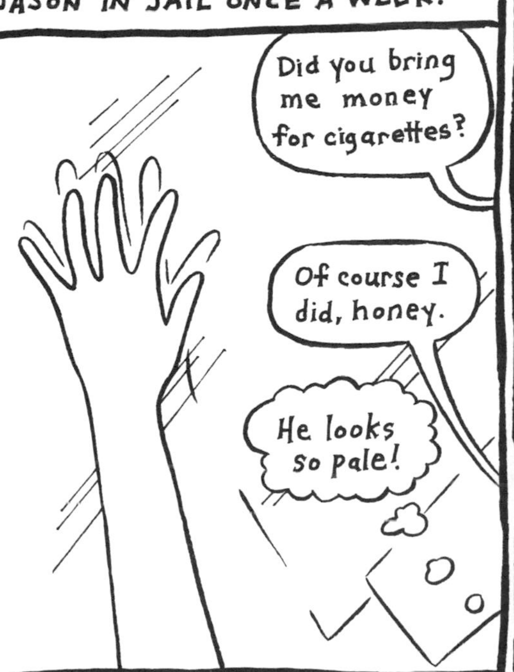

EVERY DAY HE WROTE ME LONG, PROFOUND LETTERS ABOUT THE MISTAKES HE'D MADE AND HOW HE WANTED TO BETTER HIMSELF.

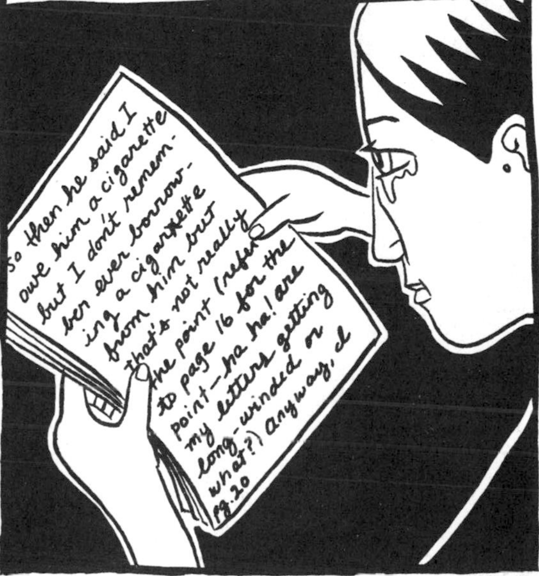

HIS TRIAL KEPT GETTING DELAYED. WE HAD NO IDEA HOW LONG HE WAS GOING TO BE STUCK IN THERE.

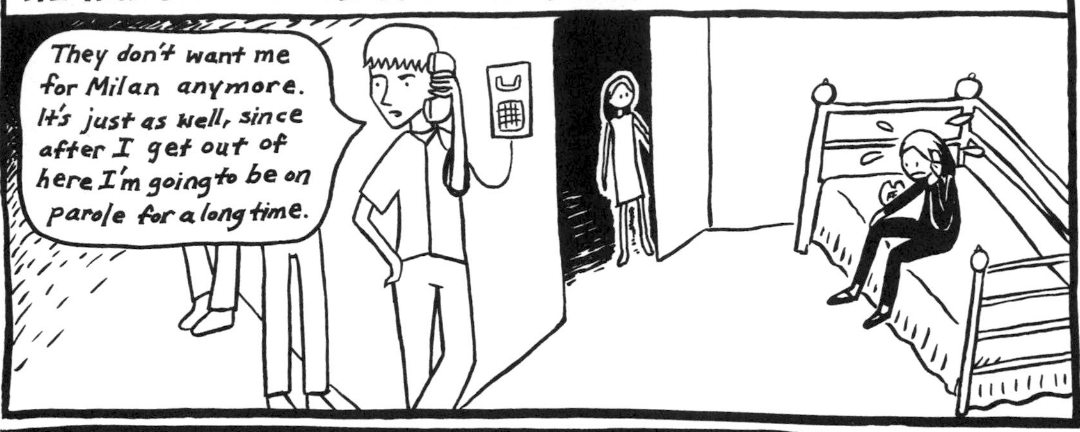

MY FRIENDS HAD GROWN DISTANT FROM ME. THEY HAD NORMAL HIGH SCHOOL SCHEDULES WHEREAS I WAS UP ALL NIGHT, WORKING AND WRITING. MY LIFE WAS SO DIFFERENT NOW, I HAD LITTLE IN COMMON WITH THEM. THUS, I HAD NO ONE TO TURN TO.

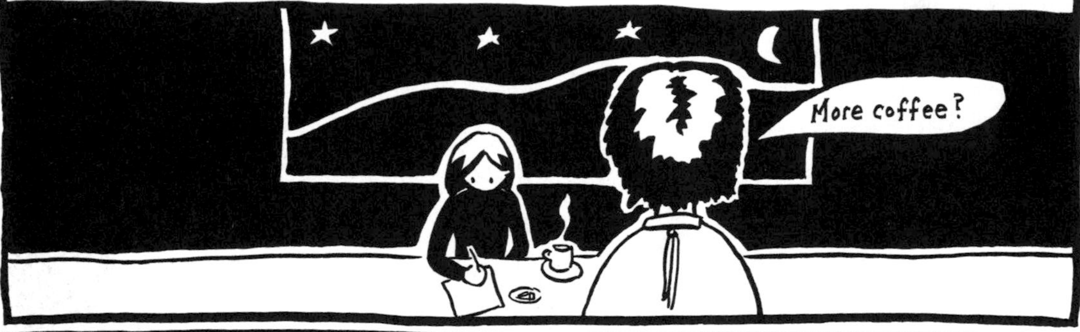

SO I TRIED TURNING TO HIS FRIENDS FOR SOLACE.

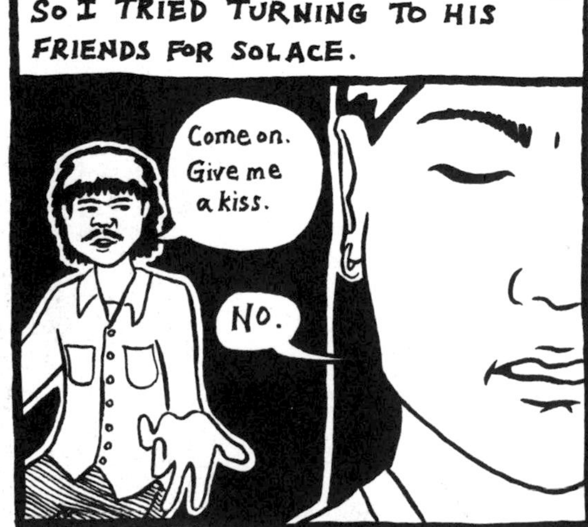

ALL MY MALE FRIENDS SUDDENLY WANTED TO SLEEP WITH ME.

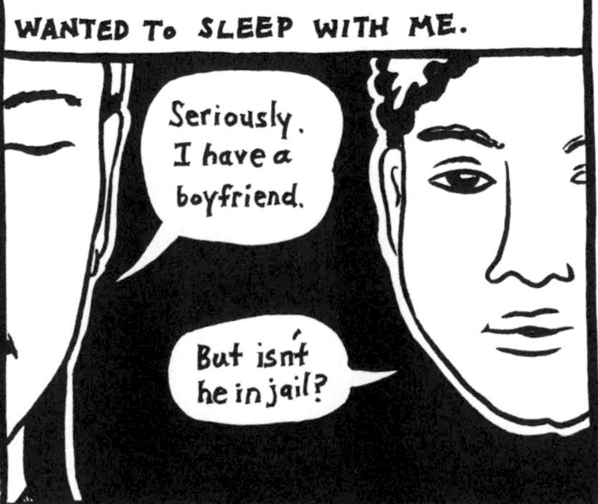

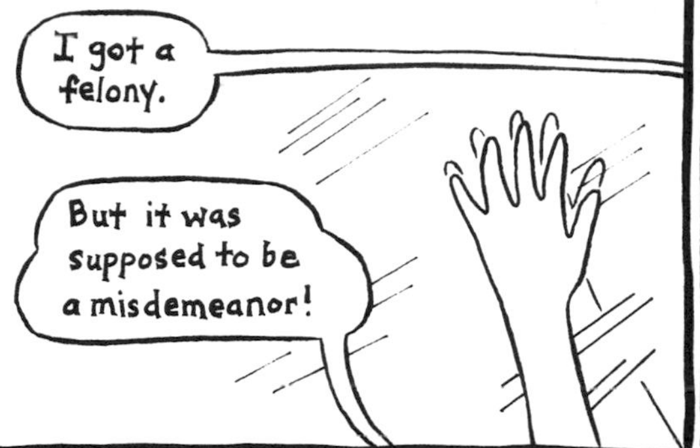
HIS TRIAL CAME AND HIS COURT-APPOINTED LAWYER DID ABSOLUTELY NOTHING FOR HIM.
I got a felony.
But it was supposed to be a misdemeanor!

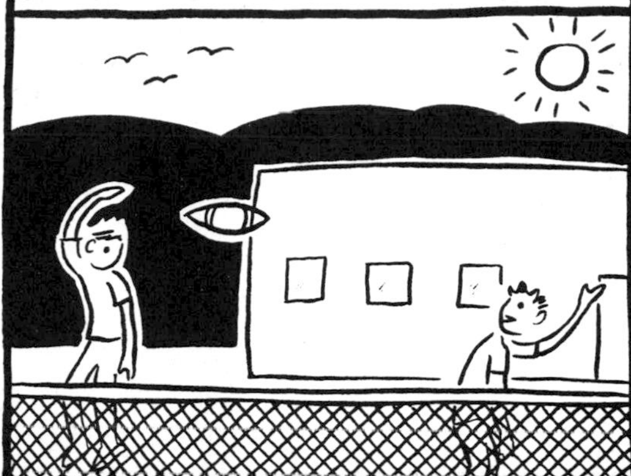
THEY TRANSFERRED HIM TO A MINIMUM-SECURITY PRISON.

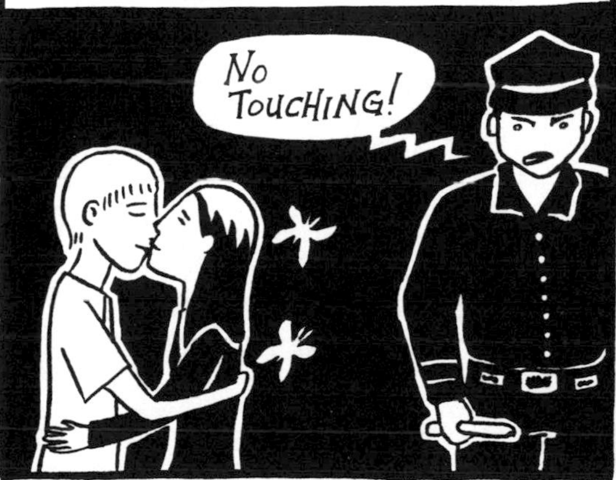
I GOT TO SEE HIM, SMELL HIM, TOUCH HIM.
No TOUCHING!

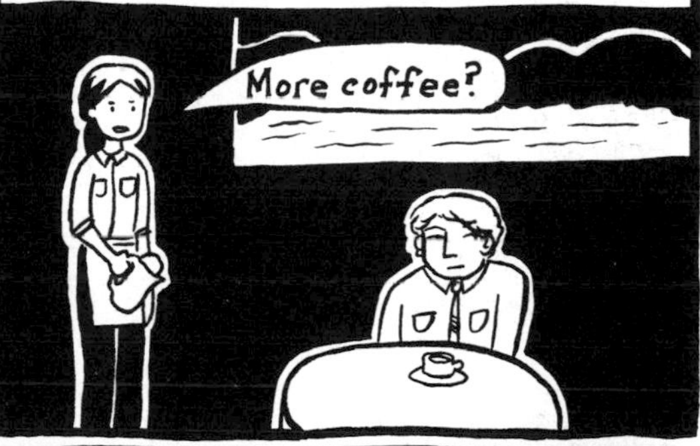
BUT WE STILL HAD NO IDEA HOW LONG HE WAS GOING TO BE INCARCERATED. I FELT LIKE MY LIFE WAS IN LIMBO AND COULD BE ETERNALLY SO.
More coffee?

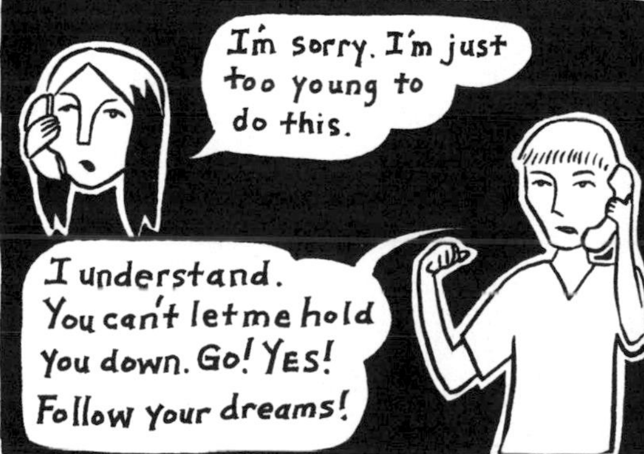
AFTER MONTHS OF HEAVY THOUGHT AND LISTS OF PROS AND CONS, I DID WHAT I HAD TO DO.
I'm sorry. I'm just too young to do this.
I understand. You can't let me hold you down. Go! YES! Follow your dreams!

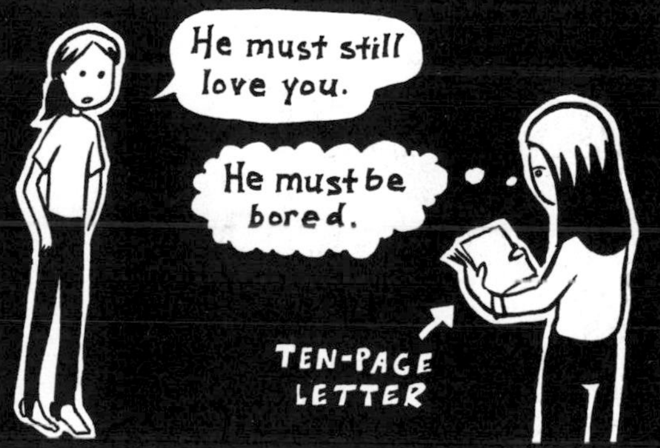
WE ENDED OUR PHONE CALLS SO I COULD MOVE ON BUT HE STILL SENT ME THE OCCASIONAL LETTER.
He must still love you.
He must be bored.
TEN-PAGE LETTER

MONTHS LATER, I HAD A DREAM. DURING PUBERTY I'D HAD A RECURRING NIGHTMARE OF BEING CHASED BY A MUMMY. I HADN'T HAD THIS NIGHTMARE IN YEARS, BUT SUDDENLY THERE IT WAS AGAIN.

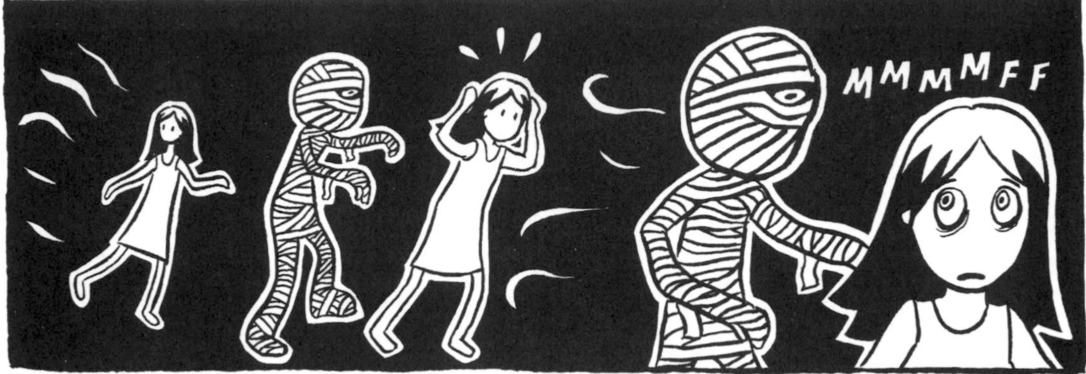

BUT THIS TIME THE MUMMY CAUGHT UP TO ME. IT GRABBED ME BY THE SHOULDER WITH ITS GAUZED HAND. WHEN I TURNED TO FACE IT, I REALIZED IT WAS JASON, ONLY HIS FACE WAS ALL MUTILATED.

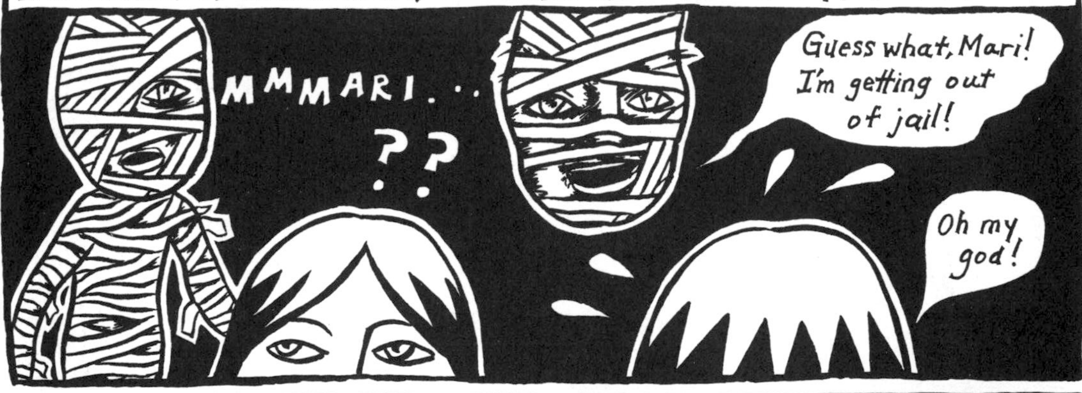

THE RINGING OF THE TELEPHONE WOKE ME UP.

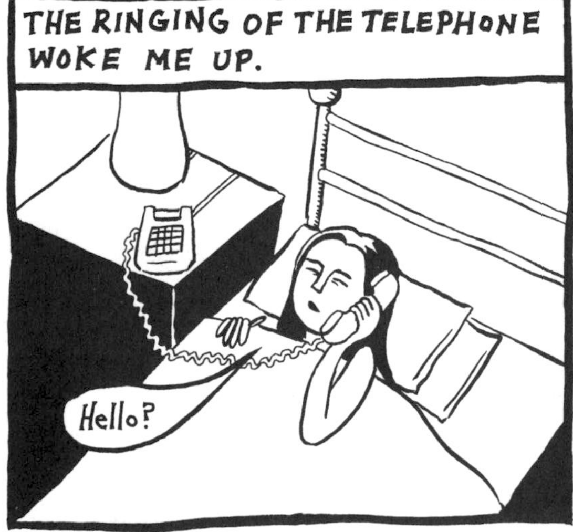

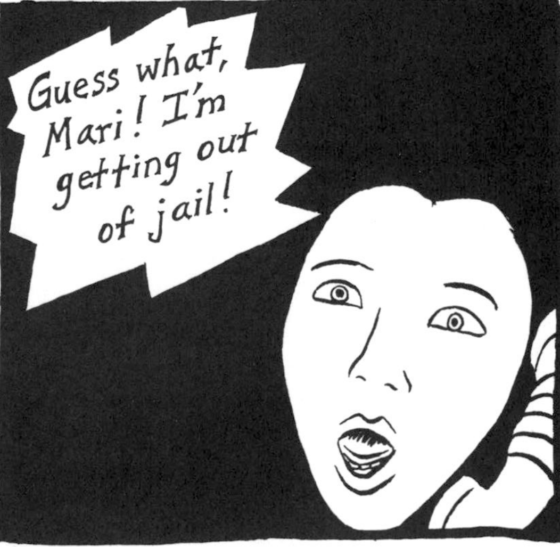

HE'D BEEN PUNCHED IN THE FACE BY A FELLOW INMATE. THEY HAD TO DO RECONSTRUCTIVE SURGERY.

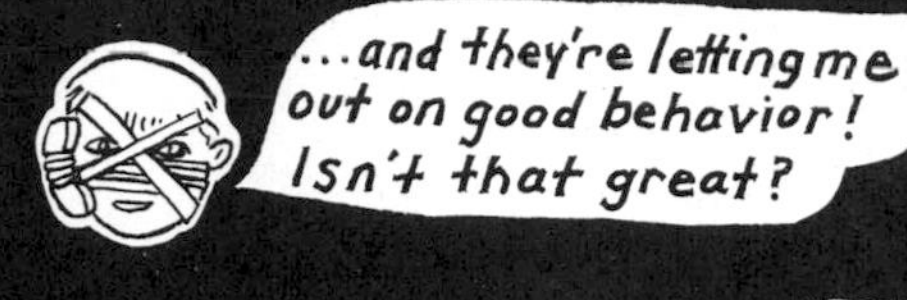

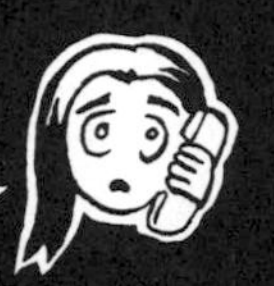

WHEN HE WAS RELEASED, HE WAS PUT UNDER HOUSE ARREST. HE STAYED WITH A PHOTOGRAPHER WHO HAD A CRUSH ON HIM.

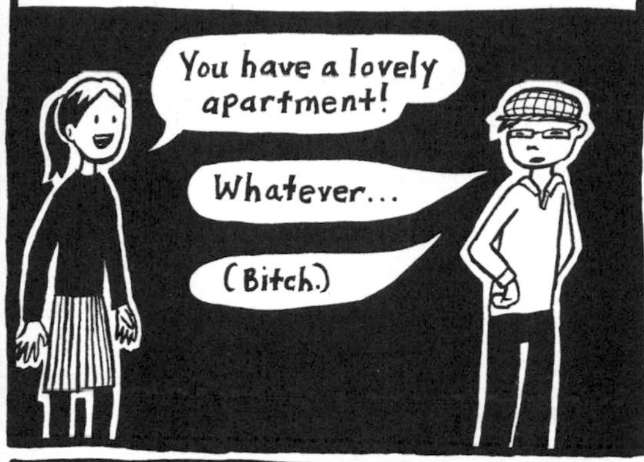

IT WAS STRANGE SEEING HIM AGAIN. THERE WAS TOO MUCH HISTORY AND NOT ENOUGH RESOLUTION.

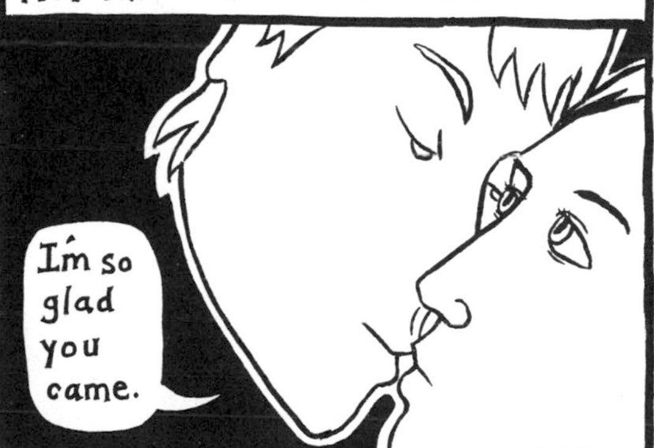

I DIDN'T SEE HIM AGAIN FOR A LONG TIME, BUT OCCASIONALLY HE TRACKED ME DOWN.

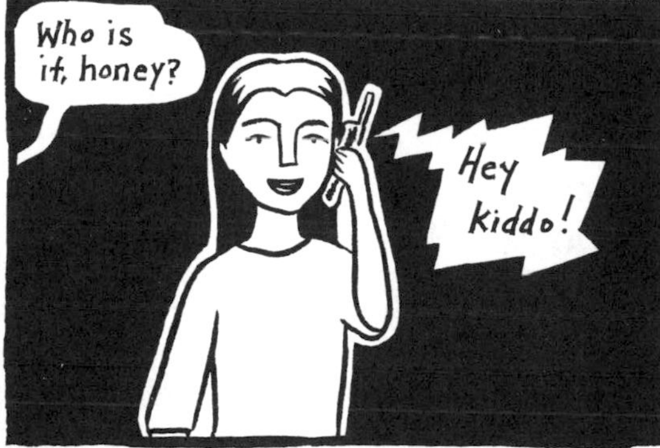

HE ALWAYS HAD INTERESTING STORIES.

And when I got to Athens I discovered that commercials aren't so glamorous after all. They dressed me up like Pee-wee Herman! It was so humiliating! So then I had to resort to male stripping. And let me tell ya, those Greek goddesses can be quite the handful! I'm lucky to still be alive after all that drama!

HA! HA!

I GOT TO SEE HIM ONE LAST TIME. HE CAME TO VISIT ME IN MARIN.

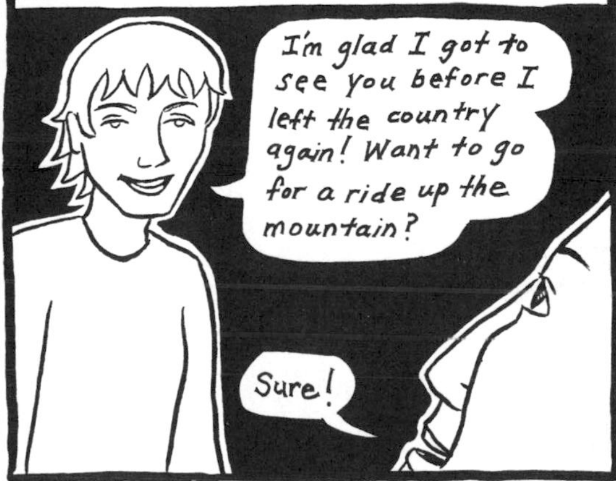

OUR RAPPORT WAS FANTASTIC, JUST LIKE IN THE OLD DAYS. AND EVEN THOUGH I WAS HAPPY IN ANOTHER RELATIONSHIP, I REALIZED I MISSED HIM LIKE CRAZY AND ALWAYS WANTED HIM IN MY LIFE.

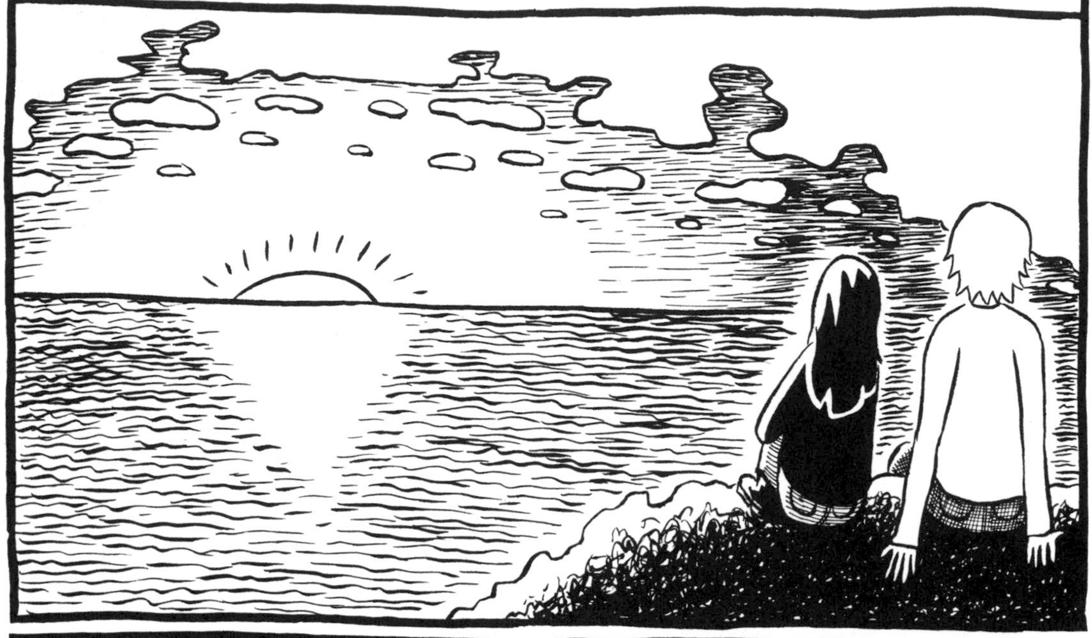

YEARS LATER, I SENT HIM A DRAMATIC LETTER.

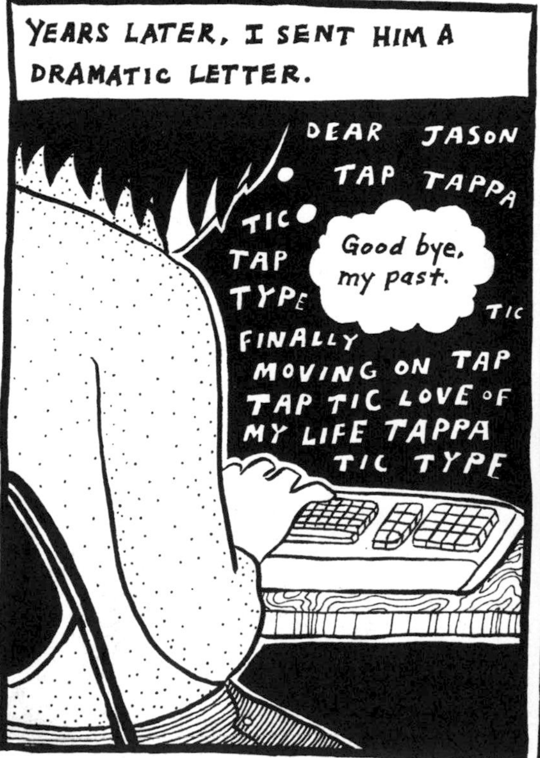

HE NEVER CONTACTED ME AGAIN AND I WAS UNABLE TO FIND HIM.

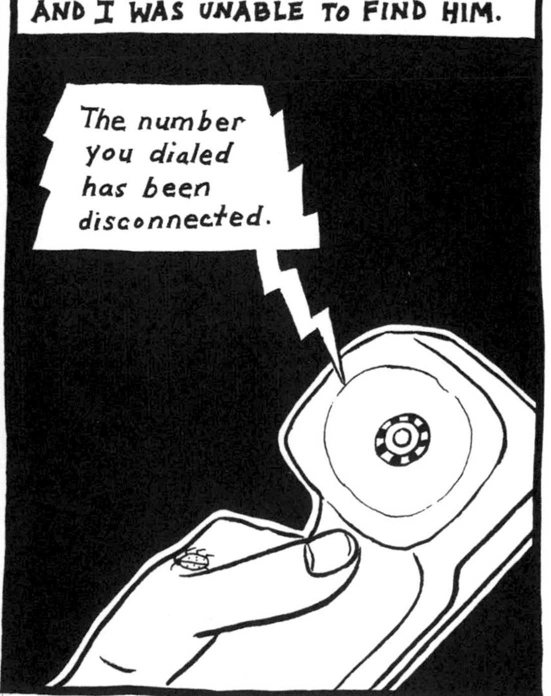

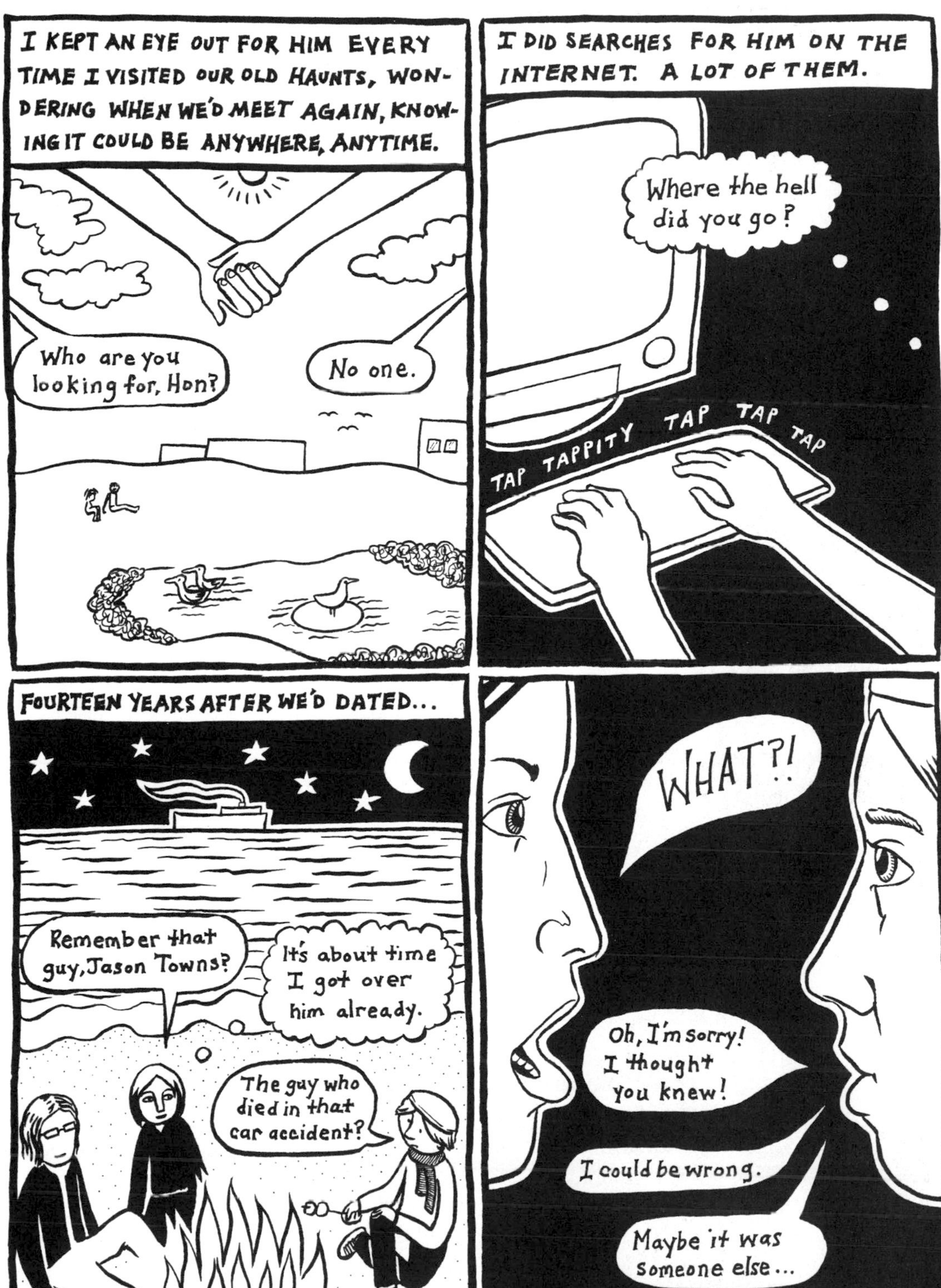
I KEPT AN EYE OUT FOR HIM EVERY TIME I VISITED OUR OLD HAUNTS, WONDERING WHEN WE'D MEET AGAIN, KNOWING IT COULD BE ANYWHERE, ANYTIME.
Who are you looking for, Hon?
No one.
I DID SEARCHES FOR HIM ON THE INTERNET. A LOT OF THEM.
Where the hell did you go?
TAP TAPPITY TAP TAP TAP
FOURTEEN YEARS AFTER WE'D DATED...
Remember that guy, Jason Towns?
It's about time I got over him already.
The guy who died in that car accident?
WHAT?!
Oh, I'm sorry! I thought you knew!
I could be wrong.
Maybe it was someone else...

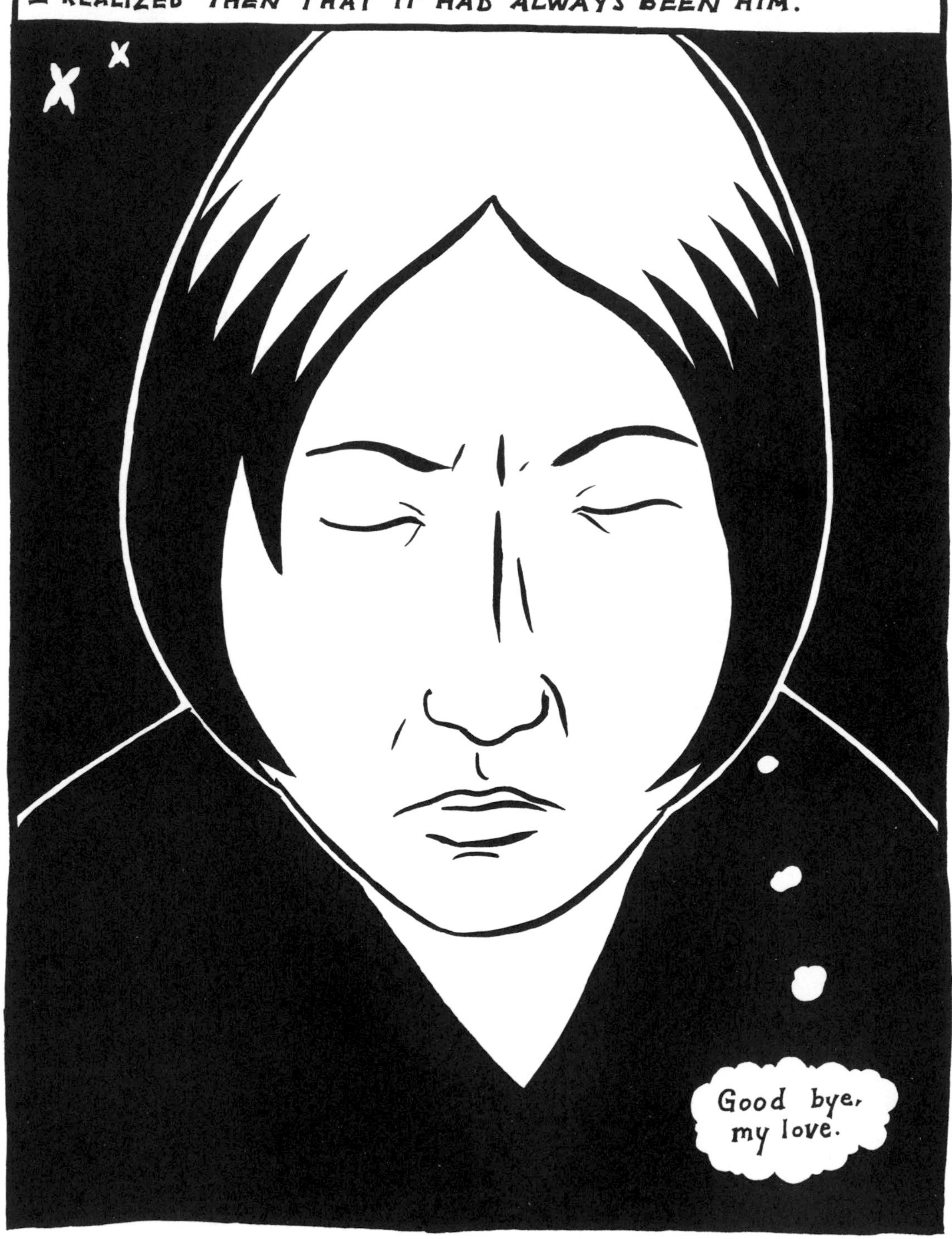
HE WAS THE ONLY PERSON I HAD EVER TRULY LOVED AND TRUSTED UNABASHEDLY. I'D NEVER THOUGHT I BELIEVED IN "THE ONE." I REALIZED THEN THAT IT HAD ALWAYS BEEN HIM.
Good bye, my love.

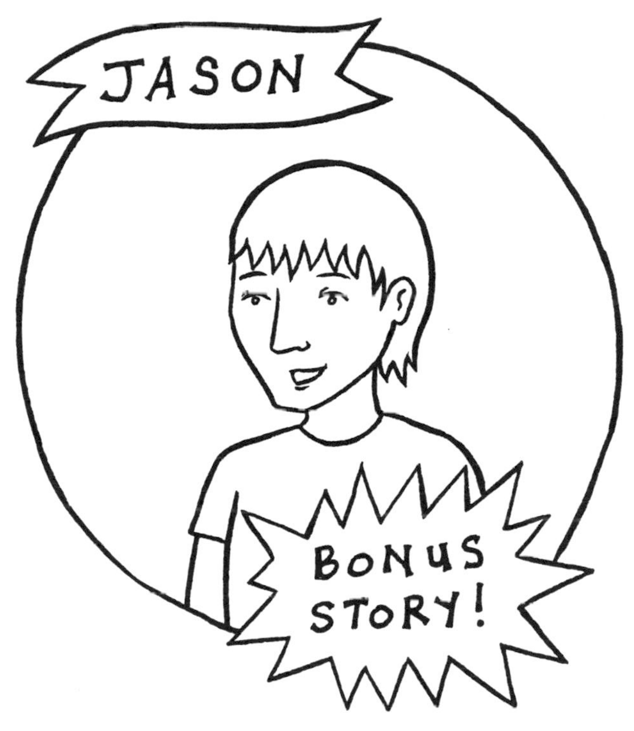
JASON
BONUS STORY!

WE DROVE TO RENO TO TRY OUR LUCK AT GAMBLING. I WAS SIXTEEN BUT MY I.D. SAID I WAS TWENTY-SIX.

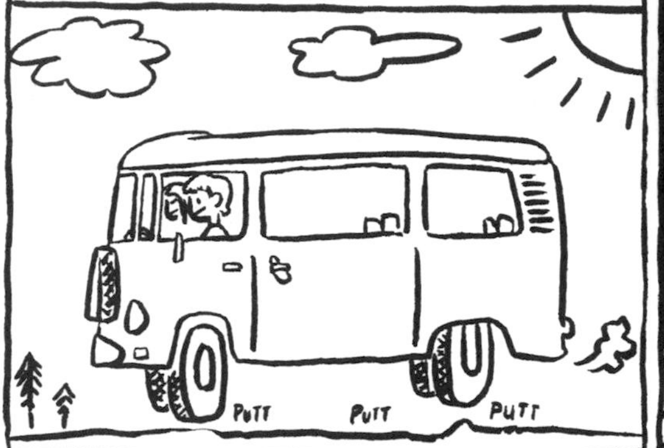

I WAS DOING REALLY WELL.

Wow, Mari! You've got the touch!

AFTER I'D WON A FEW HUNDRED DOLLARS I THOUGHT I SHOULD CALL IT QUITS.

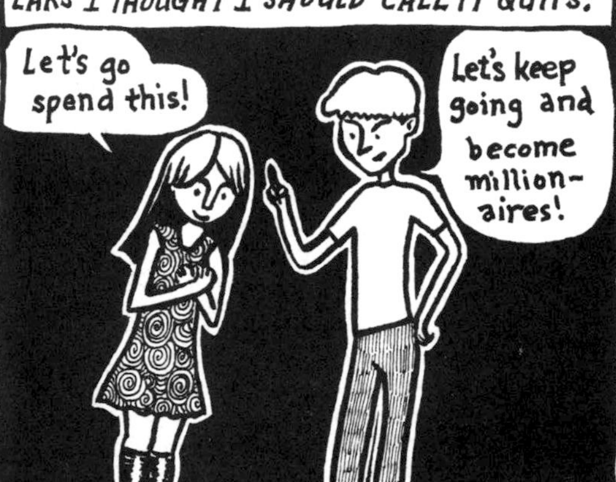

HE WAS SO INSISTENT. HE WON THE ARGUMENT, WHICH EFFECTIVELY LOST US ALL OUR DOUGH.

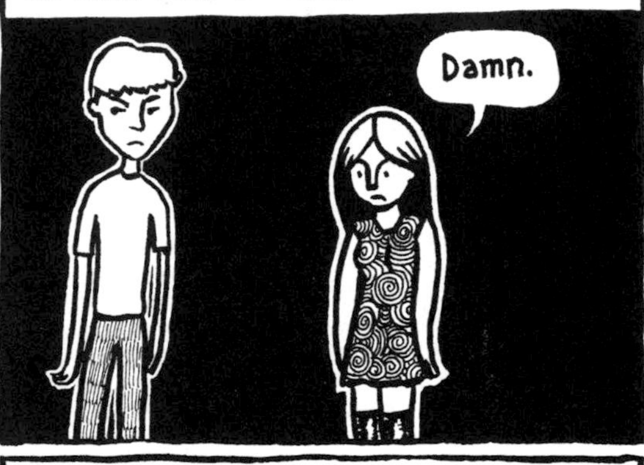

EXCEPT OUR GAS MONEY, UNTIL...

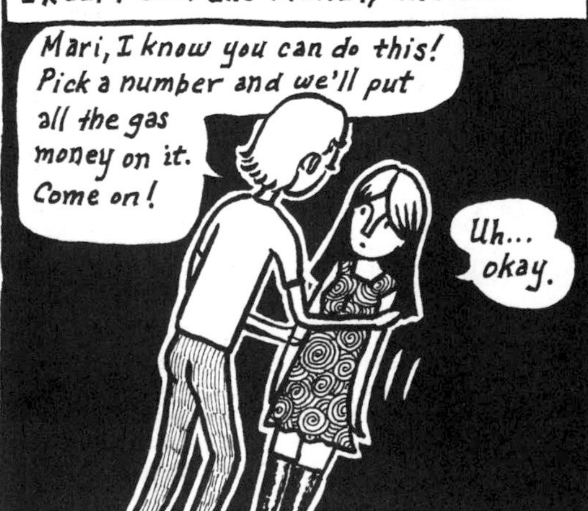

I SCANNED THE TABLE CAREFULLY.

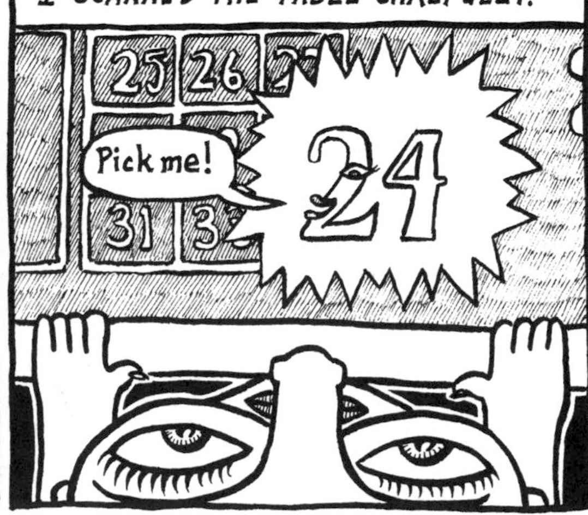

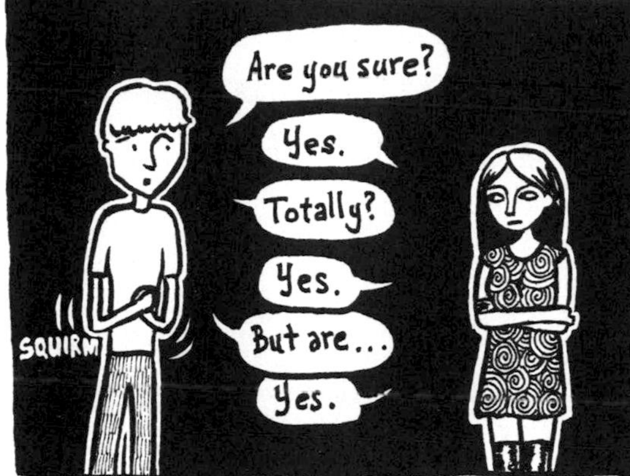
CEREMONIOUSLY, HE PUT ALL OUR GAS MONEY ON 24.
Are you sure?
Yes.
Totally?
Yes.
But are...
Yes.
SQUIRM

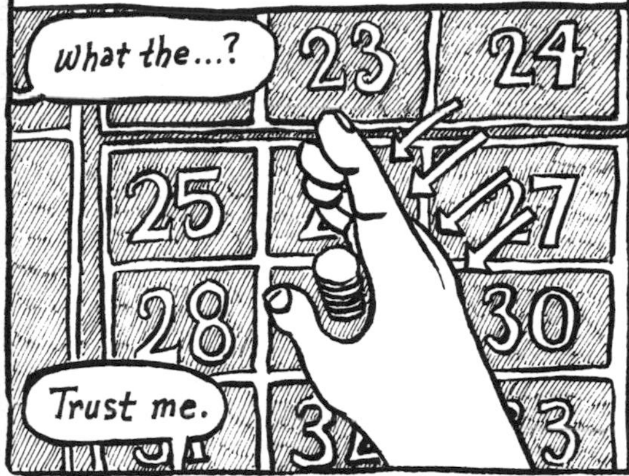
BUT HE GOT SCARED AT THE LAST MOMENT AND MOVED IT TO ANOTHER NUMBER.
What the...?
Trust me.
23
24
25
27
28
30

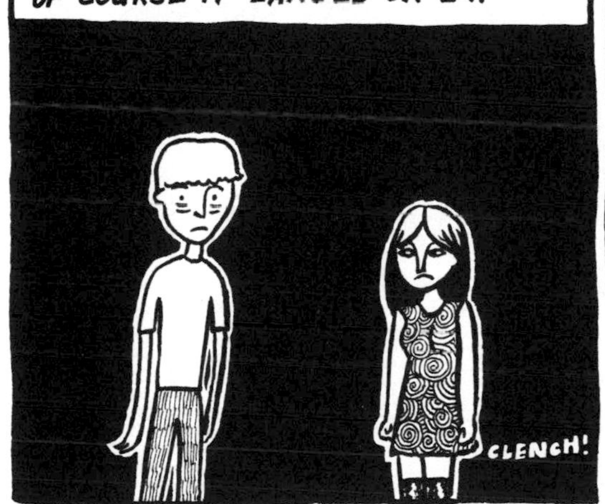
OF COURSE IT LANDED ON 24.
CLENCH!

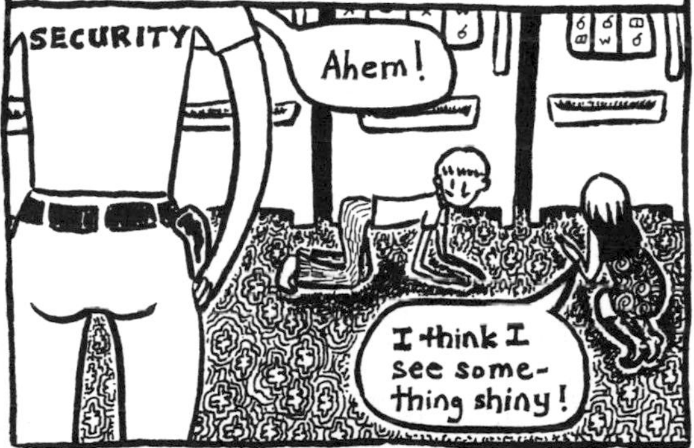
WE WERE SCREWED. THEY BOOTED US OUT OF THERE FOR SCROUNGING FOR CHANGE ON THE FLOOR.
SECURITY
Ahem!
I think I see something shiny!

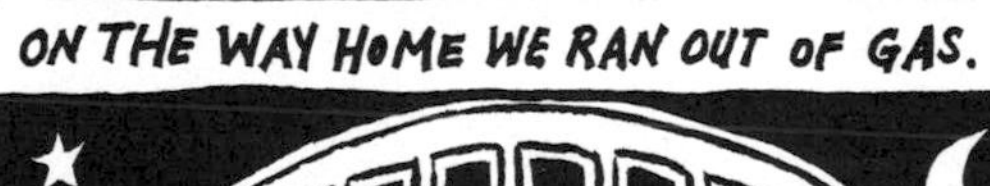
ON THE WAY HOME WE RAN OUT OF GAS.

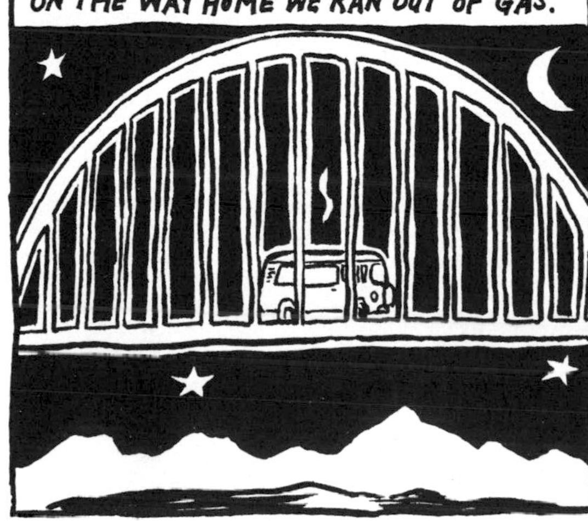

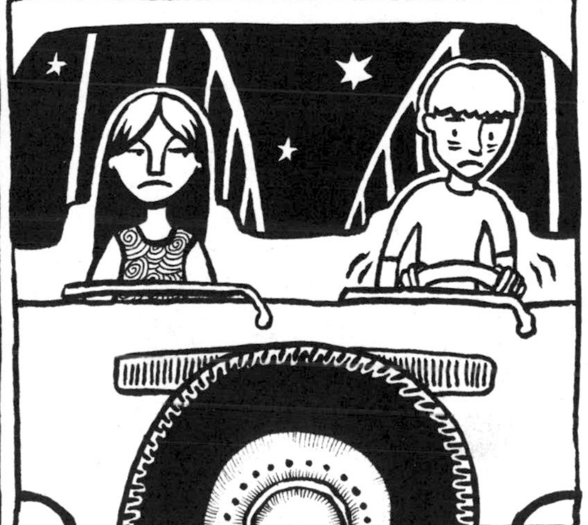

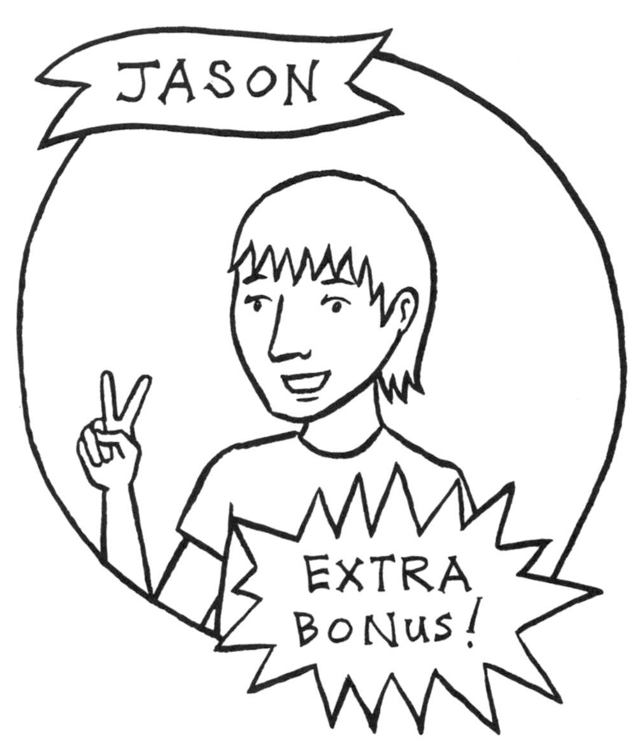
JASON
EXTRA BONUS!

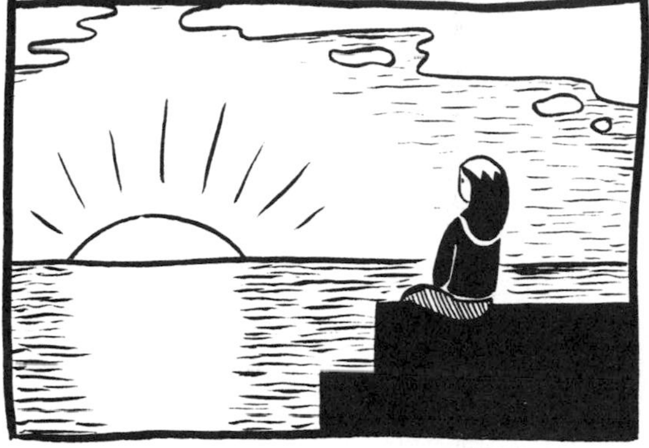
WHEN MY FIRST LOVE, JASON, WENT AWAY TO JAIL, I SPENT A LOT OF TIME SITTING AROUND AND MISSING HIM.

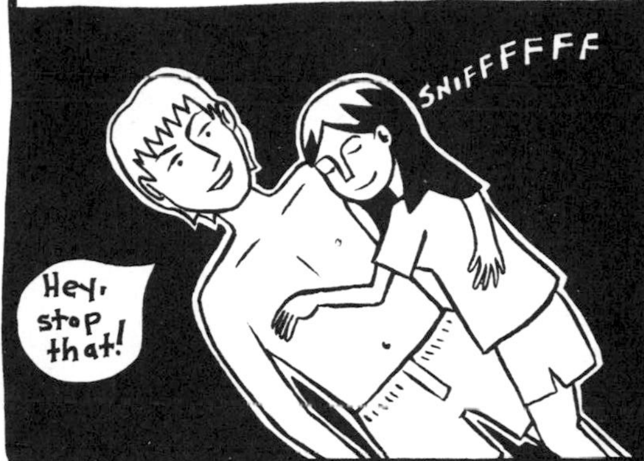
WHAT I MISSED MOST WAS HIS WARMTH AND SCENT. HIS BODY EXUDED A MUSKY, SWEET ODOR THAT MADE ME FEEL SAFE.
SNIFFFFFF
Hey, stop that!

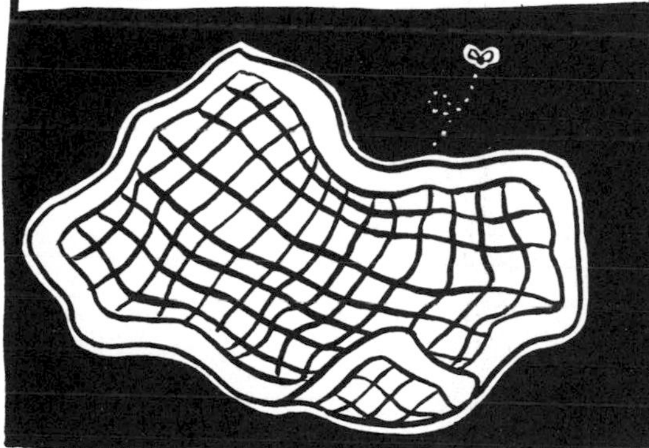
HE'D LEFT BEHIND HIS FAVORITE OLD ORANGE VELOUR BLANKET THAT HAD CAPTURED HIS SCENT PERFECTLY.

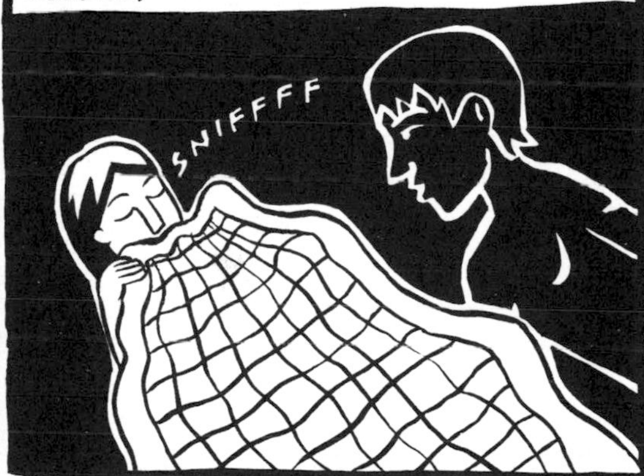
I SPENT HOURS INHALING HIS SCENT DEEPLY, IMAGINING HE WAS THERE.
SNIFFFFF

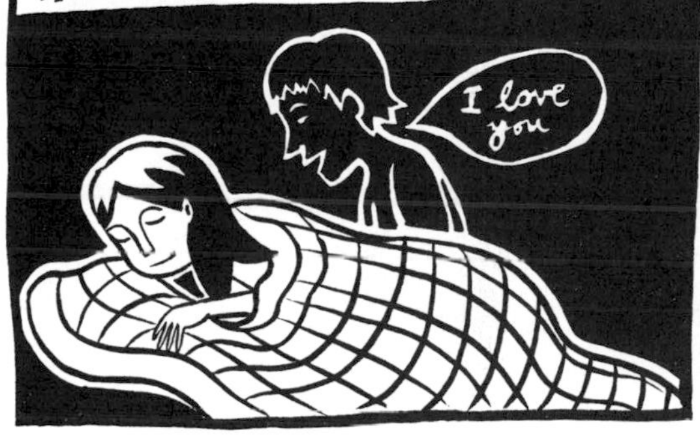
I COULD ALMOST FEEL HIS WARM BREATH AS I DRIFTED OFF TO SLEEP EACH NIGHT WITH THE BLANKET HELD TIGHT IN MY ARMS.
I love you

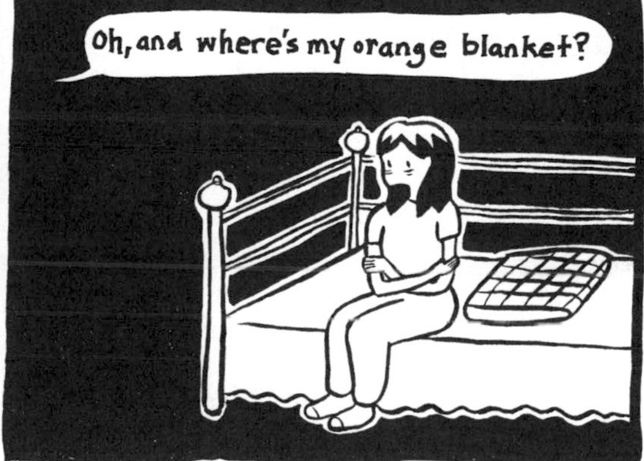
EVENTUALLY HE GOT OUT OF JAIL AND TOOK HIS BLANKET BACK. I MISSED IT.
Oh, and where's my orange blanket?

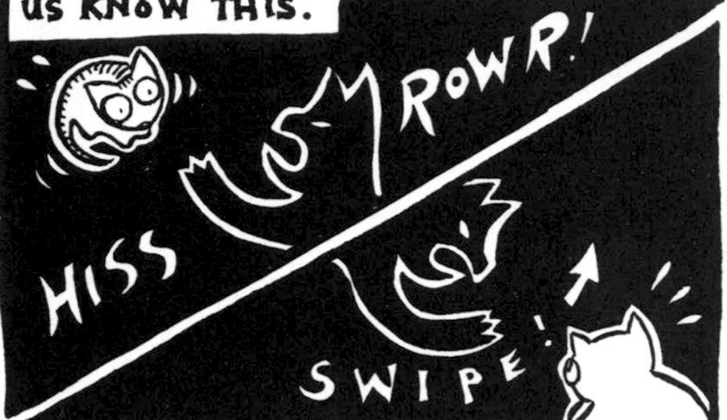
FAST-FORWARD TO TWENTY YEARS LATER. MY CAT WAS PISSED OFF THAT MY NEW MAN'S CATS HAD MOVED IN AND SHE TOOK EVERY OPPORTUNITY TO LET US KNOW THIS.
MROWR!
HISS
SWIPE!

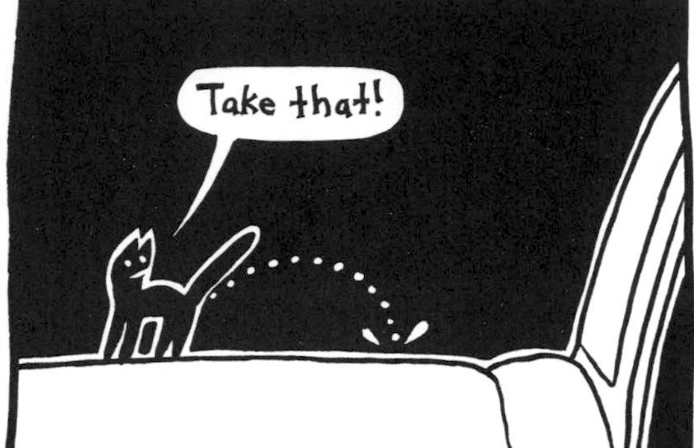
AND WHEN HISSING AND ATTACKING FAILED TO GET HER POINT ACROSS, SHE TOOK IT TO THE NEXT LEVEL.
Take that!

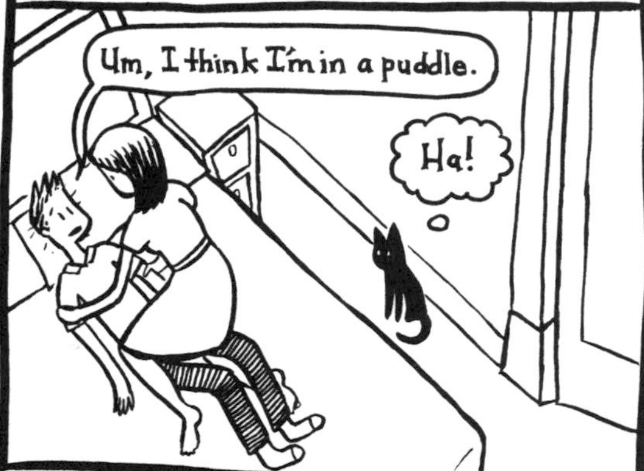
UNFORTUNATELY, WE DISCOVERED THIS DURING A VERY INAPPROPRIATE MOMENT.
Um, I think I'm in a puddle.
Ha!

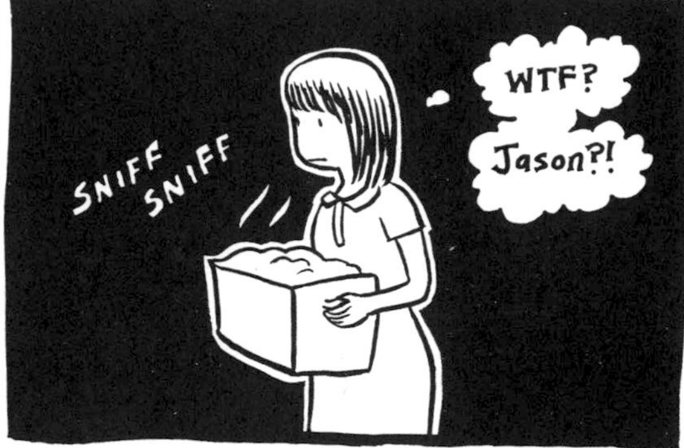
TAKING THE LAUNDRY DOWN, I RECOGNIZED THAT WARM, SWEET SMELL, LIKE VISITING AN OLD FRIEND.
SNIFF
SNIFF
WTF?
Jason?!

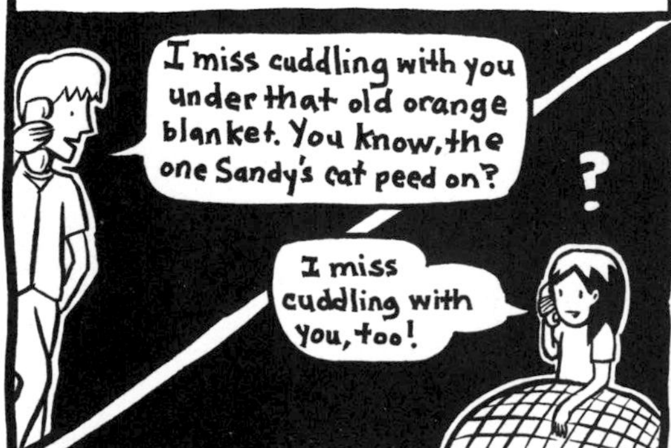
SUDDENLY, ANOTHER MEMORY CAME RUSHING BACK TO ME OF A CONVERSATION I HAD WITH JASON WHILE HE WAS IN JAIL.
I miss cuddling with you under that old orange blanket. You know, the one Sandy's cat peed on?
?
I miss cuddling with you, too!

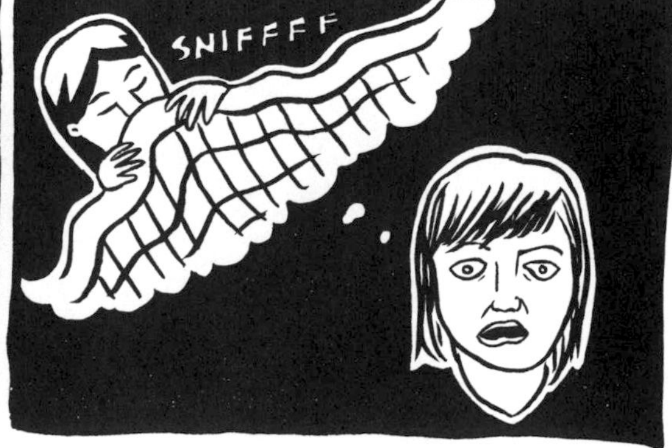
IT HIT ME LIKE A TON OF BRICKS WHAT IT HAD BEEN THAT I'D SPENT SO MANY NIGHTS SMELLING IN MY YOUTH.
SNIFFFF

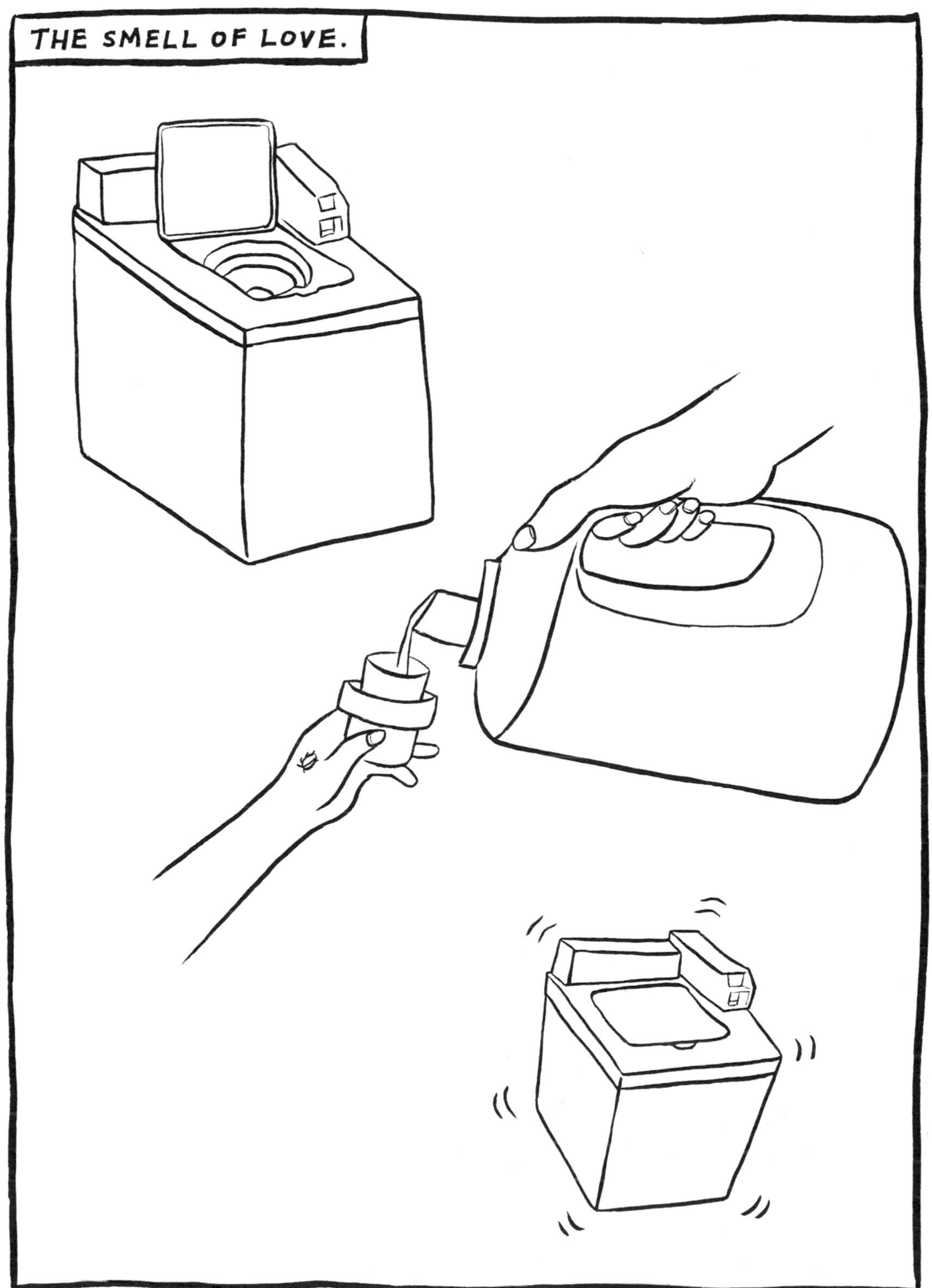
THE SMELL OF LOVE.

Sympathy from the folks

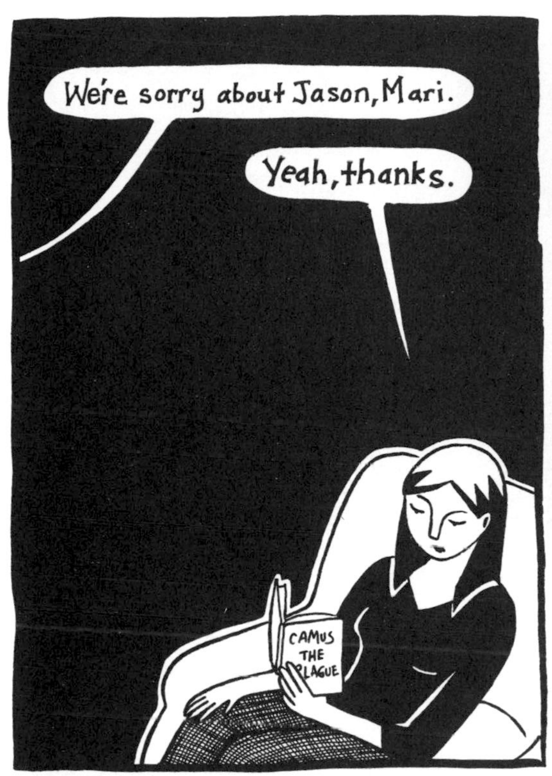
We're sorry about Jason, Mari.
Yeah, thanks.
CAMUS THE PLAGUE

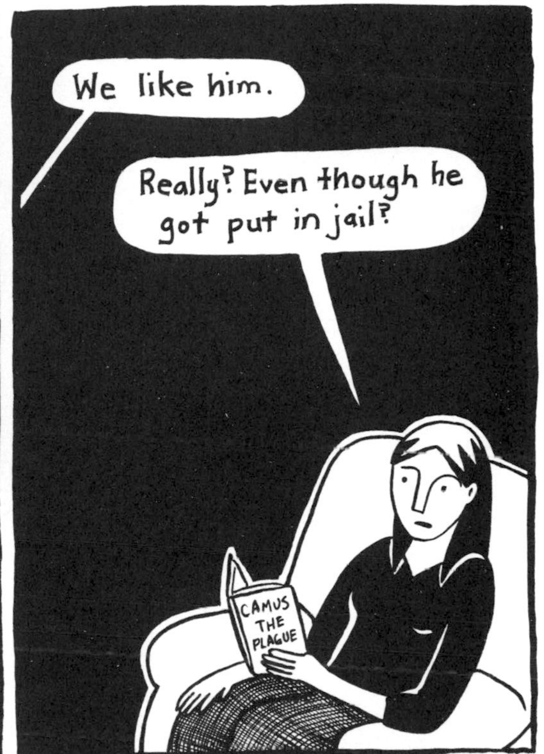
We like him.
Really? Even though he got put in jail?
CAMUS THE PLAGUE

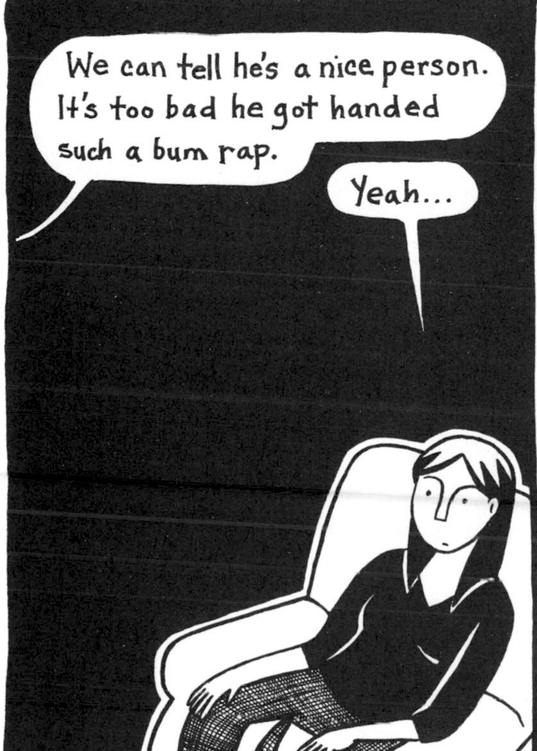
We can tell he's a nice person. It's too bad he got handed such a bum rap.
Yeah...

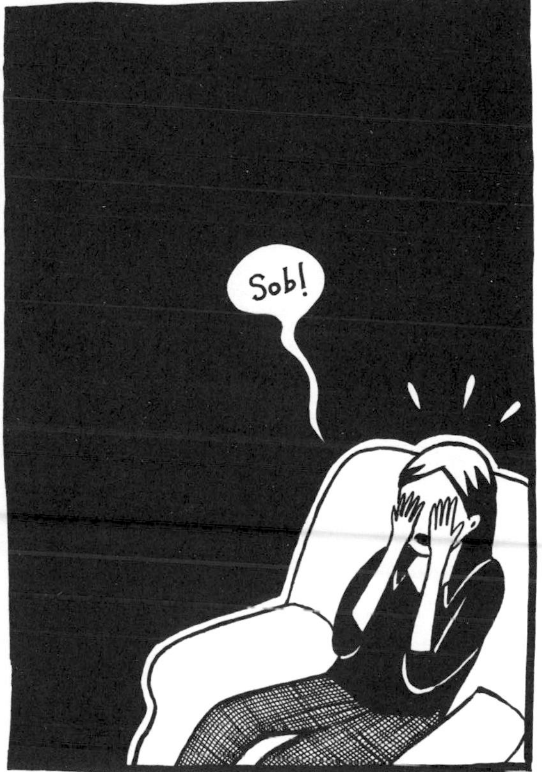
Sob!

1990

ages 16 ~ 17

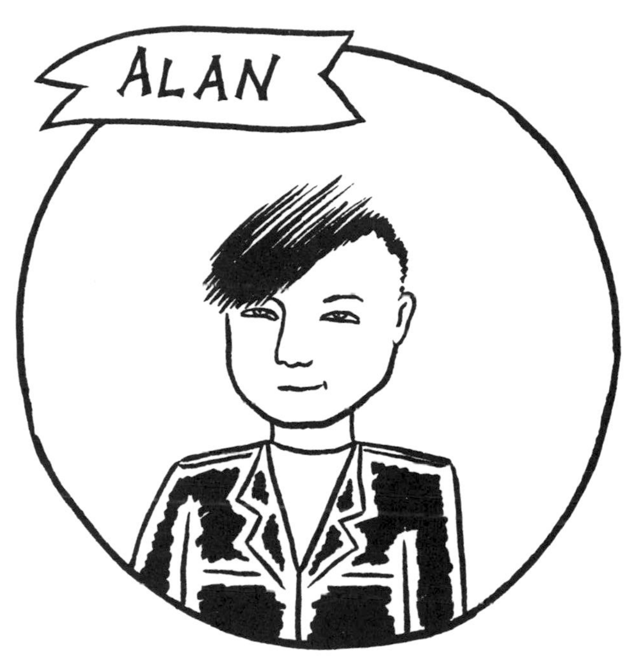
ALAN

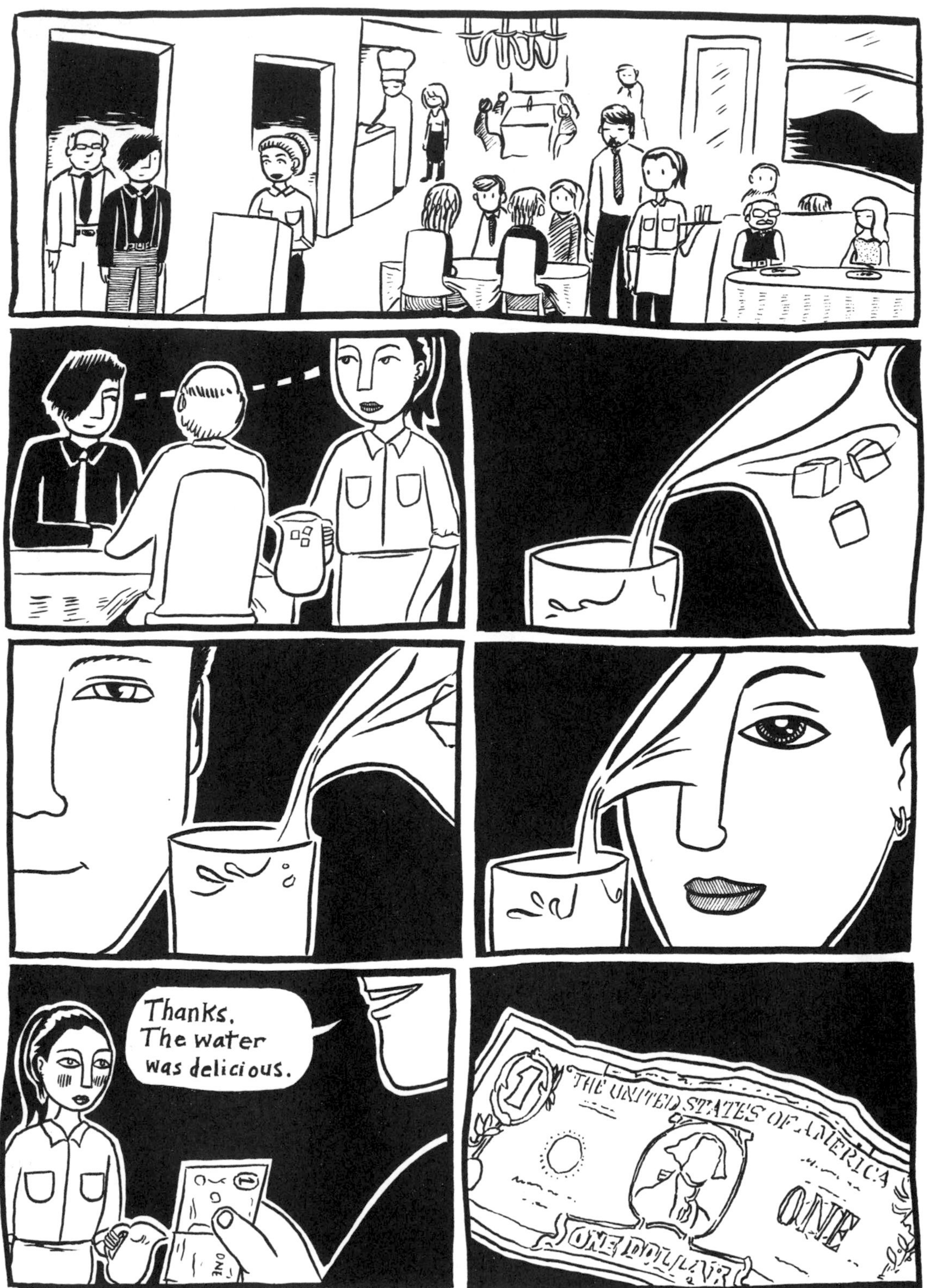
Thanks. The water was delicious.
THE UNITED STATES OF AMERICA
ONE
ONE DOLLAR

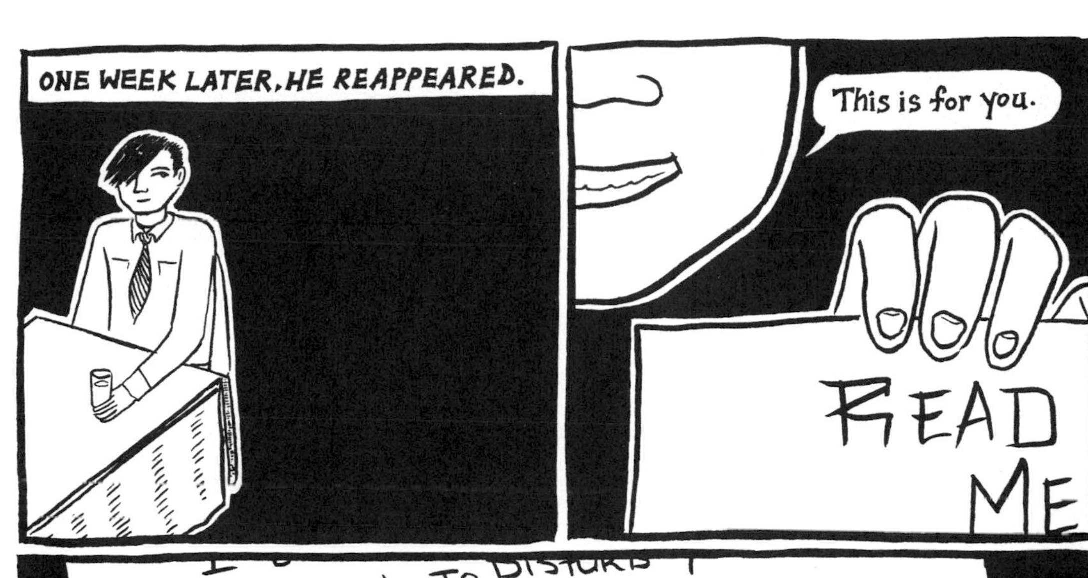

Do Not wish To DISTURB
OVERMuch.
LAST WEEK My PARENTS BRought ME
TO DINE At Butlers ON THE EVE of MY
Twentieth BirthDAY
YOUR IMMENSE BEAUTY GAVE ME PAUSE.
I Hope This is Not too Bold of ME,
But TRUTH BE TOLD, I DID NOT COME
BACK for THE fINE fooDS, OR THE
'Delicious WATER,' (HA HA) IN FACT THE
fORMER IS A little Rich for MY BLOOD,
But I CAME IN THE Hopes of SEEING you
AgAIN.
I REAlize This is RATHER ABRUPT
AND PERhAPS You GET This SORT of
Thing Alot, But This is A first for
ME. So I hope you will GIVE ME YOUR
PHONE NUMBER, OR At LEAST INDulge
ME with YOUR NAME AND CONSIDER
ME TOMORROW EVENING.

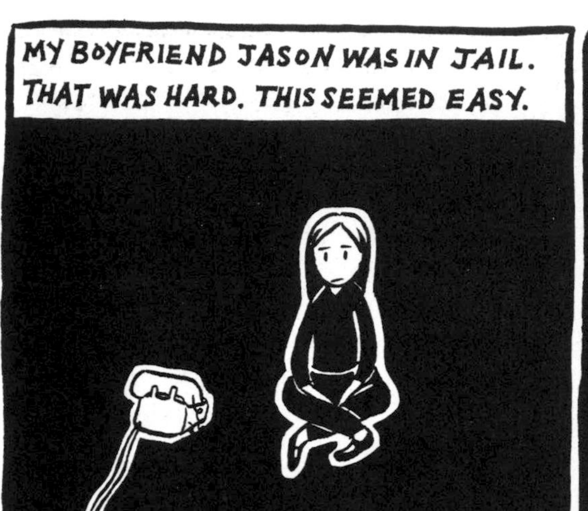
MY BOYFRIEND JASON WAS IN JAIL. THAT WAS HARD. THIS SEEMED EASY.

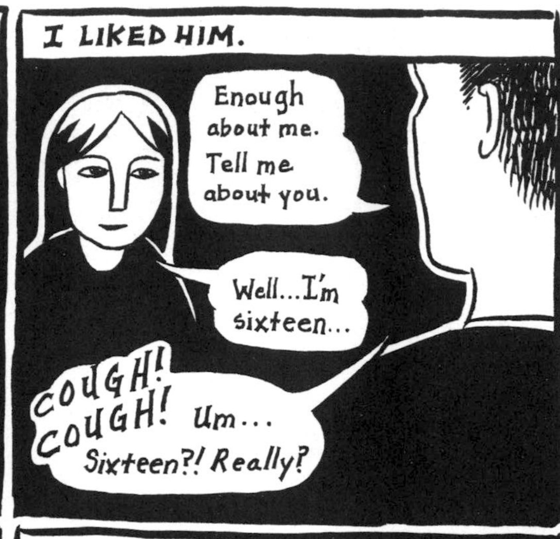
I LIKED HIM.
Enough about me. Tell me about you.
Well... I'm sixteen...
COUGH! COUGH! Um... Sixteen?! Really?

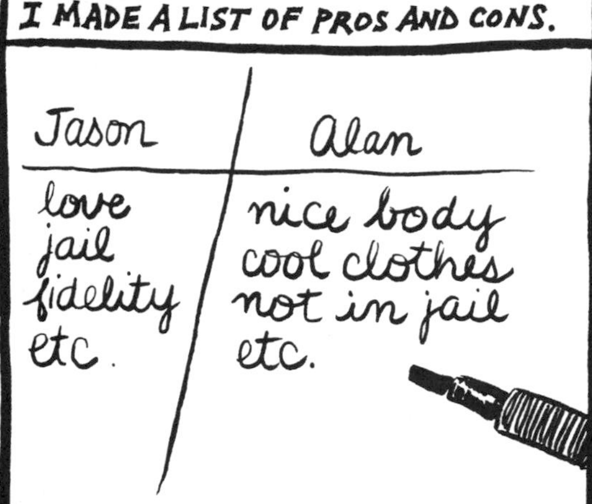
I MADE A LIST OF PROS AND CONS.
Jason
Alan
love
jail
fidelity
etc.
nice body
cool clothes
not in jail
etc.

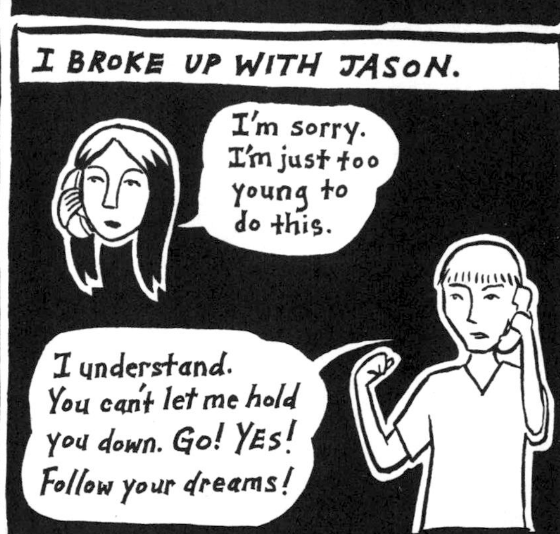
I BROKE UP WITH JASON.
I'm sorry. I'm just too young to do this.
I understand. You can't let me hold you down. Go! YES! Follow your dreams!

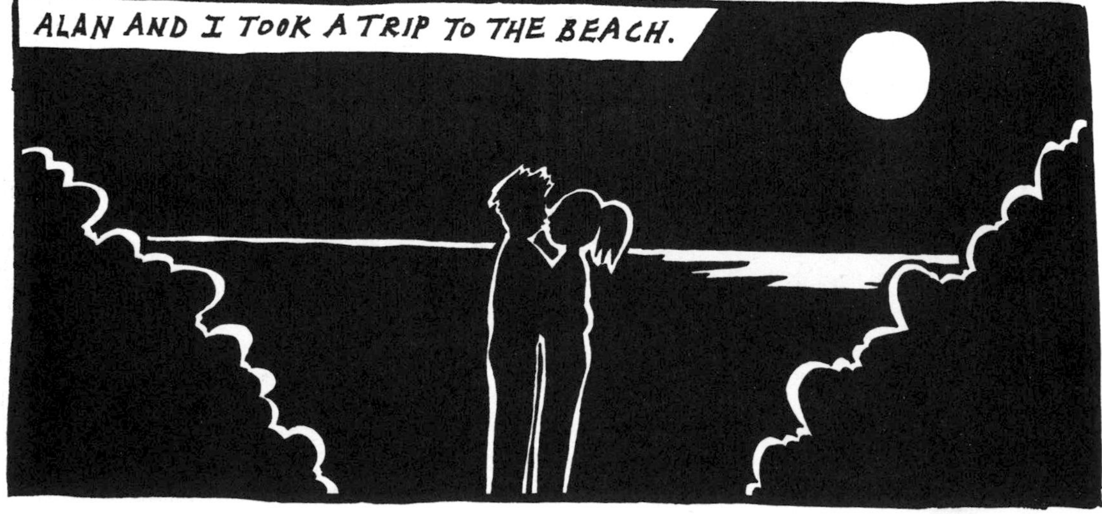
ALAN AND I TOOK A TRIP TO THE BEACH.

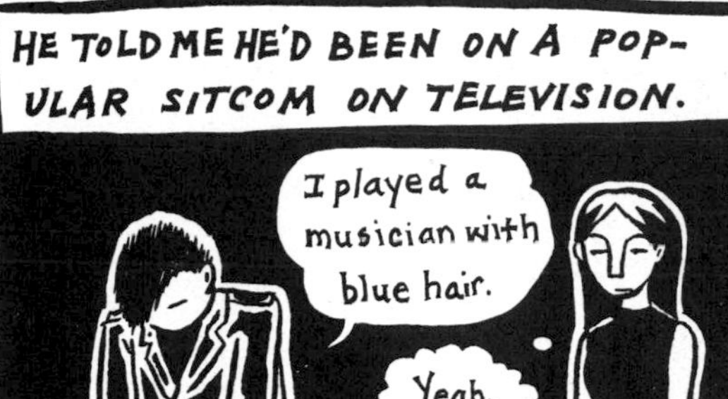
HE TOLD ME HE'D BEEN ON A POPULAR SITCOM ON TELEVISION.
I played a musician with blue hair.
Yeah, right.

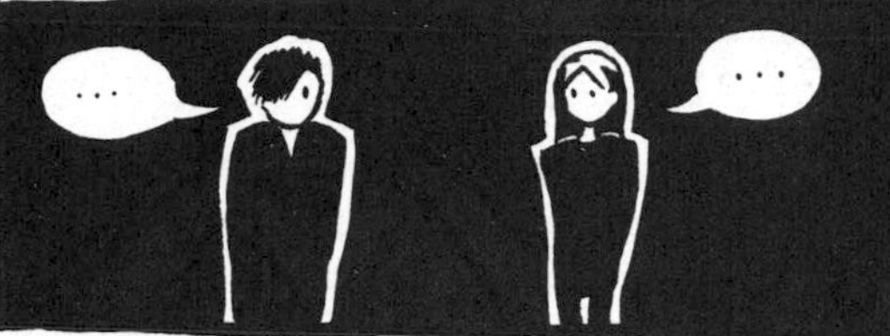
WE DIDN'T HAVE MUCH IN COMMON. HE DIDN'T GET MY SENSE OF HUMOR AND I DIDN'T UNDERSTAND HIS OBSESSION WITH BONE COLLECTING.
...
...

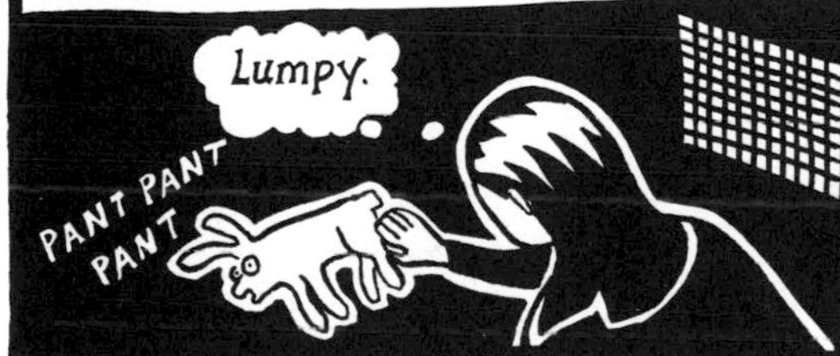
ON EASTER MORNING, MY PET RABBIT CRAWLED UNDER MY PARENTS' HOUSE TO DIE.
Lumpy.
PANT PANT PANT

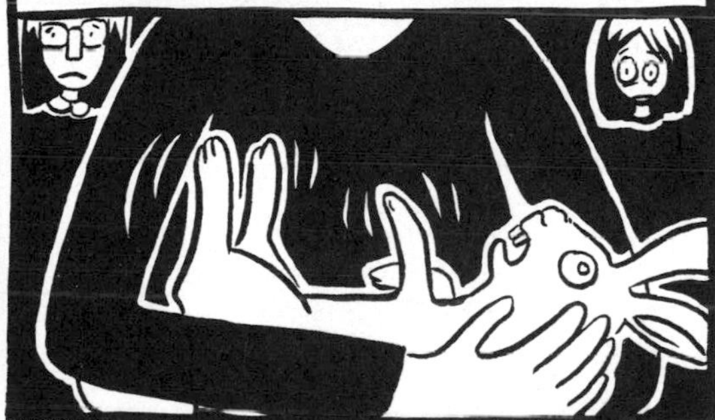
SHE DIDN'T LIKE TO BE TOUCHED.

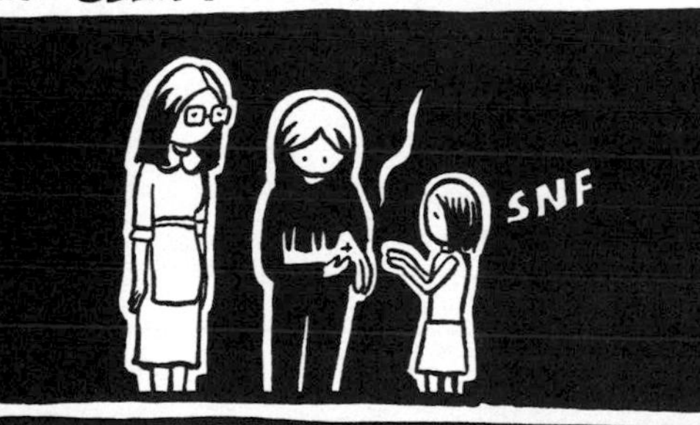
WE HADN'T REALIZED THAT SHE HAD BEEN FULL OF TUMORS.
SNF

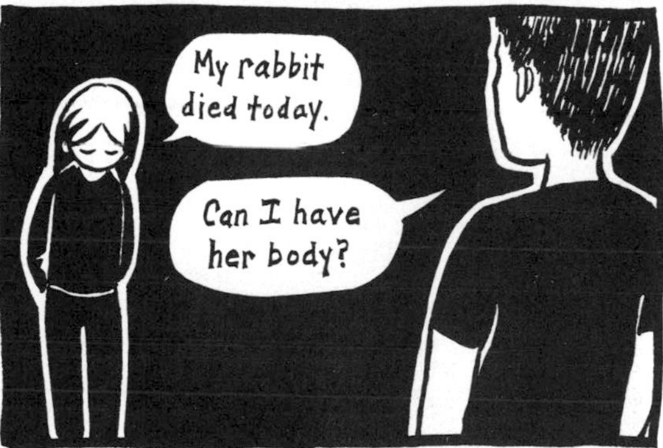
My rabbit died today.
Can I have her body?

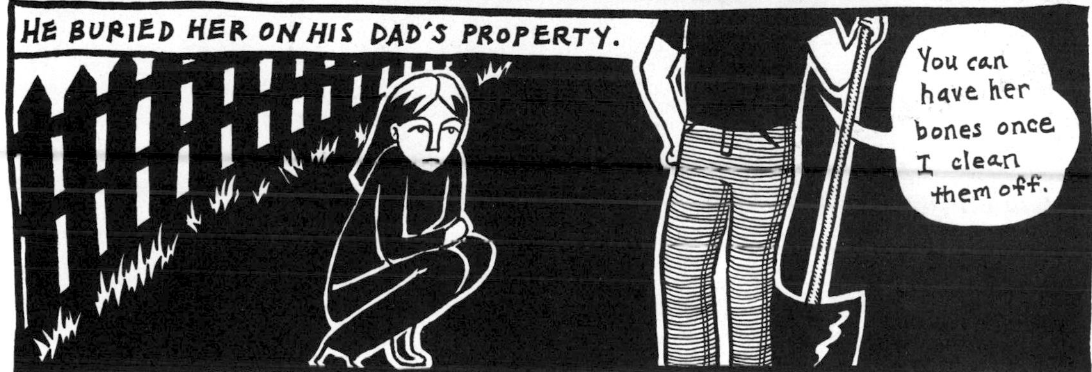
HE BURIED HER ON HIS DAD'S PROPERTY.
You can have her bones once I clean them off.

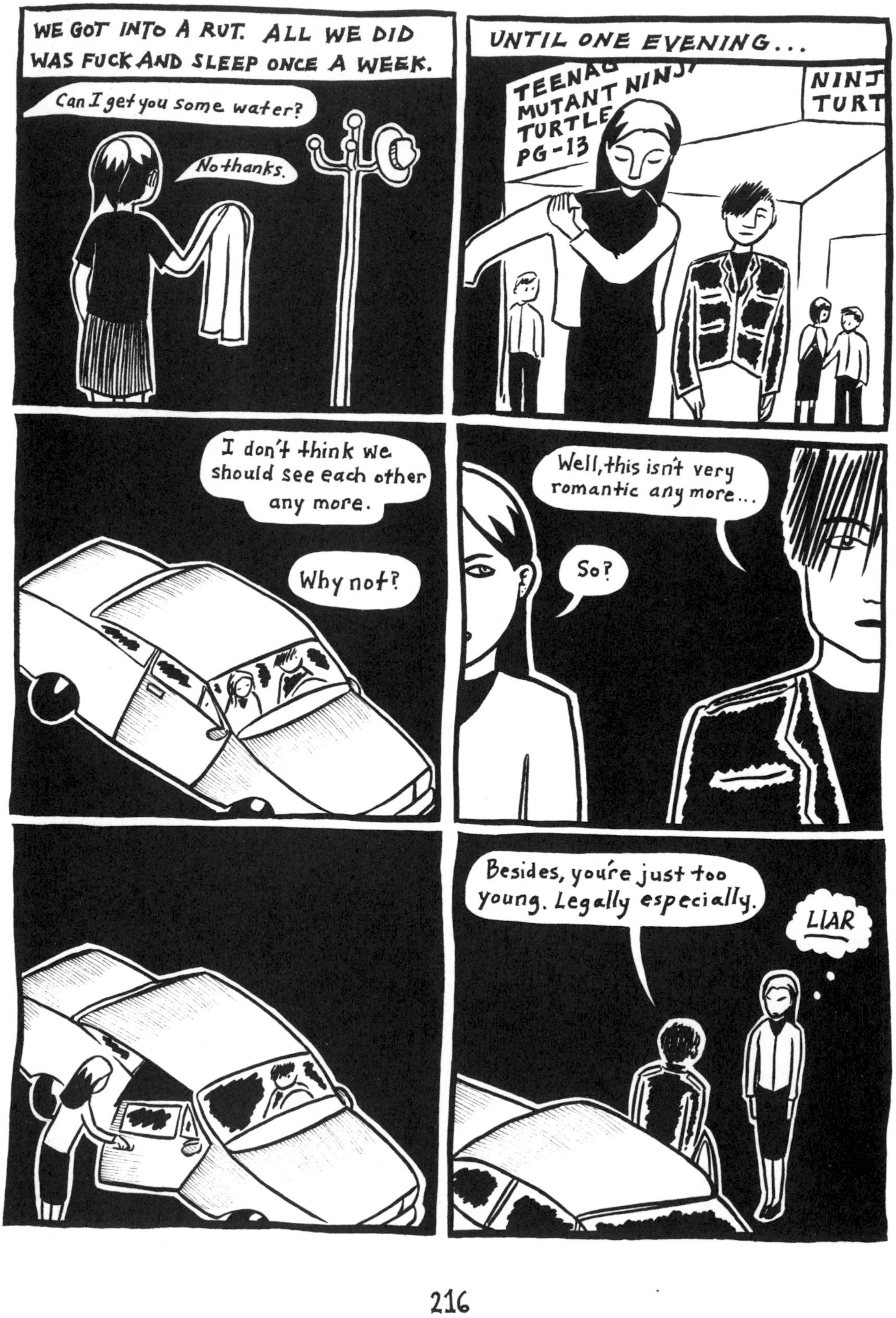

WE GOT INTO A RUT. ALL WE DID WAS FUCK AND SLEEP ONCE A WEEK.

Can I get you some water?

No thanks.

UNTIL ONE EVENING...

TEENAG MUTANT NINJ TURTLE PG-13

NINJ TURT

I don't think we should see each other any more.

Why not?

Well, this isn't very romantic any more...

So?

Besides, you're just too young. Legally especially.

LIAR

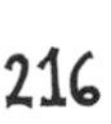

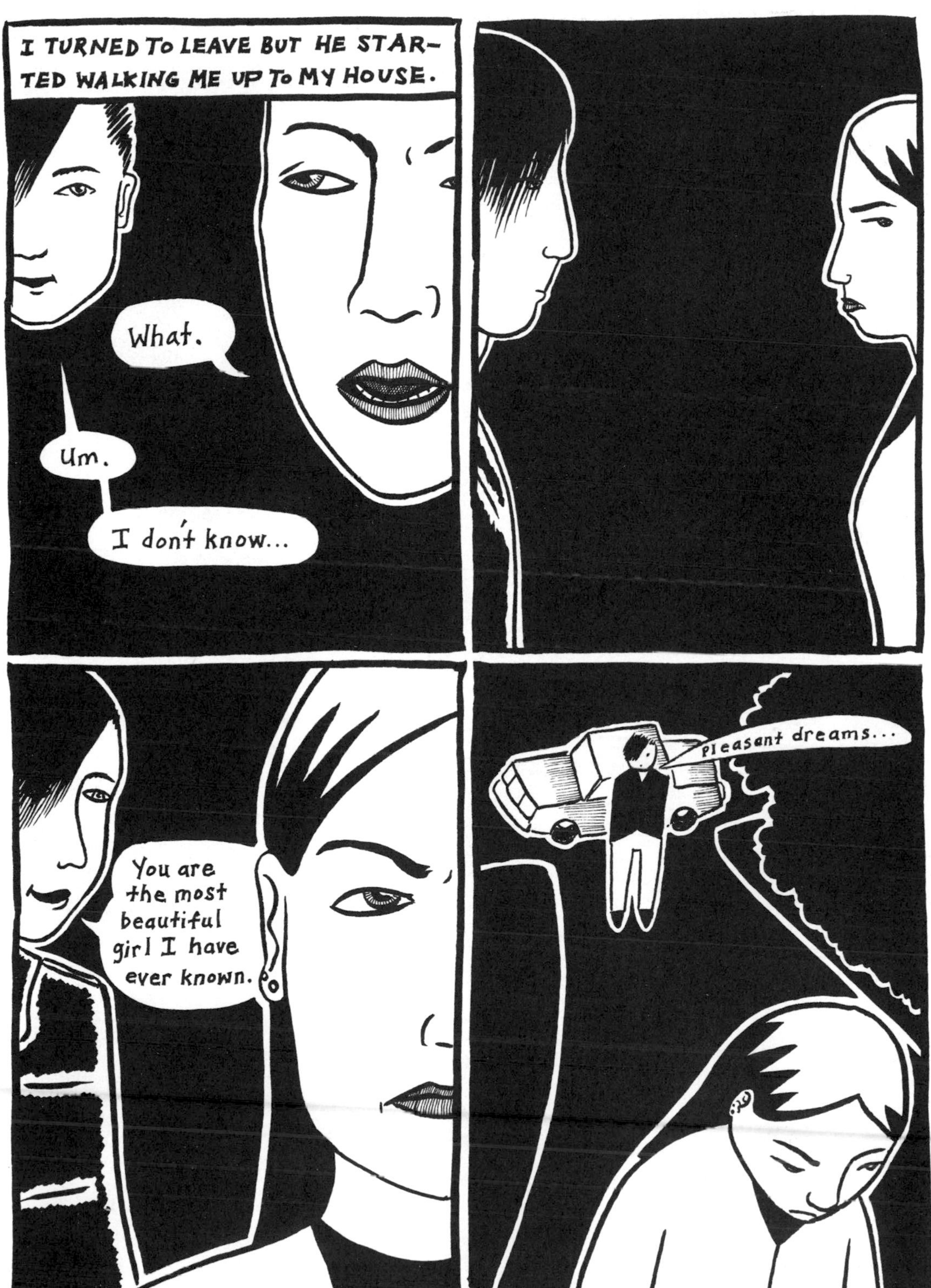
I TURNED TO LEAVE BUT HE STARTED WALKING ME UP TO MY HOUSE.
What.
Um.
I don't know...
You are the most beautiful girl I have ever known.
Pleasant dreams...

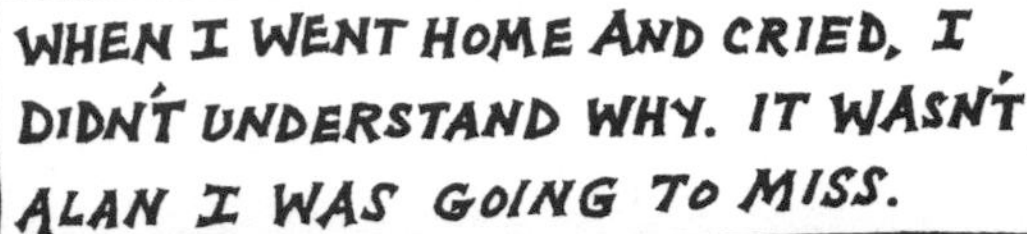
WHEN I WENT HOME AND CRIED, I DIDN'T UNDERSTAND WHY. IT WASN'T ALAN I WAS GOING TO MISS.

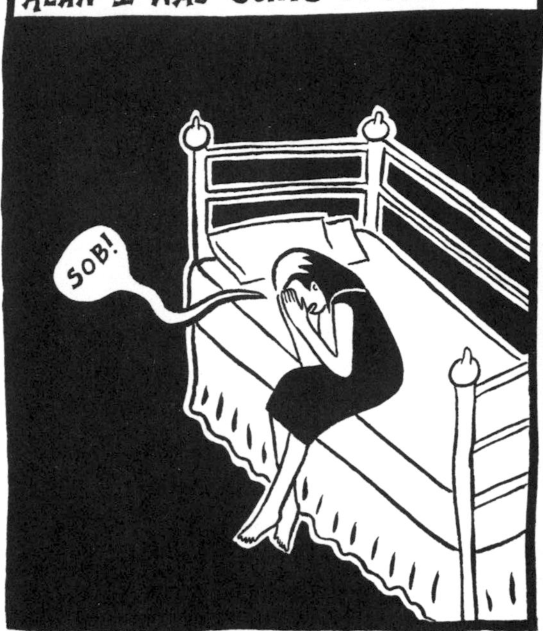
SOB!

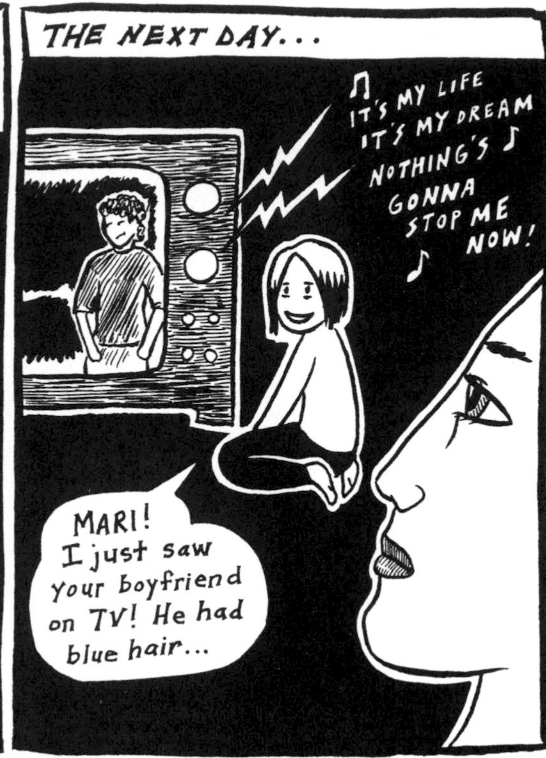
THE NEXT DAY...
♫ IT'S MY LIFE IT'S MY DREAM NOTHING'S ♪ GONNA STOP ME NOW! ♪
MARI! I just saw your boyfriend on TV! He had blue hair...

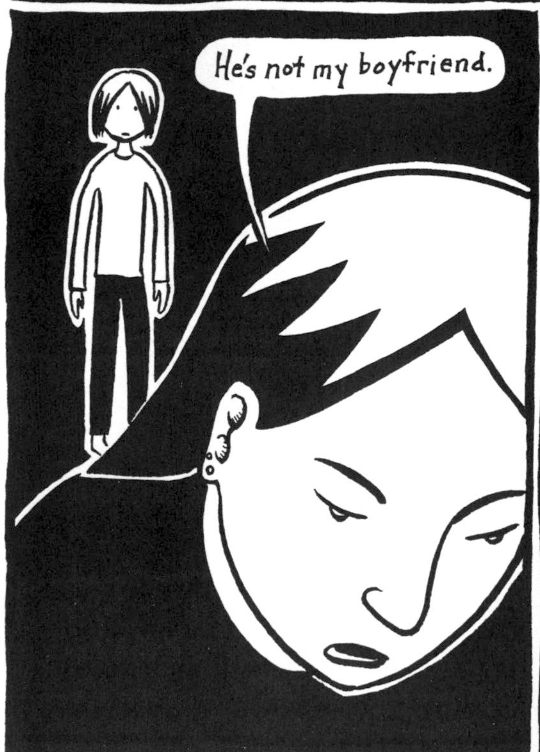
He's not my boyfriend.

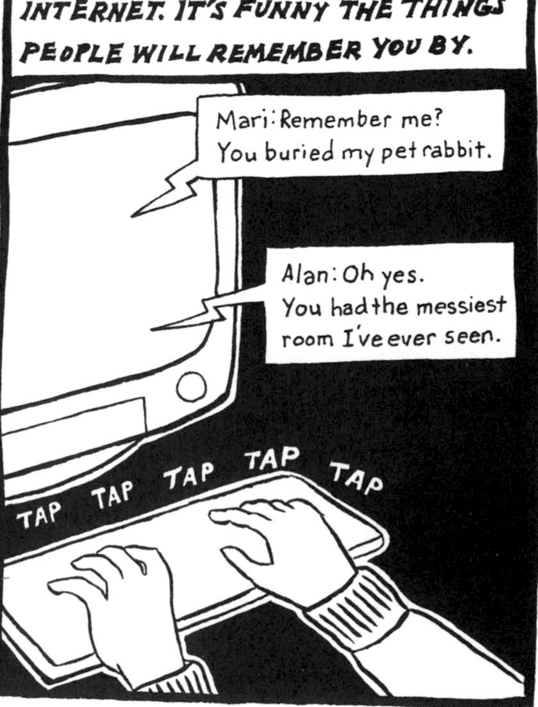
YEARS LATER, I FOUND HIM ON THE INTERNET. IT'S FUNNY THE THINGS PEOPLE WILL REMEMBER YOU BY.
Mari: Remember me? You buried my pet rabbit.
Alan: Oh yes. You had the messiest room I've ever seen.
TAP TAP TAP TAP TAP

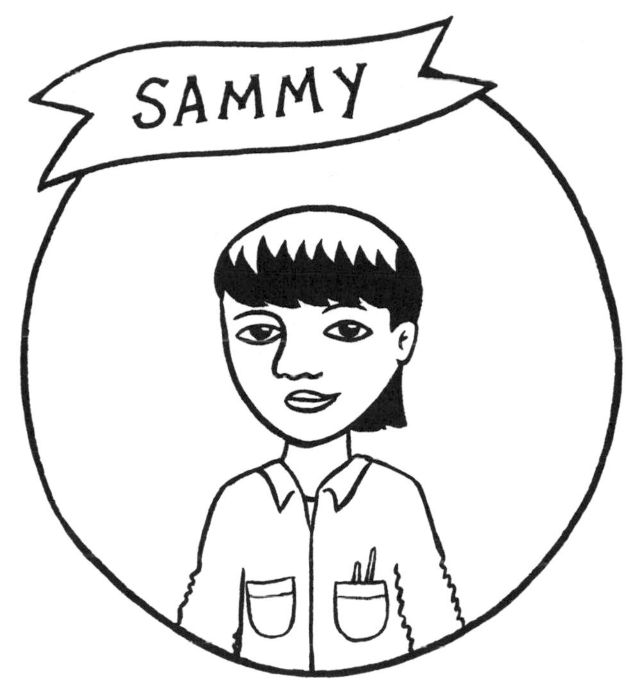
SAMMY

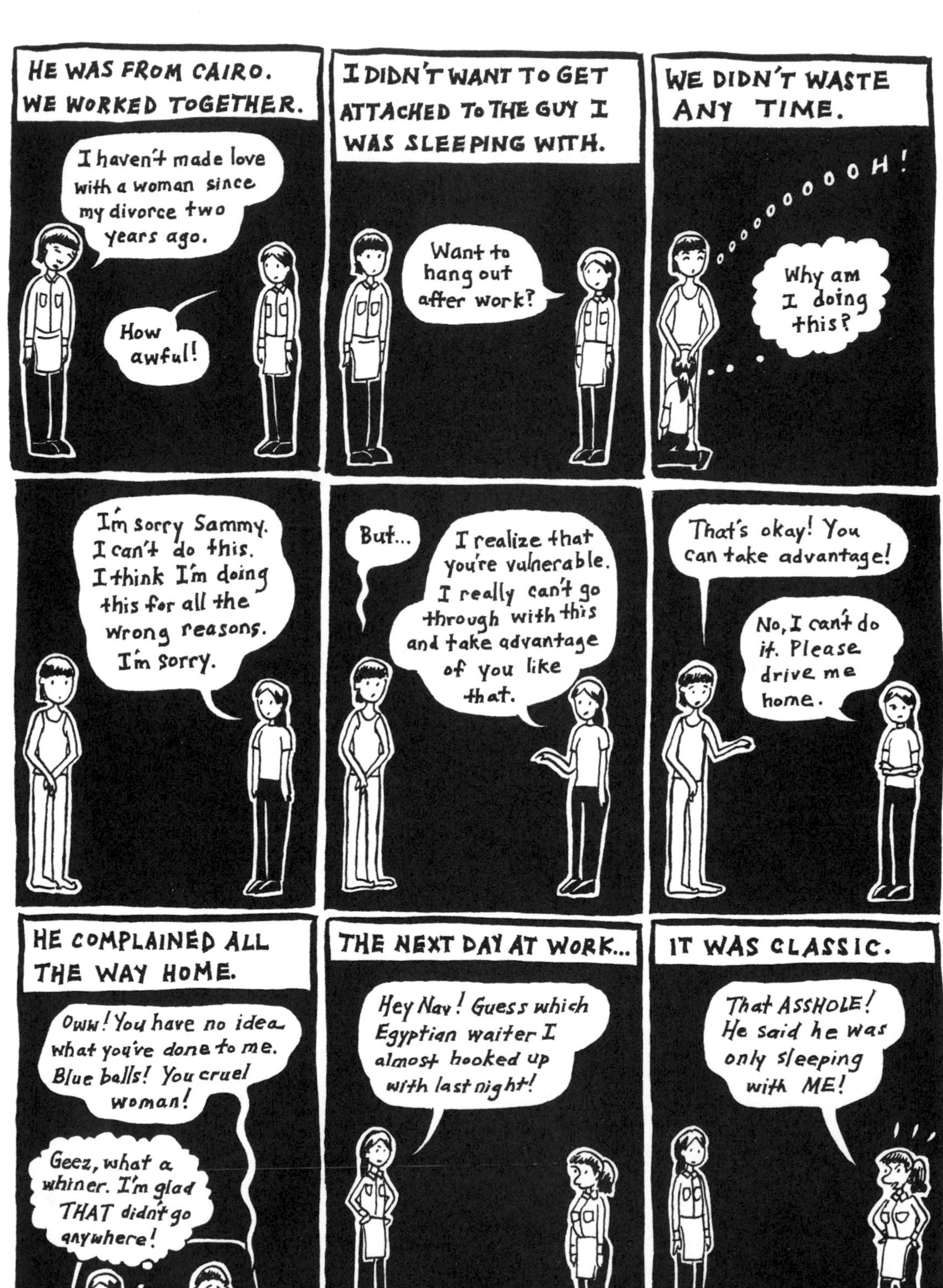
HE WAS FROM CAIRO. WE WORKED TOGETHER.
I haven't made love with a woman since my divorce two years ago.
How awful!
I DIDN'T WANT TO GET ATTACHED TO THE GUY I WAS SLEEPING WITH.
Want to hang out after work?
WE DIDN'T WASTE ANY TIME.
OOOOOOOOOOOH!
Why am I doing this?
I'm sorry Sammy. I can't do this. I think I'm doing this for all the wrong reasons. I'm sorry.
But...
I realize that you're vulnerable. I really can't go through with this and take advantage of you like that.
That's okay! You can take advantage!
No, I can't do it. Please drive me home.
HE COMPLAINED ALL THE WAY HOME.
Oww! You have no idea what you've done to me. Blue balls! You cruel woman!
Geez, what a whiner. I'm glad THAT didn't go anywhere!
THE NEXT DAY AT WORK...
Hey Nav! Guess which Egyptian waiter I almost hooked up with last night!
IT WAS CLASSIC.
That ASSHOLE! He said he was only sleeping with ME!

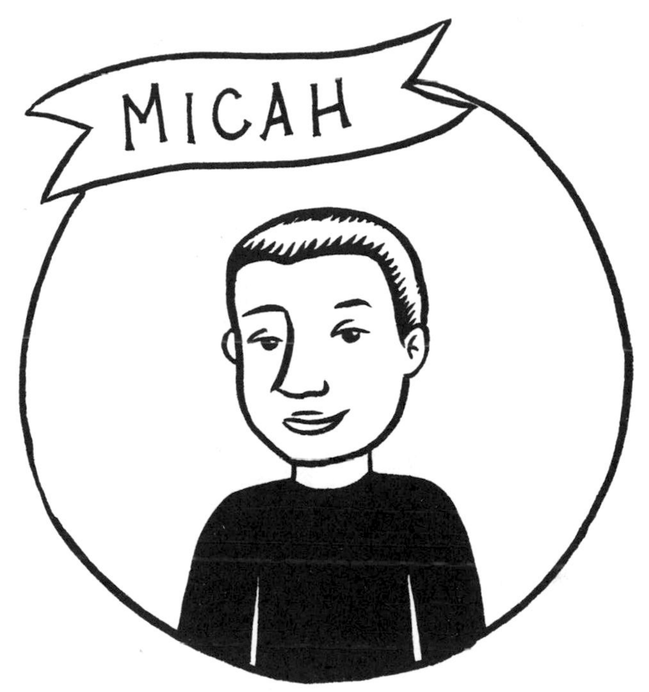
MICAH

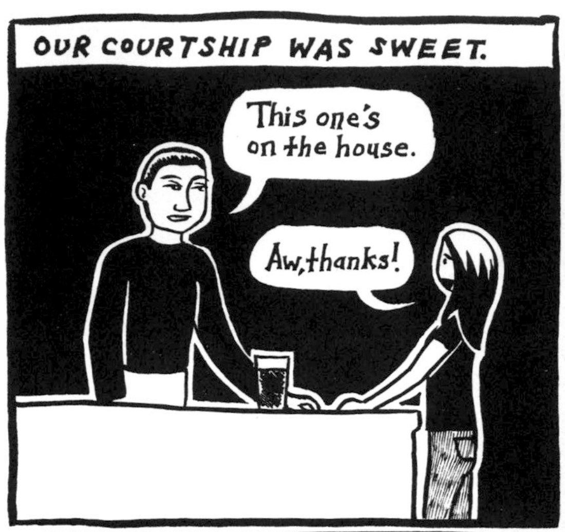
OUR COURTSHIP WAS SWEET.
This one's on the house.
Aw, thanks!

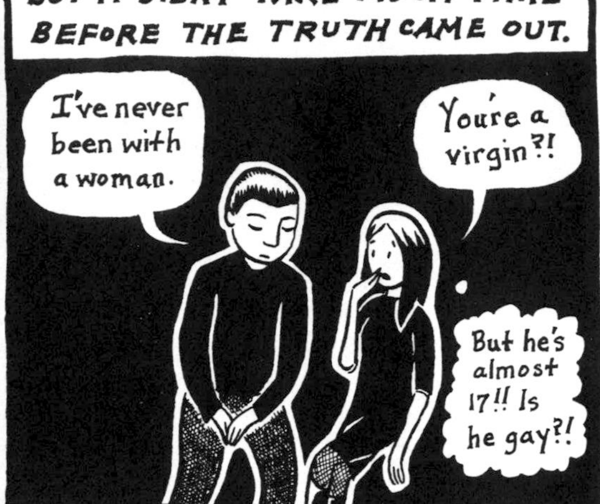
BUT IT DIDN'T TAKE MUCH TIME BEFORE THE TRUTH CAME OUT.
I've never been with a woman.
You're a virgin?!
But he's almost 17!! Is he gay?!

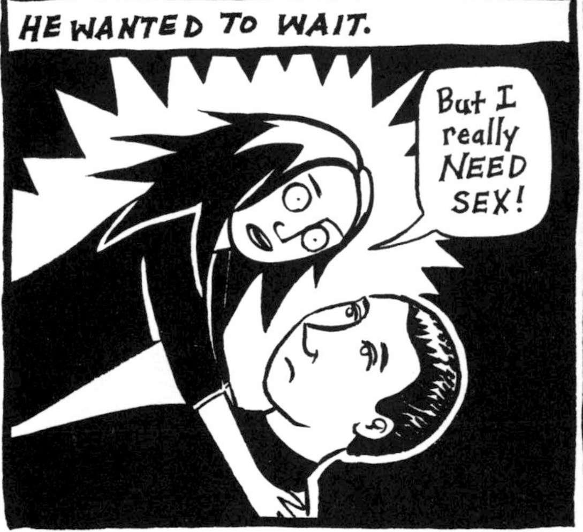
HE WANTED TO WAIT.
But I really NEED SEX!

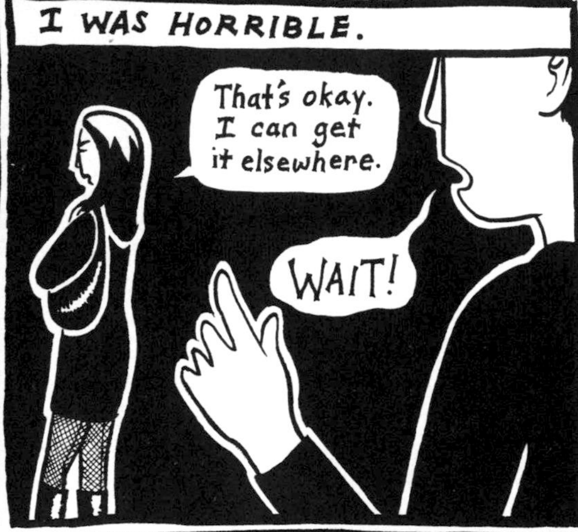
I WAS HORRIBLE.
That's okay. I can get it elsewhere.
WAIT!

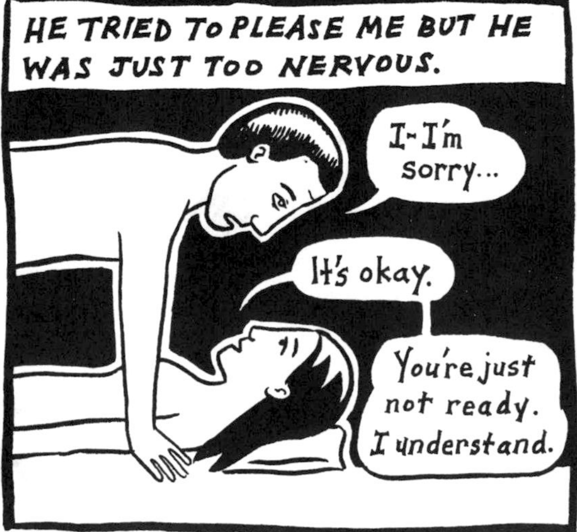
HE TRIED TO PLEASE ME BUT HE WAS JUST TOO NERVOUS.
I-I'm sorry...
It's okay.
You're just not ready. I understand.

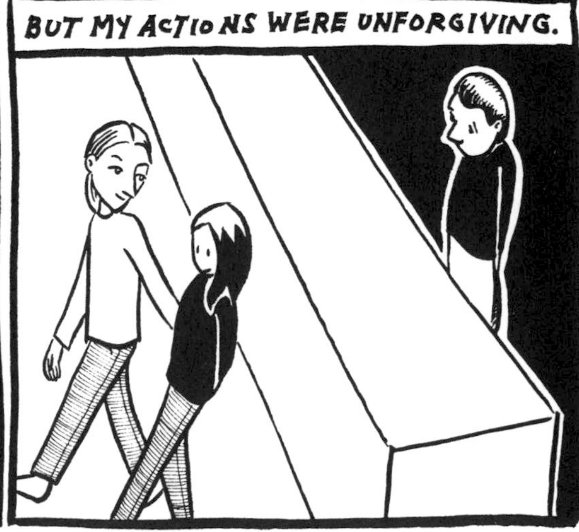
BUT MY ACTIONS WERE UNFORGIVING.

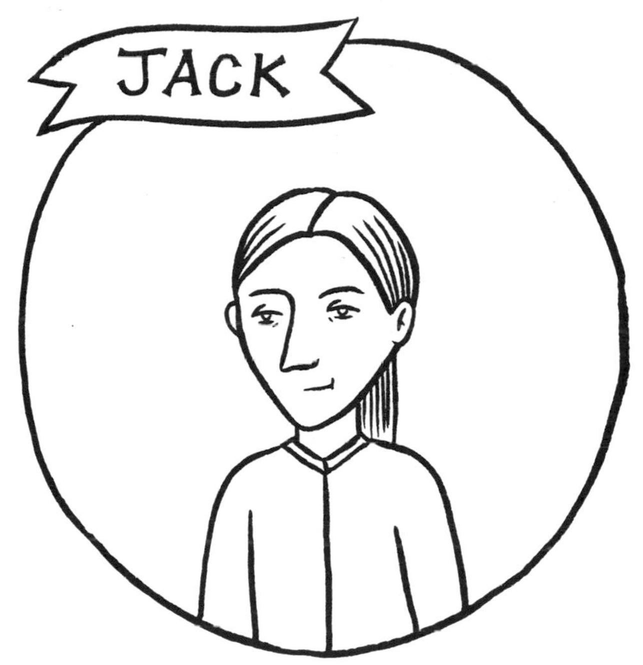
JACK

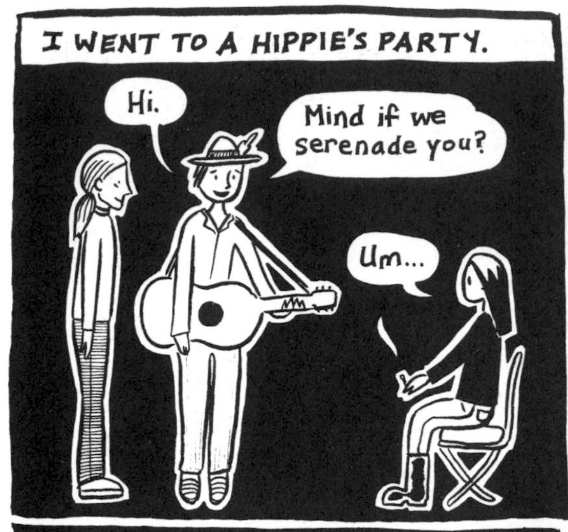
I WENT TO A HIPPIE'S PARTY.
Hi.
Mind if we serenade you?
Um...

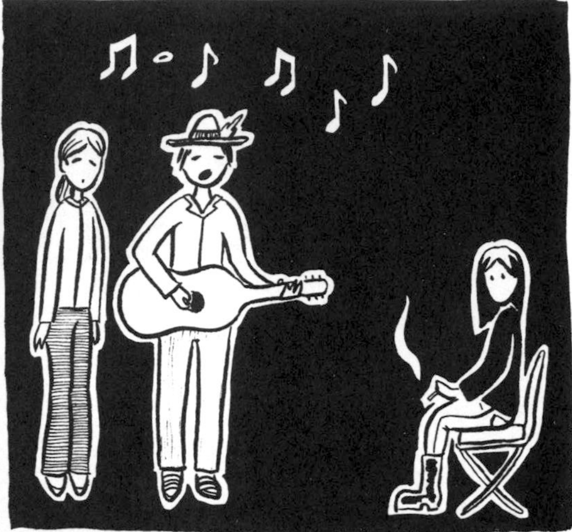

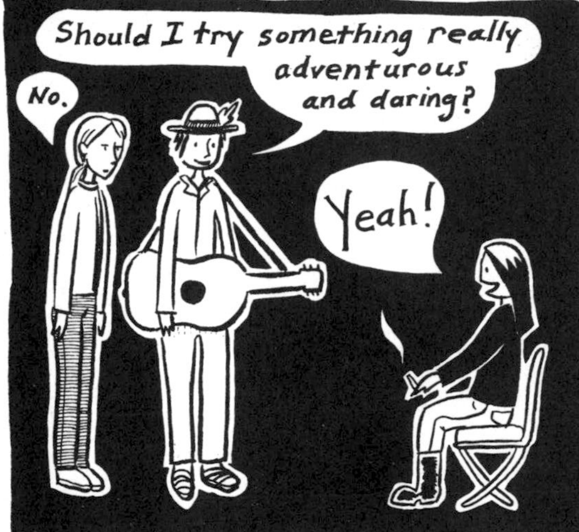
Should I try something really adventurous and daring?
No.
Yeah!

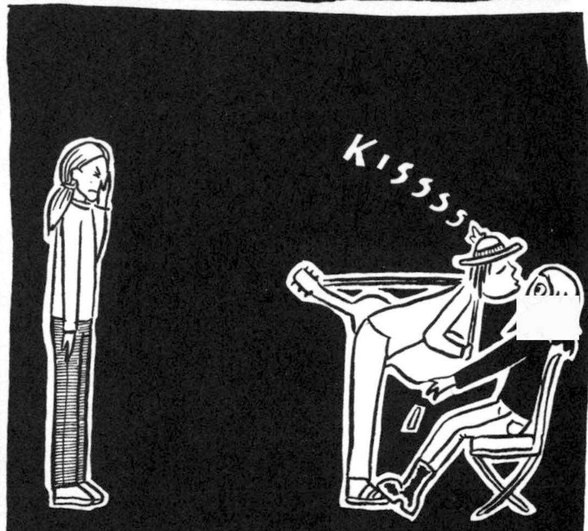
KISSSSS

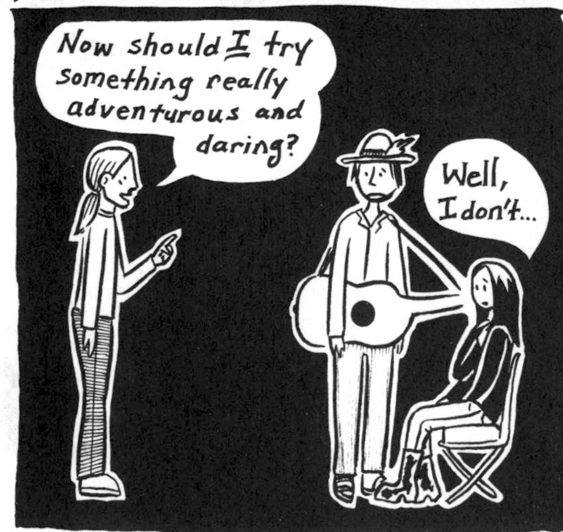
Now should I try something really adventurous and daring?
Well, I don't...

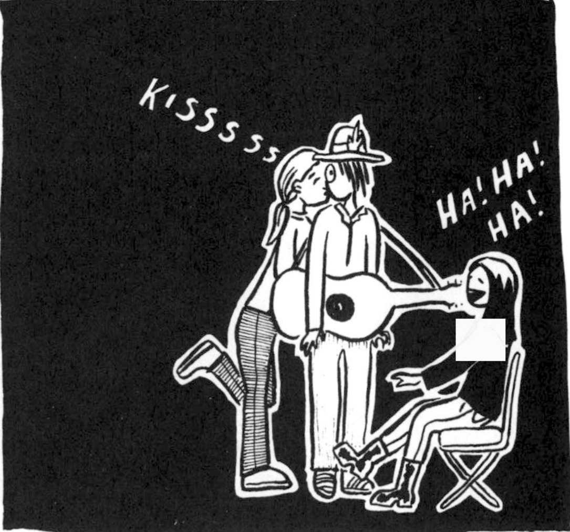
KISSSSSS
HA! HA! HA!

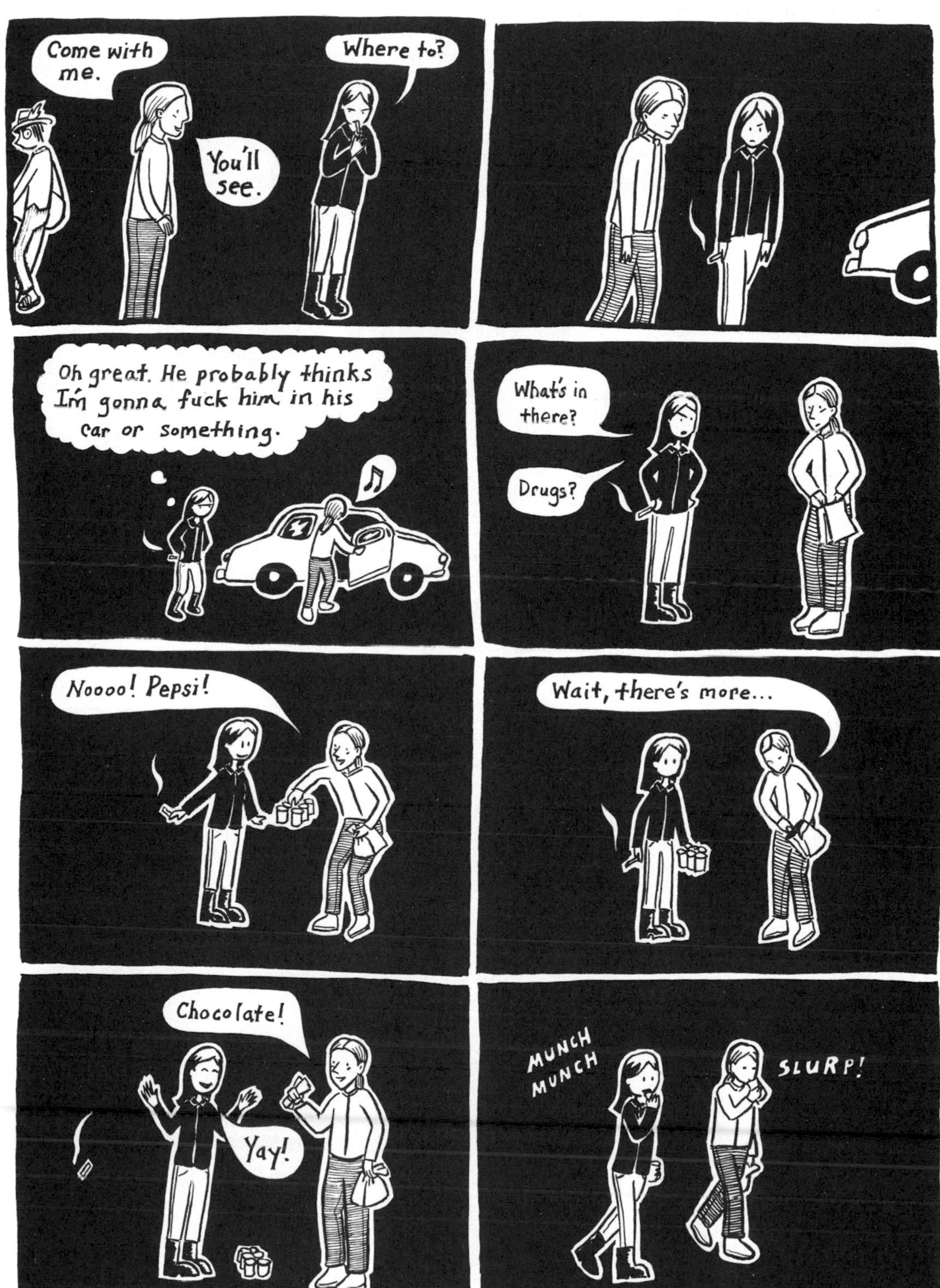
Come with me.
Where to?
You'll see.
Oh great. He probably thinks I'm gonna fuck him in his car or something.
What's in there?
Drugs?
Noooo! Pepsi!
Wait, there's more...
Chocolate!
Yay!
MUNCH MUNCH
SLURP!

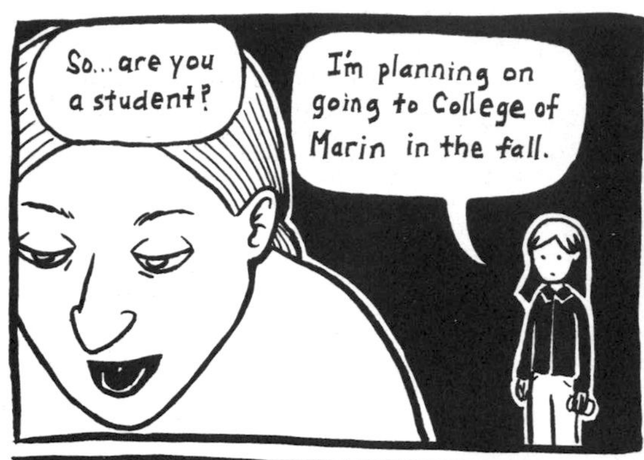
So... are you a student?
I'm planning on going to College of Marin in the fall.

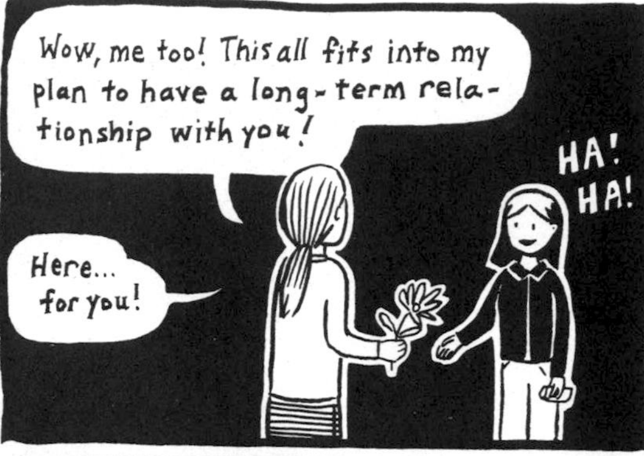
Wow, me too! This all fits into my plan to have a long-term relationship with you!
HA! HA!
Here... for you!

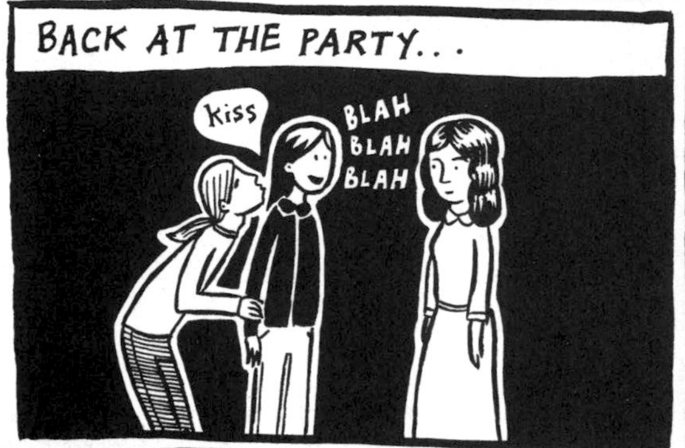
BACK AT THE PARTY...
Kiss
BLAH
BLAH
BLAH

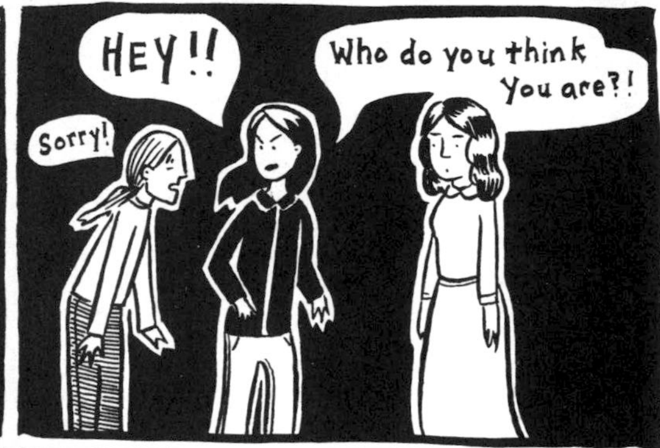
HEY!!
Who do you think You are?!
Sorry!

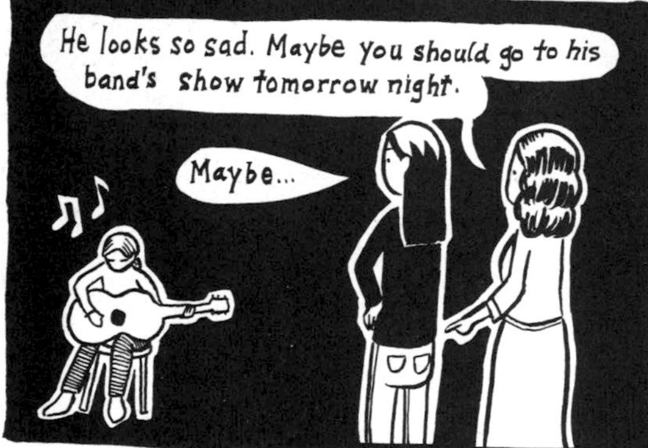
He looks so sad. Maybe you should go to his band's show tomorrow night.
Maybe...

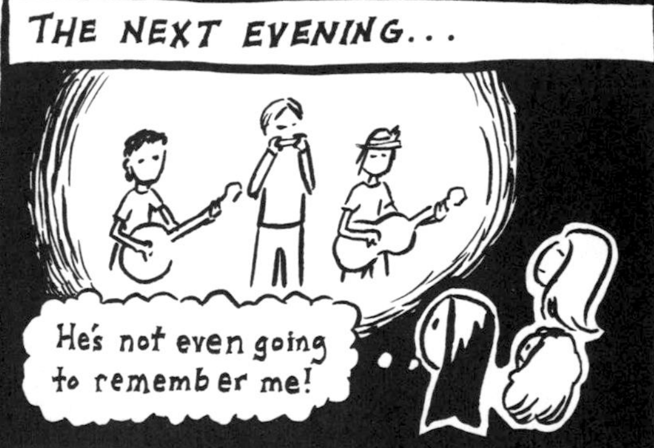
THE NEXT EVENING...
He's not even going to remember me!

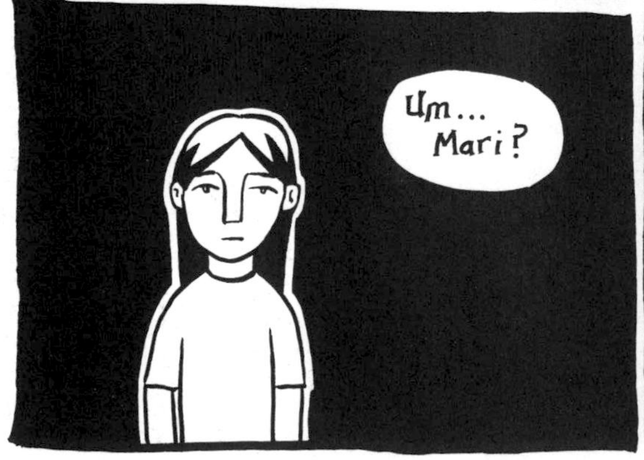
Um... Mari?

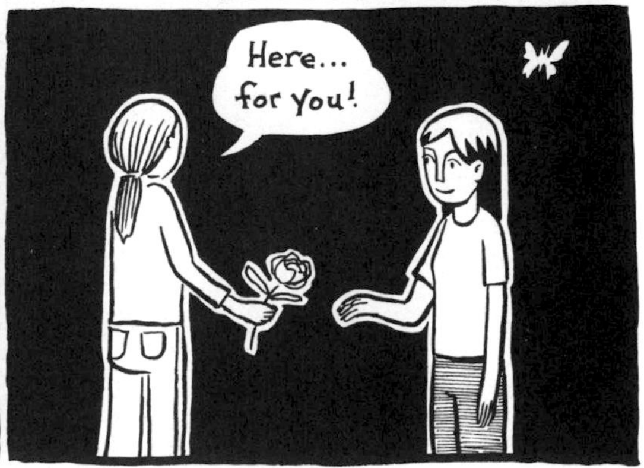
Here... for you!

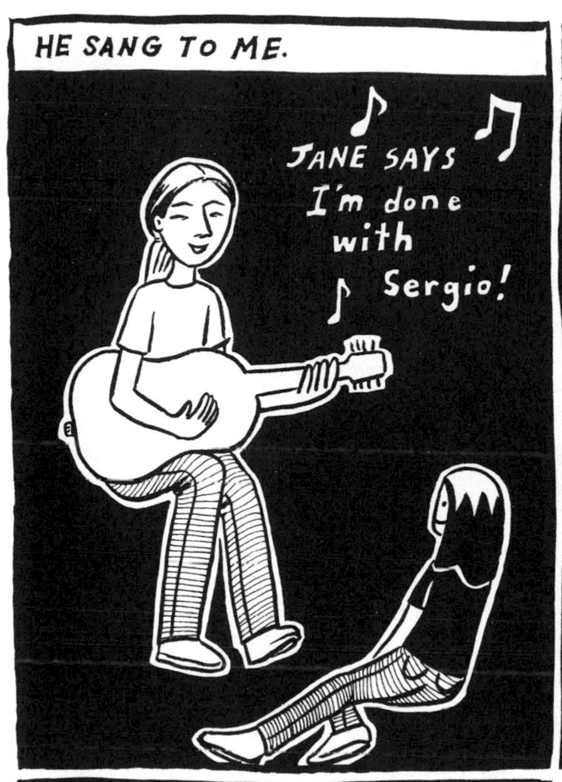
HE SANG TO ME.
JANE SAYS I'm done with Sergio!

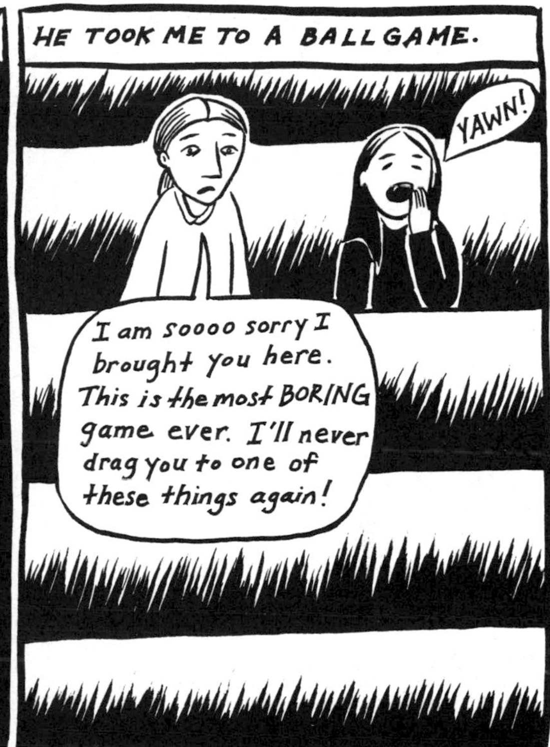
HE TOOK ME TO A BALLGAME.
YAWN!
I am soooo sorry I brought you here. This is the most BORING game ever. I'll never drag you to one of these things again!

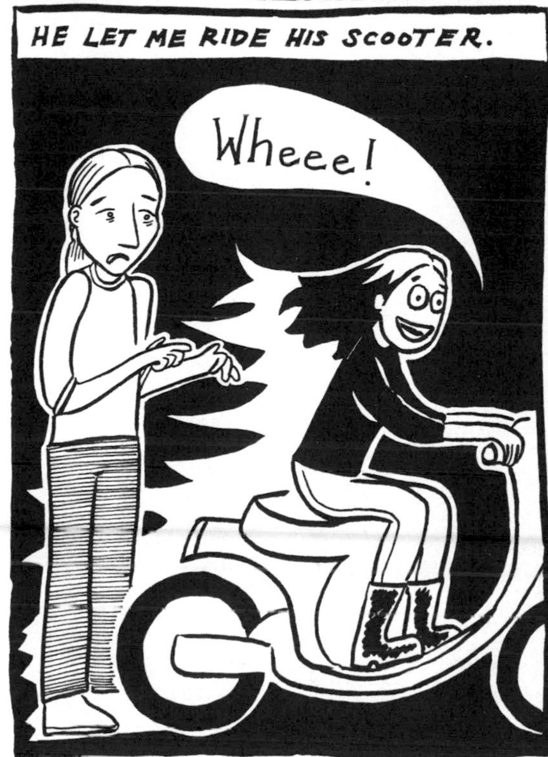
HE LET ME RIDE HIS SCOOTER.
Wheee!

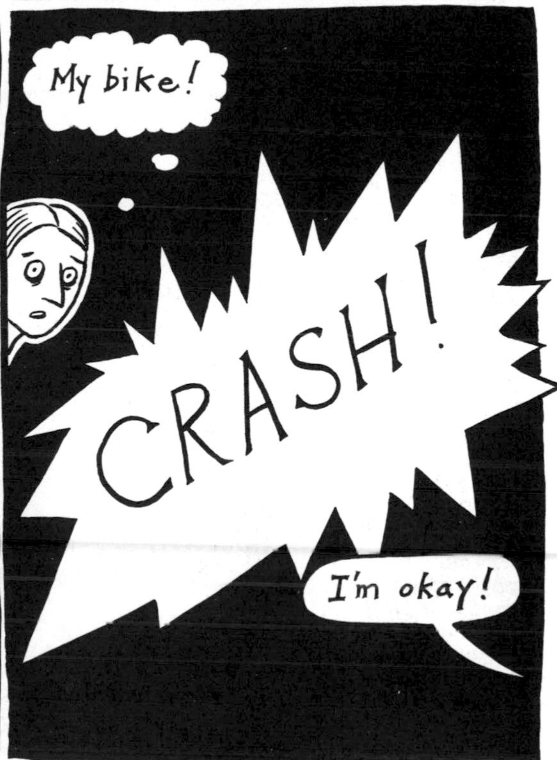
My bike!
CRASH!
I'm okay!

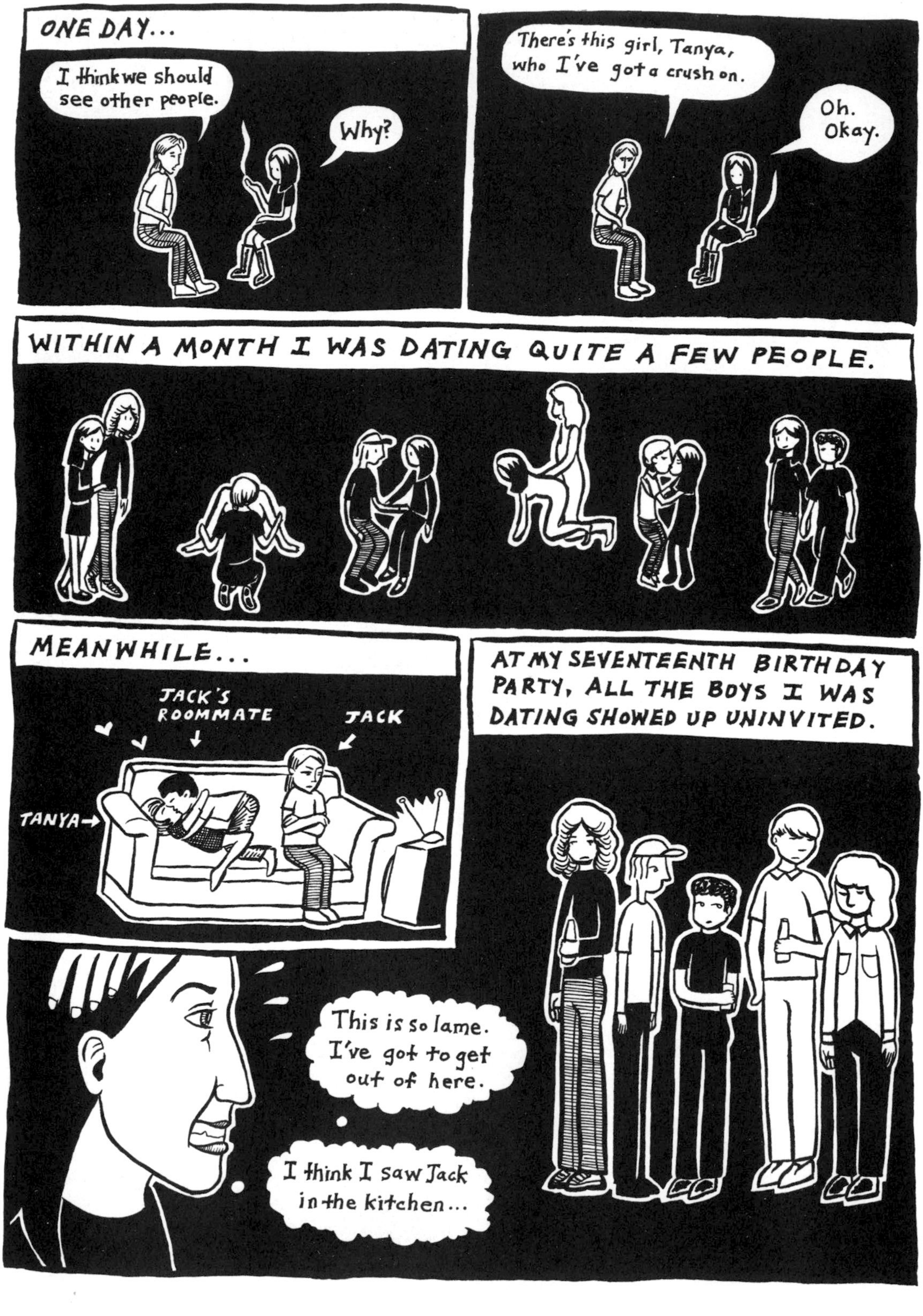

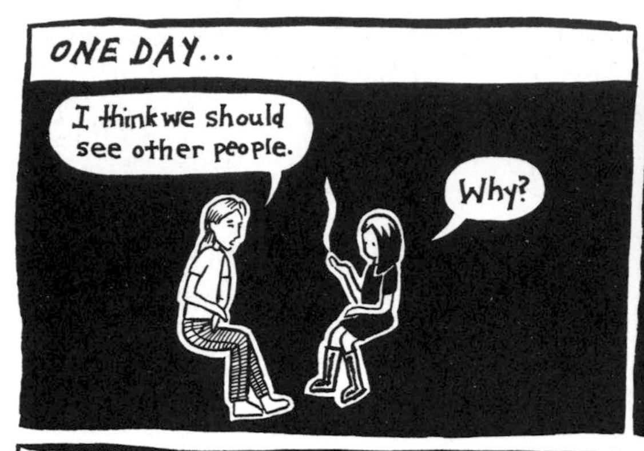

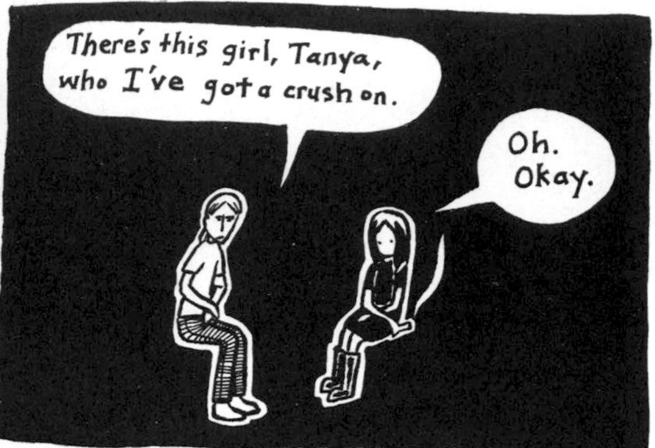

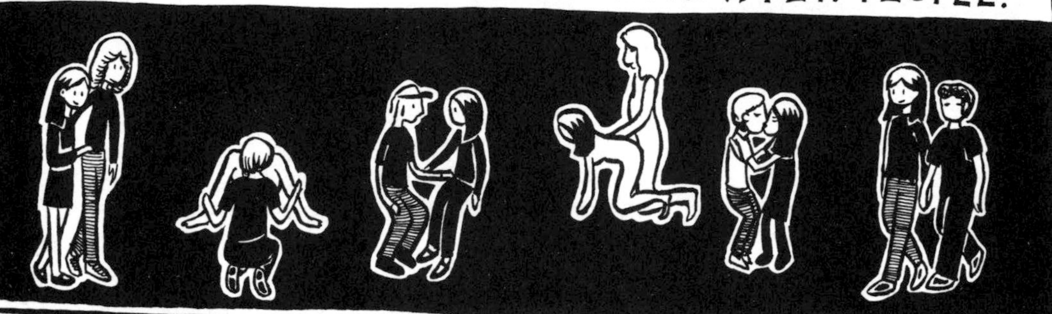

MEANWHILE...

JACK'S ROOMMATE

JACK

TANYA

AT MY SEVENTEENTH BIRTHDAY PARTY, ALL THE BOYS I WAS DATING SHOWED UP UNINVITED.

This is so lame. I've got to get out of here.

I think I saw Jack in the kitchen...

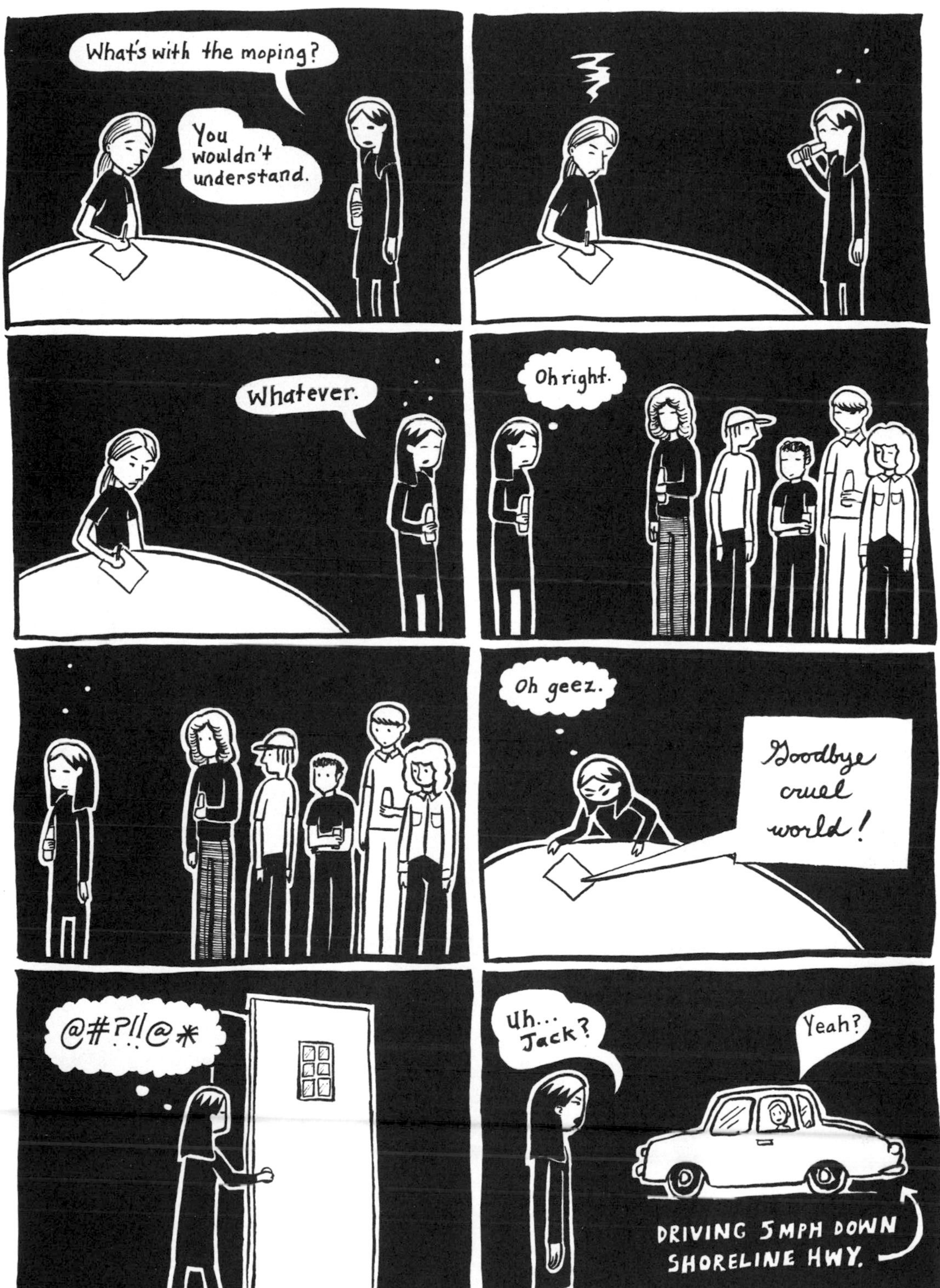
What's with the moping?
You wouldn't understand.
Whatever.
Oh right.
Oh geez.
Goodbye cruel world!
@#?!!@*
Uh... Jack?
Yeah?
DRIVING 5MPH DOWN SHORELINE HWY.

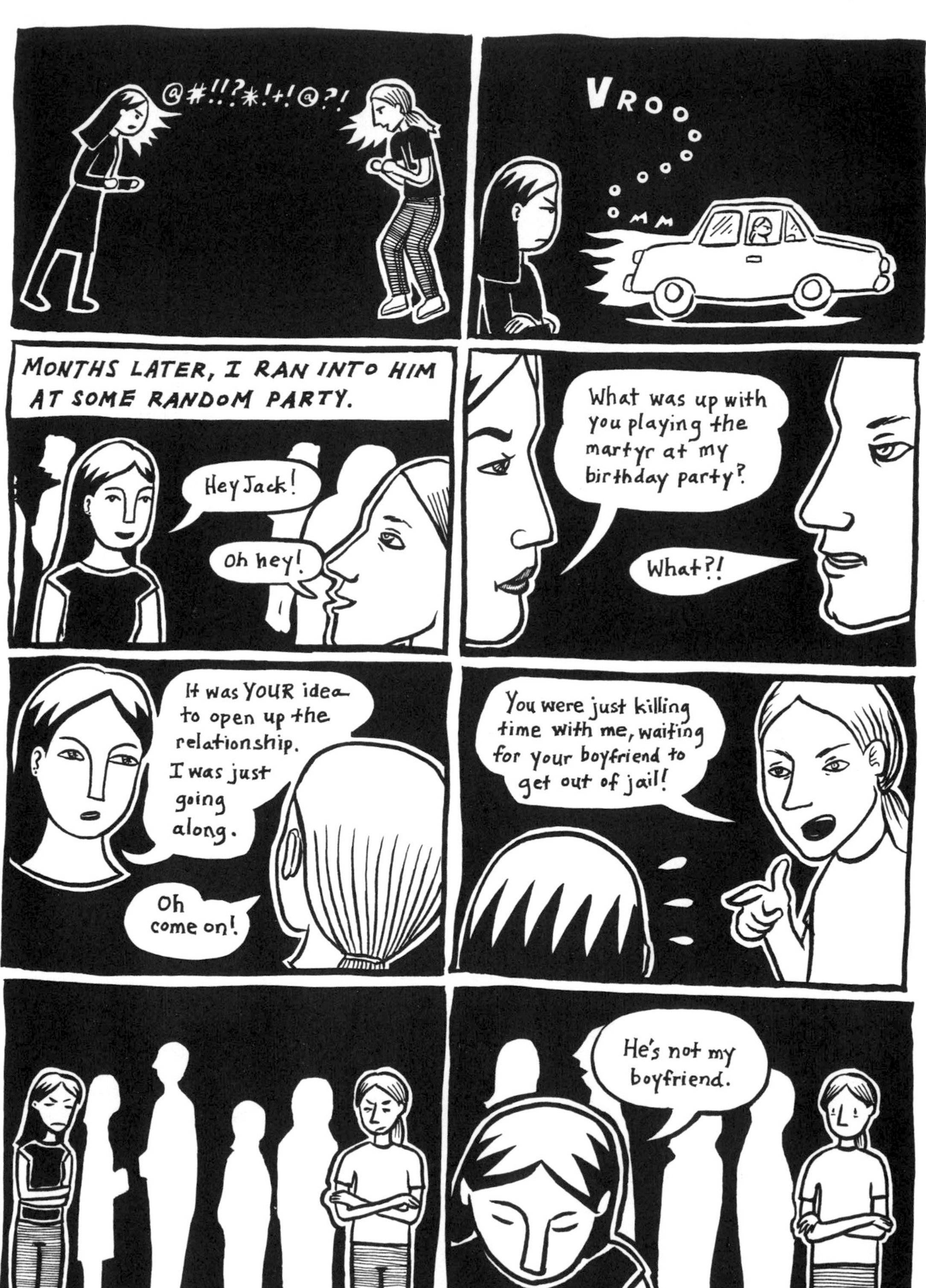
@#!!?*!+!@?!
VROOOOOOOOOMM
MONTHS LATER, I RAN INTO HIM AT SOME RANDOM PARTY.
Hey Jack!
Oh hey!
What was up with you playing the martyr at my birthday party?
What?!
It was YOUR idea to open up the relationship. I was just going along.
Oh come on!
You were just killing time with me, waiting for your boyfriend to get out of jail!
He's not my boyfriend.

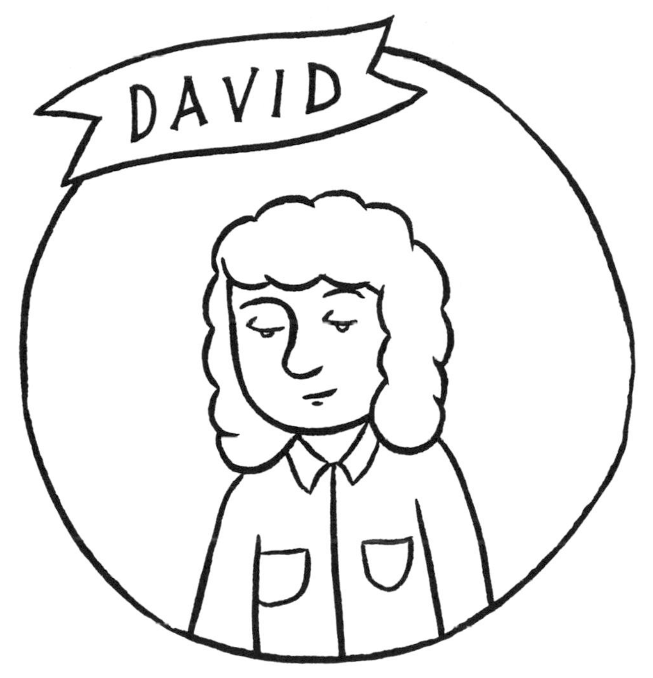
DAVID

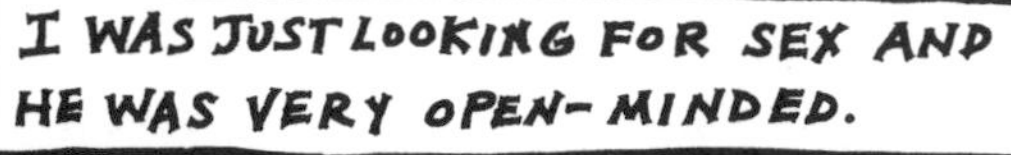
I WAS JUST LOOKING FOR SEX AND HE WAS VERY OPEN-MINDED.

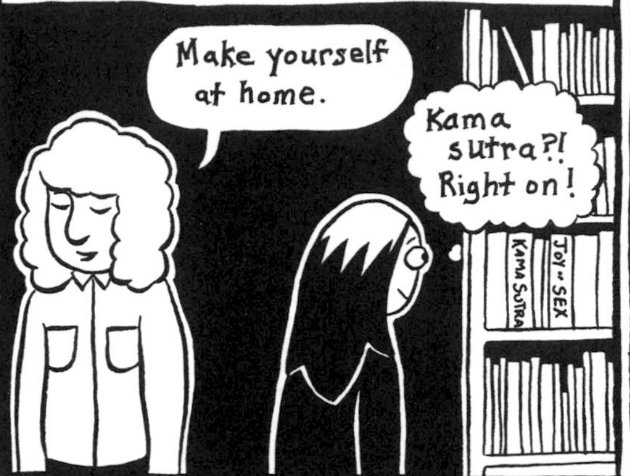
Make yourself at home.
Kama sutra?! Right on!
JOY of SEX
KAMA SUTRA

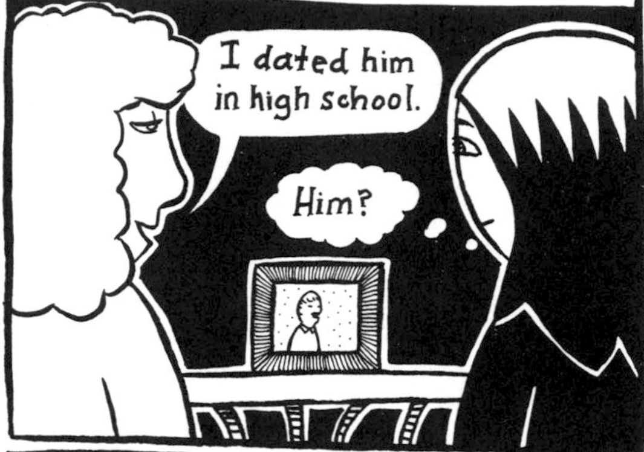
WE DIDN'T TALK MUCH, BUT WHEN WE DID, HE SOMETIMES ALLUDED TO A MYSTERIOUS PAST.
I dated him in high school.
Him?

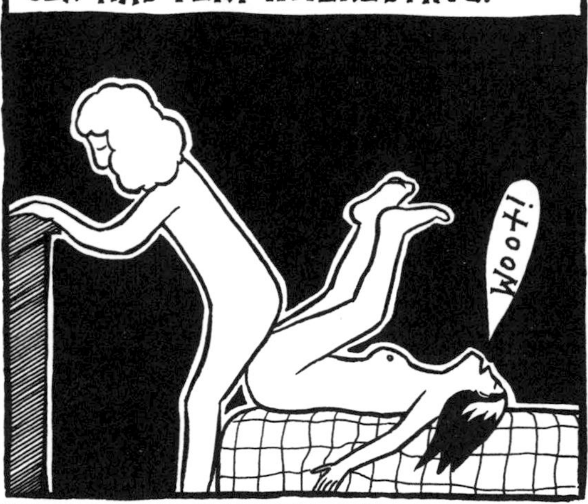
SEX WAS VERY INTERESTING.
Woo!

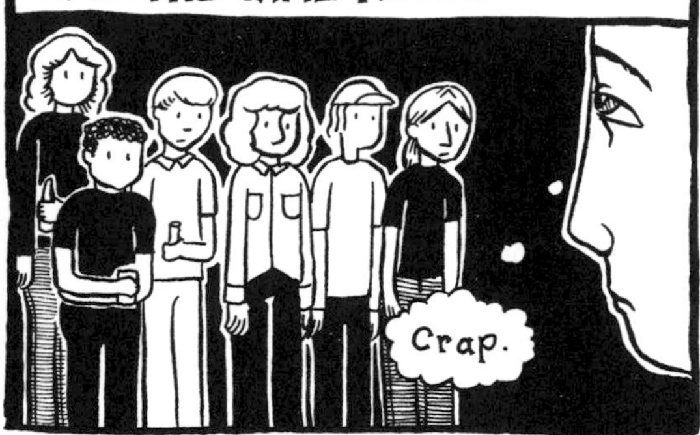
ONE NIGHT I WAS UNEXPECTEDLY THROWN INTO A SITUATION WHERE ALL OF THE MEN I WAS SEEING ENDED UP IN THE SAME ROOM.
Crap.

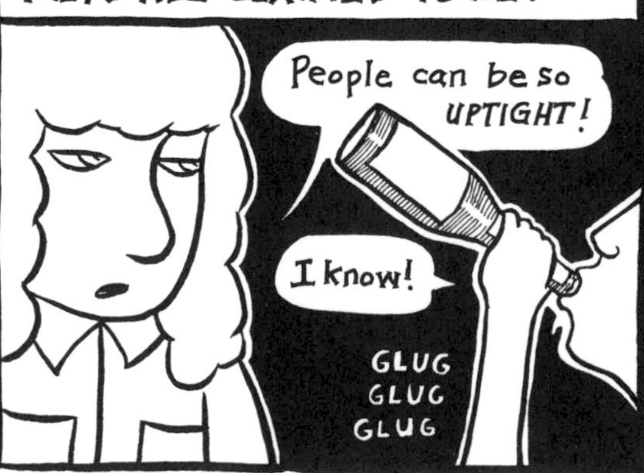
HE WAS THE ONLY ONE WHO WAS COOL WITH IT, EVEN THOUGH THEY'D ALL CLAIMED TO BE.
People can be so UPTIGHT!
I know!
GLUG
GLUG
GLUG

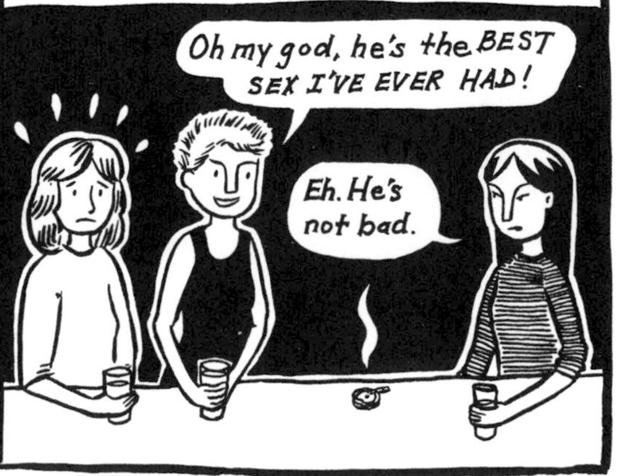
MONTHS LATER, MY BEST FRIEND'S LESBIAN LOVER SLEPT WITH HIM.
Oh my god, he's the BEST SEX I'VE EVER HAD!
Eh. He's not bad.

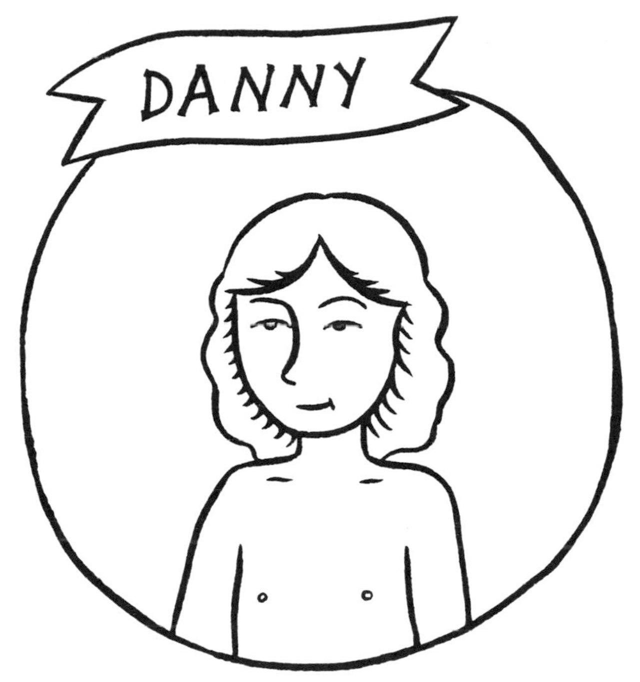
DANNY

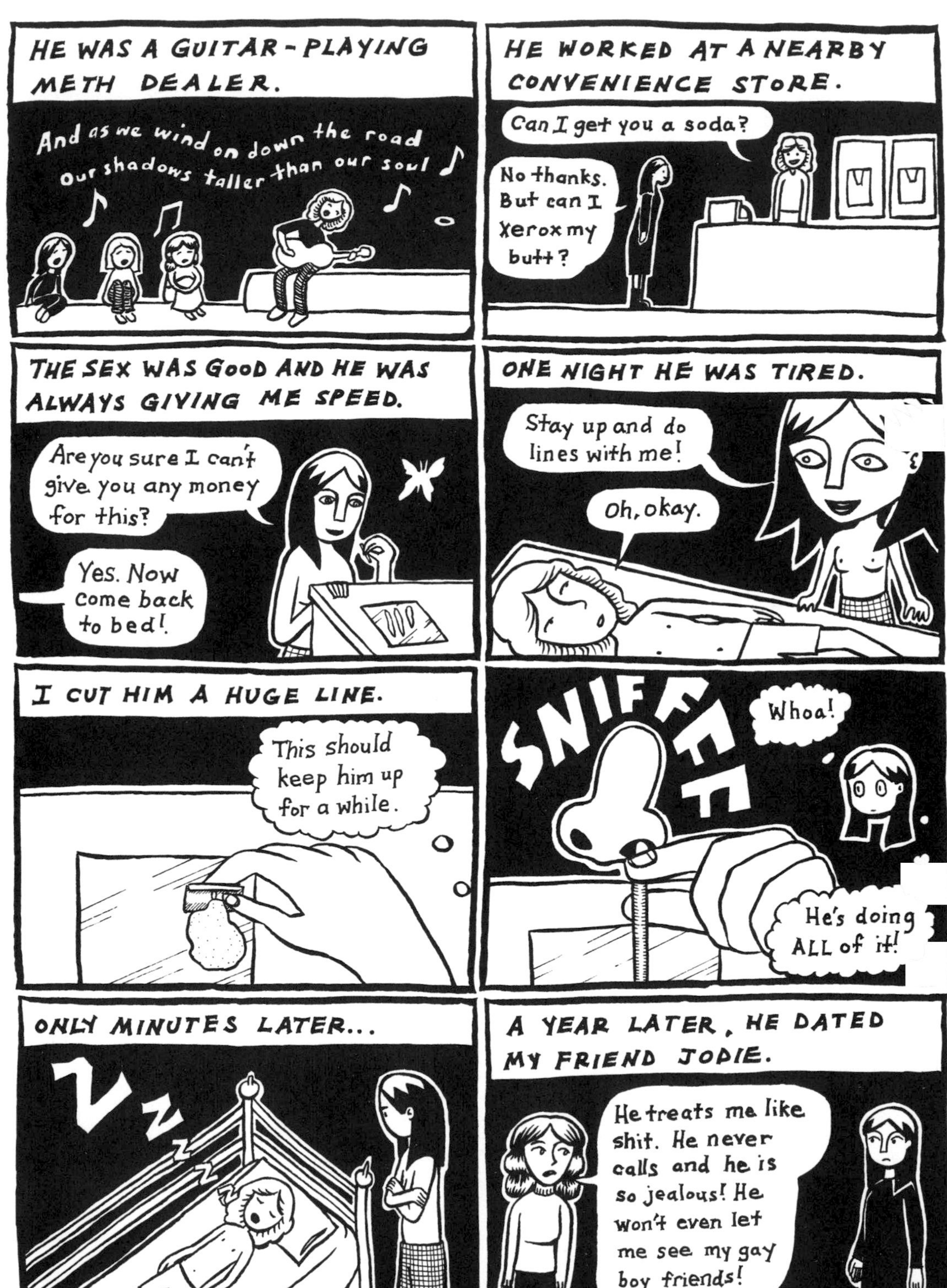
HE WAS A GUITAR-PLAYING METH DEALER.
And as we wind on down the road our shadows taller than our soul
HE WORKED AT A NEARBY CONVENIENCE STORE.
Can I get you a soda?
No thanks. But can I Xerox my butt?
THE SEX WAS GOOD AND HE WAS ALWAYS GIVING ME SPEED.
Are you sure I can't give you any money for this?
Yes. Now come back to bed!
ONE NIGHT HE WAS TIRED.
Stay up and do lines with me!
Oh, okay.
I CUT HIM A HUGE LINE.
This should keep him up for a while.
SNIFFFF
Whoa!
He's doing ALL of it!
ONLY MINUTES LATER...
Z Z Z Z
A YEAR LATER, HE DATED MY FRIEND JODIE.
He treats me like shit. He never calls and he is so jealous! He won't even let me see my gay boy friends!

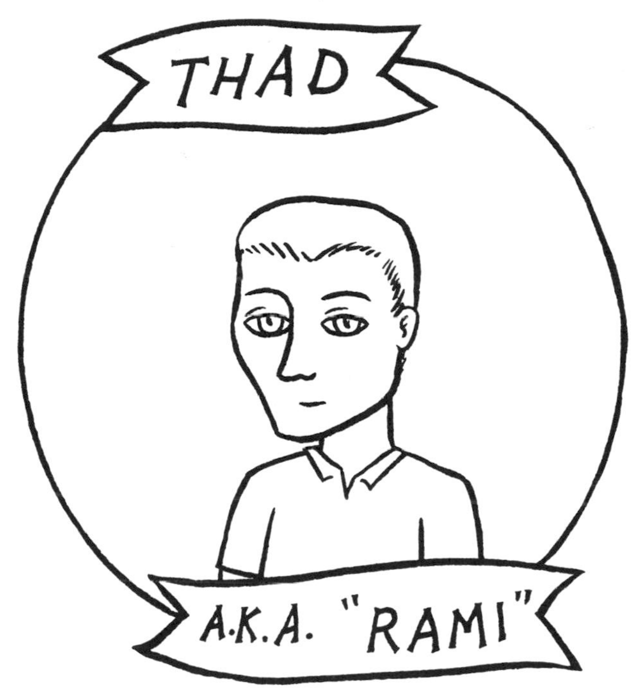
THAD
A.K.A. "RAMI"

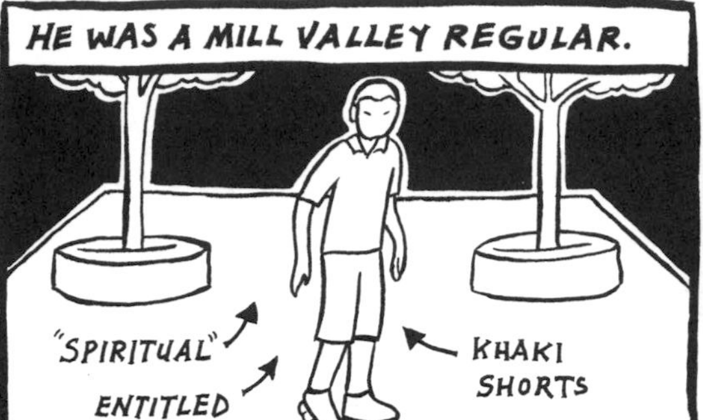
HE WAS A MILL VALLEY REGULAR.
"SPIRITUAL"
ENTITLED
KHAKI SHORTS

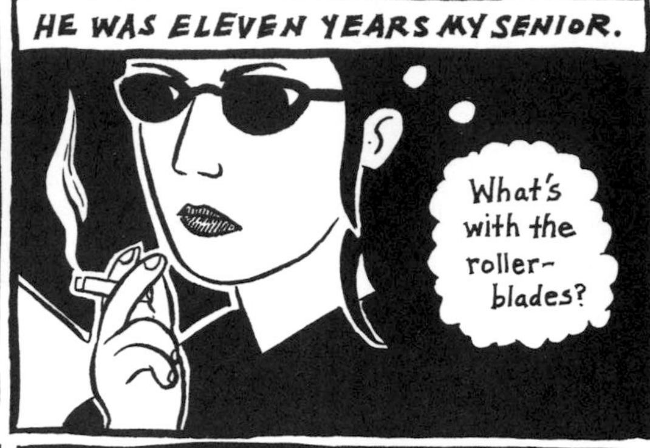
HE WAS ELEVEN YEARS MY SENIOR.
What's with the roller-blades?

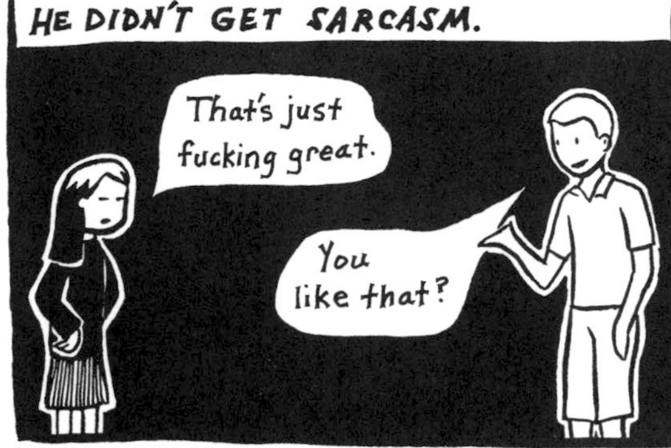
HE DIDN'T GET SARCASM.
That's just fucking great.
You like that?

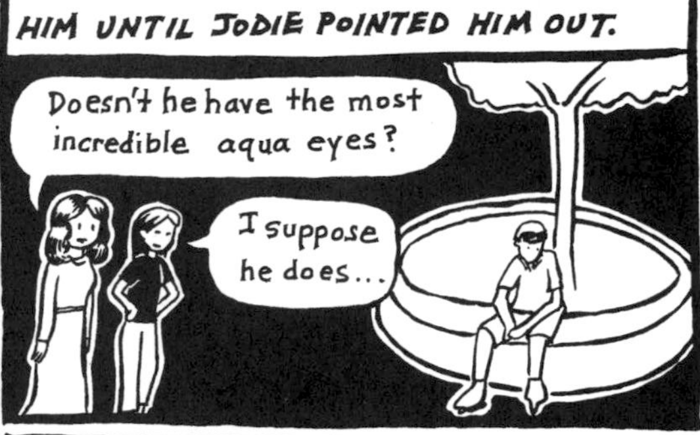
I NEVER REALLY THOUGHT ABOUT HIM UNTIL JODIE POINTED HIM OUT.
Doesn't he have the most incredible aqua eyes?
I suppose he does...

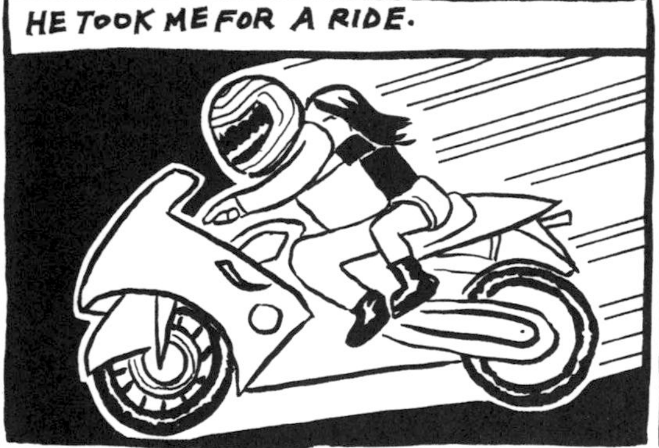
HE TOOK ME FOR A RIDE.

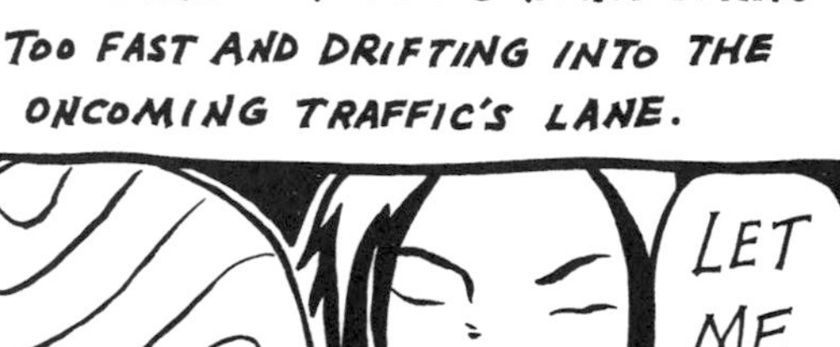
HE SHOWED OFF, TAKING BLIND TURNS TOO FAST AND DRIFTING INTO THE ONCOMING TRAFFIC'S LANE.
LET ME OFF!

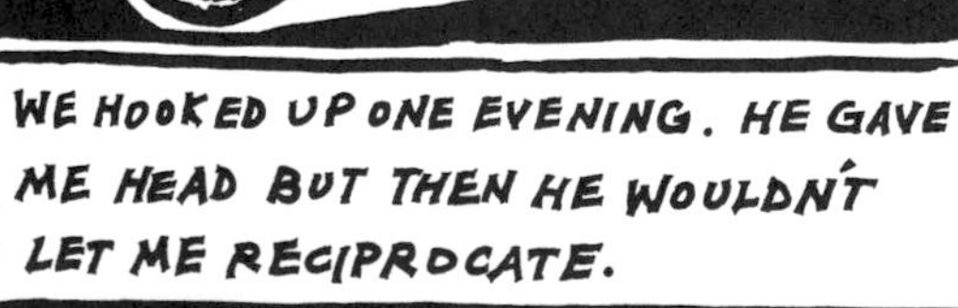
WE HOOKED UP ONE EVENING. HE GAVE ME HEAD BUT THEN HE WOULDN'T LET ME RECIPROCATE.

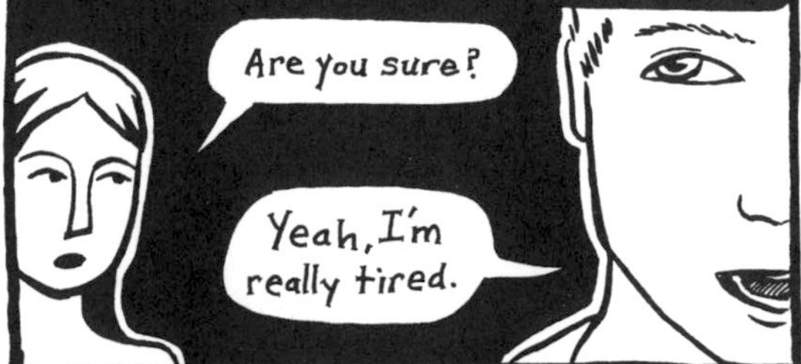
Are you sure?
Yeah, I'm really tired.

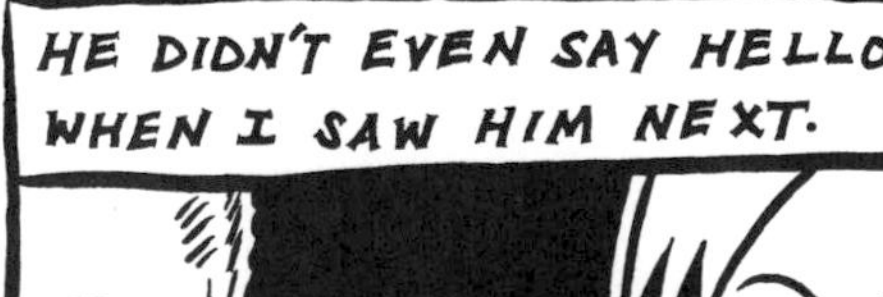
HE DIDN'T EVEN SAY HELLO WHEN I SAW HIM NEXT.
WTF?

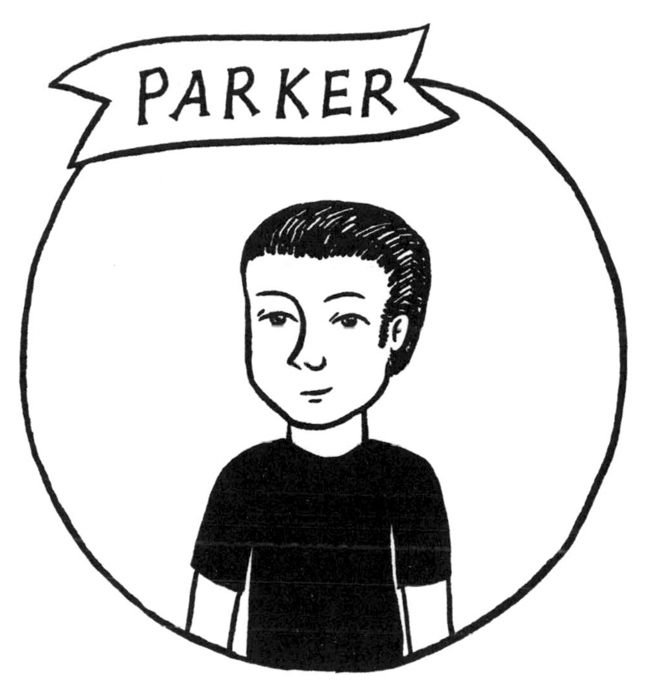
PARKER

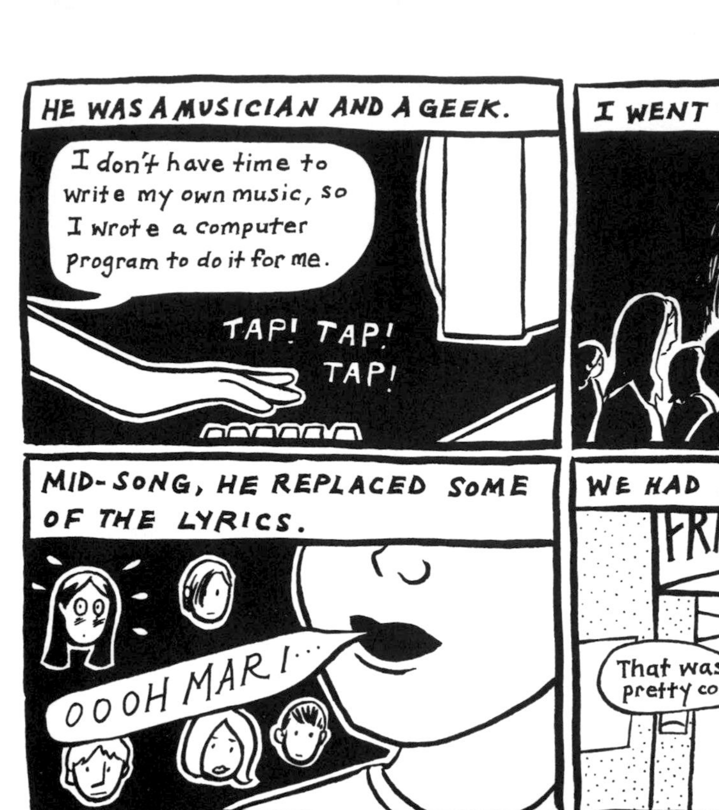
HE WAS A MUSICIAN AND A GEEK.
I don't have time to write my own music, so I wrote a computer program to do it for me.
TAP! TAP! TAP!
I WENT TO ONE OF HIS SHOWS.
MID-SONG, HE REPLACED SOME OF THE LYRICS.
OOOH MARI...

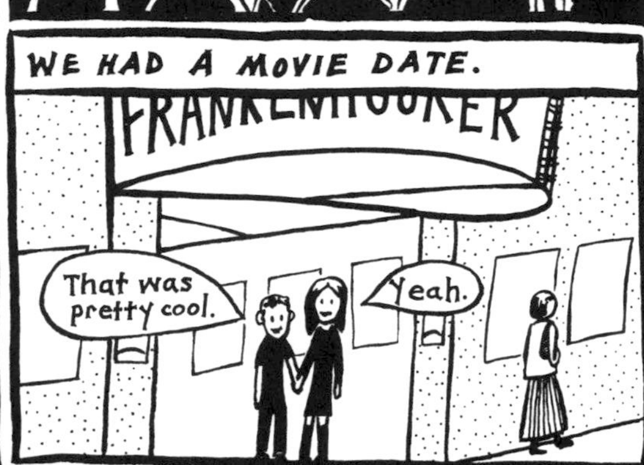
WE HAD A MOVIE DATE.
That was pretty cool.
Yeah.

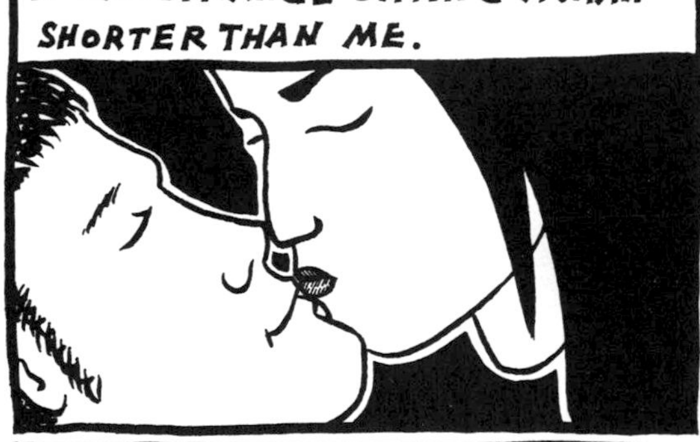
IT WAS STRANGE DATING A MAN SHORTER THAN ME.

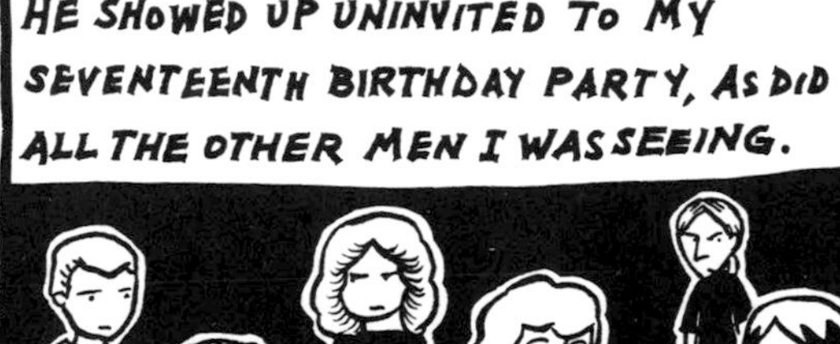
HE SHOWED UP UNINVITED TO MY SEVENTEENTH BIRTHDAY PARTY, AS DID ALL THE OTHER MEN I WAS SEEING.

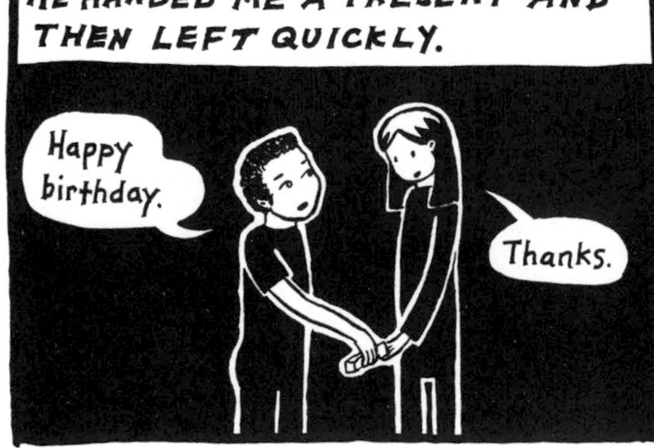
HE HANDED ME A PRESENT AND THEN LEFT QUICKLY.
Happy birthday.
Thanks.

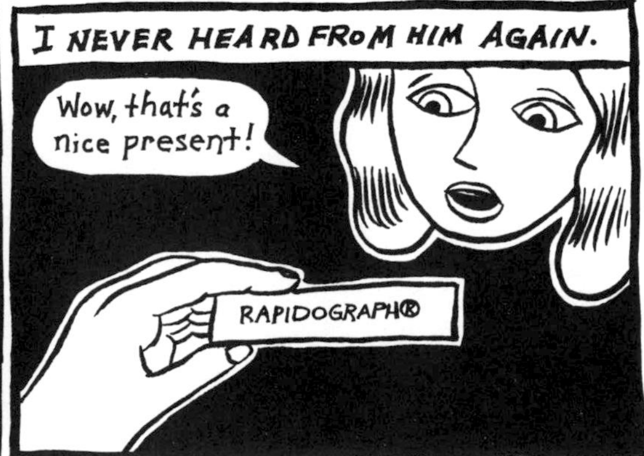
I NEVER HEARD FROM HIM AGAIN.
Wow, that's a nice present!
RAPIDOGRAPH®

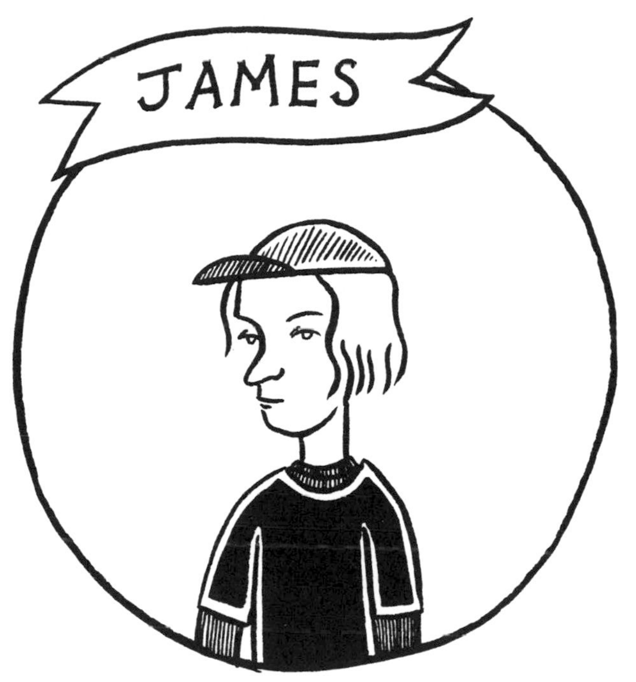
JAMES

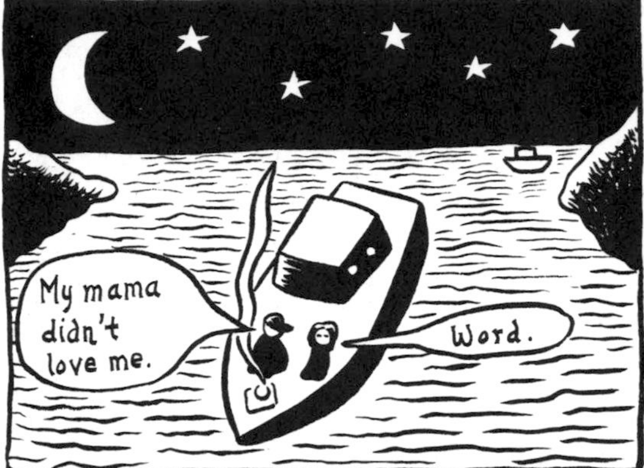
I MET HIM IN 1988. WE WERE BOTH TEENAGE RUNAWAYS.
My mama didn't love me.
Word.

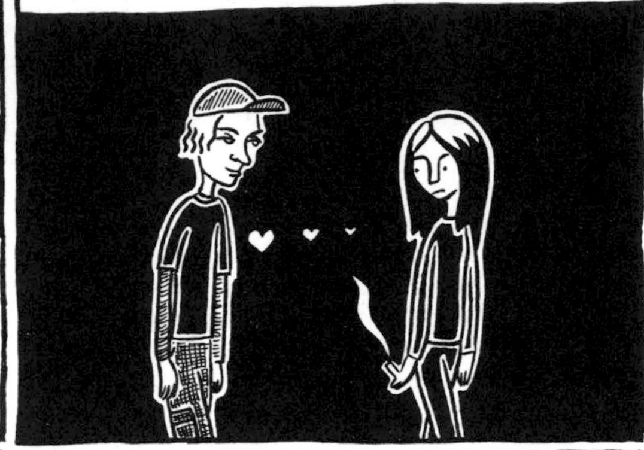
HE WAS GREAT: SMART AND FUNNY WITH A DARK SIDE. BUT I DIDN'T GO OUT WITH YOUNGER BOYS.

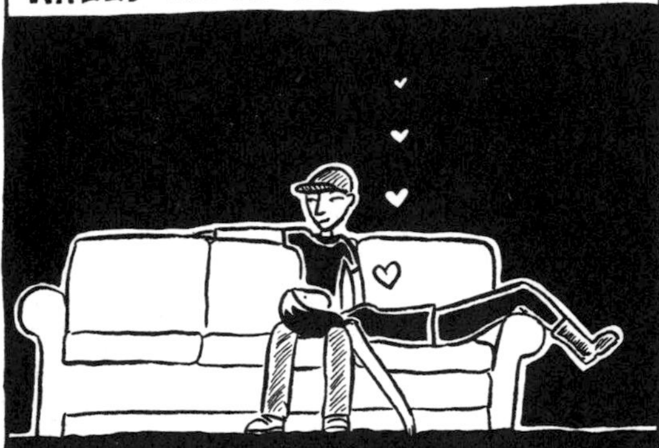
OVER SOME TIME A FLIRTATION DEVELOPED, BUT BY THIS TIME HIS WALLS WERE IMPENETRABLE.

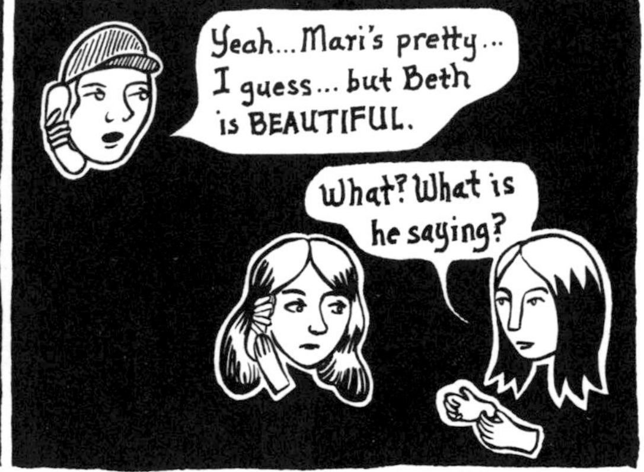
HE HAD A CRUSH ON A FRIEND OF MINE.
Yeah... Mari's pretty... I guess... but Beth is BEAUTIFUL.
What? What is he saying?

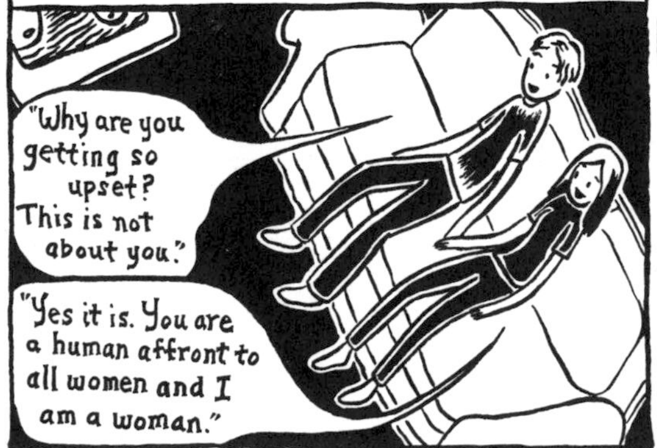
IN THE SUMMER OF 1990, WE SPENT EVERY SINGLE DAY WATCHING THE MOVIE "WHEN HARRY MET SALLY."
"Why are you getting so upset? This is not about you."
"Yes it is. You are a human affront to all women and I am a woman."

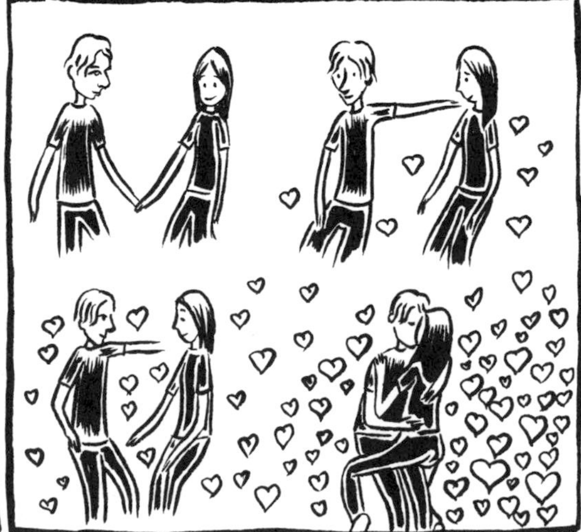

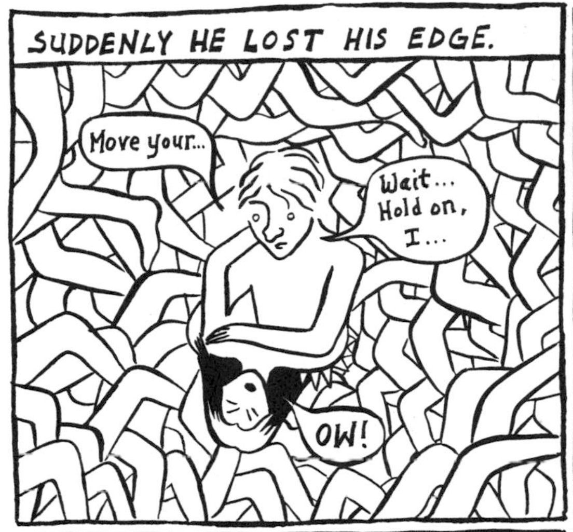
SUDDENLY HE LOST HIS EDGE.
Move your...
Wait... Hold on, I...
OW!

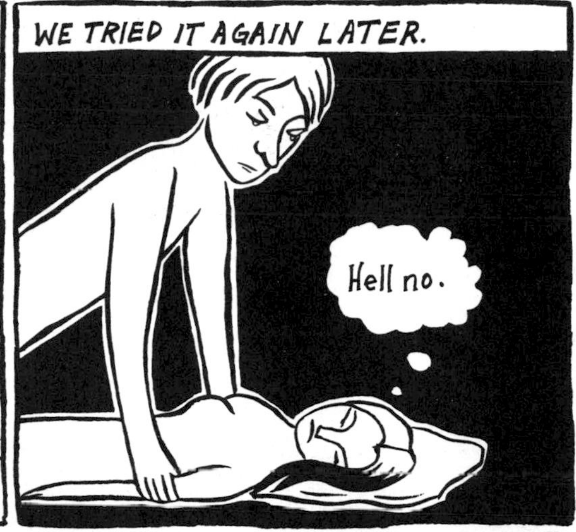
WE TRIED IT AGAIN LATER.
Hell no.

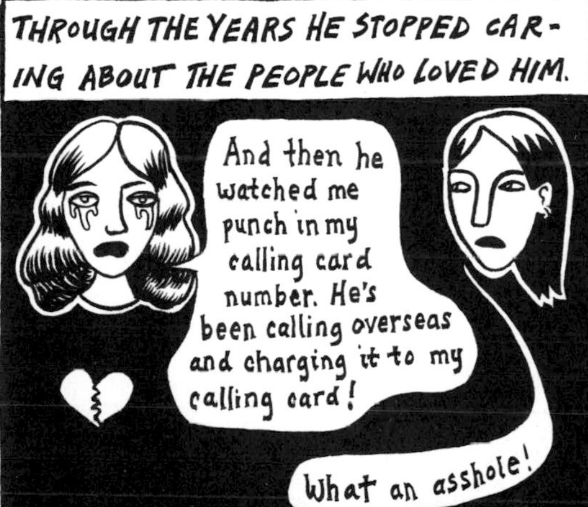
THROUGH THE YEARS HE STOPPED CARING ABOUT THE PEOPLE WHO LOVED HIM.
And then he watched me punch in my calling card number. He's been calling overseas and charging it to my calling card!
What an asshole!

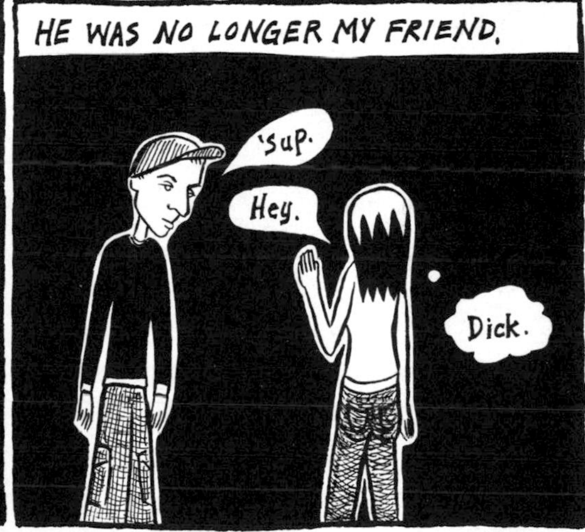
HE WAS NO LONGER MY FRIEND.
'Sup.
Hey.
Dick.

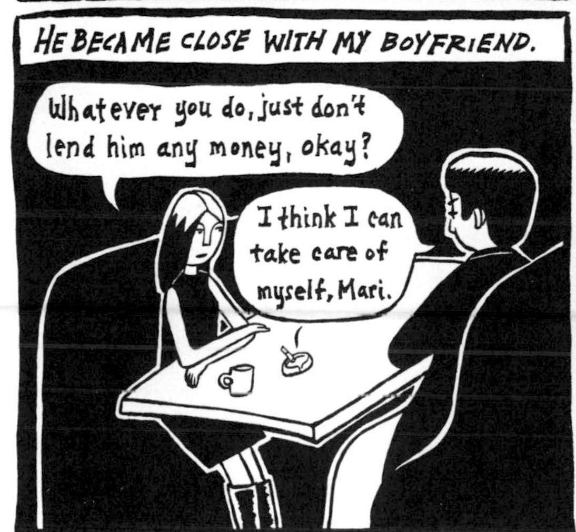
HE BECAME CLOSE WITH MY BOYFRIEND.
Whatever you do, just don't lend him any money, okay?
I think I can take care of myself, Mari.

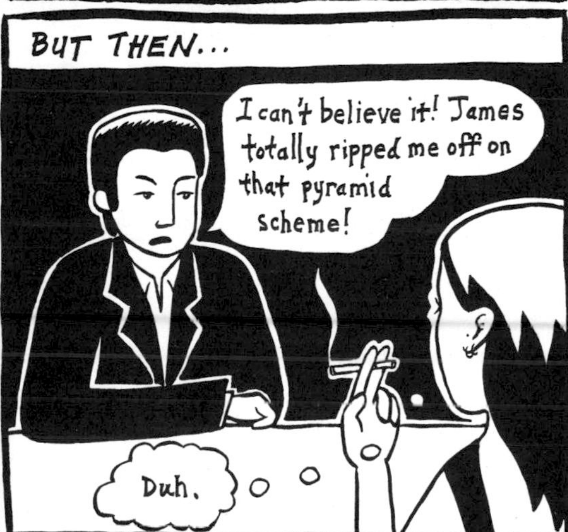
BUT THEN...
I can't believe it! James totally ripped me off on that pyramid scheme!
Duh.

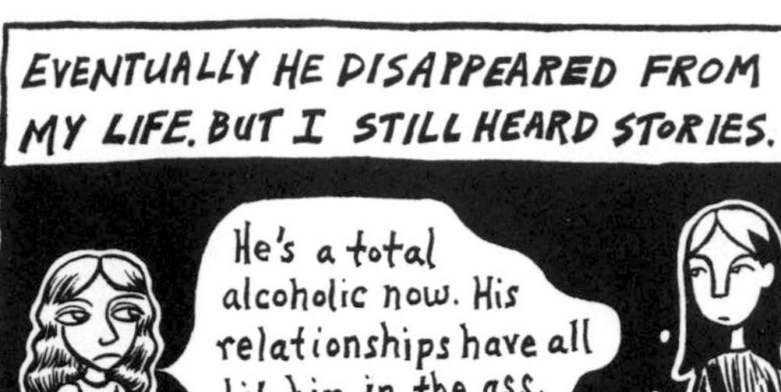
EVENTUALLY HE DISAPPEARED FROM MY LIFE. BUT I STILL HEARD STORIES.
He's a total alcoholic now. His relationships have all bit him in the ass.
Serves him right.

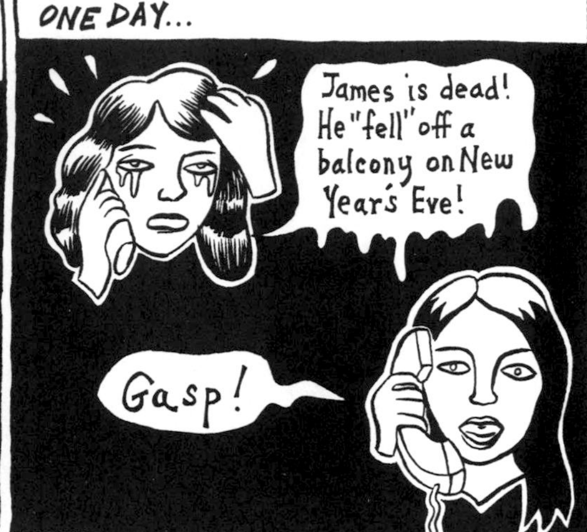
ONE DAY...
James is dead! He "fell" off a balcony on New Year's Eve!
Gasp!

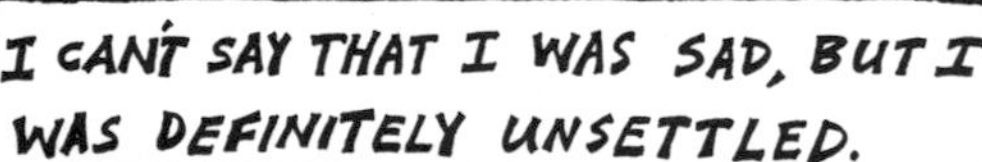
I CAN'T SAY THAT I WAS SAD, BUT I WAS DEFINITELY UNSETTLED.

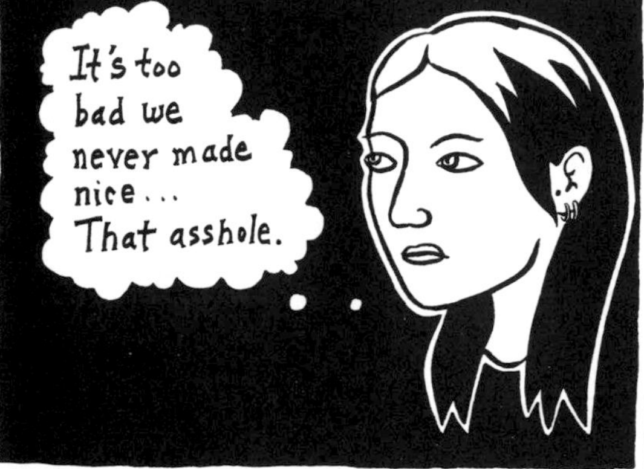
It's too bad we never made nice... That asshole.

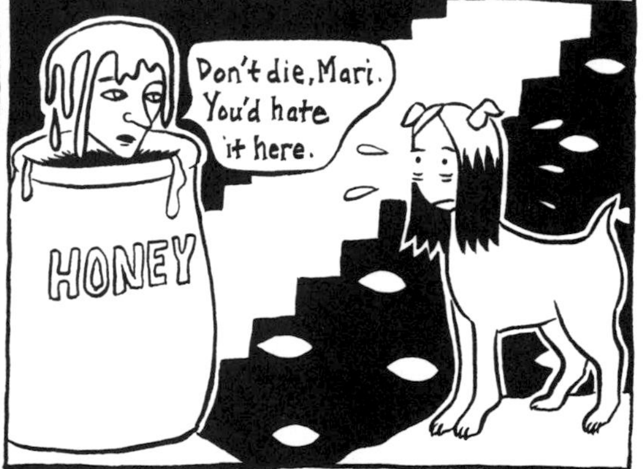
IN THE WEEKS THAT FOLLOWED, I HAD SOME DISTURBING DREAMS.
Don't die, Mari. You'd hate it here.
HONEY

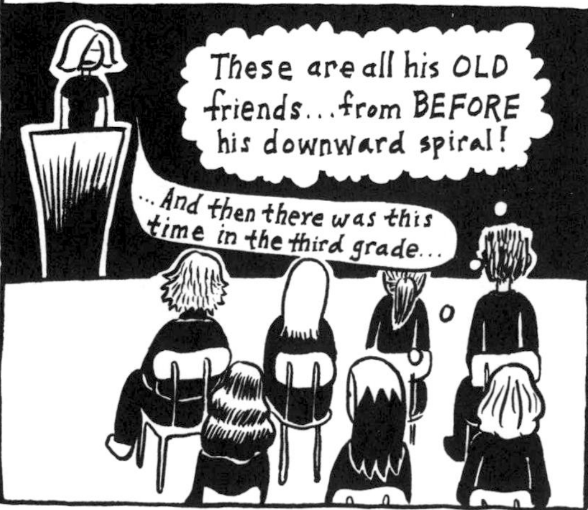
I GOT DRAGGED TO HIS WAKE.
These are all his OLD friends... from BEFORE his downward spiral!
...And then there was this time in the third grade...

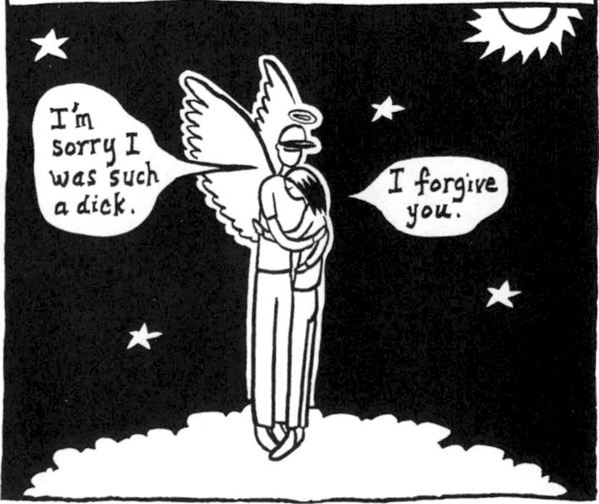
THEN ONE NIGHT I HAD A DREAM.
I'm sorry I was such a dick.
I forgive you.

Book Two

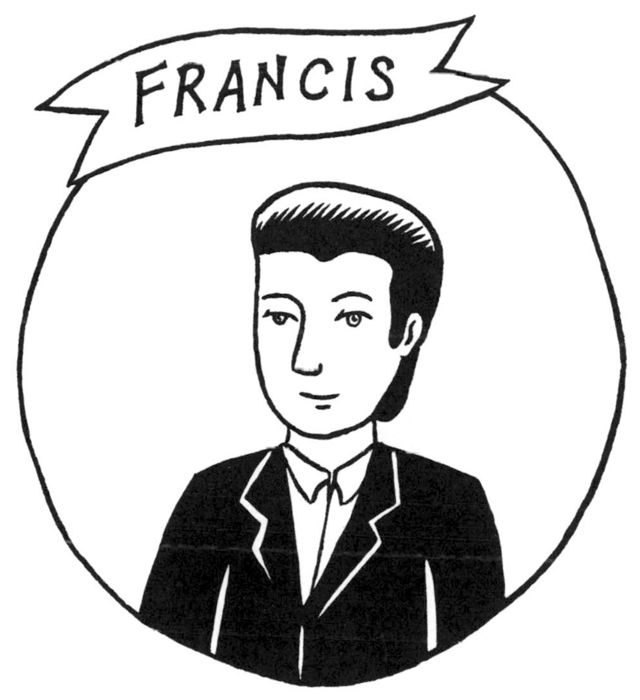
FRANCIS

IN SEVENTH GRADE, I HAD A DREAM I WAS THE FUTURE MOTHER OF JESUS CHRIST REBORN. SOME EVIL-LOOKING CHARACTERS WERE CHASING ME THROUGH A MATTRESS FACTORY.

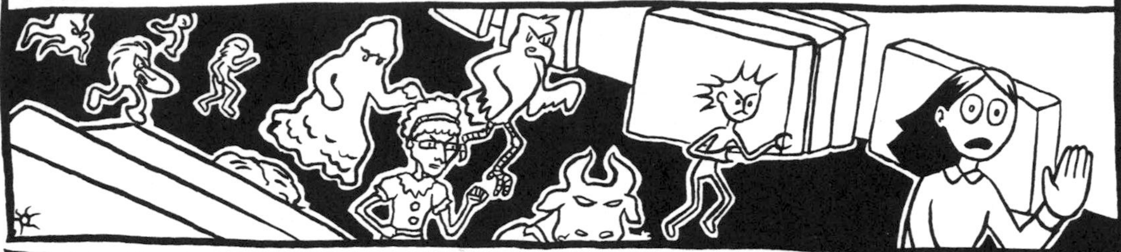

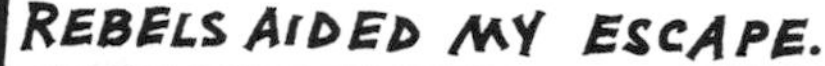

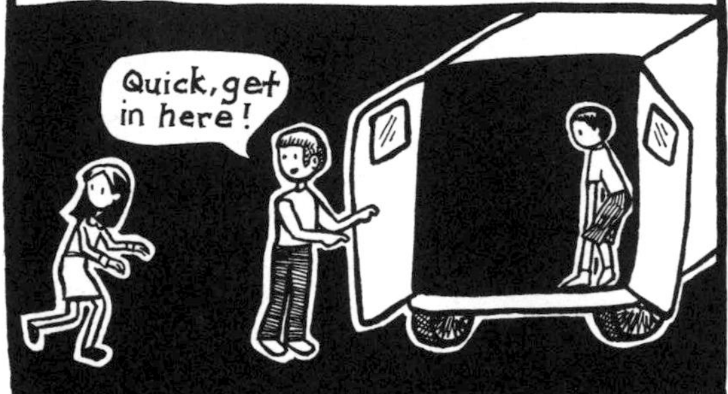

A BOY AWAITED ME IN THE VAN.

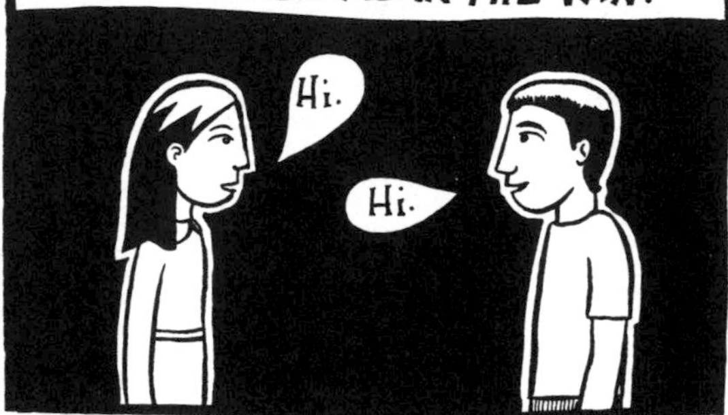

WE HELD EACH OTHER TIGHT.

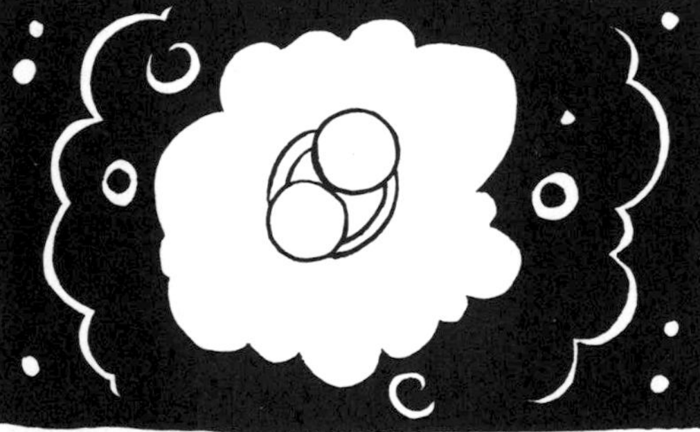

AFTER MANY ADVENTURES, I GAVE BIRTH TO A BLOND, BLUE-EYED QUIET BABY JESUS.

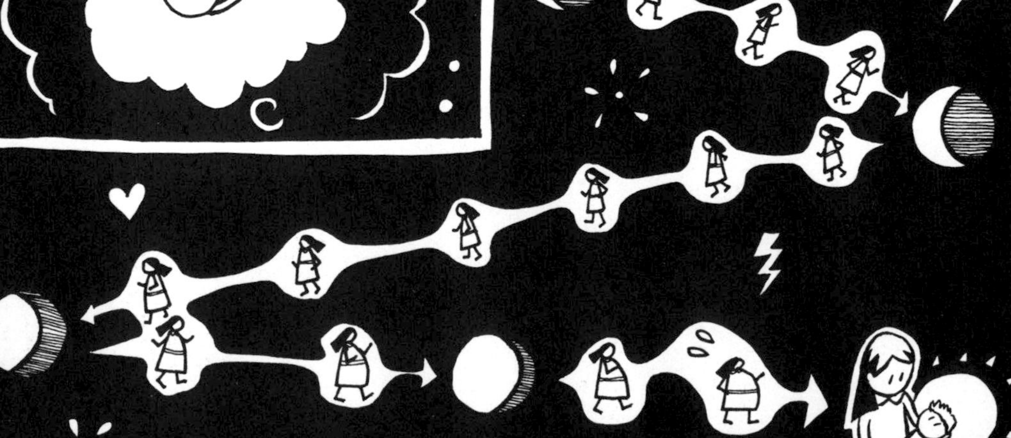

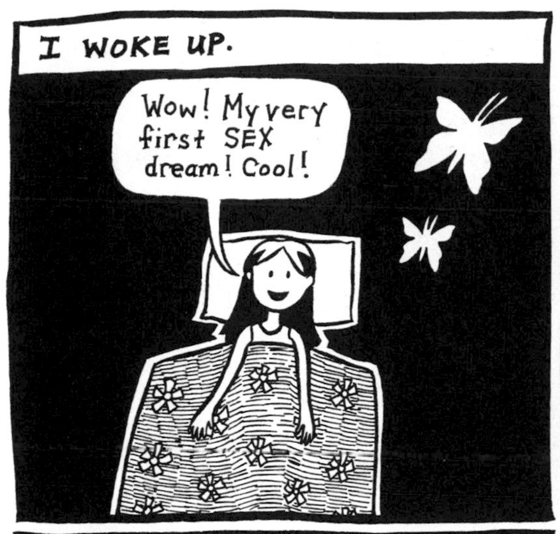
I WOKE UP.
Wow! My very first SEX dream! Cool!

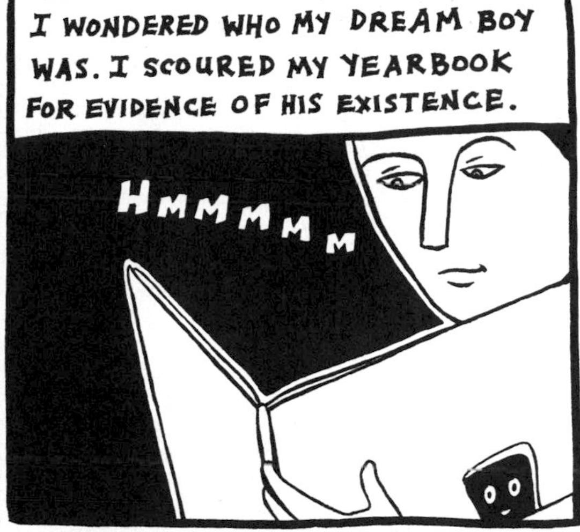
I WONDERED WHO MY DREAM BOY WAS. I SCOURED MY YEARBOOK FOR EVIDENCE OF HIS EXISTENCE.
HMMMMMM

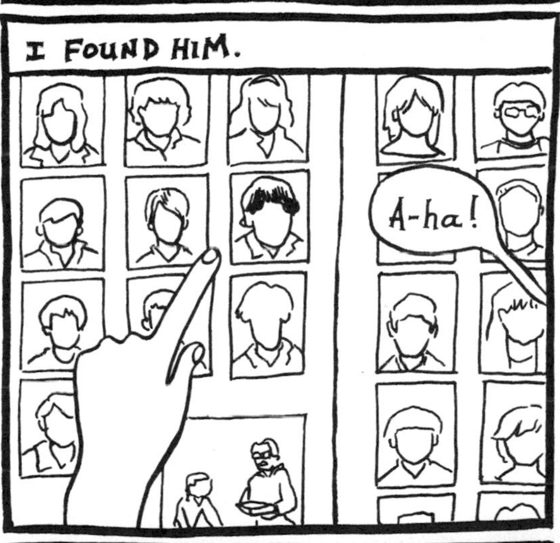
I FOUND HIM.
A-ha!

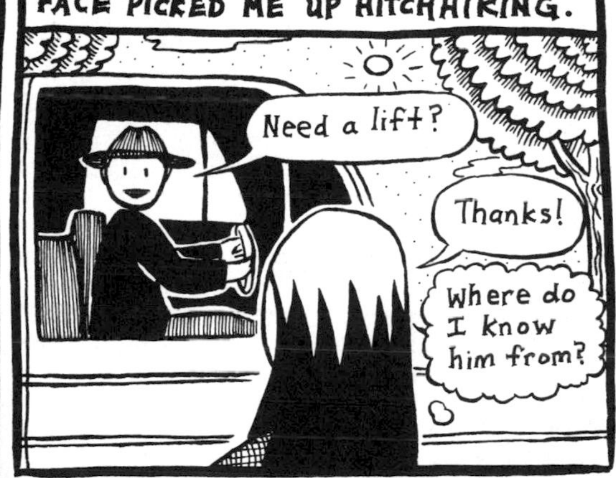
FOUR YEARS LATER, A FAMILIAR FACE PICKED ME UP HITCHHIKING.
Need a lift?
Thanks!
Where do I know him from?

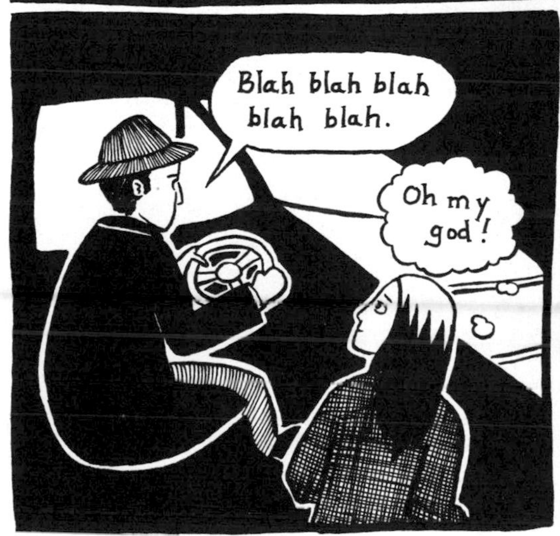
Blah blah blah blah blah.
Oh my god!

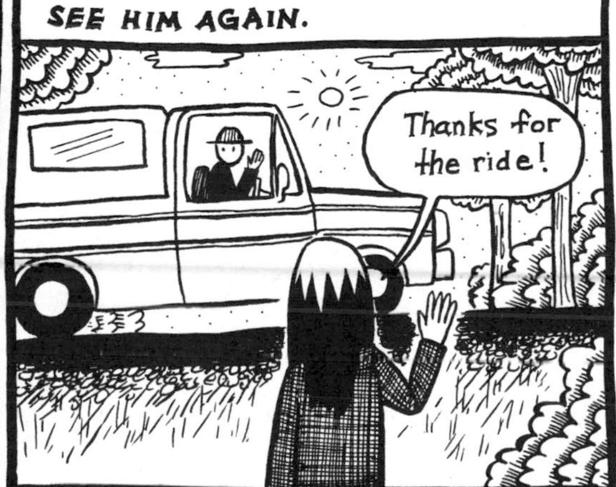
I NEVER REALLY EXPECTED TO SEE HIM AGAIN.
Thanks for the ride!

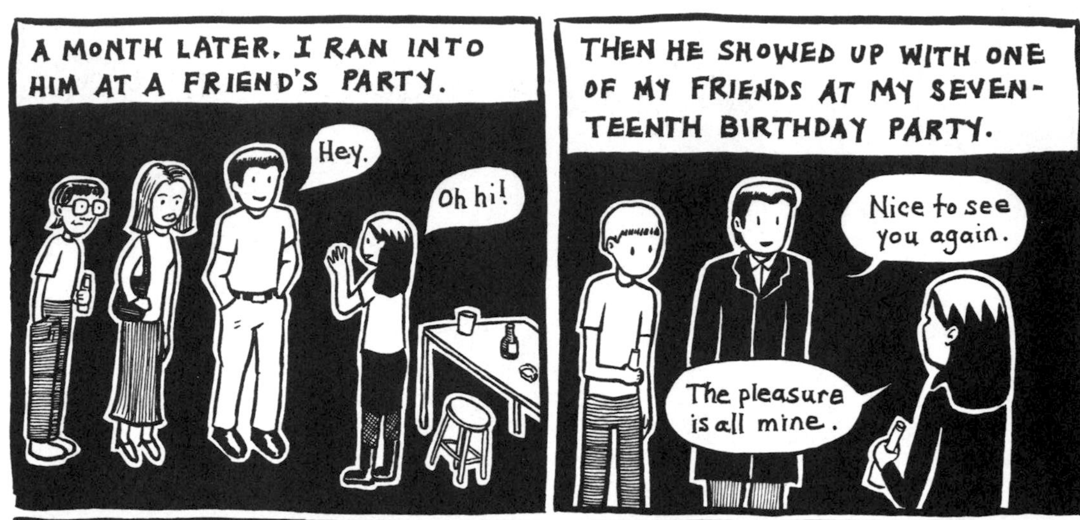

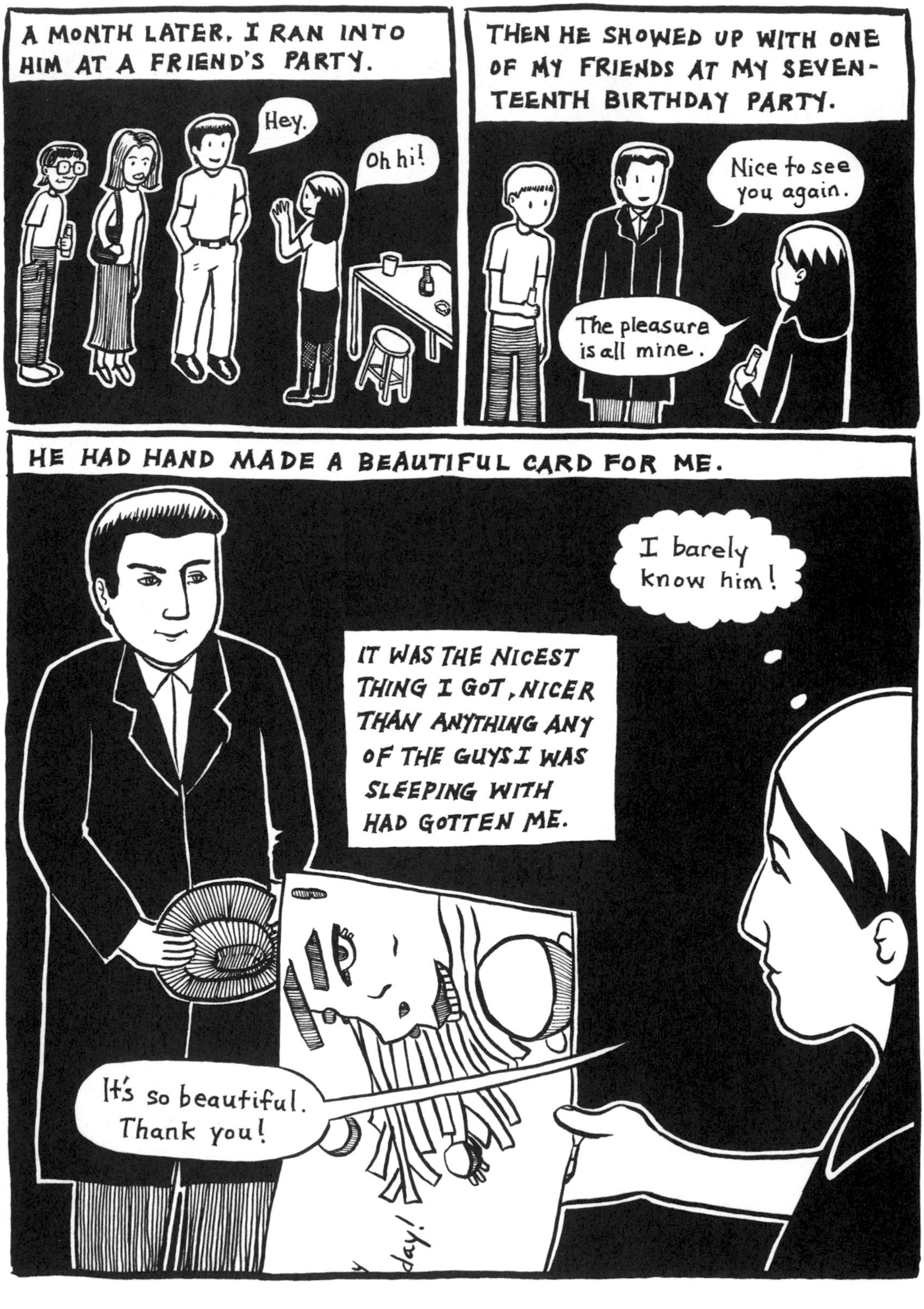

HE HAD HAND MADE A BEAUTIFUL CARD FOR ME.

I barely know him!

IT WAS THE NICEST THING I GOT, NICER THAN ANYTHING ANY OF THE GUYS I WAS SLEEPING WITH HAD GOTTEN ME.

It's so beautiful. Thank you!

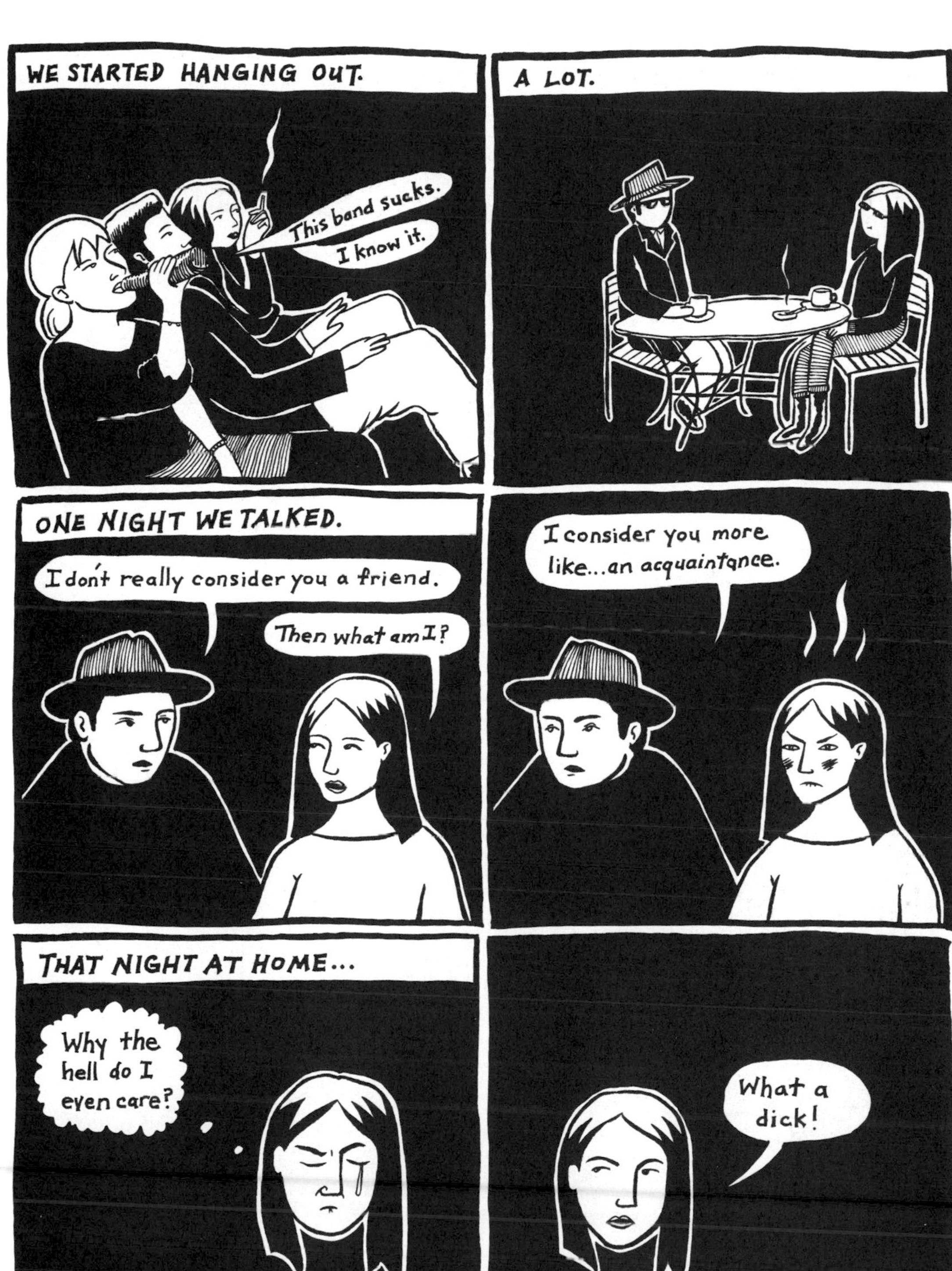
WE STARTED HANGING OUT.
This band sucks.
I know it.
A LOT.
ONE NIGHT WE TALKED.
I don't really consider you a friend.
Then what am I?
I consider you more like...an acquaintance.
THAT NIGHT AT HOME...
Why the hell do I even care?
What a dick!

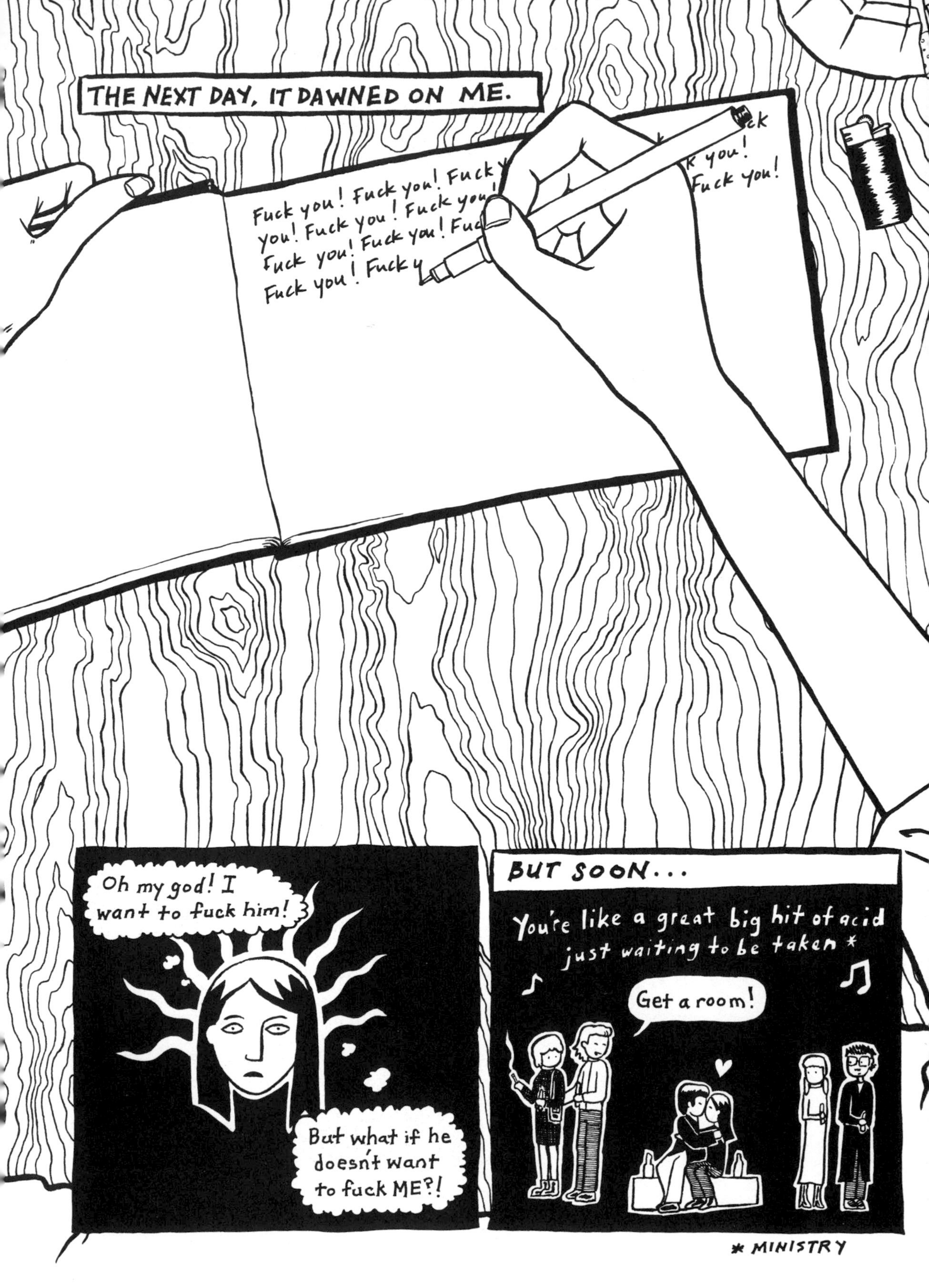
THE NEXT DAY, IT DAWNED ON ME.
Fuck you! Fuck you! Fuck you! Fuck you! Fuck you! Fuck you! Fuck you! Fuck you! Fuck you! Fuck
you! Fuck you!
Oh my god! I want to fuck him!
But what if he doesn't want to fuck ME?!
BUT SOON...
You're like a great big hit of acid just waiting to be taken *
Get a room!
* MINISTRY

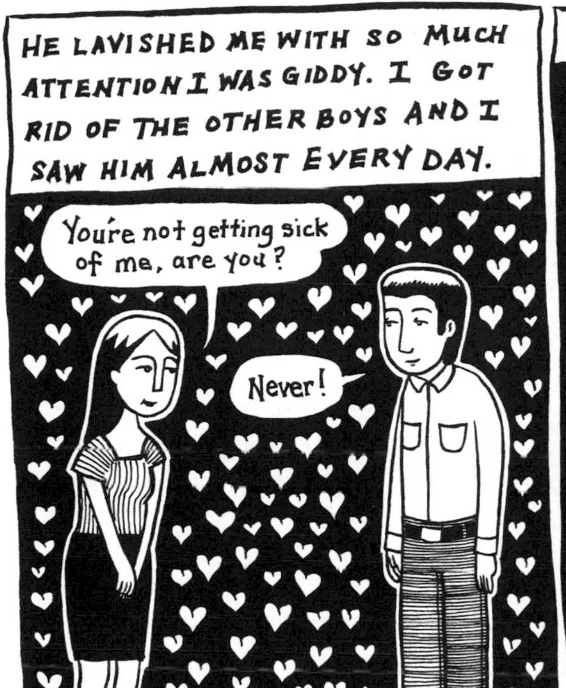
HE LAVISHED ME WITH SO MUCH ATTENTION I WAS GIDDY. I GOT RID OF THE OTHER BOYS AND I SAW HIM ALMOST EVERY DAY.
You're not getting sick of me, are you?
Never!

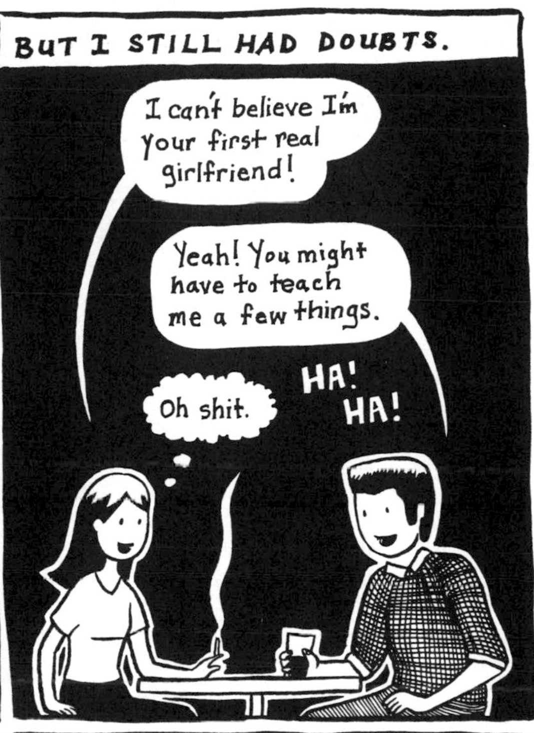
BUT I STILL HAD DOUBTS.
I can't believe I'm your first real girlfriend!
Yeah! You might have to teach me a few things.
Oh shit.
HA! HA!

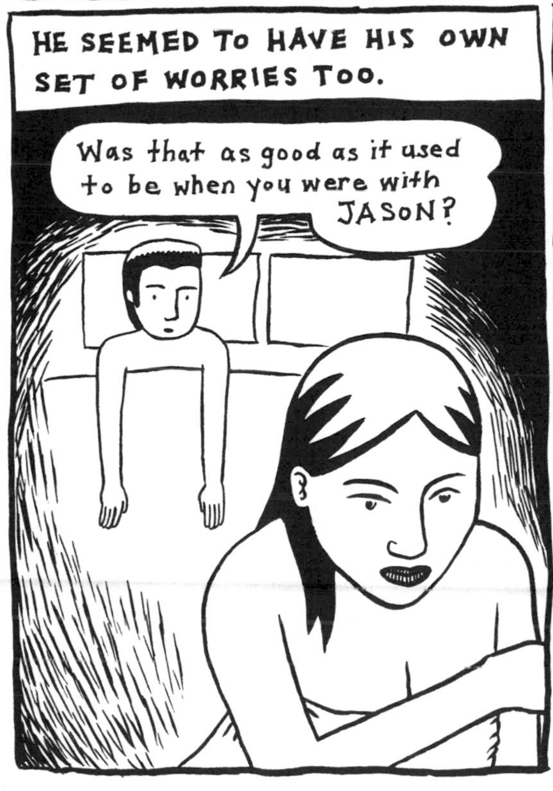
HE SEEMED TO HAVE HIS OWN SET OF WORRIES TOO.
Was that as good as it used to be when you were with JASON?

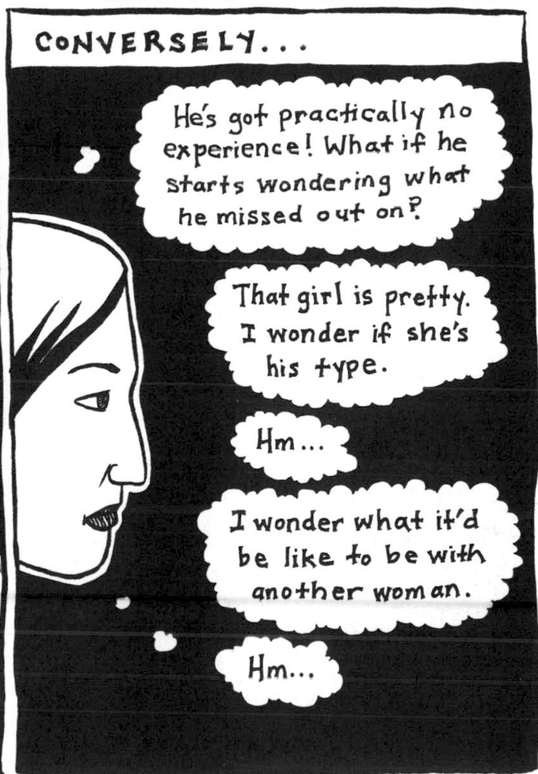
CONVERSELY...
He's got practically no experience! What if he starts wondering what he missed out on?
That girl is pretty. I wonder if she's his type.
Hm...
I wonder what it'd be like to be with another woman.
Hm...

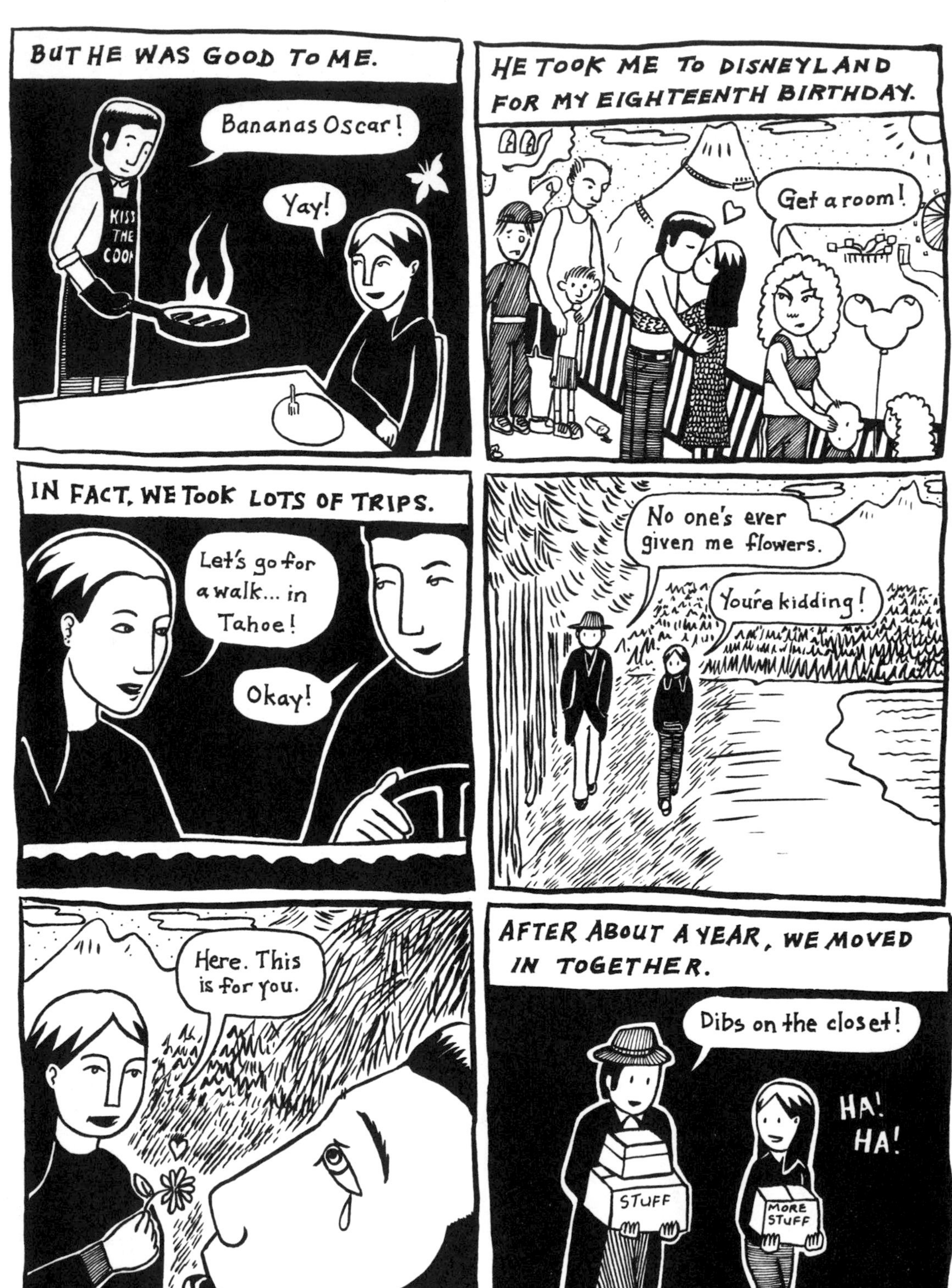
BUT HE WAS GOOD TO ME.
Bananas Oscar!
KISS THE COOK
Yay!
HE TOOK ME TO DISNEYLAND FOR MY EIGHTEENTH BIRTHDAY.
Get a room!
IN FACT, WE TOOK LOTS OF TRIPS.
Let's go for a walk... in Tahoe!
Okay!
No one's ever given me flowers.
You're kidding!
Here. This is for you.
AFTER ABOUT A YEAR, WE MOVED IN TOGETHER.
Dibs on the closet!
HA! HA!
STUFF
MORE STUFF

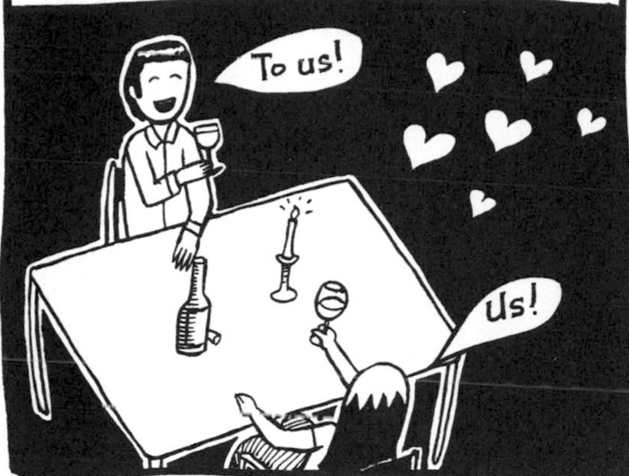
MOST OF THE TIME, THINGS WERE VERY GOOD.
To us!
Us!

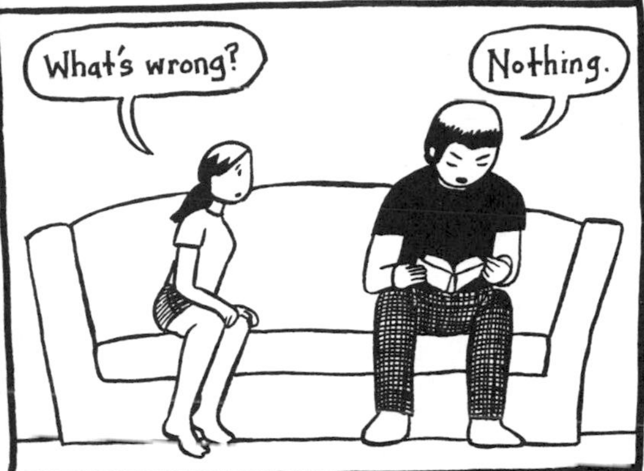
BUT SOMETIMES THEY JUST WEREN'T. I DIDN'T KNOW WHY.
What's wrong?
Nothing.

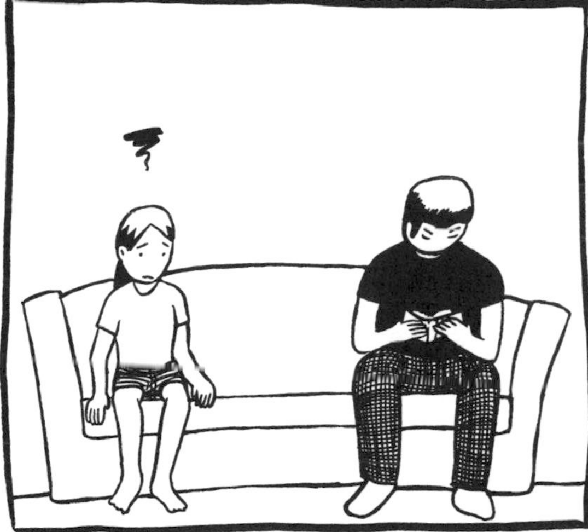

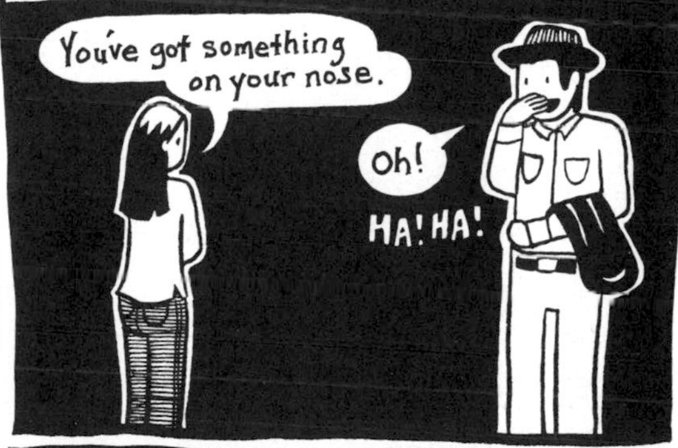
HE WORKED AT A MEXICAN RESTAURANT AND OFTEN CAME HOME REEKING OF REFRIED BEANS AND COKE.
You've got something on your nose.
Oh!
HA! HA!

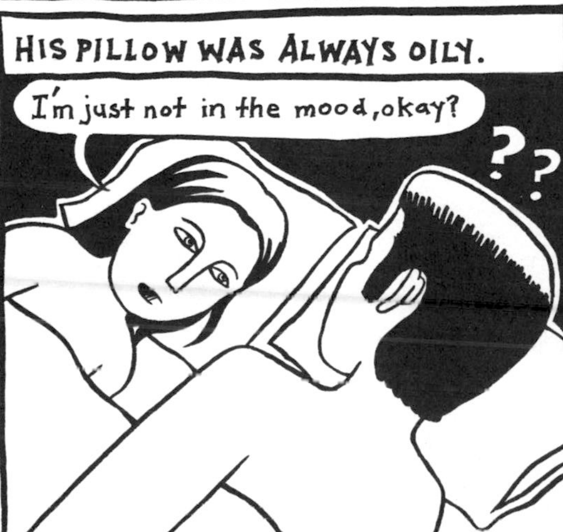
HIS PILLOW WAS ALWAYS OILY.
I'm just not in the mood, okay?
??

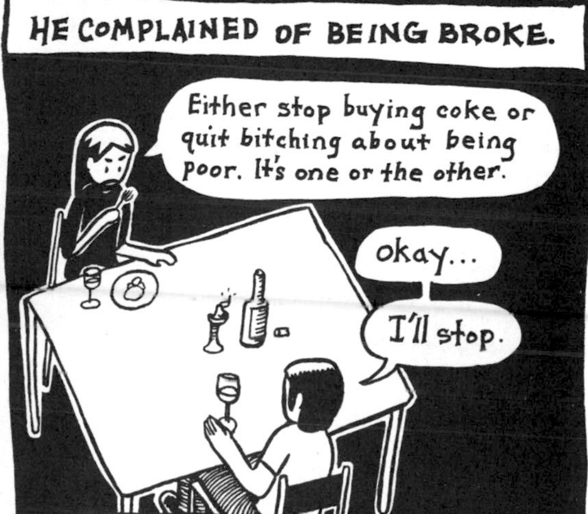
HE COMPLAINED OF BEING BROKE.
Either stop buying coke or quit bitching about being poor. It's one or the other.
okay...
I'll stop.

ONE DAY HE BLEW UP AT ME OVER NOTHING.

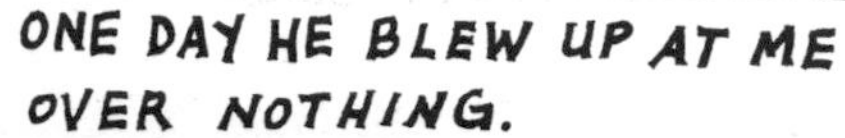

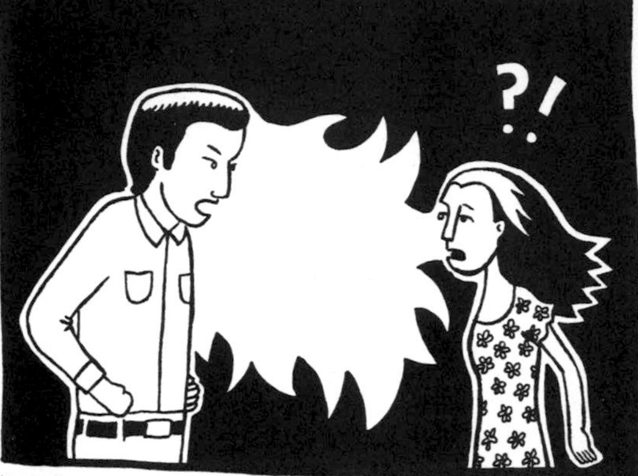

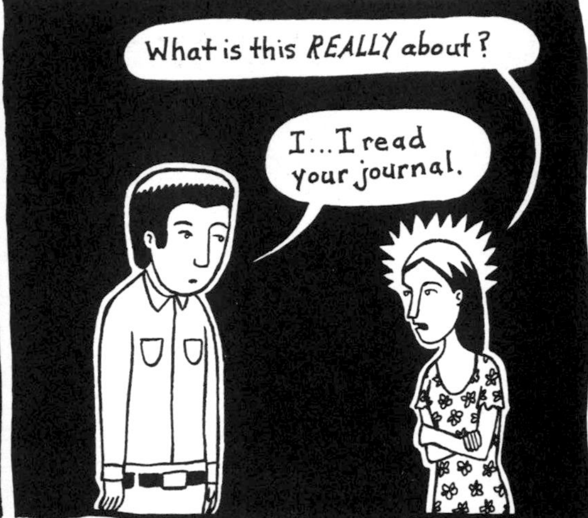

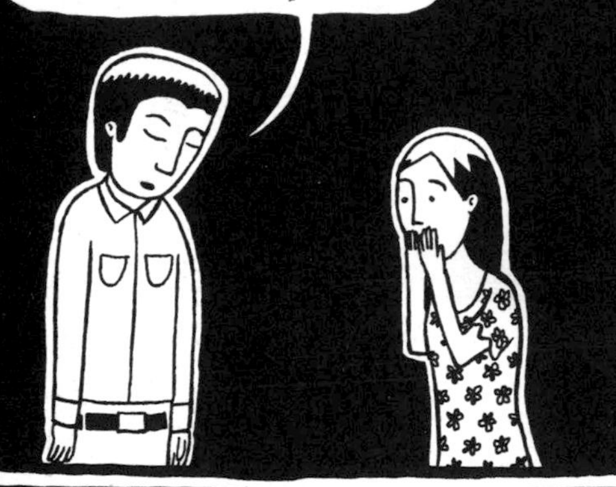

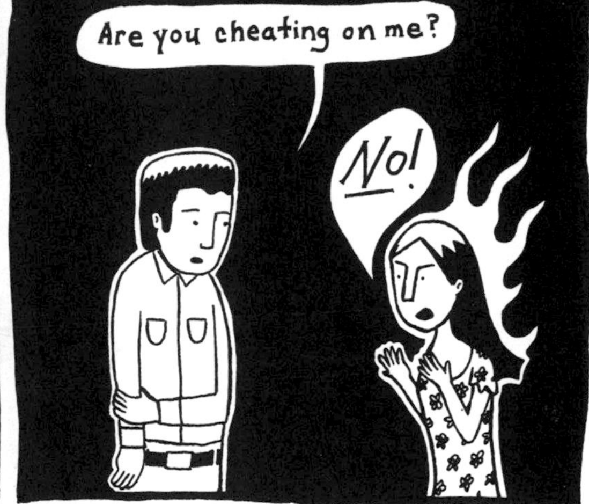

I EXPLAINED AS BEST I COULD THAT I WAS TOTALLY FAITHFUL AND DEVOTED TO HIM.

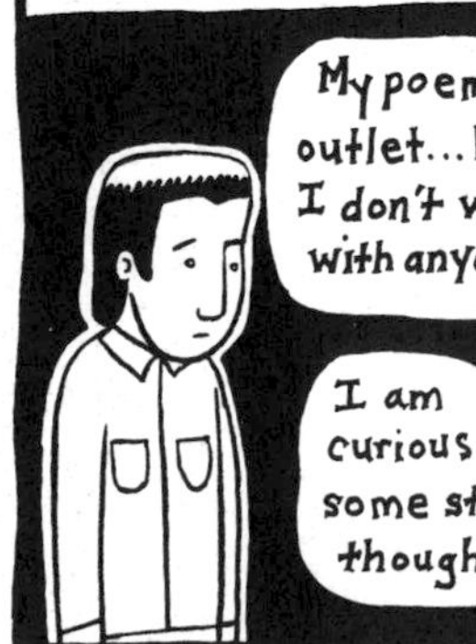

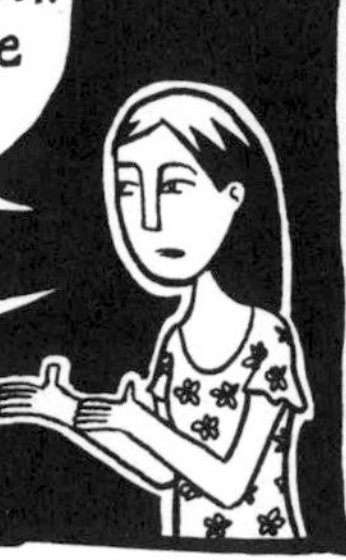

IT WAS ONE OF THOSE LONG, EXHAUSTING TALKS THAT MIGHT BE ULTIMATELY BETTER FOR THE RELATIONSHIP, BUT FEEL WORSE AT THE TIME.

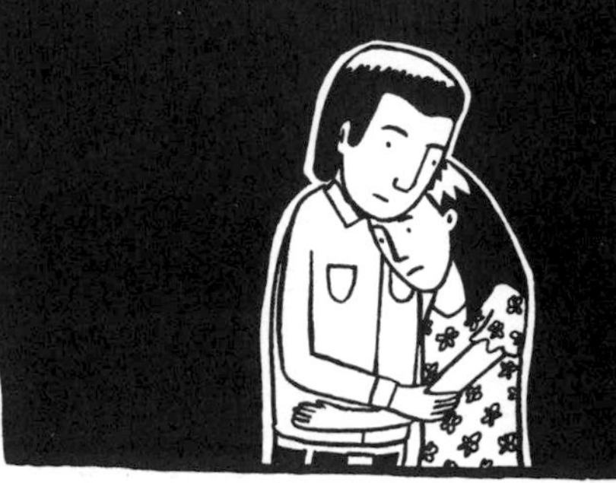

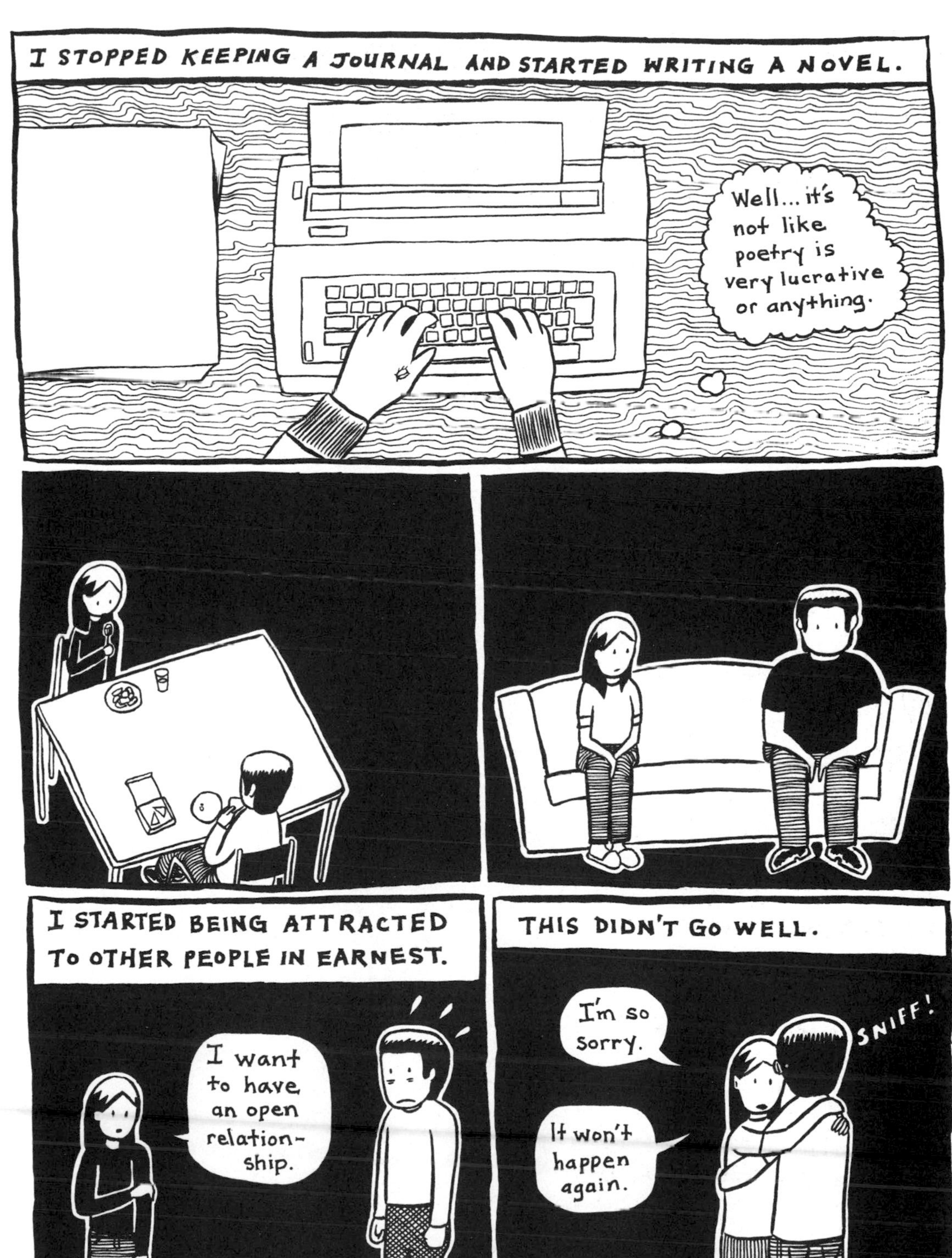
I STOPPED KEEPING A JOURNAL AND STARTED WRITING A NOVEL.
Well... it's not like poetry is very lucrative or anything.
I STARTED BEING ATTRACTED TO OTHER PEOPLE IN EARNEST.
I want to have an open relation-ship.
THIS DIDN'T GO WELL.
I'm so sorry.
It won't happen again.
SNIFF!

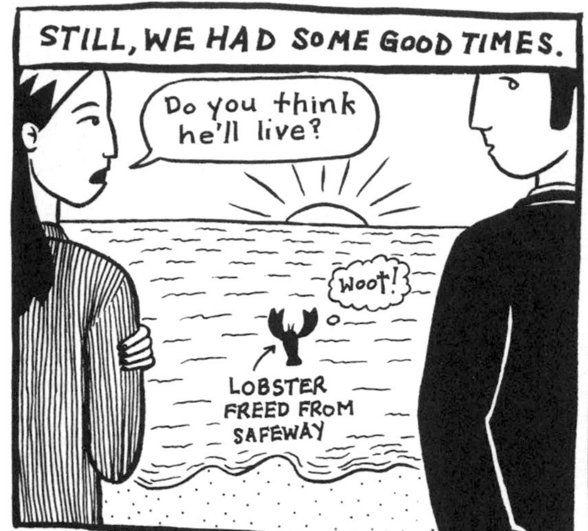
STILL, WE HAD SOME GOOD TIMES.
Do you think he'll live?
Woot!
LOBSTER FREED FROM SAFEWAY

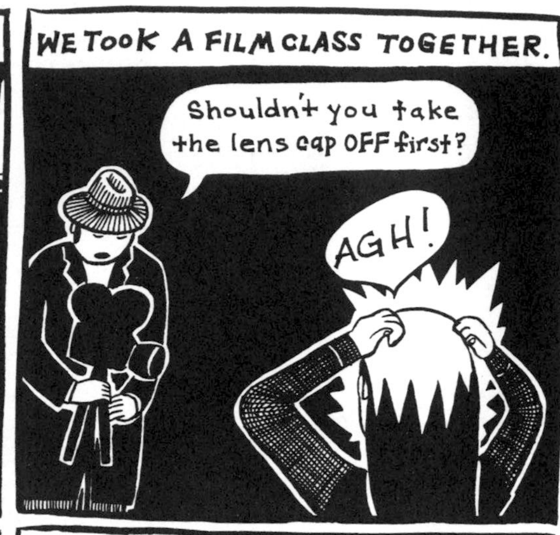
WE TOOK A FILM CLASS TOGETHER.
Shouldn't you take the lens cap OFF first?
AGH!

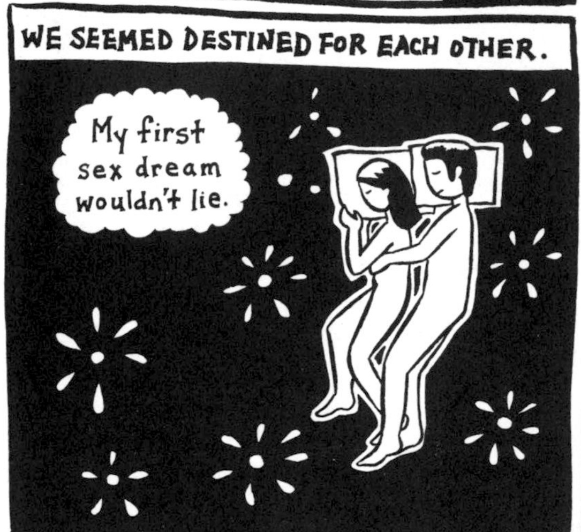
WE SEEMED DESTINED FOR EACH OTHER.
My first sex dream wouldn't lie.

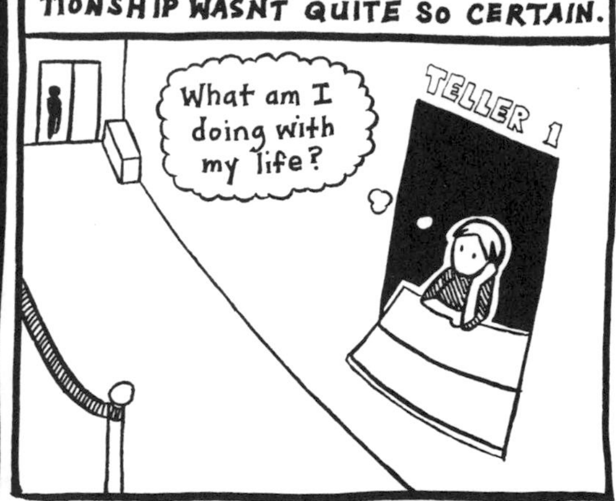
BUT LIFE OUTSIDE OF THE RELATIONSHIP WASN'T QUITE SO CERTAIN.
What am I doing with my life?
TELLER 1

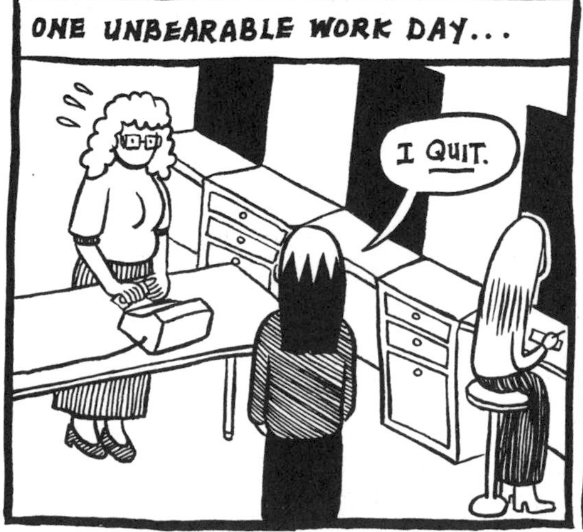
ONE UNBEARABLE WORK DAY...
I QUIT.

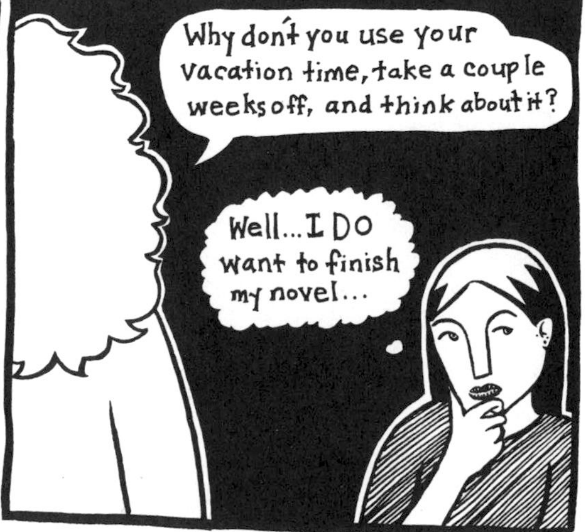
Why don't you use your vacation time, take a couple weeks off, and think about it?
Well... I DO want to finish my novel...

IT WAS REWARDING TO HAVE A FINISHED PIECE OF WORK IN MY HANDS BUT IT DIDN'T CHANGE THE FACT I WAS UNHAPPY.

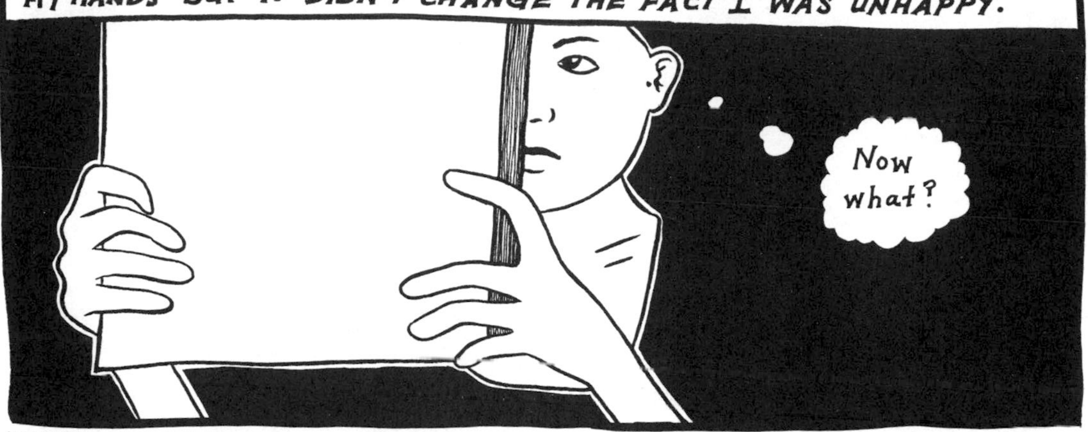

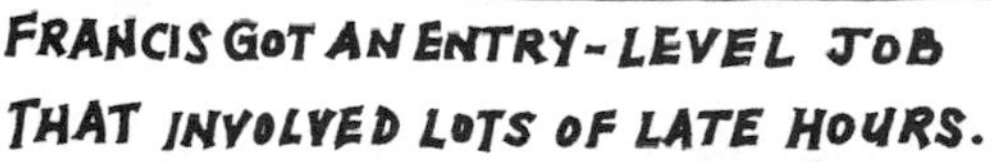

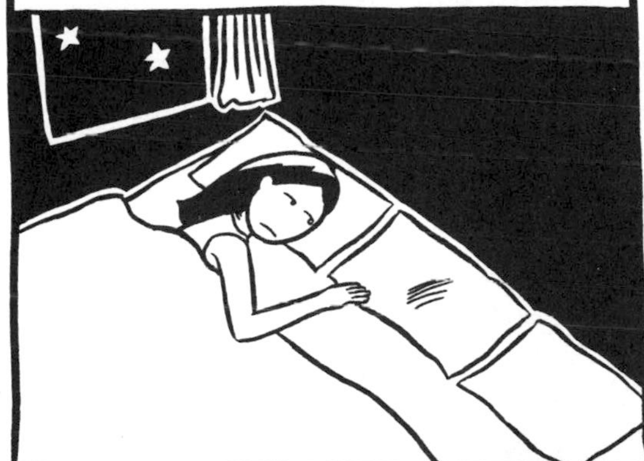

I BECAME INCREASINGLY UNHAPPY AT MY JOB AND FOUND NO SOLACE IN MY HOME LIFE.

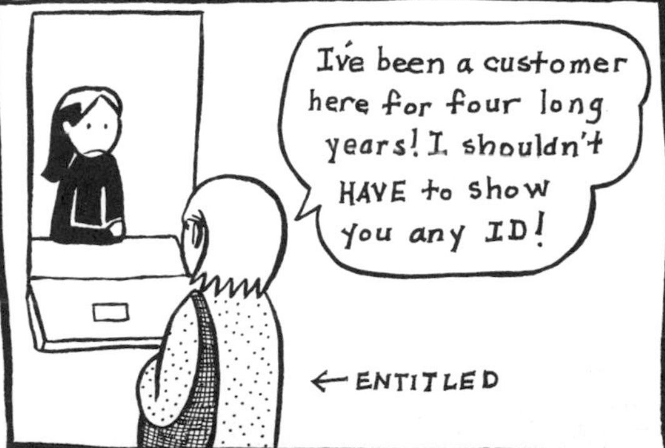

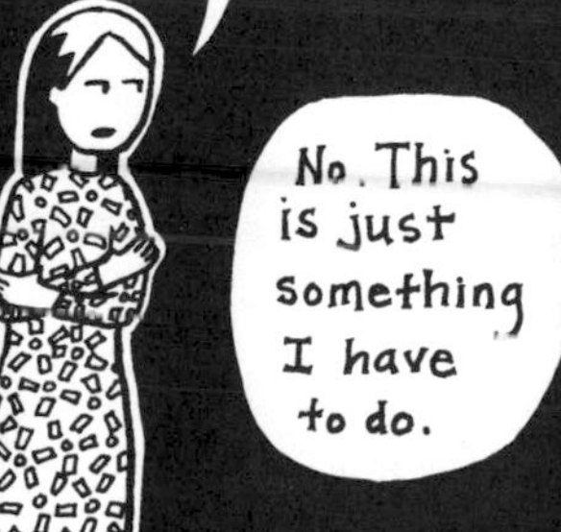

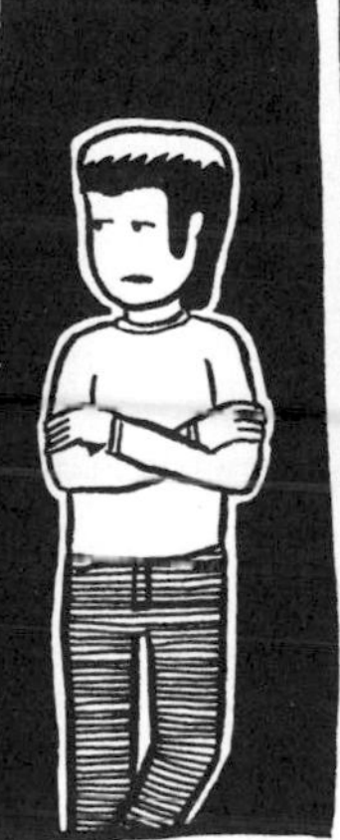

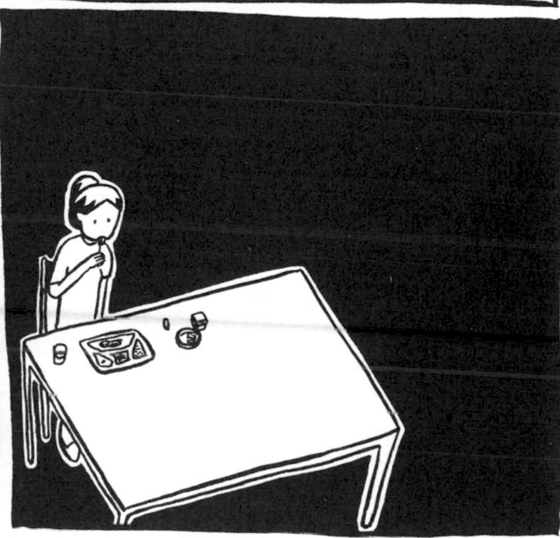

BUT FRANCIS TRIED TO MAKE ME HAPPY IN OTHER WAYS.

THIS OFTEN AMOUNTED TO HIM SACRIFICING HIS OWN HAPPINESS TO DO SO.

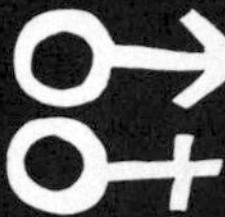

WHEN THESE ATTEMPTS WERE UNSUCCESSFUL, HE BECAME RESENTFUL.

What's wrong?

Nothing.

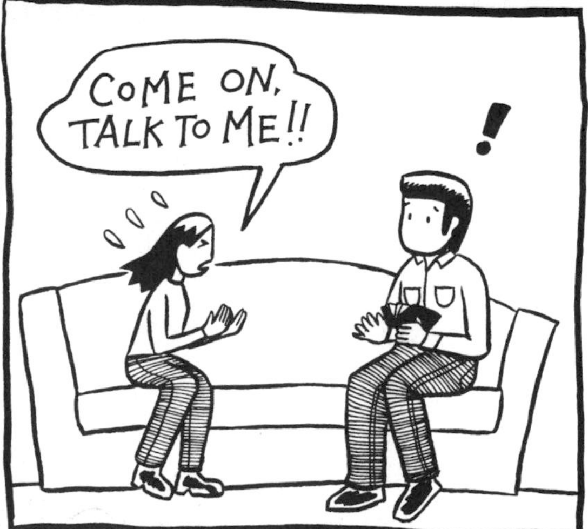

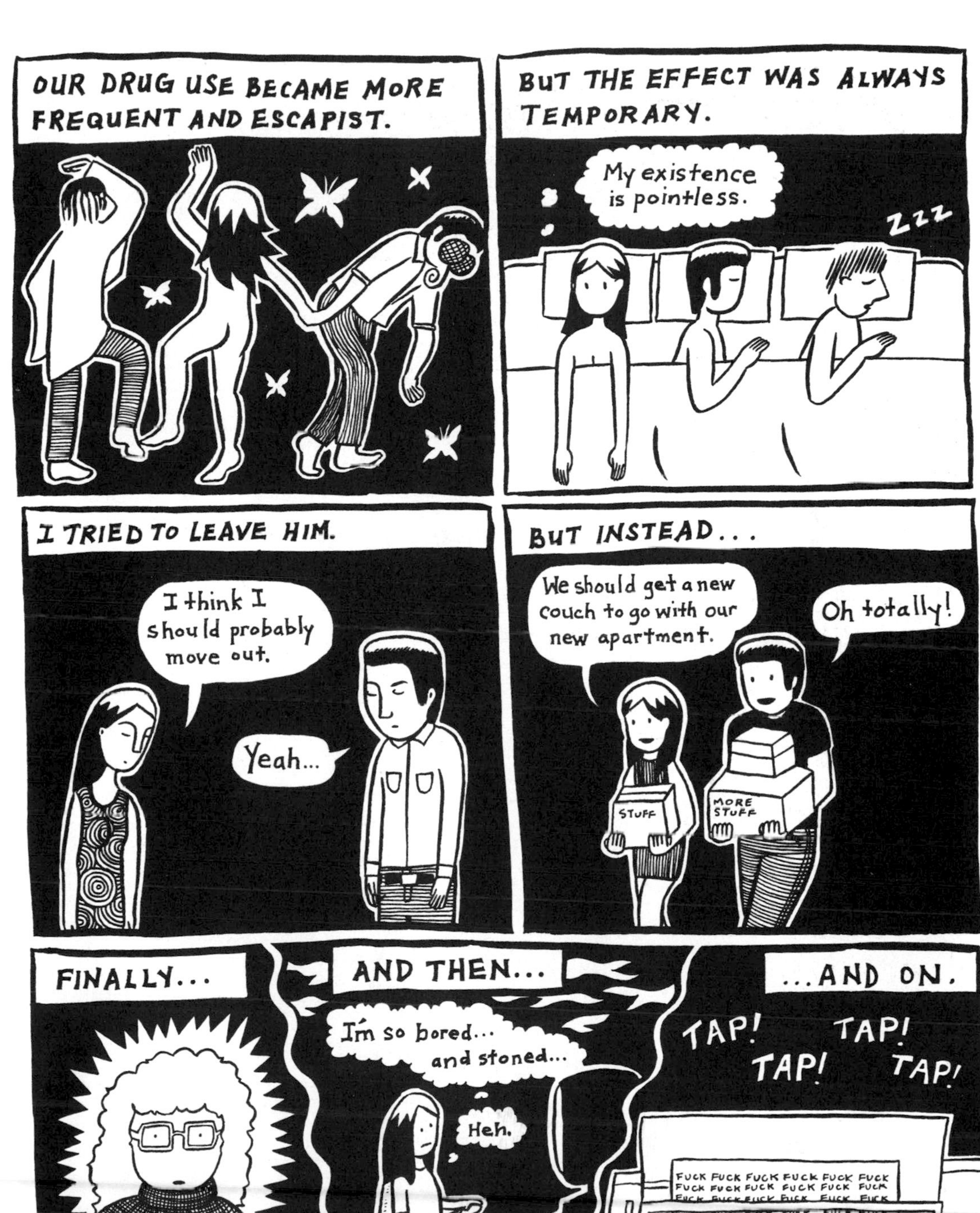
OUR DRUG USE BECAME MORE FREQUENT AND ESCAPIST.
BUT THE EFFECT WAS ALWAYS TEMPORARY.
My existence is pointless.
ZZZ
I TRIED TO LEAVE HIM.
I think I should probably move out.
Yeah...
BUT INSTEAD...
We should get a new couch to go with our new apartment.
Oh totally!
STUFF
MORE STUFF
FINALLY...
I'm sorry but I can't work here anymore.
AND THEN...
I'm so bored... and stoned...
Heh.
...AND ON.
TAP! TAP! TAP! TAP!
FUCK FUCK FUCK FUCK FUCK FUCK
FUCK FUCK FUCK FUCK FUCK FUCK

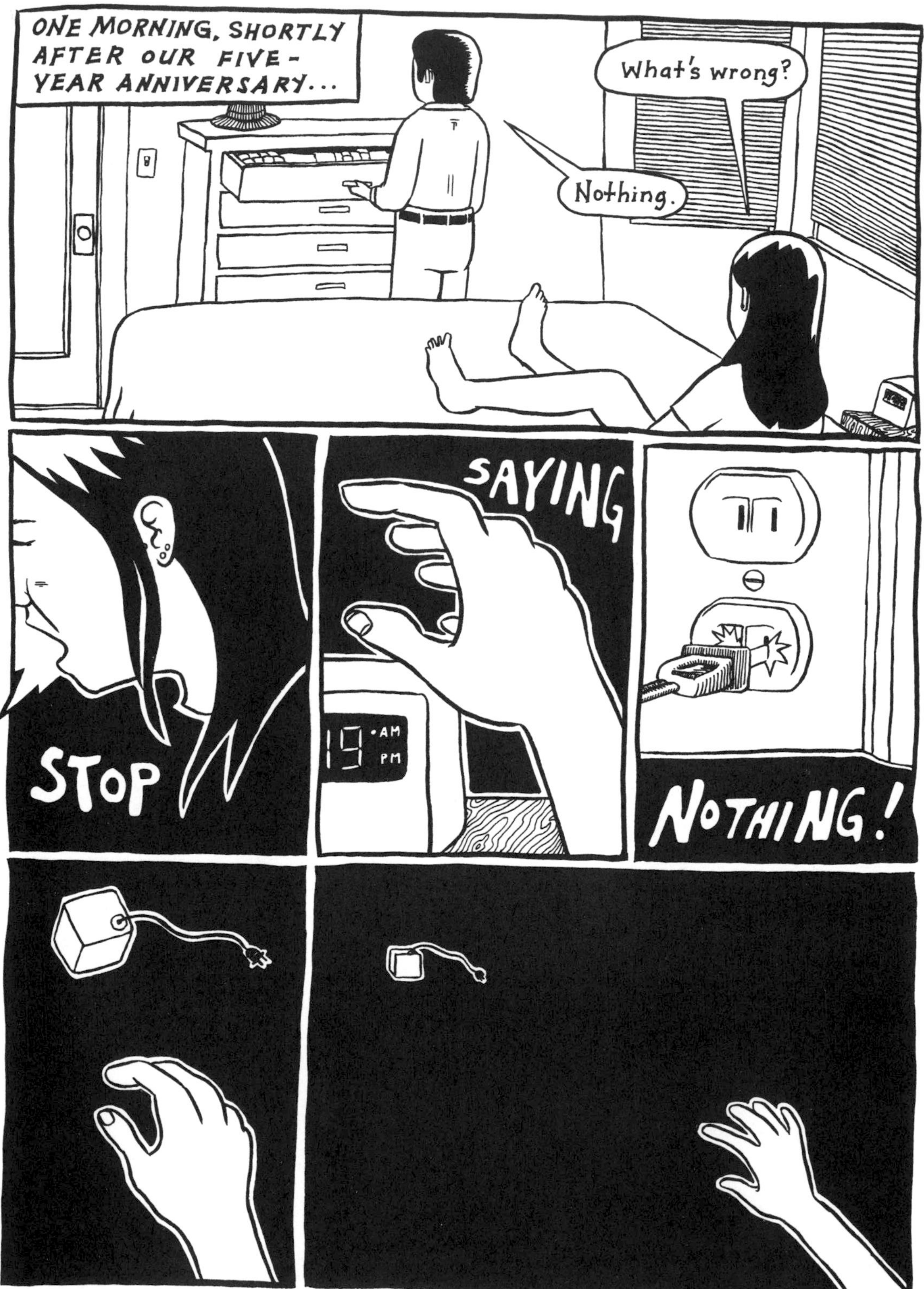
ONE MORNING, SHORTLY AFTER OUR FIVE-YEAR ANNIVERSARY...
What's wrong?
Nothing.
STOP
SAYING
NOTHING!

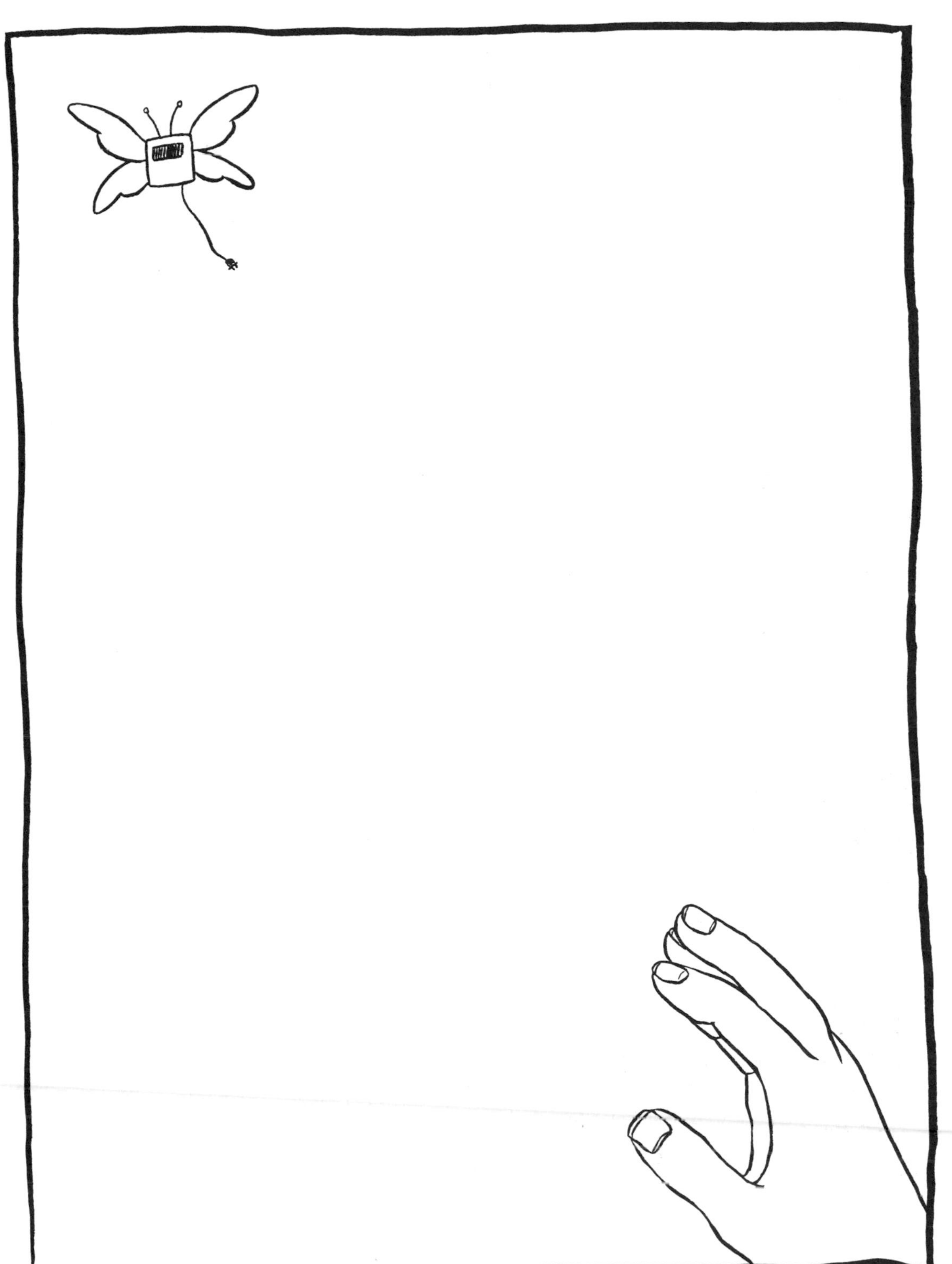

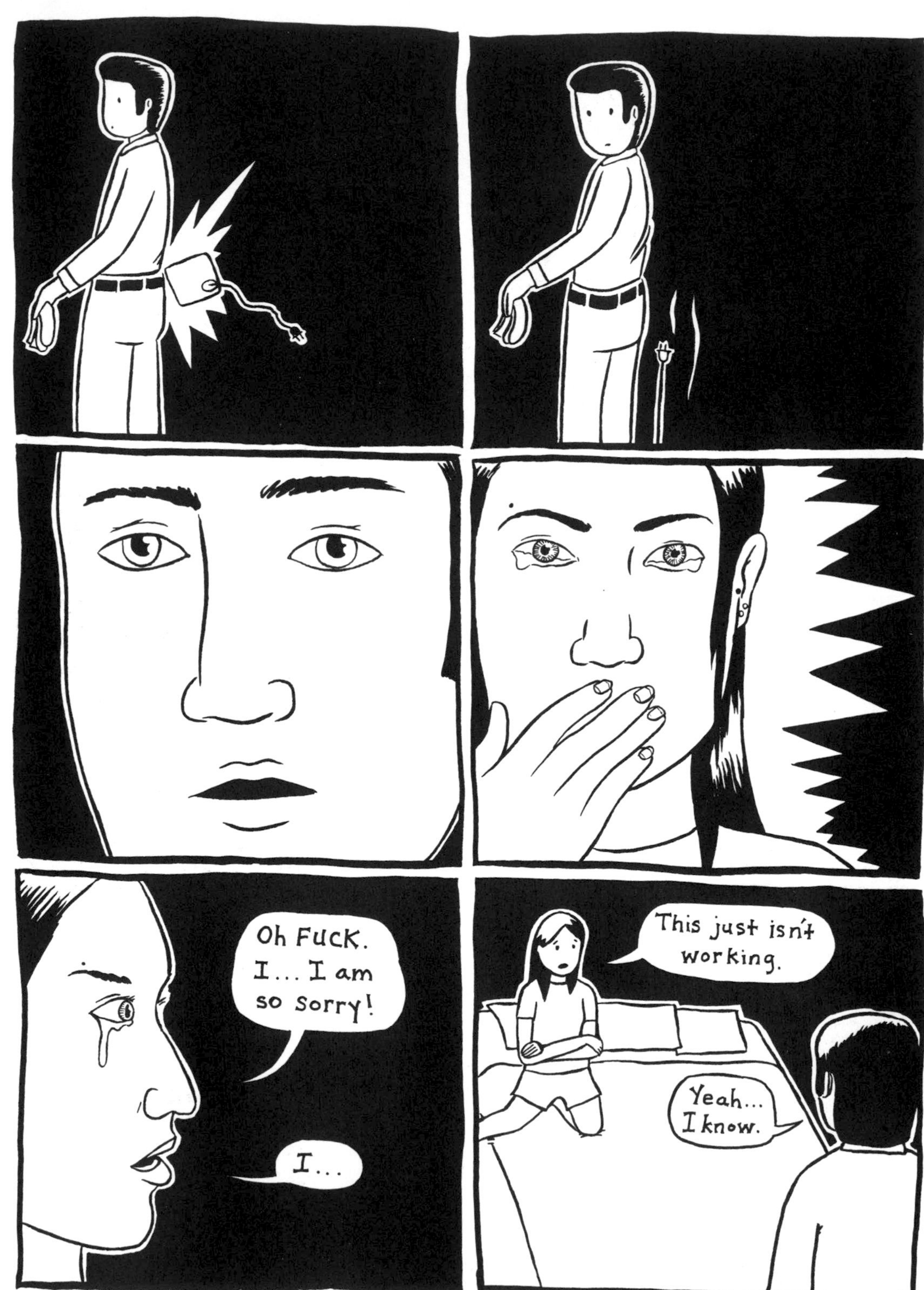
Oh FUCK.
I... I am so sorry!
I...
This just isn't working.
Yeah... I know.

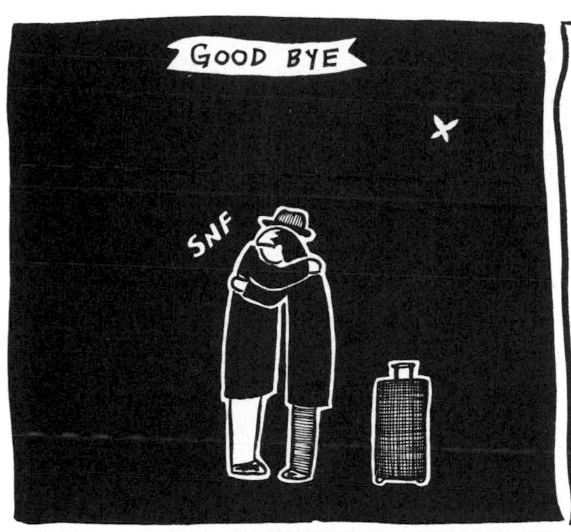
GOOD BYE
SNF

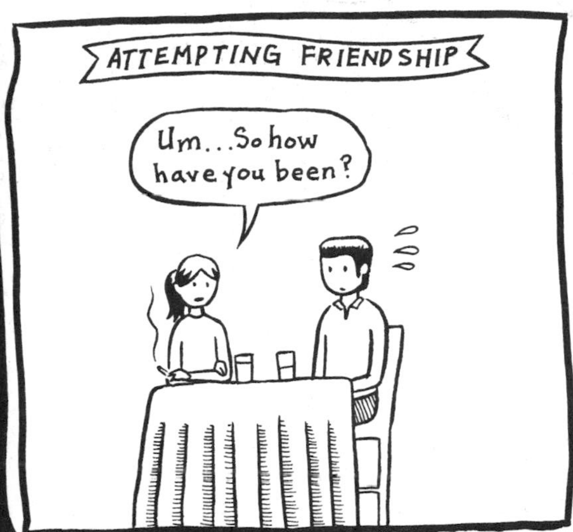
ATTEMPTING FRIENDSHIP
Um... So how have you been?

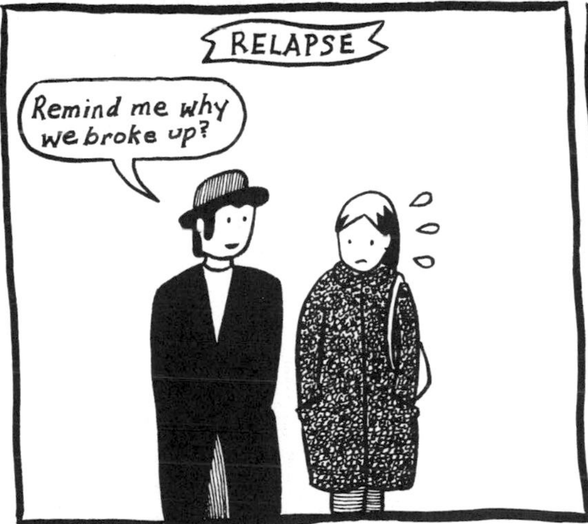
RELAPSE
Remind me why we broke up?

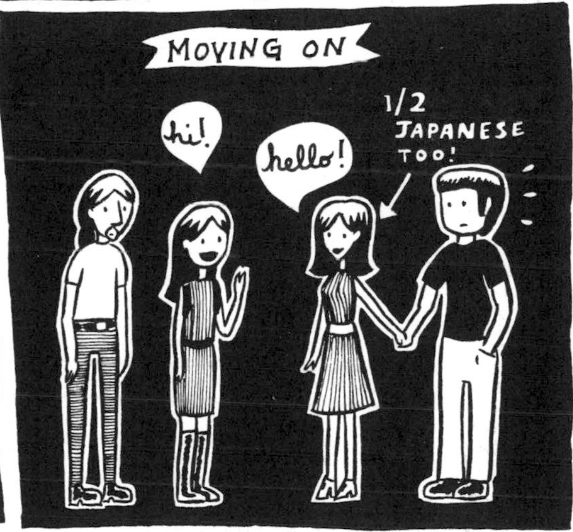
MOVING ON
hi!
hello!
1/2 JAPANESE TOO!

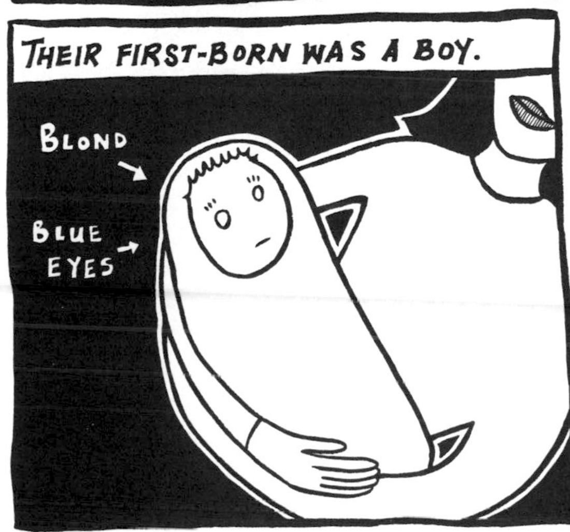
THEIR FIRST-BORN WAS A BOY.
BLOND
BLUE EYES

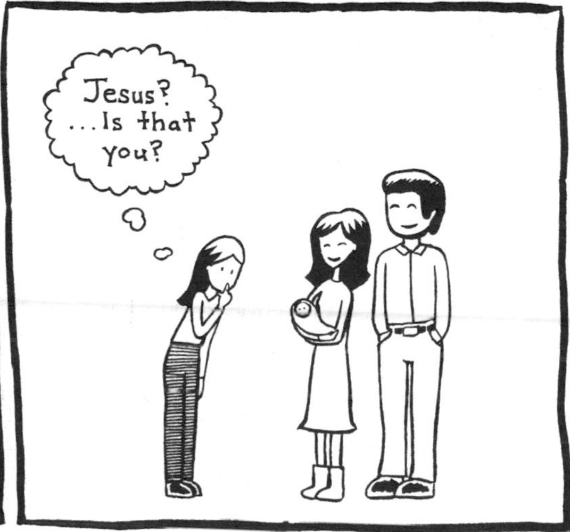
Jesus? ...Is that you?

1991

age 18

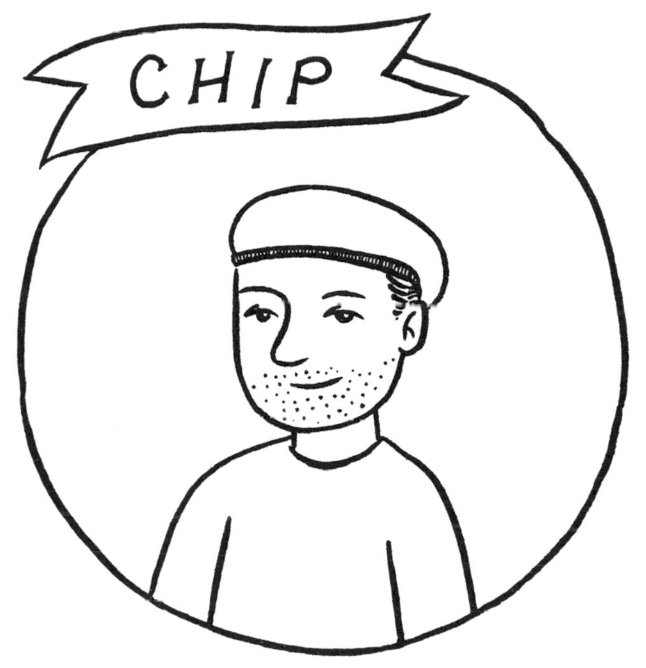
CHIP

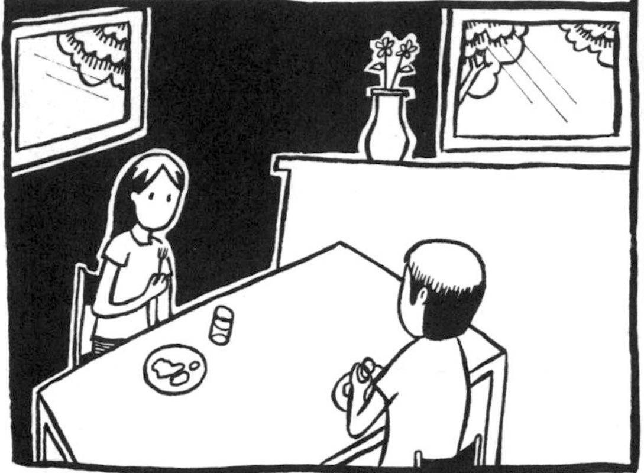
FRANCIS AND I DECIDED TO ATTEMPT AN OPEN RELATIONSHIP.

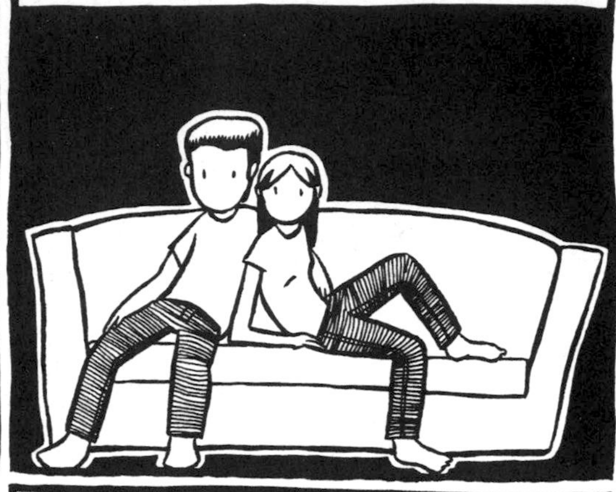
AFTER AN INTENSE YEAR TOGETHER WE'D RECENTLY COHABITATED.

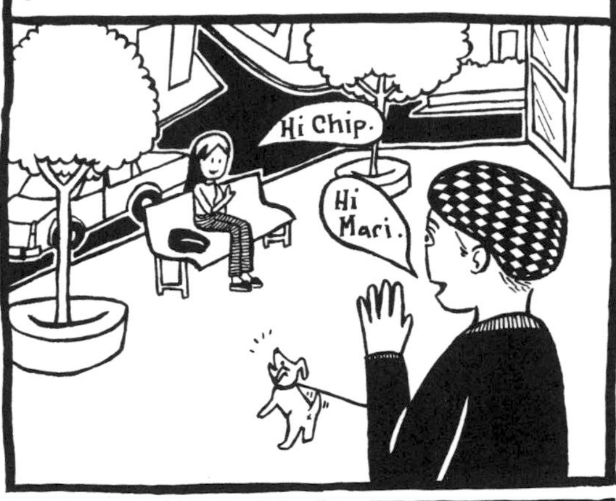
AN OPPORTUNITY QUICKLY PRESENTED ITSELF WITH AN OLD PAL.
Hi Chip.
Hi Mari.

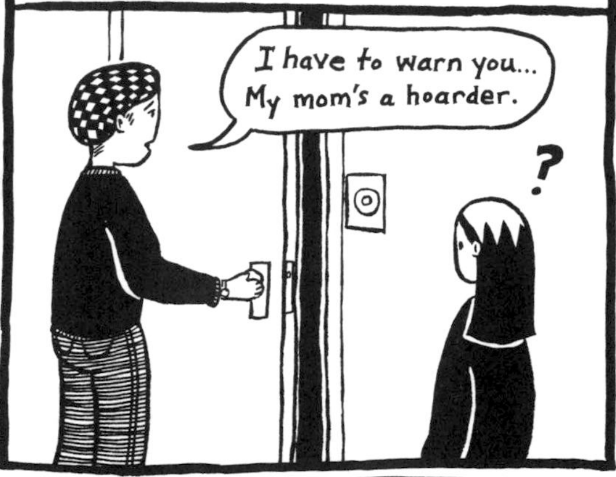
HE BROUGHT ME TO HIS MOTHER'S HOUSE.
I have to warn you... My mom's a hoarder.
?

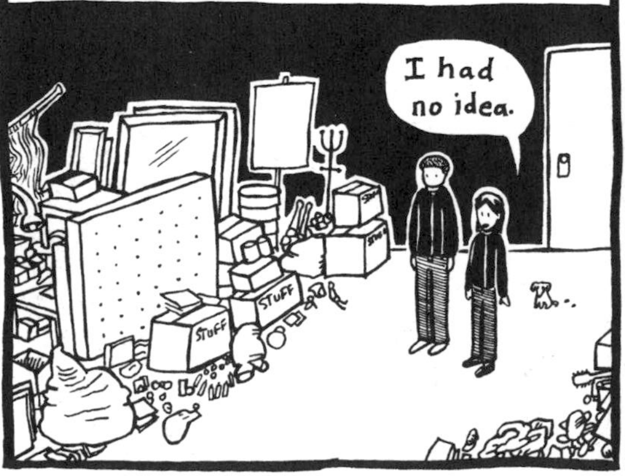
THE PLACE WAS A TATTERED MUSEUM OF KITSCH AND GARBAGE.
I had no idea.
STUFF
STUFF

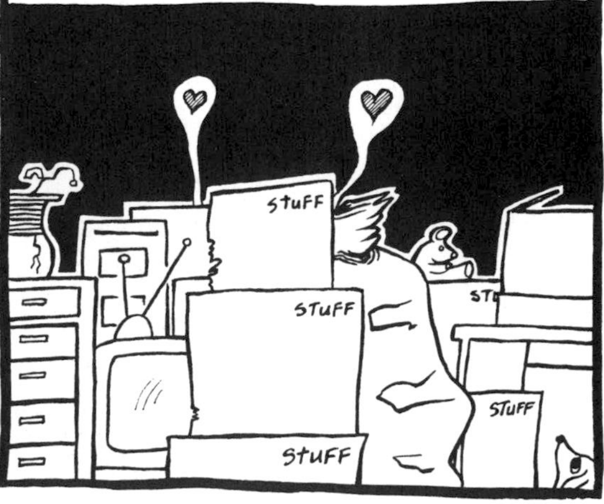
BUT THAT DIDN'T STOP US.
STUFF
STUFF
STUFF
STUFF

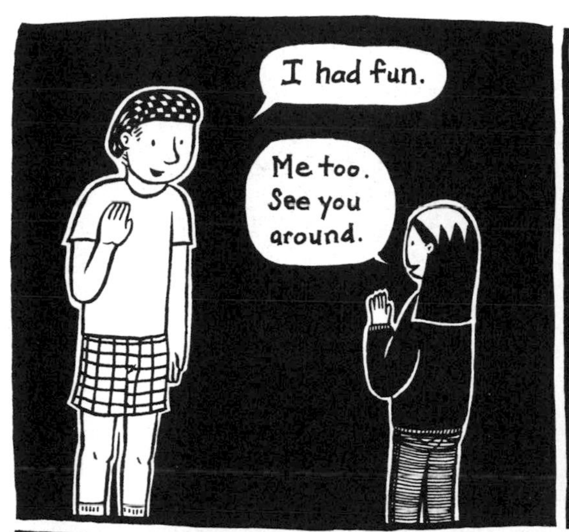
I had fun.
Me too. See you around.

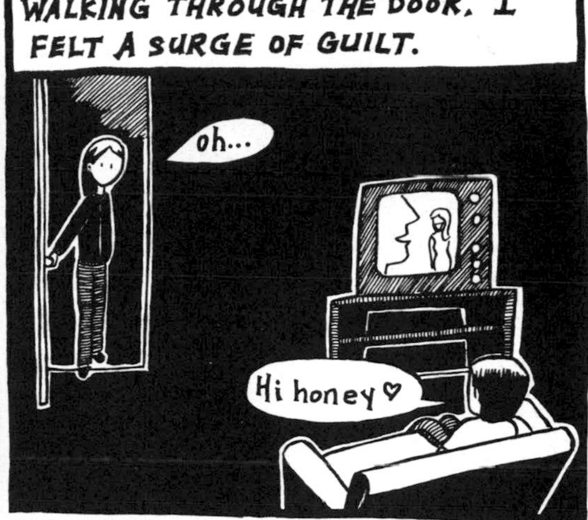
WALKING THROUGH THE DOOR, I FELT A SURGE OF GUILT.
oh...
Hi honey♡

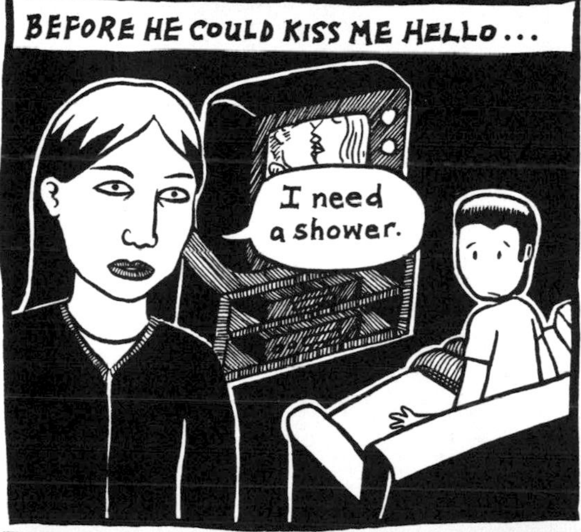
BEFORE HE COULD KISS ME HELLO...
I need a shower.

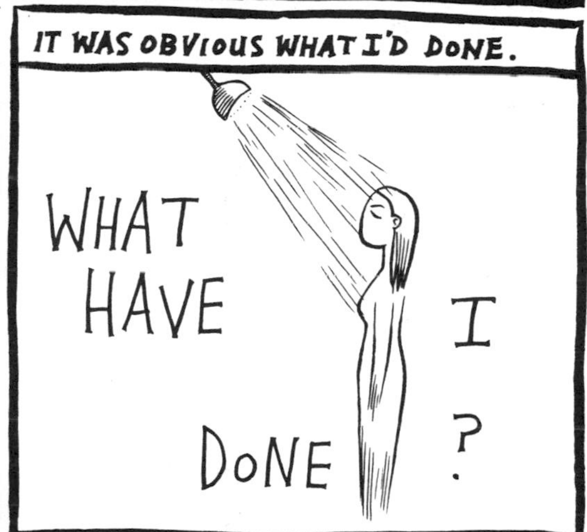
IT WAS OBVIOUS WHAT I'D DONE.
WHAT HAVE I DONE?

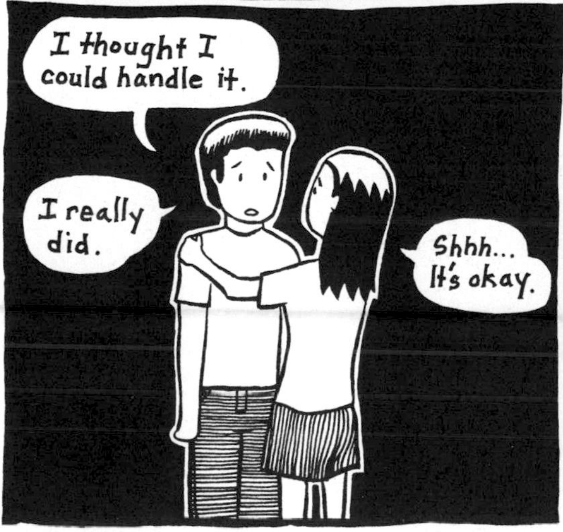
I thought I could handle it.
I really did.
Shhh... It's okay.

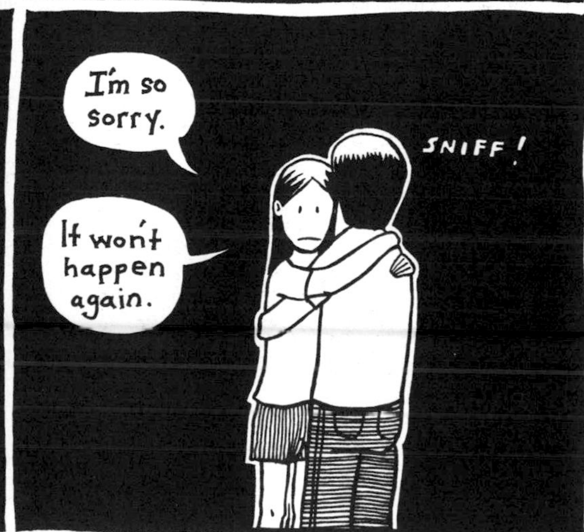
I'm so sorry.
SNIFF!
It won't happen again.

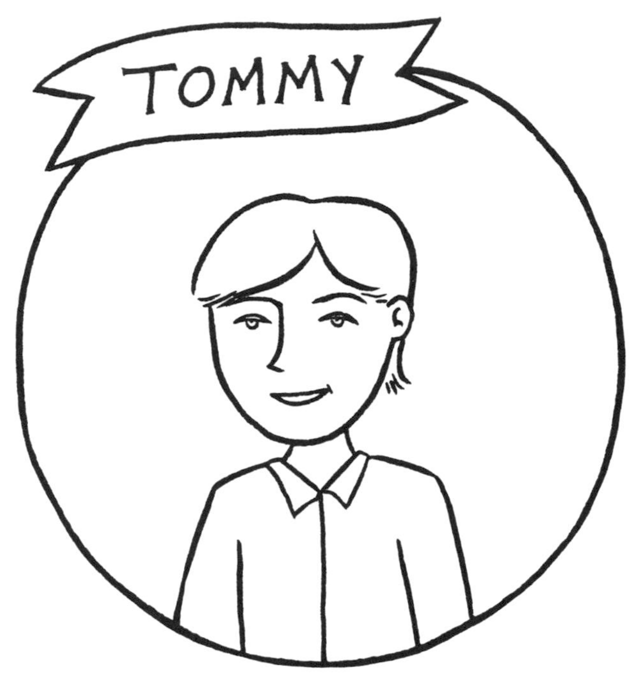
TOMMY

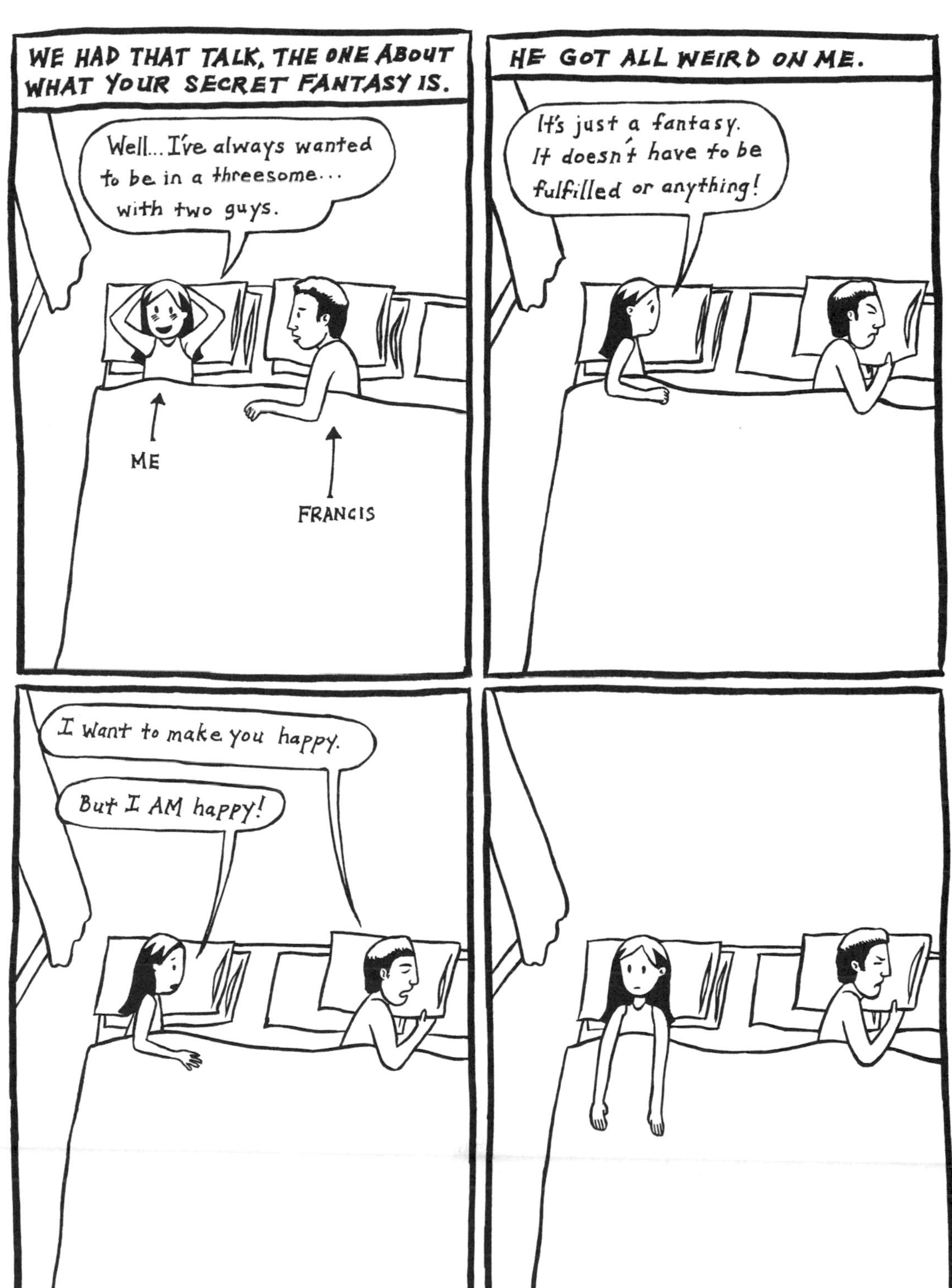
WE HAD THAT TALK, THE ONE ABOUT WHAT YOUR SECRET FANTASY IS.
Well... I've always wanted to be in a threesome... with two guys.
ME
FRANCIS
HE GOT ALL WEIRD ON ME.
It's just a fantasy. It doesn't have to be fulfilled or anything!
I want to make you happy.
But I AM happy!

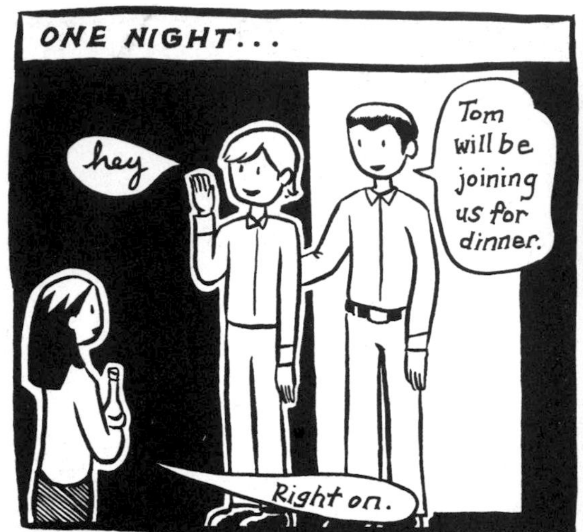
ONE NIGHT...
hey
Tom will be joining us for dinner.
Right on.

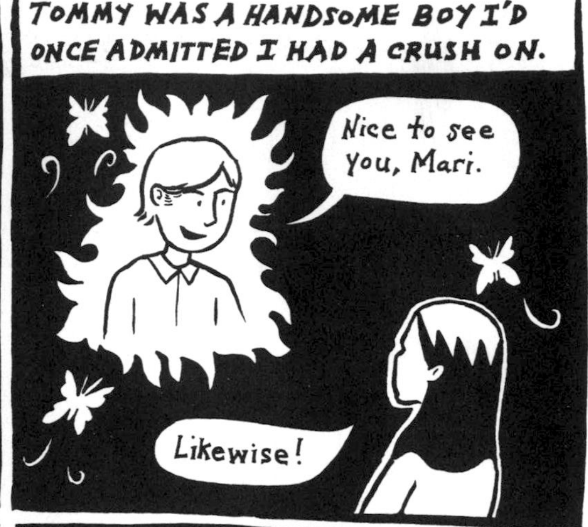
TOMMY WAS A HANDSOME BOY I'D ONCE ADMITTED I HAD A CRUSH ON.
Nice to see you, Mari.
Likewise!

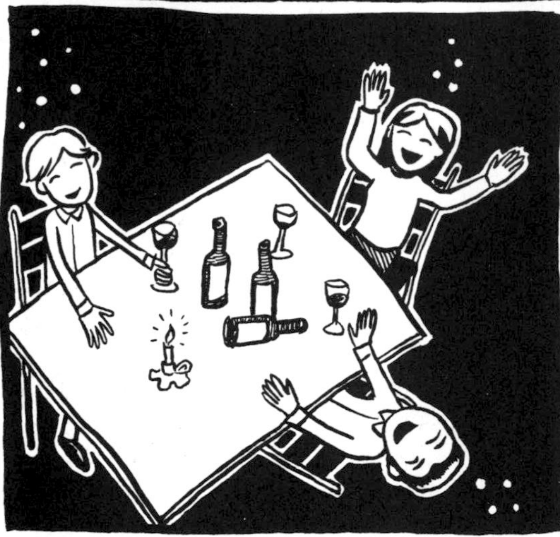

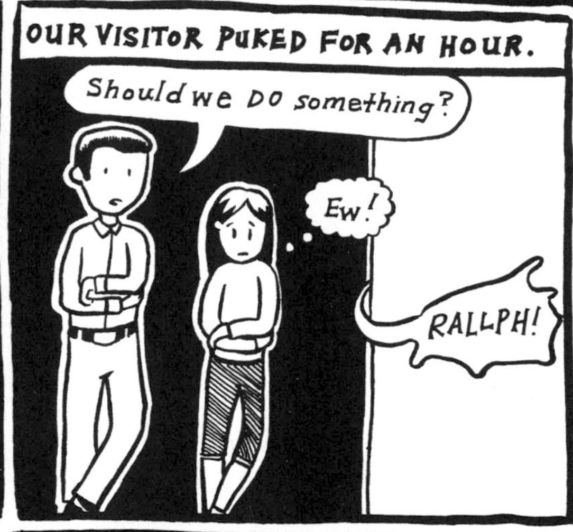
OUR VISITOR PUKED FOR AN HOUR.
Should we DO something?
Ew!
RALLPH!

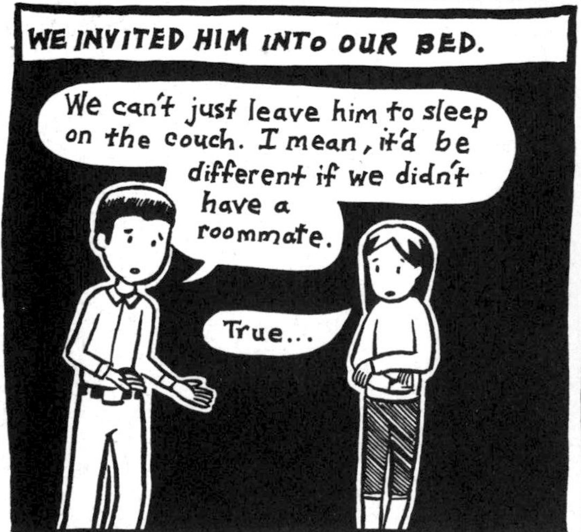
WE INVITED HIM INTO OUR BED.
We can't just leave him to sleep on the couch. I mean, it'd be different if we didn't have a roommate.
True...

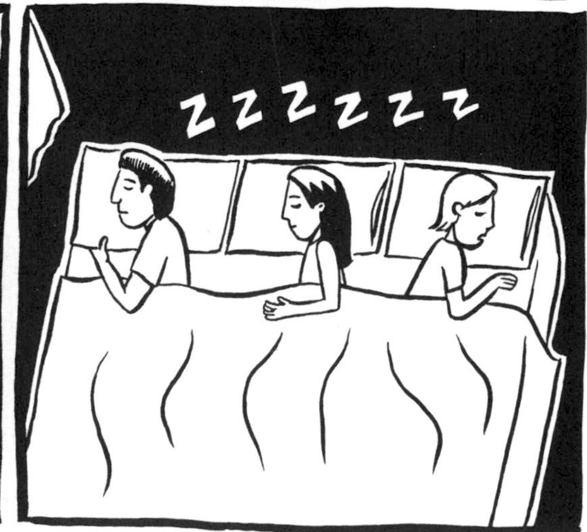
ZZZZZZZ

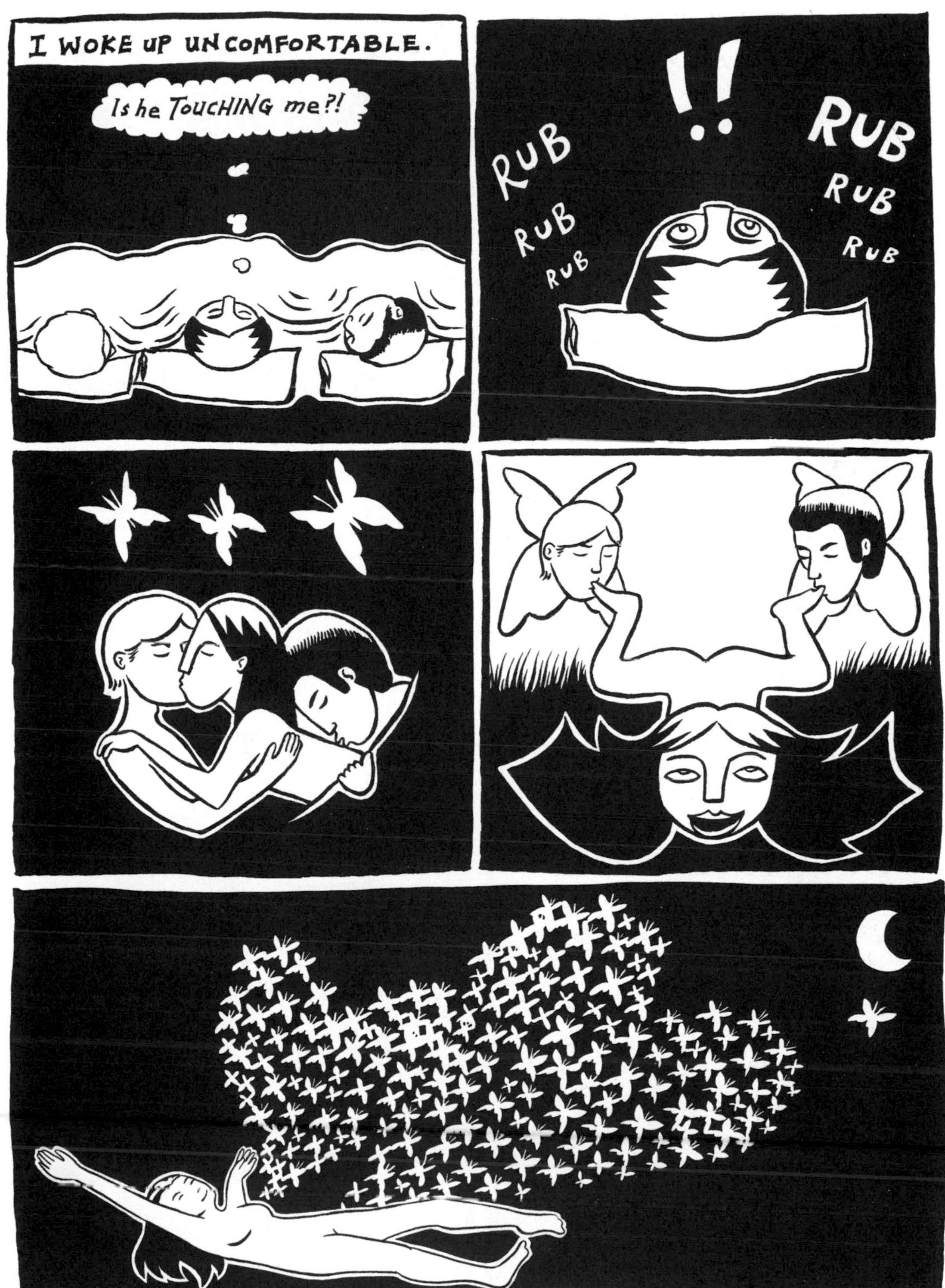
I WOKE UP UNCOMFORTABLE.
Is he TOUCHING me?!
!!
RUB
RUB
RUB
RUB
RUB
RUB

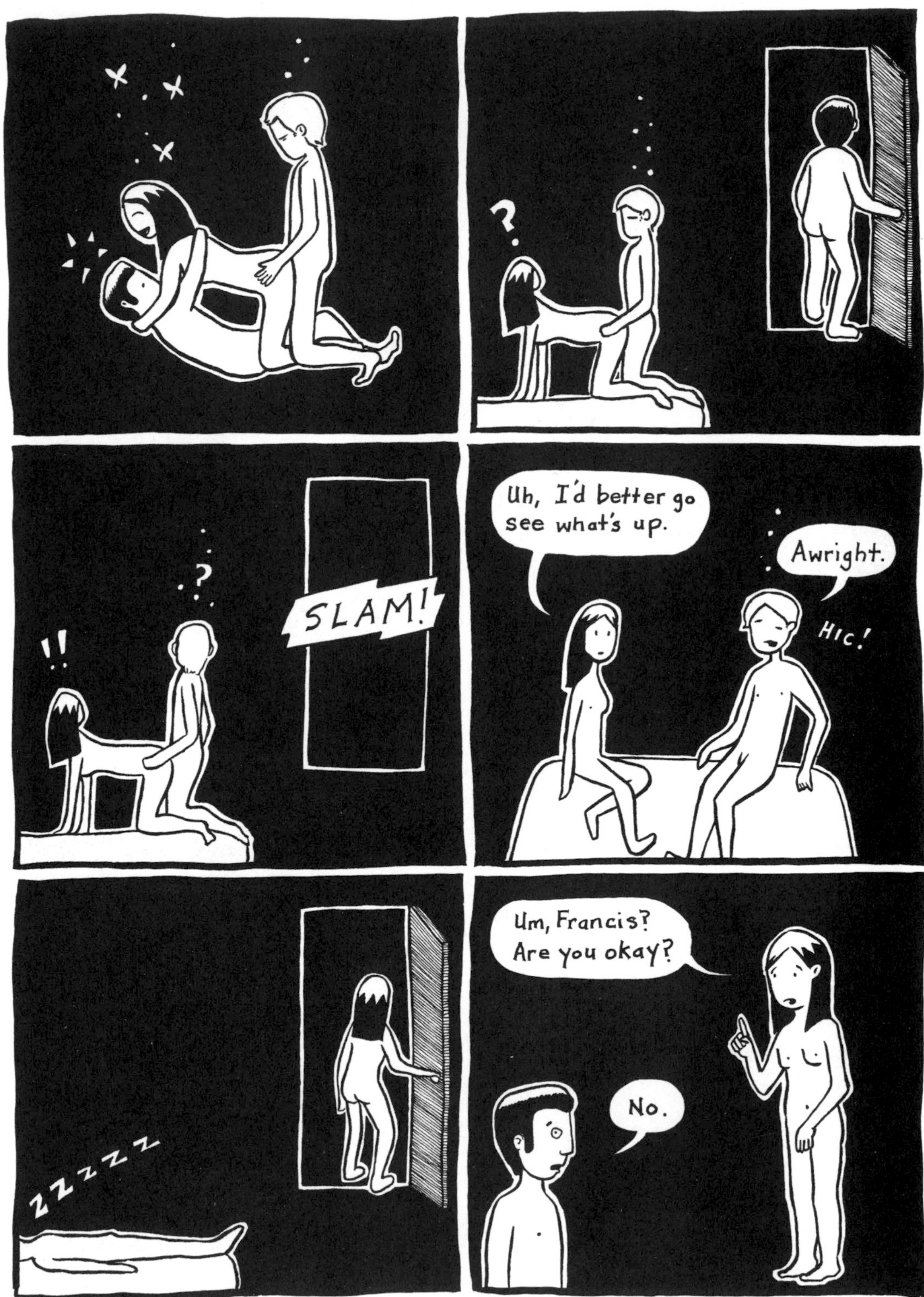
?
!!
?
SLAM!
Uh, I'd better go see what's up.
Awright.
HIC!
ZZZZZZ
Um, Francis? Are you okay?
No.

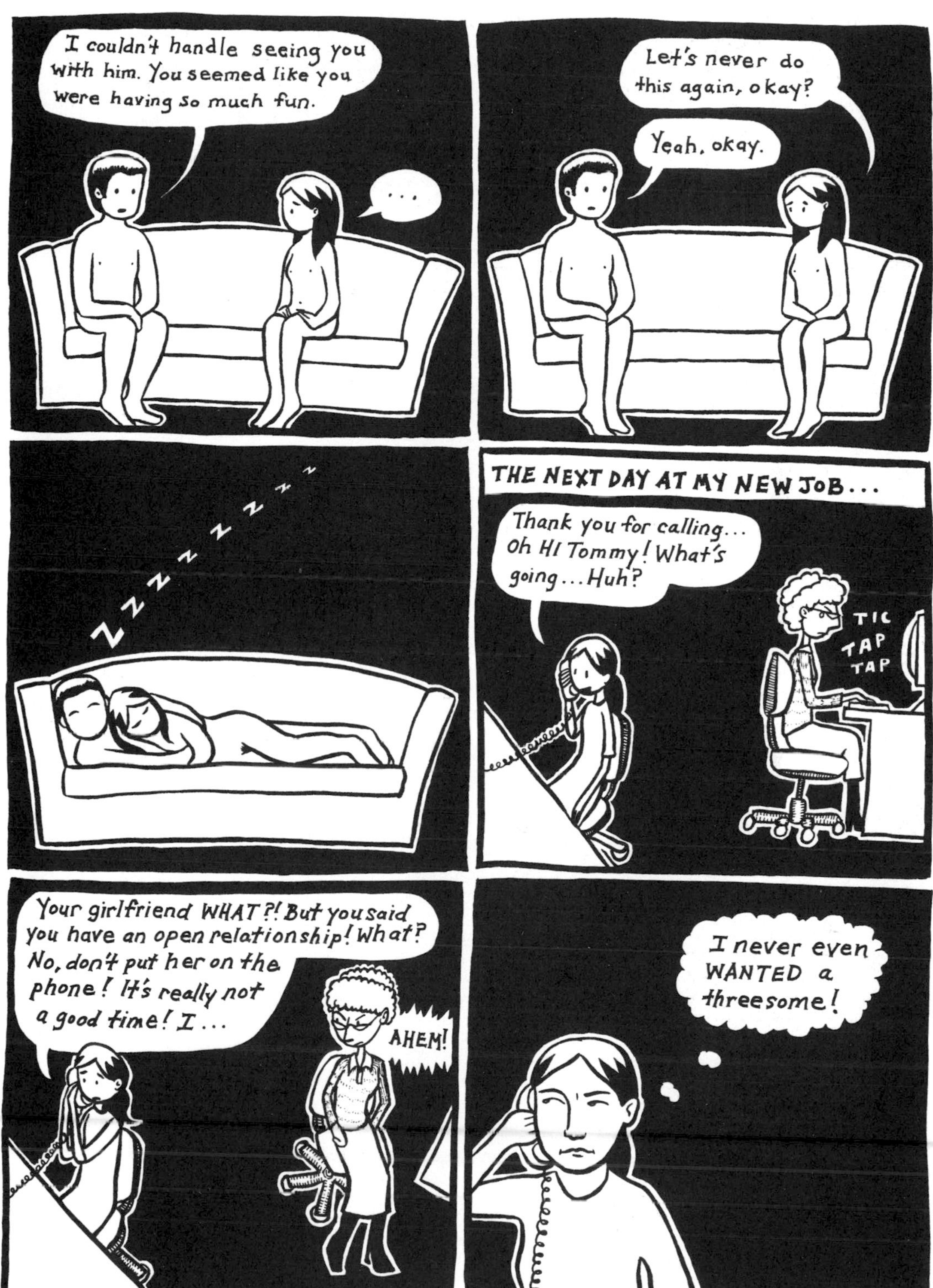
I couldn't handle seeing you with him. You seemed like you were having so much fun.
. . .
Let's never do this again, okay?
Yeah, okay.
Z Z Z Z Z Z Z Z Z Z
THE NEXT DAY AT MY NEW JOB...
Thank you for calling... Oh HI Tommy! What's going... Huh?
TIC TAP TAP
Your girlfriend WHAT?! But you said you have an open relationship! What? No, don't put her on the phone! It's really not a good time! I...
AHEM!
I never even WANTED a threesome!

1993

age 20

Thanksgiving dinner

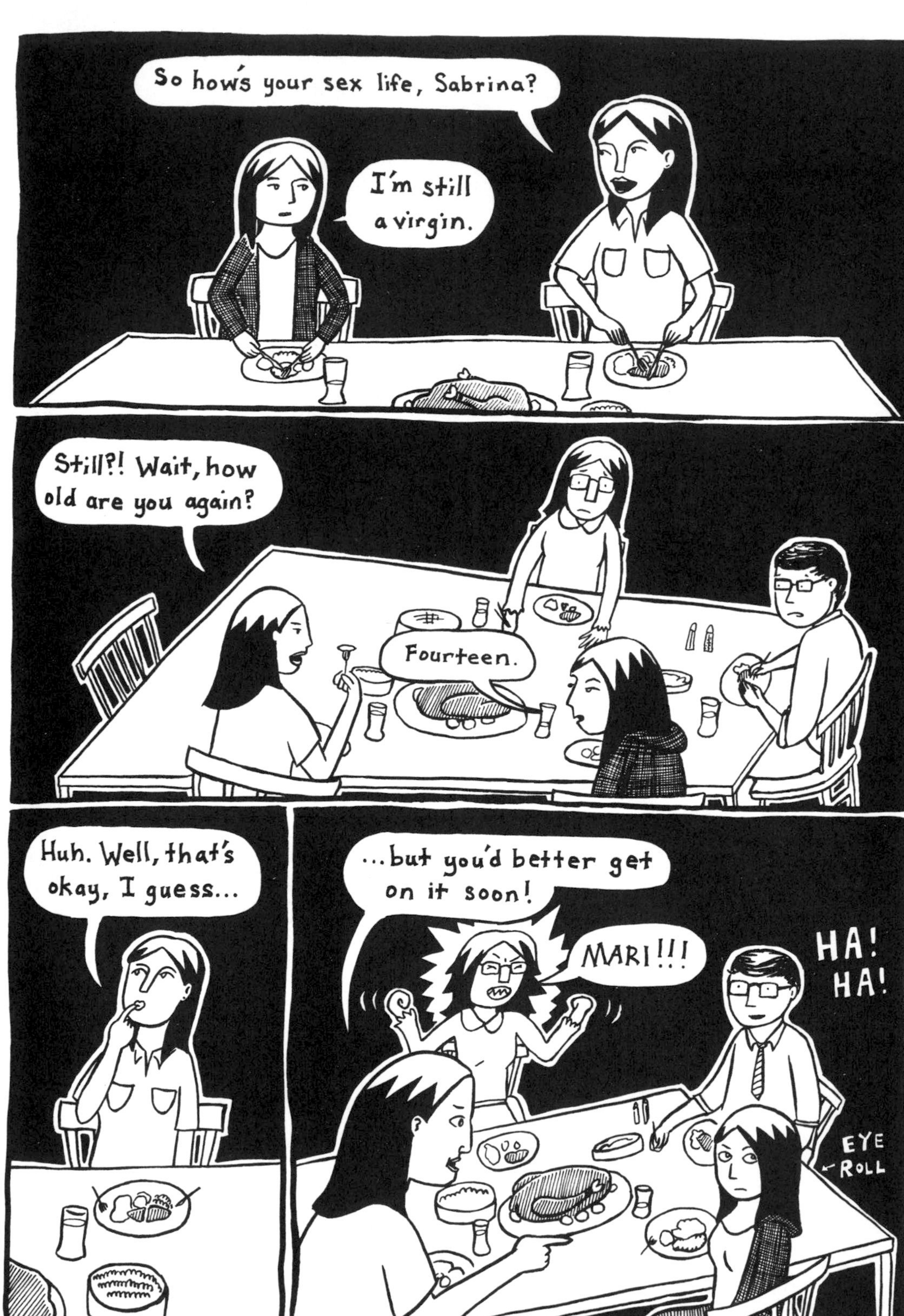
So how's your sex life, Sabrina?
I'm still a virgin.
Still?! Wait, how old are you again?
Fourteen.
Huh. Well, that's okay, I guess...
...but you'd better get on it soon!
MARI!!!
HA! HA!
EYE ROLL

1994
age 21

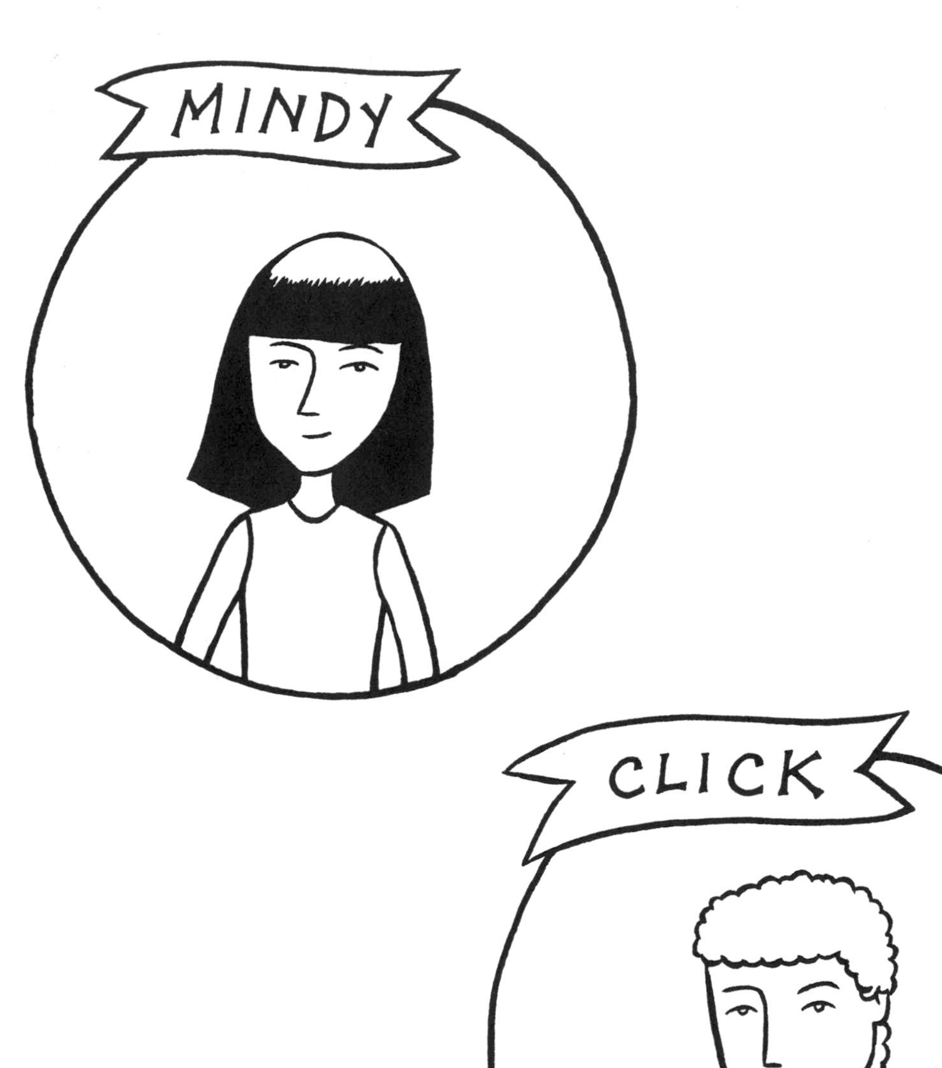
MINDY
CLICK

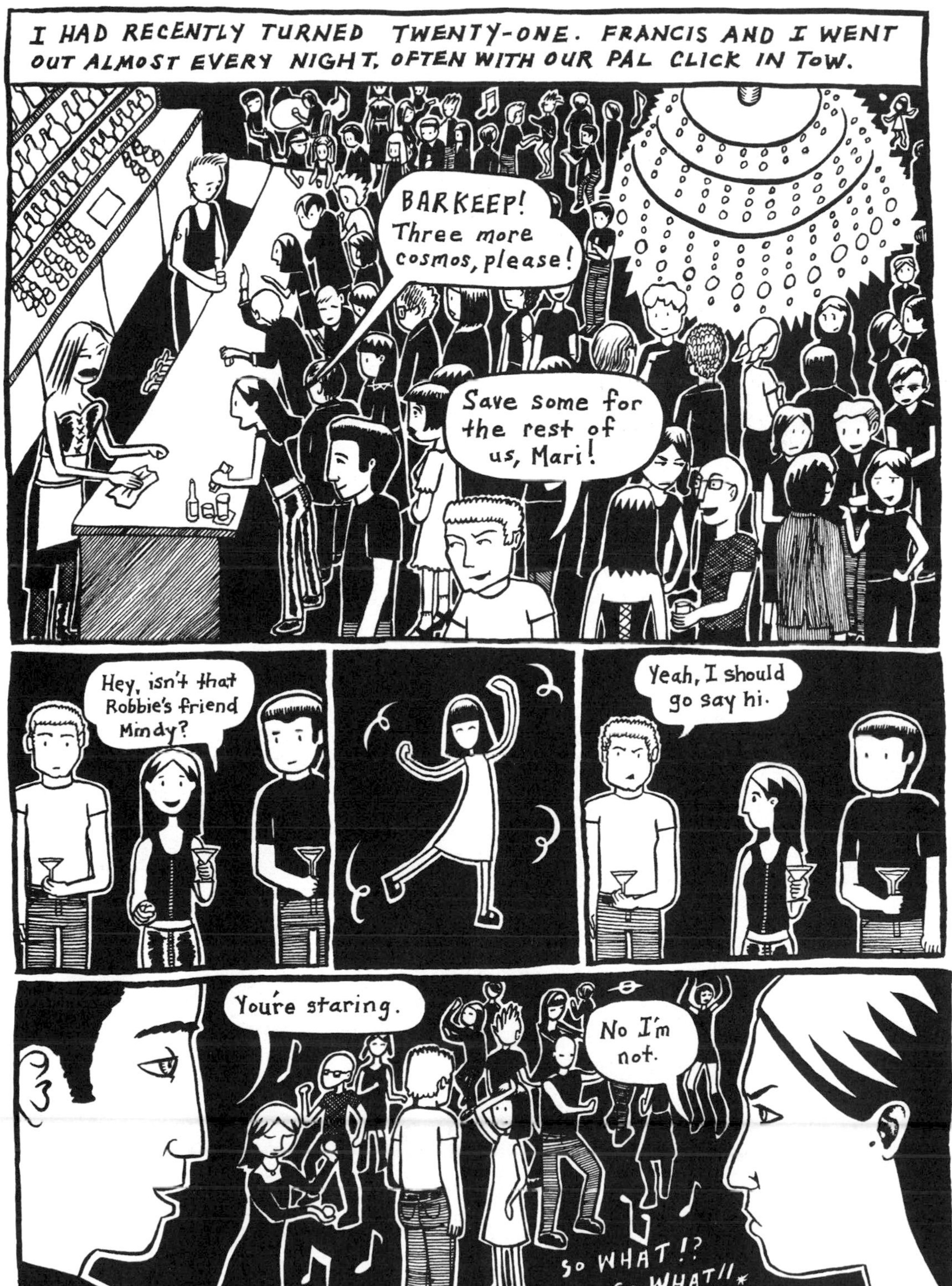
I HAD RECENTLY TURNED TWENTY-ONE. FRANCIS AND I WENT OUT ALMOST EVERY NIGHT, OFTEN WITH OUR PAL CLICK IN TOW.
BARKEEP! Three more cosmos, please!
Save some for the rest of us, Mari!
Hey, isn't that Robbie's friend Mindy?
Yeah, I should go say hi.
You're staring.
No I'm not.
SO WHAT!? SO WHAT!! *
* MINISTRY

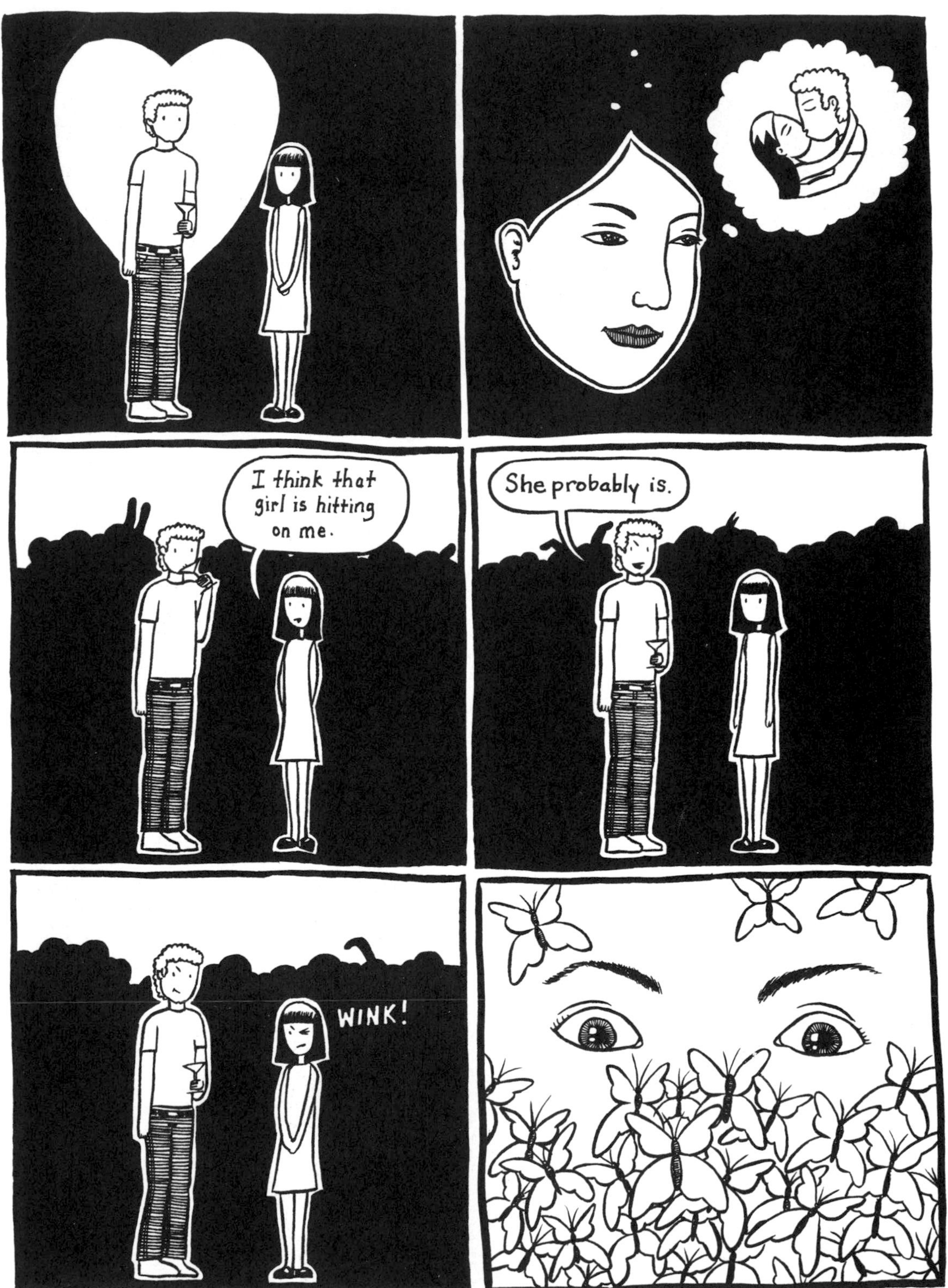
I think that girl is hitting on me.
She probably is.
WINK!

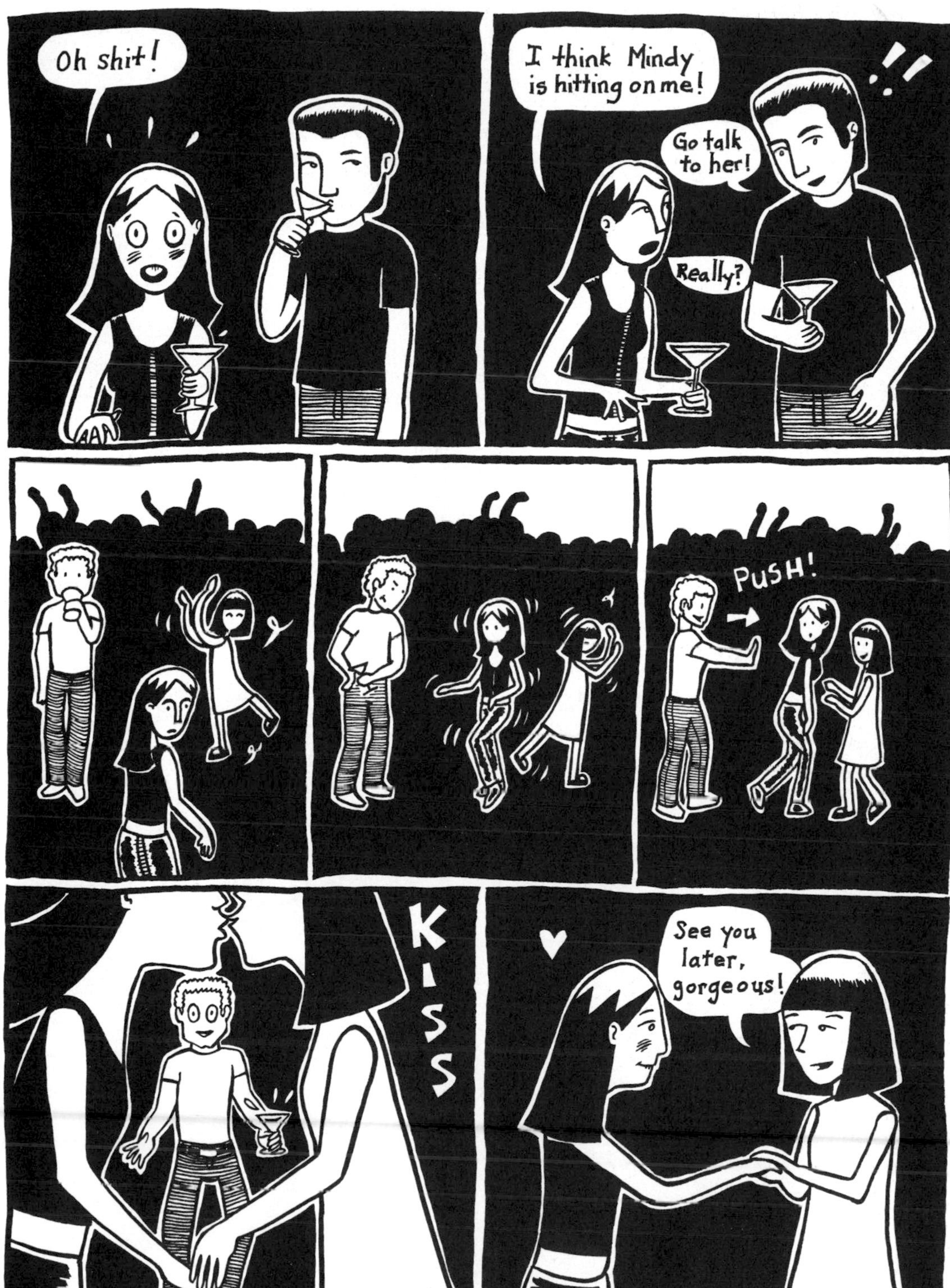
Oh shit!
I think Mindy is hitting on me!
Go talk to her!
Really?
PUSH!
KISS
See you later, gorgeous!

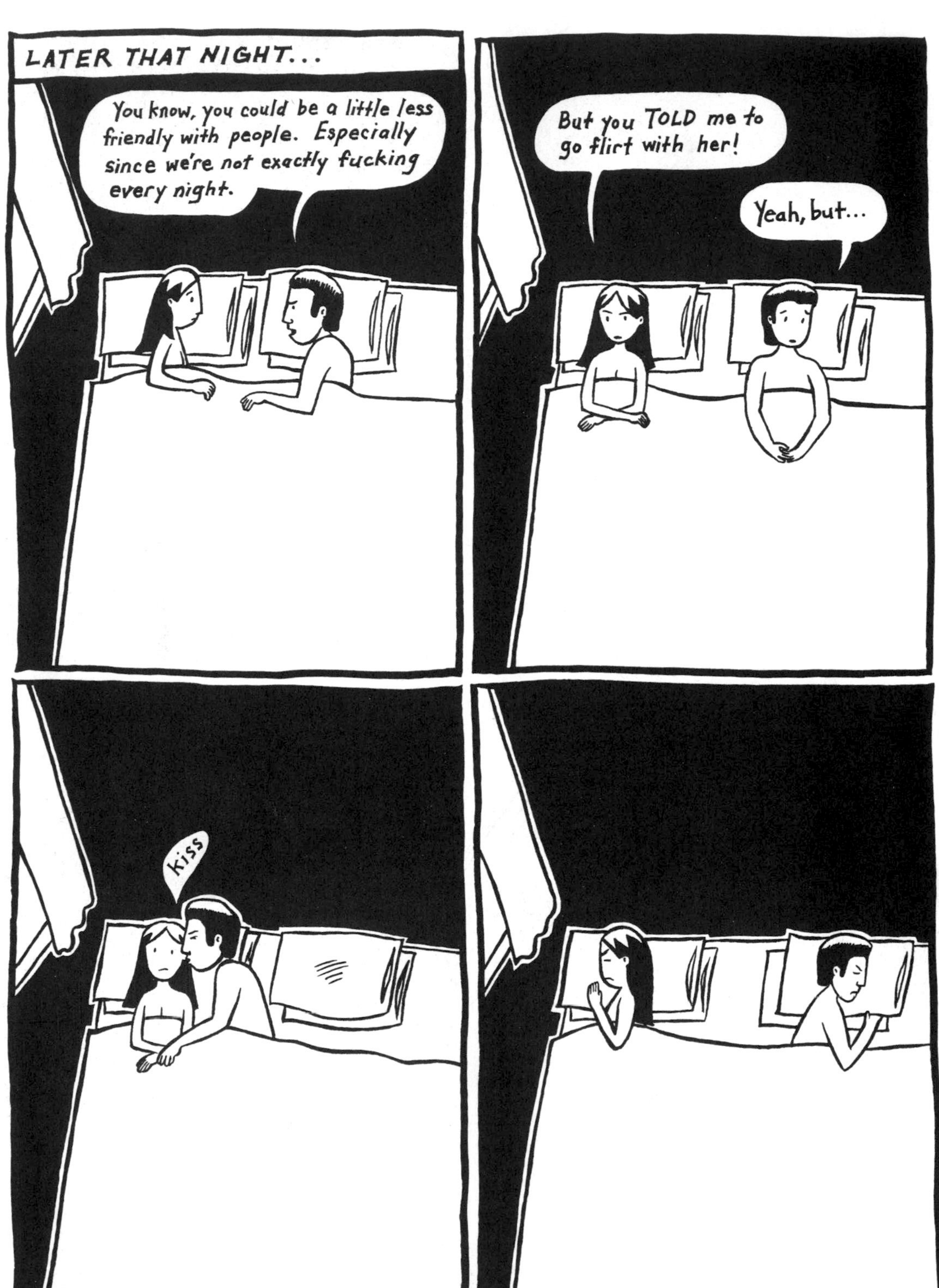
LATER THAT NIGHT...
You know, you could be a little less friendly with people. Especially since we're not exactly fucking every night.
But you TOLD me to go flirt with her!
Yeah, but...
kiss

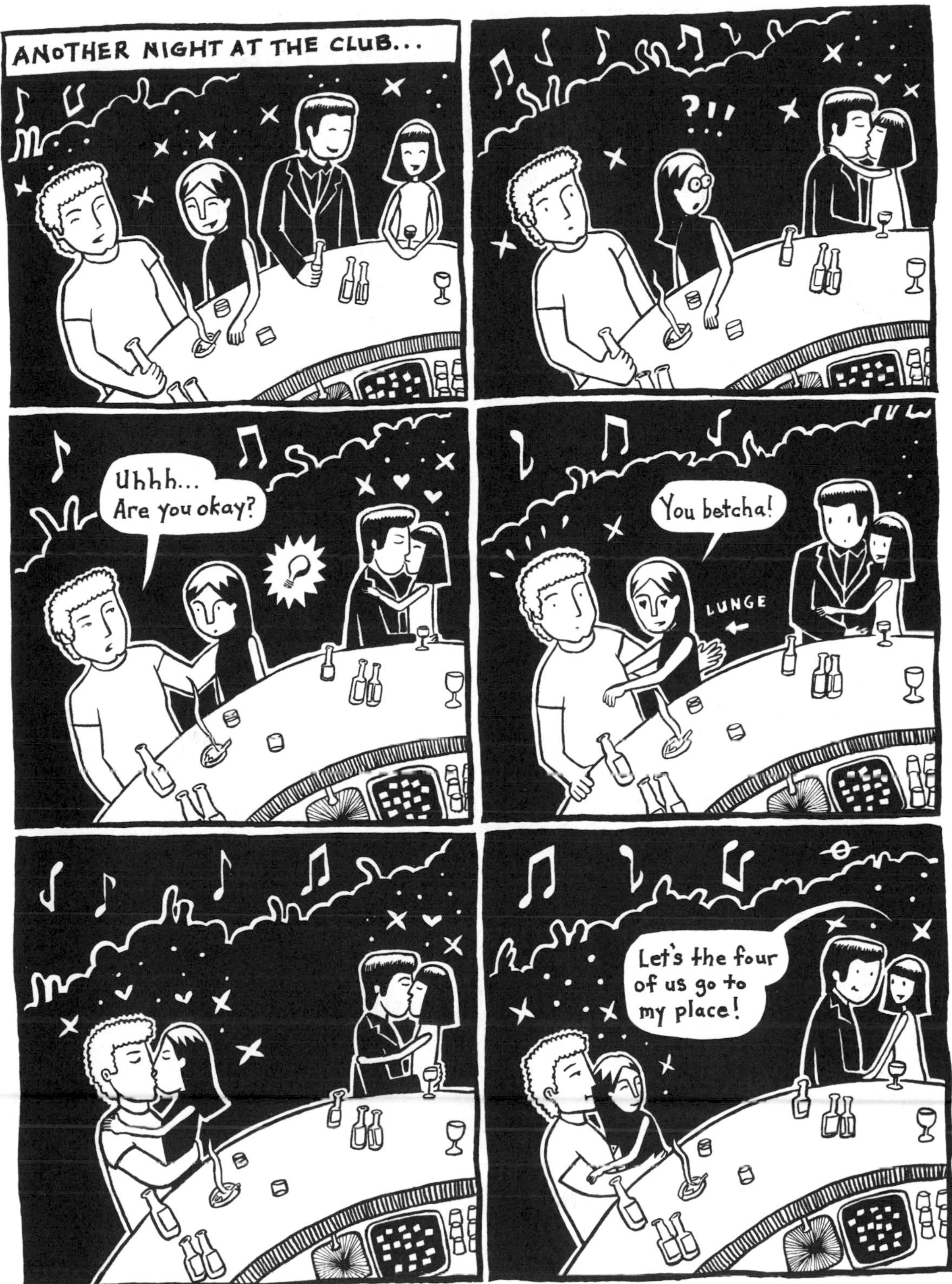
ANOTHER NIGHT AT THE CLUB...
?!!
Uhhh...
Are you okay?
You betcha!
LUNGE
Let's the four of us go to my place!

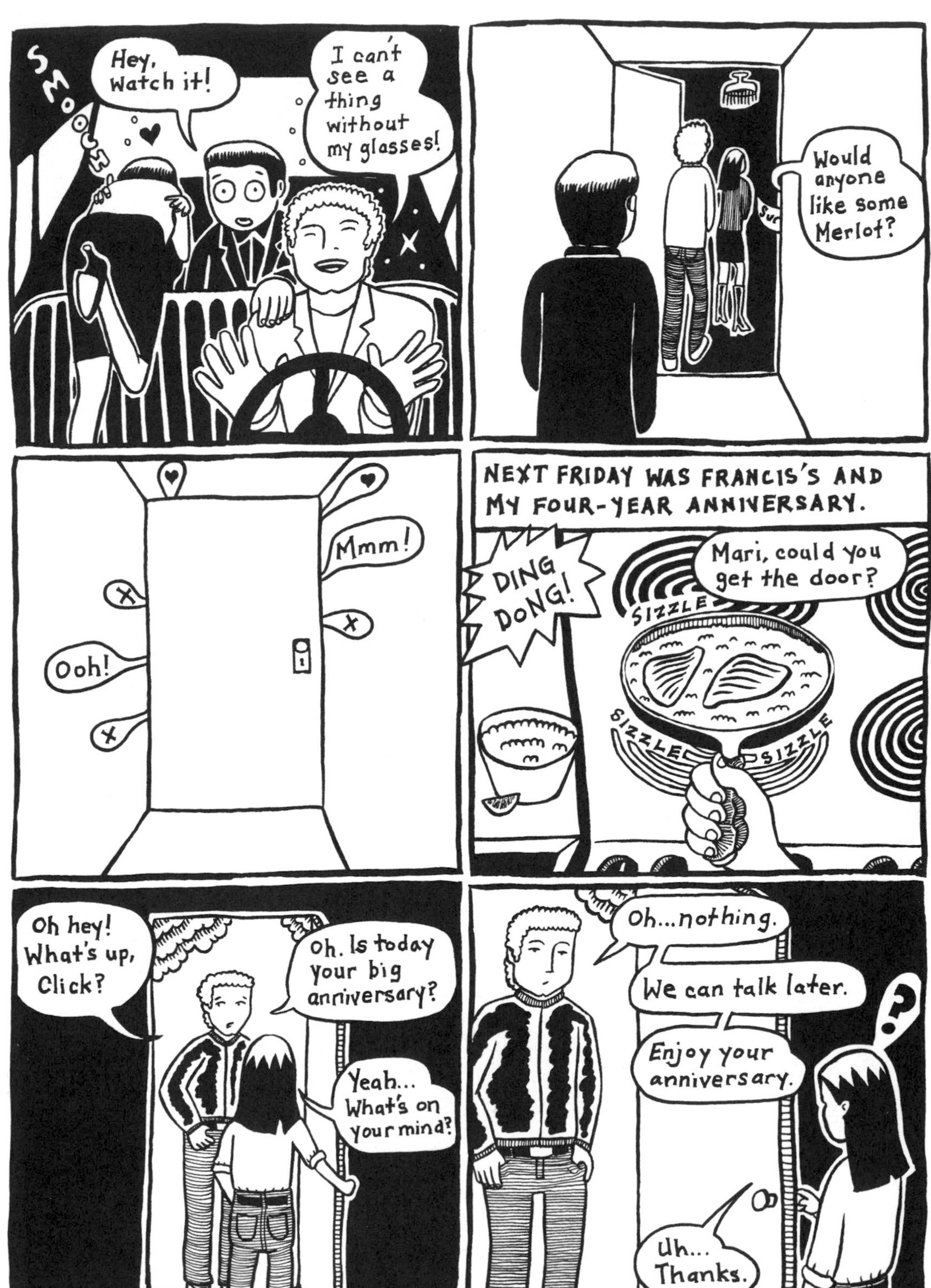
SMOOCH
Hey, Watch it!
I can't see a thing without my glasses!
Would anyone like some Merlot?
Mmm!
Ooh!
NEXT FRIDAY WAS FRANCIS'S AND MY FOUR-YEAR ANNIVERSARY.
DING DONG!
Mari, could you get the door?
SIZZLE
SIZZLE
SIZZLE
SIZZLE
Oh hey! What's up, Click?
Oh. Is today your big anniversary?
Yeah... What's on your mind?
Oh...nothing.
We can talk later.
Enjoy your anniversary.
Uh... Thanks.

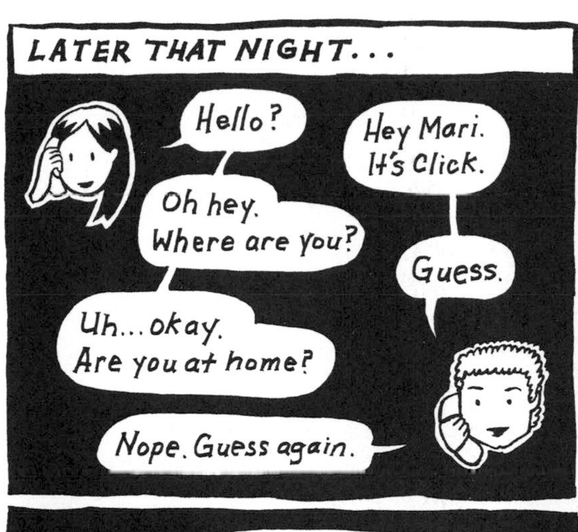
LATER THAT NIGHT...
Hello?
Hey Mari. It's Click.
Oh hey. Where are you?
Guess.
Uh...okay. Are you at home?
Nope. Guess again.

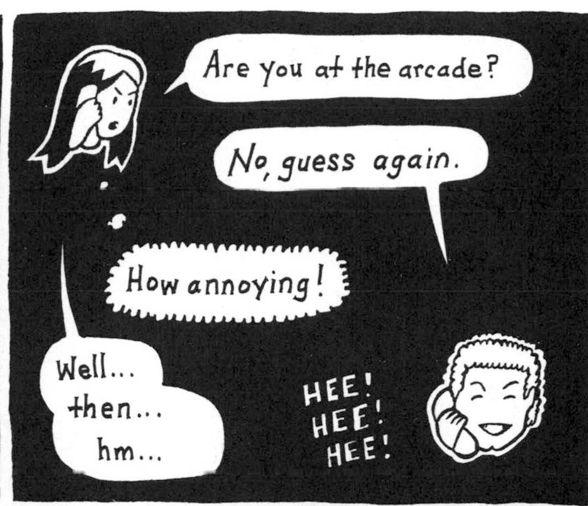
Are you at the arcade?
No, guess again.
How annoying!
Well... then... hm...
HEE! HEE! HEE!

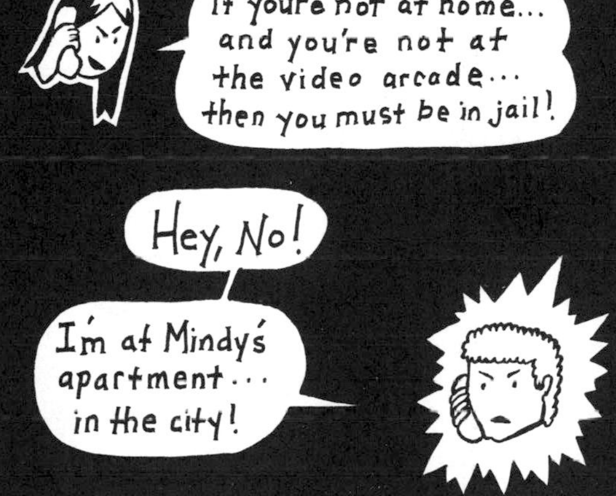
If you're not at home... and you're not at the video arcade... then you must be in jail!
Hey, No!
I'm at Mindy's apartment... in the city!

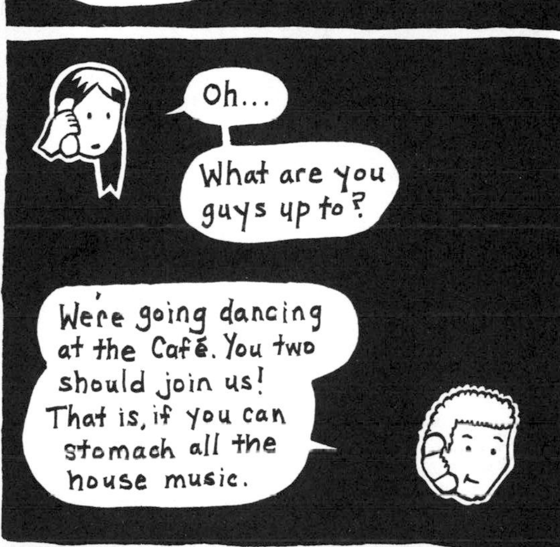
Oh...
What are you guys up to?
We're going dancing at the Café. You two should join us! That is, if you can stomach all the house music.

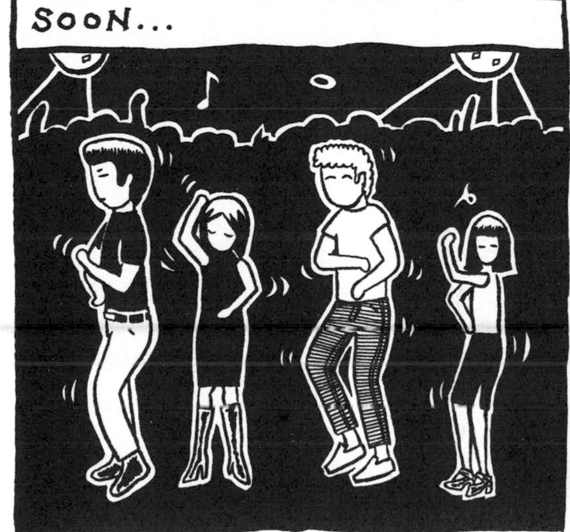
SOON...

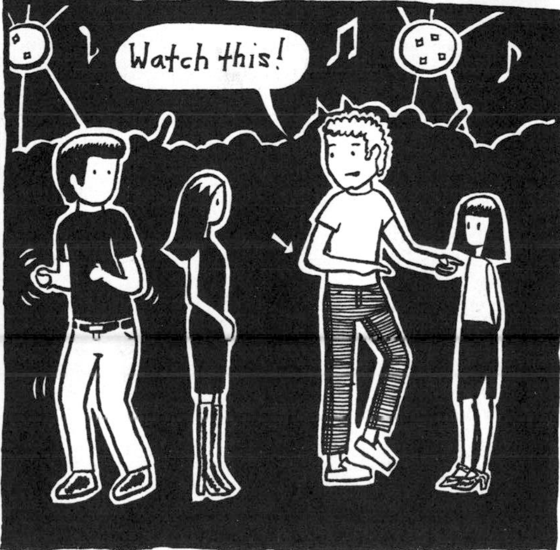
Watch this!

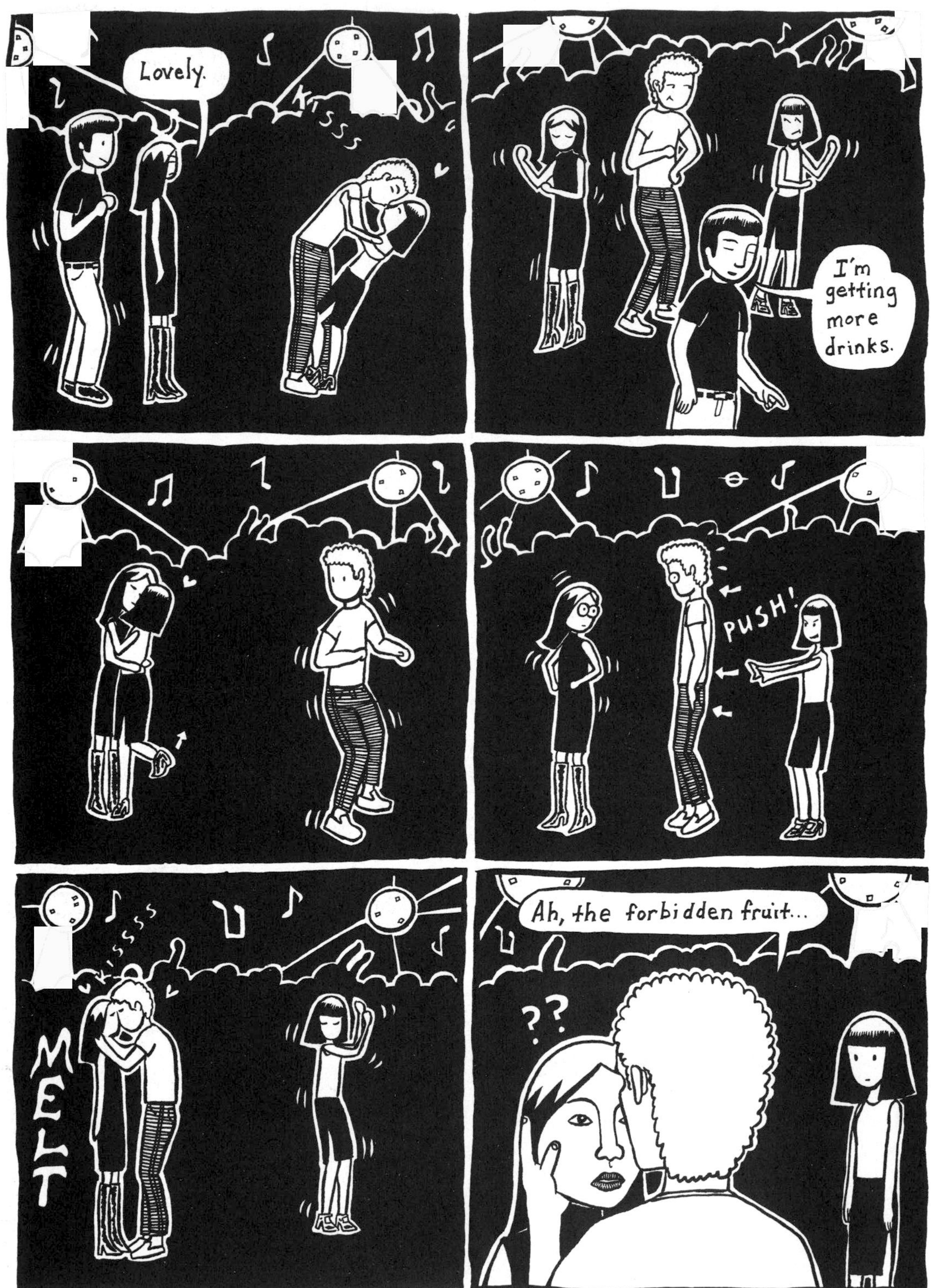
Lovely.
KISSS
I'm getting more drinks.
PUSH!
KISSSSS
MELT
Ah, the forbidden fruit...
??

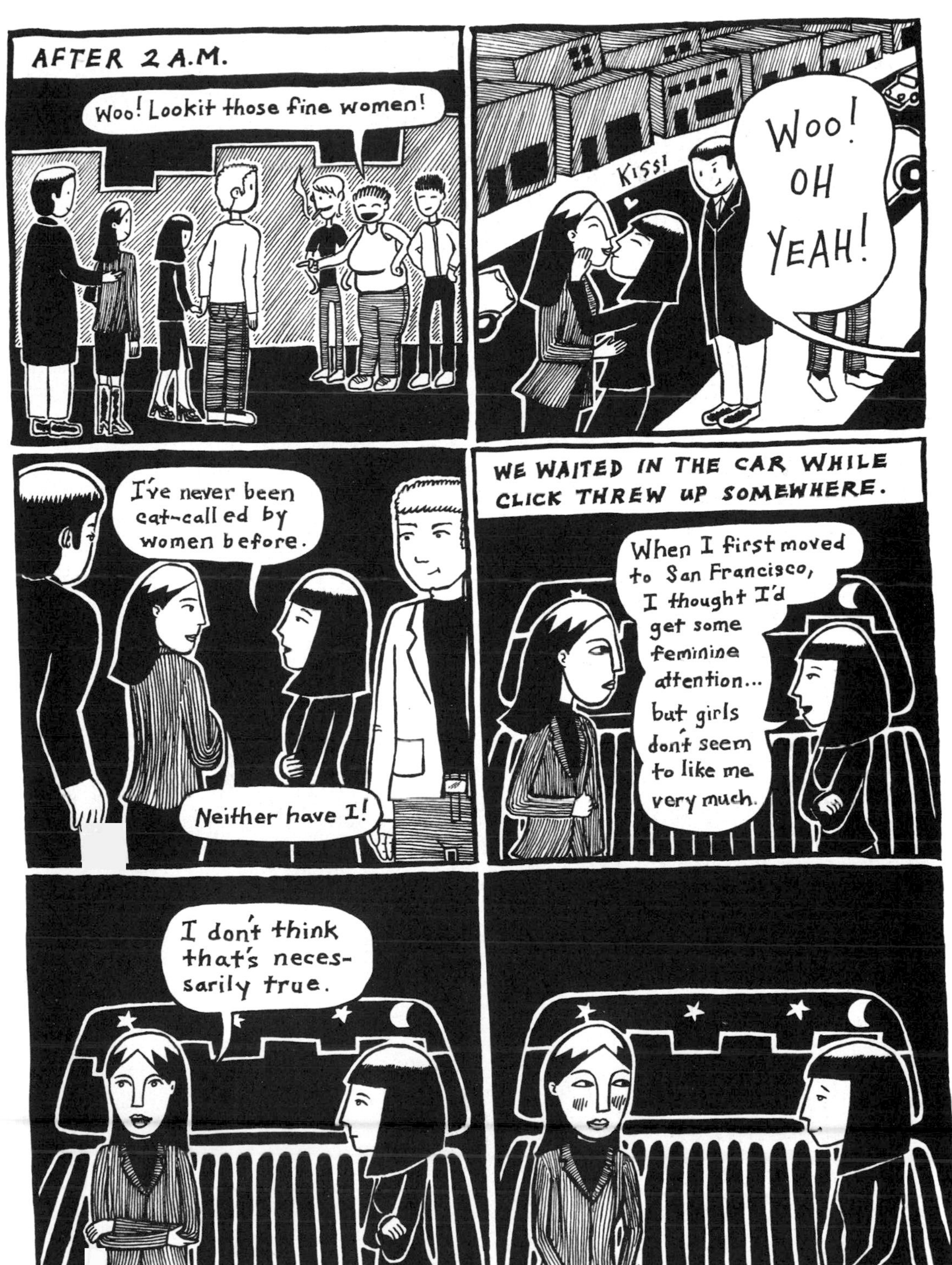
AFTER 2 A.M.
Woo! Lookit those fine women!
KISS!
Woo! OH YEAH!
I've never been cat-called by women before.
Neither have I!
WE WAITED IN THE CAR WHILE CLICK THREW UP SOMEWHERE.
When I first moved to San Francisco, I thought I'd get some feminine attention... but girls don't seem to like me very much.
I don't think that's necessarily true.

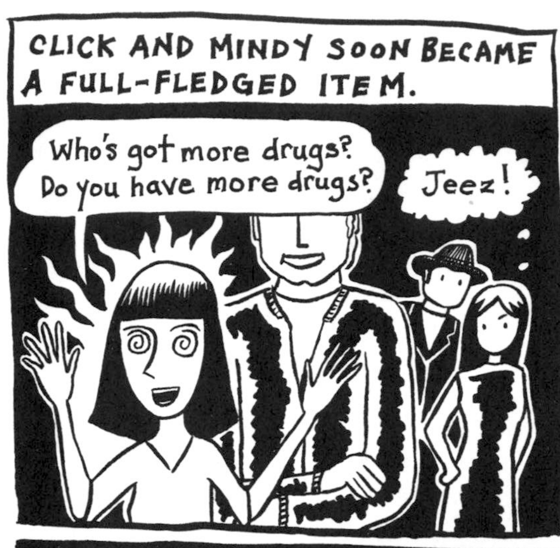
CLICK AND MINDY SOON BECAME A FULL-FLEDGED ITEM.
Who's got more drugs? Do you have more drugs?
Jeez!

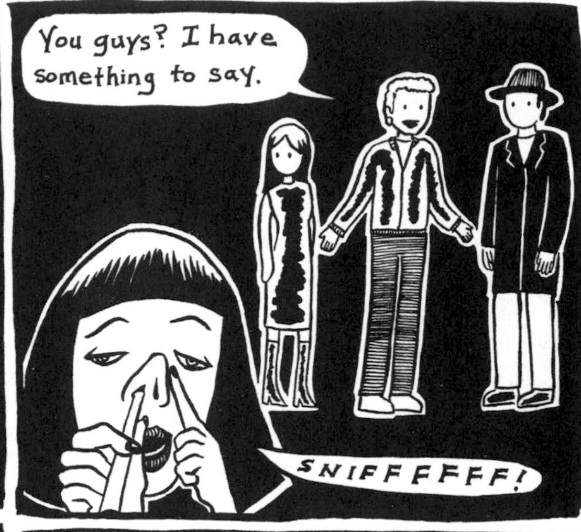
You guys? I have something to say.
SNIFFFFFFF!

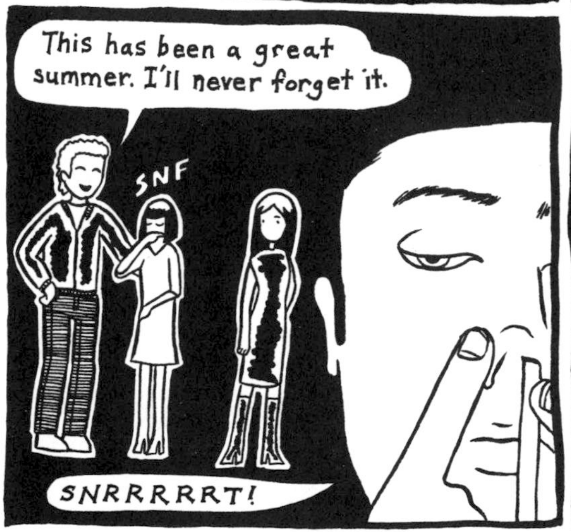
This has been a great summer. I'll never forget it.
SNF
SNRRRRRT!

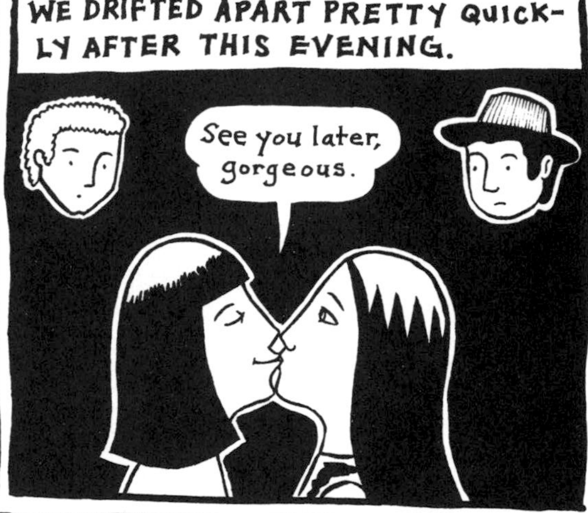
WE DRIFTED APART PRETTY QUICKLY AFTER THIS EVENING.
See you later, gorgeous.

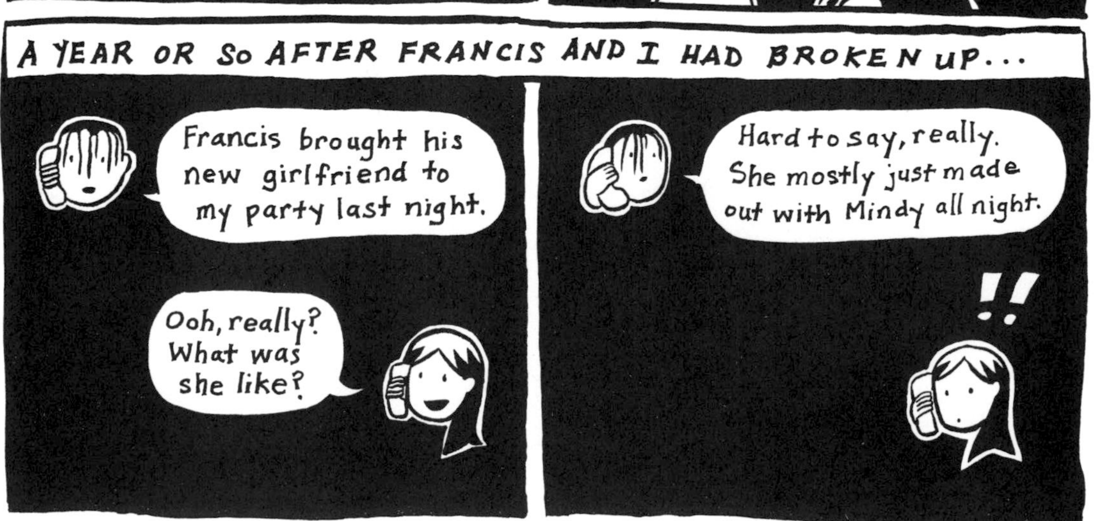
A YEAR OR SO AFTER FRANCIS AND I HAD BROKEN UP...
Francis brought his new girlfriend to my party last night.
Ooh, really? What was she like?
Hard to say, really. She mostly just made out with Mindy all night.
!!

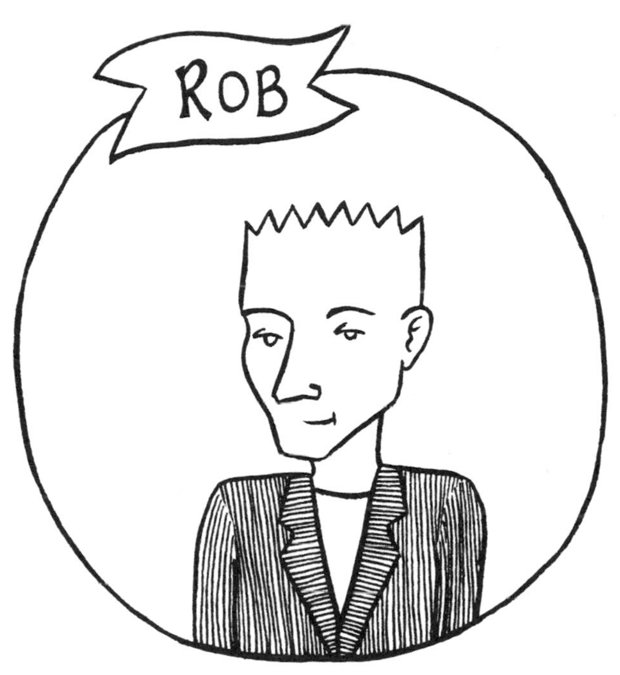
ROB

HE WAS THE ARCHETYPAL BEST FRIEND FOR FRANCIS AND ME. NEXT-DOOR NEIGHBOR, LATE-NIGHT PHILOSOPHER—FOR YEARS WE COULD ALWAYS DEPEND ON HIM AS A FRIEND, CONFIDANT, PARTY-GOER, WING MAN, YOU NAME IT.

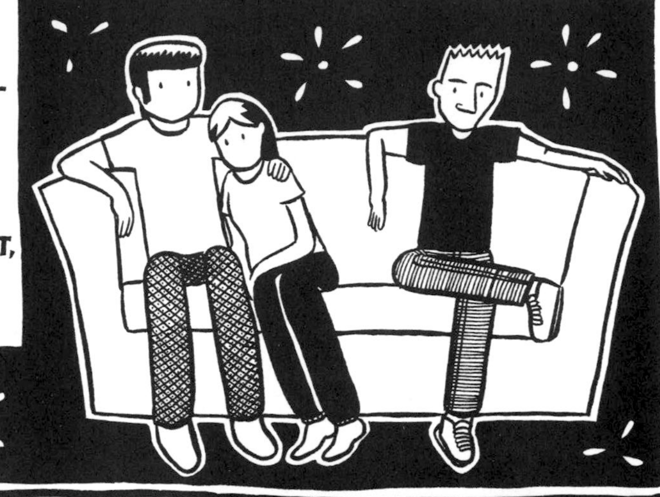

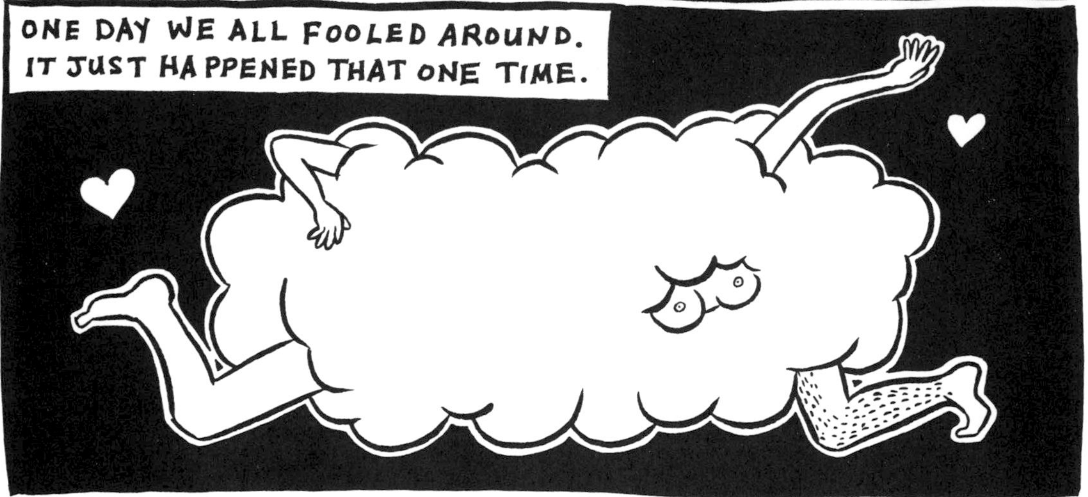

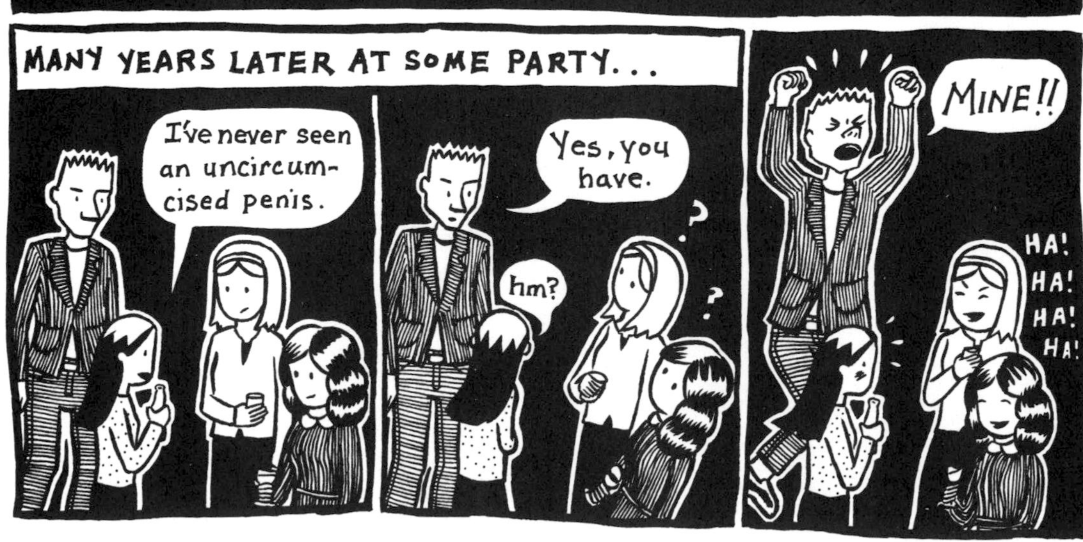

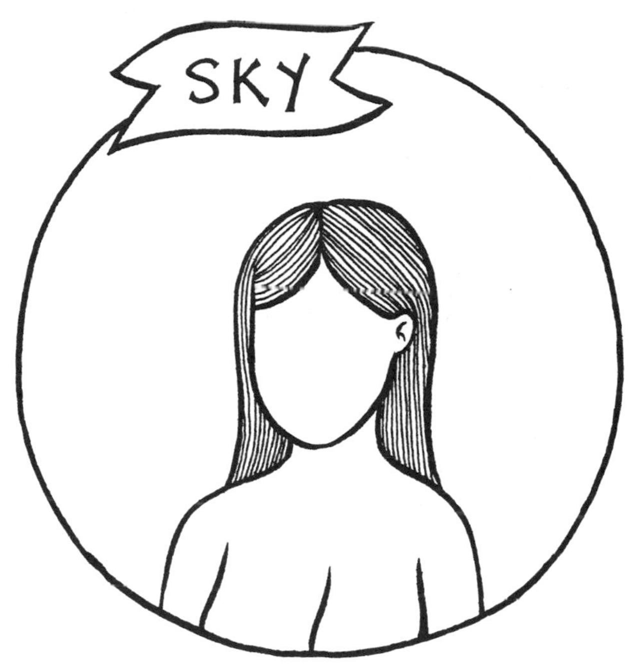
SKY

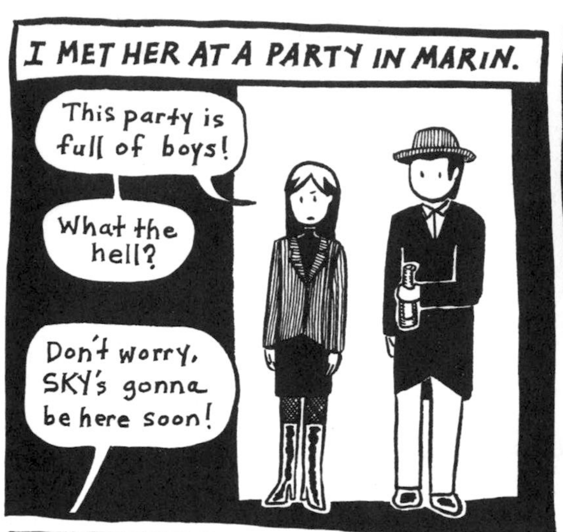
I MET HER AT A PARTY IN MARIN.
This party is full of boys!
What the hell?
Don't worry, SKY's gonna be here soon!

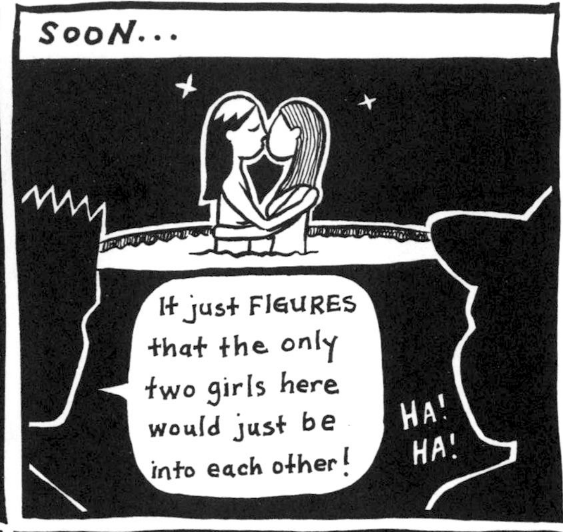
SOON...
It just FIGURES that the only two girls here would just be into each other!
HA! HA!

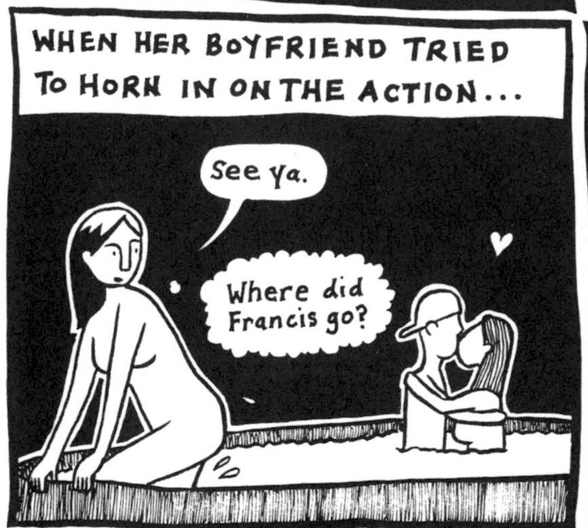
WHEN HER BOYFRIEND TRIED TO HORN IN ON THE ACTION...
See ya.
Where did Francis go?

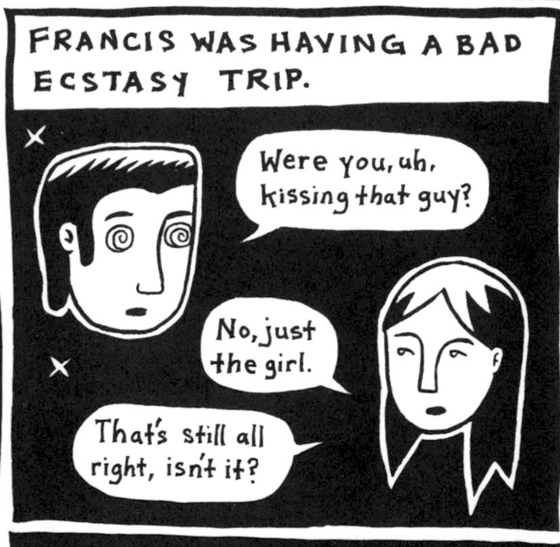
FRANCIS WAS HAVING A BAD ECSTASY TRIP.
Were you, uh, kissing that guy?
No, just the girl.
That's still all right, isn't it?

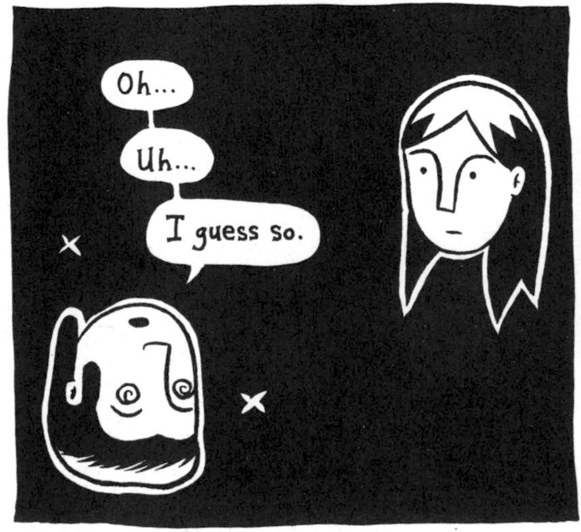
Oh...
Uh...
I guess so.

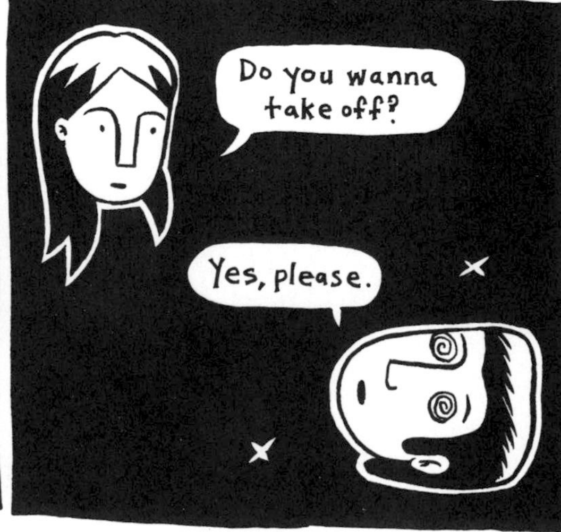
Do you wanna take off?
Yes, please.

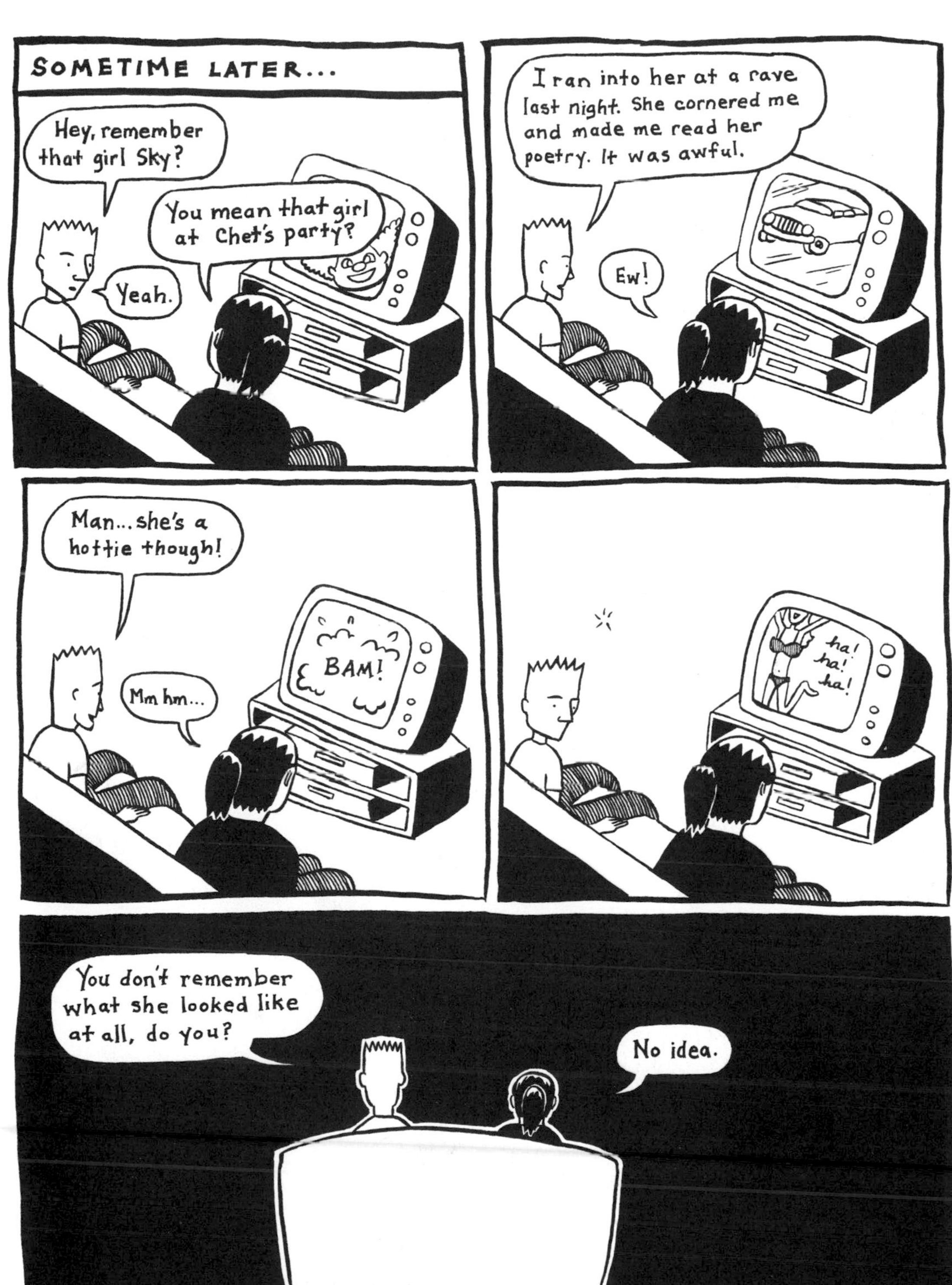
SOMETIME LATER...
Hey, remember that girl Sky?
You mean that girl at Chet's party?
Yeah.
I ran into her at a rave last night. She cornered me and made me read her poetry. It was awful.
Ew!
Man...she's a hottie though!
Mm hm...
BAM!
ha! ha! ha!
You don't remember what she looked like at all, do you?
No idea.

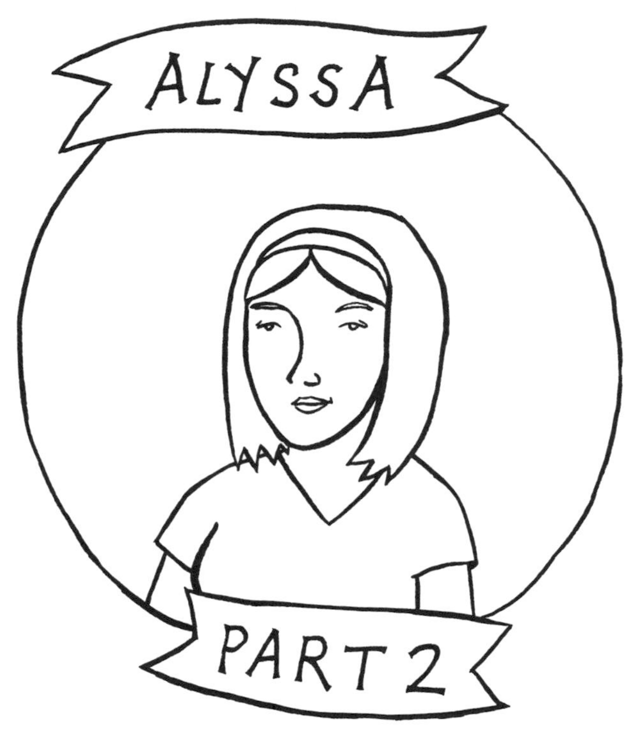
ALYSSA
PART 2

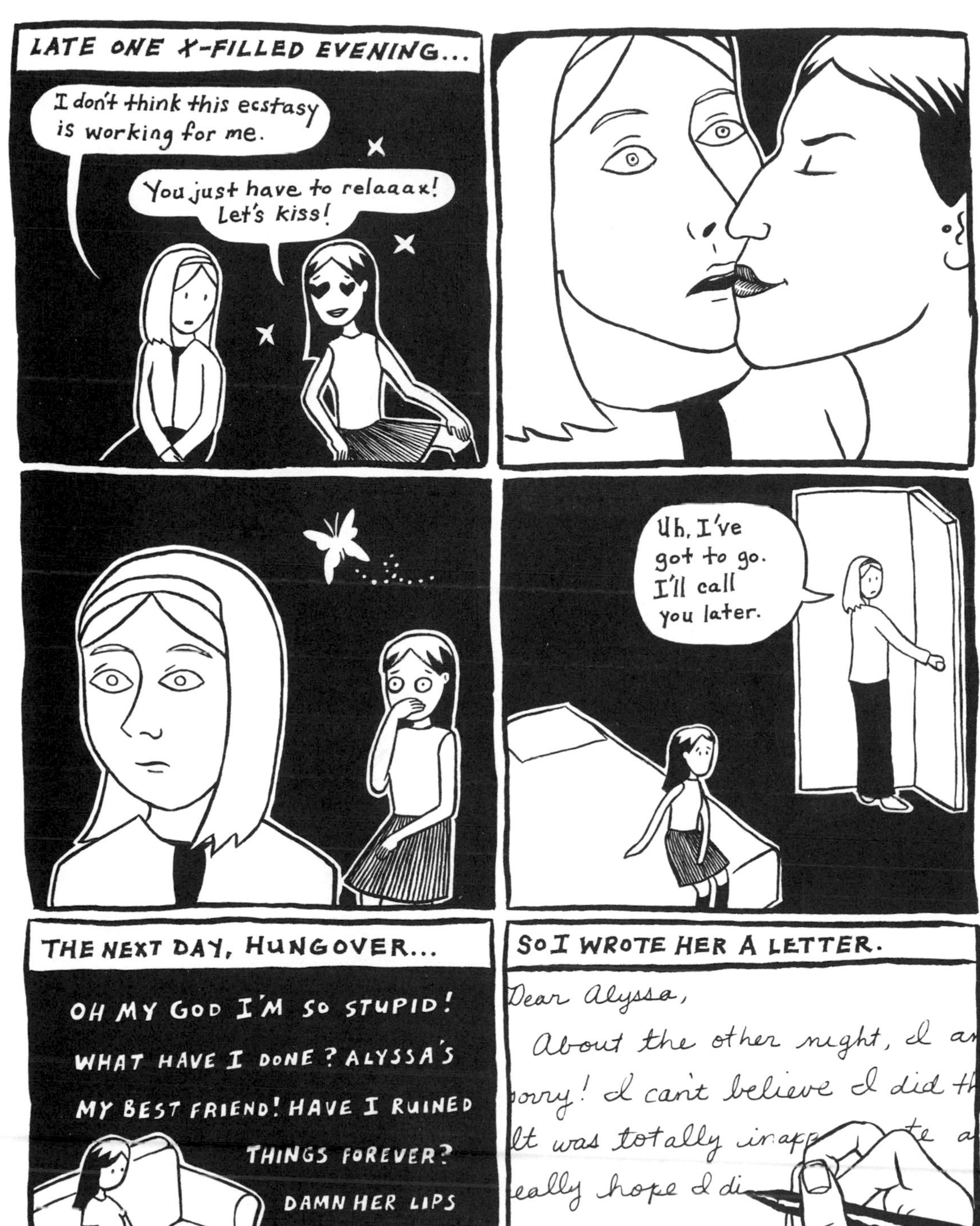
LATE ONE X-FILLED EVENING...
I don't think this ecstasy is working for me.
You just have to relaaax! Let's kiss!
Uh, I've got to go. I'll call you later.
THE NEXT DAY, HUNGOVER...
OH MY GOD I'M SO STUPID! WHAT HAVE I DONE? ALYSSA'S MY BEST FRIEND! HAVE I RUINED THINGS FOREVER? DAMN HER LIPS WERE SO SOFT... FUCK FUCK FUCK
SO I WROTE HER A LETTER.
Dear Alyssa,
About the other night, I a
sorry! I can't believe I did th
It was totally inapp te a
eally hope I di

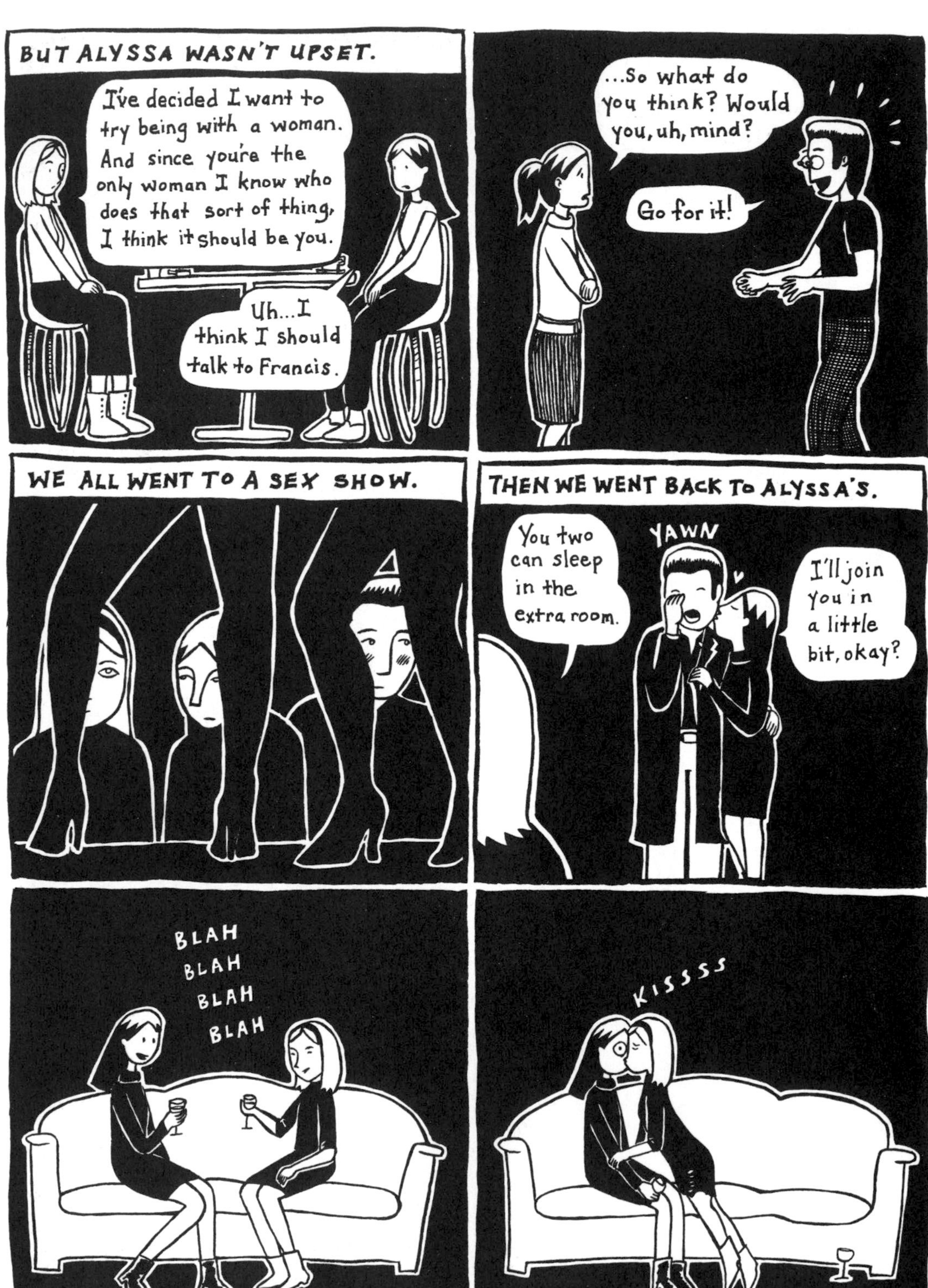
BUT ALYSSA WASN'T UPSET.
I've decided I want to try being with a woman. And since you're the only woman I know who does that sort of thing, I think it should be you.
Uh...I think I should talk to Francis.
...So what do you think? Would you, uh, mind?
Go for it!
WE ALL WENT TO A SEX SHOW.
THEN WE WENT BACK TO ALYSSA'S.
You two can sleep in the extra room.
YAWN
I'll join you in a little bit, okay?
BLAH
BLAH
BLAH
BLAH
KISSSS

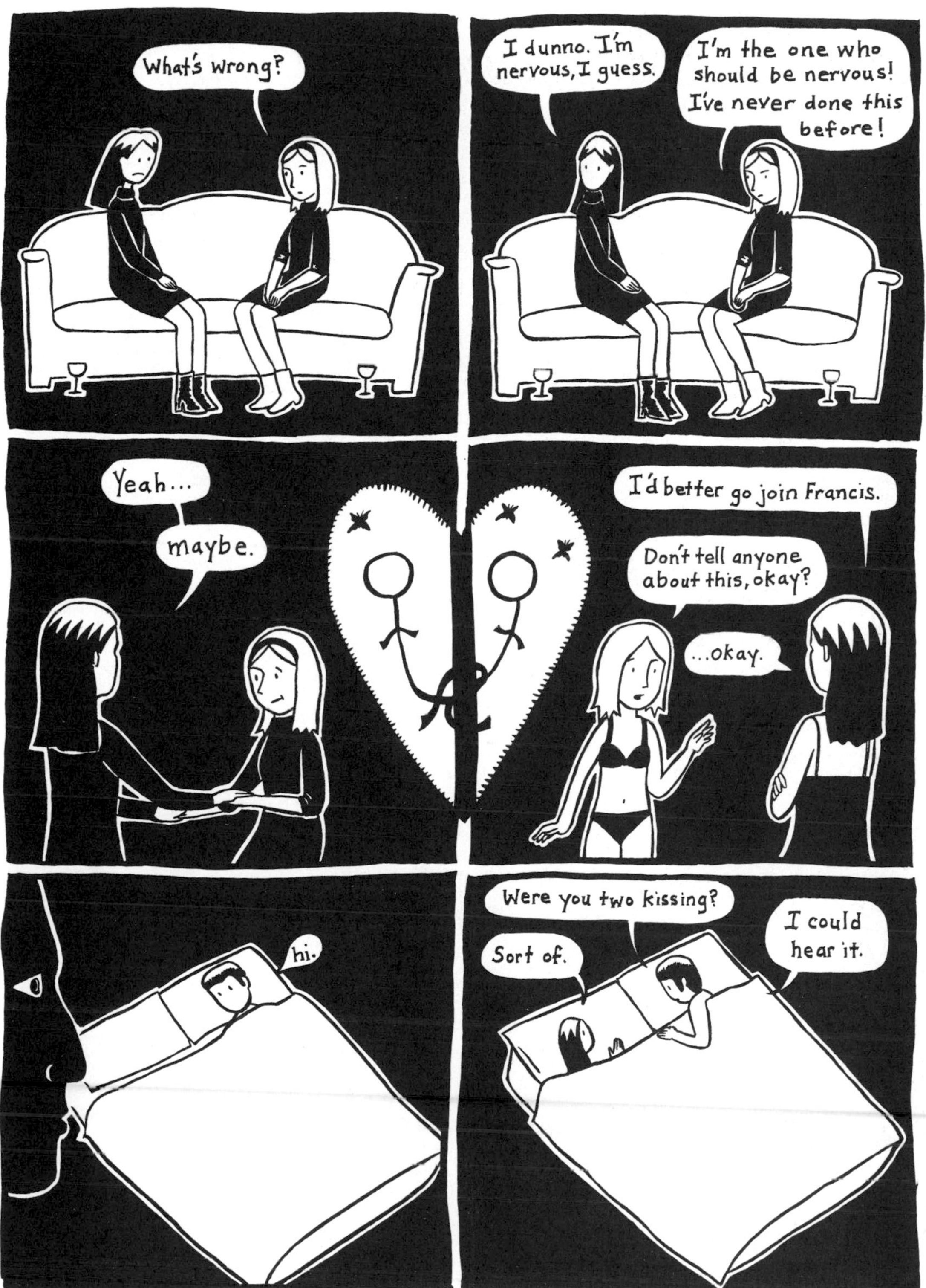
What's wrong?
I dunno. I'm nervous, I guess.
I'm the one who should be nervous! I've never done this before!
Yeah...
maybe.
I'd better go join Francis.
Don't tell anyone about this, okay?
...okay.
hi.
Were you two kissing?
Sort of.
I could hear it.

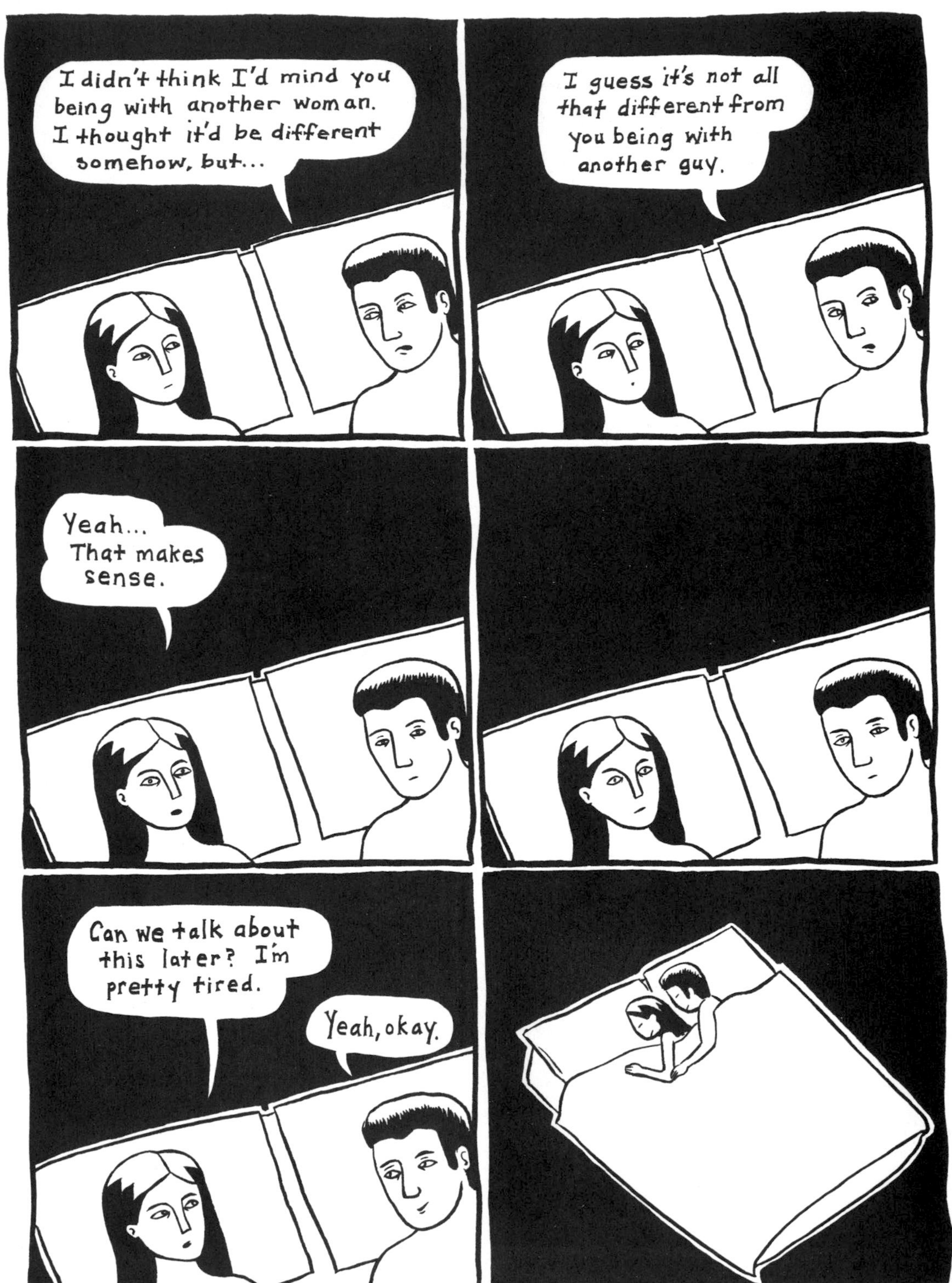
I didn't think I'd mind you being with another woman. I thought it'd be different somehow, but...
I guess it's not all that different from you being with another guy.
Yeah... That makes sense.
Can we talk about this later? I'm pretty tired.
Yeah, okay.

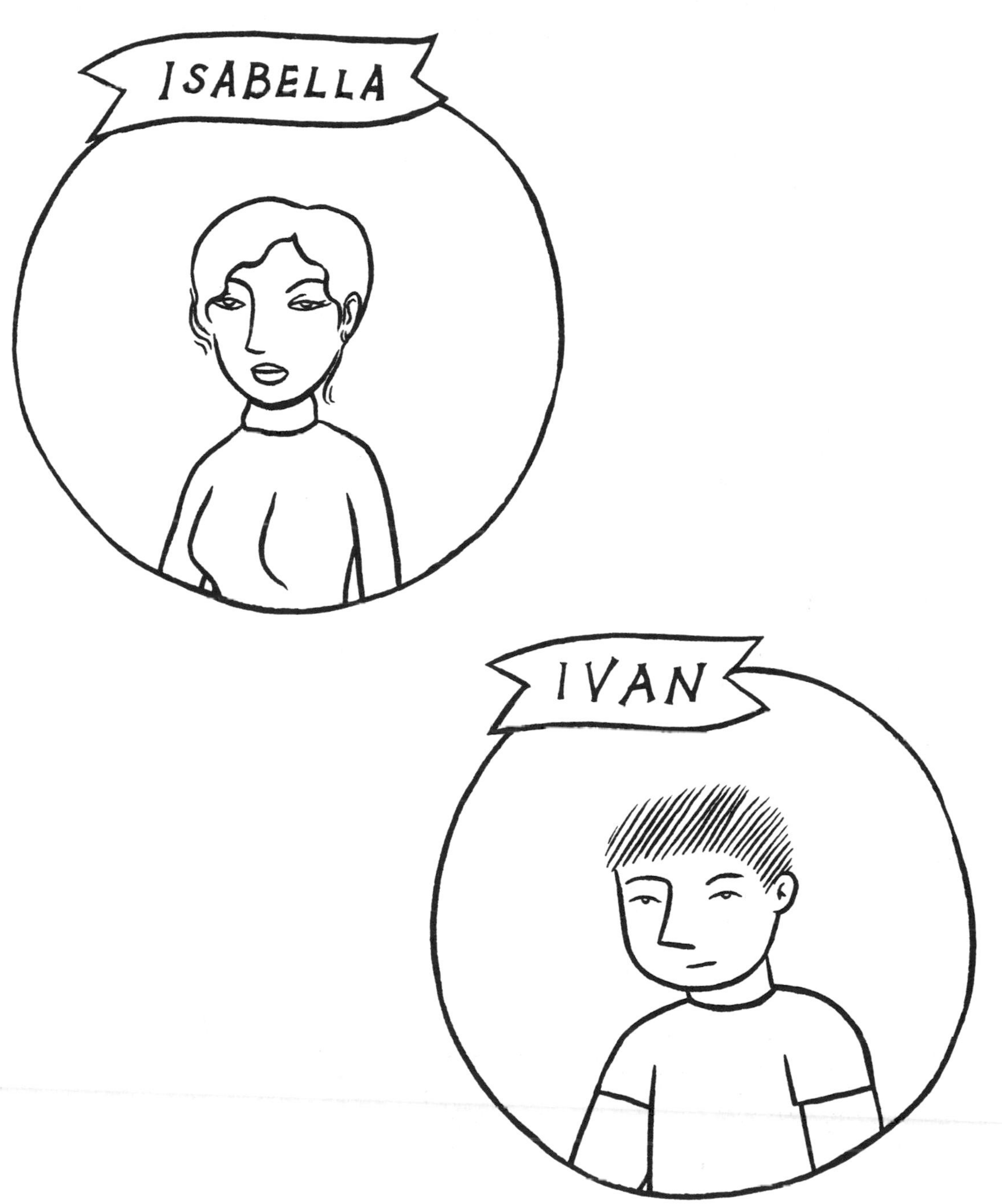
ISABELLA
IVAN

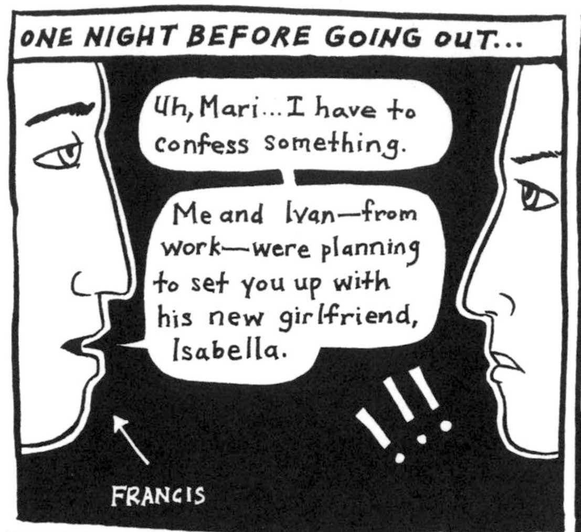
ONE NIGHT BEFORE GOING OUT...
Uh, Mari... I have to confess something.
Me and Ivan—from work—were planning to set you up with his new girlfriend, Isabella.
!!!
FRANCIS

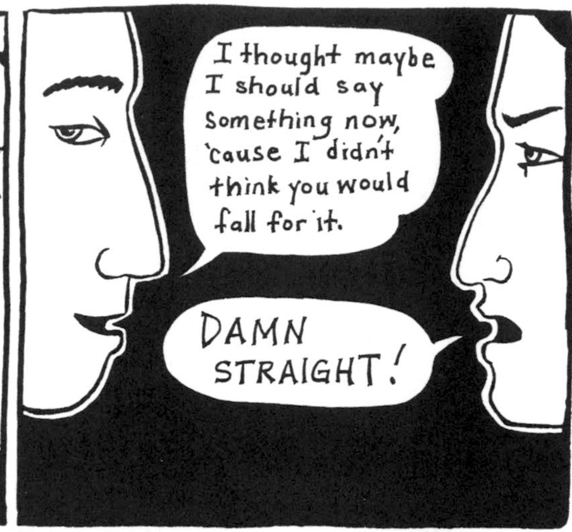
I thought maybe I should say something now, 'cause I didn't think you would fall for it.
DAMN STRAIGHT!

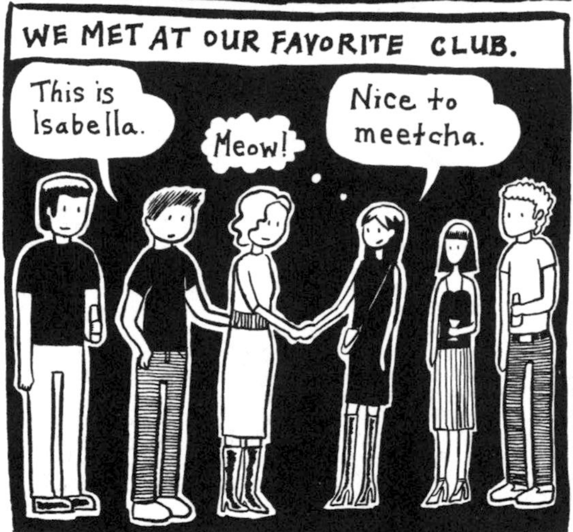
WE MET AT OUR FAVORITE CLUB.
This is Isabella.
Meow!
Nice to meetcha.

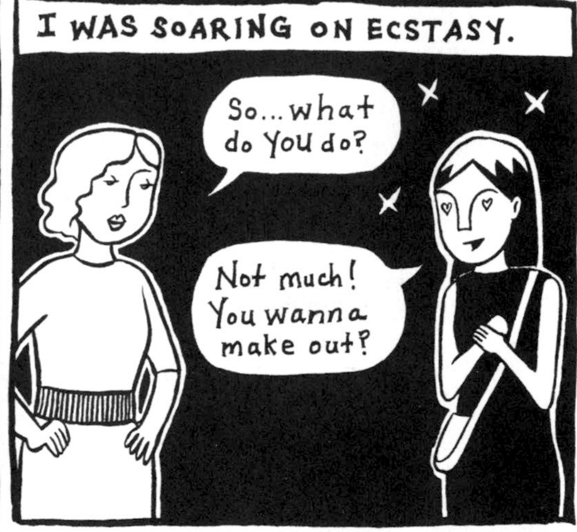
I WAS SOARING ON ECSTASY.
So... what do you do?
Not much! You wanna make out?

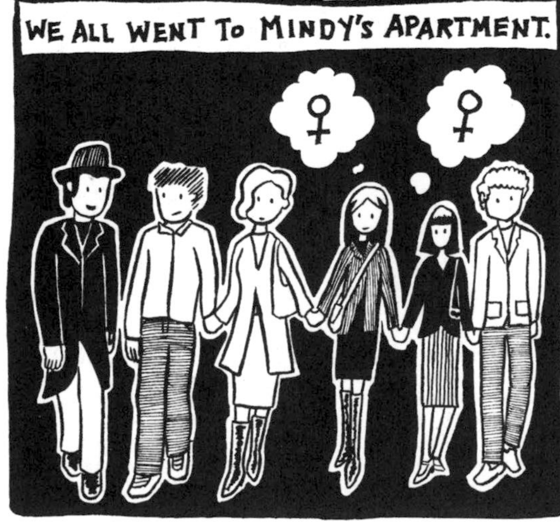
WE ALL WENT TO MINDY'S APARTMENT.

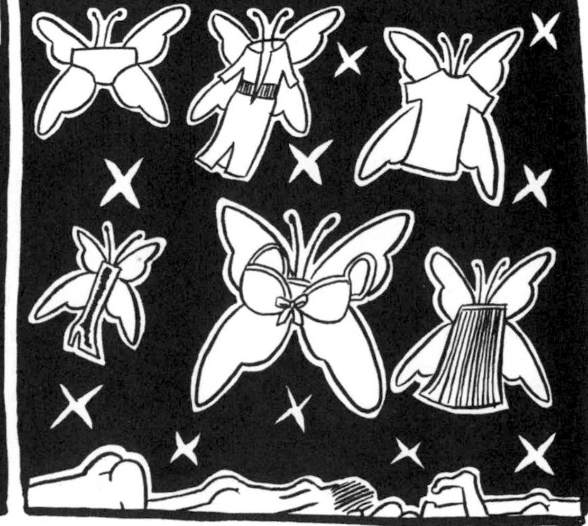

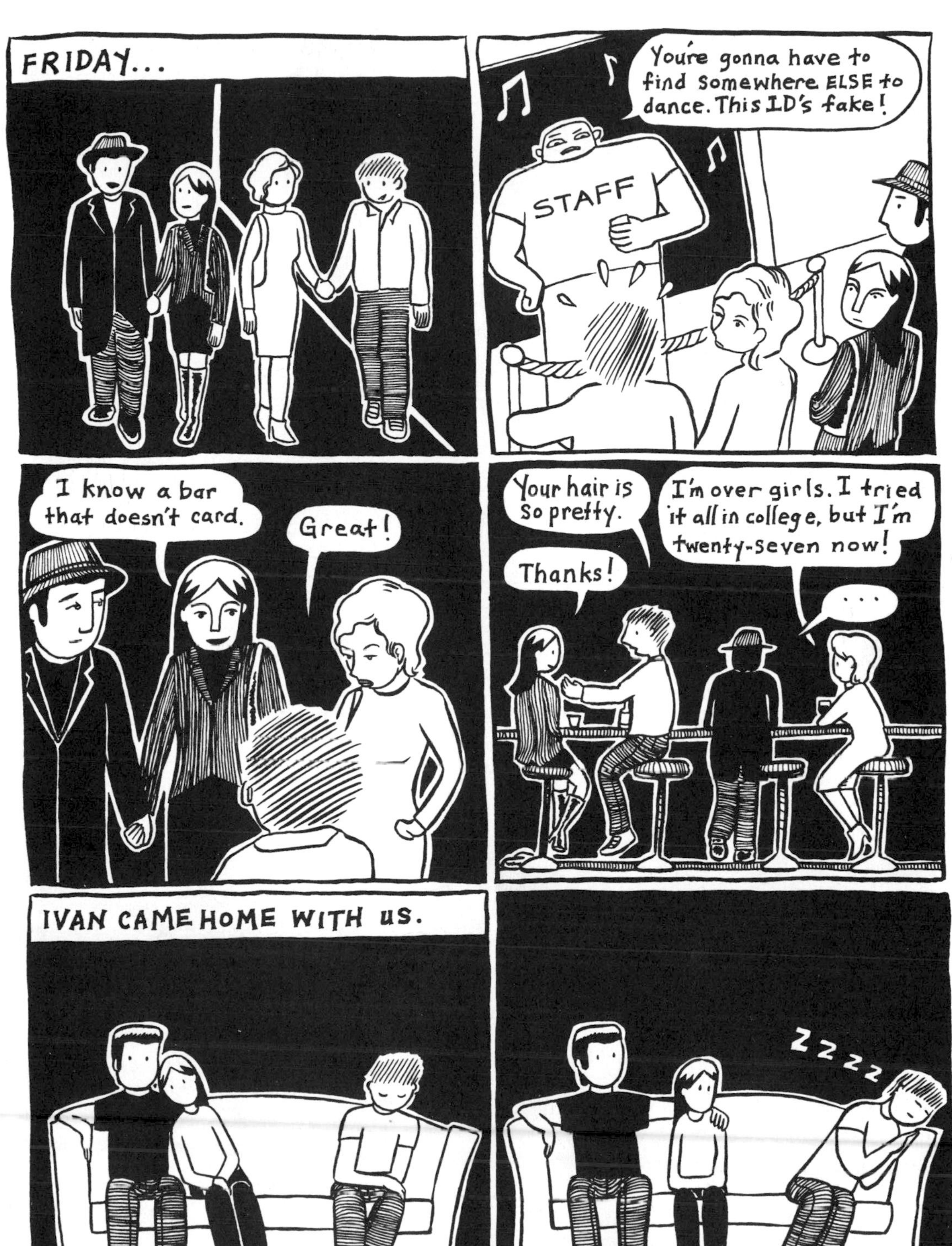
FRIDAY...
You're gonna have to find somewhere ELSE to dance. This ID's fake!
STAFF
I know a bar that doesn't card.
Great!
Your hair is so pretty.
Thanks!
I'm over girls. I tried it all in college, but I'm twenty-seven now!
...
IVAN CAME HOME WITH US.
ZZZZ

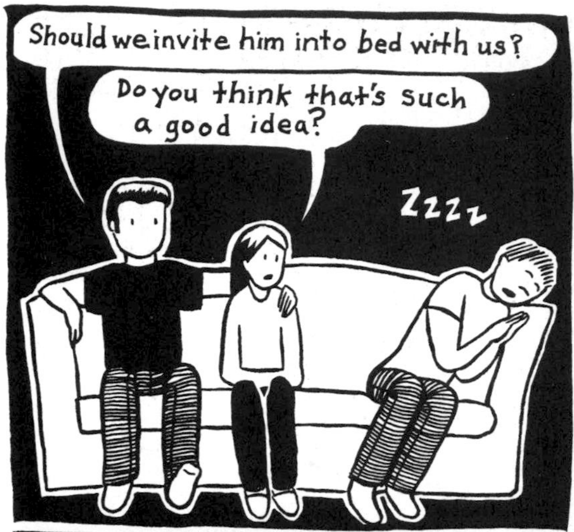

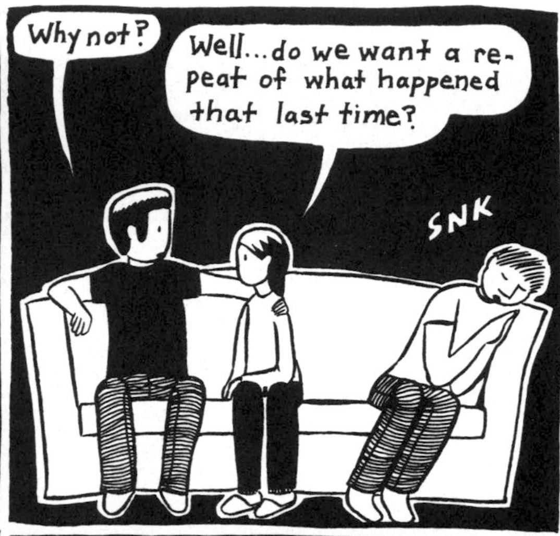

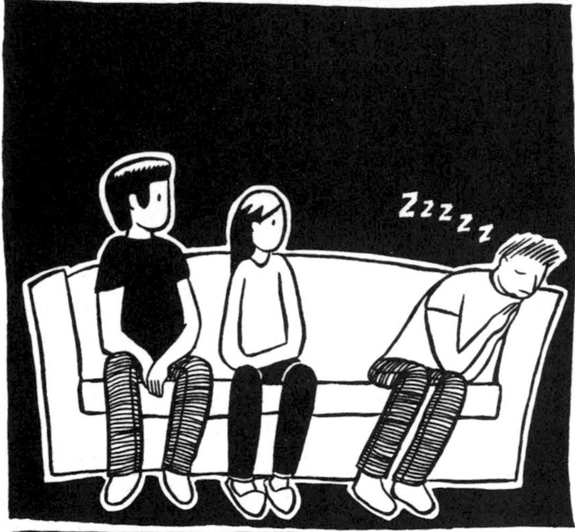

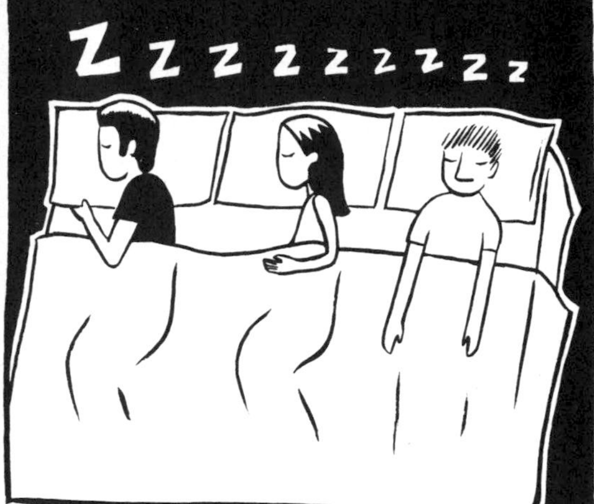

I DREAMT I WAS SCROLLING DOWN A LONG LIST OF NUMBERS TRYING TO FIND THE CODE THAT WOULD UNLOCK MY SEXUALITY.

AS I CAME TO, THE CODE WAS HIT AND I AWOKE TO HOT KISSES AND BODIES ON EITHER SIDE OF ME.

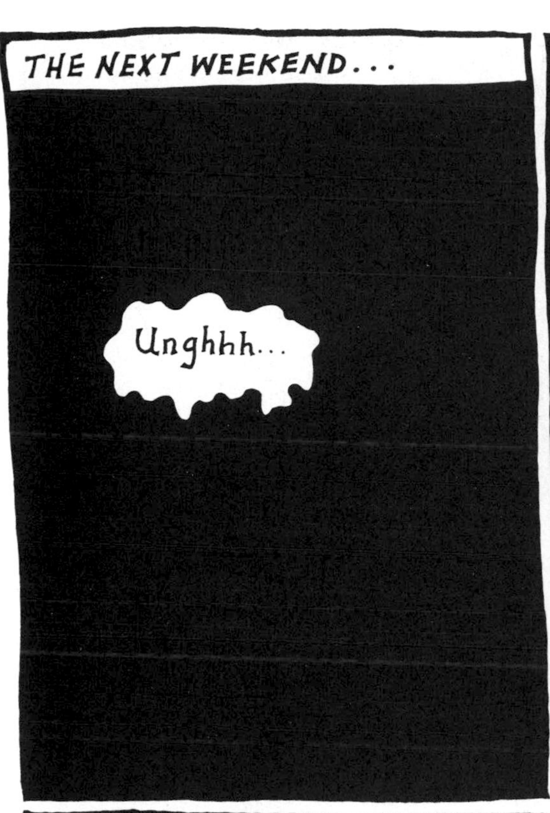
THE NEXT WEEKEND...
Unghhh...

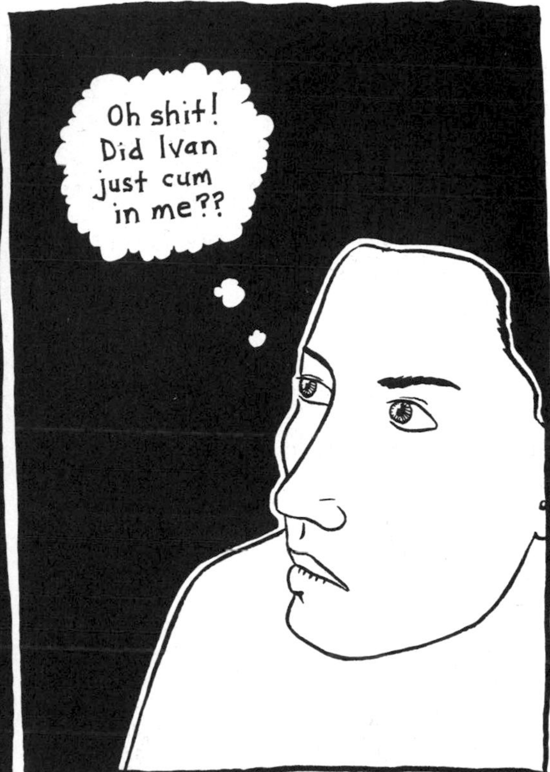
Oh shit! Did Ivan just cum in me??

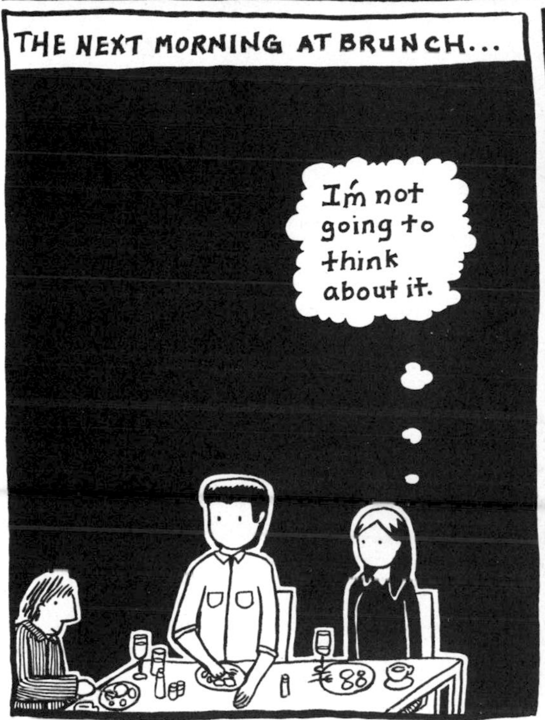
THE NEXT MORNING AT BRUNCH...
I'm not going to think about it.

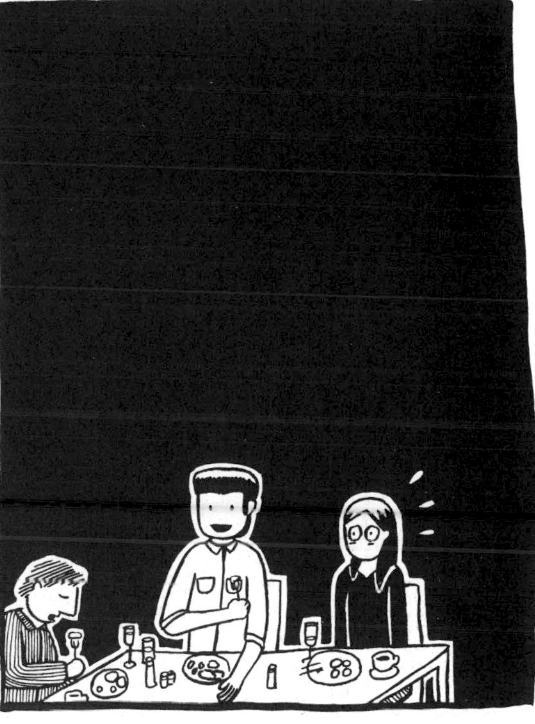

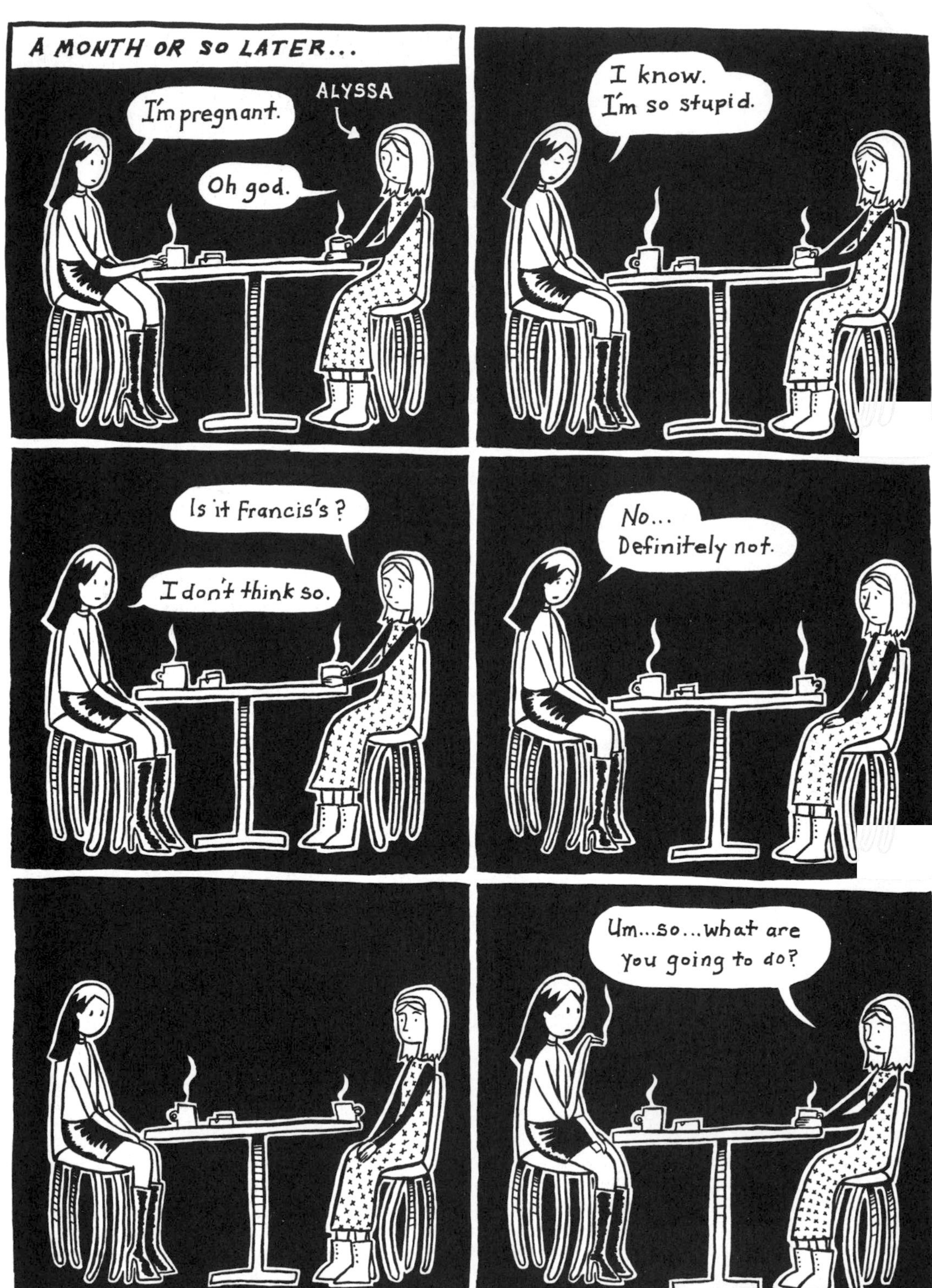
A MONTH OR SO LATER...
I'm pregnant.
ALYSSA
Oh god.
I know.
I'm so stupid.
Is it Francis's?
I don't think so.
No...
Definitely not.
Um...so...what are you going to do?

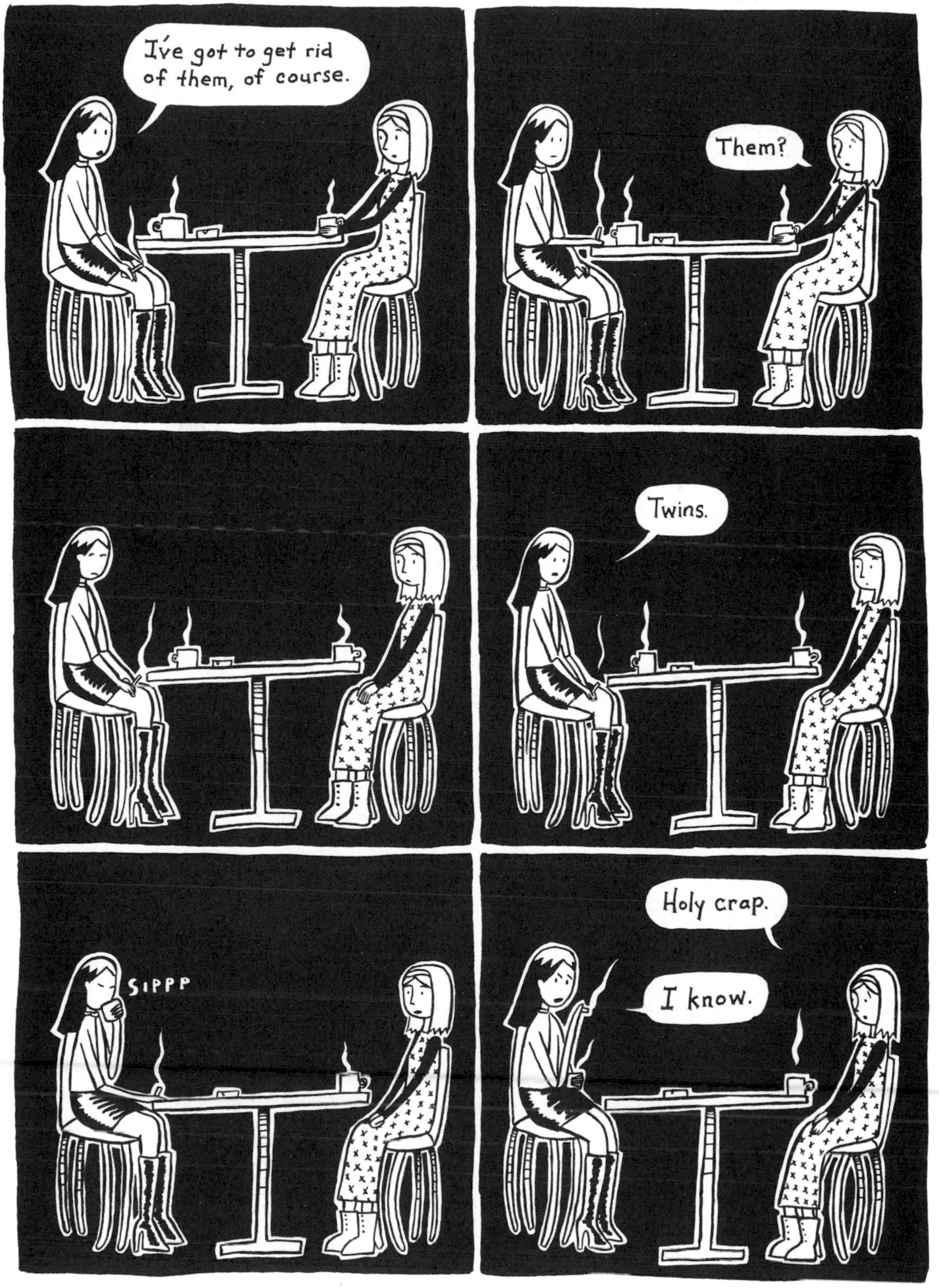

I've got to get rid of them, of course.

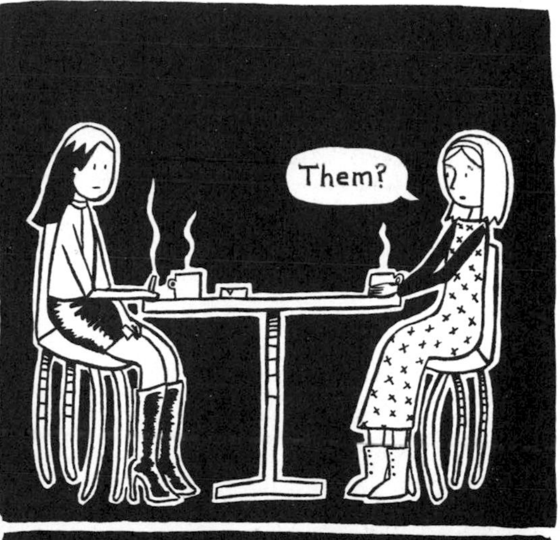

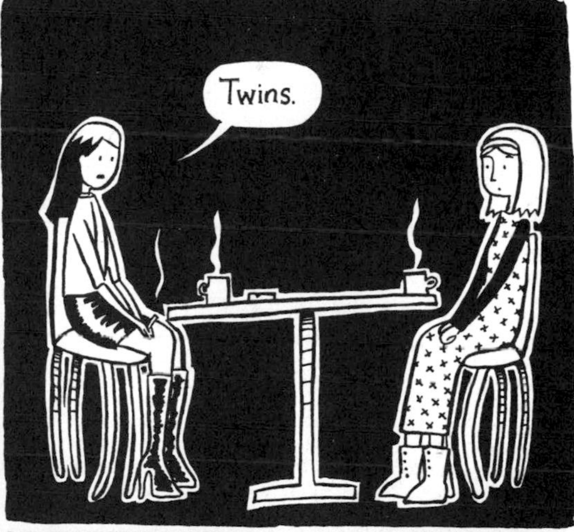

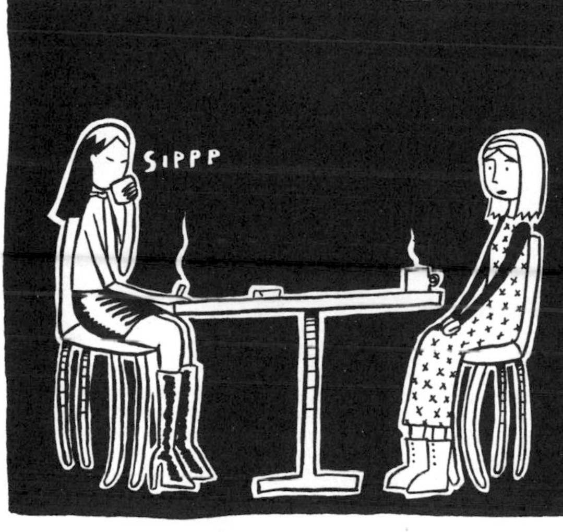

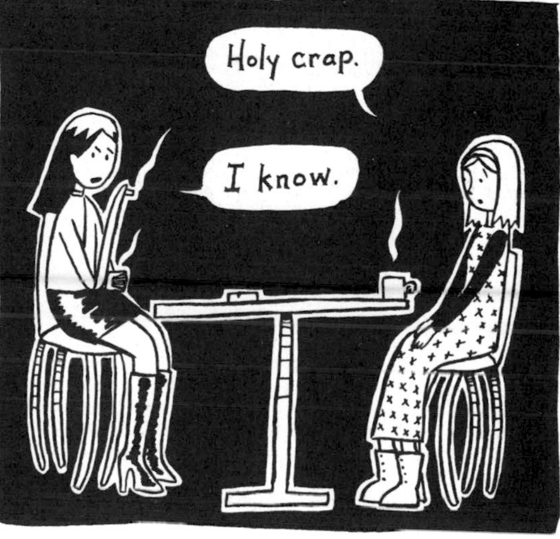

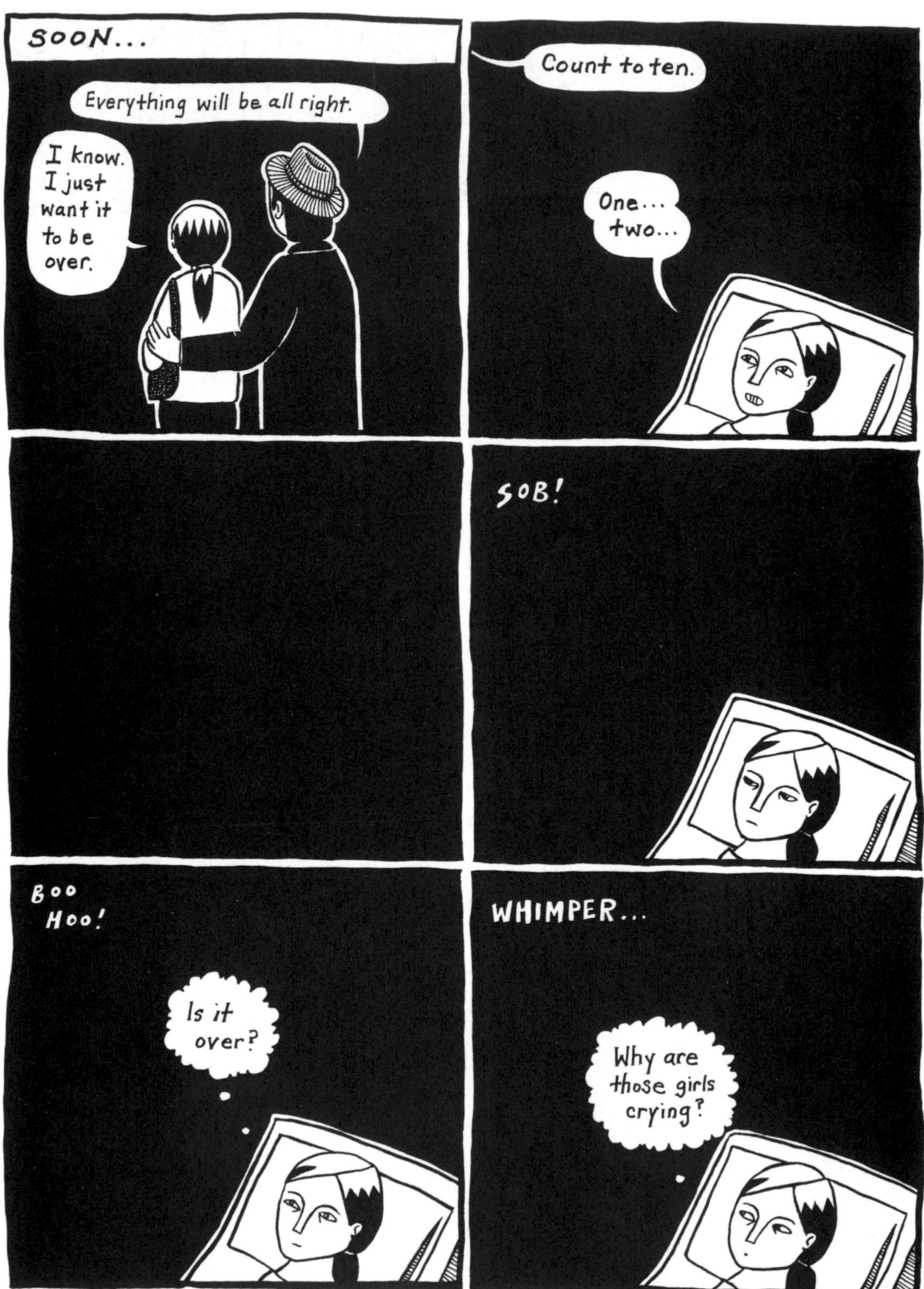
SOON...
Everything will be all right.
I know. I just want it to be over.
Count to ten.
One... two...
SOB!
BOO HOO!
Is it over?
WHIMPER...
Why are those girls crying?

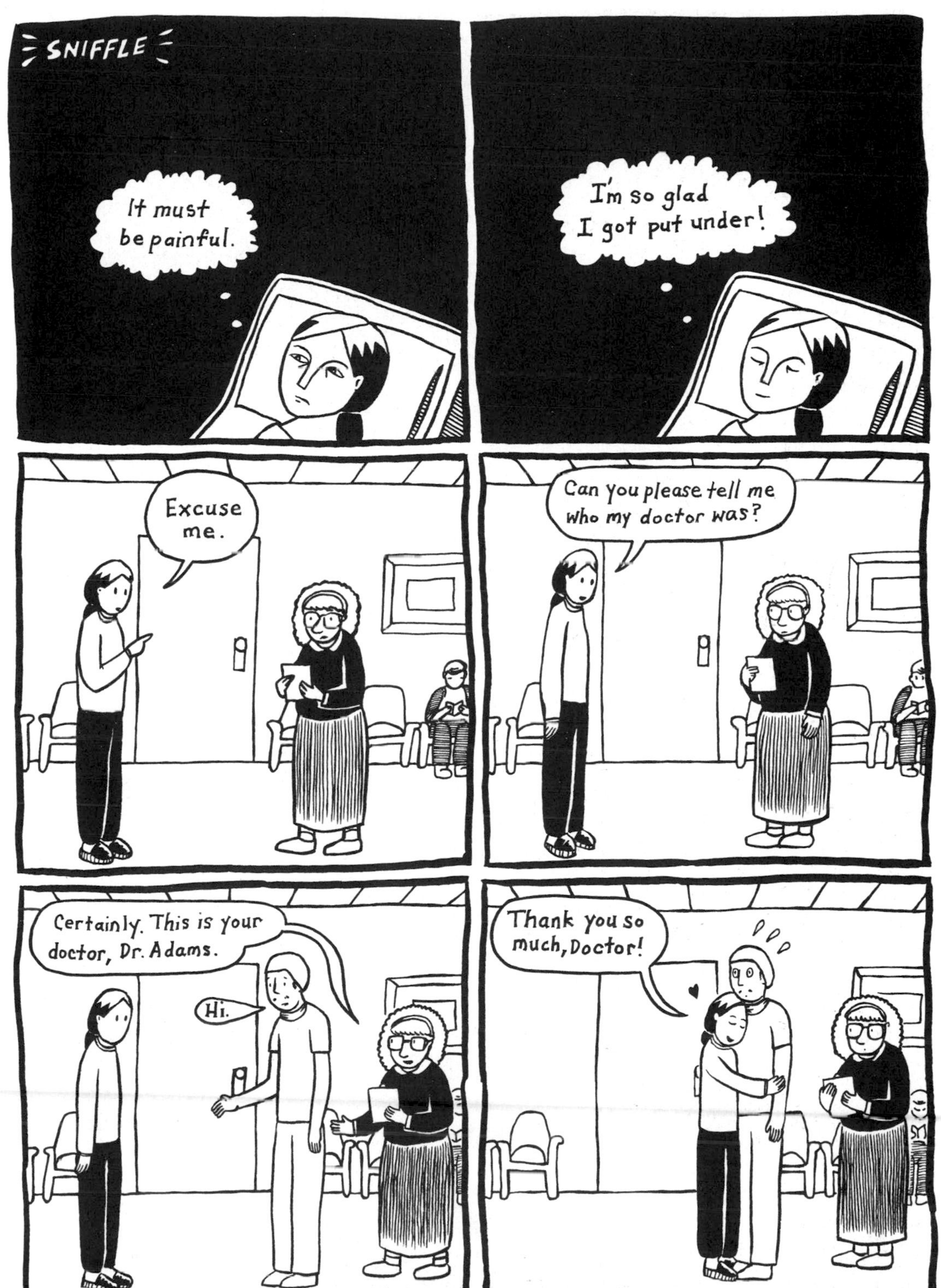
SNIFFLE
It must be painful.
I'm so glad I got put under!
Excuse me.
Can you please tell me who my doctor was?
Certainly. This is your doctor, Dr. Adams.
Hi.
Thank you so much, Doctor!

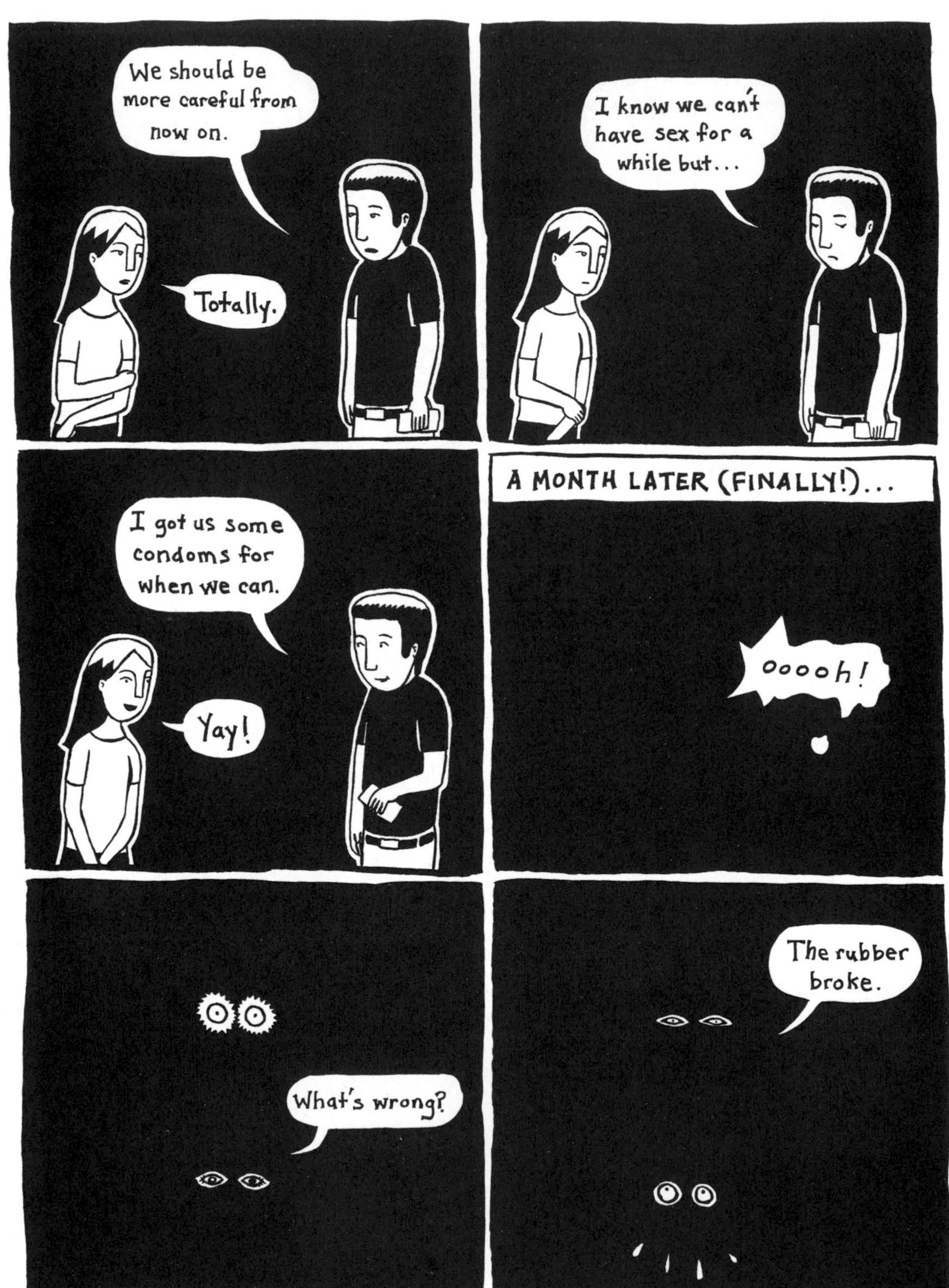
We should be more careful from now on.
Totally.
I know we can't have sex for a while but...
I got us some condoms for when we can.
Yay!
A MONTH LATER (FINALLY!)...
ooooh!
What's wrong?
The rubber broke.

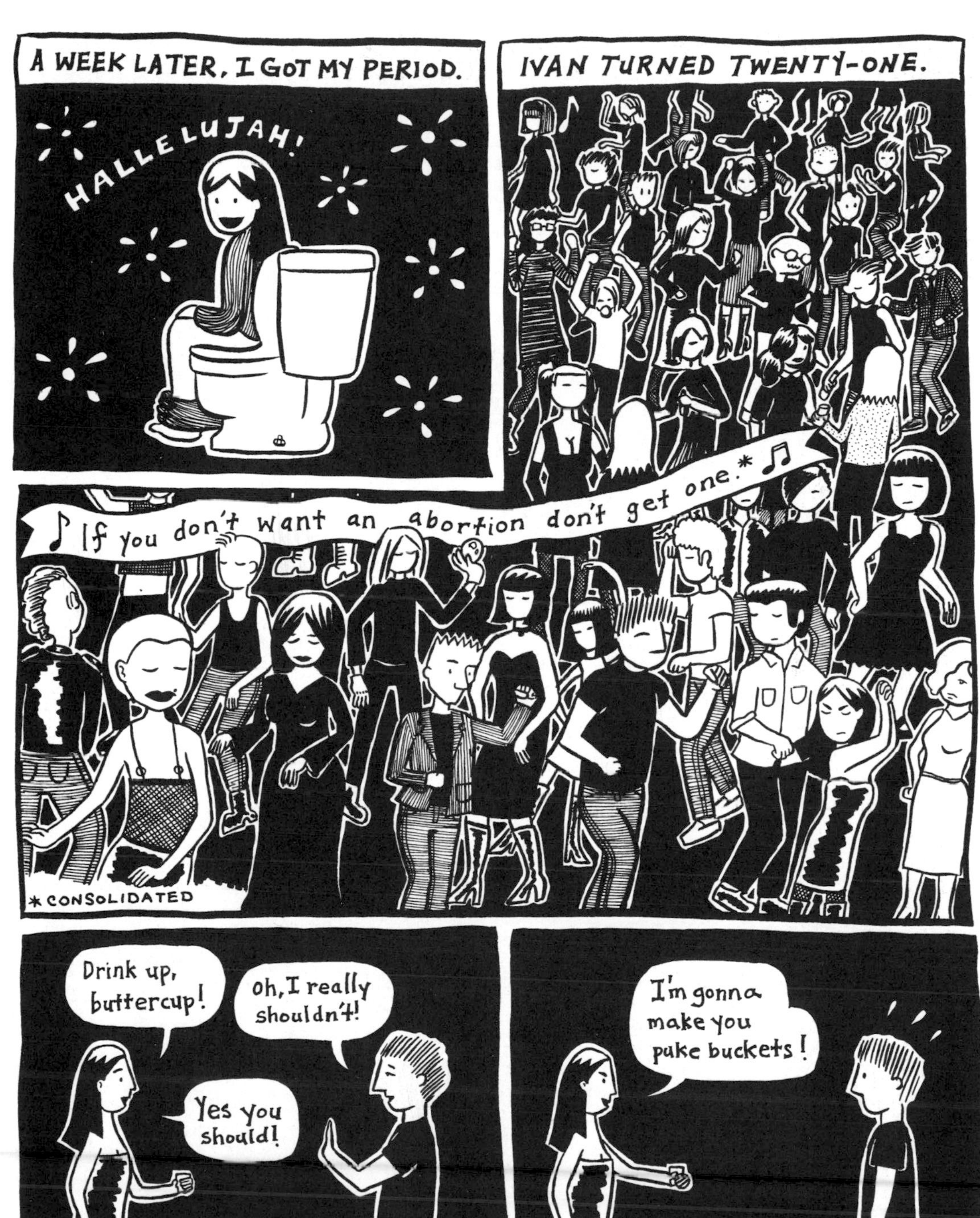

A WEEK LATER, I GOT MY PERIOD.
HALLELUJAH!
IVAN TURNED TWENTY-ONE.
♪ If you don't want an abortion don't get one.* ♫
* CONSOLIDATED
Drink up, buttercup!
Oh, I really shouldn't!
Yes you should!
I'm gonna make you puke buckets!

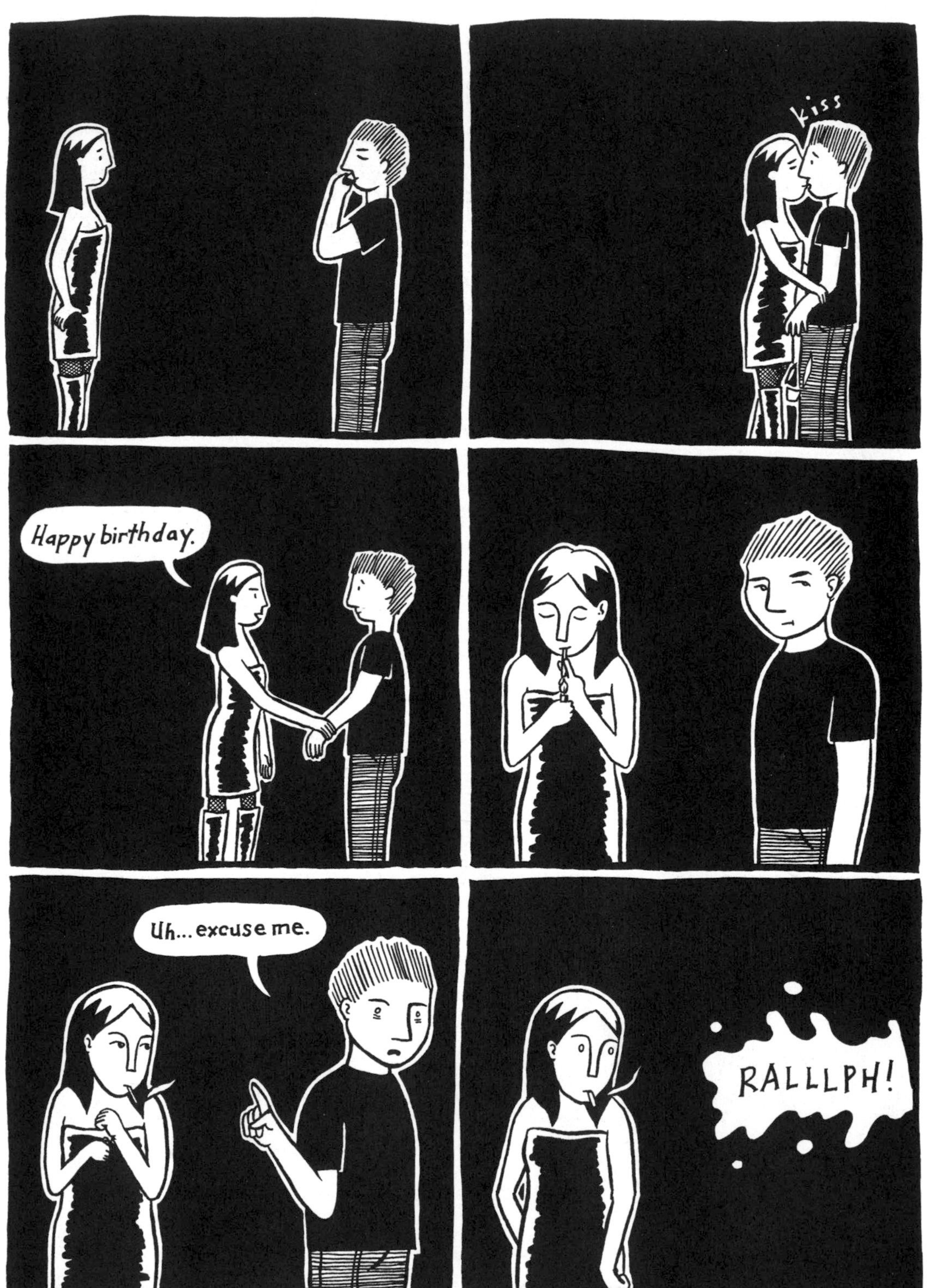
kiss
Happy birthday.
Uh... excuse me.
RALLLPH!

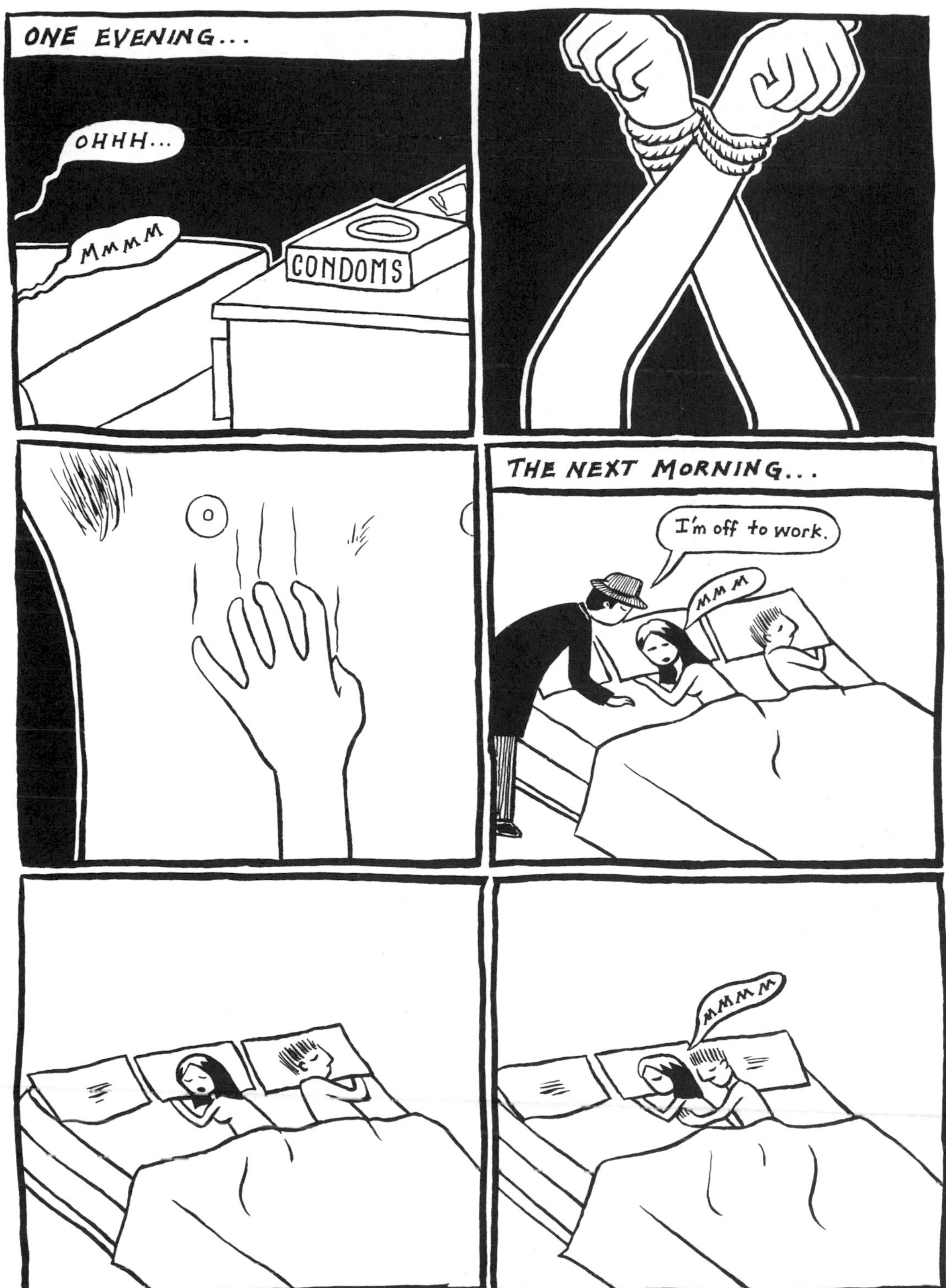
ONE EVENING...
OHHH...
MMMM
CONDOMS
THE NEXT MORNING...
I'm off to work.
MMM
MMMM

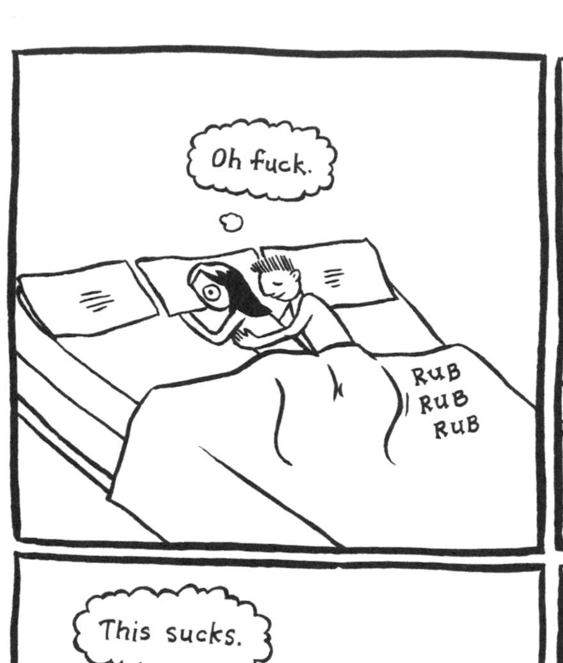
Oh fuck.
RUB
RUB
RUB

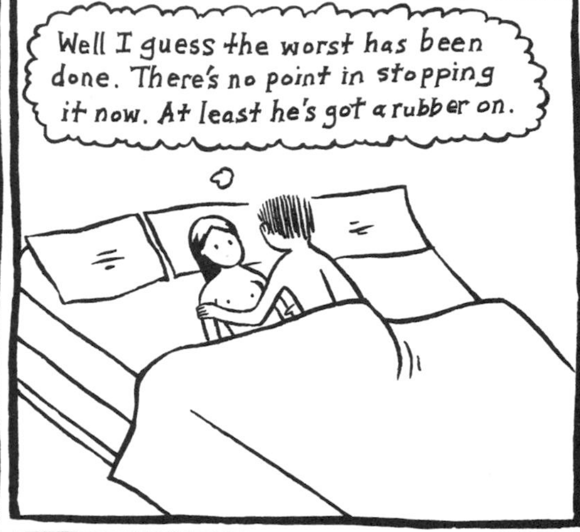
Well I guess the worst has been done. There's no point in stopping it now. At least he's got a rubber on.

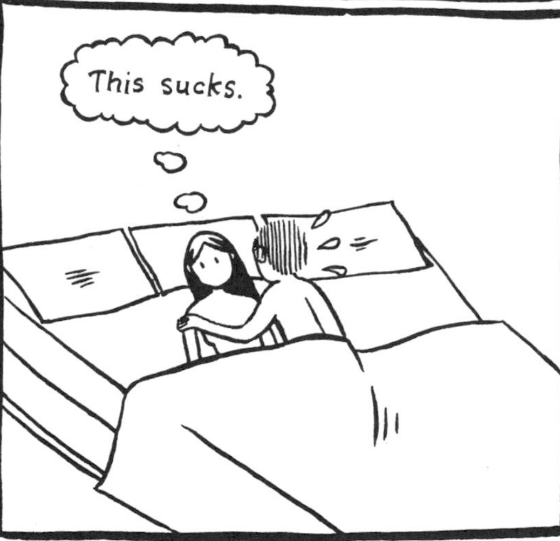
This sucks.

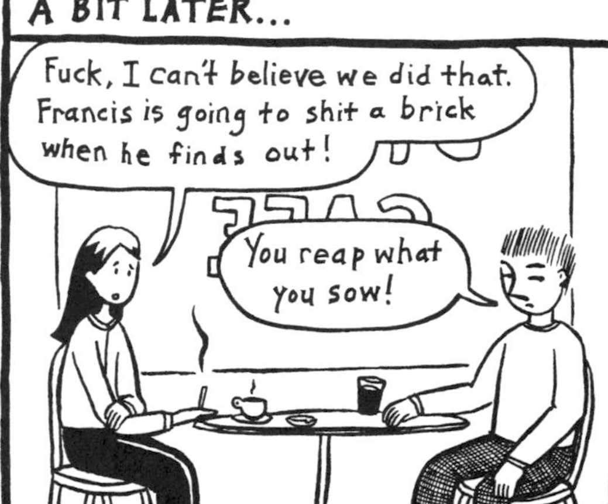
A BIT LATER...
Fuck, I can't believe we did that. Francis is going to shit a brick when he finds out!
You reap what you sow!

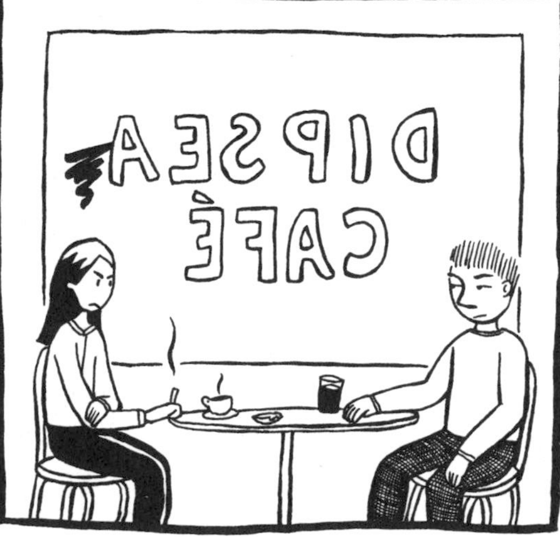
DIPSEA
CAFÉ

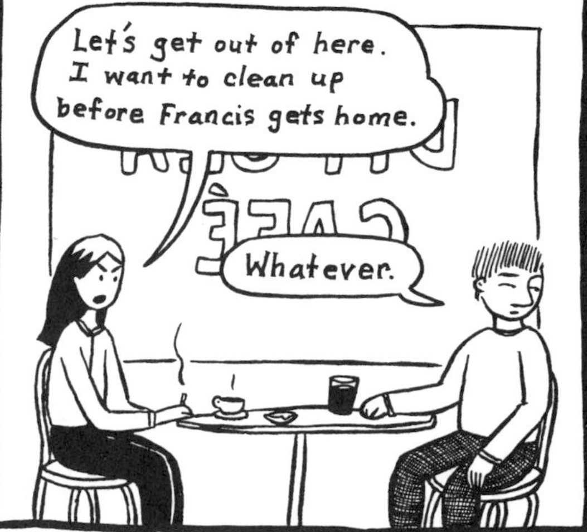
Let's get out of here. I want to clean up before Francis gets home.
Whatever.

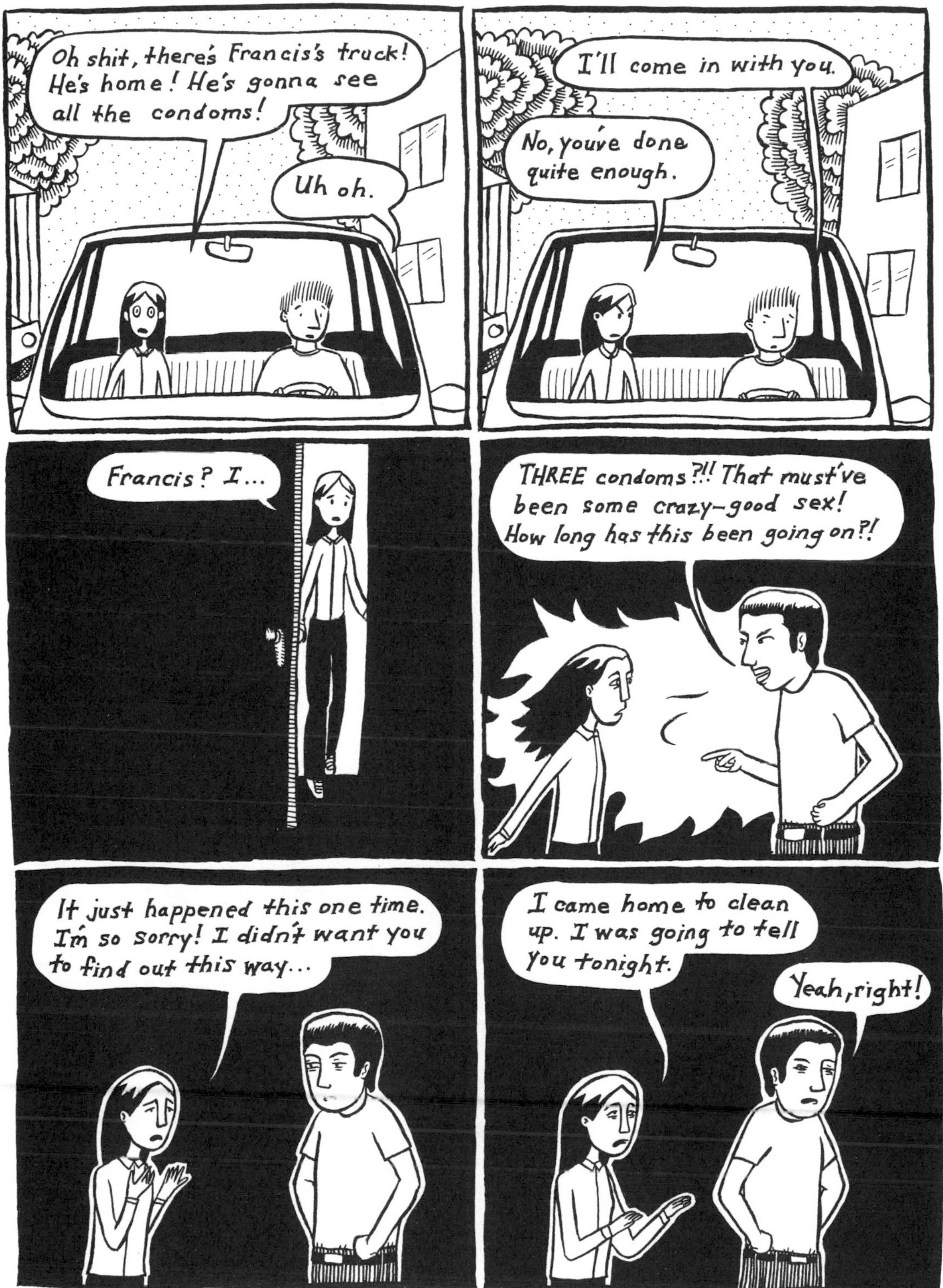
Oh shit, there's Francis's truck! He's home! He's gonna see all the condoms!
Uh oh.
I'll come in with you.
No, you've done quite enough.
Francis? I...
THREE condoms?!! That must've been some crazy-good sex! How long has this been going on?!
It just happened this one time. I'm so sorry! I didn't want you to find out this way...
I came home to clean up. I was going to tell you tonight.
Yeah, right!

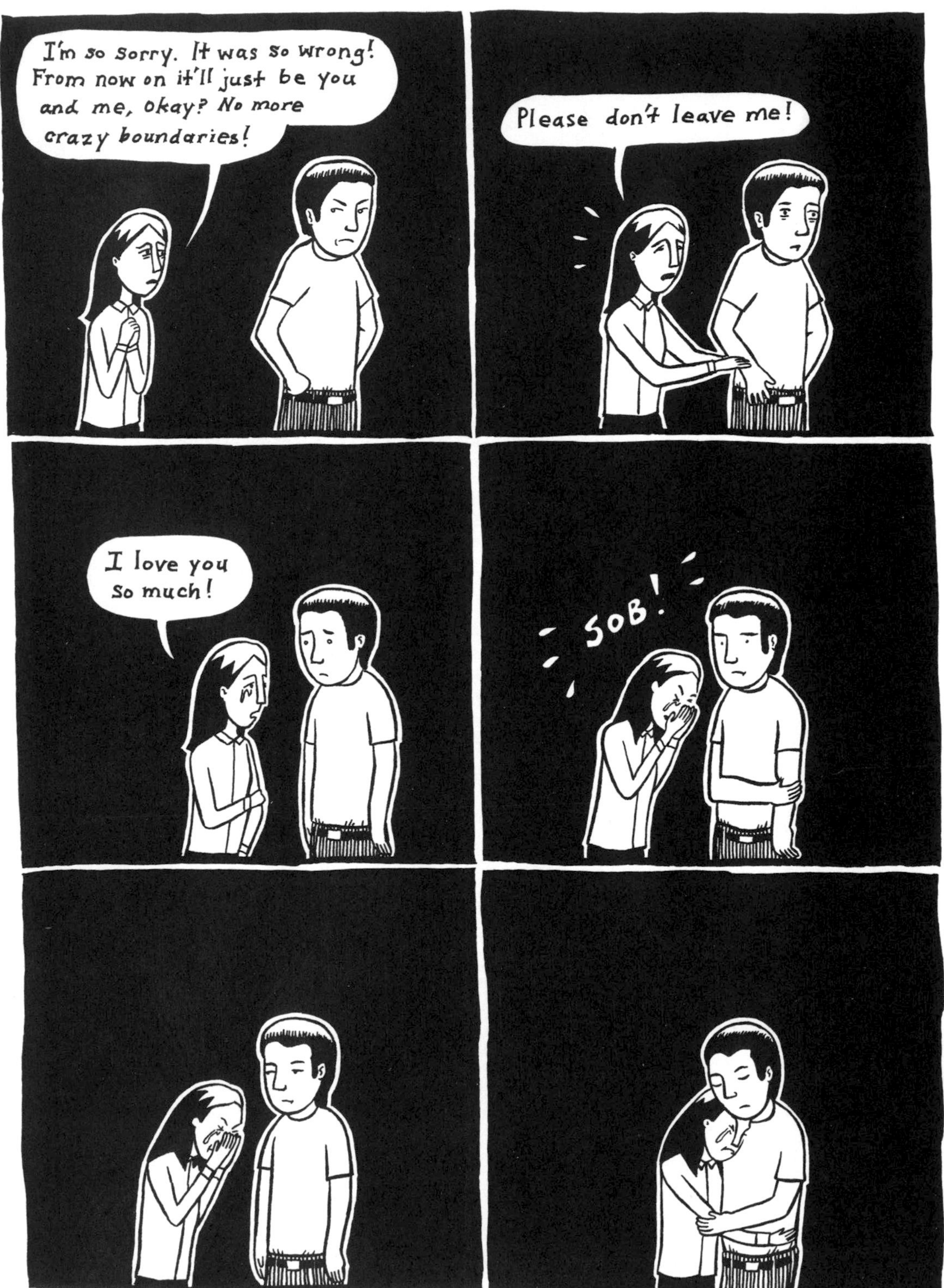
I'm so sorry. It was so wrong! From now on it'll just be you and me, okay? No more crazy boundaries!
Please don't leave me!
I love you so much!
SOB!

1995

ages 21 ~ 22

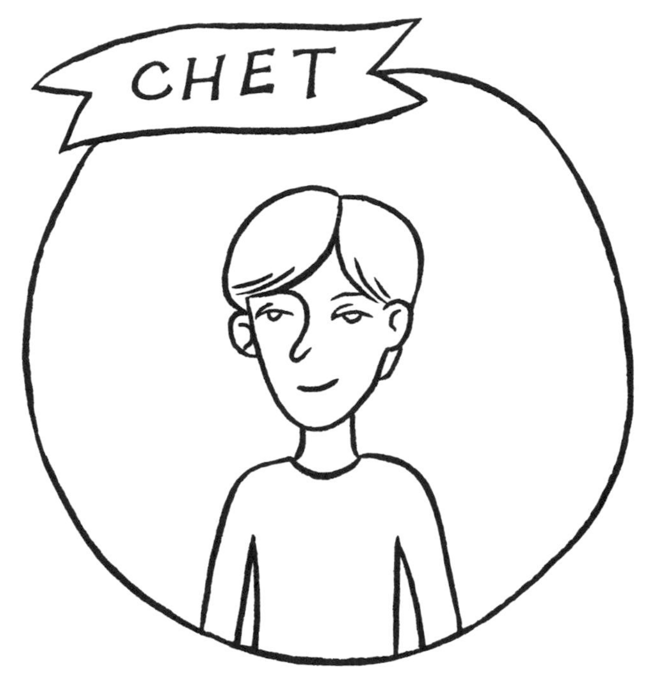
CHET

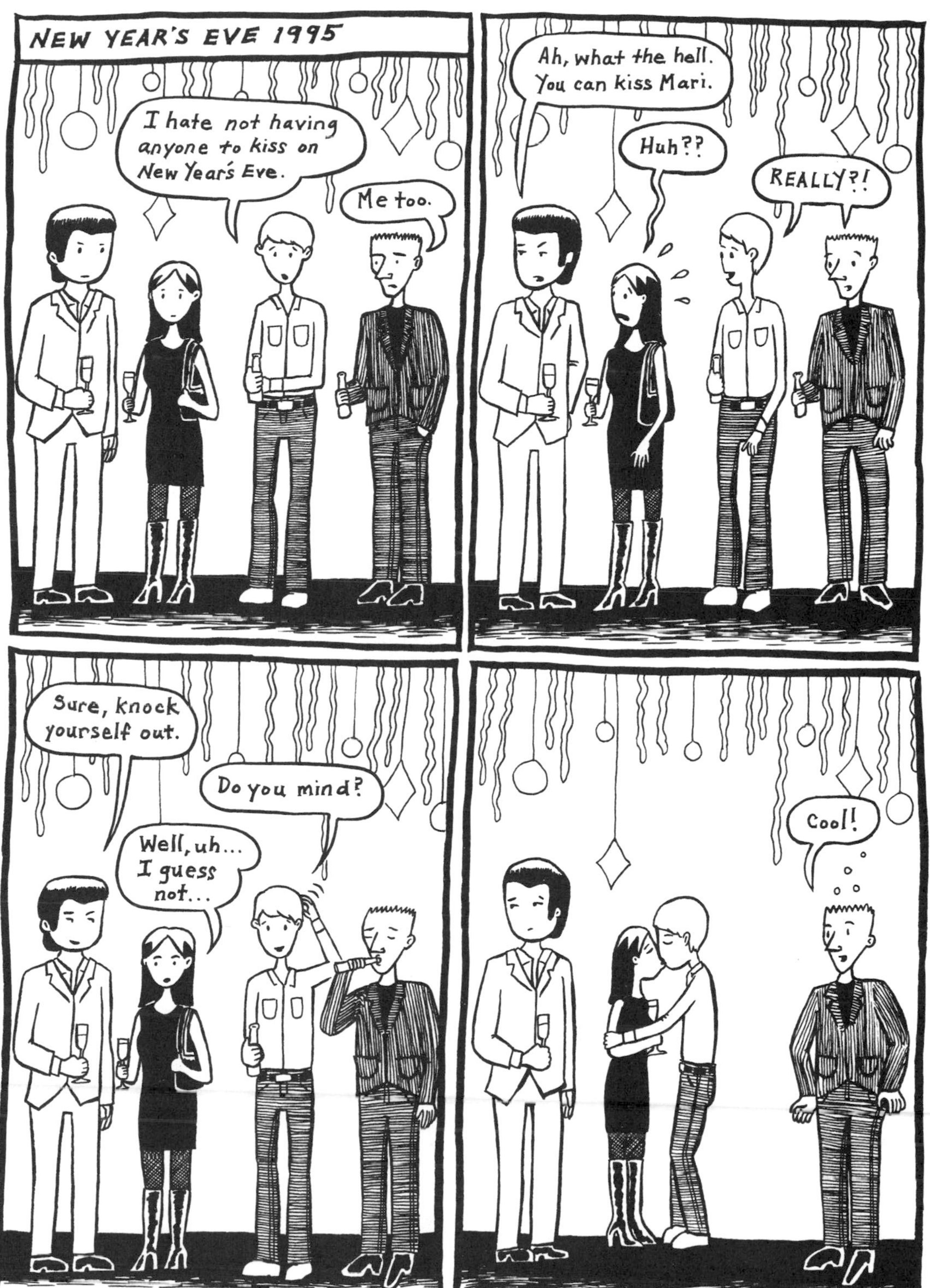
NEW YEAR'S EVE 1995
I hate not having anyone to kiss on New Year's Eve.
Me too.
Ah, what the hell. You can kiss Mari.
Huh??
REALLY?!
Sure, knock yourself out.
Do you mind?
Well, uh... I guess not...
Cool!

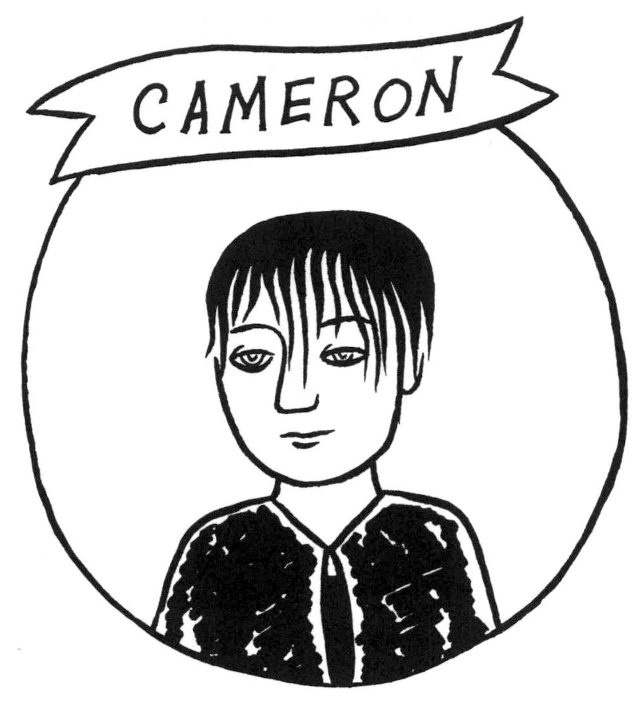
CAMERON

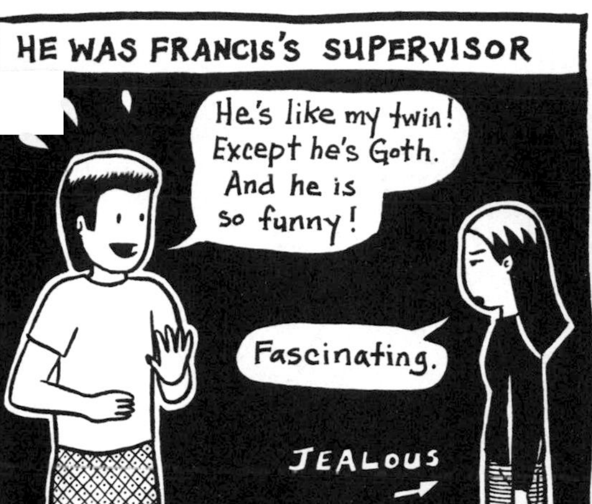
HE WAS FRANCIS'S SUPERVISOR
He's like my twin! Except he's Goth. And he is so funny!
Fascinating.
JEALOUS

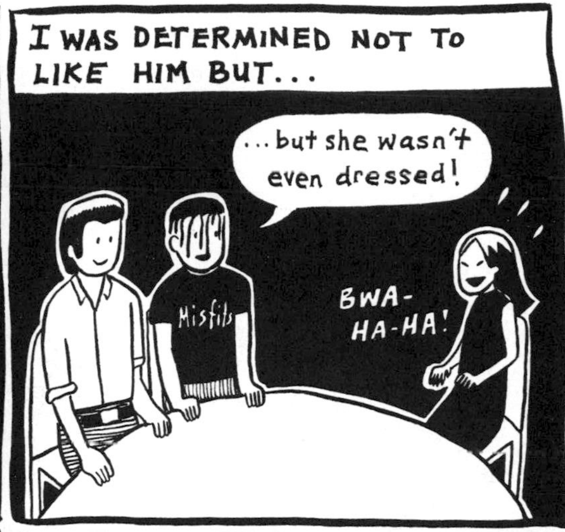
I WAS DETERMINED NOT TO LIKE HIM BUT...
...but she wasn't even dressed!
Misfits
BWA-HA-HA!

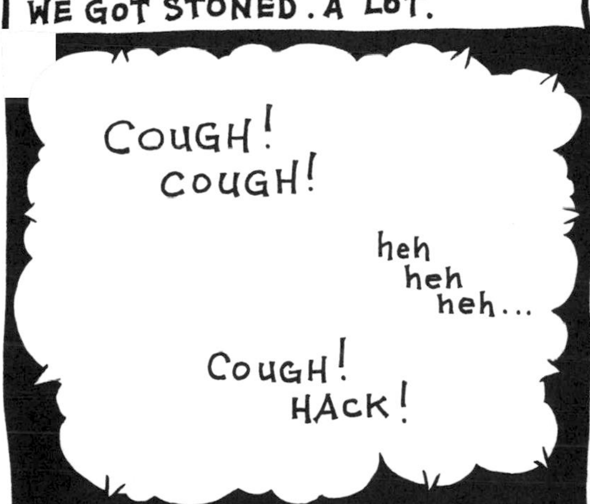
WE GOT STONED. A LOT.
COUGH! COUGH!
heh heh heh...
COUGH! HACK!

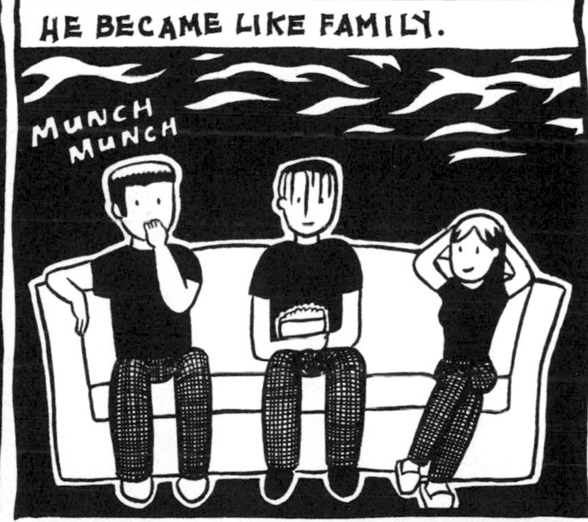
HE BECAME LIKE FAMILY.
MUNCH MUNCH

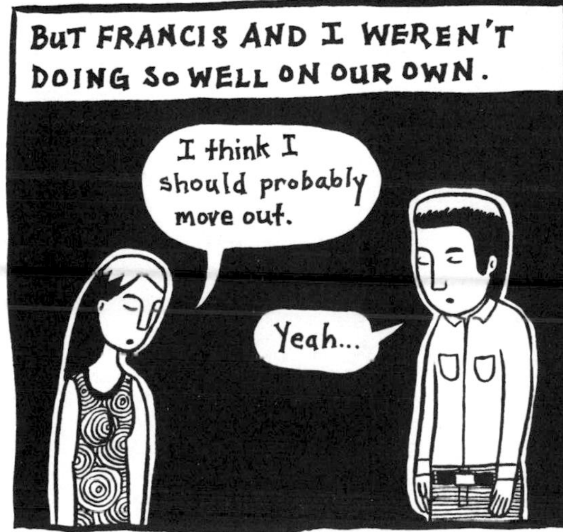
BUT FRANCIS AND I WEREN'T DOING SO WELL ON OUR OWN.
I think I should probably move out.
Yeah...

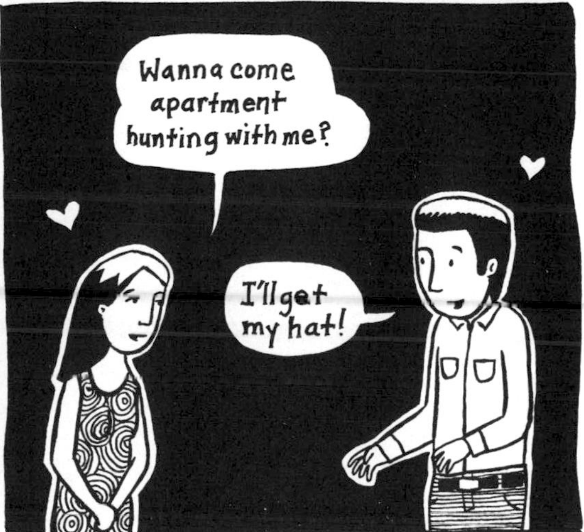
Wanna come apartment hunting with me?
I'll get my hat!

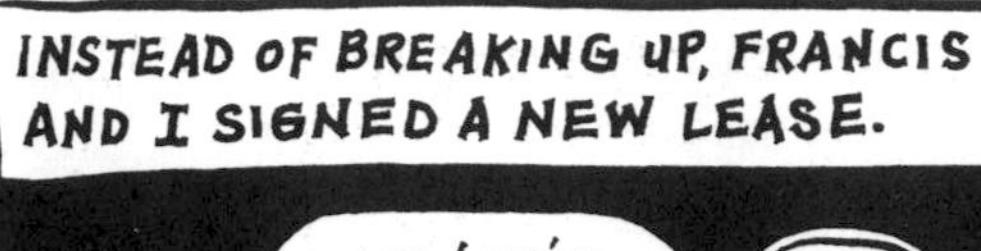
INSTEAD OF BREAKING UP, FRANCIS AND I SIGNED A NEW LEASE.

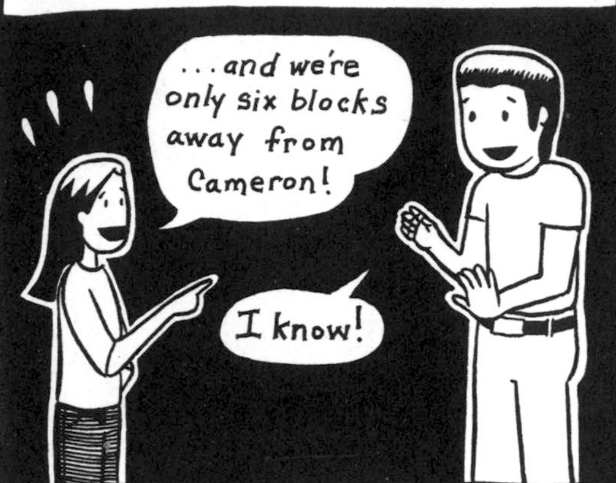
...and we're only six blocks away from Cameron!
I know!

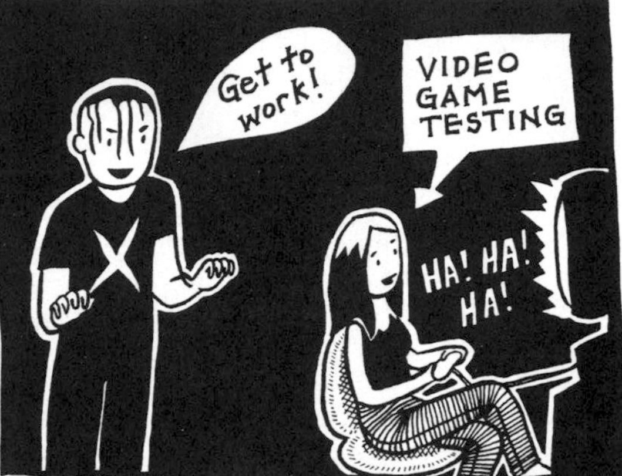
I QUIT MY JOB SO I COULD WORK WITH CAMERON TOO.
Get to work!
VIDEO GAME TESTING
HA! HA! HA!

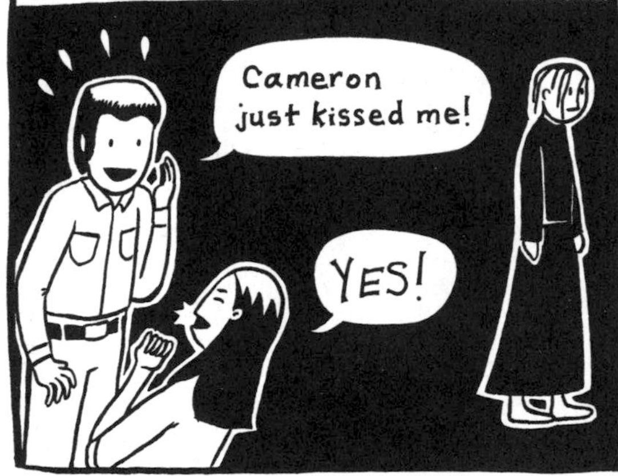
OUR RELATIONSHIP BECAME MORE AND MORE NEBULOUS.
Cameron just kissed me!
YES!

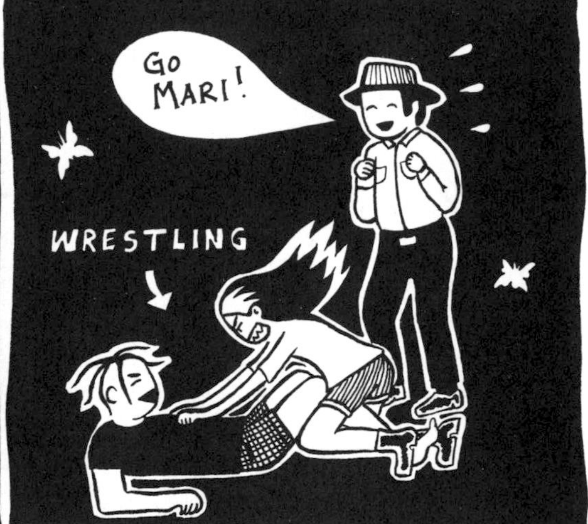
GO MARI!
WRESTLING

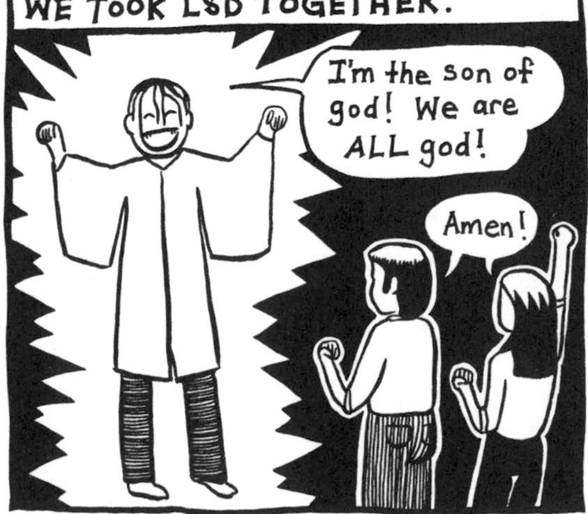
WE TOOK LSD TOGETHER.
I'm the son of god! We are ALL god!
Amen!

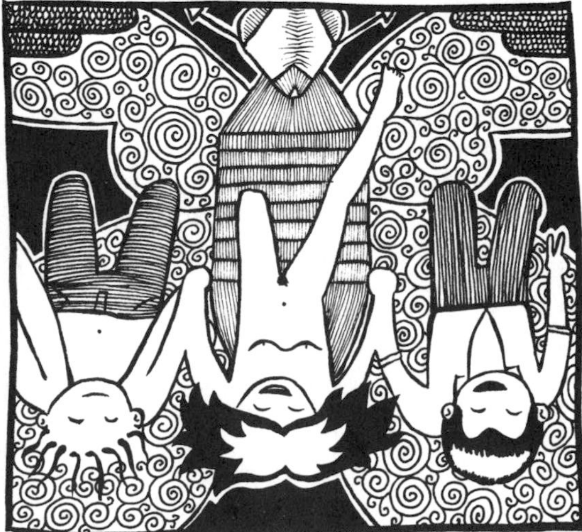

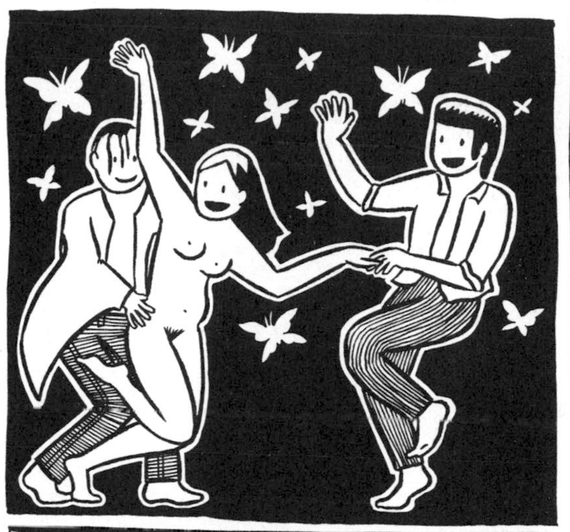

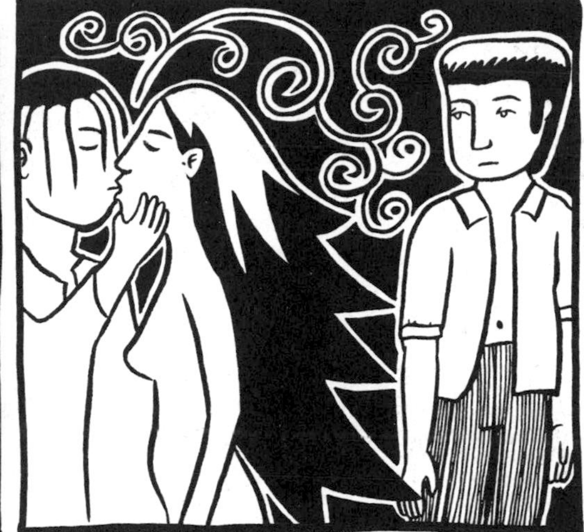

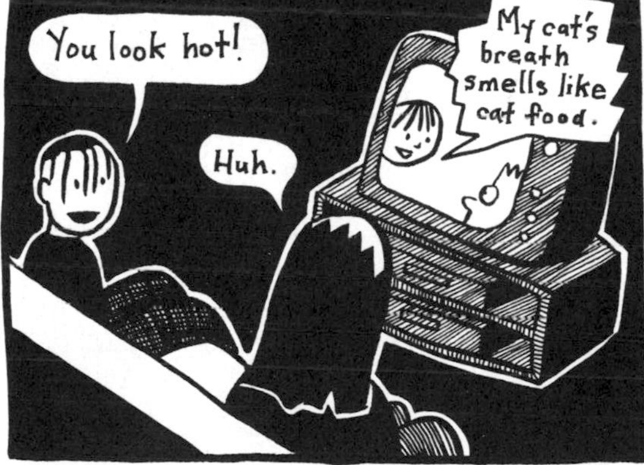
BUT WHEN FRANCIS WASN'T THERE, I BECAME ALOOF, DISINTERESTED.
You look hot!
Huh.
My cat's breath smells like cat food.

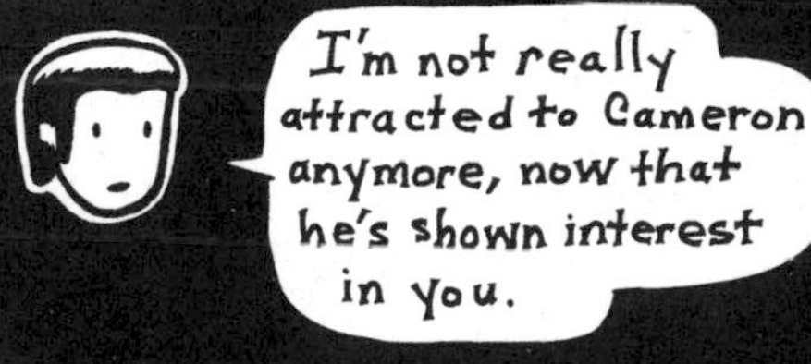
EVENTUALLY I UNDERSTOOD.
I'm not really attracted to Cameron anymore, now that he's shown interest in you.

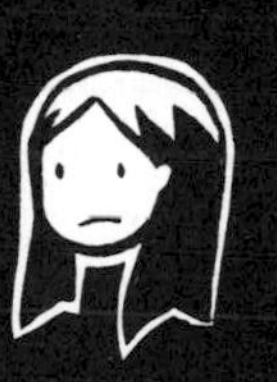
Nothing can save us.

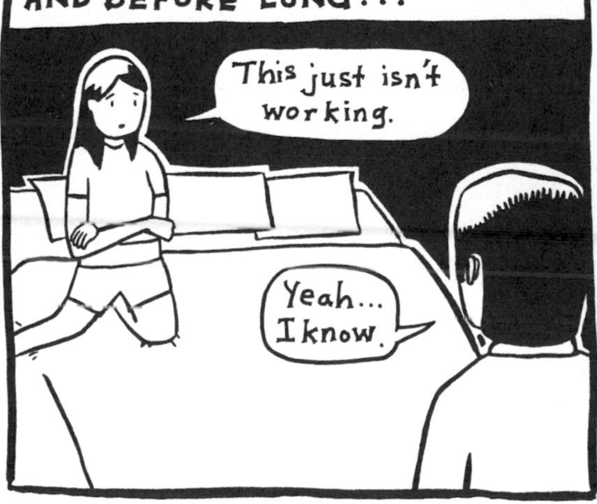
AND BEFORE LONG...
This just isn't working.
Yeah... I know.

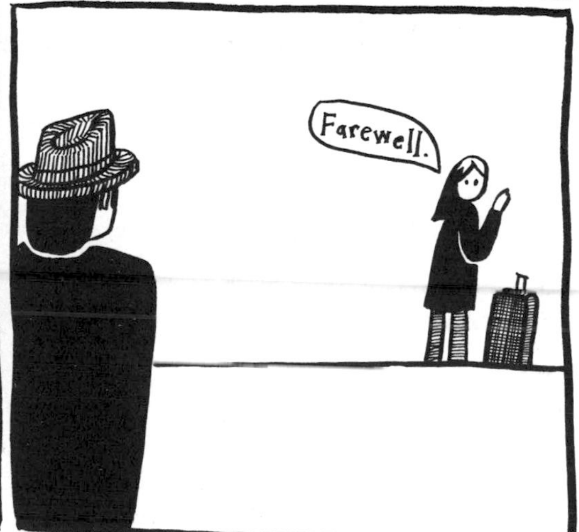
Farewell.

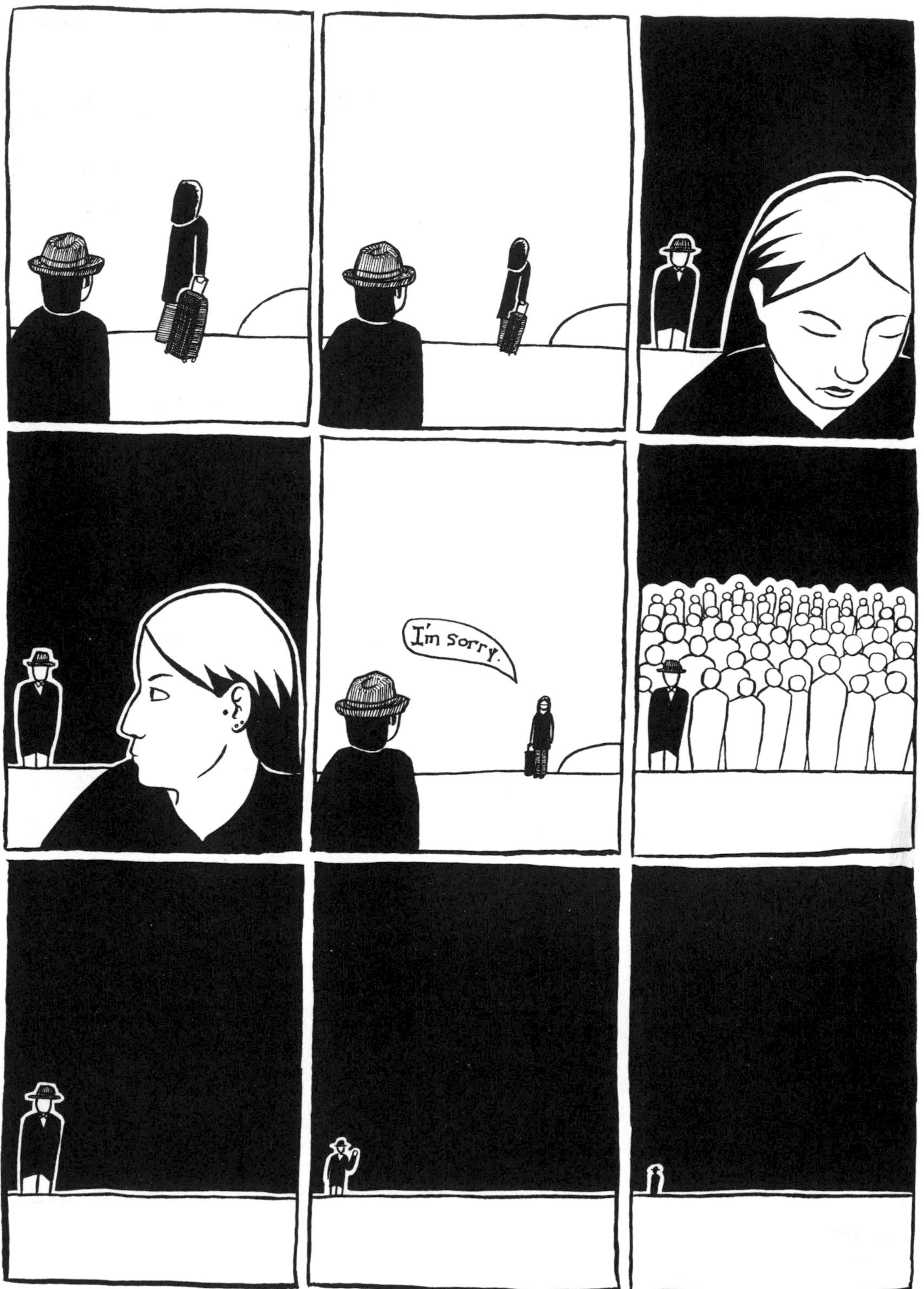
I'm sorry.

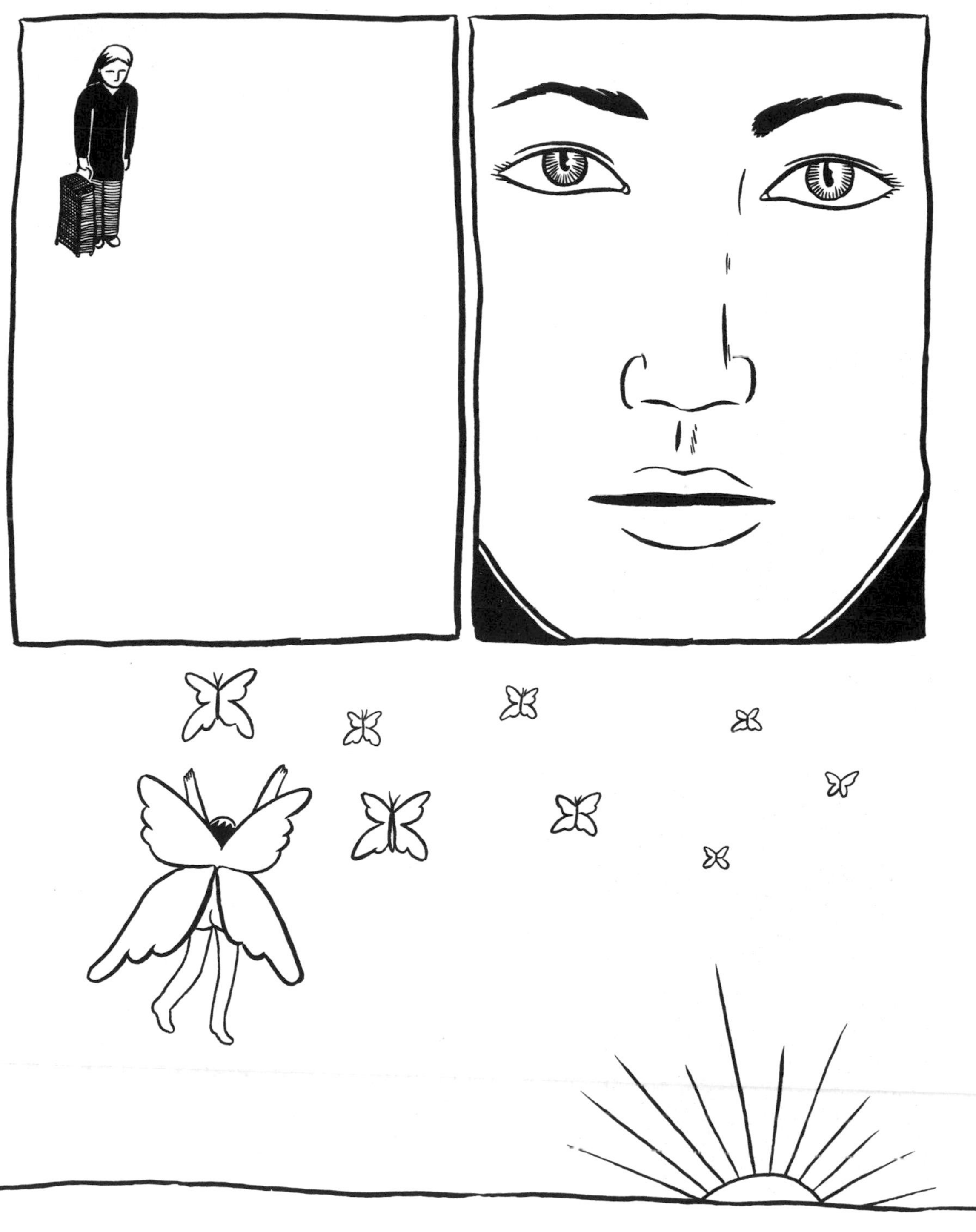

Epilogue

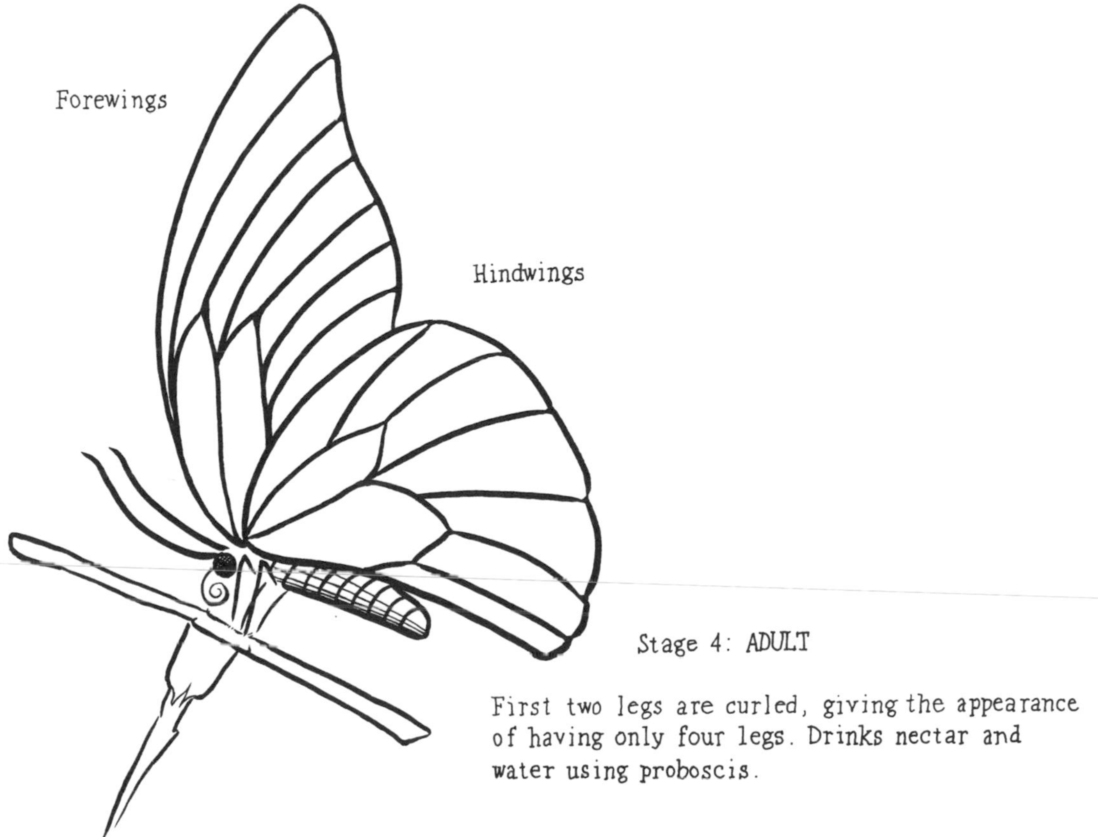
Forewings
Hindwings
Stage 4: ADULT
First two legs are curled, giving the appearance of having only four legs. Drinks nectar and water using proboscis.

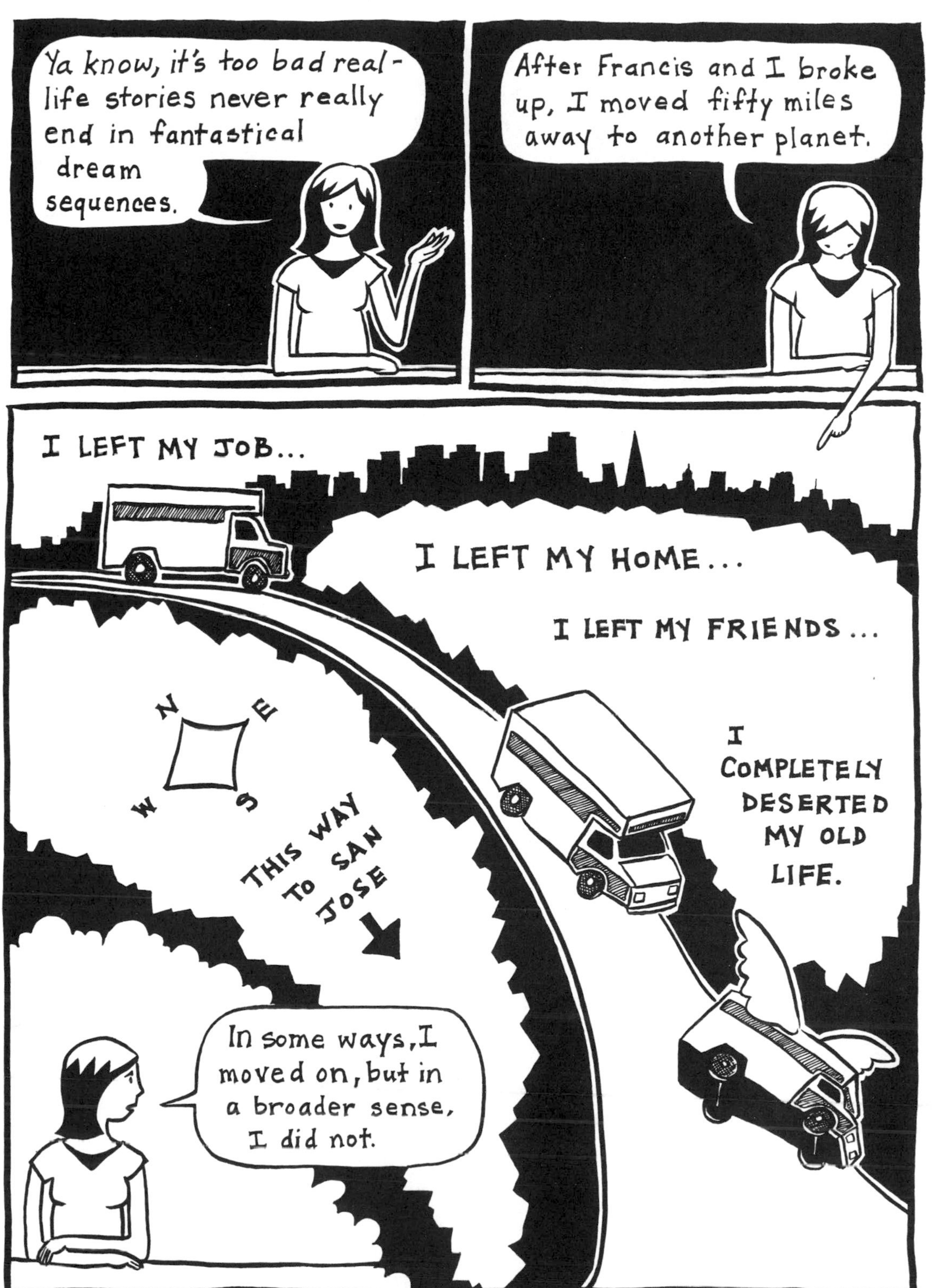
Ya know, it's too bad real-life stories never really end in fantastical dream sequences.
After Francis and I broke up, I moved fifty miles away to another planet.
I LEFT MY JOB...
I LEFT MY HOME...
I LEFT MY FRIENDS...
I COMPLETELY DESERTED MY OLD LIFE.
N
E
W
S
THIS WAY TO SAN JOSE
In some ways, I moved on, but in a broader sense, I did not.

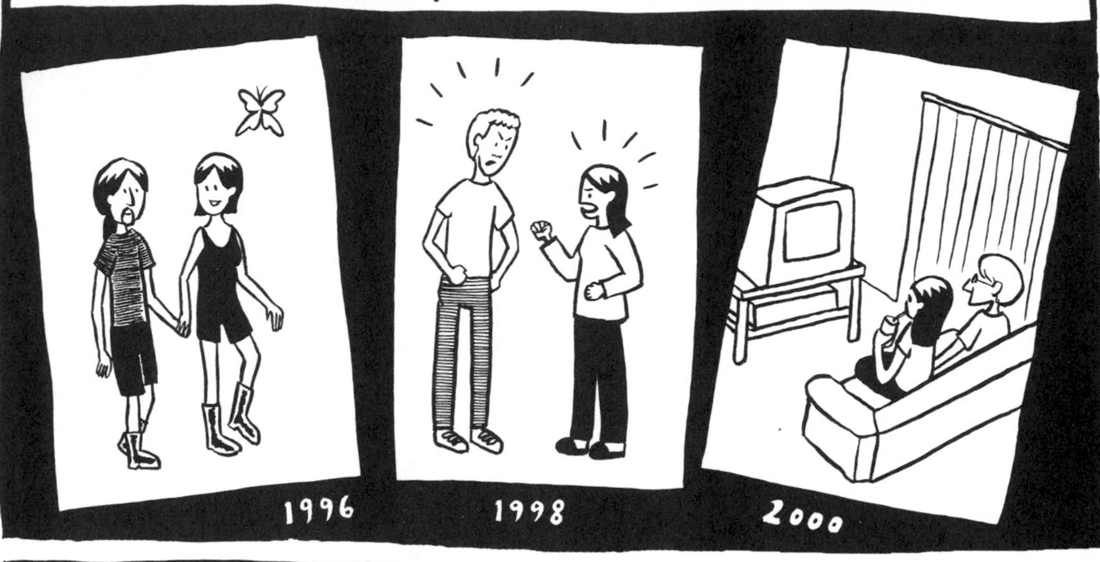

EVENTUALLY I REALIZED THAT THE ME I KNEW WAS MOSTLY A WOMAN REFLECTED THROUGH THE EYES OF OTHER PEOPLE. IT TOOK A LONG TIME BEFORE I GOT TO KNOW MYSELF BY MYSELF.

Opinionated
Devoted
Worrywart
Monogamous
Sensitive
Ambitious
Truthful
Responsible
Independent (but sometimes needy)
Empathetic
Nosey
Shy
Impatient
Open-minded
Forthright

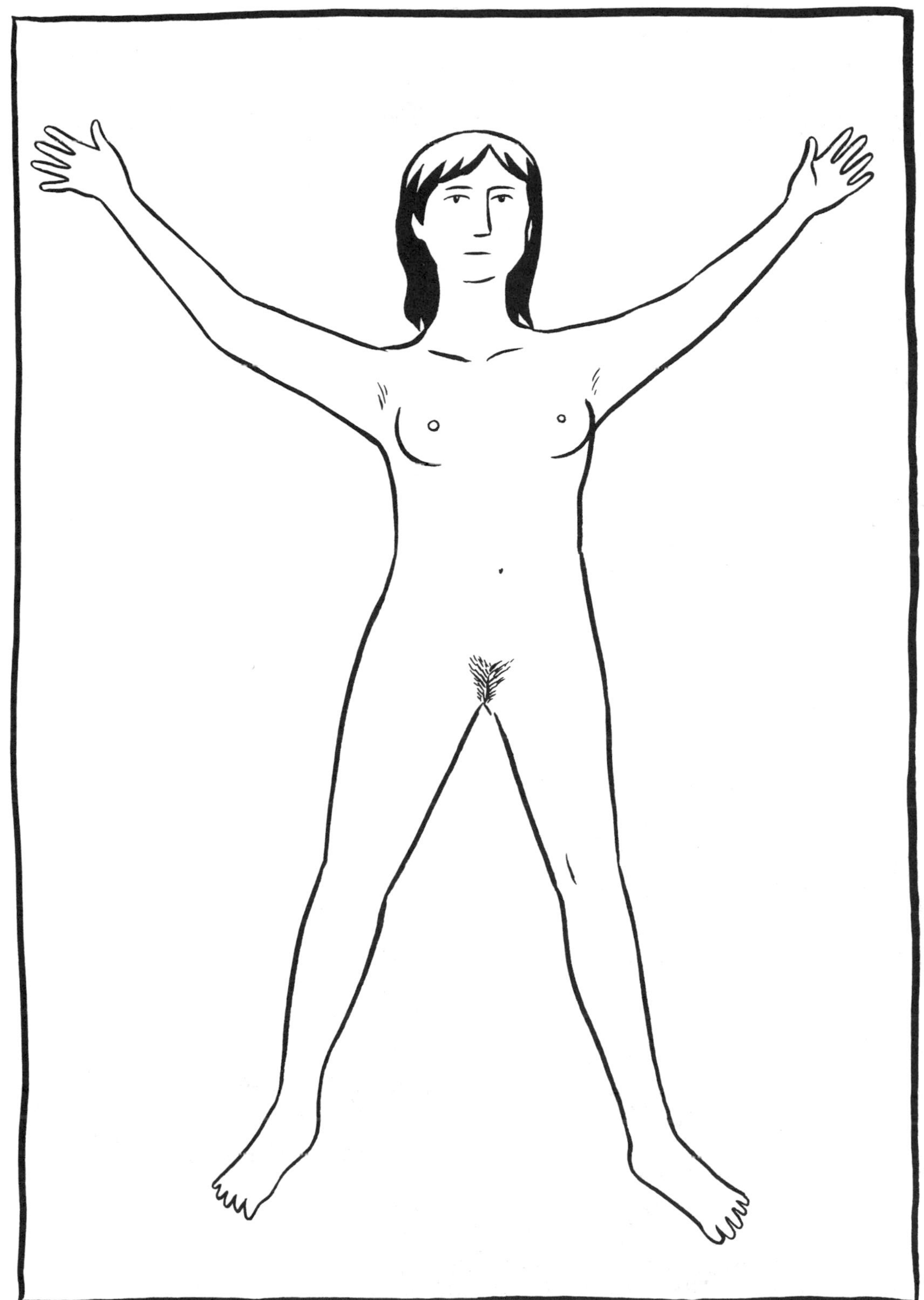

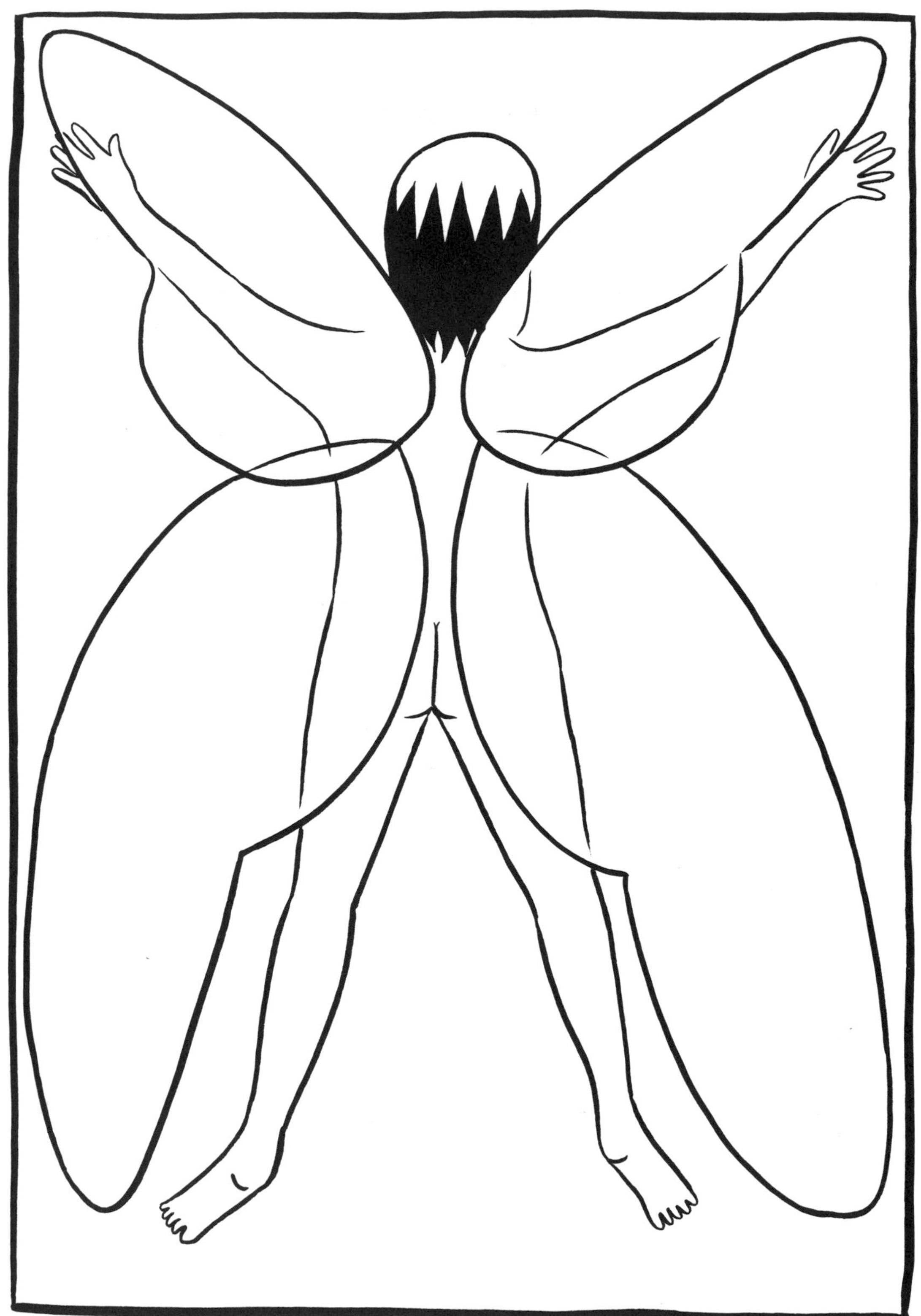

Acknowledgements

A big fat thank you to my amazingly patient, helpful and sexy husband Gary, to my awesome friends Lisa Thomson and Fiona Taylor, who were essential to the creation of this book, and to Christopher Pappalardo, Joey Sayers and Ric Carrasquillo, for their creative input and helping me keep moving forward.

Extreme thanks to my agent PJ Mark, and to editor extraordinaire Jeanette Perez for making this the best book that it could be.

Grateful shout-outs to those who helped support and inspire me throughout this process, especially AAWAA, Andrea Hyson, Bill Dunlap, Brian Kaaaaas, Bucky Sinister, the Cartoon Art Museum, Chris Lucich, Christina Loff, Derek Kirk Kim, the Dirty Drawers (notably Damien Jay, Eli Bishop of Global Hobo, Geoff Vasile, Justin Hall and Minty Lewis), Dylan Williams of Sparkplug, the Hagers, Heather Griggs, Jameel Din, Jason Shiga, Jason Thompson, Jenny Schwam, Jesse Harold, Julia Wertz, Katie McMurran, Kelly Dhillon, Kiyoshi Nakazawa, Lainie Baker, the Lakes, Lark Pien, Maryalice, Melaina Eller, Microcosm, Osamu Shibamiya, Robert Kirby, Rob Kunkle, Samay Israel and Shannon O'Leary.

Most of all, thanks to my seester Sabrina, and all the people who appear in my stories, for being in my life and for keeping it interesting.

Sincerely,

PS. If anyone knows the whereabouts of Jason Towns, tell him to call me, wouldja?